Cognitive Psychology

Cognitive Psychology

Ken Gilhooly, Fiona Lyddy & Frank Pollick

London   Boston   Burr Ridge, IL   Dubuque, IA   Madison, WI   New York   San Francisco
St. Louis   Bangkok   Bogotá   Caracas   Kuala Lumpur   Lisbon   Madrid   Mexico City
Milan   Montreal   New Delhi   Santiago   Seoul   Singapore   Sydney   Taipei   Toronto

Cognitive Psychology
Ken Gilhooly, Fiona Lyddy & Frank Pollick
ISBN-13 9780077122669
ISBN-10 0077122666

Published by McGraw-Hill Education
Shoppenhangers Road
Maidenhead
Berkshire
SL6 2QL
Telephone: 44 (0) 1628 502 500
Fax: 44 (0) 1628 770 224
Website: www.mheducation.co.uk

British Library Cataloguing in Publication Data
A catalogue record for this book is available from the British Library

Library of Congress Cataloguing in Publication Data
The Library of Congress data for this book has been applied for from the Library of Congress

Executive Editor: Natalie Jacobs
Development Editor: Kiera Jamison
Senior Production Editor: James Bishop
Marketing Manager: Geeta Kumar

Text Design by Kamae Design
Cover design by Adam Renvoize
Printed and bound in Great Britain by Ashford Colour Press Ltd

ISBN-13 9780077122669
ISBN-10 077122666

Dedication

To Mary

KG

To Adam

FL

With love to my son Josh, and gratitude to the late
Vince Brown for kindness and generosity in sharing his
fascination with Cognitive Psychology

FP

Brief Table of Contents

Detailed Table of Contents

Preface

During a typical day we all handle a vast amount of information, mostly smoothly and effortlessly. In fact, the running of our complex technological societies depends on the reliable way in which people doing safety-critical jobs such as air traffic controllers, nuclear power workers, surgeons and train drivers, to name a few, correctly perceive situations and efficiently decide on suitable actions. Most of the time, the cognitive processes underlying complex behaviours, in both safety-critical and less hazardous conditions, run very effectively. However, sometimes, things do go wrong, as when we misperceive the outside world, fail to notice important pieces of information, forget previous correct representations of what has happened, make faulty predictions about what will happen next or make poor decisions, even when all the needed information is in front of us. As the good or bad consequences of our behaviour are dependent on accurately dealing with information, it is important to understand not only how we (mostly) do so, but also how errors can arise. This is the subject matter of cognitive psychology – one of the most dynamic areas of psychology.

Much research in cognitive psychology is laboratory based and uses pared down situations to uncover basic processes; such as, using word lists in carefully controlled studies to examine whether forgetting involves simple decaying away of memories or whether it is more a matter of later memories interfering with earlier memories and thus making them hard to remember. The use of laboratory situations in studying cognition can make it seem lacking connection with the real world. This book aims to overcome that apparent gap between real life and laboratory studies by providing an accessible account of the key cognitive topics through not only theory and pure research, but also through applications. Our approach is that relevance to the real world can make all the difference in understanding something and engaging examples will bring the subject to life.

As will become apparent to readers, cognitive psychology is relatively young as a scientific endeavour. There is not always agreement on how each process should be understood or what methods of investigation are best. This is in the nature of a developing science but we believe that the bases for assessing explanations, in terms of clarity, logic and evidence, emerge and become clear as we progress through the chapters.

We've done our best to ensure that this text offers a student-friendly, integrated and up-to-date introduction to cognition. Naturally, the historical progression of theories and research is included as this is the basis for modern research, but the newer contributions of information processing approaches and cognitive neuroscience are also integrated throughout to provide a multi-disciplinary approach.

The order of the chapters reflects the flow of information through the mind and thus after a general introduction (Chapter 1) we deal with topics in the following order: perception and attention (Chapters 2 & 3), short-term (Chapter 4) and long-term memory (Chapter 5), learning and forgetting (Chapter 6), knowledge and imagery (Chapter 7), motor control and action (Chapter 8), problem solving (Chapter 9), decision making (Chapter 10), reasoning (Chapter 11), language understanding and production (Chapters 12 & 13) and cognition and emotion (Chapter 14). This sequence of topics covers all the key areas of cognition and for UK readers has the benefit of meeting the British Psychological Society (BPS) requirements for cognitive psychology teaching in BPS accredited Psychology degrees in the UK.

PEDAGOGY

A key component of the content is the integration of well structured pedagogic features throughout each chapter, with a focus on research and application.

Preview and Review Questions – Each chapter opens with a set of preview questions highlighting the key coverage for that chapter and intended as a more interactive version of learning objectives. The review questions link back to these and challenge student understanding, application and evaluation.

Research Close Ups – going back to real research is always important to understand methodology and theories. In these features, we take notable experiments that are relevant to the topics and provide an overview of the original research in a format and style similar to real papers. This helps to provide an emphasis on methodology and its importance to the subject, but also familiarises students with reading real research.

Practical Applications – whilst pure research is key to the development of the field, applications of key research and theories can help to provide relevance and context for topics. Cognitive psychology is crucial for our understanding of how we perceive, interpret and act upon the world; it has real benefit to the world at large and research doesn't simply stop in the lab. Discoveries can be applied in the real world to help us improve the way things work. For example, we can use research on attention and memory to determine whether it is safe to drive while using a mobile phone.

When Things Go Wrong – a lot of what we know about the mind, comes not from research into how things work well but into investigation of what happens when things go wrong. This has been a key approach in cognitive psychology and one which continues to provide insight through behavioural and brain imaging studies. These features focus on what we have learnt about a topic by considering things that have gone wrong and what that tells us about the mind. For example, in language we discuss loss of language abilities (aphasia) brought about by brain damage and how studies of aphasia help to identify the different functions and brain areas involved in speech production.

AND FINALLY . . .

We hope that this book will stimulate your curiosity about the cognitive workings of the mind and that some of you may go on to contribute to the field yourselves as cognitive psychologists of the future!

Ken Gilhooly, Fiona Lyddy and Frank Pollick

Guided tour

Preview questions

1 How do we make decisions?
2 Why take out insurance when the insurance companies always win?
3 Why bet on lottery tickets when the lottery always wins?
4 When does deciding on the basis of 'gut feelings' help? And when does it hind
5 How do experts make decisions in critical situations?
6 Can brain studies help explain how we decide?

Preview questions

Linked to the end of chapter Review Questions, these questions provide clear learning objectives to guide you through each chapter.

Broca's area is an area located in the left temporal lobe, damage to which is associated with aphasia (speech deficits).
Localization is the view that specific mental functions are tied to specific brain areas; this also appears as the modularity hypothesis and may be contrasted with the Distributed view, that functions are realized by joint action of many areas.
Neuropsychology is the study of psychological effects of brain damage and disease.

of lesion in the inferior part of the left frontal gyrus. This region, now named Broca's area, is vital for speech production (see Figure 1.6, and Chapter 12 for more detail).

Since Broca's finding it has become well established that in 90 per cent of right-handed people, and in the majority of left-handed people, language functions are strongly localized in the left hemisphere.

Broca's study exemplifies the basic ideas of neuropsychology which are that most, if not all functions, are linked closely to the healthy working of specific brain areas and t... indicate which areas are i... about how broad functions... patient showed that the b... language production and l... the patient could understa... of localization had been...

Key terms

These are highlighted and defined in the relevant chapters, providing ease of reference. All definitions can also be found in the Glossary at the end of the book.

Box 5.6 Practical Application: Remembering passcodes

In the past few years, a number of high profile hacks have revealed prolific use of overly simplistic online passwords, with many computer users choosing names of family members, partners, or pets and with the sequences 'password', 'password1', and '123456' featuring amongst the most frequently used items (Burnett & Kleiman, 2005). Personal identification number (PIN) codes would seem to be no better. A survey by Bonneau et al. (2012) found that common PIN codes included birthdays, years of birth and the sequences 1234 and 1111. (Given that most people carry some form of identification along with their ATM card, a thief who acquires the ATM card will likely also have access to the birthday.) Bonneau et al. estimate that, based on reported passcodes, a thief could gain use of an ATM card once every 11 or so stolen wallets, using birthday information and other common codes. P... also showed limited variety, with 'love' and its corresponding PIN 5683, frequ...

In selecting a passcode, there is a trade-off between security and memorabili... and random passcode will be secure, it is only useful if you can remember it...

Practical Application boxes bring research, theories and concepts to real-world, practical situations.

Box 13.7 Research Close Up: The Stroop effect

Source: Stroop, J. R. (1935). Studies of interference in serial verbal reactions. *Journal of Experimental Psychology*, 18, 643–662.

INTRODUCTION

In 1935, J. R. Stroop published a research article describing an effect that continues to form the basis for many diverse experiments today. A typical Stroop colour-naming the colour in which a word is printed, when the word is itself a c... agrees with the print colour (for example, the word BLUE printe... 'blue'), response times are faster than when naming a neutral co... word (one that is not associated with a particular colour), an effec... word colour and meaning do not concur (e.g., the word RED writ...

Research Close Up boxes introduce you to the format of real research in cognitive psychology. Each box summarizes an important research paper, explaining the methods the authors used, the results they obtained and a discussion to help you think critically about the significance of the study.

Box 12.4 When Things Go Wrong: The split brain

We are unaware of the division of labour between the left and right hemispheres because the two hemispheres of our brains communicate so effectively via a number of connecting bands of fibres between the hemispheres, called commissures. The largest of these is the corpus callosum. This band of over 200 million fibres is surgically severed in a *commissurotomy*, a rare surgical procedure which is performed in order to reduce the effects of a type of intractable epilepsy that is unresponsive to drug therapy.

After the procedure the 'split-brain patient' behaves surprisingly normally, considering such a radical operation has been performed. However, on careful testing, it is apparent that the left and right hemi

When Things Go Wrong boxes look at what we have learned by examining cases where things went wrong, both in terms of errors and unexpected results in testing, and in lessons from psychopathology.

Summary

This chapter examined long-term memory. Cases such as that of H.M. have shown that LTM processes are not distributed throughout the brain; damage to particular areas within the temporal lobes will cause profound LTM loss. H.M. and other cases with the characteristic deficits of amnesia show that memory consists of a number of different systems, some of which are unaffected by amnesia. Amnesia is associated with intact short-term memory, as measured by digit span, for example; memory for language, and concepts, is relatively unaffected; but there is severe amnesia for events that onset of the illness/injury. Skill learning, conditioning and priming will be unaffected. also be able to engage in skills acquired prior to the onset of amnesia (e.g. play a music

It is generally agreed that there is a distinction in LTM between implicit or non-declarati explicit or declarative memory, a distinction described as 'knowing that' as opposed to Explicit memory involves conscious recollection of information, whereas implicit me when performance that does not require conscious recollection is facilitated by prior

Chapter summary

This briefly reviews and reinforces the main topics you will have covered in each chapter to ensure you have acquired a solid understanding of the key topics.

Review questions

1 What evidence is there supporting the main components of Baddeley's working memory model?
2 What are the functions of the phonological loop?
3 How has evidence from brain injury contributed to our understanding of normal memory?
4 What is the relationship between short-term and working memory?
5 How might we best measure the capacity of short-term memory?

Review questions

Each chapter is followed by a range of questions to check your understanding of the material and challenge you to think critically.

FURTHER READING

Goldin-Meadow, S. (2003). *Hearing gesture: How our hands help us think.* Cambridge, MA: Belknap Press of Harvard University Press.

Haggard, P., Rossetti, Y., & Kawato, M. (2008). *Attention and performance XXII: Sensorimotor foundations of higher cognition.* Oxford: Oxford University Press.

Jeannerod, M. (2006). *Motor cognition: What actions tell the self.* Oxford: Oxford University Press.

Jordan, M. I. (1997). Chapter 25 Serial order: A parallel distributed processing approach. In J. W. Donahoe & V. Packard Dorsel (Eds.), *Neural-network models of cognition* (pp. 471–495). Amsterdam: Elsevier Science.

Lashley, K. S. (1951). The problem of serial order in behavior. In L. *ior.* New York: Wiley.

Scott, S. H. (2004). Optimal feedback control and the neural ba *Neuroscience,* 5(7), 534–546.

Further reading

A selection of further reading suggestions are provided which are designed to act as a springboard into further or more detailed study.

Online Resources

Please visit **www.mheducation/textbooks/gilhooly1** today!

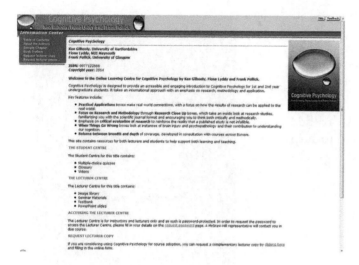

Online Learning Centre (OLC)

After completing each chapter, log on to the supporting Online Learning Centre website. Take advantage of the study tools offered to reinforce the material you have read in the text, and to develop your knowledge of economics in a fun and effective way.

Resources for students include:
- Multiple-choice quizzes
- Glossary
- Videos
- Web links
- Sylvius Brain Dictionary

Also available for lecturers:
- Image library
- Instructor's Manual
- Testbank
- PowerPoint slides
- Seminar Materials

Test Bank available in McGraw-Hill EZ Test Online

A test bank with hundreds of questions is available to lecturers adopting this book for their module. A range of questions is provided for each chapter including multiple choice, true or false, and short answer or essay questions. The questions are identified by type, difficulty and topic to help you to select questions that best suit your needs and are accessible through an easy-to-use online testing tool, **McGraw-Hill EZ Test Online**.

McGraw-Hill EZ Test Online is accessible to busy academics virtually anywhere – in their office, at home or while travelling – and eliminates the need for software installation. Lecturers can chose from question banks associated with their adopted textbook or easily create their own questions. They also have access to hundreds of banks and thousands of questions created for other McGraw-Hill titles. Multiple versions of tests can be saved for delivery on paper or online through WebCT, Blackboard and other course management systems. To register for this FREE resource, visit www.eztestonline.com.

connect®
PSYCHOLOGY

McGraw-Hill Connect Psychology is a learning and teaching environment that improves student performance and outcomes whilst promoting engagement and comprehension of content.

You can utilize publisher-provided materials, or add your own content to design a complete course to help your students achieve higher outcomes.

PROVEN EFFECTIVE

INSTRUCTORS

With McGraw-Hill Connect Psychology, instructors get:

- ☐ Simple **assignment management,** allowing you to spend more time teaching.

- ☐ **Auto-graded** assignments and quizzes including interactive excercises.

- ☐ **Detailed visual reporting** where students and section results can be viewed and analysed.

- ☐ Sophisticated **online testing** capability.

- ☐ A **filtering and reporting** function that allows you to easily assign and report on materials that are correlated to learning outcomes, topics, level of difficulty, and more. Reports can be accessed for individual students or the whole class, as well as offering the ability to drill into individual assignments, questions or categories.

- ☐ **Instructor materials** to help supplement your course.

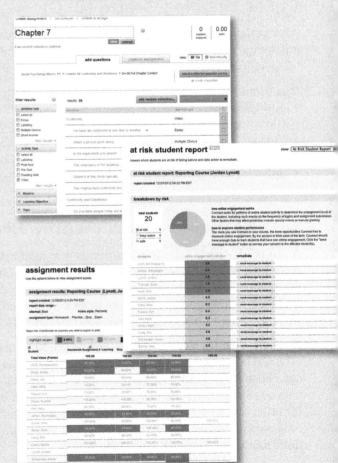

Get Connected. Get Results.

STUDENTS

With McGraw-Hill Connect Plus Psychology, students get:

Assigned content

- ☐ Easy **online access** to homework, tests and quizzes.
- ☐ **Immediate feedback** and 24-hour tech support.

eBook

- ☐ An integrated ebook, allowing for anytime, anywhere access to the textbook.
- ☐ Dynamic links between assigned materials and the location in the eBook where that content is covered.
- ☐ A powerful search function to pinpoint key concepts.
- ☐ The ability to highlight, note-take and bookmark content.

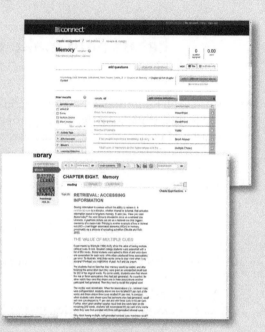

MATERIALS

Interactive Activities

Interactive Activities are designed to reinforce textbook concepts and aim at a higher level of understanding and application. The activities provided feature seamless assignability and automatic grading capabilities, and a variety of assessment types including click-and-drag and interactive quizzes are available.

Quizzes

These quizzes help to test the concepts and theories from each chapter to ensure that students understand and learn the key components from the chapter coverage. They take a multiple choice format so that they can be automatically marked and students can receive immediate feedback if desired.

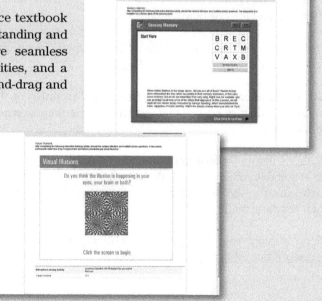

Let us help make our <u>content</u> your <u>solution</u>

At McGraw-Hill Education our aim is to help lecturers to find the most suitable content for their needs delivered to their students in the most appropriate way. Our custom **publishing solutions** offer the ideal combination of content delivered in the way which best suits lecturer and students.

Our custom publishing programme offers lecturers the opportunity to select just the chapters or sections of material they wish to deliver to their students from a database called CREATE™ at

http://create.mheducation.com/uk/

CREATE™ contains over two million pages of content from:
- textbooks
- professional books
- case books – Harvard Articles, Insead, Ivey, Darden, Thunderbird and BusinessWeek
- Taking Sides – debate materials

Across the following imprints:
- McGraw-Hill Education
- Open University Press
- Harvard Business Publishing
- US and European material

There is also the option to include additional material authored by lecturers in the custom product – this does not necessarily have to be in English.

We will take care of everything from start to finish in the process of developing and delivering a custom product to ensure that lecturers and students receive exactly the material needed in the most suitable way.

With a **Custom Publishing Solution**, students enjoy the best selection of material deemed to be the most suitable for learning everything they need for their courses – something of real value to support their learning. Teachers are able to use exactly the material they want, in the way they want, to support their teaching on the course.

Please contact your local **McGraw-Hill representative** with any questions or alternatively contact e: <u>custom.publishing@mheducation.com</u>

Acknowledgements

AUTHOR ACKNOWLEDGEMENTS

First, we would like to thank our students, whose curiosity into how the mind works, provides a constant inspiration for developing these materials. We'd also like to thank the anonymous reviewers for their constructive comments throughout the process which have helped to shape our writing.

We are grateful to colleagues at the University of Hertfordshire, the National University of Ireland Maynooth and the Perception, Cognition and Action group and associated colleagues at the University of Glasgow for providing a supportive intellectual environment to work on this project. Helpful advice from Mike Burton, Sang Chul Chong, Frank Durgin, Peter Hampson, Mitsuo Kawato, Keith Laws, Scott Love, Pascal Mamassian, Mike Page, Richard Roche, Anne Ryan and Gert van Tonder has been greatly appreciated.

Finally, great thanks go to Natalie Jacobs, Kiera Jamison, Alexander Krause and Jennifer Rotherham at McGraw-Hill whose insight and constructive criticism helped to guide this project.

PUBLISHER'S ACKNOWLEDGEMENTS

Our thanks go to the following reviewers for their comments at various stages in the text's development:

James Anderson, University of Stirling

Susan Anthony, University of Hertfordshire

C. Philip Beaman, University of Reading

Tim Brennan, University of Oslo

Yvonne Broom, University of the Witwatersrand

Caroline Brown, University of the West of England

Marc Buehner, Cardiff University

Gary Christopher, University of the West of England

Kate Cockcroft, University of the Witwatersrand

Hans Crombag, University of Sussex

Simon Davies, Liverpool Hope University

Bo Edvardsson, Örebro University

Martijn Goydbeek, Tilburg University

James A. Grange, Keele University

Kirston Greenop, University of Witwatersrand

Anne Hillstrom, University of Portsmouth

Neal Hinvest, University of Bath

Lennart Högman, Stockholm University

Måns Holgersson, University of Kristianstad

Jeannette Hommes, Maastricht University

Chris Janeke, University of South Africa

Steve Jones, Leeds Trinity University

Beena Khurana, Sussex University

Emiel Krahmer, Tilburg University

Torstein Låg, University of Tromsö

Stephen R. H. Langton, University of Stirling

Magnus Larsson, Lund University

Michael Lewis, Cardiff University

Nick Lund, Manchester Metropolitan University

Jon May, University of Plymouth

Phillip L. Morgan, University of South Wales

Wayne Murray, University of Dundee

Jeroen G. W. Raaijmakers, Universiteit van Amsterdam

Romke Rouw, Universiteit Amsterdam

Charlotte Russell, Brunel University

Mark Scase, De Montfort University

Kenneth Scott-Brown, University of Abertay

Camilla Siotis, Kristianstad University

Eric Soetens, Vrije Universiteit Brussel

Stefan van der Stigchel, Utrecht University

Gert Westermann, Oxford Brookes University

Richard Wilkie, University of Leeds

Gezinus Wolters, Leiden Universiteit

We'd also like to thank those who participated in other forms of feedback which contributed to this project:

Adrian Banks, University of Surrey

Dawn Behne, NTNU

Robert Biegler, NTNU

Lorraine Boran, Dublin City University

Rosalind Crawley, University of Sunderland

Tom Dickins, Middlesex University

Ebba Elwin, Uppsala University

Philip Fine, University of Buckingham

Lisbeth Harms, Copenhagen University

Nigel Holt, Aberystwyth University

Casper Hulshof, Utrecht Universiteit

Eric Raymond Igou, University of Limerick

Åse Innes-Ker, Lund University

Wido La Heij, Leiden University

Peter Lovatt, University of Hertfordshire

David Maree, University of Pretoria

Andy Morley, University of Central Lancashire

Eva Neidhardt, Universitat Luneburg

Rüdiger Pohl, University of Mannheim

Timothy Ritchie, University of Limerick

Richard Roche, NUI Maynooth

Jennifer Rodd, University College, London

Noam Sagiv, Brunel University

Peter Starreveld, Universeit van Amsterdam

Gijsbert Stoet, University of Glasgow

Anna Stone, University of East London

Nina Svensson, Karlstad University

Lydia Tan, City University, London

Maria Uther, University of Winchester

Daniel Vastfjall, Linköping University

José van Velzen, Goldsmiths, University of London

Frans Verstraten, University of Sydney

Willem Verwey, University of Twente

David Westley, Middlesex University

Lee Wickham, University of Manchester

We would like to thank Eamon Fulcher for his contributions to the digital materials; he has produced our Connect learning materials as well as our instructor support materials:

We would also like to thank Elaine Bingham and James Bishop for their work on the text during production.

Finally, we would like to thank the following people for permission reproduce materials:

APA   Dirk Bernhardt-Walther

Elsevier   Instituto Italiano di Tecnologia

iStock   Mike Burton

Laura Taverna

About the authors

Professor Ken Gilhooly has joint appointments at the University of Hertfordshire, where he is Emeritus Professor of Psychology and at Brunel University, London, where he is Research Professor in Quantitative Gerontology. Having completed undergraduate studies at the University of Edinburgh and postgraduate studies at the University of Stirling, he went on to work at the University of Aberdeen before taking a Chair at Brunel, followed by another at University of West of Scotland. Ken then moved to a Chair at Hertfordshire in 2004. He's served as the Chair of the Cognitive Section of the British Psychological Society (BPS) and has served on a number of Research Council panels and boards. He is a Fellow of the BPS and was recently elected to the Academy of Social Sciences and to Fellowship of the Royal Society of Arts.

Dr Fiona Lyddy is a senior lecturer in psychology and Dean of the Faculty of Science and Engineering at the National University of Ireland Maynooth. She completed a bachelor's degree in Applied Psychology and a PhD in Psychology at University College Cork. She lectured at University College Cork and at the University of Wales Institute Cardiff before joining National University of Ireland Maynooth in 2001. She is a chartered psychologist, a Fellow of the Psychological Society of Ireland and an Associate Fellow of the British Psychological Society. She was founding chair of the Psychological Society of Ireland's Division of Teachers and Researchers in Psychology.

Professor Frank Pollick is a professor at the University of Glasgow. He completed undergraduate studies in Physics and Biology at MIT, and masters studies in Biomedical Engineering at Case Western Reserve University before obtaining his PhD in Cognitive Sciences from The University of California, Irvine. He then moved to Kyoto, Japan where he worked at the Advanced Telecommunication Research Institute (ATR) as a researcher in the Human Information Processing laboratory. Since 1997 he has been at the University of Glasgow.

Cognitive Psychology

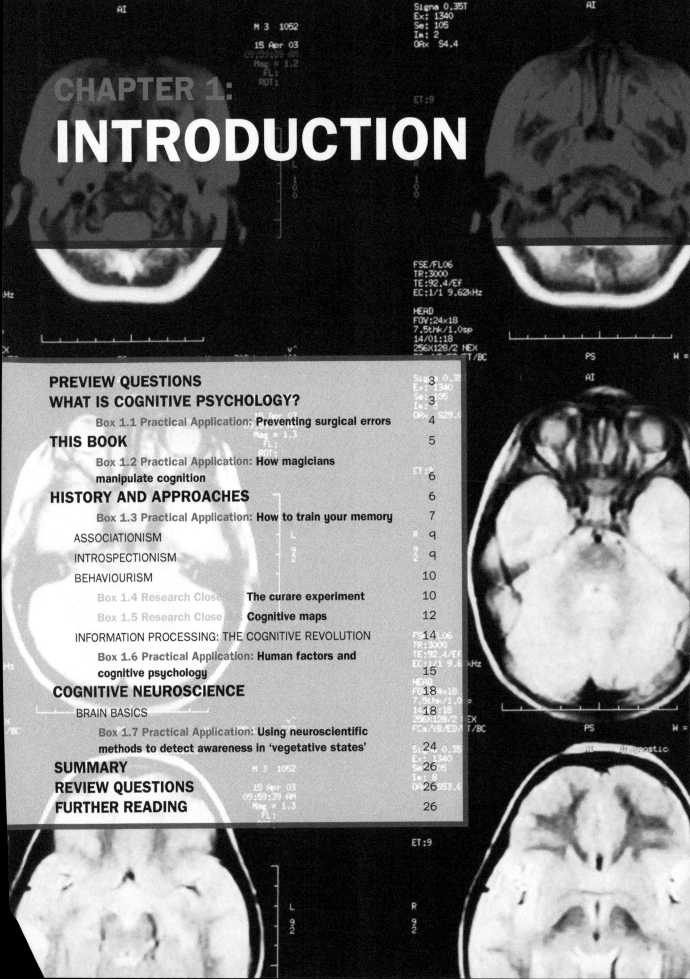

CHAPTER 1:
INTRODUCTION

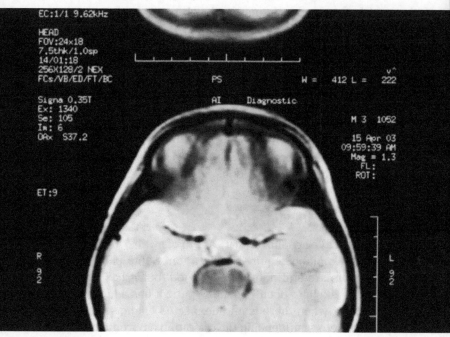

Preview questions

1 What topic areas does cognitive psychology address?
2 What are the main approaches to cognitive psychology?
3 When did cognitive psychology emerge as a sub-discipline within psychology?
4 What is distinctive about the cognitive approach?
5 What can studies of brain injury tell us about how we think, remember and forget?
6 What can we learn from neuroimaging studies of brain function?

WHAT IS COGNITIVE PSYCHOLOGY?

Psychology may be broadly defined as the study of mind and behaviour in humans and animals. Within the general field of psychology, cognitive psychology is concerned with how the mind represents and uses information about the outside world. During a typical day we all handle a vast amount of information, mostly smoothly and effortlessly, but sometimes things go wrong as when we misrepresent the outside world, forget previous correct representations, make faulty predictions about what will happen next or make poor decisions. As all of our behaviour is dependent on accurately dealing with information, it is important to understand how we do so and how errors can arise. For example, imagine you are crossing a road. You must attend to moving traffic, ignore distractions, make a judgement as regards the velocity of an approaching vehicle, estimate how quickly you can cross to the other side, and effect the motor sequence that will see you safely across. An error in judgement or a misperception could be catastrophic (see Box 1.1 for a further example). Fortunately, most of the time we execute such manoeuvres without error.

Cognitive psychology is the scientific study of how people and animals process information.

Each day, we carry out a range of cognitive functions without great effort, allowing us to focus on matters of current importance. Think about an imaginary day you might experience as a student. On waking, you might look out of your window and see that it is raining and looks set to continue all day. This representation of the world can be later retrieved from memory and used to decide whether to carry an umbrella or not when you go out. You may then remember that you have a statistics tutorial at noon and decide to solve problems from the set book before going out. You begin attending to the first problem. You read the set question carefully but do not understand it and go back to your lecture notes for an explanation. Alternatively, you may forget that you have a statistics tutorial and reason that it would be best to focus on your essay due tomorrow. As the day goes on you are constantly dealing with information from many sources, from memory, and also from the environment, from other people via speech and reading and from assorted media. How do you deal with all this information?

Cognitive psychology seeks to answer that broad question and is the study of how humans (and other animals):

- acquire information;
- store information in memory;
  - retrieve information;
  - work with information to reach goals.

Mental representations are inner representations such as an image or a verbal concept of some external reality.

In all these cases, we are dealing with internal or mental representations. How such representations are formed, stored and used is the essential business of cognitive psychology.

Box 1.1 Practical Application: Preventing surgical errors

Every year, some surgical patients leave hospital with a variety of swabs, instruments and other objects accidentally left inside their bodies. Many require re-operation. Some patients do not survive. The risk factors for such medical errors are still poorly understood, but it has been established that the retention of foreign bodies is more likely to occur when the patient has a high body-mass index, when a patient has emergency surgery or when there is an unexpected change in their surgical procedure (Gawande et al., 2003). Cognitive factors influencing the operating environment are increasingly being considered.

Counting procedures are the main method used to guard against retained foreign bodies, with theatre nursing staff playing a key role in keeping track of swabs, instruments and other items during surgery. The task requires sustained attention while multiple tasks are handled, and in emergency situations the cognitive workload can increase dramatically, leading to human error. How do nurses allocate attention in such situations? And how can applied cognitive psychology reduce this type of medical error?

A study by Koh et al. (2011) examined the relationship between experience and visual attention in 10 experienced and 10 novice scrub nurses working in an obstetrics theatre. These participants wore a mobile eye tracker during caesarean section surgeries. Four areas of interest were established: the operation site itself; the patient's lower body; the surgical tray placed near the patient's lower body; and the main instrument trolley, which was located to the side of the surgical tray, away from the patient. The eye tracker recorded the focus of visual attention and scanning patterns in each of these areas of interest throughout the surgical procedure, from initial incision to dressing. A detailed analysis of the counts (of swabs, instruments, etc.) was conducted, with frequency of counts, duration of counts, number of interruptions during counts, and the stage in the surgery noted.

The eye tracking data showed that the more experienced nurses directed their visual attention considerably more to the incision area than the novice group. This suggests that they would be better prepared to anticipate the surgeon's needs as the surgery progressed, for example, reacting to a request for a surgical instrument. The nurses performed an average of seven counts per surgery, spending on average 9 per cent of their time counting, and they were interrupted, on average, on two occasions during their counts. The experienced nurses had fewer interruptions, and in particular did not allow interruptions other than from the surgeon, again suggesting an ability to prioritize the surgeon's needs. The experienced nurses also showed fewer attention switches during their counting tasks and required less time for their final count. The study highlights the key role of experience in counting fluency and efficiency, and suggests that training nurses on the optimal patterns of attentional focus, and threats to that focus, may be effective in reducing errors.

THIS BOOK

This textbook examines aspects of how representations are formed, retained and used and includes topics such as perception and attention (Chapters 2 and 3), short-term (Chapter 4) and long-term memory (Chapter 5), learning and forgetting (Chapter 6), knowledge and imagery (Chapter 7), complex motor skills (Chapter 8), problem solving (Chapter 9), decision making (Chapter 10), reasoning (Chapter 11), language understanding and production (Chapters 12 and 13) and emotional cognition (Chapter 14). To sum up: this book is about the systematic, scientific study of the cognitive processes that handle mental representations.

The order of topics in this book reflects the flow of information through the mind. Information is taken in through perceiving what is attended to, and is stored initially in short-term or working memory. Then selected items are retained in long-term memory through learning processes and form knowledge that can be represented in a variety of ways. Later, stored information may be retrieved if it has been retained, or it may turn out to have been forgotten. Perceived and recalled information shapes skilled actions on the environment and enters into problem solving, reasoning and decision processes. Information can be shared with others via language and frequently involves an emotional aspect.

As will become apparent, cognitive psychology is relatively young as a scientific endeavour. There is not always agreement on how each process should be understood or what methods of investigation are best. This is in the nature of a developing science and we hope that the bases for assessing explanations, in terms of clarity, logic and evidence, will emerge and become clear as we progress through the chapters.

In the remainder of this introductory chapter we will set out briefly the historical context for the discipline. Today's cognitive psychology deals with questions that have surely been raised since before written history began, when people first began to wonder about questions such as: why do we sometimes remember things very clearly and sometimes not?; why do we remember faces better than names?; why do we find some decisions and problems easy and others hard?; why do our senses sometimes deceive us? (e.g. when we fall for visual illusions; see Box 1.2).

First, we will review the main historical approaches, which are those of the eighteenth century associationist philosophers, the nineteenth century introspectionists, the early twentieth century behaviourists and the still dominant mid-twentieth and early twenty-first century information processing theorists. Finally, in this chapter, we also introduce the increasingly prominent neuroscientific approach to understanding cognition.

Box 1.2 Practical Application: How magicians manipulate cognition

A skilled magician has a sophisticated understanding of human cognitive functioning and its limits. Macknik et al. (2008), in a review of the neuroscientific basis of magicians' techniques, note that: 'Insofar as the understanding of behaviour and perception goes, there are specific cases in which the magician's intuitive knowledge is superior to that of the neuroscientist' (p. 871). Throughout its long history, magic has relied on the magician's ability to identify and manipulate the limits of human memory, perception and attention. Among other devices, magicians make use of visual and cognitive illusions to achieve their aims.

A visual illusion occurs when the subjective experience of a visual stimulus differs from physical reality. In the Spoon Bending Illusion, for example, the magician, using 'only the power of the mind', seems to bend a spoon by shaking it or rubbing the metal near the neck of the spoon. The spoon is held horizontally and shaken up and down; it appears pliant, as if had turned into rubber. This classic magic trick relies on differential responding of motion detecting neurons in the visual system, giving rise to the illusion of flexibility (Macknik et al., 2008).

A second magicians' trick makes use of misdirection, which involves drawing the spectator's attention away from an action. In the Vanishing Ball Illusion, a ball thrown upwards seems to vanish midair. In setting up this trick, the magician throws a ball into the air and catches it several times before pretending to throw the ball. Most spectators will think they have seen the ball being thrown, when in fact it remained in the magician's hand (see Macknik et al., 2008). Timing of gaze changes plays an important role in detecting the trick (Kuhn et al., 2008).

Verbal suggestion can also be used to trick the mind. An example is provided by Wiseman and Greening (2005). They showed participants a video clip of a 'psychic' performer picking up a key and apparently bending it using his psychokinetic powers. The key was then placed on a table in front of him, and shown in close up for 60 seconds. Some participants heard the performer say that the key was continuing to bend, while participants in a control condition heard no such comment. Participants who heard the performer's commentary were significantly more likely to agree with the statement 'After the key was placed on the table, it continued to bend' with approximately 40 per cent of participants in that condition agreeing, compared to 5 per cent of control participants. In this case, it would seem that the verbal suggestion alone was enough to give rise to the misperception.

Magic acts demonstrate how the cognitive system can be fooled and highlight some of the natural vulnerabilities within the perceptual, memory and higher cognitive processes. These processes, and vulnerabilities, will be examined over subsequent chapters.

HISTORY AND APPROACHES

Wondering about cognition leads to theorizing about the processes involved, and such theorizing started at least as far back as the Greek philosophers, Plato and Aristotle, over two and a half thousand years ago (Murray, 1988). Plato compared memory for information to writing on a wax tablet, which if not rubbed smooth by time could be read off, as in recall. Forgetting was the equivalent of the wax tablet becoming illegible. Alternatively he suggested that memory was like an aviary in which the birds flying about correspond to specific memories and remembering was like catching a particular bird. Often we recall a memory which is nearly right, but not quite, just as we might grab a nearby bird but miss the target bird among a flock of birds flying in an aviary.

The ancient world was much concerned with the art of rhetoric (that is persuasive speaking) and during that time a very practical way of remembering long lists of facts or points to make in a speech was developed. This is known as the method of loci (or 'places) by which vivid images are formed linking the objects to be remembered to a sequence of familiar places such as rooms in your house. See Box 1.3 and Chapter 6 for more on mnemonics or methods of boosting memory. The method of loci and variations are still used today. For example, a student learning a timeline of scientific discoveries, might picture a path through their house from their front door to the bedroom, with a sequence of images recreating the list. The student might visualize planets revolving around the sun at the front door (Copernican Heliocentric Theory), then an apple falling from a tree on their stairs (Universal Law of Gravitation), and the familiar face of Albert Einstein at the top of the stairs. Intermediate events could then be added along the timeline. Other date-based lists, such as lists of prime ministers or laws, might be remembered in the same way. A similar method is used by competitors in memory contests. Journalist Joshua Foer's book *Moonwalking with Einstein* (2011) recounts how he trained from scratch to become a US Memory Champion in a contest which included remembering the order of playing cards in a number of merged packs after one exposure, and up to 500 random words in sequence. Some further examples are discussed in Box 1.3.

> **Mnemonic** is a learning device used to aid memory.

Box 1.3 Practical Application: How to train your memory

In modern life, much memory work is handled by external devices; we note family birthdays in a calendar; we store telephone numbers in our mobile phones; we record travel directions and routes in our satellite navigation systems. The use of such tools may lead us to underestimate the capabilities of our memories. In 2005, a science journalist named Joshua Foer visited the USA Memory Championship as part of his preparation for an article on 'savant memory'. He returned and won the championship a year later, setting a new record for the 'speed cards' event in the process, by memorizing the order of 52 cards in 1 minute and 40 seconds. Foer's year-long quest to develop his memory is charted in his 2011 book *Moonwalking with Einstein: The Art and Science of Remembering Everything*, and he recounts a number of techniques he used to expand his memory capabilities (for example, see Figure 1.1).

Figure 1.1   How to memorize names. To remember the name Edward Bedford (1), we might picture the man lying on a truck bed (2), or see him fording a river on a bed (3). Adding an image of Edward Scissorhands provides a link to the man's first name (4).

Source: Foer, J. (2011). Secrets of a mind-gamer. *New York Times*, 15 February 2011.

Many such mnemonic (or memory facilitating) techniques rely on the use of mental imagery and spatial memory. The method of loci, as described in the previous section, relies on associating a visual image with the object to be remembered, and placing these images in a familiar location or along a familiar route. Let's say, for example, that you want to remember 10 items on a shopping list. You visualize a familiar route, such as from your bedroom to the front door of your house, and you place each object on your list at a location along that path. So, you might 'see' a loaf of bread on your bed, a jar of coffee hanging on your bedroom door, an apple at the top of your stairs, and so on. Remembering the list then simply involves working your way along the route, mentally, and seeing what object is at each location. This method is also useful for remembering items in a particular order, such as lists of historical figures.

Another method, the keyword method, is used when learning foreign language (second language or L2) vocabulary and has been shown to be effective, albeit under some circumstances (see De Groot & Van Hell, 2005). The learner makes an association between the unfamiliar L2 word and a familiar word in the native language (L1) that sounds like the L2 word. For example, to remember the French word *église* (church), an English speaker might use the keyword 'egg', and then picture a church carved out of an egg to remember the English translation. The use of an interactive visual image underlies the mnemonic effect. Imagery can be a useful mnemonic device. For example, say you need to remember someone's name. If you are shown a photograph of a man and told his names is 'Baker', memory for that association is poorer than if you were told he is a 'baker'. The occupation 'baker' is embedded in a network of other associations in memory – bread, tall white hat, hot ovens – and provides a richer memory for retrieval. The name Baker on the other hand is linked only to the photograph, and does not carry such a rich network of associations. Mnemonists make use of this paradox, using imagery to make names more memorable (see Figure 1.1).

Another system, called the phonetic number system or major system, which is commonly used by memory experts, increases memory capacity for numbers. This system converts numbers into consonant sounds, which can then be made into words, and potentially viewed as mental images. Long digit strings can be remembered in this way. For example, the number 2 converts to the /n/ sound, because the letter n has two downstrokes. The number 3 converts to an /m/ sound on the same basis. The number 0 is a /z/ sound, for zero, and so on. (The convention of placing a letter between slash marks, as in /n/, denotes a speech sound.) This system can be used to aid memory for PIN numbers or passcodes consisting of digit sequences. (See also Chapter 5 for more on mnemonics for passcodes.)

The use of spatial learning strategies seems to be of particular importance for such techniques. Maguire et al. (2003) using neuropsychological tests and brain imaging, tested eight memory experts who had been placed highly at the World Memory Championships. They found that their superior memory did not seem to be related to superior intellect or structural differences in the brain; rather, the participants' use of a spatial learning strategy seemed to underlie their memory advantage. Such studies highlight the role of learning and experience, as opposed to innate abilities, in superior memory.

Mnemonic techniques such as those described above allow us to create associations between unrelated pieces of information (such as items on your shopping list, or strings of digits) but, as Ericsson (2003) notes, they are less likely to help us complete meaningful and task specific memory tasks, and correspondingly World Memory champions do not show superior performance on everyday memory tasks. Despite superior memory for vast sequences of playing cards or number strings, they may still forget their mother's birthday or forget where they have left their keys.

Turning from the ancients to a more recent period, from the seventeenth until the early nineteenth century the dominant approach to cognition was that of associationism, which we will now outline.

ASSOCIATIONISM

Empiricist philosophers, such as John Locke, David Hume and John Stuart Mill, held that all knowledge came from experience and that ideas and memories were linked by associations. Locke (1690) for instance, pointed out that two unrelated ideas could become associated if they often were actively considered close together in time. So, if a bell is always followed by dinner, soon the idea of 'bell' will tend to arouse the idea of 'dinner'. Closeness (proximity) in space as well as in time fosters associations also. Thus, roof and chimney tend to be found close together and those ideas would become associated. Relationships of similarity will also cause associations to be formed. By that route, cup and mug will tend to be associated as they are very similar objects in general shape and function.

> Empiricism is the philosophical school which holds that all knowledge comes from experience. Association is a linkage between mental contents such that activation of one content activates linked content e.g. table → chair

Locke, Hume and the other Associationists relied on their own intuitions and introspections to guide their theorizing and did no experiments on others; the use of experiments had to wait until 1879 with the founding of the first psychology laboratory by Wilhelm Wundt in Leipzig, Germany. Wundt was the leading proponent of the introspectionist approach, which we turn to next.

INTROSPECTIONISM

Wundt and his associates in the second half of the nineteenth century focused on the nature of conscious experience and sought to break down complex experiences into elementary sensations. The approach might be described as a form of 'mental chemistry'. Just as chemists in the nineteenth century were analysing compounds into chemical elements, Wundt tried to analyse normal perceptions (e.g. of a table) into simpler sensations (brownness, straight lines, textures) which combined to give the perception.

The method favoured was 'Classical Introspection' (or 'Self-Observation') in which specially trained participants gave a verbal account of their sensations in terms of *mode* (visual, auditory, tactile etc.), *quality* (colour, shape, texture, etc.), *intensity, duration* and *feeling* (positive, negative, relaxed, tense). Introspective reports were generally backed up by reaction times or other behavioural measures.

The method was of limited application as extensive training was required (c. 10,000 trials were judged just sufficient to master the technique) and clearly could not be used by some groups of interest, including children, and people with reduced capacity or mental illness. It could not be applied to study cognition in non-human animals. So, data could only be gathered on a very limited population. Introspection could only be applied to some mental processes. It is reasonable to assume that a trained observer might be able to recount something useful regarding his or her problem solving progress. But it is unlikely that an account of how he or she perceives visual illusions could be generated. Introspectionism was also problematic because the process of introspection might well confound the cognitive process of interest. If you are engaged in a mathematics problem, and you are required to give an account of your progress in solving the problem, does its additional cognitive demand alter the nature of processing of the primary task (i.e. solving a maths problem). It may well do so.

In addition, differences in results between laboratories were difficult to resolve. For example, Wundt's pupil Edward Titchener, at Cornell, reported that faint imagery was always present in verbal tasks such as in answering general knowledge questions (e.g. 'What is the capital of France?'), while Wundt's laboratory supported the existence of thought without images (Miller, 1960).

BEHAVIOURISM

Partly in reaction to the drawbacks and limitations of introspectionism, James Watson (1913), Edward Thorndike (1898) and others, mainly in the USA, developed the Behaviourist approach. This approach abandoned the attempt to look inside the mind and took only observable behaviour and stimuli as its data. This approach essentially aimed to be a psychology without reference to internal cognitive processes. The focus was on learning and particularly about how behavioural responses could be predicted from knowing the history of rewards and punishments following behaviour in response to particular stimuli. Much of the research in this tradition was carried out with animals, particularly the laboratory rat and pigeon, as it was assumed that learning processes were the same in animals and humans.

Watson (1913, p. 158) stated the behaviourist manifesto very starkly as follows: 'Psychology as the behaviorist views it is a purely objective natural science. Its theoretical goal is the prediction and control of behavior. Introspection forms no essential part of its methods, nor is the scientific value of its data dependent on the readiness with which they lend themselves to interpretation in terms of consciousness. The behaviorist, in his efforts to get a unitary scheme of animal response, recognizes no dividing line between man and brute. The behavior of man, with all its refinement and complexity, forms only a part of the behaviorist's total scheme of investigation.'

Watson proposed that all apparently mental phenomena could be traced to behavioural activity. So, for example, he argued that 'thinking' was actually slight movements of muscles in the tongue and larynx (see Box 1.4). Interestingly, this idea has been partially revived in recent 'embodied' approaches to mental representation (Barsalou, 2008) which include motor areas of the brain as involved even in abstract concepts (see Chapters 2, 7 and 8 for more on embodied approaches). Continuing in the behavioural tradition, Watson's work was expanded on by B.F. Skinner, who brought to the fore the importance of consequences (that is, rewards or punishments) for behaviour (e.g. Skinner, 1938).

Box 1.4 Research Close Up: The curare experiment

Source: Smith, S. M., Brown, H. O., Toman, J. E. P., & Goodman, L. S. (1947). The lack of cerebral effects of D-tubocurarine chloride. *Anesthesiology*, *8*, 1–14.

INTRODUCTION

For Watson (e.g. 1913), thinking was no more than inner speech, a sub-vocal type of speaking whereby muscles moved as they would in speech but with no sound being emitted. For Watson, thinking depended crucially on articulation. Thus thinking was behaviour. However, an unusual experiment by Smith et al. (1947) showed that this was not the case. Smith et al. (1947) set out to examine the cerebral effects of curare, a plant-derived poison that had been used for centuries by Amazonian tribes when hunting. The poison was rubbed on arrow tips and known as 'flying death', because once it entered the blood stream of the prey, death was inevitable. The poison worked by paralysing the skeletal muscles; a bird struck by the arrow would fall to the ground dead. A land animal would become immobile and death would follow from suffocation because the breathing muscles would no longer be effective. The meat could be safely eaten: curare was only poisonous if it entered through the skin, it was harmless if eaten in small quantities.

When curare was brought to Europe, it attracted the attention of the medical profession and, in particular the burgeoning field of anaesthesia. In the early 1900s curare was used for a number of purposes, but its precise effects on the central nervous system remained unclear. In 1946, a 34-year-old anaesthesiologist named Scott M. Smith set out to investigate its effects, volunteering himself as subject for the experiment. Smith and his team set out to establish the effects of curare on the sensation of pain and on consciousness (see Altman, 1998).

METHOD AND RESULTS

A detailed account of the procedure is provided in Smith et al. (1947). The experiment took place on 10 January 1946. At 2pm in the afternoon, Smith was prepared for the experiment and basic observations such as pulse and blood pressure were taken. Eleven minutes later, curare, in the form of D-tubocurarine chloride was administered, at a dose two and a half times that normally required to induce complete muscle paralysis. Over the next 15 minutes, Smith reported feeling 'a little bit dizzy and quite a glow' (p. 4)! His jaw muscles became weak and he had difficulty speaking, swallowing and keeping his eyes open. By 2.20pm, he could not speak. He could hear, however, and could nod his head in answer to questions. A breathing bag was used to aid respiration. By 2.24pm, he could no longer move his head or open his eyes, but he could still indicate that he understood questions by wrinkling his forehead. He could also signal that he felt pain, heat and cold. By 2.32pm, slight movement was possible only in the left eyebrow. By 2.45pm that movement was gone. Artificial respiration was applied. Smith et al.'s report notes that the 'subject stated on recovery he was "clear as a bell" all this period' (p. 6). An antidote was applied and Smith began to recover. By 6pm he was almost back to normal, with some remaining weakness lasting throughout the evening.

DISCUSSION

If thought is inner speech and if inner speech relies on some form of the movements made during speech, then Smith should not have been capable of thinking when the muscles were completely and utterly paralyzed. However, this is not what happened. Even when Smith could not communicate at all, thinking, inner speech, continued as normal, as the report notes (p. 7):

> various statements were made, questions asked, stimuli presented, objects placed in the line of gaze and so forth, on which the subject was requested to report when speech returned. In each instance the report was accurate in all details and properly oriented as to temporal sequence.

Smith's experiment showed that curare did not reduce the sensation of pain or affect consciousness and so it could not be used alone as an anaesthetic. But this study also contributed to cognitive psychology by showing that movement of the speech muscles is not necessary for inner speech or thought. Such findings suggested that psychology needed an alternative to the behaviourist approach to thinking. However, Watson may not have been altogether wrong. A recent study by Oppenheim and Dell (2010), for example, showed that inner speech differs when it is articulated compared to when it is not, and so while inner speech *can* occur without any movement of the speech musculature, it is not entirely independent of the movements that would be used if that thought were uttered.

Other behaviourists, such as Tolman, were less extreme than Watson on the status of mental activity and allowed that rats and other animals could be usefully seen as having goals and mental representations or mental maps that aided in learning the layout of mazes containing food rewards (see Box 1.5).

Mental maps are mental representations of a spatial layout.

BOX 1.5 Research Close Up: Cognitive maps

Source: Tolman E. C. (1948). Cognitive maps in animals and man. *Psychological Review, 55*, 189–208.

INTRODUCTION

Although the behaviourist approach had many successes in accounting for basic animal learning, some studies raised the possibility that animals could be usefully seen as having goals and using some form of mental representations or 'mental maps'. Edward C. Tolman made a significant contribution to our understanding of learning and motivation by showing that learning could occur in the absence of an obvious source of reinforcement, supporting the notion of a 'cognitive map' or abstract mental representation underlying performance. Tolman's studies involved maze-running in rats.

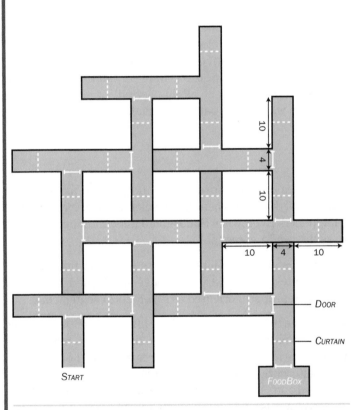

Figure 1.2   Tolman's 14 unit T maze. The 14 unit alley maze used by Tolman contains a number of T junctions leading to true path segments or blind alleys which the rat must navigate in order to find the food.

Source: Tolman E. C. (1948). Cognitive maps in animals and man. *Psychological Review, 55*, 189–208. APA; reprinted with permission

METHOD AND RESULTS

In one set of studies, three groups of rats were exposed to a maze task once a day for 22 days. The maze was a 14-unit T maze (see Figure 1.2). The food-deprived rats had to run from the starting unit to the end unit, where, in some cases, a food reward was waiting. Rats in Group A found a food reward when they got to the end of the maze each day. This group quickly learned the location of the food, and the number of errors (wrong turns) made decreased steadily over the duration of the experiment. Group B rats were placed in the maze but they received no food reward. This group showed relatively little change in the number of 'errors' made for the duration of the experiment. Group C received no reward for the first 10 days, but on Day 11, food was placed at the end of the maze. Rats in this group performed similarly to Group B for the first ten days, but they showed a sudden decrease in errors once the food reward was introduced. Group C's errors dropped quickly such that their performance matched that of Group A, who had received the food reward all along (see Figure 1.3).

DISCUSSION

These data suggested that learning had occurred in Group C, but that this learning was not apparent until the food reward was provided. The term latent learning is used to describe a situation where learning occurs but is not immediately demonstrated in performance. The fact that learning had occurred only became evident when the reward was introduced. Of course, reinforcement may still be involved, as something is motivating the rat to explore the maze, even in the absence of the food reward. As Cole

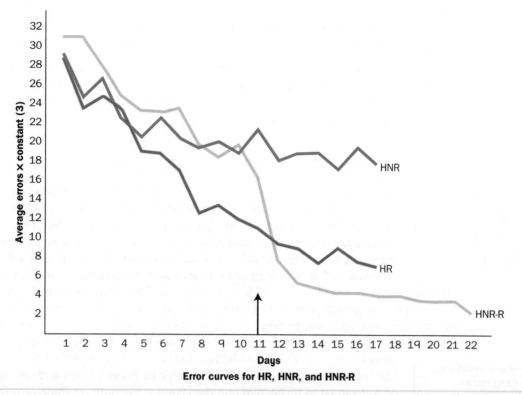

Figure 1.3 Error curves for Group A (HR: Hungry, reward), Group B (HNR: Hungry, no reward), Group C (HNR-R: Hungry, no reward until Day 11). The experiment used two control groups, a group that never found food in the maze (HNR) and a group that found food throughout (HR). The experimental group (HNR-R) found food on reaching the end of the maze from Day 11 on.

Source: Tolman E. C. (1948). Cognitive maps in animals and man. *Psychological Review*, 55, 189–208. APA; reprinted with permission

(1953) notes: 'The moral does not seem to be that learning takes place without any reinforcement, since there was reinforcement in the sense that some events regularly followed others even in the preliminary runs before food was brought in' (p. 337).

Although the behaviourist approach had many successes in accounting for basic animal learning, it was less applicable to complex mental phenomena such as reasoning, problem solving, decision making and language. To tackle these areas, an approach which stressed the role of internal mental representations and processes was required. The information processing approach, outlined next, fully met these requirements.

Tolman (1948) argued that an abstract mental representation of the maze had been acquired, a 'cognitive map', and that stimuli encountered by the rat 'are usually worked over and elaborated . . . into a tentative, cognitive-like map of the environment. And it is this tentative map, indicating routes and paths and environmental relationships, which finally determines what responses, if any, the animal will finally release' (p. 193).

Furthermore, the rats' behaviour in the maze is not limited to its initial responses. This was demonstrated effectively by D.A. Macfarlane (1930), who flooded his maze once the rats had learned the route to the food. If learning involves the acquisition of motor responses, then rats that had learned to run the maze should show a performance decrement when they are now required to swim the maze. Macfarlane showed that this was not the case; rats swam to the food instead of running to it. This supported the idea that the rat had acquired an abstract mental representation of some kind that was independent of the specific movements that allowed it to complete the maze (Rosenbaum, 2006).

Tolman's work predated the cognitive revolution by several decades, but shows how cognitive factors, and issues of mental representation, were already being considered within psychology, even if his findings were not entirely inconsistent with behavioural principles suggested by B.F. Skinner.

INFORMATION PROCESSING: THE COGNITIVE REVOLUTION

Information processing approach is a metaphor for understanding mental activity, based on computing.

The information processing approach, which brought mental representations back to centre stage, was inspired by the development of programmable digital computers that began to appear in the mid-1940s. It was quickly realized that computers could be programmed to carry out any kind of symbol manipulation that could be specified in detail. The obvious problems and procedures that computers could carry out were numerical, such as calculating trajectories of missiles or working out payrolls. More interestingly for cognitive psychology, computers could also be programmed to tackle non-numerical problems such as playing chess, suggesting medical diagnoses given symptoms and (although still not perfectly) automatic translation between natural languages. Computer programs to solve suitable problems could be seen as comparable to strategies

Strategies are systematic ways to carry out a cognitive task such as solving a problem.

that humans might use to solve the same problems. In both cases there are definite steps to be carried out, decisions to be made, storage of new information and retrieval of old information from memory. For example, to solve an anagram problem ('What word can be made from PECNOCT?') a human strategy might be to pick two letters as possible starting letters, then search long-term memory for words that have those two starting letters and check each retrieved word in turn, to see if it matches the letters in the anagram; when a complete match is found the problem is solved. A computer with a list of all English words stored in memory could be readily programmed to follow the same strategy (Answer: Concept). Thus, a well-specified theory or model for how people tackle some task or set of tasks could be expressed as a program.

Simulation involves programming computers to solve problems in a similar way to humans.
Artificial intelligence is the attempt to program computers to carry out complex tasks such as medical diagnosis, planning, using natural language.
Internal representations are mental representations of external objects and events.
Mental operations are inner actions manipulating mental representations.

A program which expresses a model of human thinking would be labelled a simulation program and should be distinguished from an artificial intelligence program which seeks to solve the problem as effectively as possible without any attempt at mimicking human strategies. Despite this distinction, many ideas developed in artificial intelligence research have been adopted in the information processing approach to human cognition (particularly in the area of problem solving, as we will see in Chapter 10).

The information processing approach has been dominant in cognitive psychology since the early 1960s and is still the major framework in the area. Theorists attempt to explain performance in cognitive tasks by using concepts of internal representations which are transformed by mental operations using both long-term and working (short-term) memories (see Chapters 4 & 5). The theories are usually stated in verbal terms or with the aid of 'box and arrow' diagrams that illustrate the flow of information and the kind of operations being carried out. The chapters that follow this one contain many examples of such theories or models. One example is Baddeley's analysis of short-term working memory into separate stores for phonological and visuo-spatial information in which information is preserved by rehearsal (e.g. Baddeley, 2007; see Chapter 4). This model has been explored and tested by experimental methods, for example by having participants perform tasks that load one or other memory system and observing the effects, rather than by computer simulation. This reflects a general fact that although the information processing approach was inspired by computers, most work in the field does not involve computer modelling but progresses through experimental testing of model predictions. At times, however, the approach might be accused of reducing cognition to information flow, whereas people process information, of enormous variety, in a complex and at times unpredictable environment. The field of human factors (see Box 1.6) developed from a need to consider more centrally the human element in information processing.

Box 1.6 Practical Application: Human factors and cognitive psychology

During the Second World War, interest in 'human factors' increased, as a number of technologies came into use that raised concerns about performance issues. The field of human factors is concerned with how human capacities and limitations influence performance when interacting with technology. A classic example is provided by radar operators.

Early radar involved what initially seemed to be a straightforward task of the type that might be explained by behaviourist accounts. The radar screen looked like a series of concentric disks, with a line sweeping across them corresponding to the direction of the radar antenna. As the line moved across the screen, dots or 'blips' representing objects detected by the radar would briefly appear and then disappear. The blips on the radar screen could be caused by objects in the environment (a mountain, or a flock of birds, for example) or by atmospheric or weather effects such as heavy rain, or they could signal the presence of an aircraft. The radar operator's task was to detect enemy aircraft and to alert the relevant authorities so that the plane could be intercepted. It quickly became clear that a number of factors influenced the accuracy of detection by the operator. First, the task is ambiguous. There is much 'noise', that is blips that do not represent enemy aircraft, and a signal may or may not appear in amongst that noise. Second, this task requires sustained attention and vigilance over a period of time, and we do not sustain attention well over time. Third, the operator was often alone and had to make an immediate and accurate decision without further information. Fourth, the stakes were high. Failure to detect a threat would allow enemy access, while a false alarm would waste time and resources chasing an enemy aircraft that did not exist. This was a stressful and difficult task to perform and yet it was also monotonous. It was clear that cognitive factors would have to be investigated if we were to understand how such a task might be performed reliably.

Table 1.1 shows the possible decisions the radar operator might make in the presence or in the absence of an enemy signal. The operator is correct if he or she correctly detects an enemy aircraft when there is one (1), or does not react to a blip that is actually innocuous (2). There are two types of error: (3) failure to detect an enemy signal, and (4) thinking there is an enemy presence when there is not, that is, a false alarm. While at face value the task may seem to be a simple one with a response that is either 'yes' or 'no', in fact, the information feeding into the decision may be ambiguous or incomplete and different factors affect which of the two types of errors might be made. Examining hit rate alone will not give a full picture of performance. This approach has been influential when considering decision making in real-life situations, which usually brings conditions of uncertainty.

Table 1.1 Signal detection in the radar task

		Signal: Is an enemy aircraft present?	
		Yes	No
Decision: Is the dot an enemy aircraft?	Yes	1. Hit	4. False alarm
	No	3. Miss	2. Correct rejection

Table 1.1 summarizes an approach known as signal detection theory, which adds a cognitive dimension to the question of how we detect a signal, such as a noise, or a visual cue. Signal detection theory is a mathematical theory of decision making in conditions of noise, separating perceptual sensitivity from response bias.

There are many contexts in which people have to make important decisions under conditions of uncertainty and cognitive psychology is helping us understand how these tasks can best be performed: the radiologist examining a mammogram for breast cancer; the lifeguard watching a crowded seafront; the intensive care nurse monitoring patients for prodromal symptoms; the long distance lorry driver watching lights on the road ahead. Cognitive psychology can help us understand how reliable performance of these and many other, tasks, might be supported.

Although, as we shall see in later chapters, most work in cognitive psychology does not involve computer modelling, information processing modelling often made use of computer models. For example, initially, the main examples of progress in the field involved simulation models such as Newell et al.'s (1958) General Problem Solver, which could tackle problems such as logic tasks and simple games, in ways similar to humans, by breaking them down into goals and sub-goals. A more recent example is that of Anderson's ACT-R model (2004) which can be applied to a wide range of laboratory tasks in memory and problem solving (see Chapter 10's discussion of the Tower of Hanoi). ACT-R is built up from simple IF-THEN rules that check a working memory to see if their condition is met, in which case they fire and replace the contents of working memory. For example, 'IF goal is to solve anagram, THEN pick two letters from anagram and place in working memory'; 'IF goal is to solve anagram AND 2 letters in working memory, THEN retrieve word from long-term memory that starts with the 2 letters'; and so on.

Connectionism is an approach to cognition in terms of networks of simple neuron-like units that pass activation and inhibition through receptor, hidden and output units.
Backwards propagation is a way of modifying weights on the links between units in a connectionist network, in response to errors, to obtain the desired output.

An alternative style of Information Processing modelling that can be explored through simulation is known as connectionism (Rumelhart & McClelland, 1986). Connectionist models simulate basic learning and perceptual phenomena by means of a large network of simple units organized into input, output and internal (also known as 'hidden') units. The units are connected by excitatory or inhibitory links of varying strengths through which activation flows. Link strengths are modified through learning rules such as backwards propagation. These models are arguably more 'brain like' and utilize parallel distributed processing rather than the strictly serial processing of traditional symbolic models. However, although brain like, the units in such models are much simpler in their properties and functioning than the real neural units or neurons that constitute the brain (Figure 1.4) and so the similarity of a connectionist network to real neural networks is limited.

The basic components of a connectionist network are:

- a set of processing units;
- weighted connections between units;
- a learning strategy.

The processing units can be input, output or hidden units (between input and output). The network's architecture is determined by the way in which the units are connected. In a feedforward network, input units are connected to output units such that information flows in one direction

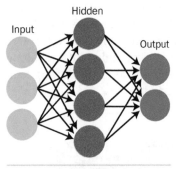

Figure 1.4   A connectionist network. A simple three-layer feedforward connectionist network showing input, hidden and output layers and the connections between them.

from input to hidden to output layers (see Figure 1.4 for example). In a recurrent network, some of the connections feed back to earlier layers. For example, some of the output units might send information back to the input layer, in order to take account of the previous output when processing the next input. Input units take in information as an input pattern from outside the network or from other parts of the network. Hidden units communicate with input and output units but are cut off from the external environment. They do the computational work of the network and pass activation to the output units. The output units produce the response that can be characterized as the 'behaviour' of the network.

All units have some level of activity, denoted by their activation value. This determines how much activation or output a unit passes onto connected units. Often, activation values are expressed in the range from 0 to +1, where 0 is 'off' and +1 is 'on'. Units affect each other by excitation or inhibition, that is a unit can act to cause a neighbouring unit to 'fire' or it can act to subdue the neighbouring unit's activation so that it is less likely to fire.

The functional level of analysis

Overall, the information processing approach can be said to focus on our 'mental software'. It asks 'What strategies are followed in processing information? How is information encoded during perception, stored in memory during learning and retrieved by remembering for further processing in thinking?' Essentially, these questions are about *functions* and *functional properties* and can be answered without referring to any underlying hardware, just as we can describe a computer program in terms of its processing steps without needing to say anything about the computer hardware that the programs run on. Some cognitive theorists are indifferent to the hardware of the brain, in which human strategies are executed, saying that, for them, the brain may as well be made of porridge – which is an interesting choice of word, as the English word 'brain' seems likely to be derived from the same root as 'bran', which the brain resembles in appearance (Liberman, 2009)! On the functionalist view, the nature of the brain and the details of underlying neural processes are of no concern for analyses at the cognitive level (Turing, 1950). Fodor (1999), for example, has an entertaining paper entitled 'Let your brain alone', in which he argues against the relevance of brain science for psychology and writes, 'If the mind happens in space at all, it happens somewhere north of the neck. What exactly turns on knowing how far north?'

However, despite such scepticism among functionalists (see also Page, 2006), there has been a growing trend within cognitive psychology that pays attention to the findings of neuroscience and considers the underlying brain hardware that allows cognition. We will now outline and discuss some key aspects of neuroscience being considered by cognitive psychologists.

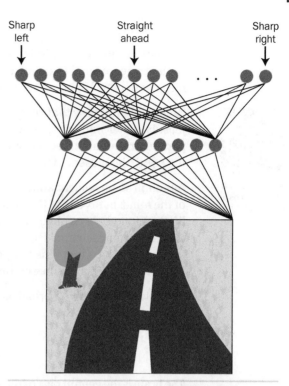

Figure 1.5   A connectionist network for navigation. An example of a simple three-layer feedforward connectionist network showing input, hidden and output layers and the connections between them. In this example, input is in the form of a visual scene presented to the input units. The network learns to steer left, right or straight ahead, over a series of trials.

Source: Pomerleau, D. A. (1990). Neural network based autonomous navigation. In C. Thorpe (ed.), *Vision and navigation: The CMU Navlab*, pp. 83–92. Kluwer Press.

COGNITIVE NEUROSCIENCE

The notion that the brain is the source of mental activities and experience is a very ancient one. Around two and a half thousand years ago, the Greek thinker and pioneer medical doctor, Hippocrates, gave this idea a very clear statement:

Scan to watch the video "Neuroscience meets magic"

'Men ought to know that from the brain, and from the brain alone, arises our pleasures, joys, laughter and jests, as well as our sorrows, pains, griefs and tears. Through it, in particular, we think, see, hear, and distinguish the ugly from the beautiful, the bad from the good, the pleasant from the unpleasant.'

Although some ancient authorities, such as Aristotle, argued against the brain as the seat of the mind, in favour of the heart, the basic notion that the brain is necessary for mental life has long been widely accepted. As Francis Crick (1994, p. 3) put it more recently in terms reminiscent of Hippocrates: 'You, your joys and sorrows, your memories and your ambitions, your sense of personal identity and free will, are in fact no more than the behaviour of a vast assembly of nerve cells and their associated molecules.'

We will now try to give a broad picture of the brain before discussing particular approaches and methods.

BRAIN BASICS

The brain is the central part of the body's nervous system; the peripheral parts of the nervous system feed sensory information from external and internal sources into the brain which in turn sends motor signals to the muscles in order to cause actions, from walking to talking.

Corpus callosum is the thick band of nerve fibres that connects the left and right cerebral hemispheres.

If the brain is removed from the skull it does indeed look rather porridge-like, as has often been remarked. However, unlike a bowl of porridge, it is actually highly structured into distinct parts and subparts. At a very broad level, it is clearly divided into left and right hemispheres (connected by the corpus callosum). As you can see in Figure 1.6, four main sections (lobes)

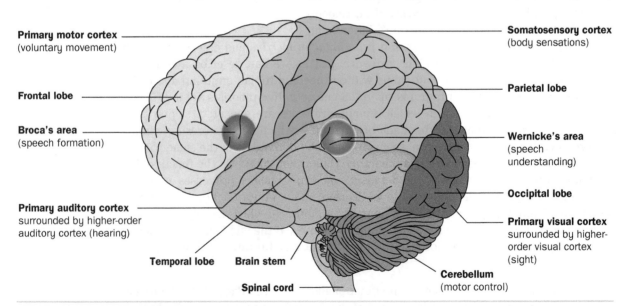

Primary motor cortex (voluntary movement)

Frontal lobe

Broca's area (speech formation)

Primary auditory cortex surrounded by higher-order auditory cortex (hearing)

Temporal lobe   Brain stem

Spinal cord

Somatosensory cortex (body sensations)

Parietal lobe

Wernicke's area (speech understanding)

Occipital lobe

Primary visual cortex surrounded by higher-order visual cortex (sight)

Cerebellum (motor control)

Figure 1.6 **Lobes of the brain.** The four lobes of the brain are shown along with some key areas for vision, hearing, language and motor function. The frontal lobes are shown in blue, temporal in orange, occipital in purple and parietal in green.

Source: Adapted from Holt, N. et al. (2012). *Psychology: The science of mind and behaviour*. McGraw-Hill Education.

are apparent in the outer layer (the cerebral cortex) in both hemispheres: the frontal lobes, the parietal lobes, the occipital lobes and the temporal lobes.

Deeper inside the brain are distinct structures such as the *thalamus* (from Greek: inner room), *hippocampus* (from Greek: seahorse) and *amygdala* (from Latin and Greek: almond). At the base of the brain is the *cerebellum* (from Latin: little brain) that is important in movement control. The names reflect the shapes of the structures (see Figure 1.7).

Finally, the following terms are often used to indicate locations in the brain: *Dorsal* meaning towards the top (Latin: back); *Ventral* meaning towards the bottom (Latin: belly); *Anterior* meaning towards the front (Latin: before); *Posterior* meaning towards the back (Latin: coming after); *Lateral* meaning at the side (Latin: a side) and *Medial* meaning in the middle (Latin: middle).

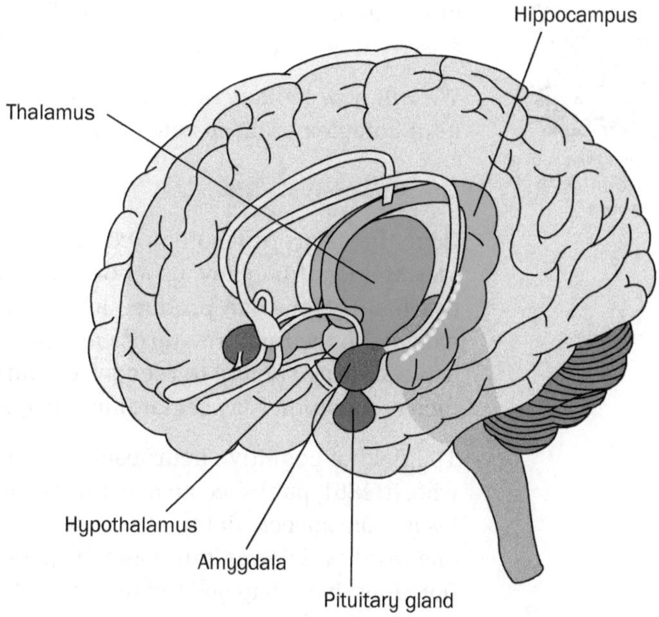

All these structures in the brain are composed of the same building blocks, that is, the neurons. These are specialized cells that exchange information by transmitting electrical impulses. Neurons are somewhat varied but typically have a soma or cell body, dendrites which receive signals, and an axon which transmits signals to other neurons by chemical transmission across synaptic gaps (see Figure 1.8 for a typical neuron structure).

Neurons are the basic units of the nervous system, principally consisting of a cell, axon and dendrites.

Figure 1.7 Key sub-cortical structures of the human brain. The thalamus, hypothalamus, amygdala and hippocampus are shown.

Source: Adapted from Holt, N. et al. (2012). *Psychology: The science of mind and behaviour*. McGraw-Hill Education.

The human brain is a fantastically complex structure composed of approximately one billion neurons each of which may connect with up to ten thousand other neurons. Thus the theoretical number of possible patterns of connections is of the order of ten trillion different patterns. This huge number of possible patterns of connections underlies the

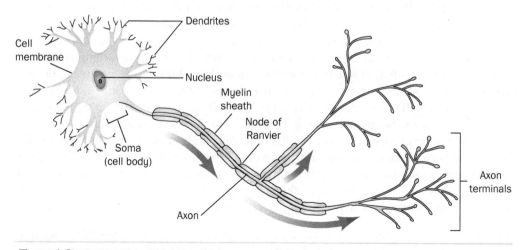

Figure 1.8 Schematic outline of a neuron.

Source: Holt, N. et al. (2012) *Psychology: The science of mind and behaviour*. McGraw-Hill Education.

Scan to watch of a video on a map of the brain

brain's ability to encode an essentially indefinite range of knowledge. The question then arises – how can we possibly understand such a complex system as our own brains?

We will now look at two main approaches to gaining some understanding of how the ultra-complex brain system generates cognitive activity.

Cognitive neuropsychology

Cognitive neuropsychology examines the effects of brain damage on behaviour, with a view to identifying how psychological functions are organized. Brain damage confined to small regions can produce informative breakdowns in performance; for example, damage to the fusiform gyrus can lead to loss of ability to recognize familiar faces but leave a normal ability to recognize familiar objects (Grüter et al., 2008) suggesting that face recognition is a special function distinct from general object recognition.

The field of cognitive neuropsychology can be traced back to the work of Paul Broca, who, in 1861, published an account of a 51-year-old patient called Leborgne who had lost his normal speech ability after a stroke many years before and was left able to say just one word, which was 'tan'. Only the patient's speech was affected and all other cognitive functions, including understanding spoken language, were unaffected. At a post-mortem examination, 30 years after the stroke, Broca found that there was a small area of damage or lesion in the inferior part of the left frontal gyrus. This region, now named Broca's area, is vital for speech production (see Figure 1.6, and Chapter 12 for more detail).

Broca's area is an area located in the left temporal lobe, damage to which is associated with aphasia (speech deficits).
Localization is the view that specific mental functions are tied to specific brain areas; this also appears as the modularity hypothesis and may be contrasted with the distributed view, that functions are realized by joint action of many areas.
Neuropsychology is the study of psychological effects of brain damage and disease.
Phrenology was an early form of localization that attempted unsuccessfully to link psychological functions to bumps in the skull taken to reflect growth of brain in specific areas.

Since Broca's finding it has become well established that in 90 per cent of right-handed people, and in the majority of left-handed people, language functions are strongly localized in the left hemisphere.

Broca's study exemplifies the basic ideas of neuropsychology which are that most, if not all functions, are linked closely to the healthy working of specific brain areas and that impairments following localized damage can indicate which areas are important for which functions and be informative about how broad functions are organized into narrower functions. Thus, Broca's patient showed that the broad language function could be split into spoken language production and language perception as separate abilities (because the patient could understand speech but could not himself speak). The notion of localization had been developed earlier by Gall and the phrenological school which tried to tie a host of very complex functions, such as 'prudence', 'acquisitiveness', 'destructiveness', 'sense of justice' and so on, to particular underlying brain areas. Phrenologists, such as Gall, sought to infer from bumps in the skull how well developed the underlying brain areas had become, and suggested for example, that a large bump just above the right ear indicated destructive tendencies. Although the detailed project of phrenology failed, in that skull bumps were not in fact linked to the complex functions as hypothesized, the notion of localization of function has persisted strongly. In recent times, the idea has become labelled as 'modularity' (Barret & Kurzban, 2006; Fodor, 1983). The notion of modularity proposes that cognition involves a large number of independent processing units that work separately from each other and apply to fairly narrow domains (e.g. face processing; shape perception; perceiving word meanings; speech generation and so on).

The opposite perspective to modularity is that mental functions, especially complex functions, are not localized but are distributed through the brain. On this view, impairments of mental functions due to brain damage depend on the quantity of tissue destroyed (Law of Mass Action, Lashley, 1929) and not on the specific site of the damage.

Experimental studies on the effects on animal learning of the amount of brain tissue removed lent support to the distributed, or Mass Action, hypothesis (Lashley, 1929). Interestingly, the famous case of Phineas Gage (Harlow, 1868) who suffered the passage through his left frontal lobe of a metre long, three and a half pounds weighted iron bar, in an explosive industrial accident, was initially taken to support mass action, as he showed no intellectual impairments. However, the personality changes in Gage that became evident over time, from a conscientious careful railroad worker, to an impulsive individual who lacked perseverance, were later interpreted as indicating localization of executive, controlling functions in the frontal lobes. (For more on the Gage case, see Chapter 14.)

Overall, human cognitive neuropsychology has found the localization assumption useful in interpreting effects of brain damage, and the general notion of localization underlies much neuropsychological research.

Of particular interest for neuropsychology are cases of double dissociation in which patients can be found with opposite patterns of impairment in two functions. For example, one case may have impaired short-term memory but normal long-term memory and another may have the opposite pattern. This would suggest that long- and short-term memory are indeed separate functions and not just aspects of a unitary single memory system. Simple dissociations where patients show an impairment in one function but not in other functions can also be informative, particularly regarding localization (this was the position with Broca's famous case, discussed above).

> Double dissociation of function arises when, following brain injury, some people do well on one Task 'A' and poorly on a second Task 'B' while others with different brain injuries show the opposite pattern. Then the two tasks are said to be doubly dissociated.

Recently neuropsychology has benefited from the development of imaging or scanning techniques which enable researchers to see and accurately measure the location and extent of damage in living patients (rather than having to rely on information gleaned at autopsy). We will now outline some of the main imaging methods.

Brain imaging

Broadly there are two main categories of brain scanning or imaging. These are (1) structural imaging, which shows the static anatomy of the brain and (2) functional imaging which represents brain activity over time.

Over recent years a number of structural imaging methods have been developed such as X-ray computed tomography and computerized axial tomography (CAT) scans which require highly focused X-ray beams to be passed through the body. Magnetic resonance imaging (MRI) is the dominant method currently and provides high-resolution anatomical images. This technique does not involve possibly damaging radiation but uses radio waves and a strong magnetic field which surrounds the person being scanned as he or she lies in a narrow tunnel like apparatus.

Turning to functional methods, electroencephalography (EEG) and event-related potentials (ERPs) give a record of function as a summary of electrical activity over a wide area of cortex, measured though sensors on the scalp. The resulting wave forms following particular stimuli are different, depending on factors such as how expected the stimulus was, and so the method is useful in assessing expectancy (and other) effects. For example,

> Structural imaging methods show brain anatomy.
> Functional imaging methods detect brain activity.
> Magnetic resonance imaging is a high-definition method for structural imaging using strong magnetic fields.
> Electroencephalography (EEG) is a functional brain imaging method showing waves of electrical activity from scalp recorders.
> Event-related potentials (ERPs) are a functional brain imaging method recording electrical activity during repeated stimulus presentations.

ambiguous words (e.g. 'bank') are presented and are then disambiguated as, for example, 'place money is kept' or 'side of a river'. If the disambiguation is expected from the context then the waveform will differ from when it is unexpected. The great advantage of EEG and ERP is that they are able to measure the electrical activity of the brain with the precision of milliseconds. However, sophisticated techniques are needed to be able to localize the part of the brain that is the source of the electrical activity and even then the precision is in the order of centimetres due to the fact that the skull and scalp effectively smear the original electrical signal.

Positron emission tomography (PET) is a functional imaging method which uses positron emissions from radioactive glucose to indicate areas of increased blood flow in the brain.

An early functional method that gives a more localized picture than does ERP or EEG is positron emission tomography (PET). This requires injection of a radioactive compound into the blood stream. The scans then measure the blood flow to different regions of the brain. Interpretation is based on the finding that when a brain area is active, more blood flows into it and thus there is increased chemical activity involving the radioactive compound. Interestingly, a nineteenth-century Italian physiologist, Angelo Mosso, first reported this fact, long ago, in the 1870s, from studies of patients whose skulls had been opened up by accidents, so that the cerebral arteries had been exposed to view and the increased blood flow could be seen, as it happened (Legrenzi & Umilta, 2011, p. 12). Although useful, PET scans only show activity averaged over about 90 seconds or longer, thus giving a very crude picture of the sequence of activity. This along with the need for an invasive injection of a radioactive material has discouraged the widespread use of PET for general experimental purposes.

Functional Magnetic Resonance Imaging (fMRI) is a method of imaging brain activity that uses oxygenation levels of blood flow and has good temporal and spatial resolution.

The currently favoured technique for functional imaging is functional Magnetic Resonance Imaging or fMRI. This method does not require injection of radioactive substances and measures the degree to which oxygen in the blood flow is depleted in many areas simultaneously. The more the activity, the more oxygen is taken from the blood by the neurons. What is measured in fMRI is known as the BOLD or blood-oxygen-level-dependent contrast signal. It can show effects over quite a short time scale (1–3 seconds) relative to what is possible with PET and in small areas (approximately 3 cubic mm) known as 'voxels'. (However, it should be noted that many cognitive processes as measured by reaction times, seem to take 300–400 milliseconds and so are much faster than the 1–3 seconds required for BOLD signal changes; and a single voxel contains hundreds of thousands of neurons, so the temporal and spatial resolution of fMRI is not yet as high as would be wished.)

Scan to watch a video comparing brain scan types of

In recent years results from fMRI brain scans have been frequently reported (or misreported, some would say!) in the media. In such reports, typically a brain outline is shown on which red blobs are superimposed reflecting areas of high activation and sometimes blue blobs to indicate de-activation. In newspapers, magazines and websites, we are told such blobs show centres for altruism, criminal tendencies, love, wisdom and religion, among many other complex functions (Vrecko, 2010), including according to one claim, actual true romantic love for iPhones (Lindstrom, 2011). An internet search with a key phrase such as 'Brain scans show. . . .' will yield many more examples for the curious reader. However, to really understand fMRI results, it is important to be aware of how these images arise. They are not simple snapshots of brain activity but rather are highly computed images based on many assumptions.

The images are frequently arrived at by a task subtraction method in which the brain activity of all the voxels in the control condition (measured by BOLD signal) are statistically compared to the brain activity in the corresponding voxels in the experimental condition. If the activity is greater in the experimental condition than the control condition then it is common to call this an 'activation'. Some of the complexity of dealing with fMRI data is shown in Figure 1.9, which shows the probability that a given brain voxel will be more active when a participant listens to a human voice than when they listen to other sounds (see also Chapter 2). While there is a relatively small region where the majority of listeners will show a difference in activation, this region is surrounded by an extensive area where some listeners will show a difference. Why there is this large region where some participants will show an activation remains an open challenge for fMRI. It has been suggested that the reliability of repeated scans is not high (Kong et al., 2007). There has also been debate over some commonly used statistical procedures, which have been criticized as overstating the significance of obtained differences by Vul et al. (2009) who pointed to the risks of capitalizing on chance. A typical brain volume obtained with fMRI involves tens of thousands of voxels and when activity in these voxels is compared

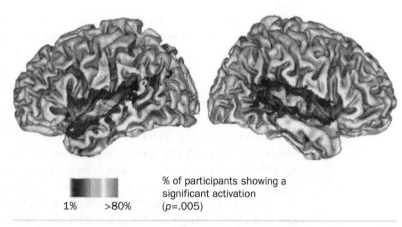

% of participants showing a
significant activation
(p=.005)

1%   >80%

Figure 1.9 **Probabilistic map of fMRI activity for a listening task.** An 'activation' is defined as greater activation for the experimental condition (human voice) than the control conditions (other sounds). From performing the experiment on many participants one develops a model of the probability that a voxel will show an activation.

Source: Reprinted from Chartrand, J.-P., Peretz, I., & Belin, P. (2008). Auditory recognition expertise and domain specificity. *Brain Research*, *1220*, 191–198, with permission from Elsevier.

between experimental and contrast conditions many differences will prove significant by chance alone. Even when conventional methods of dealing with multiple comparisons are applied, a tendency to report the mean effect sizes for the voxels above threshold significance will lead to spuriously high effects being reported.

Some further difficulties with generalizing fMRI results arise from the fact that the environment in which the measurements are carried out is very specific and highly unusual. Lying flat on one's back, while keeping perfectly still, in the claustrophobic noisy tunnel typical of fMRI machines, may well affect how tasks are tackled as compared to typical laboratory or real life situations. There is evidence that posture affects problem solving; for instance, Lipnicki and Byrne (2005) found that being supine, that is, lying on one's back, facilitated anagram solving but hindered mental arithmetic compared to upright postures, so results from supine participants as in fMRI studies could well be specific to that posture.

What might imaging studies tell us about cognitive processes?

Despite all the difficulties just outlined, fMRI is now a much used method, and it is hoped that consistent results will emerge over laboratories as studies accumulate and the implications become clearer. Suppose I had devised a new spatial reasoning task and wondered if people might use verbal reasoning to solve it. I might make an argument from scans to processes along the following lines:

1 Broca's area is known to be activated in tasks independently classed as involving implicit speech.
2 Broca's area is activated in my new spatial reasoning task.
3 Therefore, my new spatial task involves implicit speech.

Here is a real example, which takes things a few steps further (Ferris et al., 2005):

1 The striatum is activated when animals receive pleasure through rewards.
2 The striatum is activated when rats suckle their young.
3 Therefore, suckling is pleasurable to rats.
4 The striatum is activated less by cocaine injection than by suckling in rats.
5 Therefore, suckling is more pleasure inducing in rats than is cocaine.

In these arguments we have examples of 'reverse inference' (Poldrack, 2006), that is going from 'If a task involves cognitive function F1 then brain area Y is active' and 'In task B, brain area Y is active' to 'In task B, function F1 is involved'. In strict deductive logic this is not a valid argument. It is the equivalent of saying, 'If it's Friday, then Smith eats fish at noon' and 'Smith is eating fish at noon today', 'Therefore, today is Friday'. But perhaps Smith eats fish at noon on Tuesdays and Wednesdays as well as on Fridays. The conclusion that today is Friday is not necessarily true. Similarly, brain area Y may be active when many different cognitive functions are involved. The reverse inference only works when the 'if' means 'if and only if'. This inference pattern is known in logic as 'affirming the consequent' and is an invalid argument or 'fallacy', which we will discuss more fully later in Chapter 11. However, although reverse inference arguments are not conclusive or *necessarily* correct, they can be seen as generating plausible hypotheses for later testing and this is a useful role that imaging results can play. In our mini example, if brain area Y is active, then function F1 cannot be ruled out, but further independent evidence would be needed to conclude that function F1 is indeed involved in Task B. (The negative case, in which brain area Y is not active would support the valid inference that function F1 is not involved in Task B.) Overall, then, imaging results often suggest hypotheses for further research rather than being decisive in particular cases. However, for cases when there is controversy over which cognitive model might more accurately reflect human capabilities it is sometimes possible to design an fMRI experiment to critically evaluate these theories. Furthermore, for specific cases such as retinotopy, fMRI data has been fairly decisive in mapping out the visual field in the visual cortex.

Imaging methods can also make practical contributions, as is indicated in Box 1.7 on the use of imaging in identifying patients in persistent vegetative states who may well be conscious although unable to respond overtly to stimuli.

Box 1.7 Practical Application: Using neuroscientific methods to detect awareness in 'vegetative states'

Following severe brain injuries, some patients emerge from a coma and appear to be awake but show no signs of awareness and no signs of purposeful behaviour in response to external stimulation. In circumstances such as this, there is no guarantee that the patient is not actually aware and just unable to respond normally. Given the application of imaging methods to see specific responses in the brain, these techniques are being investigated as a way of communicating with patients unable to respond in any other way. For example, Owen and colleagues (Owen et al., 2006) used fMRI methods with a female patient who met all the criteria for the diagnosis of being in a vegetative state. While being scanned, the patient and normal control participants were asked to imagine (a) playing tennis and (b) visiting all the rooms in their houses starting from their front door. The results were striking, as shown in Figure 1.10. The patient and normal controls showed essentially identical patterns of activation (compared to resting periods) to the two instructions. Imagining playing tennis activated the supplementary motor area and imagining visiting all rooms at home activated parahippocampal gyrus, posterior parietal lobe and lateral premotor cortex to similar extents in both the patient and controls. Owen et al. concluded that the patient did have awareness of instructions and could demonstrate this by her neural response.

The study attracted some criticism in that the patient's response could have been automatically cued by the words 'tennis' and 'house' (Greenberg, 2007; Nachev & Husain, 2007). However, Owen et al. (2007) were able to show that simply presenting the words without the instruction to imagine the activities did not produce any significant response. The results were confirmed in a larger follow up with 54 patients and 16 healthy controls (Monti et al., 2010).

More recently, Owen and colleagues (Cruse et al., 2011) have found similar evidence for awareness in some patients in a vegetative state using the more portable (and more affordable) EEG methods. This work could lead to ways of communicating with patients who can respond to instructions. Patients could be asked to imagine wiggling their right thumb to signal 'Yes' and their right big toe to signal 'No' and then answer yes/no questions. This method generates distinctive EEG traces in both patients and healthy controls. Thus, a questioner could read off their yes/no answers from the EEG trace. Another application might be to control machines modified to accept such binary thought signals. In Chapter 3, we consider the implications of this work for our understanding of consciousness.

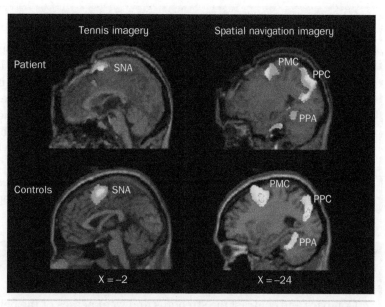

Figure 1.10   fMRI scans of patient in vegetative state and normal controls when undertaking imagery tasks. SMA = supplementary motor area. PPA = parahippocampal gyrus. PPC = posterior parietal lobe. PMC = lateral premotor cortex.

Source: Owen, A. M., Coleman, M. R., Boly, M., Davis, M. H., Laureys, S., Jolles, D., & Pickard, J. D. (2006). Detecting awareness in the vegetative state. Science, 313, 1402. Reprinted with permission from AAAS.

Networks

Paying more heed to *networked* as against highly localized activity may yield useful results (Dobbs, 2005). For example, it has become apparent from imaging studies that in a resting state many brain areas are active. The use of 'resting' states as control or contrast conditions yielded the unexpected finding of 'deactivation' across a range of brain areas when active tasks were worked on. Subtracting the resting activation levels from the task activation levels often produced negative patterns. That is, large areas of the brain were more active during 'rest' than when a focused task was begun. From these results it was inferred that there is a Default Mode Network (DMN) reflecting internal tasks such as daydreaming, envisioning the future, and retrieving memories (Buckner et al., 2008). Activity in the DMN is negatively correlated with activity in brain systems when people focus on external visual signals. In the infant brain, there is limited evidence of the default network, but default network activity is more consistently found in children aged 9–12 years, suggesting that the default network undergoes developmental change (Raichle & Snyder, 2007).

Summary

In this chapter we have indicated the main areas that cognitive psychology deals with. These are: perception, motor action, attention, learning, memory and forgetting, language, decision making, reasoning and problem solving. These topics all involve the processing of information and cognitive psychology can be seen as the study of how we and other animals acquire, store, retrieve and use information. These functions are carried out ultimately by brain processes and so neuroscience studies of the brain, involving functional and structural imaging and case studies of brain damage are relevant to cognitive psychology. A number of approaches to understanding cognition have been explored over the centuries including associationism, introspectionism and behaviourism. The dominant approach today is the information processing approach which derives from analogies with computers and computer programs. In this analogy the brain is the hardware on which the cognitive software runs.

Review questions

1 What topics are the focus of cognitive psychology?
2 Compare and contrast the strengths and weaknesses of the behaviourist and information processing approaches.
3 What is meant by a functional level of analysis?
4 What can brain imaging methods tell us about cognition?
5 To what extent can we draw conclusions from fMRI scans about cognitive processes?
6 What can studies of people with brain injuries tell us about cognitive functions?

FURTHER READING

Baddeley, A. D. (2007). *Working memory, thought and action*. Oxford: Oxford University Press.

Foer, J. (2011). *Moonwalking with Einstein: The art and science of remembering everything*. New York: Penguin Books.

Frankish, K., & Ramsey, W. (2012). *The Cambridge handbook of cognitive science*. Cambridge: Cambridge University Press.

Roche, R. A. P., & Commins, S. (Eds.). (2009). *Pioneering studies in cognitive neuroscience*. London: McGraw-Hill.

Ward, J. (2010) *The students' guide to cognitive neuroscience* (2nd ed.). Hove: Psychology Press.

CHAPTER 2:
PERCEPTION

INTRODUCTION

Perception is the remarkable set of processes that organize sensory experience into an understanding of our surrounding world. The study of perception gives us insight into how properties of the physical world are transformed into our mental world and informs our understanding of behaviours like navigation and recognition. For example, consider being given a complicated set of directions in a dimly lit and noisy environment like a nightclub. If later you cannot find your destination, it is possible that you failed because you (1) did not properly hear the directions, (2) did not see the relevant landmarks, or (3) were somehow incapable of understanding and executing the directions. The study of perception examines these first two points of hearing and seeing the world. It provides us with an understanding of what information about the world is available to our cognitive systems.

> Perception is our sensory experience of the world.

We can view perception standing in the continuum between sensation – where physical energy is transformed into brain signals, and cognition – where mental representations of the world and our goals are used to reason and

> Sensation entails the processes by which physical properties are converted to neural signals.

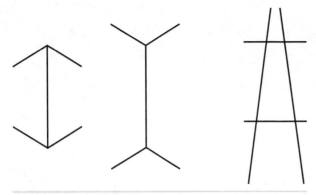

Figure 2.1   Illusions show perception is not always accurate.
To the left is an example of the Muller-Lyer illusion where the two vertical lines are the same length but are not perceived to be identical. A similar effect is seen to the right in the Ponzo illusion where the horizontal lines are the same physical length but not perceived as such. These and other illusions illustrate the fact that perception is not always accurate.

Somatic perception refers to perception of the body through touch and sensing the orientation of limbs in space.

plan behaviour. The study of perception emphasizes how physical properties of the world are represented mentally and although it does not have sharp, distinct boundaries with either sensation or cognition it forms a unique field of study. Perceptual information can come in many forms – sight, sound and bodily perception will be considered in this chapter. This perceptual information is essential to inform us about our surroundings and guide our interactions with the physical and social world. If all relevant information about the physical world were captured in our perceptual representations then the study of perception might be extremely straightforward. However, visual illusions (Figure 2.1) provide clear evidence that our perceptual systems do not always faithfully represent the physical world.

This chapter is organized into four sections. The first section describes basic principles and theory that would be relevant to any perceptual system. The second section outlines the capabilities of visual, auditory and somatic perceptual processes, and how basic principles shape perceptual experience. The remaining two sections of the chapter describe how perception leads to recognition. In the third section we consider general recognition of objects, scenes and events, while in the final section we consider the case of social perception where faces, voices and bodies are recognized. The understanding of perceptual processes is increasingly finding application in new areas of technology, and we discuss one such advance in Box 2.1.

Box 2.1 Practical Application: Cognitive robotics and human-robot interaction

In the past the field of robotics was largely concerned with industrial robots confined to repetitive tasks in predictable environments. However, cognitive robotics (Vernon et al., 2010) and human-robot interaction (Goodrich & Schultz, 2007) are two new fields of robotics that are defining the move of robots from these restricted environments to everyday scenes. One basis for the advancement in robotics has been an explosion in the availability of high-performance sensors, actuators, computers and power systems which make it possible to develop and control increasingly sophisticated mechanisms. However, to realize the potential of these devices one needs to know how to make a system that can sense and adapt to its environment and cooperate with other agents in the world. Given that biological systems, in particular humans, excel in their ability to perceive information about their environment and to adapt, they have become models for the development of robot systems at many levels. This has provided an important link between the results of past decades of research into perception and cognitive science and the development of new robots.

Goals of these new robots include the ability to achieve tasks in an unstructured environment and to be able to efficiently interact with humans so that task goals can be effectively communicated and

Figure 2.2   (top) Roomba and (bottom) iCub

Source: (Top) Beano5/iStock; (bottom) Reproduced with permission from IIT (Istituto Italiano di Tecnologia). Photo by Laura Taverna.

controlled. Within this framework a variety of robots have been developed. At one end of robot design are basic robots such as Roomba (Figure 2.2a), which faces the challenge of navigating an unpredictable and unstructured environment to make your home tidy. At another end are robot designs that mimic the form and function of humans and animals. Early examples were the dog Aibo from Sony or Asimo from Honda and recent examples include Nao, Robonaut2 and iCub (Figure 2.2b). One motivation for mimicking human form is that if these robots are going to help us in our own environment then they should be able to navigate these environments, by, for example, having legs to climb stairs. Moreover, if we want to be able to teach the robot by copying our own actions then it is convenient for the robot and human to share the same structure.

This chapter includes many connections with current robotics research, which will be useful to reflect upon as you read through it. For example, we discuss fundamental concepts in perception and cognition, and the most fundamental concepts are those that apply to both human and robot perception. We discuss human perceptual systems; these are useful for providing an existence proof that there is sufficient information in the perceptual world for the task to be achieved. Moreover, robots that mimic human form and structure make a fascinating test bed for exploring ever more complex theories of perception. Finally, we discuss recognition and social perception, and while reaching human levels of performance is still far in the future, even rudimentary skills could aid the performance of robots placed in care situations.

FUNDAMENTAL CONCEPTS

FROM PHYSICAL WORLD TO PERCEPTUAL REPRESENTATION

The essential problem of perception is that the physical world is 'out there' and our mental world has its home base inside our head. To address this problem we will emphasize an information-processing approach that looks at how the senses provide information about the world and how this information is transformed into understanding (for an introduction to the information processing approach, see Chapter 1). A primary question is whether enough information comes in through our senses to accurately represent the physical world, and if not, why? One simple answer to this question is 'no', for the reason that our sensory organs have limited ranges. Dogs provide an illustration of this since they can hear in ranges that humans cannot. However, there is a deeper information-processing issue known as the inverse-problem that describes why even for the best sensory organs perception cannot typically guarantee a faithful representation of the physical world (Pizlo, 2001). The nature of the inverse-problem can be illustrated with an example from vision. The world is three-dimensional, and this three-dimensional world is projected onto our eyes to become two-dimensional images. The

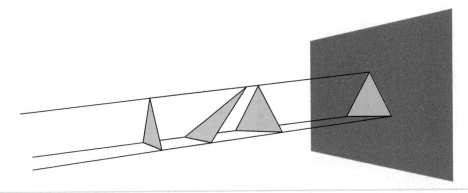

Figure 2.3   Different shapes in the world can produce the same image. The image of a triangle with sides of equal length can be created by an infinite number of possible triangles in the world provided we orient them in a particular way. This demonstrates the inverse problem: the image on the eye has lost information and the brain must somehow recover this information.

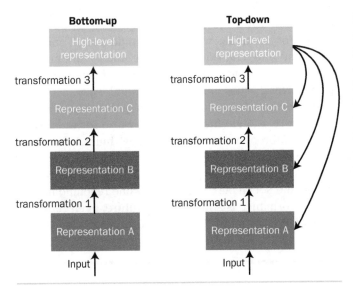

Figure 2.4   The flow of information in purely bottom-up and top-down processing. (Left) In a bottom-up (data-driven) system, the answer bubbles up through a series of transformations that are not affected by factors such as expectancies. (Right) In a top-down system, the rising flow of information is filtered by the influence of information held higher in the processing hierarchy.

inverse problem is that typically these two-dimensional images do not have enough information to specify the exact three-dimensional world that created them. The images have lost a dimension and there is no way, given just the images and nothing more, to invert the image creation process from the two-dimensional images back to a unique three-dimensional scene (Figure 2.3). The crucial realization here is that there are fundamental ways that information is lost in the sensory encoding of the physical world. Thus, the fidelity of our mental representations of the physical world cannot wholly depend upon the incoming information. Crucially, it must depend upon the ability of perceptual processes to use assumptions about the structure of the world to analyse incoming sensory information in a way that we can overcome the inverse problem to build plausible interpretations of what is out there.

The previous paragraph asserted that perception does not guarantee us a faithful representation of the physical world, due to the inverse-problem and the intrinsic loss of information as the physical world is transformed into a mental representation. However, the fact that most of us have success with the great majority of our interactions with the physical world demonstrates that our perceptual systems have evolved effective principles to overcome theoretical limitations to the processing of perceptual information. We will discuss these general principles in the coming sections.

PRINCIPLES AND THEORIES OF PERCEPTION

The inverse problem suggests that the solution to how we perceive the world will not be simple, however it does not prescribe any particular solution. To tackle this problem we will focus on how best to characterize the flow of information in the fully developed perceptual system and what principles might be at work to organize this information.

The flow of information: bottom-up and top-down processing

A fundamental distinction in perceptual processing is whether we achieve an understanding of the world through bottom-up or top-down mechanisms. In bottom-up processing, the original sensory input is transformed in an uninterrupted cascade of transformations feeding forward the information, one transformation following the other until the final representation is obtained. Bottom-up processing, also known as data-driven processing, is characterized by perceptual mechanisms that can independently create increasingly complex representations. In contrast to this is top-down processing, which crucially involves connections between the higher levels and the lower ones. Instead of an uninterrupted cascade of feed-forward transformations there are feedback connections that mediate the transformations with higher-level information. These two styles of information processing are shown in Figure 2.4. An example of the distinction between the two styles of information can be given in recognizing an orange. In bottom-up processing the individual surface dimples would organize into a texture that could be combined with perception of the spherical shape and the orange colour, and from these separate processes the orange could be recognized. In top-down processing, it is critical that we start out with some expectation of what we are looking for, and this knowledge exerts influence on lower-level processes that will interact with the processing of colour, shape and texture. At the extremes, bottom-up processing holds that what we experience is an inevitable consequence of what sensation strikes our eyes, ears or skin and top-down processing holds that this perception will be substantially changed by what we expect to experience.

Evaluation

The bottom-up and top-down processing approaches provide contrasting views of theoretical principles behind how we process incoming sensory information. It is possible to debate whether bottom-up or top-down processing predominates. For example, that bottom-up processing would dominate for unambiguous perceptual input and top-down processing would dominate for situations where the perceptual input is ambiguous. However, for many situations the two can be seen to work together as demonstrated by research by Kawano and colleagues that measured the response of visual neurons in monkeys. They found that information about the emotional expression of a face could be encoded and transmitted faster than other information (Sugase et al., 1999). They proposed that an initial facial representation could be rapidly transmitted to centres that would begin to determine emotion. This emotional judgement could then be used to refine the further processing of information. Such a system might be important for quickly identifying friend or foe (happy or angry) and to use this to shape the interpretation of the incoming information for deciding about other factors such as identity (Figure 2.5). This example used faces and emotion to illustrate the interplay of bottom-up and top-down processing and we will further discuss faces later in this chapter and emotions in Chapter 14.

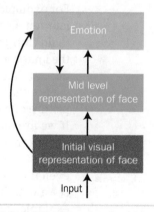

Figure 2.5   Example of top-down processing of faces. In this example based on neurophysiology, data informative about facial emotion is transmitted ahead in the processing stream so that emotional information can be used to influence mid-level processing of facial information.

Perceptual organization: likelihood principle

The direction of information flow is one aspect of information processing, and another is how the incoming data is transformed. An important concept to discuss in this regard is the likelihood principle (Pomerantz & Kubovy,

> **Likelihood principle**
> states that the preferred organization of a perceptual object or event will be the one which is most likely.

1986). The likelihood principle states that the likelihood that an object or event will occur is important for the perceptual processing of that object/event. Indeed, it proposes that we will perceive the object/event that was most likely to have occurred, and this idea historically goes back to discussions of Helmholtz in the 1800s about unconscious inference (Helmholtz & Southall, 1962). The importance of the principle can be seen in light of the fundamental problem discussed earlier that perceptual input is typically not sufficiently rich in information to uniquely specify what will be perceived. Thus, something additional is necessary for us to infer the properties of the world. The likelihood principle suggests a statistical view is appropriate for evaluating our perceptual input to determine what we are experiencing. One statistical approach to perception is provided by a computational theory called Bayesian Decision Theory (Geisler & Kersten, 2002; Jazayeri & Shadlen, 2010; Mamassian & Landy, 2010; Mamassian et al., 2002). Other views of Bayesian approaches are given in Chapters 8 and 11.

From a Bayesian point of view, perception is an inference problem: what is the most likely event responsible for my perception? For vision this becomes: given the image on my retina, what is the most likely scene to have caused it? In Bayesian Decision Theory there are three components involved in answering this question. First, there is the *likelihood*, that represents all the uncertainty in the image. The larger the number of scenes consistent with the image, the larger the uncertainty. The second component is the *prior* and it represents the knowledge one has about the scene before even looking at the image. The stronger the prior, the less one is subject to the uncertainty of the likelihood. Finally, the third component is the *decision rule*. Depending on the task and the objectives of the observer, one might be interested in finding the most likely interpretation given all the information available (from the likelihood and prior), or instead explore randomly one of the possible interpretations every time the same image is presented. The decision rule thus adds flexibility to the general framework to model behaviour.

For example, let us assume we have built a cat detector to look for photos of cats on the internet. Our (hypothetical) cat detector examines each input image to look for something fluffy with pointy ears. However, the ears of the cat may not always be visible in the image and to get the likelihood we need to know how many other photos might get our cat detector to fire in a similar way. The likelihood thus represents how uncertain we are that our detector is actually viewing a cat. The prior is the chances of seeing a picture of a cat on the internet and might change depending on where we are browsing. If we are on a random web page then the prior is just the probability of seeing a cat on the internet – the number of cat pictures on the Internet divided by the total number of photos on the internet. However, if we are on a super-cute cat picture website then, even if the image has a small likelihood of being a cat, the large prior would guide us to see a cat. Finally, the decision rule lets us take into account various other factors. For example, if we desperately need a picture of a cat and we were on a website with fuzzy and ambiguous photos (low likelihood) of many kinds of animals (low prior) we would change to a website with clear photos of only cats (high likelihood and high prior). However, if we were relaxed and seeking entertainment or a novel view we might explore further on the low likelihood and low prior website.

Information processing approach

Invariants in vision are properties of the three-dimensional object being viewed that can be derived from any two-dimensional image of the object.

In his book, *Vision*, David Marr (1982) proposed an information processing approach to perceptual processing in vision. This built upon earlier work led by the ecological psychologist Gibson (1979). Ecological psychology holds that perception works in a largely bottom-up fashion by exploiting regularities in the visual world that are termed invariants. By studying how perception works in the actual environment (not the lab) and uncovering these invariants we can understand how the perceptual system directly transforms perception into an interpretation of the world. This process was termed direct perception. Marr questioned how 'direct' this process could be and tried to understand the fundamental nature of information processing necessary for transforming perceptual input into an interpretation of the world. He suggested that for any information-processing device to be completely understood it must be understood at three different levels. The first level is the computational theory to understand the purpose of the computation and to demonstrate its appropriateness for the task at hand. The second level is the choice of representation for the input and output, and the algorithm to achieve the transformation between input and output. The third level is how to realize these computations, for example in a human or a digital computer. The generality of this three-level approach was influential in opening boundaries between researchers working in computer vision, visual psychology and the physiology of vision.

> Direct perception, also termed event perception and ecological perception, refers to the bottom-up process by which objects and their function are recognized.

First level – computational theory

At the first level, the question is what is the purpose of a computation and why does it do what it does? In the broadest sense, the purpose of the perceptual processes of vision, hearing and touch are to keep us aware of our external world and support our adaptability to the changing world. Why these processes exist can take on a more philosophical perspective, but as a matter of practical significance these processes exist to ensure our survival. Marr used the example of theorizing about a cash register to illustrate computational theory. At the computational level what a cash register does is add and why it does it is that this is appropriate for the task of summing a total. While this might seem overly simplistic, it has been noted that approaches based in physiology or psychology sometimes missed this basic consideration or did not keep it distinct from other details.

Second level – choice of representation

The second level is the choice of representation for the input and output and the algorithm to achieve the transformation between input and output. To explain this level we can continue with the cash register example. With the cash register we can represent numbers using the Hindu Arabic system where four is represented as '4' or with the Roman system where four is represented as 'IV'. Moreover, our choice of representation will motivate the use of different algorithms to achieve addition. This second level is an essential aspect of cognitive science. Light energy hits the eye, or energy from air vibrations hits the ear or mechanical energy is applied to the skin. This input is transformed to an output; so with light we consider the transformation from light to output representations such as colour, edges and motion, while for sound we consider the transformation of air pressure into representations of pitch and volume. Although these transformations are in one sense transformations of physical energy from one form to another, a fundamental view of cognitive science is to consider them as transformations from one information state to another. With this perspective we will model human behaviour, and experience of the world, as the result of algorithms operating on representations of information.

Third level – achieving the computations

The earlier discussion about how faces might be processed in the monkey visual system raises the final point in Marr's hierarchy. Namely, the final level to discuss is the actual way in which the computations are achieved, whether by man, machine, monkey or banana slug. Every organism or machine will have its own limitations imposed by the device performing the computations, whether a brain or a computer chip. These limitations introduce practical considerations on the second-level of what representation and type of algorithm is optimal to use but they will not impact the first-level computational theory of what is the goal of the computation. Thus, keeping this choice of device as a separate consideration allows us to discuss perception in terms of transforming incoming stimulus energy into appropriate representation of information without worrying about the specific implementation. To return to our example, a cash register, an electronic calculator and an abacus can all be seen to solve the computational problem of adding the value of items. However, the particular hardware we choose to do the calculation can motivate different representations and different algorithms to solve the identical problem.

The approach of Marr to emphasize computational theory and keep the three levels of description distinct has enabled perceptual scientists in psychology, neurophysiology, computer science and engineering to communicate with each other and facilitated a cross-fertilization of research ideas.

THE BODY AND PERCEPTION

Up to now in this chapter we have conceived of perception as providing us with an internal mental representation of the physical world. In a traditional view of cognitive science this representation would effectively be symbolic and the goal of cognition would be to appropriately manipulate the symbols. However, such a view leaves out how our own physical body and the actions it produces might influence perception.

Embodied cognition holds that cognition is about the experiences arising from a perceptual system tightly linked to an action system rather than the manipulations of abstract representations.

As a way to incorporate consideration of these physical and environmental factors, one can take an embodied view of cognition (Barsalou, 1999; Gomila & Calvo, 2008). Such a view of how perception and cognition interact draws upon, among others, the theories of Gibson and the ecological psychologists that to understand a cognitive system we need to take as the unit of analysis the 'system' embedded into its surrounding environment. Crucial to the embodied view of perception is that what one perceptually experiences of the world is related not only to the perceptual input but also to one's purpose, physiological state and emotions. For example, when wearing a heavy backpack it has been reported that hills appear steeper and their distances appear greater (Proffitt, 2006). The claim is that perceiving spatial layout combines the geometry of the world with behavioural goals and the costs associated with achieving these goals. However, this claim remains controversial. In several cases embodied perception effects previously attributed to physical burdens or manipulations of behavioural potential have instead been shown to depend on participants' spontaneous beliefs about the goals of the experimenter (e.g. Durgin et al., 2009, 2012; Shaffer et al., 2013) or on instructions that lead participants to consider non-visual information relevant to their reports (Woods et al., 2009).

The embodied view of cognition has philosophical implications for our understanding of cognition (Clark, 1997; Haugeland, 1998; Hurley, 1998; Noë, 2004; Shapiro, 2004) that are beyond the scope of this current chapter. However, it is relevant to review six claims that form a basis for embodied cognition (Wilson, 2002):

1 Cognition is situated – it takes place in the real world and inherently involves perception and action.

2 Cognition is time-pressured – we need to evaluate our situation in the environment as quickly as it changes and this is essential to consider.

3 We off-load cognitive work onto the environment – whether counting on our fingers or organizing a hand of cards in poker we actively change our environment to reduce cognitive workload.

4 The environment is part of the cognitive system – given the continuous dense flow of perception and action it is not meaningful to study the mind alone.

5 Cognition is for action – perception and memory must be considered in terms of how they contribute to action.

6 Off-line cognition is body based – even when the mind can be separated from the environment it is grounded in mechanisms involving perception and action such as using metaphor based on physical relations.

While there is still active discussion of these six claims (Gomila & Calvo, 2008) they provide a basis for considering the essential role of perception (and action) in cognition. In the next section we discuss perceptual systems and include evidence, consistent with an embodied approach, that vision incorporates special systems designed for integrating perception with action. Related discussions of embodied cognition are provided in Chapters 7 and 8.

HUMAN PERCEPTUAL SYSTEMS

In this section we briefly review the systems that produce perceptual features such as orientation, colour, motion, timbre, pitch and pressure. Features are important since the modelling of high-level perception and cognition is often focused on the information provided by particular features. For example, the colour of an object might be key to a memory or the tonal variation of a voice might signal aspects of meaning in the language being spoken. Consistent with the discussion of Marr's three levels of information processing, it is worth reminding ourselves that the human brain is just one particular implementation of an information-processing device. However, the human system provides a good starting point for understanding other organisms as well as for the design of biologically inspired machines.

We will organize our discussion of perceptual systems to first focus on separate systems and then on the combination of information across senses. While there are advantages for combining across the senses, discussing the systems separately helps for a simpler explanation and is also consistent with the view that perceptual systems are functionally organized in a modular fashion. Moreover, the human brain exhibits a large degree of modularity in its arrangement of sensory processing areas for audio, video and somatosensory processing (Figure 2.6). This modularity principle can even

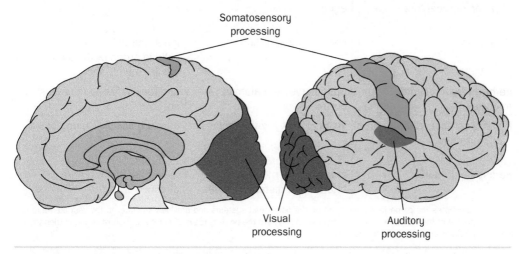

Figure 2.6   Primary sensory areas for sight, hearing and touch in the human brain. Processing of vision, audition and somatoperception is supported by cortical areas, which are largely dedicated to that single sensory modality. Loss of any of these primary sensory areas results in a profound loss of sensory awareness in that modality.

Synaesthesia is an uncommon condition where stimulation of one perceptual modality results in experiencing a percept in a typically unrelated modality, e.g. tasting a sound.

be extended further to subdivide processing within a sensory modality. For example, different perceptual features, such visual shape and location can be attributed to different regions of the visual brain. However, it is worth mentioning that there are some instances where modularity appears violated and one of these cases is synaesthesia (Cytowic, 2003; Hubbard & Ramachandran, 2005; Ward, 2008). Individuals with synaesthesia appear to combine the senses in a way that appears to cross over modular boundaries. For example, colour-grapheme synaesthetes see colours and other vivid visual patterns when viewing particular forms such as letters and numbers.

Scan to watch a video explaining synaesthesia

A final point before discussing the individual perceptual systems is that there is a degree of structural similarity across the visual, auditory and somatosensory systems. The basic organization is a hierarchy from specialized receptors, through dedicated neural pathways to centres in the brain with specialized patterns of organization. These centres in the brain can either be found in the cortex for information requiring elaborate processing and conscious awareness or in brain tissue at subcortical levels if the perceptual information is needed for immediate monitoring without conscious awareness. Table 2.1 provides a broad overview of the visual, auditory and somatoperceptual systems and provides terms useful for further study of perception. From the table it can be seen that the visual, auditory and also the touch component of somatoperception share many properties in going from specialized receptors to a systematically organized cortical structure. We include

Proprioception is the sense of how our limbs are positioned in space.
Vestibular sensation is the sense of balance and orientation in space.

proprioception and vestibular sensation within somatoperception since typically we not only need to know that a particular body part is being touched but also the orientation of that body part relative to the rest of the body (proprioception) and the orientation of the body in space (vestibular sense). Vision can also strongly contribute to a sense of the orientation of the body and limbs in space.

Table 2.1 Basic organization of perceptual systems

	Vision	Audition
Location of receptors	eyes	ears
Receptors	cones, rods in retina	inner hair cells, outer hair cells in organ of Corti on basilar membrane
Pathway from receptor to cortex	optic nerve → thalamus → cortex	auditory nerve → thalamus → cortex
Primary cortical receiving area / organization	visual cortex / retinotopic	auditory cortex / tonotopic
Perceptual features	colour, form, motion, orientation, distance/depth	loudness, pitch, timbre, distance

This table illustrates the properties common to all the perceptual systems and provides a pointer to the vast literature on each component of the table. The row and column headings are the primary focus of our discussion while the entries within the table provide terms to enable further study.

We will use the framework presented in Table 2.1 to present the visual, auditory and somatoperception systems. For each system we will discuss the flow of information from receptor to primary receiving area in cortex, further processing in related secondary sensory areas, and how damage to particular brain regions lead to systematic changes in behaviour.

VISUAL SYSTEM

The encoding of visual information begins in the retinas of the two eyes and is transmitted from there to the primary visual cortex. This process follows the basic pattern of using specialized receptors to transform light energy to a neural signal that is sent to specific brain regions with a unique functional organization (Figure 2.7). Towards the centre of each retina is a region known as the fovea that contains an abundance of receptors known as cones that encode colour and high-resolution spatial form information. Surrounding the cones are receptors known as rods that encode motion and low-resolution form information. The mapping of visual information from retina to cortex follows a systematic retinotopic organization that preserves spatial order – neighbouring regions in the retina are represented in neighbouring regions of cortex. A deeper understanding of this mapping requires consideration of the optics of how images are projected by the lens onto the eye and how the visual pathways of the optic nerve organize transmission from the two eyes. However, the result of this optics and neural wiring provide the organization shown in Figure 2.7. The right visual world ends up in the left half of the brain's primary visual cortex and the left visual world ends up in the right half of the brain's primary visual cortex. Closer inspection of Figure 2.7 also reveals that the centre of the visual field – the fovea with its abundance of high

> Cones are special neurons in the retina that are sensitive to different coloured light and densely packed to resolve fine image detail.
> Rods are special neurons in the periphery of the retina that are effective in low levels of light and to sense motion.

Somatoperception		
touch	proprioception	vestibular
skin	tendons, muscles	semicircular canals of ears
Meissner, Merkel, Ruffini and Pacinian receptors in skin	Golgi tendon organs, muscle spindles	hair cells in otolith organ
nerve fibres → spinal cord → thalamus → cortex	nerve fibres → spinal cord → cerebellum → cortex	nerve fibres → brainstem nuclei
primary somatosensory cortex (Brodmann Areas 1, 2, 3a and 3b) / somatotopic	Brodmann Areas 2 and 3a of somatosensory cortex	no dedicated area
pressure, vibration	force of muscles, joint angles	body movement and body orientation

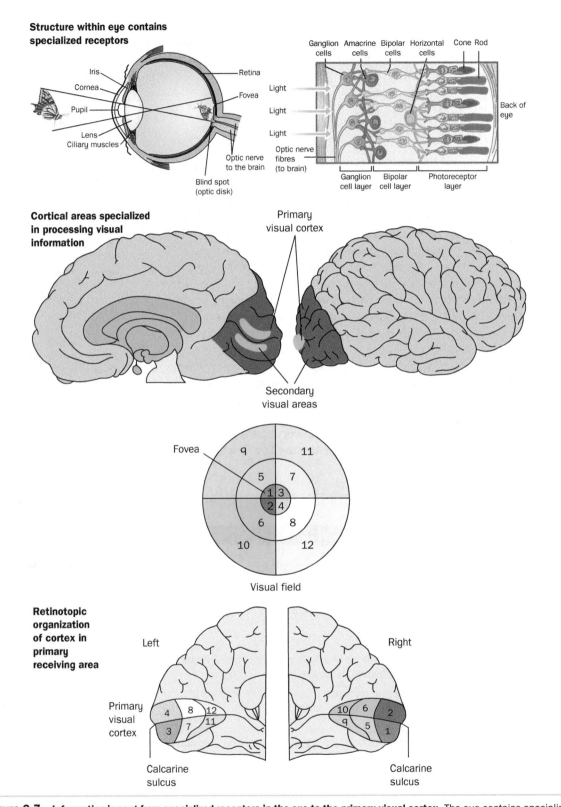

Figure 2.7   Information is sent from specialized receptors in the eye to the primary visual cortex. The eye contains specialized receptors that transduce light energy into neural signals and these neural signals make their way to the primary visual cortex. Primary visual cortex is organized in a retinotopic fashion with specific parts of the visual world represented in specific parts of the brain. Surrounding the primary visual cortex are further secondary areas that are specialized for processing visual information.

Sources: (T) Adapted from Holt, N. et al. (2012). *Psychology: The science of mind and behaviour.* McGraw-Hill Education.

spatial resolution cones – has a dispro-portionate amount of visual cortex dedicated to processing the incoming visual information. This fact explains why moving our eyes so that the image projects onto the fovea provides us with the greatest encoding of spatial and colour information. In Box 2.2 we further explore the function of primary visual cortex in describing a classic study involving the discovery of feature detectors for orientation in primary visual cortex.

From primary visual cortex there are two primary pathways for visual processing that lead into occipital cortex and beyond; these are shown in Figure 2.8 (Ungerleider & Mishkin, 1982). One pathway leads from visual cortex to the temporal lobe; it is specialized for determining what objects are in the visual world and is called by neuroanatomic convention the

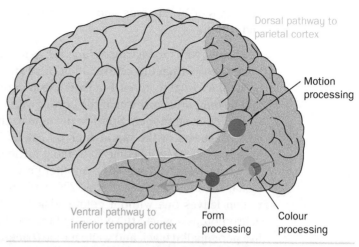

Figure 2.8 Two pathways out of primary visual cortex. The dorsal stream travels to parietal cortex and specializes in motion processing as well as being important for visually guided action. The ventral stream travels towards temporal cortex and specializes in processing of colour and form. The processing of depth is distributed across these two pathways. Due to their different functions the dorsal pathway is sometimes referred to as the 'where' or 'how' pathway and the ventral stream as the 'what' pathway.

ventral stream. The other pathway, known as the dorsal stream, leads from visual cortex towards parietal cortex and is specialized for determining where objects are in the visual world. The characterization of the ventral and dorsal streams as supporting what and where was augmented by Goodale and Milner (1992) to include the distinction of separate visual systems for perception and action. In this two visual system model the ventral stream is responsible for processes that provide conscious awareness of what an object is while the dorsal stream is responsible for processes that enable us to know how to perform actions on an object. For example, if we were in a garden admiring the style of flower arrangements, the ventral stream would be involved in perceiving detailed shapes and colours and recognizing flowers, but if a wasp were about to land on our arm the dorsal stream would be involved to swat it away.

Ventral stream is the visual pathway from occipital cortex to temporal cortex that is involved in recognition of the object being viewed.
Dorsal stream is the visual pathway from occipital cortex to parietal cortex that is involved in locating and guiding how to use an object.

Evaluation

The idea that two independent visual streams from visual cortex form the basis of our further visual information processing for perception and action has met with some controversy. One question is whether there are examples of behaviour in typical individuals which provide evidence that these two streams are independent. Evidence consistent with the view that the streams are independent came from experiments suggesting that viewing a particular object might be influenced by a visual illusion but that directing an action towards the object will not be influenced by the illusion (Aglioti et al., 1995; Carey, 2001). However, subsequent experiments examining motor behaviour towards visual illusions yielded somewhat mixed results that the vision and action systems are independent (Brenner & Smeets, 1996; Bruno, 2001; Franz, 2001). An additional complication to the two-stream approach is that Glover (2004) suggested that a more complete understanding is available if we divide the dorsal, action stream into two separate components of planning and control. Planning was modelled to take place in the inferior parietal lobe and control in the superior parietal lobe. Debate on these issues continues with resolution complicated by the inherent complexity in modelling large

Scan to see a video on colour perception

networks of brain areas and in conducting experiments that involve both perception and action.

Consistent with modularity of function as an organizing principle, it is possible to localize brain areas within the ventral and dorsal streams that are responsible for representing particular visual features. For example, a brain region in the dorsal stream located in the middle temporal cortex near the border with visual cortex has been shown to be responsible for seeing motion. Specific damage to this region leaves an individual capable of seeing aspects of the world such as colour and shape but not motion; activities like crossing the street become extremely difficult as it is impossible to tell the motion of oncoming traffic (Zeki, 1991). Another brain region, this time from the ventral stream of visual cortex (Bouvier & Engel, 2006), is responsible for seeing colour. Damage to this region leaves one without colour vision and leads to a condition known as cerebral achromotopsia where the colours of the world are replaced with shades of grey such as in a poor quality black and white movie (Sacks, 1997). However, some perceptual features like depth are not precisely localized in the brain and thus our impression of depth must come from a combination of depth cues. This is due to the variety of ways in which information in an image could signal depth. For example, depth cues include (1) pictorial cues such as interposition where we see depth because one object obstructs view of an object behind, (2) motion parallax where we see a faster moving surface as closer than a slower moving surface (for example out the window of a moving vehicle where distant objects move slowly compared to those nearby), and (3) stereo depth where the difference in position of the two eyes yields differences in the two images that carry depth information (an effect exploited to create 3D movies). How we see depth thus raises the issue of how different sources of depth information are combined, and at the end of this section we will discuss how different sources of sensory information are combined.

Box 2.2 Research Close Up: Discovery of feature detectors in primary visual cortex

Source: Hubel, D. H., & Wiesel, T. N. (1959). Receptive fields of single neurones in the cat's striate cortex. *Journal of Physiology*, *148*(3), 574–591.

INTRODUCTION

Although conducted over 50 years ago, the 1959 study by Hubel and Wiesel (1959) marks a fundamental advance in visual science that is still relevant today. The body of work associated with this finding resulted in the 1981 Nobel Prize for Hubel and Wiesel. Here, we will emphasize how this study gave a critical starting point for explaining what features the visual system uses to represent incoming information. Although much was known about vision by 1959, physiological evidence was lacking of how visual information is initially represented and subsequently transformed in primary visual cortex (also known as striate cortex). The study of Hubel and Wiesel changed this, as the introduction to their paper makes clear: 'In the central nervous system the visual pathway from retina to striate cortex provides an opportunity to observe and compare single unit responses at several distinct levels. Patterns of light stimuli most effective in influencing units at one level may no longer be the most effective at the next. From differences in responses at successive stages in the pathway one may hope to gain some understanding of the part each stage plays in visual perception' (p. 574).

METHODS

Hubel and Wiesel presented visual stimuli to an anaesthetized cat while measuring the electrical activity of neurons in its visual cortex. They achieved these measurements by placing an electrode at different locations of visual cortex and measuring the response properties of neurons. Their methods for presenting stimuli, though effective, lacked the precise computer control of visual stimuli that is now standard. A specialized projector was mounted upon an adjustable tripod and shone upon a screen. When measuring a particular neuron, sheets of paper were affixed to the screen and marked with whether the neuron was excited or inhibited by a particular pattern of light placed at that location. In this way it was possible to map out the response properties of the neuron and the sheets of paper formed the experimental record. Hundreds of neurons were mapped out in this way, each taking 2–9 hours, and the results of 45 were presented in the paper.

RESULTS

An example from the study of a mapping with a very small diameter disk of light is shown in Figure 2.9. The results use 'x' to mark regions where the neuron was excited by the light and triangles to mark where the neuron was inhibited by the light. It can be seen that the overall pattern is consistent with an optimal response by a vertically aligned bar. The results of testing this same neuron with bars of different orientation are shown in two columns to the right with the bar's orientation shown in the left column and the neuron response in the right column. As can be seen in how the number of spikes in the right column changes with orientation this particular neuron is maximally stimulated by vertical lines. This example showed a neuron sensitive to vertical lines and examination of other neurons revealed ones sensitive to other orientations.

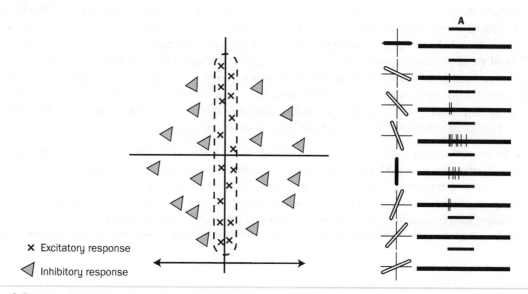

Figure 2.9 Orientation specificity in response of a neuron in visual cortex. (Left) An example of a mapping of the receptive field indicates that this neuron is optimally responsive to a vertical bar. (Right) An example of this orientation tuning. When a bar approaches vertical the firing of the neuron is greatest as shown by the large number of spikes in the trace in the right column. When the bar is horizontal the neuron does not fire.

Source: Hubel, D. H., & Wiesel, T. N. (1959). Receptive fields of single neurones in the cat's striate cortex. *The Journal of Physiology*, *148*, 574–591.

DISCUSSION

The significance of these findings are that they suggest short oriented line segments as primary visual features. This motivated a view of the visual system as taking a picture of the world and transforming it into a line drawing for subsequent analysis. An important further development of this finding involved considering how these line detectors could be created from basic neural mechanisms. At the time it was already known that neurons earlier in the visual pathway, in the retina and thalamus, had shown

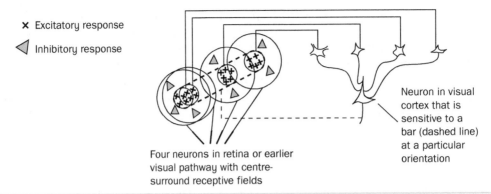

✗ Excitatory response

◁ Inhibitory response

Four neurons in retina or earlier
visual pathway with centre-
surround receptive fields

Neuron in visual
cortex that is
sensitive to a
bar (dashed line)
at a particular
orientation

Figure 2.10 **Simple detectors can be combined to make more complex feature detectors.** From Hubel and Wiesel (1962) we can see how four centre-surround circular receptive fields can be wired together in cortex to form a feature detector that is sensitive to an oriented bar. Four such centre-surround receptive fields are shown with each being excited by light shone on the centre and inhibited by light shone in the annulus surrounding the centre. Combination of these receptive fields by a neuron in visual cortex produces a neuron that is sensitive to a bar at a particular orientation.

Source: Hubel, D. H., & Wiesel, T. N. (1962). Receptive fields, binocular interaction and functional architecture in the cat's visual cortex. *The Journal of Physiology*, *160*, 106–154.

sensitivity only for spots of light (not oriented lines) in a manner known as a centre-surround receptive field. In this centre-surround design either a bright spot surrounded by a dark annulus or a dark spot surrounded by a light annulus is the best visual arrangement to stimulate a neuron. An insight of Hubel and Wiesel was that theoretically one could wire together arrays of these earlier centre-surround receptive fields as input to produce a neuron that was sensitive to an oriented line (see Figure 2.10). Moreover, it was possible to wire together these oriented line detectors to explain more sophisticated neural responses. Thus, this result launched an understanding of feature detectors in vision that were built upon increasingly complex arrangements of basic feature detectors.

A wealth of both experimental and theoretical studies followed on from the 1959 experiment. For example, it was shown by Hubel and Wiesel that development of these feature detectors depends upon having an adequately rich visual experience. This result was of great practical significance in demonstrating that there are sensitive periods in the development of sensory processing and resulted in more insightful treatment of infants and young children with sensory deficits.

AUDITORY SYSTEM

The encoding of auditory information begins within a special structure in the ear known as the cochlea and is transmitted from there to a part of the brain known as primary auditory cortex (Figure 2.11). The cochlea contains a band of nervous tissue known as

Basilar membrane is a stiff structural element located in the inner ear which contains specialized fluids as well as the hair cells that are key in transducing sound energy into neural impulses.

the basilar membrane on which hair cells are located, and these hair cells move in response to sound pressure to transduce vibration into a nervous signal to be sent along the auditory nerve. The perceived pitch of a sound depends in a complex way on the frequency of the sound pressure vibrations and one way that pitch is encoded is that different sections of the basilar membrane are sensitive to different pitches of sound. Aspects of the basilar membrane near to the base of the cochlea encode high-frequency sound and aspects at the apex of the cochlea encode low frequency. For example, if we listen to a choir we can imagine the voices of the sopranos being encoded at the base and the voices of the bass singers being encoded at the apex. In the primary auditory

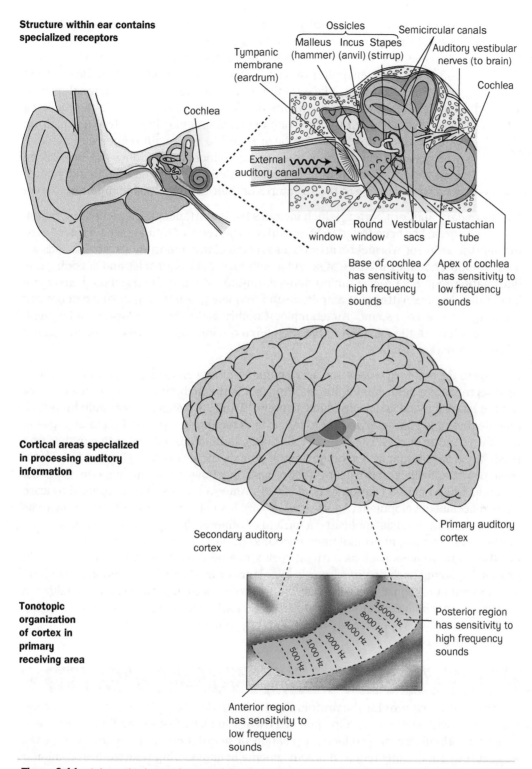

Structure within ear contains specialized receptors

Cochlea

Ossicles

Malleus (hammer) Incus (anvil) Stapes (stirrup)

Tympanic membrane (eardrum)

Semicircular canals

Auditory vestibular nerves (to brain)

Cochlea

External auditory canal

Oval window Round window Vestibular sacs Eustachian tube

Base of cochlea has sensitivity to high frequency sounds

Apex of cochlea has sensitivity to low frequency sounds

Cortical areas specialized in processing auditory information

Secondary auditory cortex

Primary auditory cortex

Tonotopic organization of cortex in primary receiving area

16000 Hz
8000 Hz
4000 Hz
2000 Hz
1000 Hz
500 Hz

Posterior region has sensitivity to high frequency sounds

Anterior region has sensitivity to low frequency sounds

Figure 2.11   Information is sent from specialized receptors in the basilar membrane to the primary auditory cortex. The ear contains specialized receptors that transduce sound waves into neural signals and these signals make their way to the primary auditory cortex. The primary auditory cortex is organized in a tonotopic fashion with specific frequencies of sound represented in specific parts of the brain. Adjacent to the primary auditory cortex is the secondary auditory cortex that is also involved in processing sound information

Source: (T) Adapted from Holt, N. et al. (2012). *Psychology: The science of mind and behaviour*, McGraw-Hill Education. (B) adapted from Kandel et al. (2000). *Principles of neural science*.

Tonotopic map is where the auditory processing of different tones is arranged in an orderly layout in cortex. Firing rates is a term from neurophysiology where the activity of a single cell or group of cells is recorded. A high firing rate indicates great activity of the cell due to sensitivity to the incoming information.

cortex this segregation of pitches is preserved with pitches of similar frequencies neighbouring each other. This arrangement in auditory cortex, known as a tonotopic map, is similar to that obtained in vision where there is a retinotopic mapping of visual space onto visual cortex. Besides the encoding of pitch by place on the basilar membrane, an additional mechanism for pitch encoding exploits the fact that firing rates in the auditory nerve can vary with higher pitch sounds creating higher-frequency firing rates. Firing rates have also been found to vary with perceived loudness, with greater firing rates corresponding to increased loudness. In Box 2.3 we explain how cochlear implants can be used to restore hearing to individuals who have damage to the structures of their ear but an intact auditory nerve.

The secondary auditory cortex, which includes the important speech perception region Wernicke's area, has been found to be sensitive to patterns of timing (see Chapter 13 for further discussion of Wernicke's area). This is particularly important as most sounds we hear contain a complex mixture of sound amplitudes and frequencies and decoding this information requires precise timing. Indeed, timbre, which is the psychological correlate of the complex patterns of amplitude and frequency, is possibly the most important property of perceived sound. An example of timbre is that both a clarinet and a piano can play a tone of the same pitch but they have obvious differences in sound quality; this corresponds to timbre.

Scan to watch a video explaining amusia and what it is like for a sufferer

Damage to the auditory cortex and surrounding regions can lead to a variety of deficits such as receptive aphasia and amusia. Aphasia is the inability to use either verbal or written language and is discussed in Chapters 12 and 13. Amusia, commonly known as tone deafness, is characterized by a deficit in detecting fine-grained pitch changes in melodies (Ayotte et al., 2000; Peretz et al., 2002). Individuals with amusia can thus find music to be an unorganized arrangement of sounds that is even unpleasant to hear. In some cases, amusia is a transient effect of a stroke, however it can sometimes persist for an extended period (Sarkamo et al., 2009). Amusia has also been reported to arise from abnormal development (Ayotte et al., 2002). Recent examination of the brain areas implicated in amusia has implicated a variety of other brain regions and thus it appears to not involve simply abnormal pitch encoding (Stewart et al., 2006). The involvement of other brain regions such as parietal cortex has been implicated in other deficits in processing sound such as phonagnosia (Vanlancker et al., 1989). In phonagnosia individuals cannot recognize the sound of familiar voices although they can discriminate a variety of other sounds. These individuals suffer particularly in not being able to recognize the identity of a speaker when talking on the phone.

Box 2.3 Practical Application: Cochlear implants

Cochlear implants are devices that provide the profoundly deaf with the ability to hear and understand speech and other sounds. Cochlear implants rely upon electrical stimulation of the auditory nerve, and attempts to use electrical stimulation to produce a sensation of hearing go back hundreds of years. However, producing successful designs required advancements in engineering (electronics, computer technology and compatible materials for implantation) as well as advances in understanding the relationship between physiology of the ear and the psychology of hearing and speech perception. Modern research into cochlear implants started in the 1950s with the first devices implanted in the 1980s, and research is still ongoing to improve performance.

A cochlear implant has two essential components (Figure 2.12). One component is external and includes a microphone, sound processor and a transmitter system. The other component is an implanted receiver

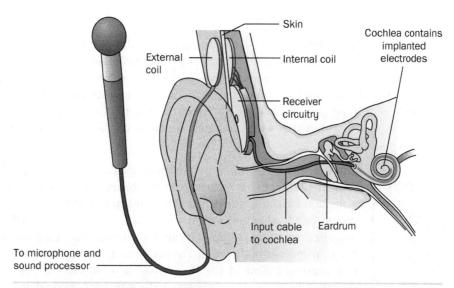

Figure 2.12   Ear with cochlear implant.

Source: Holt, N. et al. (2012). *Psychology: The science of mind and behaviour*. McGraw-Hill Education.

and an electrode array system to transmit signals to the auditory nerve. The implantation procedure requires a special surgery to secure the receiver and to place the electrode array along the winding length of the cochlea. From the perspective of psychology, the two most relevant aspects are the external sound processor and the internal electrode array. Together, the sound processor and electrode array must act to replace the complex acoustics of the inner ear and the complex transduction properties of the receptors in producing a signal to be sent along the auditory nerve that the brain can decode.

The sound processors have the job of taking as input the full audio signal and reducing that to the critical acoustic information for a user to function in the world. An example of a simple sound processor is the telephone that takes our voice and only transmits the sound frequencies from around 400 to 3400 Hz (the full range of human hearing for a typical adult is around 15 to 15,000 Hz) and this is why voices sound different on the telephone. Limiting the amount of information transmitted is an important design constraint as the sound processor has limited computing power and there are only a small number of electrodes to stimulate the auditory nerve. (There are tens of electrodes in a cochlear implant and this is small compared to the thousands of receptors along the basilar membrane in the healthy ear.) The electrodes are spaced along the length of the cochlea to take advantage of the place encoding of pitch and the sound processor can also exploit firing rate encoding of sound by varying the frequency of the stimulation.

In some cases cochlear implants are given to children and they develop with this experience of sound. Adults who receive cochlear implants typically require an extended period of time before the sound experience can organize itself into a useful signal. However, once this is achieved they are typically able to clearly understand speech in a relatively quiet environment. Once there is noise, performance at understanding speech can diminish. In particular, it has been noted that background music can produce a background noise that makes it difficult to understand speech. Indeed, there are complaints among adults that listening to music becomes unpleasant after a cochlear implant. At least part of this results from the fact that the cochlear implants cannot fully reproduce properties such as the timbre of a sound. Thus, one might be able to detect different pitches of a sound but not appreciate the difference between a piccolo and a violin playing the same pitch. Perception of music is one example of the challenges that remain for advancing the state of the art in cochlear implants and understanding auditory perception will play an essential part of these advancements.

SOMATOPERCEPTION SYSTEM

The somatoperception system as revealed by Table 2.1 is a combination of several different subsystems including proprioception, vestibular sensation and touch. Proprioception and vestibular sensation give us a sense of the position of our limbs relative to our body and our body in space. Both of these are important factors for producing and controlling action (Chapter 8). Touch is used to obtain information about objects in the world and in this way functions similarly to vision to enable us to recognize objects.

Central sulcus is a major anatomical landmark on the brain that forms the boundary between parietal cortex and frontal cortex. Brodmann areas were developed in 1909 by Korbinian Brodmann, a German neurologist, who divided the brain into approximately 50 regions distinguished by the structural properties of the neuronal architecture.

The processing of touch begins in specialized receptors in the skin, which project pathways of neurons to the brain. These pathways terminate in a portion of the brain called the primary somatosensory cortex and also known as SI, which is located next to the central sulcus. (Figure 2.13). The organization of this region is somatotopic with local regions of cortex dedicated to specific body parts. The somatosensory homunculus ('little human') is a representation of the amount of somatosensory cortex dedicated to different body parts. It shows body size proportional to size of cortical representation and is a convenient way to visualize the allocation of somatosensory processing over the body (Figure 2.13). As can be seen, body areas like the lips and fingers, which are highly sensitive to touch, are large in the homunculus. A further organizing principle of the somatosensory system is the subdivision of processing specialization that run in strips along the length of the primary somatosensory cortex. These different strips can be identified by the anatomic convention of brain areas defined by Brodmann areas (Figure 2.13). This division includes area 3A, which involves proprioception, and area 3B, which involves simple representations of touch. Areas 1 and 2 show sensitivity to more complex features, such as particular directions of skin stimulation in area 1 and particular shapes in area 2. Brain regions adjacent to the primary somatosensory cortex such as the secondary somatosensory area (SII) and the posterior parietal cortex have been shown to be involved in further elaboration of somatosensory representations.

Damage to the somatosensory cortex typically results in a loss of proprioception and fine touch. This can lead to deficits in the ability to know where on the body one is being touched or to be aware of being touched at all (Head & Holmes, 1911; Longo et al., 2010). However, one of the more profound examples of dysfunction of the somatosensory system arises from phantom limbs that can occur when an individual loses a limb. Here, it is not damage to the cortex itself but to the body that creates unique perceptual experiences. Individuals with phantom limbs can report a clear perceptual awareness of their missing limb (Melzack, 1990, 1992) even though they are aware that the limb is missing. The primary issue is that the perceptual apparatus of the brain to represent the

Figure 2.13 *(opposite)* **Information is sent from specialized receptors in the skin to the primary somatosensory cortex.** The skin contains specialized receptors that transduce mechanical energy into neural signals which make their way to the somatosensory cortex. The somatosensory cortex is organized in a somatotopic fashion with different parts of the body represented along its length. The homunculus shows how this representation of body surface is distributed in the brain, with greater brain area dedicated to body parts like the tongue and hand. Another organizational principle in the somatosensory cortex is found along its width, with simple representation of touch in Brodmann area 3 and more fine-tuned processing in Brodmann areas 1 and 2. Adjacent areas in the secondary somatosensory cortex and parietal cortex are also engaged in processing somatosensory information.

Source: (M) Adapted from Kandel et al. (2000). *Principles of neural science*; (B) Holt, N. et al. (2012). *Psychology: The science of mind and behaviour*. McGraw-Hill Education.

Skin contains specialized receptors

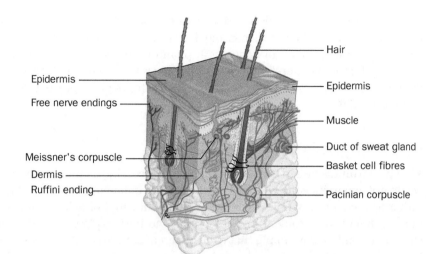

- Hair
- Epidermis
- Muscle
- Duct of sweat gland
- Basket cell fibres
- Pacinian corpuscle

- Epidermis
- Free nerve endings
- Meissner's corpuscle
- Dermis
- Ruffini ending

Cortical areas specialized in processing somatosensory information

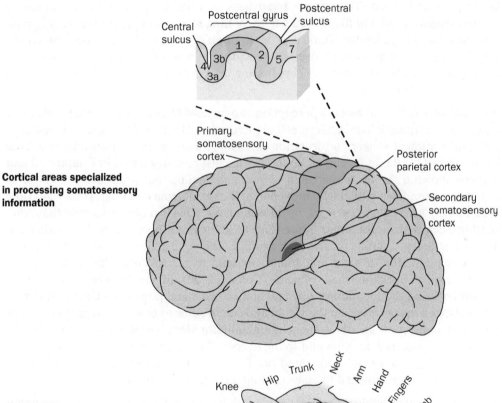

Central sulcus
Postcentral gyrus
Postcentral sulcus
4 3b 1 2 5 7
3a

Primary somatosensory cortex

Posterior parietal cortex

Secondary somatosensory cortex

Somatotopic organization of cortex in primary receiving area

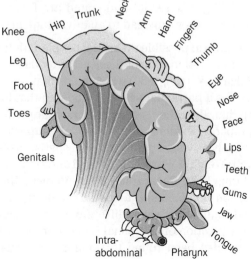

Knee Hip Trunk Neck Arm Hand Fingers
Leg   Thumb
Foot   Eye
Toes   Nose
                                       Face
Genitals   Lips
                                       Teeth
                                       Gums
                                       Jaw
Intra-abdominal   Pharynx   Tongue

lost part of the body still exists and the resulting activity appears to override any cognitive awareness that the limb is missing. Debate still surrounds the treatment of the often painful sensations that can occur with phantom limbs. However, it is acknowledged that a key factor in understanding the condition is to reveal how the adult cortex remaps the regions of somatosensory cortex which are no longer represented (Ramachandran & Hirstein, 1998).

MULTISENSORY INTEGRATION

We have so far discussed the senses and their processing channels separately. However, we do not experience the world as a collection of independent pieces of information but rather as a coherent whole. How we combine information within and across senses is thus an important problem in perception. The best explanation of why information should be combined is simply that each different source of information about the world has its own particular strengths and weaknesses and thus combining the information should provide benefit. This is true regardless of whether information is combined within a sensory modality like vision where motion, stereo and pictorial cues might all be incorporated to judge the shape and depth of an object or whether visual and auditory information might both be used to indicate the location of an object. Combining sensory information has practical benefits for the construction of multisensory interfaces, as is described in Box 2.4.

Two examples from audiovisual perception can be used to demonstrate that sights and sounds are integrated. The McGurk effect (McGurk & MacDonald, 1976) demonstrates that combination of sensory information can lead to a perception that is different from that produced by the independent sources. This effect is discussed in Chapter 13 and involves showing the lip movements of someone saying 'ga' while the sound 'ba' is played synchronously with the lip movement. The result from combining this visual 'ga' and auditory 'ba' is the experience of the sound 'da'. This is a clear example that combination occurs since the vivid impression of 'da' cannot be explained by either the visual or auditory component. The next example, the ventriloquist effect, demonstrates that the combination of sight and sound can lead to improved intelligibility. Acts of ventriloquism go back thousands of years (Connor, 2000) and are the related phenomena of misattributing the location of a sound source. This is a powerful effect and Driver (1996) showed that even when the visual and sound sources of a person speaking were presented at different locations speech intelligibility increased when participants mistakenly fused together the sight and sound to come from a common origin. This increase in intelligibility when sight and sound are fused together illustrates how integrating sensory information can lead to an advantage in understanding the world.

There are several possible theoretical explanations of how the perceptual system might combine information. One of these is the modality appropriate hypothesis (Welch et al., 1986; Welch & Warren, 1980) which holds that for each physical property of the environment there is a particular sensory modality that has a higher acuity for estimating this property than the other senses; this modality will *always* dominate bimodal estimates of the property. Evidence for the modality appropriate hypothesis comes from experiments that show vision dominating on spatial tasks (Bertelson & Radeau, 1981; Warren et al., 1981; Welch & Warren, 1980) and audition dominating on temporal tasks (Gebhard & Mowbray, 1959; Recanzone, 2003; Shipley, 1964; Welch et al., 1986). An example, where vision dominates in a spatial localization task, is when a flash and sound are presented simultaneously at different locations, and the location of the sound is attributed to the position of the visual flash (Bertelson & Radeau, 1981; Warren et al., 1981). Vision has also been found to dominate a visual-somatoperception estimate of the straightness of lines (Easton & Moran, 1978; Hay, Pick & Ikeda, 1965). When distorting glasses are worn to make straight line objects look curved participants tend to feel the straight object yet feel/experience it as curved. These examples of vision dominating other senses are termed 'visual capture'. Hay et al. (1965) reported a large influence of vision on the other sense involved but very little, if any, influence of the other senses on vision. There is, however, evidence of an auditory corollary to 'visual capture', auditory driving. Whereas evidence for 'visual capture' comes from spatial tasks, evidence for auditory driving comes from cases where the rate of a visual stimulus is distorted by the rate of an auditory stimulus (Gebhard & Mowbray, 1959; Recanzone, 2003; Shipley, 1964; Welch et al., 1986). For example, using tempo discrimination experiments Recanzone (2003) showed conclusively that, even when asked to discriminate tempo solely on the basis of a visual cue (e.g. flashing light), the presence of a discrepant auditory cue (e.g. beeping tone) has a profound biasing influence on visual estimates of tempo; there was 'no measurable influence' from discrepant visual cues on auditory estimates of tempo.

Recent research, however, suggests that the idea that the most appropriate modality (i.e. the one with the highest acuity for the physical property) will *always* dominate bimodal estimates is incomplete. For example, Ernst and Banks (2002) found that, depending on information quality, either visual or somatosensory information could dominate a visual-somatoperception bimodal estimate of height. Alais and Burr (2004) also showed that despite vision under normal circumstances having a higher acuity for spatial estimates than audition, an auditory click can dominate a bimodal audiovisual location estimate ('an inverse ventriloquist effect'). These results have been described in terms of a maximum-likelihood estimation strategy (Clark & Yuille, 1990; Ernst & Banks, 2002; Landy et al., 1995). In this strategy the more reliable perceptual information is weighted more heavily than the less reliable perceptual information. In this way the perceptual system actively monitors the reliability of the incoming information and attaches more significance to the reliable input.

Evaluation

The maximum likelihood model of cue integration explains that the cues will be combined in accordance with their reliability, and that this weighting can dynamically respond to environmental conditions. This finding does not necessarily contradict the previous modality-appropriate hypothesis, but instead adds a dynamic aspect to what had been considered a static view of how cues would combine. However, recent work is only beginning to address this problem of dynamic cue weighting (Sheppard et al., 2013). Relatively little is known about the particular mechanisms that monitor reliability and how responsive they can be in changing cue weights. This points out the issue that as one moves from static to dynamic theories of perception and cognition there is a challenge to understand these dynamics.

Box 2.4 Practical Application: Multisensory warning signals in driving

Driving is a highly visual task and thus when we take our eyes off the road ahead we are taking a risk. Indeed, the importance of vision was highlighted in a recent naturalistic driving study (Klauer et al., 2006), in which it was found that 78 per cent of all crashes and 65 per cent of all near-misses involved the driver looking away from the forward roadway in the moments just prior to the incident. While such a result is not surprising, it does raise the question of whether anything can be done to prevent the situation. If an upcoming dangerous situation could be automatically detected then some kind of warning would be helpful. It has been suggested that an extra 500 milliseconds would lead to a 60 per cent

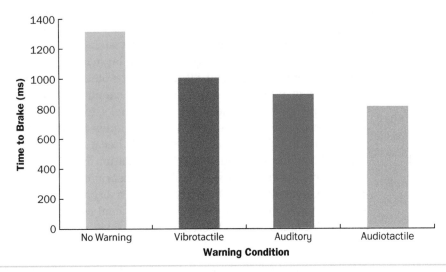

Figure 2.14   Latencies for audio, vibrotactile, audiotactile and no warnings. Participants in the experiment had the task of braking in response to adverse conditions. If we take baseline performance as the time it takes when given a vibrotactile warning, then participants were around 30 per cent slower when given no warning, and 20 per cent faster when given a warning signal that contained both audio and tactile information in combination.

Source: Data from Ho, C., Reed, N. & Spence, C. (2007). Multisensory In-Car Warning Signals for Collision Avoidance. *Human Factors*, *49*(6), 1107–1114.

reduction in the incidence of front-to-rear end collisions, which accounts for approximately 25 per cent of all accidents (Spence & Ho, 2008; Suetomi & Kido, 1997).

If we assume that an incident detection technology exists already or could be developed in the near future, then the question arises, what is the best way to provide a warning signal? The driving environment has already become overloaded with technology producing sensory information (Sivak, 1996). Thus, the design of a warning signal would benefit from utilizing clear principles based on cognitive psychology. Although traditional models of sensory processing in driving hold that independent sensory channels are processed largely independently (Wickens, 1980, 1992, 2002), it has been proposed recently that multisensory signals are of greater benefit than unisensory signals in providing warning (Spence & Ho, 2008). These claims arise from studies such as that by Ho et al. (2007) which examined the latencies (time from warning to putting foot on the brake) for an audio, a vibrotactile (vibrating buzzer), and an audiotactile (vibrating buzzer plus sound) warning as well as no warning. The results are shown in Figure 2.14 and we can see that the greatest benefit is found for the audiotactile warning.

Although further questions remain, such as how best to provide the vibrotactile stimulation (in the seat, the seatbelt or the steering wheel) and where best to localize the audio sound source in space, the case is clear that multisensory warning signals hold great promise. Such findings could be of benefit to particular groups of drivers. For example, Laurienti and colleagues (Laurienti et al., 2006) reported that the elderly participants in their study (mean age of 71 years; ranging from 65–90 years) responded to auditory and visual targets 15 per cent more slowly than did a group of younger participants (mean age of 28 years; ranging from 18–38 years). However, the older participants were able to respond to multisensory targets (consisting of the simultaneous presentation of the auditory and visual targets) as rapidly as the younger participants could respond to either of the unimodal targets. As driving technology capabilities increase, there is a need for an associated increase in our understanding of perceptual and cognitive factors that allows us to design a driving environment to help drivers focus on relevant information without distracting them with irrelevant information.

RECOGNITION

A straightforward view of how recognition works is that general perceptual processes produce an object representation that can be compared to a stored internal representation. If the perceptual representation matches an internally stored representation in memory then the object is recognized. While many potential recognition schemes have been examined, it has turned out to be a difficult problem to capture the essence of human recognition capabilities. The key capability in which human recognition excels is the robust way it can evaluate many different perceptual inputs and recognize these different inputs as the same thing. For example, take a moment to imagine all the ways a simple letter 'A' can be written and you can begin to appreciate the issue. If you include

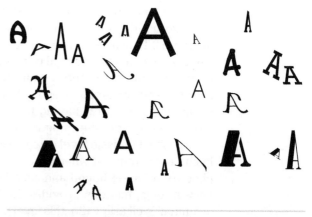

Figure 2.15 Many different shapes can have the same identity. All these figures represent the letter 'A'; however, it is difficult to quantify the essential, invariant property of the figures which allows them all to be recognized as an 'A'.

all the possible ways to transform these different versions of 'A' such as rotation and scaling (shrinking or enlarging) that still allow recognition the capability becomes all the more impressive (Figure 2.15). Moreover, this recognition capability is not isolated to vision and in Chapter 13, when covering speech understanding, we will see there is the equivalent capability to recognize the sound of a letter despite the many ways it is produced by different voices. This robustness of our perceptual systems to such variability shows that we cannot be using a simple template matching system where, like the children's toy, the round peg goes in the round hole and the square peg in the square hole.

One property of effective recognition systems is that they are able to represent the information in a way that preserves the essence of the object upon different transformations. To examine this property further we return to our example of recognizing an 'A' with the goal of finding a representation that preserves the essential information upon transformation. One approach, known as a feature analysis, involves deconstructing an object into a set of component features that can be compared to a library. Inside this library each object is described by a unique set of features. The list of features could include the number of line segments and their patterns of connectivity, such as the types of angles between the different segments. The difficulty with such an approach is coming up with a unique feature list that could capture all the different versions of an 'A' and would be applicable after all possible transformations. One way to overcome such challenges was the Pandemonium model proposed by Selfridge (1958). In this model, so-called demons are arranged in a hierarchy, with lower demons assigned to evaluate the utility of individual features and higher-level demons assigned with evaluating the success of these sub-demons. This hierarchy could be extended to include demons for recognition of words, and higher still to recognize phrases. For example, to model how this sentence is read and understood we can imagine one set of demons that puts the line-shapes into letters, another set that puts the letters into words, a set that assigns meaning to the words and a final set that arranges the individual meanings into a coherent idea.

We have been using the example of an 'A' to motivate our explanation of recognition. One essential issue discussed was that there is a large variety of shapes we might call an 'A' and this posed the challenge of how to come up with a distinct feature list that would capture the essence of an object. Another approach to solving this challenge is provided by prototype theory (Rosch, 1973), where the goal is to find what member of a category is the best example of that category. For example, although all of the letters in Figure 2.15 can be seen as an 'A', some are rarer and more exotic examples of an 'A' while others are more typical or central to the category. Determining what members of a category are more central than others allows a more graded response to distinguish across the members of a category. For example, if we take the features of a bird to include (1) having a beak, (2) having feathers, (3) able to fly, we see that a robin is a more typical exemplar of the category of birds than a penguin. A further notion of prototype theory is that of basic level categorization, which is defined as the response that is most likely to be produced when asked to categorize an object. Thus, when presented with a photo of a basset hound and asked what you see, most people will respond with the answer 'dog', and this provides the basic level of categorization. While the response 'mammal' is clearly valid, this level is superordinate to the basic level of categorization; 'basset hound' is valid at a subordinate level of categorization. The boundaries between different basic level categories are not fixed since we are dynamically taking on new information that might cause us to rearrange our category boundaries. However, a basic assumption is that categorization works to come up with basic level categories that maximize the difference between other basic level categories and minimize the variability within elements of the same basic level category. Such an approach leads to maximally informative categories, and while we can expect these to be largely similar among a population, differences would be predicted. For example, an expert dog breeder when shown the photo of the basset hound will likely respond 'basset hound' rather than 'dog'. A reason for this is that within their rich knowledge of dog breeds they possess subordinate categories to distinguish between the Basset Artesian Normand and the Basset Bleu de Gascogne. Thus, 'basset hound' becomes the basic level response.

OBJECTS

We are going to discuss two cases of object recognition, the first involving the visual system and the second the somatoperception system. Although different in many ways, both illustrate the selection of features used for recognition. Defining the features used and how they can be obtained and computed is an essential aspect of object recognition.

Visual object recognition

Most objects in the natural world are three-dimensional; this is problematic for vision since it faces the task of recognizing a three-dimensional object with only the two-dimensional information on the retina. An influential paper from Binford (1981) provided a series of assumptions about how to relate lines in an image or line drawing to the possible three dimensional configurations that could have caused them to occur. For example, consider Figure 2.16 and the following statement made about it: 'If a true edge e of a solid is truncated by a visible surface S, the result is a vertex whose image is an arrow junction or Y junction.' This observation is critical in that it tells us that from whichever viewpoint we observe the object, when the world is projected onto our retina and the depth

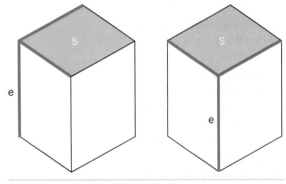

Figure 2.16 Truncating an edge with a surface creates a 'Y' junction that is viewpoint invariant. Binford (1981) demonstrated that if an edge 'e' were truncated by a surface 'S', then the image would contain a 'Y' junction. This is demonstrated in the figure by showing two different views of the edge 'e' truncated by 'S'.

Source: Adapted from Binford, T. O. (1981). Inferring surfaces from images. *Artificial Intelligence, 17*(1), 205–244.

dimension lost, the Y junction will be formed. Thus the Y junction is known as a viewpoint invariant relationship. Following on from this logic, numerous other viewpoint invariant relations were derived and their significance to human object recognition explored (Jacobs, 2003; Pomerantz & Kubovy, 1986).

> Viewpoint invariant relationship is any aspect of an object that is preserved no matter the direction from which we view the object.

One way to exploit these viewpoint invariant relations for object recognition is to create a set of volumetric primitives that have unique combinations of viewpoint invariant relations. These volumetric primitives can serve like the letters of an alphabet do to generate words. If we can model objects as created by a set of volumetric primitives then we can recognize an object from arbitrary viewpoints since each part of the object is recognizable by its unique collection of viewpoint invariant properties. An example of such a volumetric primitive is a brick (Figure 2.17a), which is specified by its arrangement of arrows and Y junctions as well as parallel lines. The use of viewpoint invariant features for recognition was further advanced by Biederman (1987), who named his volumetric primitives 'geons'. At the heart of his recognition by components (RBC) approach was that objects could be thought of as composed of a collection of geons. Since every individual geon in an object could be recovered by its unique collection of viewpoint invariant properties, this allowed the entire object to be recognized (Figure 2.17b).

> Geons are the elements of a set of volumetric primitives or shapes that can be recognized from any viewpoint, proposed by Biederman in his recognition by components (RBC) theory.

This RBC approach was demonstrated to reflect human performance on a variety of object recognition experiments. One such experiment used systematic deletion of particular parts of a line drawing to demonstrate that geon recovery was crucial for

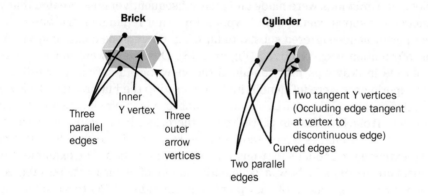

(a)

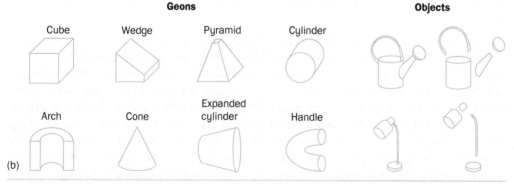

(b)

Figure 2.17 Geon properties and objects composed of geons. (a) Viewpoint invariant properties of two different geons. (b) These and other geons are used to make a number of different objects.

Source: (a) Biederman, I. (1987b). Recognition-by-components: A theory of human image understanding. *Psychological Review*, 94(2), 115–147. APA; reproduced with permission. (b) Adapted from Gobet et al. (2011). *Foundations of cognitive psychology*. McGraw-Hill Education.

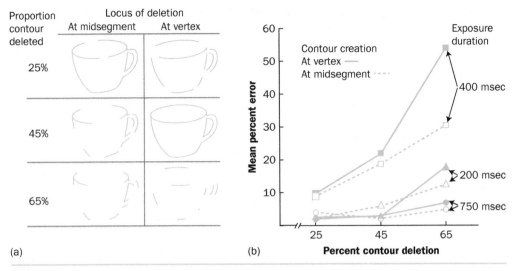

Figure 2.18   Visual stimuli and contour deletion. (a) Portions of line drawings were removed either at a midsegment location or at a vertex location to impair recovery of the geon structure of the object. (b) Results show that removal of vertices has a greater impact on object recognition than at midsegment, particularly for short exposure to objects with extensive contour deletion.

Source: Biederman, I. (1987b). Recognition-by-components: A theory of human image understanding. *Psychological Review*, 94(2), 115–147. APA; reproduced with permission

recognition. Line drawings were made and then subsequent versions created that were either deleted at regions containing viewpoint invariant regions or elsewhere. It was found that performance suffered substantially when the regions containing viewpoint invariant information were removed (Figure 2.18). Observers were much quicker to identify objects in drawings that contained the viewpoint invariant properties. This and other experiments were influential in demonstrating the importance of viewpoint invariant relationships and how RBC could account for viewpoint independent recognition of objects from line drawings. However, there has been some criticism of its ability to perform on images generated from the real world and doubts that it could be flexibly extended to model subordinate level categorization. For example, RBC is clearly adequate to explain how a schematic model of a bird can be created for recognizing birds independent of viewpoint, but extending RBC to account for the ability to distinguish between the shape of a robin, a wren and a raven becomes more complicated.

One theory of object recognition, known as multiple views theory, rose to challenge the RBC approach, asserting that recognition is fundamentally image-based (Tarr & Bulthoff, 1998). It argued that object recognition could be achieved by storing representations of a few select views of the object that had been learned. From these select views, sophisticated mechanisms could fill in representations of the intermediate views. Thus, when one observed a novel view of an object it could be recognized by mechanisms that matched the viewed image to the select and intermediate filled-in versions. This method predicted that recognition would be better when viewing objects from directions more similar to the learned views. Several series of experiments using stimuli containing bent paperclips or other novel objects provided evidence that recognition was not always viewpoint invariant, but instead could depend importantly on viewpoint (Logothetis & Sheinberg, 1996). This dependence on viewpoint ran counter to the claims of the RBC approach, which held recognition to be viewpoint independent.

Training images   Informative image fragments

Figure 2.19   Learning features for recognition. Ullman and colleagues (2002) developed a system that used the most informative image fragments to obtain recognition. Here we show on the left a set of horse images that the system was trained to recognize. The most informative image fragments are shown to the right and recognition of an image was obtained on the basis of how it matched this set of informative fragments.

Source: Ullman, S., Vidal-Naquet, M., & Sali, E. (2002). Visual features of intermediate complexity and their use in classification. *Nature Neuroscience*, 5(7), 682–687.

A spirited debate ran between the RBC and view-based camps as to which approach was more appropriate to model human object recognition (Biederman & Gerhardstein, 1995; Tarr & Bulthoff, 1995). Ultimately, several researchers obtained evidence that the object recognition system shows flexibility in being able to utilize both view-dependent and view-independent properties to recognize objects (Foster & Gilson, 2002; Hayward, 2003). In addition, variants of these two approaches were developed. For example, an approach by Ullman and colleagues (2002) used information theory to show that patches of images with intermediate complexity were optimal to encode a set of images for subsequent recognition tasks (Figure 2.19). This approach shares with RBC the use of a set of informative image features but does not require them to be informative about three-dimensional structure, only that they optimally describe the objects to be recognized.

In a final note about visual object recognition we address a question that you might have considered already. This is whether object recognition also relies upon factors such as colour, or does shape dominate? Clearly for tasks such as picking ripe fruit it would seem that colour is essential. However, it appears that for human object recognition colour comes into play only when shape is ambiguous, though long-term colour knowledge can play a role in top-down mechanisms (Mapelli & Behrmann, 1997). It is remarkable that shape alone is so influential, and that even simple line drawings can convey rich information about the object depicted. Possibly this can be explained by the human visual system's generous allocation of brain resources to the representation of spatial properties of the visual world.

Somatoperceptive object recognition

The second case of object recognition we will discuss is how the somatoperception system is used to recognize objects. Free exploration of an object, for example with the hands, will engage subsystems of the somatoperceptual system that involve estimating the weight and texture of an object as well as the position of the body parts touching the object. Collectively these subsystems contribute to what is called haptic perception (Lederman &

Haptic perception is the combination of abilities that allow us to represent the material characteristics of objects and surfaces for recognition.

Klatzky, 2009; Woods & Newell, 2004). When trying to identify an object using haptics it has been shown that frequently a single grasp is sufficient to recognize the object (Klatzky et al., 1985). However, when more detailed aspects are required, the hand engages in stereotypical 'exploratory procedures' that are shown in Figure 2.20 along with a table providing the hypothesized functions of these different procedures (Lederman & Klatzky, 1986). These exploratory procedures have been shown to be effective in recognizing surfaces, and it has been shown that a single hand sweep over a surface enables detection of roughness independent of the complexity of the surface (Plaisier et al., 2008). What appears crucial for these exploratory procedures is that the hand actively engages with the surface. The importance of active engagement could be predicted by ecological psychologists. They argued that touch movements made by an active observer provide the phenomenal experience of *touching* an object, while the same physical contact made by placing an object with a passive observer provide the experience

Exploratory procedure

Knowledge about object				
Substance-related properties	texture		Lateral motion	
	hardness		Pressure	
	temperature		Static contact	
	weight		Unsupported holding	
Structure-related properties	weight		Unsupported holding	
	volume		Enclosure	Contour following
	global shape		Enclosure	
	exact shape		Contour following	
Functional properties	part motion		Part motion test	
	specific motion		Function test	

Figure 2.20   Exploratory procedures used in haptic recognition. Exploratory procedures describe the way we manipulate and move our hands over an object to determine its properties and function. For each of the three different categories of object properties (substance-related, structure-related and functional) there are exploratory procedures that provide specific information. For example, lateral motion over the surface provides texture information, which is a substance-related object property,

Source: Adapted from Lederman, S. J., & Klatzky, R. L. (1987). Hand movements: A window into haptic object recognition. *Cognitive Psychology, 19*(3), 342–368.

of *being touched* (Gibson, 1962). However, physiological experiments have shown that when the body is moving, sensory transmission of touch is diminished, and when this is taken into account, substantial differences between active and passive touch are not necessarily revealed (Chapman, 1994). Although some complex recognition tasks might require extensive exploration of the object, this is not always necessary.

Visual agnosia and prosopagnosia

In our discussion of the visual system we mentioned how particular lesions of the brain in occipital cortex and along its border with temporal cortex could destroy one's sense of colour vision or motion perception. Lesions can also occur in the inferior region of temporal cortex that selectively impact the ability to recognize objects (Konen et al., 2011). This condition is known as visual agnosia, and what sets it apart from a condition like blindness is that patients with visual agnosia appear able to extract a reasonably intact perception of what they see but are unable to assign any meaning to this percept (Farah, 1990; Humphreys & Riddoch, 1987). The evidence that visual agnosia is restricted to assigning meaning to vision is striking when observing an interviewer interact with a patient. For example, if we were to interview a patient about recognizing a spoon we could expect the following: we would expect a visual agnosic to be able to pick it up while blindfolded and correctly identify that it is a spoon by using haptic perception. Similarly, if we asked them to tell us what a spoon was, they could provide a rich description of its shape and uses. In addition, if we showed them a metal spoon they would be able to describe its basic visual features – shiny, rounded at one end, etc. However, if we show them a spoon and ask them what it is we will get a confused response that reveals a profound inability to recognize visual objects.

Different forms of visual agnosia can be extremely specific to the type of visual stimuli. Evidence for this is given by a condition known as prosopagnosia (Mayer & Rossion, 2007) where the recognition of faces is severely impaired after brain damage. As with visual agnosia in general, individuals suffering from prosopagnosia can still recognize the identity of individuals by properties such as voice, hairstyle or glasses. However, when presented with just the face of someone familiar they are unable to recognize it. Since there are numerous other routes people use to recognize identity (e.g. voice, hair) it is thought that prosopagnosia might be under-reported due to the success of these alternative recognition strategies. Consistent with this is the recent finding that one form of prosopagnosia can be inherited (Grueter et al., 2007), suggesting that a certain proportion of the population does not naturally develop the talent to recognize faces.

SCENES

The recognition of scenes provides a natural extension of studies in object recognition. In object recognition one typically studies how a single, precisely displayed object in isolation is recognized. Scene recognition involves perception of an environment and includes not only perception of individual objects but also the nature of all the objects taken together. For example, a typical scene of a city is different from a typical scene in a forest and, as we describe in Chapter 3, making this discrimination does not necessarily rely on the recognition of any specific object. Scene recognition is important for understanding how recognition works in the typical cluttered scenes we view when outside of perception labs. The study of scene recognition can even be extended, as we see in Box 2.5, to the question of why we find pleasure in viewing particular scenes.

Box 2.5 Research Close Up: Visual aesthetics and structure of a landscape design

Source: Van Tonder, G. J., Lyons, M. J., & Ejima, Y. (2002). Visual structure of a Japanese Zen garden – The mysterious appeal of a simple and ancient composition of rocks is unveiled. *Nature, 419*(6905), 359–360.

INTRODUCTION

The stone landscape garden of Ryoanji temple was created during the Muromachi era (AD 1333–1573) and despite its sparse design comprised of 15 stones, the enigmatic appeal of the Zen garden, similar to other famous works of art, continues to invite speculation about what peculiar structural properties make this composition special. The intentions of the designer are lost to history, and while various symbolic interpretations of the artwork have been offered, Van Tonder and colleagues analysed the structure of the garden to reveal its perceptual significance (Van Tonder, 2006; Van Tonder et al., 2002). The quantitative property they examined was the medial axis transform (Blum, 1973) of the structure of the garden. The medial axis is like the skeleton of a shape and an example of the medial axis transform of a human contour is shown in Figure 2.21a. One intuitive way to think of the medial axis is

© geWildNatuurfotografie/iStock

to imagine a contour drawn in a field of dry grass that is set alight; the medial axis is where the inward flames meet. There are two reasons why the medial axis is an appropriate choice for examination of the structure of the garden: first, the medial axis has previously been implicated as an important property in the perception of shape (Kovacs & Julesz, 1994) and second the medial axis itself, particularly at branch junctions are those parts of a landscape which afford the most informative views of a landscape (Leyton, 1989). This second point is important since there has become a preferred viewpoint for the garden and it was hypothesized that the medial axis would relate to this point.

METHOD

The primary analysis of Van Tonder and colleagues was to take the location of the 15 stones within the garden and input them to a computer. From this it was possible to compute the medial axis transform of the garden structure and note any special properties. A secondary analysis was performed to see if the properties of the medial axis of the existing garden would still be obtained if changes, such as moving a stone, were performed. This second analysis enables one to determine if the properties obtained were special and unique to the existing garden structure.

RESULTS

The result of the primary analysis is shown in Figure 2.21b where the medial axis can be seen as a black underlay in the form of a branching tree structure, with the main hall in white and the outline of the garden in a black rectangle. The preferred viewing position is shown with a larger red circle and a smaller circle indicates the location of an altar with a statue of Buddha. These medial axis results show that the structure of the empty space between the rock formations is arranged into a hierarchical branching structure that (1) follows proportional rules found in biological branching systems and (2) converges onto the viewing area of the garden, passing nearly through the preferred viewing location.

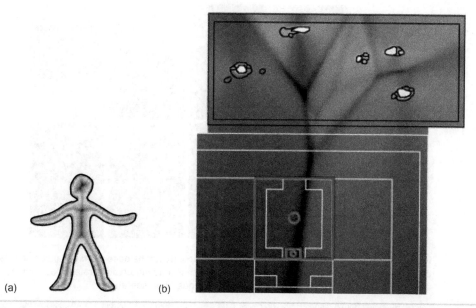

Figure 2.21   (a) The medial axis of a human contour. (b) The medial-axis transformation of the layout of the Zen garden, showing the rock clusters (top) and building plan (AD 1681) of the temple (outlined in white). The main hall is indicated by the larger red square; the larger red circle indicates the preferred viewing point for the garden. The smaller red rectangle and enclosed circle indicate the alcove containing a Buddhist statue.

Source: Van Tonder, G. J., Lyons, M. J., & Ejima, Y. (2002). Visual structure of a Japanese Zen garden. *Nature*, 419(6905), 359–360.

The results of the secondary analysis showed that most or all of the special structural properties of the garden would be lost if a stone were moved. At best (dividing the garden into a grid of 1 square metre units), one needs to randomly cast the fifteen stones into this garden a hundred trillion times before a similar convergent branching network will appear.

DISCUSSION

The results both indicate the principles used by the garden designer in placing the stones and by observers in finding a preferred viewing location. This is exciting because it suggests that we can develop perceptual theories of how landscape garden scenes or other artefacts appeal to our sense of beauty. In particular, the preferred viewing position is at a point where the maximal configuration of the stones would be visible and thus would require the least cognitive resources to view the scene. Additionally, the natural hierarchical branching structure of the medial axis created by this configuration of the stones attests to the garden designer's skill in creating a naturalistic composition since our human perceptual inclination is towards creating symmetry and alignment, the opposite of what is found here. Finally, there is the puzzling observation that the entire medial axis pattern converges exactly onto the Buddhistic altar at the back of the viewing room – from where no human, but only the statue of Buddha can view the garden.

Early research into recognition of a sequence of photographs of complex scenes indicated that presentation times of 250 milliseconds or less was adequate for participants to accurately judge whether or not they had seen a photo in the rapidly presented sequence (Potter & Levy, 1969). More recent studies examining recognition of whether or not an animal was present in a scene presented for 20 milliseconds (Figure 2.22) showed that manual key responses were produced in approximately 400 milliseconds. However, EEG data showed distinctive patterns of electrical activity that indicated correct recognition was obtained in under 150 milliseconds from stimulus presentation (Thorpe et al., 1996). These and other results (Kirchner & Thorpe, 2006; Van Rullen & Thorpe, 2001) confirm that humans are very good at rapidly processing visual scenes.

Figure 2.22   Recognizing whether an animal is present can be done rapidly. Various scenes and animals of the type used in the experiments by Thorpe and colleagues demonstrated that humans could encode whether an animal was present within 150 milliseconds of presentation.

Source: Reprinted from Kirchner, H., & Thorpe, S. J. (2006). Ultra-rapid object detection with saccadic eye movements: Visual processing speed revisited. *Vision Research, 46*(11), 1762–1776, with permission from Elsevier

When we discussed the visual system we stated that an abundance of cortical area was dedicated to processing the fovea (the centre of the retina). For this extra processing power to be effective the eye must place the centre of the retina at the point of interest and keep it fixed to this location. The eyes change where they fixate approximately every 1/3 second and are poor at capturing information when they are not fixated. Figure 2.23 shows an example of a pattern of fixations to a natural scene. What becomes evident is that the pattern of eye movement is complex and that not every part of the scene will be fixated (Henderson & Hollingworth, 1999; Tatler et al., 2010; Yarbus, 1967). An important question then is when presented with a random photo, why do we look where we do? What is driving our eye movements? The two basic possibilities are the familiar bottom-up and top-down explanations. The bottom-up explanation is that novel image properties such as brightness, colour or distinctive shape make particular image locations salient and this image salience is capturing our eye movements. Evidence that this is true comes from biologically inspired models of image salience which use novelty to successfully predict image salience (Itti & Koch, 2001). The top-down explanation is that our goals and expectations are at work to direct the eye movements (Rao et al., 2002; Torralba et al., 2006). (See Chapter 3 for more on this topic.)

Vision is not alone in providing valuable information about the layout of a scene. Audition provides information about the distance, location and number of objects in a scene as well as the general openness of the space. Although amplitude of the sound wave is one obvious cue to distance, the timbre of the incoming sound wave contains distance information. Much as the atmosphere absorbs and scatters light to make distant scenes hazy and thus appear distant, the atmosphere filters sound waves so the high frequencies are attenuated, and this change in the distribution of sound frequencies also signals distance. Similarly, what we hear is a combination of both the sound wave taking a direct path to our ear as well as all the reflections (echoes) of that sound wave. Comparison of the direct and the reflected waves is especially relevant indoors where walls provide multiple reflecting surfaces. Thus, with our eyes closed the sound quality of our footsteps can inform us whether we are walking in a small or large room. A proof of the richness of sound information is given by bats' abilities to use echolocation to navigate, and there is even evidence from some blind humans that

Figure 2.23   Eye scan path of an observer as they view an image of a scene for 10 seconds. The circles represent points where the eye fixed on a visual location and the diameter of the circle is proportional to the time spent looking at that point (fixating). The lines represent the eye movements (saccades) as the eye scans the image. If you are curious about what a scan path might look like to one of your own images visit http://solutions.3m.com/wps/portal/3M/en_US/VAS-NA/VAS/

Image courtesy of Jeff B. Pelz, Carlson Center for Imaging Science, Rochester Institute of Technology

Photo Credit: Madeline Pelz (photograph taken in Prospect Park Dog Run, Brooklyn, NY USA)

Source: Henderson, J. M. (2007). Regarding scenes. *Current Directions in Psychological Science, 16*(4), 219–222.

similar strategies can provide valuable information about the layout of an auditory scene (Rosenblum et al., 2000; Schenkman & Nilsson, 2010).

Segregation of sound streams is a fundamental ability of auditory scene analysis (Bregman, 1990). For example, rhythm can be used in a bottom-up fashion to segregate different sound streams. However, top-down effects allow what we expect to hear based on knowledge about the speaker and situation to shape what we hear. For example, if we are listening to a speaker in a noisy environment we do not hear just a bland mixture of all the sound but our knowledge of language and the context of what we expect to hear guides our abilities to discern the sound and meaning of the speaker. (See Chapter 13 for more on this topic.)

EVENTS

So far, our presentation of the visual recognition of objects and scenes has treated the visual world as static and unchanging. However, motion and change are everywhere. A classic example of how actions unfolding over time are perceived comes from studying how observers interpret the interactions of physical objects. Studies conducted by Albert Éduard Michotte examined simple displays in which one geometric object approached another one that then itself began moving (Michotte et al., 1990; Michotte, 1946, 1963). The nature of the contact between the two objects and subsequent direction and speed of motion of the two objects was studied, and Michotte characterized a range of conditions in which a sequence gives rise to the impression that one object has launched the other into motion (Figure 2.24). Critical variables to see a launching event include the objects' proximity when the second object begins moving, the timing of the motion change, and the relative velocities of the objects' motions (Scholl & Tremoulet, 2000). Related work on perceiving objects in motion showed that even very simple displays composed of geometric objects could, when animated correctly, evoke the perception of complex narratives of social interactions (Heider & Simmel, 1944). The motion properties that make a display be seen as animate or alive include speed changes, direction changes and the relative non-rigid motion of different parts of an object

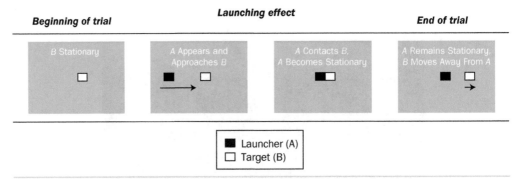

Figure 2.24 Launching phenomenon explored by Michotte. When a moving launcher (object A) contacts a stationary target (object B) it is perceived as A launching B if the time between contact and object B moving is short enough and the speed of object A is sufficiently greater than the velocity of B.

Source: Hubbard, T. L., & Favretto, A. (2003). Naïve impetus and Michotte's 'tool effect': Evidence from representational momentum. *Psychological Research*, 67(2), 134–152. With kind permission from Springer Science and Business Media.

(Schlottmann et al., 2006; Tremoulet & Feldman, 2000). An example of an inanimate object appearing animate is the plastic bag scene from the movie *American Beauty* (Mendes, 1999) where the motion of a plastic bag blowing in the wind is described as 'dancing with me. Like a little kid begging me to play with it'.

The term event perception has been defined in ecological psychology as changes in layout, changes in surface existence or changes in colour and texture (Gibson, 1979). Another definition holds that an event is 'a segment of time at a given location that is conceived by an observer to have a beginning and end' (Zacks & Tversky, 2001, pp. 4–5). This deconstruction of ongoing activity into discrete events with beginning and end can be used to organize our perception of the world. Furthermore, Shipley (2008) observed that these two definitions of events can be related to one another within the context of the perceptual cycle (Neisser, 1976). The perceptual cycle is defined as the cyclic process comprised of the following steps: (1) memory in the form of schema drives exploration, which (2) leads to information pick-up of the kind described by ecological psychology, which (3) leads to potential modification of schema and subsequent repetition of the steps of this cycle. The important situation arises when the happenings of the world do not unfold to match expectations (i.e. our schema do not produce reliable predictions about what happens next). The time that these prediction errors occur can be used to define the time of the boundary of one event finishing and the next one beginning (Zacks et al., 2007). The importance of predictability resonates with earlier experiments by Newtson (1973) who investigated how observers divided action streams into events when they contained different numbers of occurrences where prediction errors occurred. Results showed that action streams with more frequent occurrence of prediction error were divided into more events than action streams where prediction was more successful.

> **Schema** is a framework that represents a plan or a theory, supporting the organization of knowledge.

SOCIAL PERCEPTION

The study of social perception is significant for several reasons. At a basic level, understanding what perceptual information signals social meaning will inform our understanding of human-human interaction at a deeper level. Moreover, as computing and robotics technologies advance rapidly, a precise understanding of how social signals are processed can inform human-computer and human-robot interfaces (Pentland, 2007; Vinciarelli et al., 2009). Another reason is simply that although human activity is complex, it is constrained by our biology. Our faces, bodies and voices limit what sights and sounds we can produce, and how these special signals are perceived informs us about our basic cognitive capabilities. Finally, there is the unique link between perceiving others and our social and emotional responses. For example, following the suggestion of Marr (1982) we can ask, what is the computational theory behind social perception? In other words, what is social perception used for, and why does it do what it does? An answer to this is that social perception informs us about the thoughts, emotions and internal states of others and this is useful information to help us navigate our social world (Frith & Frith, 2003). Following on from this and consistent with Marr's second level, we can view an important aspect of social perception as the transformation from social signals to representation of emotion. Emotion and cognition are covered in Chapter 10 when we discuss decision making and extensively in Chapter 14, but the importance of emotional evaluation to social perception is illustrated when we discuss Capgras syndrome in Box 2.6.

Box 2.6 When Things Go Wrong: Capgras syndrome

An example of the complexity of human recognition within a social context is given by a condition known as Capgras syndrome. Capgras syndrome is a relatively rare condition where the sufferer believes that people, or in some instances things, have been replaced with duplicates (Ellis et al., 1994). Typically the people who the sufferer believes to be duplicates are close family members. These duplicates are rationally accepted to be identical in physical properties but the irrational belief is held that the 'true' entity has been replaced with something else. Some sufferers of Capgras syndrome have even claimed that the duplicate is a robot. Ellis and Lewis (2001) describe the recent situation of a man who after a car accident believed that his wife had died in the accident, and the woman he currently lived with (his wife) was a duplicate. Naturally, he found this situation to be uncomfortable. Similarly Hirstein and Ramachandran (1997) reported a man who after an automobile accident believed that his parents were imposters. Interestingly, this delusion was limited to the visual modality since when speaking on the phone he always thought that he was speaking to his true parents.

While on the surface the Capgras delusion might seem to be a very special case of prosopagnosia, there is evidence that it is in fact quite different from prosopagnosia (Young & Ellis, 1989). The explanation for this begins with the fact that some prosopagnosia patients demonstrate an emotional response to familiar faces that they say they cannot recognize. The psychophysiological evidence for this emotional recognition is from skin conductance measures similar to that of lie detectors (Bauer, 1984). Thus, it is thought that when we see a face there are at least two processes occurring. One is overt recognition, and it corresponds to our ability to name and recall conscious properties related to the face. The other process is a covert emotional response and corresponds to visual information being sent to brain areas that are involved in emotions. Ellis and Lewis (2001) argue that Capgras syndrome arises from an intact system for overt recognition coupled with a damaged system for covert emotional recognition (whereas in prosopagnosia one has a damaged system for overt recognition and a sometimes spared covert system for emotional recognition). It is argued that this leads to a conflict arising from knowing the identity of the person you see but failing to connect any emotional response to this identity. Resolution to the conflict of recognizing a family member but not having any emotional indication of emotional familiarity leads to the delusion that the person is some sort of impostor.

FACES

Faces are important sources of social information that we use to recognize person properties such as emotion, gender, age, attractiveness and identity. Indeed, with the common use of photo IDs our face can become our identity. What makes recognizing faces challenging is that although properties of the face, such as its shape, remain stable

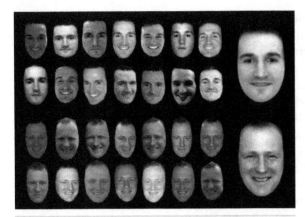

Figure 2.25   Familiar faces are recognized despite great variability in appearance. If you were familiar with Rob Jenkins or Mike Burton then you would easily recognise the top two rows as all images of Rob and the bottom two rows as all images of Mike. This is accomplished despite a variety of ages, expressions, lighting and camera angles represented by the images. How humans compensate for this great variability in image appearance is a challenging problem for face recognition research; one possible explanation is that the average face image, shown at the right helps to form a stable face representation.

Source: Jenkins, R. & Burton, A. M. (2001). Stable face representations. *Philosophical Transactions of the Royal Society of London. Series B: Biological Sciences*, 366(1571), 1671–1683.

over years, any particular view of a face will be affected by lighting, viewpoint, makeup, health, expression, etc. that drastically alter its appearance moment by moment (Figure 2.25). However, despite this multitude of complicating factors, recognition of faces can be surprisingly accurate. The literature on how we recognize faces is vast and reflects over 30 years of intense interest. From this, we can uncover some general properties of face recognition. First, humans are exquisitely tuned to recognize *familiar* faces and can do so under many adverse conditions (Johnston & Edmonds, 2009), that would defeat the best automatic computer recognition systems (Sinha et al., 2006). Second, recognition of *unfamiliar* faces tells a different story and for unfamiliar faces recognition performance can be surprisingly poor (Hancock et al., 2000). This fact has implications for eyewitness testimony (see Box 2.7). Third, there are specialized brain areas and networks for facial recognition (Allison et al., 1994; Haxby et al., 2000; Kanwisher et al., 1997; Rossion et al., 2000). Finally, the mechanisms of facial recognition are holistic, meaning that the particular way a configuration of facial features makes up a face is important in its own right, and one cannot deconstruct facial recognition into any simple collection of how individual facial features are recognized.

An early cognitive model of face recognition (Bruce & Young, 1986) that has come to be known as the Bruce and Young model, set a framework for many of the subsequent studies in face perception. It outlined how the primary encoding of faces must feed into processes of recognition (*I know this person*), identification (*I know who this person is*), analysis of emotion through facial expression and the combination of additional information such as voice to augment facial processing. The Bruce and Young model predicts that recognition of identity and expression should be independent of one another and, although this is largely supported by behavioural data, the separation is not complete (Calder & Young, 2005). The influence of the Bruce and Young model was widespread because it considered both basic mechanisms of facial processing as well as the important social questions such as, are we with someone familiar? who are they? and what is their emotion?

Box 2.7 Practical Application: Eyewitness identification

Eyewitness identification of an individual during a trial can have great impact on a jury. Given the importance of being able to correctly identify the perpetrator of a crime, and the dire consequences of making an error, the topic of eyewitness identification has seen considerable research to understand the conditions in which it can and cannot produce reliable results (for a review see Lindsay et al., 2011). The impact of this research can be seen in how it has influenced policies and procedures of various governments around the world, such as in the UK (Police and Criminal Evidence Act 1984 Code D, 2010) and the USA (Technical Working Group for Eyewitness Evidence, 1999). Elsewhere in this book we will cover topics in eyewitness performance that are related to memory (Chapters 5 and 6) as well as the emotional state of the eyewitness (Chapter 14).

While it might seem straightforward that an observer would recognize a face that they have seen, recall that while our ability to recognize familiar faces is remarkably robust, our ability to recognize *un*familiar individuals can be surprisingly poor. Thus, if an eyewitness to a crime would see someone unfamiliar it is not certain how reliable they will be to make an identification. Numerous factors have been studied to see how they influence the reliability of eyewitness testimony and from a practical standpoint these factors fall into two categories:

1 Situational factors that are beyond the scope of what can be controlled by the legal system, including the duration the eyewitness observed the event, the race of the individuals involved and the state of the eyewitness at the time.

2 System factors that are under the control of the legal system, such as what instruction is provided to the witness and the process of identification from photos, composites or line-ups.

Across the broad variety of situational and system factors studied the results have not always been consistent. However, some factors have gained a general consensus that they influence eyewitness performance, and we will discuss one situational and one system factor.

The situational factor we will discuss is race. An individual is more likely to correctly identify, and less likely to incorrectly identify, a person of the same race than a person of a different race (Brigham et al., 2007; Meissner & Brigham, 2001). This is called the cross-race effect and has been found to be consistent across different ethnicities (Brigham, 2002). For example, Hispanics were found to be better at recognizing other Hispanics compared to Blacks across different encoding and decoding times as well as arousal and attentional demands (MacLin et al., 2001).

The system factor we will discuss is the manner in which a potential suspect is identified. A standard procedure of a police line-up has been to present one or more suspects, along with other individuals who serve as foils, and have the eyewitness indicate whether any of the individuals is the one they saw. However, line-up identification appears to be sensitive to subtle aspects of the line-up process and has proven to be a substantial source of wrongful conviction in cases where DNA evidence has exonerated innocent people (Connors et al., 1996). Wells and Turtle in 1986 studied the composition of line-ups and used a Bayesian probability analysis to show that a line-up composed of all suspects was greatly inferior to a line-up with a single suspect or a mixed model using both target-present and target-absent line-ups. While they acknowledged that practical considerations sometimes preclude using an optimal design of line-ups, they stressed that eyewitnesses have a high probability of selecting an individual from a line-up without a target and thus the potential for misidentification is high when no members of the line-up are suspects. Probability of selection is also increased for a member of the line-up who stands out, and thus care is needed to ensure that the suspect does not stand out on the basis of the witness description. Finally, effects of investigator bias have shown that when the investigator knows which line-up member is a suspect there is a higher chance of a member of the line-up being chosen (Phillips et al., 1999). For this reason it is recommended that a line-up is administered by an individual who does not know the suspect (Lindsay & Wells, 1985).

A neural model of human face recognition was provided by Haxby and colleagues (2000) and comprised multiple regions spread throughout the brain (Figure 2.26). The organization of this distributed system emphasizes a distinction between the representation of invariant and changeable aspects of faces. The representation of invariant aspects of faces is responsible for the recognition of individuals, whereas the representation of changeable aspects of faces, such as eye gaze, expression and lip movement, facilitate social communication. The model divides facial processing into a core system and an extended system. In the core system, primary face processing occurs in the inferior occipital gyrus and representation of invariant aspects is mediated by face-responsive neurons in the fusiform gyrus, whereas the representation of changeable aspects is

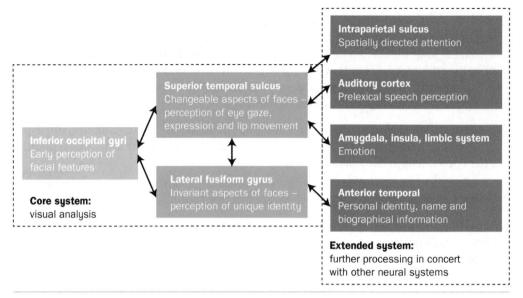

Figure 2.26   A neural model of face recognition. Haxby and colleagues proposed a hierarchical model of face perception. The model incorporates a core system involving three brain regions for visual analysis and an extended system that complements these visual functions.

Source: Reprinted from Haxby, J., Hoffman, E., & Gobbini, M. (2000). The distributed human neural system for face perception. *Trends in Cognitive Sciences, 4*(6), 223–233, with permission from Elsevier.

mediated by face-responsive neurons in the superior temporal sulcus (Figure 2.26). The extended system includes other brain areas that aid face processing with functions of attention, emotion and identification as well as providing supplementary information from speech processing.

In the time since Haxby and colleagues proposed their model (2000) there has been much critical evaluation of the model (Atkinson & Adolphs, 2011). We will discuss one particular component of the model, the fusiform face area (FFA) located in the lateral fusiform gyrus, that has attracted particular scrutiny. The FFA was identified as a face selective area using fMRI by comparing the brain response to faces with the response to other objects (Kanwisher et al., 1997). One criticism of this result was that the activity found in FFA is also consistent with a general-purpose recognition mechanism involving subordinate level classification. That is to say that faces are just one particular example of an object category upon which we can recognize subordinate elements (Gauthier et al., 2000). With this view, FFA activity reflects perceptual expertise in subordinate classification rather than a face specific mechanism, and there is still active debate on this issue. One other dimension to understanding the role of the FFA in face recognition has been raised by Weiner and Grill-Spector (2012) who argue that more sophisticated analyses of brain anatomy and function reveal that FFA is not a single cluster sensitive to faces, but instead appears to have a more complex structural organization.

VOICES

Like faces, the voice provides another important cue to our social environment. In this section we will discuss the voice as simply a sound cue that carries social information. For example, imagine staying in a hotel room where the walls are thin enough to hear the voices of your neighbours, but not so thin that you can understand any words. From

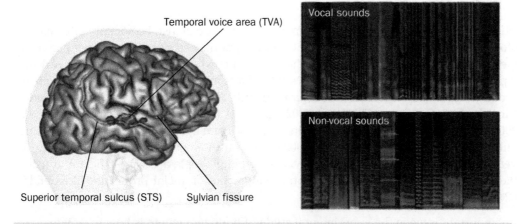

Figure 2.27 Voice-sensitive brain regions revealed by comparison of vocal and non-vocal sounds. (a) Specific regions in temporal cortex known as the temporal voice area are more active when listening to speech sounds. (b) Frequency-time spectrograms of the vocal (top) and non-vocal (bottom) sounds used in an fMRI experiment to reveal brain regions involved in voice processing.

Source: Reprinted from Latinus, M., & Belin, P. (2011). Human voice perception. *Current Biology*, 21(4), R143–5, with permission from Elsevier.

just the sound of the voices we can make out the nature of their social interaction, whether our neighbours are fighting or having a party. Similarly if you overhear two people speaking a language you do not understand, although you do not understand the language you will, without looking, be able to guess at the gender, age and size of the speakers (Ko et al., 2006; Latinus & Belin, 2011). Of course the voice also produces language, and this important property of voice is covered in Chapter 13. One way that voice carries information independent of linguistic content is found in the fact that the emotional content of an utterance can be carried in the prosody of the speech. For example, an extensive comparison of how emotion is perceived from music and voice showed that both use largely the same patterns of auditory information to convey specific emotions (Juslin & Laukka, 2003).

> Prosody is the rhythm, intonation and stress patterns in speech.

The sound quality of a voice is constrained by the combination of the folds of the larynx, which provide a sound source, and the vocal tract including the tongue, nasal cavity and lips that filter the sound. The resulting sound of each individual's voice is made unique by not only the size and shape of these physical structures but also the manner in which individuals form and articulate their vocal tract. Thus, voice contains an important source of identity information (Bachorowski & Owren, 1999; Baumann & Belin, 2010). As discussed earlier in the chapter, loss of the ability to recognize identity from voice is known as phonagnosia (Vanlancker et al., 1989). In phonagnosia individuals can understand the content of speech but are unable to identify the speaker.

Studies using fMRI in humans have found distinctive regions outside the primary auditory cortex, in the upper bank of the superior temporal sulcus (STS) that appear sensitive to human voice (Belin et al., 2000, 2004; Binder et al., 2000) (see Figure 2.27). This temporal voice area has been found to more actively respond to human voice sounds than to a variety of other sounds including animal vocalizations and assorted non-vocal sounds. In addition, recent results from an fMRI experiment that examined training effects in learning prototypical voices has shown that a distributed system exists for independently representing acoustics and identity from voice (Andics et al., 2010).

BIOLOGICAL MOTION

Observing the actions of others, like faces and voices can also be socially informative (Johnson & Shiffrar, 2013). For example, looking at the activity of a group of people in the distance gives us an idea of what they are doing, whether they are angry or sad and if possibly we know them. A variety of studies have indicated the ability of observers to use displays of human action to recognize identity (Cutting & Kozlowski, 1977), gender (Kozlowski & Cutting, 1977; Troje, 2002), emotion (Dittrich et al., 1996; Pollick et al., 2001), the action being carried out (Dittrich, 1993) and even whether a person appears vulnerable to attack (Gunns et al., 2002). It has been shown that even when there is very little information available in a visual display, people are very efficient at using the limited information present to obtain judgments of social properties like gender (Pollick et al., 2005).

An important issue in the experimental study of body movement is how to isolate body movement from other person properties. This is important since facial attractiveness, clothes, haircut and body shape all add some extra information about the person being viewed, and if you are interested in just the effect of body motion then these other factors need to be eliminated. A solution to this problem was introduced into the psychology literature by Gunnar Johansson (1973) who filmed actors in dark rooms with points of light attached to their joints. He subsequently showed films of these actions where the contrast was adjusted so only the points of light could be seen. Rather than seeing this as a cloud of unorganized points, observers were able to vividly see a human form in action. The ability to perceptually organize these point-light displays into the percept of a specific human action has been termed biological motion perception. The utility of point-light displays is illustrated in Figure 2.28, which shows two frames from a point-light display of a man pushing an object. These individual frames (as well as all the frames together) provide little information about the actor or the action when viewed singly. However, when viewed in animation the action is vividly seen.

How we can effortlessly process these sparse displays into a rich perception of action is still under debate. One theory holds that body-structure and body-motion information are independently processed before being recombined (Giese & Poggio, 2003) in the

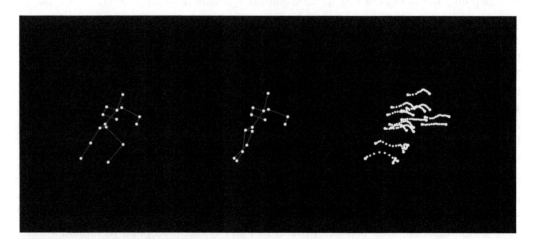

Figure 2.28   Point-light display of human movement. Point-light displays depict a human as a collection of lights located at the main joints. The left and middle images show individual frames of a point-light display of an individual pushing a heavy weight. The links between joints are shown in grey but are not shown in actual experiments. To the right is a set of overlaid frames which when viewed sequentially gives a vivid impression of the action being performed.

posterior region of the superior temporal sulcus (pSTS) (Grossman & Blake, 2002). In this theory the pSTS is a key area specialized for the perception of human activity. A somewhat opposing theory from Lange and Lappe (2006) holds that structural information from a single 'snapshot' is sufficient to inform the recognition of many properties of point-light displays. In this view motion is still important to enhance the perception of human activity, but the processing of static information is a vital first step. Consistent with neural mechanisms dedicated to the processing of static human form is the finding of an occipitotemporal brain region known as the extrastriate body area (EBA) which represents body postures (Peelen et al., 2006).

Evaluation

In this section on social perception, as well as elsewhere in the book, we have attributed function to particular brain areas. The case of pSTS and EBA provide a useful example that in some cases these attributions of function to specific brain location can still be considered work in progress. The current standard view is that while the EBA is involved in processing static images of bodies, the pSTS is the key region for biological motion perception due to being at the convergence of body-structure and body-motion information. However, increasingly there is awareness that the extended EBA region is sensitive to motion information (Ferri et al., 2013; Jastorff & Orban, 2009; McKay et al., 2012; Thompson & Baccus, 2012). Thus, while there seems little doubt that the pSTS is involved with converging information of social relevance (Allison et al., 2000) there is increasing interest in how body-form and body-motion information might be combined prior to arriving at pSTS (Vangeneugden et al., 2009).

Summary

Perception is an important topic in the study of cognition since it provides insight into the mechanisms that inform us about the external world. Although there is a vast literature on the detailed workings of perceptual capabilities, perception can be thought of as simply the early input stages of an information processing system. The first section of this chapter described fundamental concepts in perception and pursued the view that perception can be described as information processing. A great benefit of this approach is that it allows us to define concepts of perception that apply generally to man, machine and other organisms. The second section of the chapter examined human perceptual systems as a special case and provided examples of how perceptual systems are implemented in the human brain. We also explored the relationship between brain and perception, and how damage to the brain alters perception. The different perceptual systems of vision, audition and somatoperception were examined and we discussed how different perceptual inputs might optimally be combined to form a unitary percept of objects and events. An important achievement of perception is our ability to recognize objects, and the process of recognition was explored in the third section of the chapter. Recognition allows us to relate perceptual properties to mental categories and thus provides a powerful means for organizing our perceptual world. Key for recognition is the ability to efficiently represent objects and events in a flexible manner such that the essence of an object or event can be understood across different conditions: for example, the identity of an object when seen from different viewpoints or the sound of a word spoken by different speakers. In the final section of the chapter we investigated how faces, voices and body movements inform social perception. Social perception is an important talent for a social species like humans where fluent interactions are guided by our abilities to perceive social cues.

Review questions

1 What is perception used for and how is it possible to compare perception in man and machine?

2 What properties are common to the processing of audio, video and touch information?

3 Contrast bottom-up and top-down processing in the context of interpreting sensory information.

4 What are the fundamental issues in combining information from different senses?

5 What makes recognition a difficult problem to solve?

6 What types of social perception are common across different modes of perception?

7 If you were designing a perceptual system for a robot, how important would it be to take into account the physical properties of the robot?

FURTHER READING

Bregman, A. S. (1990). *Auditory scene analysis: The perceptual organization of sound.* Cambridge, MA: MIT Press.

Calvo, P., & Gomila, T. (Eds.). (2008). *Handbook of cognitive science: An embodied approach.* Amsterdam: Elsevier Science.

Marr, D. (1982). *Vision: A computational investigation into the human representation and processing of visual information.* San Francisco: W.H. Freeman.

Palmer, S. E. (1999). *Vision science: Photons to phenomenology.* Cambridge, MA: MIT Press.

Sacks, O. W. (1997). *The island of the colorblind* (1st ed.). New York: A.A. Knopf: Distributed by Random House.

Vinciarelli, A., Pantic, M., & Bourlard, H. (2009). Social signal processing: Survey of an emerging domain. *Image and Vision Computing, 27*(12), 1743–1759.

CHAPTER 3:
ATTENTION AND CONSCIOUSNESS

Preview questions

1 Of the multitude of events happening in the world, how does attention select particular items?

2 How much of the objects and events around us can we attend to, and what happens to that which we don't attend?

3 What is the relationship between attention and consciousness?

4 Why is consciousness a difficult topic for scientific enquiry?

INTRODUCTION

In this chapter we explore the topics of attention and consciousness. What these two topics have in common is the idea of selection. We attend to particular aspects of information hitting our senses and seem consciously aware of only a limited view of the world at any one time. Despite this similarity the discussion of the topics together is not simple. Attention research within the domain of cognitive science has a rich empirical tradition over the past 50 years and provides a dense and sometimes contradictory field of evidence. Empirical research into consciousness, although gaining in momentum, is relatively sparse. Moreover, it is difficult to totally dissociate study of consciousness from its philosophical roots, and indeed the question of whether it is an appropriate topic for experimental investigation. Our particular solution is to take a path through studies of attention that lead to and support our presentation of consciousness. It is important to point out that given the sheer volume of studies on attention many other paths through the literature are possible.

Our presentation of attention first provides an overview of the scope of attention research and this serves as an introduction to the different theories of attention that vary in the where and when of attention. This background leads to the discussion of some of the more recent paradigms used to examine attention. Before leaving the topic of attention we discuss failures of attention, which emphasize that although we might think we take in all the relevant and important information in our environment, what we can miss is really quite striking. This helps to underscore the importance of selection and leads into the discussion of consciousness. For consciousness we begin with a discussion of the function of consciousness that includes insight from recent philosophical studies. Following this we relate attention to consciousness to present a model that combines the two to show how they are distinct from each other. Finally, we discuss empirical approaches to the study of consciousness that include what can be learned as a result of brain damage as well as how more standard experimental techniques can help to reveal the neural basis of consciousness.

ATTENTION

An idea which is common to nearly every model of attention is that attention is a limited resource that is deployed to facilitate the processing of critical information. This idea was in the words of William James in his *Principles of Psychology* over 120 years ago. He stated, 'Every one knows what attention is. It is the taking possession by the mind, in clear and vivid form, of one out of what seem several simultaneously possible objects or trains of thought. Focalization, concentration, of consciousness are of its essence. It implies withdrawal from some things in order to deal effectively with others' (pp. 403–404). This is a useful description of attention that will encompass all that is presented in this chapter. Attention is key to addressing the problem that at any given time there are more activities going on in the external world, and potential thoughts in our internal world than we could cope with. Attention allows us to stay on task and to select relevant information. Besides selection, attention can focus our energies on relevant aspects of the world. This final aspect of attention makes it important for understanding the boundaries of human performance.

Since the time that James wrote the words 'every one knows what attention is' there have been thousands of experiments exploring attention. However, it is difficult to distill this century of progress in attention research to a short and precise definition. It turns out that research into attention has produced numerous varieties of attention that defy a common explanation. There are several possible reasons for this state of affairs. One is that attention is pervasive and can be invoked in description of nearly every cognitive and perceptual process. Thus, how it exists as an independent topic rather than something bolted on to other cognitive and perceptual theories is not always clear. Another is that attention research at times clusters around particular controversies or experimental paradigms rather than around a general theory of attention. While this is not unique to attention research it has nonetheless not always been clear how these different clusters of research support each other (Sutherland, 1998). However, any commentary about the state of attention research aside, it is clearly a critically important topic for explaining human performance, and the number of accidents in the world that can be attributed to lack of attention show that it is of great practical importance. Moreover, as we develop artificial systems to independently interact with the world it is proving useful to provide them with attentional mechanisms (see Box 3.1 later).

OVERVIEW OF ATTENTION

A taxonomy of attention research

One way to deal with the diversity of attention research is to develop a taxonomy to organize the various studies. An example of a taxonomy is the classic work in the 1700s by Carl Linnaeus who divided the natural world into the plant, animal and mineral kingdoms and developed classification systems within these kingdoms. Taxonomies are useful for delineating the major boundaries within a large structure that helps one to see the relationship between different elements. A taxonomy of attention has recently been developed by Chun et al. (2011) (Figure 3.1). Chun and colleagues break attention down to two basic categories of external and internal attention. External attention refers to selecting and controlling incoming sensory information while internal attention refers to selecting control strategies and maintaining internally generated information such as task rules, responses, long-term memory and working memory. Internal attention involves regulating our internal mental life so we can achieve our goals. For example, if we go to the store to buy milk and a newspaper it is internal attention that keeps us on task so we do not return hours later with no money, milk or newspaper (see Chapter 5 for related discussion of prospective memory). Internal attention is crucial for jobs such as being a guard where vigilance is essential. External attention is influenced both by goal directed processes where we are searching for particular sensory information as well as stimulus driven processes where sensory events such as loud noises and bright lights draw in our attention. For example, if we have seen the friend we are to meet across a busy street with many cars and people then external attention makes us aware of the traffic signals to cross safely and enables us to keep sight of our friend in the crowd.

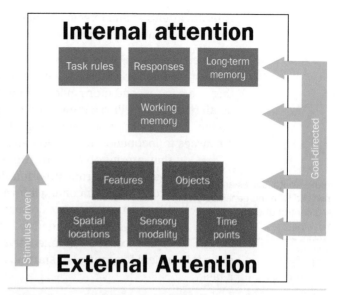

Figure 3.1   A taxonomy of attention. This taxonomy of attention was proposed by Chun et al. (2011) and has two major divisions of attention: external and internal attention. External attention includes factors such as how things in the environment capture our attention while internal attention is much more about keeping focus on internal states. Both external and internal attention are influenced by our goals. The boxes denote specific aspects of attention and many of them are covered in this chapter.

Source: Adapted from Chun, M. M., Golomb, J. D., & Turk-Browne, N. B. (2011). A taxonomy of external and internal attention. *Annual Review of Psychology, 62*, 73–101.

External attention deals primarily with sensory events external to the body.
Internal attention deals primarily with our internally generated thoughts, desires and motivations.

In the presentation of attention in the current chapter we do not cover all the areas of the taxonomy. We emphasize external attention with a concentration on the modality of vision. Our discussion of internal attention is more limited, though we do discuss proposed relationships between attention and working memory. Working memory is covered more extensively in Chapter 4 and we discuss it here only in relation to attention.

The attention system of the human brain

The taxonomy of attention had its major division between internal and external attention and thus it is not surprising that this division is key to the most influential model of the attention system in the human brain (Petersen & Posner, 2012; Posner & Petersen, 1990). This framework, proposed by Michael Posner and colleagues, has been developed extensively over the past 20 years and holds that the attention system can be seen as independent from processing systems and that it utilizes a network of anatomical areas that carry out functions that are specified in cognitive terms. The model has the three basic components of alerting, orienting and executive function whose functions are partitioned into specific brain areas. Orienting can be considered to be a type of

Attention system is a framework of the human brain containing three different systems for alerting, orienting and the executive function.

external attention and executive function to be a type of internal attention. We will discuss these components in more detail.

The alerting system is comprised of brain areas in the brainstem and frontal cortex that are responsible for achieving a state of arousal. For example, if we maintain alertness then we can respond more quickly to a signal. Similarly, if a warning signal cues us to be alert then we will respond more quickly to a signal when it arrives. The orienting system includes brain areas in frontal and parietal cortex that direct our processing resources to incoming information and includes areas such as the frontal eye fields that are involved with rapid strategic control of attention. This orienting system is external attention since it has the function of orienting our sensory processing to incoming information. The executive system originally included the anterior cingulate cortex and regions along the medial frontal cortex and this has been expanded to include parietal cortex and additional regions in frontal cortex. This executive function system is related to internal attention since it is critical for control of starting tasks and sustained maintenance of performing a task.

> Frontal eye fields are found in the frontal cortex and are involved with the generation and control of eye movements.

The alerting system is a kind of 'on' switch that organizes our behaviour for when an event might occur. The orienting and executive systems on the other hand are important for organizing our behaviour in response to what is happening in the world and what we should be doing. This contrast of what is happening and what we should be doing is reminiscent of the contrast between bottom-up and top-down processing described in Chapter 2.

Box 3.1 Practical Application: Are you talking to me?

There is a famous scene in the movie *Taxi Driver* where Robert De Niro challenges his image in the mirror over whether it is talking to him (Scorsese, 1976). Noticing that another is attending to us can be provocative in many ways. As well, not attending to someone can have unpleasant social consequences. This sensitivity to whether we are being attended has been utilized by researchers in social robotics to make interactions with robotic agents more engaging. One way in which this has been done by Kroos and colleagues is to model an attentional unit within the robot system (Kroos et al., 2011). Their system is called the Articulated Head and includes a highly realistic animation of a talking head attached to a large robot arm along with various sensors such as a camera, microphone and motion sensor (Figure 3.2a). The robot system was designed to inhabit a physical space with humans and to appear engaging and interactive to the public at the Powerhouse Museum in Sydney, Australia (at the time of writing it is still installed there).

The importance of modelling attention is apparent in previous robotics research that used attention as an essential mediator between perception and action control. This mediation includes selecting perceptual information relevant for action execution and limiting the potential actions based on the perceived context (Bachiller et al., 2008). This design principle of attention as a mediator between perception and action can be seen in Figure 3.2b, which provides a schematic of the system design for the Articulated Head. It can be observed from the diagram that attention forms a bottleneck since out of all the information being sensed and perceived, the central control system 'sees' only the information that has been selected by attention. In the Articulated Head the attention system is tuned so that the robot behaviour gives an indication that it is aware of current human actions in its vicinity. Of course, although the Articulated Head is made of state of the art sensors and computers its awareness to the physical environment is limited. However, it is adequate to provide behaviours that generate a feeling within observers that it has some intentional agency. Its behaviour appears to be neither random nor fully determined by the physical environment.

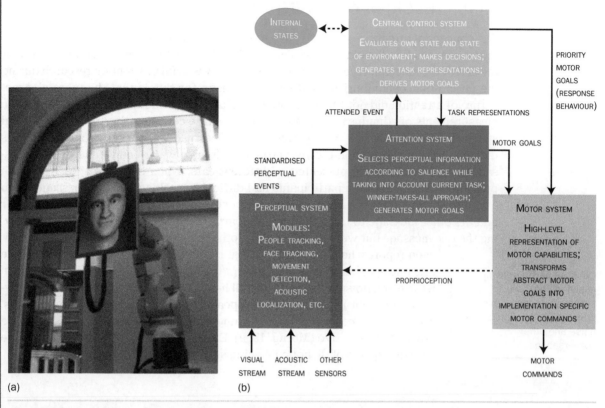

Figure 3.2 **An attention module enhances engagement between humans and a robot-activated head.** (a) The facial anima-tion presented on a flat screen is attached to a large industrial robot that allows for dynamic patterns of motion of the face and robot to engage people in a science museum setting. (b) A schematic of the robot control system includes an attentional module at the heart of the design to coordinate the activities of the perceptual, motor and central control modules.

Source: Kroos, C., Herath, D. C., & Stelarc. (2011). From robot arm to intentional agent: The Articulated Head. In S. Goto (Ed.), *Advances in robotics, automation and control* (pp. 215–240). Intech.

The attention system is crucial for driving the behaviour of the robot. If there is no environmental activi-ty strong enough to attract attention then the Articulated Head performs random scanning motions. If stimulation is not found then it goes into a sleep mode that includes increasing sensitivity to auditory events so that it is possible to awaken with a noise. Sleep mode is programmed to eventually end and if the attention system is not activated then the Articulated Head does some stretching movements. When awake, if there is a single person in the visual field then the attention system will drive pursuit of the movements of this person, but if the person stands still and does not make a sound then attention will fade. However, if the face detection software registers a face to confirm that the person is looking at the robot then it will speak a phrase from its repertoire of opening lines ('I am looking at you!', 'Did we meet before?' or 'Are you happy?') or mimic the perceived head posture. Similarly, there is a proximity sensor integrated into the information kiosk in front of the robot and if a person is standing near then this will also highly activate the attention system. If several people are detected in the vicinity then the behaviour of the Articulated Head is somewhat more difficult to characterize, but the attention system will switch its attention from person to person depending upon whether it detects their faces, move-ment, voice or other sensory input. The attention system has been demonstrated to be an important part of the Articulated Head in driving human-robot interaction and provides a clear demonstration of how attention at a conceptual level can be applied to engineering design.

EARLY THEORIES OF ATTENTION

The concept of attention – that we have the ability to select and focus our mental energies – goes back millennia, and we can see that William James was writing about it at the end of the nineteenth century. However, there was a lull in attention research during the period that behaviourism held sway. A reason for this is that the more abstract nature of attention did not fit easily into the behaviourist traditions that emphasize the measurements of stimulus and response and minimize consideration of internal mental states. However, a series of experiments by Cherry (1953) using a task known as dichotic listening showed interesting properties of how we attend when different messages are simultaneously presented to different ears. When two messages were both presented to each ear then participants had difficulty tracking any one message when asked to shadow it by speaking it aloud. However, when one message went to one ear and the other message to the other ear then participants were near perfect at shadowing the one message but were ignorant of the other message to the point they could not even report when it spoke a foreign language. This impressive skill to tune into one speaker is known as the cocktail party problem as it is like when we are at a noisy party and can still hold a conversation. Interestingly, however, our ability to tune into one speaker can be broken by certain sounds. For example, hearing your own name mentioned is something to which we are acutely sensitive (Moray, 1959). Efforts to use attention to explain these curious aspects of dichotic listening started with filter theory.

> **Cocktail party problem** describes how we successfully focus on one speaker in a background of noise and other conversations.

Filter theory

Filter theory (Broadbent, 1958, 1971, 1982) addressed issues raised by experiments in dichotic listening and can be considered the first cognitive theory of attention. The research had a direct application to issues of the day surrounding how many pilots a single air traffic controller could effectively communicate with at the same time. As discussed, a core finding was that when a listener is presented with a different message to each ear, interference between the two messages can be avoided when the listener is instructed which message was not relevant. This established the idea that a filter is used to block irrelevant information so that only the important message would reach a central channel for further processing. Filter theory used the metaphor of radio communication where the goal is to get the important information on a piece of wire so it can be transmitted to a receiver. In this case the receiver was considered to be our conscious awareness and the issue was what information attention should select to put on the wire. Prior to accessing the central channel was a buffer that contained unprocessed information such as the pitch and other physical properties of the incoming sound. However, only one signal was let through the filter and all the other information in the buffer was flushed away.

> **Early selection** describes when the filter for attention occurs early in the stream of information processing. **Late selection** describes when the filter for attention occurs late in the stream of information processing. Thus the filter eliminates some information that has already been processed.

This aspect of the model that only one signal was let through and all the other information discarded was termed early selection and proved controversial. Research by Deutsch and Deutsch (1963) proposed a model of late selection where more extensive processing was performed leading to all stimuli being identified, but only the attended ones were given access to further processing. In a similar vein, Treisman (1964) suggested modifications to the filter theory of Broadbent, replacing the total filtering of irrelevant information with one where the intensity of the irrelevant information was diminished but not totally eliminated. In this way, the diminished information might still get detected if it was of high priority to an individual. This modification would help to explain why we can hear our name being said even if we are attending to another stream of speech since it is of great personal relevance to know when we are being talked about.

Within the context of filter theory, despite extensive efforts, there was never a definitive resolution about early versus late selection. The question, however, is of general relevance since there are trade-offs between early and late selection. For example, if attention is allocated early then although there is a greater risk we might select the wrong information the information being selected will receive the maximum effect of attention and minimum cognitive resources will be expended on irrelevant information. If attention is allocated late then we will decrease the chance that attention is allocated incorrectly but we will necessarily expend cognitive resources on irrelevant information. A framework for dealing with this trade off in predicting the level of processing for unattended stimuli was provided by Lavie (2005) in load theory. The core idea of load theory is that the amount of processing an unattended stimulus will receive depends upon how difficult it is to process the attended target. If the principal target is easy to process then attention resources will overflow to irrelevant factors and these will be identified, indicative of late selection (Lavie, 1995). However, if the principal target is difficult to process then the irrelevant factors will not appear processed, indicative of early selection.

A final point to make is that regardless of whether attentional selection is early or late, filter theory imposes an important constraint on how attention functions. This constraint is that there is effectively only one channel of output to further processing and thus attention forms a bottleneck for information processing. For this reason filter theory is also known as bottleneck theory. While filter theory focused on where in attention the bottleneck occurred, the theory we will discuss next, resource theory, focused on the size of the bottleneck.

Resource theory

A new model of attention was proposed by Kahneman (1973) that also held attention to be limited; however, instead of the limit being the information capacity of a single central channel, attention was treated as a limited resource to distribute appropriately. The idea of a limited resource was motivated from the metaphor of the brain as a computer where various resources are available within the computing system and attention acts to get the right information to the central processing unit (CPU). Such a formulation allowed more flexible modelling of how attention could be allocated across single and multiple input channels. The model also incorporated aspects such as the arousal of the individual and how different tasks influenced attention. In the following paragraphs we will discuss how different research based on resource theory approached the allocation of attention across space and the challenges this presented for the theory.

The idea of attention as a resource is evident in research into vision that used the metaphor of a spotlight to describe how the resources of visual attention were distributed over space (Laberge, 1983; Laberge & Brown, 1987). Just like a spotlight can be shone on the location of a scene we want to observe, the resources of attention can be shone on specific visual locations of interest. It is important to note that this spotlight of attention

> Spotlight refers to the metaphor of attention where we can think of attention as a spotlight that illuminates locations of interest.

was shown to be able to move around the visual scene even when the eyes do not move. Movement of the eyes towards a subject signal an overt shift of attention, while moving attention when keeping the eyes fixed and attention moves is a covert shift of attention. This ability to move the spotlight of attention around is useful in certain kinds of social situations where we are interested in watching somebody but it would be awkward to look directly at him or her. One obvious question about a spotlight model is how large is the spotlight and whether, and at what cost, the size of the spotlight can be changed. This question was addressed by Eriksen and colleagues (Eriksen & St James, 1986; Eriksen & Yeh, 1985) who proposed the zoom lens model. Here the intuition is that just as a zoom lens on a camera will change how much of the scene is contained in the image, we could effectively have a zoom function for attention that zooms in and out to cover different amounts of the scene. Since attention is a limited resource then the amount of attention at any one location in the spotlight will decrease as we zoom out and attention must cover a larger area. The opposite will occur if we zoom into the scene.

Both the spotlight and zoom lens models treat attention as a resource spreading across visual space without consideration of the objects that inhabit that space. However, it turns out that there is evidence that attention can be characterized as being applied to objects, rather than simply the spatial location that the object occupies. This evidence comes from experiments by Egly, Driver and Rafal (1994) that had participants attend to the end of one of two rectangles by brightening the end of the rectangle to cue the location for 100 milliseconds (Figure 3.3). The brightness was then reduced back to the original shade and then after 200 milliseconds the target appeared. Participants were asked to detect the onset of the target. The target could appear either at the cued location, the other end of the rectangle that had been cued, or a location on the other rectangle that was equal in distance to the length of the rectangle. Participants were faster to detect the target when it appeared at the other end of the cued rectangle than on the uncued rectangle. The important point is that the two uncued locations were equidistant

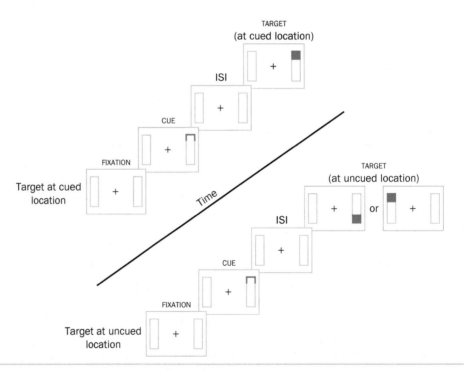

Figure 3.3 Attention can be attached to objects. Egly, Driver and Rafal (1994) showed that attention can be bound to objects. After fixation, participants are cued to a particular location on one of the objects, in this case the top of the right bar. After a delay the target comes up either at the cued location, on the other end of the same object or an equal distance away on the other object. Participants were faster to detect the target when it was on the same object than when it was an equal distance away on the other object.

Source: Adapted from Egly, R., Driver, J., & Rafal, R. D. (1994). Shifting visual-attention between objects and locations – Evidence from normal and parietal lesion subjects. *Journal of Experimental Psychology-General, 123*(2), 161–177.

from the cue and thus the results show enhanced processing of the entire rectangle. These findings support object-based attention.

The fact that the objects inhabiting visual space would influence attention makes sense from the perspective of our interactions with the world. For example, as we are navigating through the environment the spatial positions of all the objects in the world are constantly changing and thus attaching attention to the object rather than the location would be an advantage for sustaining attention. Further explorations into object-based attention investigated whether once attention is attached to an object it is attached to the entire object, or perhaps only the parts of the object that are relevant. The results are mixed with some studies revealing that there is the tendency for all the features of the object to undergo obligatory processing by attention (Duncan, 1984; O'Craven et al., 1999; Vecera & Farah, 1994). However, some recent evidence suggests that only object features that are relevant for the task to be performed are processed (Woodman & Vogel, 2008).

Consideration of both the spotlight of attention and object-based attention raises the question of how the limited resource of attention is allocated. This interest in how we can distribute attention gave rise to dual-task studies of how attention is used to perform two tasks simultaneously (see also Box 3.3 for an experiment using a dual-task paradigm). With a dual-task paradigm task performance is measured on each task by itself and for when both tasks are performed simultaneously. Typically performance is lower when performing both tasks simultaneously. Moreover, when performing both tasks and asked to invest greater percentages of effort in one of the tasks, participants are able to do so relative to the other task. These results are consistent with the notion that attention is a limited resource that is shared between tasks. When tasks are performed simultaneously, resources are split between the tasks and performance goes down due to decreased resources available for the individual tasks. Additionally, when resources are strategically diverted to one task, performance goes down in the other. This view of resource limitations was shared by theories of Norman and Bobrow (1975) involving resource limits which held that once the resource limit was reached, tasks would interfere with each other in competition for the limited central resources.

Dual-task paradigm arises when one measures performance on two tasks independently and together. If performance when performed independently and together is equal, then the two tasks do not compete for resources.

Experiments using a dual-task paradigm revealed that some task combinations systematically appeared to cause less interference between each other. When tasks were more dissimilar to each other there was less of a reduction in performance when performed together. For example, two auditory tasks or two visual tasks will show a greater negative effect than an auditory task combined with a visual task. This suggested that the idea of a single central attention resource was not fully adequate to explain human performance and motivated development of multiple resource models (Wickens, 1984, 2002). With multiple resources one assumes that there are independent pools of resources, each of which is limited. Thus, a given task will compete with some tasks for the same resources but with other tasks there will be no competition. A schematic representation illustrating Wickens' model is provided in Figure 3.4. The first dimension of the model is processing stages that include perception, cognition and responding. The second dimension includes the processing modalities of vision and auditory input. The third dimension includes the codes, spatial or verbal, for how the input will be processed and this separation is carried through to the response stage where a response will be manual/spatial or vocal/verbal. Our ability to do multiple tasks will depend on how far apart they are on the relevant dimensions. Being close along any one dimension implies competition for resources and a necessary reduction in performance. Although it has proven difficult to precisely specify the basis of the different resources, such

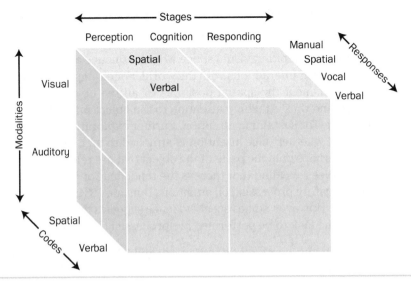

Figure 3.4   A diagram indicating how different attentional resources interact. The model of Wickens creates a space spanned by types of inputs, types of responses and processing stages to represent schematically how different tasks interfere with each other for attentional resources. If two tasks are close to each other in this space they will interfere greatly; if they are far apart they will interfere less. For example, a visuo-spatial task leading to a manual response will not compete so much with an audio-verbal task leading to a verbal response – you can talk while doing a simple jigsaw puzzle.

Source: Adapted from Wickens, C. D. (2002). Multiple resources and performance prediction. *Theoretical Issues in Ergonomics Science*, 3(2), 159–177.

models have been very influential in the applied area of designing man-machine interfaces as they provide a means for predicting how different interfaces will affect human performance.

Driving a vehicle is a common man-machine interface and we can use it to illustrate how the model of Wickens depicts which dual tasks will be taxing. For a first task let us consider driving on a familiar road with a quiet passenger with no radio or music to be our primary task. When driving we need to navigate while obeying traffic signals and this requires us to continuously be running a loop of perception, cognition and response. For the proposed condition of quietly driving a familiar route we perceive a visual world and transform it into appropriate manual commands with little cognition. If for our second task we are shown a map that is upside down and asked to point the direction to an unknown landmark then we can see that this task will compete with both vision and manual response as well as tax cognition and thus would cause a large decrease in driving performance. If instead our second task was to respond to our passenger about what we thought of the weather today then this would require verbal processing and a verbal response requiring little cognitive load would not be taxing since it didn't compete with driving. As a final point we can add that the great majority of evidence shows a decrease in performing two tasks simultaneously and the question is more whether or not the decrease will be severe rather than whether it exists or not.

Although resource theory promoted a rich body of research considering how attention could be distributed across space and modality there is one theoretical drawback to resource theory. This drawback is the problem of circularity regarding mechanisms of how attention is allocated (Allport, 1980; Navon, 1984; Navon & Miller, 2002). Namely, to maximize efficiency attention should be allocated to the most important events, but how can attention 'know' what the important sensory events are in all cases. If we give attention too much capability in evaluating the incoming stimuli then it no longer seems like attention. Moreover, studies of resource allocation generally examined how the resources were allocated across different tasks and the criticism was raised that it is possible that participants are somehow rapidly switching 100 per cent of their attention between the tasks. However, a conclusive experiment to show that this rapid switching does or does not occur has proven elusive. Despite these issues, experiments studying how a limited attentional resource might be divided has produced a useful empirical literature to illuminate limitations in human performance. The question of how many sites attention can monitor simultaneously is still controversial. Early studies indicated that only a single location can be selected at any one time (Eriksen & Yeh, 1985; Mccormick & Klein, 1990; Posner, 1980), However, recent results have indicated that viewers have greater flexibility in monitoring multiple locations, but as one expands from a single location attention provides more rudimentary processing enhancements (Awh & Pashler, 2000; Franconeri et al., 2007; Kramer & Hahn, 1995). How extensive experience with using attention in rich naturalistic environments might train attention is an interesting problem and one that has been studied in videogame play (see Box 3.2).

Box 3.2 Practical Application: Playing action video games improves attention

Recent research indicates that regular play of action video games such as *God of War, Halo, Grand Theft Auto* and *Call of Duty* appear to develop enhanced attention that enable individuals to perform faster without loss of accuracy (Castel et al., 2005; Greenfield et al., 1994; Trick et al., 2005). Most importantly, this advantage is not isolated to just the video game that they have become expert, but it transfers to general attention tasks. Enhanced performance in game players include improved spatial attention (Green & Bavelier, 2006a, 2007) as well as the number of objects that can be attended simultaneously (Green & Bavelier, 2003). While it is not known exactly why these effects come about it is conjectured that several of the unique aspects of video games are conducive to developing attention. For instance, many video games require multiple items to be processed simultaneously, a task that would benefit from enhanced attentional resources across space. Additionally, many games require effective rejection of irrelevant objects, a process that would benefit from a more proficient selection process. Moreover, the penalty for either failing to process a target or allowing non-essential information to interfere with the processing of potential targets is often great. How to better understand the changes that come about with video game play and how to adapt them to training techniques (Green & Bavelier, 2003, 2006a, 2006b) is a topic of great interest in the field known as serious gaming.

The serious gaming community is interested in using video game technologies and approaches to address real world problems. One of the domains of interest to serious gaming is training in medicine and surgery (Kato, 2010). A recent study (Schlickum et al., 2009) explored how game play influenced the ability of medical students to perform a simulated endoscopy. Three groups of medical students were involved, one group played a 3D first-person shooter game, another group played a 2D non-first-person shooter game and the remaining group played no video games. The experiment went on for five weeks and the video game participants had to play between 30–60 minutes, five days a week. Although both gaming groups performed better on one virtual endoscopy task, only the 3D first-person shooter group also performed better on a second virtual endoscopy task. These kinds of results show the potential for gaming to enhance performance on a real-world task. Other research investigated baggage screening (Hubal et al., 2010; Pavlas et al., 2008) to address the problem of how to maintain vigilance in face of the fact that the majority of bags being screened are harmless (McCarley et al., 2004). One approach to alleviating this problem is what is called threat image projection (TIP) where a 'dummy' weapon is virtually projected into the baggage. This serves the purpose of both keeping up the amount of threats presented to the screener to help maintain vigilance as well as being used to assess, and provide feedback to the screener. The technology behind virtually placing threat items and the psychology of how to best develop vigilance has been adapted into video training systems for baggage screeners (Mendes et al., 2011; Schwaninger, 2004).

ATTENTIONAL MECHANISMS IN PERCEPTION AND MEMORY

In our presentation of theories of attention we discussed attention as something separate from other perceptual and cognitive functions. It is however possible to embed attentional mechanisms within other functions and in this section we cover two such examples. The first discusses how to achieve effects of attention within mechanisms of low-level vision and the second describes similarities between attention and working memory.

A neural mechanism of attention in primary visual cortex

As an introduction we will review the time course of neural activity in the brain associated with seeing a stimulus. The first component of activity is known as the feedforward sweep (Lamme, 2003; Lamme & Roelfsema, 2000), which describes how incoming sensory information travels across the brain. The primary visual cortex responds 40 milliseconds after a stimulus onset, by 80 milliseconds most secondary visual areas are activated and by 120 milliseconds activations can be found throughout the cortex. Once an area is activated it can interact with both higher and lower brain areas in a mode of recurrent processing. However, it has been found that neural tuning properties to visual stimuli are quite sophisticated even at short times after stimulus onset. From this consideration it is evident that neural mechanisms of attention could be effective in the very first stages of encoding a visual stimulus. For example, attention has been shown to sharpen the neural tuning of single neurons (Spitzer et al., 1988) or populations of neurons (Martinez-Trujillo & Treue, 2004), and reduction in neural responses has been shown when attention is directed towards a non-preferred stimulus that is presented in the same receptive field with a preferred stimulus (Moran & Desimone, 1985; Reynolds & Desimone, 2003). Various neural models have been proposed to explain how attention can selectively amplify the visual response of neurons (Li & Basso, 2008; McAdams & Maunsell, 1999; Williford & Maunsell, 2006). Recently, a unifying model has been proposed by Reynolds and Heeger (2009) that incorporates the capabilities of many of the previous theories and explains a variety of experimental results regarding how attention operates at very early levels of the neural encoding of visual information.

Feedforward processing describes a bottom-up process where lower levels progressively stimulate higher levels of brain.
Recurrent processing, within a network, involves computations that occur in a cyclic fashion.
Receptive field of a neuron indicates the physical space that stimulates the neuron. In vision it is the region of visual field to which that neuron is sensitive if stimulated with light.

The model of Reynolds and Heeger, called the Normalization Model of Attention, focuses on two functions of attention: (1) the capacity to increase sensitivity to faint stimuli presented alone, and (2) the capacity to reduce the impact of task irrelevant distractors when multiple stimuli are presented. To achieve this they developed a computational model of early stages of image processing in the visual cortex. In the model, the input, which is termed the Stimulus Drive, is multiplied by an Attention Field and divided by a Suppressive Drive to obtain the effect of attention on perception. The Suppressive Drive includes the interaction of all the attended and non-attended elements of the visual input. An example of how the model works is shown in Figure 3.5 for the case of observing two sets of vertical lines, one set to the left of fixation that is not attended and one to the right of fixation that is attended. The Normalization Model represents the Stimulus Drive and subsequent stages as a 'neural image' (Robson, 1980) in which the brightness at every spot of an image corresponds to the response of one neuron. In this example, the brightness of the Stimulus Drive corresponds to the sensitivity of a neuron to line orientation. The Stimulus Drive is the neural image of how orientation in the image is represented if there were no effects of attention. Thus, the two light bands on the left and right of the Stimulus Drive correspond to the two targets

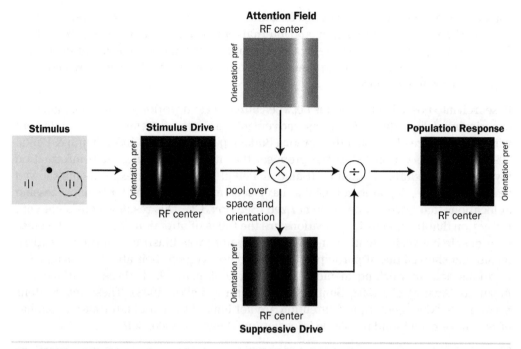

Figure 3.5   The Normalization Model of Attention. The model shows how attention can modulate the response of neurons in primary visual cortex. Details of the process are described in the text. In this example, we show an input of oriented bars with the task of attending to the three bars on the right. The area of attention is denoted by the red circle in the far left box. In the rightmost box labelled population response, the output of the system shows enhanced processing of the target on the right, as illustrated by the brighter and larger response.

Source: Reprinted from Reynolds, J. H. & Heeger, D. J. (2009). The normalization model of attention. *Neuron*, *61*(2), 168–185, with permission from Elsevier.

shown to the left and right of the centre fixation dot and are identical. In the Attention Field, a grey colour indicates no effect of attention and white indicates attention being applied. We can see that the Attention Field in this case is sensitive to the position of the stimulus but not the orientation, and its width reflects the size of the red circle around the vertical lines that denote the area to which attention is directed. It is apparent from the figure that attention is being applied to the target on the right of fixation. The result of multiplying the Attention Field by the Stimulus Drive gives the Suppressive Drive that is more broadly tuned than the original Stimulus Drive. This Suppressive Drive is then used to divide the Stimulus Drive to obtain the Population Response. This process of division is known as normalization since it takes the original input and changes it according to the surrounding context. The final result of the Population Response shows that the attended target is enhanced while the other target receives a diminished response. This simple model is capable of capturing a wide variety of phenomena about how attention can be used to modulate the activity of neurons in visual cortex.

Attention and working memory

We will discuss working memory in more detail in the next chapter, but here we would like to discuss similarities that have been discovered between attention and working memory. To appreciate the connection between attention and working memory we need first to give a brief preview of working memory. Working memory is a central cognitive mechanism coupled with separate stores for visuospatial and phonological information. Just like attention is a limited resource, the capacity of working memory is limited. The utility of working memory is that the perceptual world is constantly changing and events can be fleeting. To cope with this, working memory serves as an interface between perceptual input and internal representations (Awh et al., 2006; Chun, 2011). Working memory allows relevant perceptual information to be maintained over time and thus it is not surprising that attention to particular information would have impact in working memory.

Research into possible interactions between attention and working memory began with experiments which showed that eye movements and arm movements could interfere with maintenance of spatial information (Baddeley & Lieberman, 1980; Smyth & Pelky, 1992). This observation led to the proposal that maintenance of spatial information involves covert shifts of attention (Smyth & Pelky, 1992). Further experiments showed that visual processing at locations that have been memorized is better than processing at locations that have not been memorized (See Box 3.3). This result is consistent with the notion that the memorized locations are the focus of attention. Moreover, the close relationship between attention and working memory was illustrated in further experiments that showed that if participants were forced to direct their attention away from locations held in working memory then their ability to recall these locations was impaired (Awh et al., 1998; Smyth, 1996; Smyth & Pelky, 1992). These interactions between working memory and attention are not limited to spatial information. Similar effects have been found for shape information (Downing, 2000; Soto et al., 2005).

The relationship between attention and working memory raises interesting questions about the basis of these two cognitive functions that ongoing research is trying to resolve. The full nature of the interaction between attention and working memory is still up for debate and it has been shown that the capacity limits of working memory cannot be explained solely by attentional factors (Fougnie & Marois, 2006).

Box 3.3 Research Close Up: Using a dual task to examine attention and working memory

Source: Awh, E., Jonides, J., & Reuter-Lorenz, P. A. (1998). Rehearsal in spatial working memory. *Journal of Experimental Psychology-Human Perception and Performance, 24*(3), 780–790.

INTRODUCTION

To test the claim that spatial selective attention could be directed towards a location stored in working memory Awh and colleagues (Awh & Jonides, 2001; Awh et al., 1998) performed a dual-task experiment. Their prediction was that improved efficiency in visual processing would be obtained at locations stored in working memory. In particular they tested whether impairing the ability of participants to direct attention towards locations in working memory would result in a corresponding decrease in memory accuracy.

METHOD

The basic setup of the experiment is shown in Figure 3.6a. For the dual-task conditions individuals performed both a spatial memory and a colour discrimination task. At the beginning of the experiment participants would be presented with a cue at a particular spatial location and given the task of keeping in memory the location of this cue. They would next perform a colour classification task to a target that was either a small disk that required a shift in attention or a large disk that did not require a shift in attention since it was large enough to cover all the potential memorized locations. The colour classification task involved judging the colour from a possibility of red versus pink or blue versus purple. Finally, a probe would be presented and participants had the second task to decide whether the probe was or

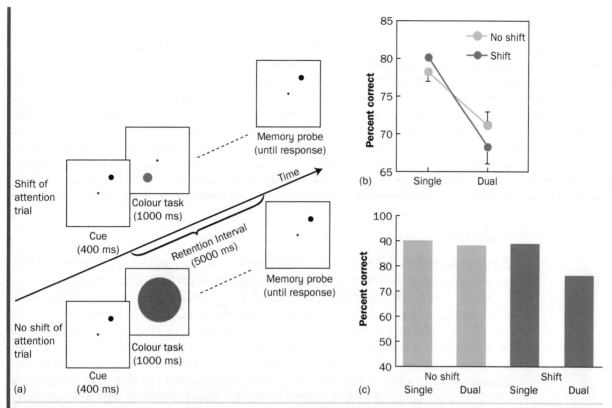

Figure 3.6   Experiment showing similarity between spatial attention and working memory. (a) Schematic of the task that participants performed during the experiment. First, a cue provided a spatial location for people to remember. Next, while maintaining fixation, they were presented either a small colour disk that required shifting attention to identify the colour (top) or a large disk that did not require shifting attention (bottom) (in control conditions participants didn't identify colour). Finally they were given a memory probe at either the same or a different location and asked to indicate if it was the same as the cue. (b) Percentage of correct responses in identifying location. (c) The percentage of correct responses in identifying colour.

Sources: (b) Adapted from Awh, E., Jonides, J., & Reuter-Lorenz, P. A. (1998). Rehearsal in spatial working memory. *Journal of Experimental Psychology-Human Perception and Performance,* 24(3), 780–790. (a) & (c) Adapted from Awh, E. & Jonides, J. (2001). Overlapping mechanisms of attention and spatial working memory. *Trends in Cognitive Sciences,* 5(3), 119–126.

was not at the same location as the cue. For the single-task conditions, the experimental conditions were identical except that more colours were used and importantly no classification of the colour was required. Thus, observers first saw a cue and were asked to keep the location in memory, second saw a small or large disk and then *only* gave a memory judgement of whether the probe was in the same location as the cue.

RESULTS

The two important results to examine are performance on the spatial memory task (Figure 3.6b) and performance on the colour discrimination task (Figure 3.6c). Performance on the spatial memory task showed decreased performance for the dual task, and in particular accuracy was worse when the small disk was used that required a shift in attention. This result shows that taking attention away from a location in working memory causes a decrement in memory performance. Performance on the colour discrimination task showed a decrement in performance for the shifting condition. This result indicates that there was interference between the colour discrimination task and maintaining the location of the cue in spatial working memory. These results are crucial in demonstrating that spatial attention plays a beneficial role in the active maintenance of location information.

DISCUSSION

In the taxonomy of attention presented at the beginning of the chapter working memory was located within internal attention while attention to spatial locations was located within external attention. However, the results of this experiment blur the boundary between internal and external attention by showing interactions between working memory and attention to spatial locations. Further experiments exploring this issue have examined whether the two systems can be considered independent but with similar operating properties or whether they are highly interdependent. The issue is not yet resolved, but brain imaging experiments have begun to reveal the overlap between brain areas related to attention and working memory (Pessoa & Ungerleider, 2004) and the details of how encoding by attention and working memory is functionally divided (Fusser et al., 2011; Mayer et al., 2007; Silk et al., 2010).

PARADIGMS FOR STUDYING ATTENTION

Both the filter theory of Broadbent (1958) and the resource theory of Kahneman (1973) were overarching theories that provided a general model of the function of attention. However, as interest in attention intensified in the 1980s the diversity of approaches and results has made it difficult to conceptualize the function of attention under a single model. Two general trends are evident since this time. The first trend is an emphasis on vision as a primary modality to explore models of attention. This has been led by recent developments in vision research that have provided an extensive set of features (colour, size, location, shape, etc.) to explore and enabled study of how attention is distributed in space. The second trend is the rich development of experimental paradigms like 'visual search', 'dual-task interference', 'inhibition of return' and 'attentional blink' which started in single studies to later become general experimental techniques. For example, we have already discussed how dual-task interference has been used to critically examine resource theory as well as the connection between attention and working memory.

Visual search

Research into visual search addresses the problem of how we use attention to search for a target in a visual display. An extremely influential approach to this problem, known as feature integration theory (FIT), was introduced by Treisman and Gelade (1980) (Figure 3.7). They considered that both the target being searched for and

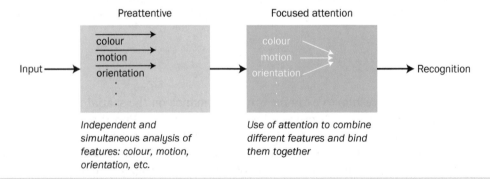

Figure 3.7   Schematic of feature integration theory (FIT) used to drive visual search. Visual input first goes to independent feature analysers that analyse the entire visual field and then pass information to a focused attention stage. With focused attention the features are joined together and passed to a recognition stage.

Source: Adapted from Treisman, A. M. & Schmidt, H. (1982). Illusory conjunctions in the perception of objects. *Cognitive Psychology*, *14*(1), 107–141.

the distractor objects would be composed of visual features such as shape, size and colour. Recognition of a target was modelled to be determined by two processes. The first process, termed preattentive, was capable of simultaneously searching the entire visual array. This preattentive process could independently examine features such as colour and form and if the item could be identified by a simple primary feature then this preattentive stage alone could lead to recognition. For example, if we are searching for a green target in a field of red distractors then we can immediately identify the green target using preattentive mechanisms. If however, recognition depends on combining multiple features then a process of focused attention is needed to combine the features. This use of attention to 'glue' together the different features helps to solve what is known as the binding problem. Namely, that from neurophysiology we know that different image features of an object such as colour and shape are not necessarily processed together, even though our subjective experience is that all these features are bound together into a unitary experience.

Preattentive visual processes can simultaneously analyse the entire scene and detect the presence of unique features.

Binding problem describes the issue that although perception works via analysis of separate perceptual features our subjective experience has all these features bound together.

Further insight into the role of focused search was provided by research into how the process of combining features could go wrong in what was termed illusory conjunctions (Treisman & Schmidt, 1982). These illusory conjunctions come about when attention is diverted or overloaded and appear as confusions between features of objects. For example, if a red square and a green triangle are presented while attention is diverted then an observer might report seeing a green square or a red triangle. This provides evidence that the features have been processed but due to the lack of attention they have not been correctly bound together.

Further research into visual search has led to a new and evolving model known as Guided Search (Wolfe, 1994; Wolfe et al., 2011). A diagram of the model is shown in Figure 3.8,

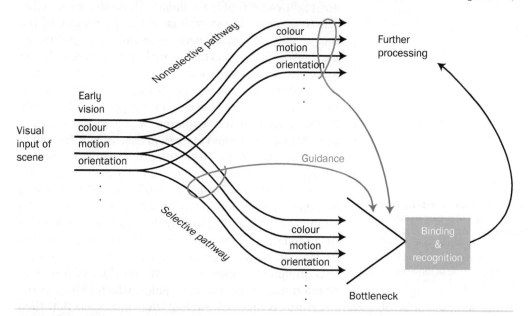

Figure 3.8   Schematic of Guided Search. Guided search is comprised of a selective pathway and a non-selective pathway that arise from early visual processing. The selective pathway leads to an attentional bottleneck that precedes the binding of features and recognition. Processing at the bottleneck is informed by guiding information based on an abstract representation of features such as colour. The non-selective pathway leads to processing of collective properties of the visual information, which can also provide guidance at the attentional bottleneck.

Source: Adapted from Wolfe, J. M., Võ, M. L. H., Evans, K. K., & Greene, M. R. (2011). Visual search in scenes involves selective and nonselective pathways. *Trends in Cognitive Sciences, 15*(2), 77–84.

in which we can see similarities and differences with FIT. The main similarity is that what Treisman and Gelade (1980) termed focused attention can be found in the selective pathway and just like with FIT it is important for binding features for recognition. Differences with feature integration theory include that although the preattentive stage still exists in the form of early visual processing, emphasis is given to how this analysis forms an abstract representation where particular features can be used to guide attention at the point of the attentional bottleneck. Another difference is the addition of a non-selective pathway, which analyses collective aspects of the visual input to guide attention. The problem of guiding attention is reminiscent of resource theory where attentional resources were managed. However, resource theory models ran into issues with circular reasoning since efficient management seemed to require knowing what was being attended before allocating the resources. To avoid this issue of circularity the guidance information is not sufficient for recognition of complex scenes or objects but can be used to facilitate processing at the attentional bottleneck. For example, the guidance arising from early visual processing can highlight the utility of a particular feature such as colour. Similarly, the non-selective pathway has access to information about the image that is insufficient for recognition but can inform the likelihood of what scene is being viewed. For example, this information might be sufficient to indicate that you are in a forest, rather than in a city (Biederman et al., 1974; Oliva & Torralba, 2001), but insufficient to tell you any other details. This capability has been termed obtaining the gist of a scene.

> Distributed attention is reminiscent of preattentive vision and allows rapid statistical analysis of the entire scene.

One of the defining characteristics of the non-selective pathway is that it uses distributed attention (Treisman, 2006). Distributed attention is in many ways similar to what was previously considered preattentive processing as it allows a rapid evaluation of the entire image. It is proposed that distributed attention works by extracting statistical properties of the objects and features present in the image. These statistics enable one to perceive the overall layout and structure of the image but are insufficient to enable recognition of particular objects. It is important to note that distributed attention acts not simply by considering the image information at a coarser scale than focused attention but rather provides a relational analysis of the whole image. Research has explored which visual features are accessible to rapid statistical assessment for use in distributed attention. These features include orientation (Dakin & Watt, 1997), contrast texture (Chubb et al., 2007) and size (Chong & Treisman, 2003), as well as velocity and direction of motion (Atchley & Andersen, 1995). An example of this ability to perceive statistical properties of an image is shown in Figure 3.9 for the perception of size. In these experiments observers were shown two groups of circles to the left and right of a central fixation and were asked to judge which side had the larger average size. Observers performed this task rapidly, demonstrating that they were able to use distributed attention to find the average size of the two groups of circles. We will return to this claim of size being available for distributed attention a little later in Box 3.4.

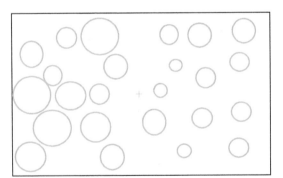

Figure 3.9   Distributed attention can rapidly determine average size. Given two groups of circles to the left and right of a central fixation cross, observers can rapidly identify which side has larger average size. This occurs via a mechanism of distributed attention that allows statistical properties of the entire image to be determined.

Evaluation

Visual search has been, and continues to be a very active field of research within the domain of attention. The diagrams presented in Figures 3.7 and 3.8 provide a schematic of the basic architectures of these systems. The heart of these approaches have been quantitative models that enable prediction of how efficient a search will be given a particular set of targets and distractors. These models have been forced to evolve as researchers developed new visual configurations that challenged existing model predictions. However, one shortcoming of this approach has been that testing precise model predictions has relied on the use of tightly controlled visual displays that are inherently artificial. Regardless of this shortcoming, there has been success in applying findings from artificial displays to everyday scenarios such as what factors influence the performance of airport baggage screeners.

Inhibition of return

If attention is attracted to an event in the visual field there will be facilitation of processing around this location. However, after attention moves away, this location suffers from delayed responding to events (Klein, 1988, 2000). This phenomenon was first described by Posner and Cohen (1984) and named inhibition of return. As the name suggests the mechanism promotes searching novel locations rather than returning to one that has already been examined. It has been proposed that inhibition of return is used in foraging behaviour to help the searcher from not returning to locations that have already been explored. Inhibition of return begins around 250–300 milliseconds after attention has been directed to a location and this inhibition appears to have a duration of around 3 seconds (Samuel & Kat, 2003). It was originally shown to exist with locations in space but it has also been shown to exist on attention directed to objects (Tipper et al., 1991). The original experiments of Posner and Cohen (1984) also showed that inhibition of return was coded in environmental coordinates rather than being fixed to the eyes' retinal coordinates. They showed this by demonstrating that eye movements could be included during the inhibitory period and the effect was still observed.

Inhibition of return has been combined with the idea of saliency maps in computer vision to search an image (Itti & Koch, 2001). Image salience indicates which parts of the image are going to draw in attention based on purely the visual features. An influential description of how bottom-up attention based on saliency might work was provided by Koch and Ullman (1985). They discussed how different visual features (size, colour, etc.) might combine to form a single map of conspicuity based on which parts of the image were most different from their surround. These conspicuous or salient parts of the image are those that are most likely to draw the attention of an observer (Figure 3.10). However, since the most conspicuous part of an image isn't necessarily the target we are looking for, inhibition of return provides a mechanism to disregard conspicuous locations for the remainder of the search as one explores less salient locations.

Figure 3.10 Examples of saliency calculated from input images. Orientation, colour and other image properties are combined in a computer algorithm to find the image locations that are most conspicuous. These conspicuous regions are indicated in the right column with the brighter shades of white indicating the more conspicuous image regions.

Source: (TopL): © mrolands/iStock (BottomL): © 4774344 sean/iStock (R): Saliency maps provided by Dirk Bernhardt-Walther. © Dirk Bernhardt-Walther.

Attentional blink

If we are watching a sequence of rapidly presented visual displays (6–20 items per second), the second of two targets cannot be identified when its presentation is close in time to that of a first target. This phenomenon is known as attentional blink. For example, if we are given the task of identifying two letters within a sequence of rapidly presented numbers, then detection will be impaired on the second letter if it is presented close in time to the presentation of the first letter. Although the phenomenon had been noted earlier (Broadbent & Broadbent, 1987), it was described as the 'attentional blink' by Raymond, Shapiro and Arnell (1992). This notion of a blink captures the intuition that after attention has obtained the first target, it 'blinks' and thus does not see the second. The basic paradigm and results of this study are shown in Figure 3.11. A sequence of visual stimuli is presented in rapid succession and if participants are instructed to identify just a single target then the proportion of correct responses is nearly identical regardless of where in the sequence it is shown. However, when instructed to identify two targets, there is a substantial reduction in performance in identifying the second target, with recognition performance below 60 per cent from 80 to 450 milliseconds after presentation of the first target. The attentional blink paradigm has been used extensively to study the availability of attention across time. It demonstrates a clear limitation of attention in showing that the best way to make a second target go unnoticed is to show it within a short time after showing the first target. It is worth pointing out that the lowest performance does not occur immediately after the first target (Figure 3.11b).

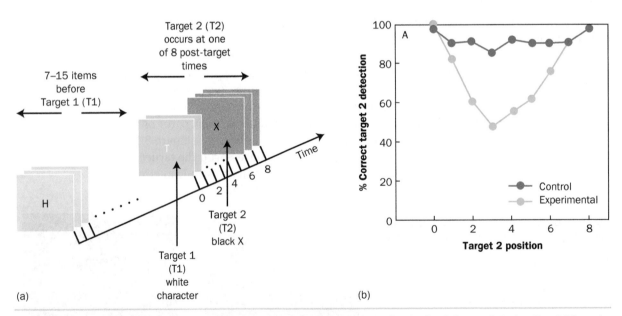

(a)   (b)

Figure 3.11   **Attentional blink shows that attention temporarily decreases immediately after being used at a location.** (a) Example of a single trial of an attentional blink experiment. After a first target (T1) is attended, then a second target (T2) is shown at the same location at different times afterwards. The closer in time T2 is to T1 then the lower the chances of correct identification. (b) Results of an attentional blink experiment show that in the control condition when only one target is shown there is no change in correct identification. However, in the experimental condition results show that when T2 is shown after T1 there is a decrease in ability to correctly identify the target.

Source: Adapted from Raymond, J. E., Shapiro, K. L., & Arnell, K. M. (1992). Temporary suppression of visual processing in an RSVP task: An attentional blink? *Journal of Experimental Psychology: Human Perception and Performance, 18*(3), 849–860.

Box 3.4 Research Close Up: Using the attentional blink to examine distributed attention

Source: Joo, S. J., Shin, K., Chong, S. C., & Blake, R. (2009). On the nature of the stimulus information necessary for estimating mean size of visual arrays. *Journal of Vision*, 9(9), 1–12.

INTRODUCTION

Distributed attention is defined as an independent mechanism of the non-selective pathway. It extracts statistical properties of objects and features to enable rapid evaluation of an image. A crucial property of distributed attention is that it should be immune to processes of focused attention. Thus, when distributed attention is used to perform a task such as judging mean size there should be no evidence of focused attention. An experiment examining this claim was performed by Joo and colleagues (Joo et al., 2009). They used an attentional blink paradigm to modulate focused attention while participants performed a distributed attention judgment of mean size.

The rationale for using the attentional blink paradigm is that during the attentional blink there is a decrease in the performance of focused attention during the period following stimulus presentation. This fact gives control over focused attention and leads to the hypothesis of Joo et al. (2009) that size estimation will not be influenced by the attentional blink since it involves distributed rather than focused attention. In other words, if size estimation is not influenced by focused attention then as focused attention changes during the attentional blink there will not be any difference in the ability of individuals to perform mean size estimation.

METHOD

The basic design of the experiment was to embed a distributed attention task of judging mean size of circles within an attentional blink paradigm. As is common in the attentional blink paradigm participants were instructed to detect a first (T1) and a second (T2) target letter within a stream of distractor letters. The stream of letters was presented with distractor letters displayed in black and target letters T1 and T2 displayed in white. An additional property of the experimental display was that T2 was surrounded by a reference circle and the three distractor letters before and after it were surrounded by circles of different sizes. The mean size of these circles was carefully controlled to be either larger or smaller than the reference circle presented at T2. An illustration of the presentation order is provided in Figure 3.12. On all trials observers were required to detect T1 and T2 and to judge whether the mean size of the presented circles were larger or smaller than the reference circle presented on T2. The timing between T1 and T2 was arranged such that either T2 occurred within the attentional blink or it did not.

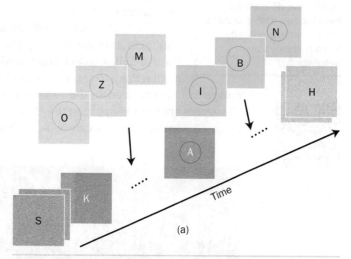

(a)

Figure 3.12   Using the attentional blink to study distributed attention. A trial consists of black distractor letters and two white target letters presented sequentially on the screen. Target 1 (T1), is shown as a white 'K', and Target 2 (T2) is shown as a white 'A'. The timing between T1 and T2 varies on different trials such that T2 does or does not fall within an attentional blink. T2 is surrounded by a reference circle and the three trials before and the three trials after T2 have the black letter surrounded by a circle of different diameters. Participants had the tasks of detecting T1 and T2 as well as judging whether the reference circle presented at T2 was larger or smaller than the average size of the presented circles.

Source: Joo, S. J., Shin, K., Chong, S. C., & Blake, R. (2009). On the nature of the stimulus information necessary for estimating mean size of visual arrays. *Journal of Vision*, 9(9), 7.

RESULTS

The authors found that the performance of identifying T2 was 84 per cent when it was outside the attentional blink and fell to 66 per cent when it fell within the attentional blink. Thus, there was clear evidence that the attentional blink was modulating focused attention. However, crucially for their hypothesis that distributed attention would be unaffected by focused attention, the judgment of mean size did not change between these two conditions.

DISCUSSION

Results confirmed the claim from distributed attention that perception of the mean size of a set of elements can be determined accurately without focused attention. Moreover, the research provided an example of how the attentional blink could be used to explore distributed attention. The results are consistent with those of Ariely (2001) that we can accurately represent the statistical properties of large groups of elements. This is an important capability since for many events in life, such as which queue to join, it is the property of the group rather than the individual elements that we need to quickly ascertain.

FAILURES OF ATTENTION

Change blindness

Change blindness is the phenomenon where substantial differences between two nearly identical scenes are not noticed when presented sequentially.

Scan to watch a demonstration of change blindness in action

Although we are very good at understanding the gist of a scene, we are not always so impressive in our capability to apprehend details of a scene. Convincing evidence of this comes from a phenomenon known as change blindness (Rensink, 2002; Rensink et al., 1997). Demonstrations of change blindness, involve showing two nearly identical photos to an observer, each for 240 milliseconds, separated by a masking image of 80 milliseconds, and asking them to say what has changed in the image. The mask is necessary so that motion is not seen in the region around where the photos have been retouched. Observers are poor at spotting the change even though the cycle of photos is shown for up to 60 seconds, and as can be seen from the example in Figure 3.13 the change is

Figure 3.13   Change blindness. Can you spot the difference? In a change blindness test, the images are shown one after another in sequence and observers are asked to spot the change. Very large changes go unnoticed and are difficult to detect even when both pictures are shown together. If you could not see the difference between images, the answer is given at the end of the chapter.

Source: © Ronald Rensink, available as a video file, along with other examples of change blindness at http://www.cs.ubc.ca/~rensink/flicker/download/index.html

extensive. These change blindness displays are prime examples that large changes can go unnoticed. Change blindness is related to a family of experimental results that have investigated how attention is related to whether or not we are able to report all aspects of what we see. In change blindness observers can freely search an image to detect the change and thus a variety of factors related to how we search and remember image properties might be at work. In the next section we will see that even under conditions when eye movements and search are not required the responses of observers are striking in what they fail to report seeing.

Inattentional blindness

The term inattentional blindness was coined by Mack and Rock (1998) to describe the rather surprising visual phenomenon that we can be looking directly at a target but will report that we do not see it if attention is not allocated. The key experimental design is shown in Figure 3.14, which shows examples of what occurred for what they called non-critical and critical trials. By contrasting the difference between non-critical and critical trials we can see the effect of inattentional blindness. On both critical trials and non-critical trials a viewer's task was to first fixate on a central target and then when a large cross came visible they were to examine it without moving their eyes to judge whether the horizontal or vertical arm of the cross was larger. Then a visual mask

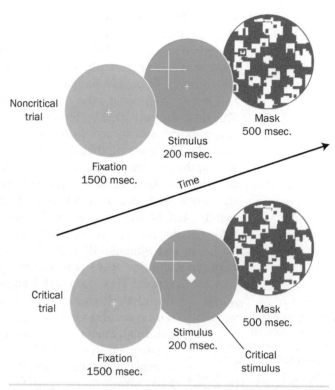

Figure 3.14   Demonstration of inattentional blindness. Participants were instructed to fixate on a central cross and after 1500 milliseconds a large cross appeared off fixation with different lengths of horizontal and vertical arms. Participants had to keep fixation while attending to the large cross and making their judgement of which arm of the cross was longer. On a small percentage of trials, termed critical trials, a small diamond unexpectedly appeared at fixation. At the end of the trials participants were asked if they saw anything different during the experiment, and 60–80 per cent of observers reported never seeing the small diamond figure appear at fixation.

Source: Adapted from Mack, A. & Rock, I. (1998). *Inattentional blindness*. Cambridge, MA: MIT Press.

appeared to eliminate any afterimage and they reported which arm was longer. On the non-critical trials nothing happened at the fixation point and on the critical trials a small, unexpected figure appeared at fixation. It would seem common sense that on these critical trials people would experience seeing this small figure, however on 60–80 per cent of trials viewers failed to detect it even though it was at fixation in the centre of their view. These unexpected results from simple stimuli in a laboratory setting clearly demonstrate that although we go through life with the feeling that we are experiencing nearly all of what is appearing before our eyes, we are systematically able to miss events that are clearly presented to us if our attention is drawn away towards something else.

Inattentional blindness is the failure to notice a clearly visible target due to attention being diverted from the target.
Afterimage occurs when vision of an object remains after presentation has ceased. For example, after staring at a bright light.

The findings of Mack and Rock (1998) demonstrated that in the lab we can miss seeing a small diamond if our attention is diverted. While one could think that this result is just a peculiar curiosity of the psychology lab, subsequent research has shown that we can miss odd and otherwise startling visuals when our attention is directed elsewhere. To see this for yourself watch the video content indicated in the margin before proceeding. These studies of inattentional blindness when viewing human activity began with the

Scan to watch an example of inattentional blindness

work of Dan Simons and colleagues. The work built upon earlier studies (Neisser & Becklen, 1975) which demonstrated that when people view two overlapping movies and are asked to attend to the activities of one movie they can miss striking changes in the other movie. For example, if a movie of people passing a basketball was overlapped with a movie of people slapping hands and people were asked to attend to the basketball movie they could miss when the hand slapping game changed to handshaking. This task was modified by Simons and colleagues (Simons & Chabris, 1999) so that a single movie was shown. In this movie there were three players in white shirts who passed the ball among themselves along with three players in black shirts who passed among themselves. The task of observers was to count the number of passes of either the white or black team. Results showed that if an unexpected event happened during the movie, such as a person in a gorilla suit walked through the crowd, only approximately half of the viewers would notice the unexpected event. Further research into how observers piece together a visual world from an edited movie was conducted by Levin and Simons (1997, 2000). They showed films with substantial differences between shots that were not detected. Examples of changes between shots include

| | scarves appearing and disappearing as well as plates changing colour. Even |

Continuity editing describes a filmmaking technique to produce a smooth continuous experience across changes in camera shot.

though these changes are obvious once informed they go virtually unnoticed during natural viewing of the film, even when viewers are asked to watch carefully. Such errors in the continuity of a scene from one shot to the next occur even in high budget films as a search for continuity errors on the internet will reveal. See Box 3.5 for discussion of psychological research into continuity editing.

A real world activity in which inattentional blindness has been reported to occur is in driving, where it can seriously contribute to accidents (National Safety Council, 2010). For example, individuals have reported driving through red lights without stopping while apparently looking directly at a traffic-light signal. Even though they could 'see' that the light was red their attention was diverted to another activity like speaking on a mobile phone and this compromised their ability to attend to the driving environment.

Box 3.5 Practical Application: Attention and continuity editing in movies

As we watch a movie, different camera shots are constantly changing our view of a scene in a way that we would never get in real life. However, we typically do not find this disturbing and cheerfully pay to see the next movie. It would be satisfying if we could state the exact scientific principles behind how this seamless viewing experience is achieved, but it turns out that it is not known. Talented editors and filmmakers are in effect applied psychologists with expertise in guiding our attention through a movie. It has even been argued that the evolution of filmmaking has led to timings of shot structures that best match the human attention system (Cutting et al., 2010).

Work by Tim Smith has discussed how attention is manipulated in cuts from one shot to the next to obtain a continuous experience (Smith, 2010). As he points out, the explanation from the early days of filmmaking about why continuity editing worked was that we do not find cuts obtrusive since we can make the cut follow the expectation of the viewer (Münsterberg, 1916). For example, if one shot ends with someone turning their head to look at a particular object, then the next shot can show that object so as to guide attention from one shot to the next. This simple trick of initiating movement before a cut enables viewers to more quickly orient to the content of the new shot and to be less aware of the editing. This phenomenon was explored by Smith and Henderson (2008) in a study that used feature films to examine how different types of edit cuts affected perception. They compared four types of edit cuts for viewers' awareness that a cut had taken place. These four types of cuts were (1) cuts between scenes,

Figure 3.15 How a cut is made influences whether a viewer will be aware it was made. Viewers watched excerpts of seven feature films for five minutes each and were asked to press a button every time they saw an edit. The data were analysed for four types of editing cuts: between scenes, within scenes, match action and gaze match. Results showed that within scene and match action cuts were most invisible. This is consistent with the fact that these guide attention and induce inattentional blindness.

Source: © Dr Tim Smith, Smith, T. J. & Henderson, J. M. (2008). Edit blindness: The relationship between attention and global change blindness in dynamic scenes. *Journal of Eye Movement Research*, 2(2), 6. Stills from *Blade Runner* (Ridley Scott, 1982).

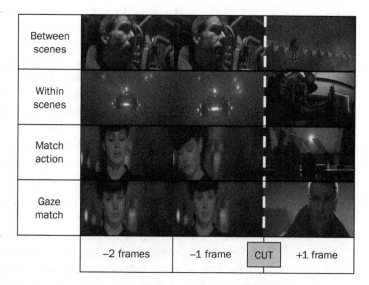

(2) cuts within a scene, (3) cuts that matched action and (4) cuts that matched gaze (Figure 3.15). Results showed that within scene and match action cuts had respectively 25 per cent and 32 per cent of cuts missed, while between scene and gaze match cuts had around 10 per cent of cuts missed. These results were consistent with the intuition used in continuity editing of film; that cuts which guide attention as well as provide a viewer with changing and optimum views of the action add interest to the viewer and engage them with the narrative. Engagement of the viewer with the narrative promotes inattentional blindness and this also helps to explain why these edit cuts are most invisible to an observer.

An interesting aspect of this research application is that the practical art of telling stories by moving images has become so advanced that most of the issues psychologists study aren't currently major practical problems since effective tools of the trade have evolved through a century of development. Nonetheless, filmmaking is a dynamic industry and both filmmakers and scientists are interested in how future practice can be shaped through a richer understanding of why current techniques are successful.

Evaluation

Our coverage of attention covered a wide range of material that both established an historical perspective on how the field has emerged and discussed current paradigms used to explore attention. Although these approaches generally treat attention as a process of its own we covered two cases where attention appears deeply embedded within other processes. These two include models of attention in the visual cortex and similarities between attention and working memory. Given this great variety of attentional phenomena it has proven difficult, if not impossible, to describe a single mechanism from which all attentional processes can be derived. There is, however, considerable structure to attention research and this is apparent in the taxonomy of attention which is useful for seeing how the many pieces of attention research fit together. That attention is an important topic to understand human performance is underscored by the various applications we discussed; these applications range from auto accidents that arise from a lack of attention to including models of attention in robotic systems so they interact better with their environment.

CONSCIOUSNESS

We now begin with a discussion of consciousness that includes the relationship between attention and consciousness and emphasizes efforts to use knowledge of neural and psychological processes to explain consciousness. Interest in consciousness within cognitive psychology goes back to the early days in the writings of Roger Sperry (1952). Moreover, aspects of consciousness have been studied in the ability to

Subliminal perception is the case where a stimulus is presented below threshold (e.g. too fast or too dim) but its effects on behaviour can still be measured.

make reliable judgements about perceptual stimuli to which we have no awareness. This research under the topic of subliminal perception has a long history in psychology (Pierce & Jastrow, 1884) and it has been argued that the modular and distributed nature of cognitive structures promotes the possibility that we would internally possess information to which we have no awareness (Erdelyi, 1974). However, there is still no precise scientific definition of consciousness. Thus a starting point is the everyday definition that to be conscious is to be aware of one's own existence as evidenced by thoughts and perception of one's surroundings. Philosophical debates into consciousness have been active for thousands of years and where appropriate we will draw upon philosophy to gain further insight.

Among the recent advocates of psychological research into consciousness was Francis Crick (1995) who expressed the view that while the topic is challenging for science to explain, it is too important a topic for science to ignore. A core difficulty is that the scientific approach is based on objective, third-person examination, while our current definition of consciousness is primarily subjective, first-person experience of 'one's own existence'. Philosophers sometimes use the thought experiment of 'Mary's Room' to explain the dilemma between first- and third-person descriptions (Jackson, 1982). Imagine Mary to be a brilliant colour scientist who, somewhat cruelly, has been born and raised in a total black and white environment. She knows everything about the colour red that it is possible to have learned. If she is allowed to leave the room and see red for the first time, will this experience of red be entirely predictable to Mary from her previous third-person, objective knowledge, or will this first-person, subjective experience of seeing red be something different?

There are many established philosophical positions that argue different outcomes for Mary. One of these is that Mary's experience of seeing red cannot possibly be explained by her previous studies of colour science. With this view it is apparent that science could never explain consciousness, and a sceptic could dismiss all efforts to scientifically explain consciousness. We believe that such a decision is premature for two reasons. Firstly, although scientific explanation might fall short of explaining all of consciousness, the limits of what it can explain are not yet known. Secondly, the conscious self appears central to a variety of psychological functions and some illumination of its function could bring practical benefits to the role of the conscious self in mental health.

FUNCTIONS OF CONSCIOUSNESS

Motivated by the three levels of explanation for an information processing system that were proposed by Marr (1982) and discussed in Chapter 2, in this section we wish to address the computational theory of consciousness – what its purpose is and why it does what it does. But before getting too deep into discussion of the functions of consciousness it would be useful for every reader to pause and contemplate their own consciousness: does it exist, and what makes it important? In addition, consider your response to my following two claims:

1 I believe that my consciousness exists and that while both myself and the computer I am using are made of physical stuff that process information, there is something about my mental life that sets me apart from the computer.

2 I cannot absolutely convince myself that those reading these words are conscious, nor do I think that I can absolutely convince a critical reader that I am conscious.

The purpose of this thought experiment is to clear the air that no matter whether you do or do not believe in consciousness or its importance, there currently is no unique, airtight, logical argument that can confirm or disconfirm these beliefs. This unsatisfying stalemate makes clear that we need to know more if we ever want to solve this problem. In the meantime we will need to be somewhat open-minded when describing the possible functions of consciousness.

Does consciousness have a function?

We start with two distinctive views of the function of consciousness. The first, conscious inessentialism, claims that consciousness is not necessary. A basis of this argument is that we can take any operation performed by a conscious agent and have it performed by something that is not conscious. Descriptions of how this might come about typically invoke what philosophers of mind call 'zombies' which can perform the same actions without being conscious (Moody, 1994). While the assertion that consciousness does not exist might not seem correct, it is hard to thoroughly disprove. Moreover, cases appear where the argument has a ring of truth. For example, you might not be able to report anything that happened while driving on a long highway journey, and thus your zombie replacement would seem equally qualified. The second view, epiphenomenalism, does not reject the existence of consciousness but holds that it has no function. T.H. Huxley likened consciousness to the whistle on a locomotive engine that makes noise but is not involved at all in the primary mechanism of moving the train (Huxley, 1896). Like conscious inessentialism, such a view is hard to disprove. For further details of the philosophical basis of this discussion see Chalmers (1996) or Dennett (1992).

Volition

Volition is defined as our ability to make conscious choices and if we can demonstrate volition then this demonstrates free will. One commonly assumed function of consciousness is that it is related to our ability to choose which action to perform. We think about moving our arm and, voilà, our arm moves. Introspectively it appears that there is a close causal link between our conscious experience and our actions. It turns out, however, there are psychological data to question this simple link. In a classic experiment, Libet and colleagues (1983, 1985) instructed participants to start with their arm resting and whenever they were ready, to move their arm. Libert measured two aspects of participants' performance in moving their arm. First, with EEG he measured what is known as the readiness potential, which indicates brain activity reflecting the initiation of preparing a movement. Second, by asking participants to report the position of a rotating dot when they first had awareness of their intent to move, he could find the time of this conscious awareness. What he found was that the readiness potential, reflecting unconscious preparatory brain activity, preceded the time of conscious awareness by around half a second. The fact that unconscious preparation precedes conscious awareness violates our intuition that our conscious decisions always precede our actions and has been taken as evidence against free will. This in turn has been used to support various claims such as that our sense of volition is merely an illusion created as we observe our own actions and assign meaning to them (Wegner, 2003; Wegner & Wheatley, 1999).

Evaluation

While Libet himself did not argue strongly against free will on the basis of these results, they are nonetheless quite striking and call into question theoretical and common sense ideas about the relationship between consciousness and achieving our desired actions. Indeed, some 20 years after the original experiments, an entire issue of the journal *Consciousness and Cognition* was devoted to the topic (Banks, 2002) and the finding continues to be a test for philosophical theories of consciousness (Searle, 2013). The interaction between science and philosophy has not been without controversy. Libet (2002, p. 292) noted that: 'It is interesting that most of the negative criticism of our findings and their implications have come from philosophers and others with no significant experience in experimental neuroscience and the brain.' One cause for this is that individuals combine the experimental results with apparently reasonable assumptions to derive conclusions that generalize past what the data support. While such 'thought experiments' are useful they are not a replacement for actual experimental verification.

Although experimental verification is elusive for complex hypotheses about consciousness there has been intense scrutiny of the basic methods employed by Libet and colleagues. These studies have revealed that the finding of a readiness potential occurring before reports of awareness is a robust finding that can be replicated (Haggard, 2005; Haggard & Eimer, 1999). However, examination of the speed of the rotating dot showed that timing estimates of the conscious decision to move one's arm will change with rotation speed (Danquah et al., 2008; Pockett & Miller, 2007), though these changes do not seem large enough to negate the basic effect. Still this research points towards one of the crucial issues of Libet's experiment, that people do not have some sort of internal clock that they can just read out to accurately provide their time of awareness. Thus timing reports will always rely upon relating the time of subjective experience to the time of external events and such judgements are vulnerable to influences of attention or sensory modality of the external event.

Other possible functions

One function proposed for consciousness is that it provides us with an executive summary of our current situation (Koch, 2004). Even with attention to limit input there is still a constant inflow of information from the world and any of a large number of personal desires we might wish to satisfy at any one time. The executive summary produced by consciousness might primarily serve to integrate this vast amount of information. This idea of consciousness performing an integrative function is similar to that proposed by the global workspace theory (Baars, 1988, 2002) where consciousness facilitates flexible context-driven behaviour. An implication of consciousness performing an integrative function is that consciousness would work across extensive brain networks with the task of creating the summary for this network. These integrative aspects of consciousness have been proposed to act over both the role of attention in providing feelings of pain, colour, etc., as well as its interpretive capabilities in constructing past and present events.

Global workspace theory proposes that consciousness requires interactions across a broad range of brain areas.

It has also been claimed that consciousness provides an important mechanism for understanding the mental states of those around us. This capability is thought to have arisen from the role of consciousness in providing us with a window into our own reasoning and decisions. From consciousness first providing us with insight into our own actions we can generalize this knowledge of ourselves to understand the actions of others (Humphrey, 2002). Other functions that have been proposed for consciousness include learning and skill acquisition, rational thought and detecting errors.

The practical importance of understanding consciousness can be seen in different domains. In Chapter 1 we discussed consciousness in relation to medicine when we need to determine if a patient is conscious. This included discussion of using fMRI to assess individuals in a vegetative state. Another practical area where consciousness is relevant is law, and in Box 3.6 we describe how the law treats our actions during sleepwalking.

Box 3.6 When Things Go Wrong: Sleepwalking and the law

Sleepwalking occurs in 2–3 per cent of adults, with 0.4 per cent of adults having a weekly sleepwalk episode; in children it is even more common with a prevalence of around 15 per cent in 5–12 year-olds (Plazzi et al., 2005; Provini et al., 2011). In most cases the sleepwalk will begin in the first hours of sleep, and the sleepwalker will move about with their eyes open but displaying a low level of arousal and awareness before returning to bed in 15–30 minutes (Provini et al., 2011). However, in some cases complex behaviour is exhibited during a sleepwalk and the extreme cases illustrate the challenging area where science and the law intersect. There is the well-known case of a man in Ontario, Canada who after falling asleep on his living room couch got up, drove 23 kilometres, took a tyre iron and a hatchet out of the boot of his car, entered the house of his wife's parents, went to their bedroom and assaulted his father-in-law and killed his mother-in-law. He then drove to a nearby police station and with a somewhat confused confession turned himself in to the police. Although it was clear what he had done, he was later acquitted of both assault and murder. To understand how this decision could have been reached we will first consider the mental states associated with sleepwalking and then how these relate to the law.

Sleepwalking is a complicated phenomenon that can be understood in terms of the basic properties of sleep. When we sleep there are the two basic states that include rapid eye movement (REM) sleep and non-rapid eye movement (NREM) sleep. Typically, during one night, we go through several cycles characterized by progressively deeper levels of NREM sleep punctuated with REM sleep. REM sleep brings about vivid dreaming that leads to a lighter level of NREM sleep and the beginning of another cycle. It turns out that sleepwalking occurs at the deepest level of NREM sleep. A general property of sleep is that by entering into the sleep cycle we are forming a disconnection between executive function in frontal cortex and the remainder of the brain (Braun et al., 1997). In other words, the evaluative and critical aspects that monitor our behaviour are not online. Intuitive evidence that this might be so is demonstrated by how uncritically we respond to some actually very bizarre events of our dreams. You might think that if the sleepwalker could move then their frontal cortex and executive function would be engaged. However, brain imaging data from a single sleepwalker indicates that although the motor systems of the brain are working, the disconnect with executive function is still in place and the mind continues to be asleep (Bassetti et al., 2000). It thus appears that sleepwalkers are in a complex state between wakefulness, deep sleep and dreaming; importantly, they do not have control over their behaviour, which includes critical evaluation of their acts.

Returning to the case of the Canadian sleepwalking killer we begin with the fact that he could not be deemed legally insane since sleepwalking is considered a sleep disorder and not a mental illness (Glancy et al., 2002). Next we consider the properties required by many legal systems to establish guilt, these include that a person's mental state in regard to the criminal act is purposeful, knowing, reckless or negligent (Hirstein & Sifferd, 2011). Thus, for his acquittal there must have been evidence that his actions weren't purposeful, knowing, reckless or negligent. We can dismiss negligence as a first step since, although he had a long history of sleepwalking, there was no reason for him to ever imagine a sleepwalk could go so wrong. To dismiss the other three conditions it is necessary to consider whether one can be purposeful, knowing, negligent or indeed conscious without the functions of executive control afforded by our frontal cortex. The global workspace theory (Baars, 1988, 2002) holds that consciousness arises from large scale integration of brain activity, and without the activity of frontal cortex and many other regions we can argue strongly that a sleepwalking individual is not conscious. Moreover, without executive function it is impossible to see how actions can be purposeful, knowing or reckless. In this way we can reach a verdict that agrees with the Canadian legal system.

ATTENTION AND CONSCIOUSNESS

Attention and consciousness share the property of involving selection of particular information above other information. In attention the selected information receives deeper processing while in consciousness the selected information receives privileged access to the stage of our mental life. Moreover, in both models of attention and consciousness there is concern over the fate of the non-selected information as both unattended and non-conscious information have been found to still be able to influence behaviour. From at least a sense of parsimony of description it appears worth considering whether attention and consciousness should be joined together into a common phenomenon. Indeed, early models of attention such as the filter theory of Broadbent had a single channel and once information was selected for transmission it became part of conscious awareness. However, studies of both attention and consciousness over the past 50 years paint a more complex picture, and in the following paragraphs we will summarize a model of how attention and conscious awareness are different (Lamme, 2003).

The model proposed by Lamme to distinguish between consciousness and attention is presented in Figure 3.16. Crucial to this model is that attention does not determine whether an input reaches consciousness but rather determines whether a conscious report about the input is possible. The distinction shown in Figure 3.16 between being conscious of an input and producing a conscious report of that input calls upon the different types of consciousness known as phenomenal consciousness and access consciousness (Block, 1995). Phenomenal consciousness is just experience (Platchias, 2010). For example, when we hear a noise like the refrigerator switch off, we feel that we have heard it all along, but without noticing it until it turns off. Access consciousness, on the other hand, is what we intuitively consider consciousness to be, as it is available for report and involved in the planning of actions. The proposed model predicts that we will be phenomenally conscious of many inputs but in the absence of attention this experience will quickly fade away and become unavailable for report. Moreover, in this model attention can be seen to act independently of awareness but is responsible for taking input from phenomenal to access consciousness.

Phenomenal consciousness includes the experiential properties of sensations, feelings and perceptions. **Access consciousness** includes representations that are broadcast for use in reasoning and control of action and can be reported.

A general framework to implement this model of attention and consciousness involves the concepts of a forward sweep of information and recurrent processing. We have previously described the feedforward sweep as the progression of activity from input brain areas to progressively more complex brain areas. This feedforward sweep corresponds to the unconscious where information is processed but we do not have access to these representations. Recurrent processing involves cyclic processing between brain areas such that the activity at both areas is dependent on each other. In this case the feedforward sweep will activate increasingly complex brain areas that will feedback their results to lower levels, which in turn modifies activity at lower levels and the ongoing information is swept forward. It is hypothesized that recurrent networks which

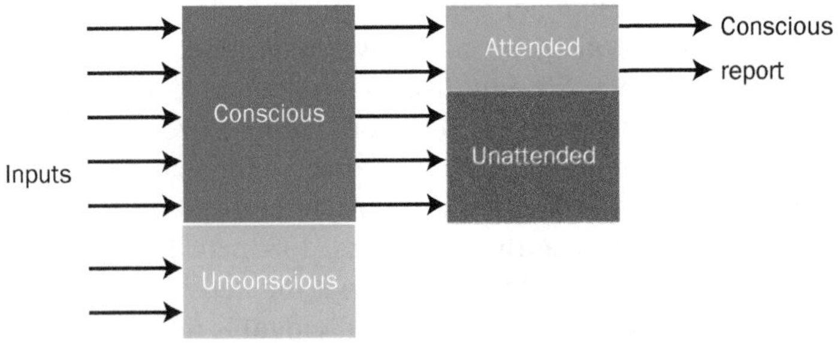

Figure 3.16   A model of how attention and consciousness work together.
In this model, different roles of attention and consciousness are distinguished in the processing of sensory input. According to the model, sensory input is first separated into conscious and unconscious streams. Only that information to which we attend will be available for conscious report.

Source: Adapted from Lamme, V. A. F. (2003). Why visual attention and awareness are different. *Trends in Cognitive Sciences*, 7(1), 12–18.

are somewhat restricted in their spatial extent will form the basis of phenomenal consciousness while widespread recurrent interactions across the brain bring about access consciousness. The role of attention in this process is to provide mechanisms to bias the recurrent processing to enable selection.

RELATING CONSCIOUSNESS TO BRAIN ACTIVITY

Through the ages philosophical investigations of consciousness have drawn from science to frame their questions, but there has traditionally been little direct, scientific testing of these questions. However, recently, there has been a sharp increase in the scientific study of consciousness. Using techniques such as brain imaging, these studies are searching for which aspects of consciousness can be related to brain function in typical individuals. Previously, scientific study of consciousness was mostly restricted to studying individuals with brain damage, and there is a tradition in neuropsychology to explore how brain damage can affect consciousness (Cooney & Gazzaniga, 2003). In this section we will first review two of these classic results from neuropsychology before moving on to more recent research paradigms.

Neuropsychology

It is basic physiology that the brain is composed of two hemispheres connected by a structure known as the corpus callosum. Our knowledge of how these two halves of the brain specialize and interact with each other was greatly enriched by the activities of Roger Sperry and colleagues in studying consciousness in individuals who had the corpus callosum severed as a last-resort medical procedure to control epilepsy (Gazzaniga, 2005; Gazzaniga et al., 1965). Early observations suggested that these patients with split brains showed little effect of having a split brain, as they were able to perform under natural conditions without evidence of deficit. However, when tested under controlled lab conditions fascinating differences emerged and it was for this research that Sperry received the 1981 Nobel Prize (Gazzaniga, 1981).

One experiment examined split-brain patients to see whether there was still a unity of consciousness between the two hemispheres. In particular, how the left hemisphere, which had language, and the right hemisphere, which did not have language, would behave when visual information was presented to only one hemisphere (see Chapter 12, Box 12.4). The left hemisphere could talk about what it was shown and thus report awareness. The right hemisphere could not talk about what it was shown but it could direct the left hand under its control to act appropriately with the object. These results led to questions about how consciousness might be distributed across these differently specialized hemispheres. However, a limitation to interpreting these results is that even with the corpus callosum severed, the two hemispheres are still connected by indirect subcortical connections which can pass information between hemispheres (Corballis, 1994). Nonetheless, the study of split-brain patients helped immensely to understand how the different parts of the brain interacted and how to address questions of consciousness.

Blindsight is another form of damage to the brain that has revealed insight into the complex relations between perception, attention and consciousness (Sahraie et al., 2006; Weiskrantz et al., 1974). Anatomically, the condition arises from damage to the primary visual cortex and can be extensive over the entire visual field due to damage in both hemispheres, or restricted to just a portion of the visual field with damage to only part of one hemisphere. The defining characteristic of blindsight is that an individual cannot provide a conscious report about what they see but they can still respond in various

Scan to watch a clip on blindsight

ways to stimuli presented in this damaged visual field. In Type 2 blindsight, individuals are able to report some attributes or feelings of knowing for stimuli such as movement or flashes, but in Type 1 blindsight there is denial of any awareness of the effected portion of the visual field. What is striking is that when an individual with blindsight is tested in their 'blind' field they can reliably discriminate factors like the orientation of lines when presented as forced yes/no types of questions. However, at the completion of testing when asked what they saw they will indicate that they did not see a thing.

The phenomenon of blindsight was not immediately accepted and early criticism raised a wealth of objections that have been examined empirically without refuting the basic claim of its existence. An explanation for how it is possible at all is that not all projections from the eye are sent to the primary visual cortex. It turns out that there are alternative pathways that bring visual information to other cortical structures. While the delivery of visual information to other brain regions explains how blindsight is possible it does not address the substantial issue of why individuals are not able to show conscious awareness of this information in any form of verbal report. Indeed, research has even shown that attention can have an effect in the blind field (Kentridge et al., 1999). More research is needed to know not only how visual information fails to reach consciousness in individuals with blindsight but also what happens to this particular visual information with intact individuals.

Neural correlates of consciousness (NCC)

The term neural correlates of consciousness (NCC) was popularized by Christof Koch (Koch, 2004; Tononi & Koch, 2008) in empirical investigations of consciousness that arose from his collaboration with Francis Crick. The term is meant not so much to be prescriptive of a particular way to conduct empirical research, but more to make the empirical NCC approach distinct from previous philosophical approaches. The essence of the approach is to examine how brain activity changes when, everything else being as equal as possible, a stimulus is experienced consciously or not. From this one can compare the brain activity between the two situations, conscious versus non-conscious, and infer the brain mechanisms related to consciousness. The goal of the NCC approach is to find the minimal neuronal mechanisms that are jointly sufficient for a conscious percept to be obtained. Implicit in this approach is an appreciation that experiments involving different stimuli might indicate different brain areas that are involved in conscious processing. While this potentially could lead to a complicated situation with conflicting results the belief is that ultimately the results will converge upon a basis for understanding how brain activity leads to consciousness.

A clear demonstration of the NCC research approach used single cell recordings in various brain areas of monkeys while they viewed different images presented to each eye (Leopold & Logothetis, 1996; Logothetis, 1998). This experimental technique

Binocular rivalry arises when different images are presented simultaneously to the two eyes and results in experiencing seeing one image and then the other alternately.

is known as binocular rivalry and previous research has shown that monkeys, like humans, when presented a different image in each eye only report that one is visible at a time (Figure 3.17). The visible image dominates the invisible one in consciousness, though both are clearly activating primary visual cortex. The results showed that in primary visual cortex only a small number of cells weakly modulated their activity based on what image was seen. However, further into visual processing, in the inferior temporal cortex, cells were found whose activity correlated with which image the monkey was currently aware. Subsequent research to these investigations explored how human primary visual cortex is related to consciousness. These studies have shown that activity in primary visual cortex is necessary for consciousness to occur, but it is not sufficient on its own (Haynes & Rees, 2005; Lee et al., 2007).

Figure 3.17 Binocular rivalry demonstrates neural correlates of consciousness. In this binocular rivalry experiment, the top row (a) illustrates the training session where a monkey is first taught to press one lever when they see the geometric figure and another lever when they see a face and to press no lever if they see both simultaneously. Next, in the actual experiment illustrated in the bottom row (b) lever presses and recordings of brain activity at different brain sites were recorded when the two pictures were simultaneously presented, one to the left and the other to the right eye. Brain activity in the inferior temporal cortex (IT) was related to the lever presses, suggesting it as a neural correlate of consciousness.

Source: Logothetis, N. K. (1998). Single units and conscious vision. *Philosophical Transactions of the Royal Society of London. Series B, Biological Sciences, 353*(1377), 1801–1818, by permission of The Royal Society.

Evaluation

We came at the problem of consciousness from two different directions. The first direction was to establish what theoretically we consider to be the functions of consciousness. This discussion drew heavily upon philosophical considerations that have long considered the problem of consciousness. A somewhat troubling aspect of these considerations is that there are arguments against a scientific description of consciousness ever being successful. Regardless of this, there are reasons to attempt to scientifically explore consciousness. The first of these is that consciousness is an important aspect of behaviour that is hard to ignore if we want a complete view of cognition. Moreover, aspects of consciousness overlap with attention, and disentangling this relationship is required to understand attention. The second reason is that for neuropsychological conditions such as split-brains, blindsight and vegetative state we need to understand consciousness to appreciate the mental life of an individual we wish to treat. A promising approach is the study of neural correlates of consciousness that are increasing our knowledge of what patterns of brain activity might be related to conscious experience.

Summary

Both attention and consciousness are areas of research that have seen an explosion of activity in the past decades, and it does not appear that this pace is decreasing. Their practical relevance is established both by the need to understand how we process information in increasingly complex, technology-driven environments as well as how to operationally define consciousness in fields like medicine and law. A key concept to both attention and consciousness is selection. For attention, selection expresses itself as how we effectively allocate resources to enhance processing of information that is currently critical for our behaviour. For consciousness, selection is involved with how some experiences arrive on our mental stage while others do not. Detailed mechanisms of how this occurs and whether deeper questions about consciousness are accessible to scientific enquiry remains an open question that is actively being addressed.

Attention research encompasses a large body of results, and it is useful to divide the topic into the domains of external attention (driven by events in the world) and internal attention (driven by events in the mind). This division of external and internal attention resonates with the neural mechanisms of orienting and executive function that have been proposed to encompass the human attention system. From an historical perspective, modern research on attention began with filter theory and resource theory. Filter theory showed how attention forms a bottleneck of processing sensory information and resource theory studied the size of this bottleneck. Various experimental paradigms have been developed to study the distribution of attention in space and time. Results show that observers can rapidly process either unique image features or some statistical properties of the entire image such as mean object size. However, when attention needs to be focused it is more time consuming and complex temporal and spatial relationships, such as the attentional blink, have been revealed. The critical importance of attention can be seen in cases like inattentional blindness where we can miss an obvious event when attention is diverted from what we are fixating our eyes upon.

There is not a consensus as to the function of consciousness, but it can generally be thought of as providing an executive summary of the current state of affairs. As such we would expect that our actions come about as a result of conscious decisions, but an interesting experiment by Libet (1985) showed that unconscious processes involved with initiating an action can appear to precede our conscious awareness of initiating the action. How attention relates to consciousness is still a topic of discussion and we presented a model which proposes that consciousness and attention make distinct contributions to our ability to report conscious experience. However, the experimental study of consciousness is still a young field and new paradigms for its study are being developed. One of these, the study of the neural correlates of consciousness, tries to relate what aspects of brain activity relate to conscious experience and holds promise for advancing our understanding of consciousness.

Review questions

1 What are the implications of attention being a limited resource?

2 What metaphors have been used to motivate different theories of attention?

3 Is attention directed towards objects or locations in space?

4 What are two paradigms used for studying attention?

5 What is the empirical evidence that our actions can be initiated by unconscious brain activity?

6 What are neural correlates of consciousness?

7 What is the relationship between attention and consciousness?

ANSWER TO FIGURE 3.13

The change is in the trees above the statue's back.

FURTHER READING

Blackmore, S. J. (2004). *Consciousness: An introduction.* Oxford, New York: Oxford University Press.

Chun, M. M., Golomb, J. D., & Turk-Browne, N. B. (2011). A taxonomy of external and internal attention. *Annual Review of Psychology, 62,* 73–101.

Pashler, H. E. (1998). *The psychology of attention.* Cambridge, MA: MIT Press.

Posner, M. I. (2012). *Cognitive neuroscience of attention* (2nd ed.). New York: Guilford Press.

Rose, D. (2006). *Consciousness: Philosophical, psychological and neural theories.* Oxford, New York: Oxford University Press.

Styles, E. A. (2006). *The psychology of attention* (2nd ed.). Hove: Psychology Press.

Wickens, C. D., & McCarley, J. S. (2008). *Applied attention theory.* Boca Raton: CRC Press.

CHAPTER 4:
SENSORY, SHORT-TERM AND WORKING MEMORY

Preview questions

1 How is short-term memory organized?
2 What are the functions of sensory memory?
3 How large is the capacity of iconic memory?
4 What is meant by 'working memory'?
5 What is happening when our mind wanders?

INTRODUCTION

Think of the last time you were standing on a street speaking with a friend. Try to remember the scene. What time of day was it? What was the weather like? What was your friend wearing? What did you speak about? Who and what else did you see? Now imagine you are told that a crime took place that day, on that street, at that time. You are asked to recall anything you saw or heard that might help with the investigation. You are asked whether you saw anything unusual. How confident would you be that you could recall a potentially significant detail?

Over the course of a single day, we encounter an environment containing a vast number of sights, sounds, smells, tastes and experiences. It is important that we remember the useful details without having to retain every piece of information that meets the senses. In this chapter and the next chapter, we look at how memory allows us to encode, store and retrieve information.

Encoding is the function by which information is coded in a form that allows it to be stored in memory.
Storage is the function by which information is retained in memory.
Retrieval is the function by which information is recollected as needed.

Short-term memory is the store where information is temporarily held in an accessible state.
Long-term memory is the system where information is held for longer periods, and can be accessed when needed.
Recollection is the act of recalling something to mind.
Working memory is the system in which information is held and manipulated in order to perform a task.

The traditional view of memory makes a distinction between short-term memory (STM) and long-term memory (LTM). LTM allows you to answer questions such as: what is the capital of Italy? What does the word 'esoteric' mean? What colour are bananas? What is your home address? Is a bat a bird? How did you celebrate your last birthday? It involves recollection of information. It also allows you to ride a bicycle, drive a car and sign your name. STM, on the other hand, allows a small amount of information to be held in mind, so that it is immediately accessible and can be used. For example, if you hear a string of digits and have to repeat them back aloud, you rely on STM to maintain that information in mind. The term working memory (WM) is used in a number of different ways, but generally refers to memory that allows us to manipulate active information, to perform mental arithmetic for example. As we will see, there is considerable overlap between the terms short-term memory and working memory, and there has been considerable debate about how they are best characterized.

The distinction between the hypothetical LTM and STM stores is long established. William James (1890), in *The Principles of Psychology*, described secondary memory as 'memory proper', while primary memory, according to James, was memory for the psychological present. This latter type of memory is the focus of the current chapter. But, according to the traditional view, before a piece of information enters short-term memory, its sensory aspects are stored temporarily in a very short-lived store called sensory memory. Sensory memory involves memory for stimuli as opposed to memory for ideas (Cowan, 2008), and there is good evidence in particular for a visual type of sensory memory, which allows a large amount of information from the eye to be held, but only for a very short period of time.

Sensory memory is a temporary sensory register that allows input from the sensory modalities to be prolonged.

SENSORY MEMORY

Have you ever been asked a question during a conversation when your mind has wandered? We can generally recover from this common experience, because we often find that, although we have not been paying attention, we can recall the last few words said and can answer the question without the other person noticing our lapse in attention. This ability reflects one aspect of sensory memory.

The sensory memory stores allow input from the sensory modalities (vision, hearing, etc.) to be prolonged briefly in order for us to process relevant aspects of that input. It is essentially a temporary sensory register, of large capacity, but which fades rapidly. Models of sensory memory assume a number of modality-specific sub-stores dealing with different types of input such as visual, auditory, haptic (that is, related to the sense of touch) and olfactory (smell) stimuli.

The idea of a brief sensory register dates back centuries. In 1740, a German physicist, Johann Andreas Segner, attached a glowing coal to a cartwheel and rotated the wheel at various speeds. He calculated that the glowing coal was perceived as a continuous circle if the wheel rotated once in about 100 milliseconds (Cowan, 2008). As early as 1899, Wundt had proposed a type of temporary visual store. Many subsequent experiments on visual memory produced anecdotal accounts suggesting that people saw far more items than they could actually report. It was Sperling's work, conducted for his doctoral thesis and published in 1960, that introduced a new methodology to this area of research, and proved what anecdotal accounts had long suggested: that people initially store a large amount of visual information but this information decays rapidly, such that only a portion of it remains available to consciousness. Sensory memory consists of a number of modality-specific stores: the term iconic memory refers to the brief storage of *visual* stimuli; the term echoic memory refers to *auditory* stimuli. Other stimulus types may also be stored, such as *haptic* sensory memory for touch-related stimuli. The sensory store prolongs sensory information so that we can attend to important parts of it; aspects that are not attended to fade away. There is considerable evidence for an iconic memory store.

ICONIC MEMORY

The iconic store (which was so named by Neisser, 1967) was investigated in a series of experiments by Sperling (1960). Sperling started out with a typical memory span experiment in which participants were presented with a visual array showing, for example, three rows of four letters (see Figure 4.1). This was presented for a brief duration of 50 milliseconds. In a 'whole report' condition, participants were asked to recall as many items as they could. They typically recalled about four or five items. However, verbal reports suggested that the participant had seen more than could be reported. Sperling introduced a 'partial report' condition, in which participants were asked to recall from only part of the array. Immediately *after* presentation of the array (that is, on stimulus offset), a tone was sounded to indicate which line the participants were to report from

> Iconic store is the sensory memory store for visual stimuli.

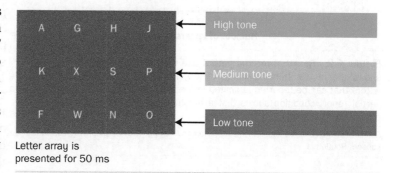

Letter array is presented for 50 ms

Figure 4.1   An array for testing visual sensory memory. This figure shows the procedure used by Sperling (1960). In the partial-report condition, after a visual array is presented, a tone indicates which line participants are to report from. In the full report condition, there is no auditory cue; participants report whatever they can.

(see Figure 4.1). A high tone signalled that they should report what they had seen within the top line of the array. A medium tone meant they should report from the middle line of the array. A low tone meant they should report from the bottom line of the array. Participants had no way of knowing in advance which line would be probed. Using the partial-report procedure, Sperling found that participants could typically recall about three items from each line; this meant that a much larger amount of information was available to participants than was suggested by the data from whole-report condition (see Figure 4.2).

Sperling varied the size of the stimulus array that participants saw, and found that as array size increased, so did the amount of information available in the partial report condition. These results confirmed that, for a short time at least, participants can potentially register a large amount of information. In a subsequent experiment, Sperling investigated the speed of decay from the store, by manipulating the length of the delay between the offset of the stimulus array and the presentation of the tone. The results showed that the partial report advantage disappears after a delay of about half a second. Sperling's data supported the idea that there was a brief memory of a visual image, which is potentially very large in capacity but which rapidly fades away: this is iconic memory.

Iconic memory allows visual input to be prolonged, which means that our visual experience is not an exact reflection of reality. This allows us to see a series of still images as moving picture sequences in motion pictures and in animation (see Box 4.1). Sperling's

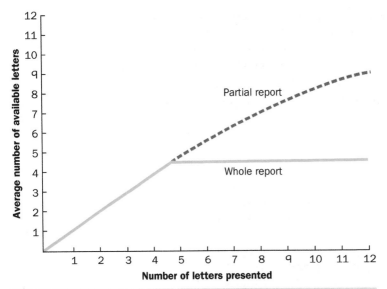

Figure 4.2   Results from the partial and whole report testing. This figure shows the results from Sperling's (1960) first experiment. The number of letters that can be reported is limited in the whole report condition, while the partial report condition shows that a much larger amount of information is potentially available.

Source: Loftus, G. R. & Loftus E. F. (1976). *Human Memory: The Processing of Information.* London: Routledge.

findings were confirmed by a number of subsequent studies; for example, Averbach and Coriell (1961) reported similar data using a version of the task that used a visual cue instead of an auditory tone.

Evaluation

Some researchers questioned whether Sperling's data might reflect use of a guessing strategy in the partial report condition (e.g. Holding, 1970). Converging evidence soon emerged that supported Sperling's notion of a temporary visual register. Haber and Standing (1969) used a task in which participants saw a series of successive circles which were presented for 10 milliseconds each and which were separated by brief intervals. They varied the duration of the interval and asked participants to report if the preceding circle had disappeared before the subsequent one was presented. They found that at intervals of less than a quarter of a second, participants reported no gap between presentation of the circles, whereas at longer intervals participants saw the first circle disappear before the second one appeared. These findings support Sperling's account and lend further support to the idea of stimulus persistence lasting about half a second.

Box 4.1 Practical Application: Making moving pictures

When we watch a movie, we perceive a continuous and moving picture. But what reaches the eye is a set of static images, flashes of light that are briefly disrupted by segments of dark screen. Visual sensory memory makes it possible to perceive a 'motion picture' from this series of stills (Baddeley, 1999).

Movies are made in such a way that our natural perceptual dispositions are exploited for maximum effect (Cutting, 2005). A movie presents images at a rate of 24 frames per second, but in order to ensure that we perceive a flicker-free, smooth moving picture each frame is presented two or three times. The human visual system is sensitive enough to detect flicker at 24 frames per second (24 Hz) but by presenting the image twice and increasing the rate to 48 frames per second (48 Hz), the flicker will not be detected (Galifret, 2006). Other animals have greater sensitivity to flicker. Birds of prey fly at great speeds to intercept their quarry and can redirect their trajectory at speed in order to do so. A bird of prey has sensitivity to flicker detection in excess of 100 Hz (Winkler, 2005). If a bird of prey could watch a modern-day motion picture, its increased sensitivity would lead it to see jerky rather than smooth moving pictures, similar to our experience of seeing older movies which had fewer frames per second. Bees' sensitivity may be as high as 300 Hz (Lea & Dittrich, 2000). Such sensitivity produces greater control over responses to visual stimuli at speed. Humans only achieve such speeds when driving a car, an activity for which the evolution of the visual system has left us under-prepared (Winkler, 2005).

When it comes to understanding how we perceive motion pictures, there are two independent issues to consider. First, how do we come to perceive a continuous picture rather than a sequence of flashes of light with intermittent darkness? Second, how do we see a scene in motion rather than a series of still frames or a sequence of jerky movements? These separate issues, the perception of constant illumination and the perception of smooth movement, reflect two separate functions of the visual system (Galifret, 2006). The first of these issues is accounted for by the tendency of sensory visual memory to prolong a brief exposure to light.

The prolonging of visual sensory input is also evident in the way people perceive lightning. A lightning bolt is perceived as continuous although it consists of a number of separate strokes which can be separated by as much as 40–50 milliseconds (Uman, 1986). High-speed video recording played back frame by frame can capture the components of a lightning strike; the human eye does not. We perceive the lightning bolt as lasting for several seconds, when it in fact is far shorter. (We also tend to perceive lightning as coming from sky to ground, when in fact the majority of the bolt's luminosity comes from the 'return stroke' travelling from the ground back to a cloud; Rakov & Uman, 2003). Similarly, we are unaware of the flicker of florescent lights (which flicker at a rate of about 100Hz) and of computer monitors with cathode ray tubes, which refresh at a rate of between 60 and 120 times per second in order to avoid flicker.

Flicker perception in humans, while less sensitive than that of some animals, is among the faster processes conducted by the visual system. Holcombe (2009) suggests that visual processes can be categorized into two groups: a fast group involving processes relating to detection of motion, depth and edges and a slower group with less sensitive temporal limits involved in higher-level perception, including high-level motion processing, word recognition and the integration of colour and motion information (see Figure 4.3).

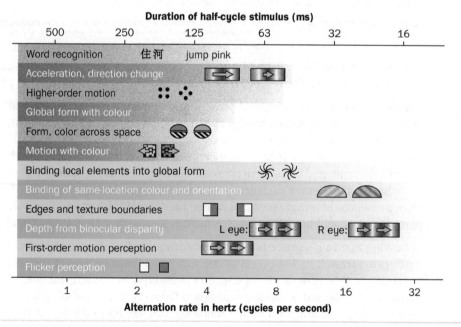

Figure 4.3 **The maximum rate at which something can be perceived.** The maximum rate at which something can be perceived differs, with processes relating to detection of motion, depth and edges showing more sensitive temporal limits than processes involved in higher level vision, including high-level motion processing, word recognition and the integration of colour and motion information.

Source: Reprinted from Holcombe, A.O. (2009). Seeing slow and seeing fast: Two limits on perception. *Trends in Cognitive Sciences*, *13*(5), 216–221, with permission from Elsevier.

ECHOIC MEMORY

Echoic memory is the auditory equivalent of iconic memory; it is sensory memory for heard information. Sperling's partial-report technique was applied

Echoic store is sensory memory specific to auditory stimuli.

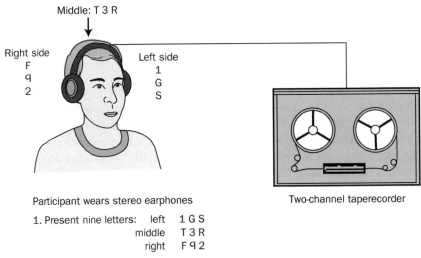

1. Present nine letters: left   1 G S
                          middle   T 3 R
                           right   F 9 2

2. Following last letters variable delay interval, 0–4000 milliseconds.

3. Signal bar presented on a screen. Bar is left of, in front of, or to right of participant.

4. Participant attempts to report channel signaled by bar.

Figure 4.4   The procedure used by Darwin et al. (1972). The figure shows the procedure used by Darwin et al. (1972). The participant hears letters and numbers presented simultaneously to one or other head-phone, or to both. A visual cue signals which location to report from.

Source: Adapted from Loftus, G. R. & Loftus E. F. (1976). *Human memory: The processing of information.* London: Routledge.

to auditory stimuli initially by Moray et al. (1965), and their procedure was extended by Darwin et al. (1972). Darwin et al.'s experimental set-up is illustrated in Figure 4.4.

The Darwin et al. study involved presenting auditory stimuli independently to each ear, or to both ears, using stereo headphones, such that the sounds would be heard from three spatial positions: from the left, right or from the 'middle' (i.e. in stereo). Nine letters and nine digits were used to form sequences; three items were presented to the left channel, three to the right, and three were presented simultaneously in stereo. They were presented such that the first item of each group was heard simultaneously; similarly, the second items were presented simultaneously, and then the third. In the example shown in Figure 4.4, participants would hear 1, T and F, simultaneously, then G, 3, 9 and finally S, R, 2.

Following Sperling's procedure, the auditory stimuli were presented and, after a delay that varied from 0 to 4 seconds, a cue indicated from which set the participants were to report. In this case, a visual cue was presented to the left, middle, or right and the participants reported what they had heard from the corresponding location. Consistent with Sperling's findings on iconic memory, Darwin and colleagues found that performance in a partial-report condition suggested a large initial memory of auditory information, which decayed rapidly. At zero delay participants could report about five of the nine items. After a delay of 4 seconds, performance had dropped to 4.25 items on average, the same number as would be expected in a whole-report condition. This suggested that there was a sensory store for auditory information that was similar in some ways to iconic memory; this became know as the echoic store (another term coined by Neisser, 1967). The echoic store provides an acoustic register, allowing auditorily presented information to be prolonged so that some aspects of the input can be retained for processing.

Shadowing is a technique that involves repeating back an auditorily presented message.

The auditory partial-report data are broadly consistent with findings using the shadowing technique, in which participants must 'shadow' or repeat back a message presented to one ear or the other. For example, Glucksberg and Cowan (1970) had participants shadow a passage of prose that was presented in one ear while another prose passage was presented to the other, 'unattended' ear. Participants were to ignore the second passage, but were warned that digits would occur in that text from time to time, and that when a light flashed, they were to report the last digit heard in the unattended message. The duration between the presentation of the digit and the light cue was manipulated. Performance on the task deteriorated at about 4 seconds. Similarly, Treisman (1964) found that if participants shadowed a message while a second unattended message was presented, they only recognized that the two messages were the same if they occurred within about 2 seconds of each other.

Evaluation

From Darwin et al.'s data, the span of echoic memory seemed to be less than that of the iconic store and its duration longer, but this may reflect a limitation of the procedure used. While Sperling could present the visual stimuli all at once without affecting the spatial relationships between the stimuli, in an auditory version of the task, all the sounds could not be presented simultaneously; three sets of temporally distinct sounds were presented. This produces some clear differences between their two procedures and may have led to an over-estimation of the duration of storage in the echoic register. Efron (1970a, 1970b, 1970c) had participants adjust the onset of a light to coincide with the offset of an auditory tone. He varied the duration of the tone and found that for very short tones (e.g. 60 milliseconds), participants adjusted the light to come on 150 milliseconds after the onset of the tone. In other words, short tones were prolonged in echoic memory so that they were perceived by participants as lasting longer than they actually were. This supports the idea of an auditory store that prolongs auditory stimuli, and provides an estimation of echoic persistence that is more accurate and more consistent with other estimates (e.g. Massaro, 1975, estimated 250 milliseconds).

What can be done with the information stored in sensory memory? In another of Sperling's experiments, he used an array that contained both letters and digits and introduced a second partial report condition, in addition to the whole and partial report conditions described above. In the new partial report condition, participants were instructed to report only the letters or only the digits within the array; a tone cued which type they were to report (letters or digits). In this partial report condition, no advantage over the whole report condition was found. Participants could report only about 4–5 items. This gives us a clue as to nature of the representation of the stimuli in the iconic store; it appears that participants have access to a visual stimulus but cannot yet categorize it or access its meaning. As Cowan (2008, p. 25) put it 'we can think of sensory memory as the memory for the knowledge-free, sensation-based characteristics of stimuli that resemble what a newborn would perceive'. Sperling's letter/digit experiment demonstrated that information held in the sensory register is not yet in a form that the cognitive system can effectively utilize and manipulate. For this, further processing and transfer to short-term memory is needed.

Sensory memory is fragile and can easily be disrupted before stimuli can be transferred into short-term memory (STM). Backward masking procedures involve the presentation of a 'masking' stimulus immediately after the target stimulus; for example, a briefly presented visual stimulus (e.g. a letter) might be followed by a row of hash marks (####). The participant is subsequently required to identify the letter in a recognition test. Recognition increases as the duration between the presentation of the target stimulus and the masking stimulus (the stimulus onset asynchrony or SOA) increases, to about 250 milliseconds. Data from backward masking also support a shorter

Masking refers to reduced perception of a visual stimulus when another stimulus is presented in spatial or temporal proximity to it.

Stimulus onset asynchrony refers to the time between the onset of a stimulus and the presentation of a mask.

duration to echoic memory than the partial-report data outlined above (see Cowan, 2008, for an overview).

Cowan (e.g. 1984, 1988) suggests that there are two stages to sensory memory in each of the modalities (see also Massaro, 1976). The first phase is a short, pre-perceptual phase lasting about 250 milliseconds while the second is longer, lasting several seconds, and involving more substantial processing and access to memory. The modality-specific differences in the partial-report data outlined above came about because Sperling's visual array data involve the first of these sensory phases while Darwin's auditory data involve the second (see Cowan, 2008).

HAPTIC MEMORY

Haptic memory is the sensory memory for stimuli sensed through touch.

It is likely that there are also sensory memory stores serving other modalities. For example, support for a haptic sensory store was provided in a study by Bliss et al. (1966) who used a tactile version of Sperling's partial-report procedure. Their participants were trained to associate a letter of the alphabet with three sections on each of four fingers of one hand. Participants then placed their hand in a device that administered a puff of air to some of these regions, and had to report which regions had been stimulated by giving the associated letter. In the partial-report condition, a visual stimulus cued whether participants were to report stimulation presented to the upper, middle or lower sections of the fingers. A small advantage for the partial-report condition was found, as long as the visual cue appeared within 800 milliseconds of termination of the tactile stimulation. These data suggest a temporary register for tactile input and are consistent with more recent data demonstrating change blindness (see Chapter 3) in the tactile modality (e.g. Gallace et al., 2007).

While sensory memory provides a temporary register that is rich in sensory detail, such memory is short-lived and cannot be manipulated. In order for effective processing to occur, information must be held in short-term memory. It is to this aspect of memory that we now turn.

SHORT-TERM MEMORY

Short-term memory (STM) holds information in consciousness; it provides temporary storage of active information. STM has a limited capacity, and information can be lost from it relatively easily. If you have ever looked up a telephone number only to forget it before you have had a chance to dial it on your phone, you will be aware of the capacity limitations affecting STM. STM allows us to complete the many daily tasks that involve active use of information, from understanding a conversation or a passage of text, to calculating a tip in a restaurant, to imagining an alternate route home when you find your usual route blocked. This last example illustrates that STM is not limited to verbal information; similarly, if you are asked how many windows there are on the front of your house, the visual image you create to address this question is also inspected in STM. Much of the information that we process in STM is not retained, and is quickly purged from STM, allowing our attention to move on to the next task. This is important for the efficiency of STM. As Bjork (1972) noted: 'We overhear conversations, we see things in newspapers and store windows, we add up numbers, we dial telephone numbers, we pay attention to advertisements, and so on – nearly all of which we have no use for beyond the point at which we attend to them' (p. 218).

William James's (1890) description of short-term memory as primary memory equated it with the psychological present, the information that is available in consciousness. Hebb (1949) also made the distinction between STM and long-term memory (LTM), and

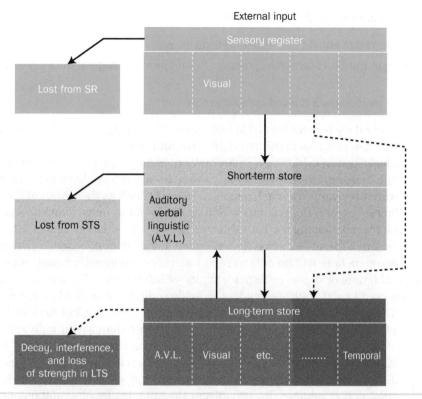

Figure 4.5 Atkinson and Shiffrin's model of memory. Atkinson and Shiffrin's model of memory treats memory in terms of a series of stages. A stimulus is processed initially in sensory memory before entering short-term memory (or in their terms the short-term store) and eventually long-term memory.

Source: Reprinted from Atkinson, R. C., & Shiffrin, R. M. (1968). Human memory: A proposed system and its control processes. In K. W. Spence (ed.), *The Psychology of Learning and Motivation: Advances in Research and Theory*, 2, pp. 89–195. New York: Academic Press, with permission from Elsevier.

a number of models in the 1950s and 1960s supported the distinction between stores of different types (e.g. Broadbent, 1958; Neisser, 1967; Waugh & Norman, 1965). Atkinson and Shiffrin (1968) introduced a model of memory that became known as the modal model ('modal' because it was similar to various other models at the time; see Norman, 1970; Waugh & Norman, 1965). It proposed three memory stores (see Figure 4.5), and made the distinction between a long-term store (similar to LTM) and a short-term store (similar to STM). The model was heavily influenced by the growing use of the computer metaphor in cognitive psychology and made a distinction between permanent, structural aspects of memory and flexible control processes, which could vary depending on task requirements.

According to the Atkinson-Shiffrin model, information is first registered in the sensory store, and salient information is transferred to STM. A number of control processes are supported by STM and the type of processing carried out will determine whether information will be stored in LTM. Rehearsal involves recycling the information (such as repeating it to yourself to keep the information refreshed in memory; maintenance rehearsal), encoding involves the extraction of some information in order to transfer to LTM (elaborative rehearsal), and retrieval strategies allow access to LTM. Information is lost from STM through decay, a time-based limitation, and displacement, a capacity-based limitation by which incoming information gains precedence over previously active information (Atkinson & Shiffrin, 1968).

Rehearsal refers to a set of processes by which we can act on currently active information.
Maintenance rehearsal retains information in STM.
Elaborative rehearsal organizes the information so that it can be integrated into LTM.
Decay is a process by which information is lost from STM over time.
Displacement is a process by which information coming into STM causes information already held there to be lost.

The basic assumptions of the modal model were that:

* there are separate short-term and long-term stores;
* processing in the short-term store determines memory storage in the long-term store; and
* short-term memory is a limited capacity store.

There was general agreement that STM had a limited capacity. Attempts to measure its capacity made use of tasks involving digit span and the recency effect in free recall

> Digit span refers to the number of digits that can be held is memory and is used as a measure of STM.

(described below). Digit span tasks present participants with digit strings of increasing lengths; participants have to repeat them back in the order they were presented. The task becomes more difficult as the length of the strings increases, and the point at which errors begin to occur indicates the limits of the participant's STM. Miller (1956) is often cited as quantifying the functional limit of STM as 7±2 items (the so-called 'magical number seven'), suggesting that, on average, people will be able to report about seven items, whether those items are individual letters or digits, or larger 'chunks' of information. For example, the digit strings on a credit card could be read as individual digits or as chunks: for example, 1010 2543 6754 2194. Taken as individual digits there are 16 digits, but read as four sets of four numbers there are four 'chunks'. Therefore more than seven individual digits

> Chunking refers to a strategy to improve memory by grouping smaller units together into a larger unit or 'chunk'.

might be recalled in this case. Chunking increases the capacity of STM; as Miller (1956, p. 95) notes: 'the span of immediate memory imposes severe limitations on the amount of information that we are able to receive, process, and remember. By organizing the stimulus input simultaneously into several dimensions and successively into a sequence of chunks, we manage to break (or at least stretch) this informational bottleneck.' Information from LTM can be used to facilitate chunking (see Chapter 1 for some examples used by world memory champions); the letter sequence CIAFBIDEADMV is more readily recalled if we organize the sequence as a series of acronyms referring to United States agencies: CIA (Central Intelligence Agency), FBI (Federal Bureau of Investigation), DEA (Drug Enforcement Administration), DMV (Department of Motor Vehicles). The larger the chunks, the more memory is required, however, and fewer will be recalled.

Miller's estimation of seven items, give or take two, was approximate (given the tone of his article it may have been meant as a rhetorical device), with various sources proposing a limit that is closer to four (e.g. Broadbent, 1975; Henderson, 1972; Mandler, 1967; see Cowan, 2000, for a review). Cowan et al. (2007) note that Sperling's research, described above, showed that, of a large amount of information in sensory memory, only a small number of items make it through to STM; when participants are shown 12 characters at once, they can typically only report around four items. A number of other sources suggest that it is the capacity of STM, rather than the decay rate of sensory memory, that is reflected in these four items (Cowan, 2010).

> Recency effect is the tendency, given a list of items to remember, to recall those from the end of the list more readily than items from the middle.
> Serial position curve is used to plot recall of a word list such that performance is examined as a function of a word's position in a list.

The recency effect in free recall refers to the fact that people recall more items from the end of a presented list than from the middle of the list. This pattern was first reported in the 1920s (Welch & Burnett, 1924), but it was only in the 1960s that it was interpreted in light of differences between STM and LTM. In the task graphed in Figure 4.6, participants hear a list of 12 unrelated words. They are then required to report the words in any order. Performance of participants is then graphed as shown in Figure 4.6 to give the serial position curve, with the word's position in the list graphed along the x-axis, and recall shown on the y-axis. The typical serial position curve shows an advantage for more recently presented items (the recency effect). Performance is also relatively good for items at the start of the list (the primacy effect). Compared to words at the end and at the start of the list, recall is relatively poor for items that were presented in the middle of the list.

The recency effect reflects items held in STM. The primacy effect reflects items that have already been transferred to LTM; as more items are added to the list, there is less time to transfer them to LTM, and so some items are not successfully transferred to LTM, and are displaced from STM. If the recency effect reflects items stored in STM, then it should be relatively straightforward to disrupt it without affecting the primacy effect, which reflects another aspect of memory (LTM). Studies have attempted to support this distinction between STM and LTM by examining the effects of distraction on the primacy and recency effects. For example, participants might be required to count backwards in threes immediately after presentation of the list: this should interfere with the information that was being held in STM by preventing the participant from rehearsing it. But the counting task should not affect recall of the items that have already been successfully transferred to LTM. In other words, the counting task should affect the recency effect but not the primacy effect. This is precisely what is found in such studies.

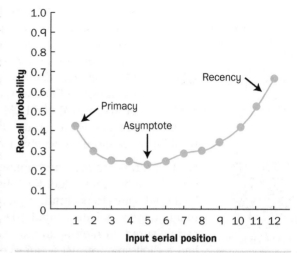

Figure 4.6 **The serial position curve.** The serial position curve shows the probability of free recall of a word as a function of the position in which it was presented in a word list. Items at the end of the list show increased recall, a pattern called the recency effect. Items at the start of the list also show better recall than those in the middle (named the asymptote), a pattern referred to as the primacy effect.

Source: Adapted from Parkin, A. (2000). *Essentials of cognitive psychology*. Psychology Press.

Primacy effect is enhanced recall of items at the start of a list compared to those in the middle.

The capacity of STM should therefore be reflected in the number of items in the recency effect, but this has proved rather difficult to estimate, as it varies depending on the nature of the information to be recalled. Glanzer and Razel (1974) conducted a series of free recall experiments and initially estimated the size of the recency effect as being 2.2 words. When they used proverbs in the recall task, they found recall of 2.2 proverbs, but for unfamiliar sentences performance dropped to 1.5 sentences. Cowan (2000), assessing the available evidence, identifies a capacity limit of on average four chunks, and outlines the task conditions under which this estimate might be predicted to differ.

The negative recency effect provides further support for separate short-term and long-term stores. Craik (1970) had participants immediately recall 19 lists of 15 words. He later had participants report any words they could remember from any of the lists in a final free recall task. If the recency effect reflects items in STM, we would expect to see a recency effect in the immediate recall task but no such effect in the final free recall task, as this task required reporting from LTM. Craik's data showed that not only was this the case, but in fact performance for list-end items was poorer than mid-list items in the final free recall task, an effect known as the negative recency effect. This pattern supports the idea of separate short-term and long-term memory stores. In the immediate recall task, participants held the list-end items in STM and did not transfer them to LTM. This meant those items were at a disadvantage in the final recall task.

Negative recency effect reflects poorer memory for list-end items compared to items from earlier input positions, in multi-list recall tasks.

If recency reflects storage in STM, we might expect to find it spared in patients who have had brain damage affecting LTM, but leaving STM intact. People with amnesic

Double dissociation of function refers to contrasting patterns of deficit in two patients or patient groups which provides evidence for functionally independent systems.

syndrome (see Chapter 5; Memory and amnesia) following brain injury show this pattern of memory impairment – they have relatively spared STM but have deficient LTM (see Chapter 5). Baddeley and Warrington (1970, 1973) found that amnesic patients had intact recall for items presented at the end of the list (a normal recency effect) while memory was impaired for other list items, reflecting the impairment of LTM. This dissociation of function between STM and LTM (that is intact STM but impaired LTM) might also be taken as evidence for separate stores; however a double dissociation of function would provide more persuasive evidence.

Scan to watch a fun clip illustrating short term memory impairment

While the reverse pattern to amnesia (i.e. impaired STM but intact LTM) is rare, such cases have been reported. KF (Shallice & Warrington, 1970) sustained severe damage to the left parieto-occipital region of his brain in a motorcycle accident. In addition to language problems (impaired speech, reading and spelling), KF had impaired STM, as measured by digit span and recency. However, KF had relatively intact LTM. He had a digit span of just 2 (an average of 1.8 on letters, 2.3 on words and digits) and yet performed normally on a paired-associate task (requiring LTM). Warrington and Shallice (1972) found that KF's STM deficit was more pronounced in auditory memory than in visual memory, which explains how he could still form long-term memories. Shallice and Warrington (1974) found that KF's problems were further limited to verbal stimuli such as words and digits, while his immediate recall of other sounds (e.g. cats meowing, a ringing telephone) was unimpaired. Since KF, a number of similar cases have been reported involving impaired STM as measured by span-type tasks and intact LTM function (e.g. Saffran & Marin, 1975; Shallice & Butterworth, 1977; Warrington et al., 1972).

Evaluation

This double dissociation of function – the fact that some patients have intact LTM but impaired STM while others have intact STM but impaired LTM – supports the notion of separate STM and LTM stores. However, the Atkinson and Shiffrin model suggests that information passes through a unitary STM in order to enter LTM. The characterization of STM as a unitary store does not explain cases of patients such as KF, who have impaired STM function, but whose LTM is relatively unimpaired. It would seem that STM is not a single, unitary store. The early models focused on the verbal aspects of STM; but are there other kinds of STM? Furthermore, short-term memory allows us to hold information in an accessible state so that we can act on it; but there are also a range of processes that we can apply to allow us to manipulate and use the information so as to set and achieve goals. What is the relationship between these processes and STM?

Miller et al. (1960) introduced the term 'working memory' to refer to memory that allows us to make plans and to keep track of goals. This concept of working memory is not entirely distinct from short-term memory, and includes storage and processing components. Miller et al. described working memory only very briefly and they did not provide any detail on its components. They wrote that when a plan is being executed it has 'special access to consciousness and special ways of being remembered. . . . We should like to speak of the memory we use for the execution of our plans as a kind of quick-access, "working memory"' (p. 65). This leaves the term 'working memory' open to interpretation so that it has come to mean different things to different theorists. The most influential account of working memory was developed and empirically tested by Baddeley and Hitch (1974). Working memory has become one of the most important and debated concepts in cognitive psychology, and it is to this concept that we now turn.

WORKING MEMORY

If LTM is dependent on STM processes, then findings from patients such as KF cannot be explained if we retain the assumption that STM is a unitary store. KF had severely deficient STM, as measured by digit span and the recency effect, and yet he showed intact long-term memory, and performed normally on tasks requiring information to be transferred to LTM, such as the paired-associate task. This finding suggests that different sub-systems must underlie tasks such as digit span and word list learning. For KF and similar patients then, the sub-system of STM underlying digit span is impaired, but some components of STM remain intact and allow relatively intact performance on tests of LTM. In other words, KF must have some intact working memory (WM) in order to demonstrate the pattern of performance he does on memory tasks.

Working memory has been described as the 'workbench' of human cognition (Klatzky, 1980), or as 'the collection of mental processes that permit information to be held temporarily in an accessible state, in the service of some mental task' (Cowan, 1998, p. 77). The term working memory means different things to different people, with researchers using the term in at least three ways (see Beaman, 2010; Cowan, 1998). Researchers may view working memory as:

- the focus of attention, consistent with James's (1890) view of primary memory (e.g. Engle, 2002);

- the information that is temporarily activated in the system, including information about our current goals and plans, consistent with Miller et al.'s original use of the term working memory;

- a sensory-specific multi-component storage system for short-term storage and processing of information (e.g. Baddeley & Hitch, 1974).

Accounts of working memory also vary in how they consider the relationship between working memory and long-term memory. Cowan's embedded processes model (e.g. 1995, 1999) views WM as consisting of a capacity-limited focus of attention and a temporarily activated subset of long-term memory (see Figure 4.7). This account places emphasis on the interaction of attention and memory and considers WM in the context of LTM. Thus, by this account, three components contribute to WM: temporarily activated information that is not yet accessible to conscious awareness; memory within the focus of attention; and information stored in LTM, which is currently inactive but could be retrieved/activated if relevant to the task (Cowan, 1999a, b; see also Oberauer's three-embedded-components model, 2002). The model proposes that these key components contribute to WM as embedded processes, with the current focus of attention being a subset of active memory and active memory presented as a subset of LTM (see Figure 4.7). By this account, information is lost from WM through processes of both decay and displacement. The focus of attention is capacity limited and information can be easily

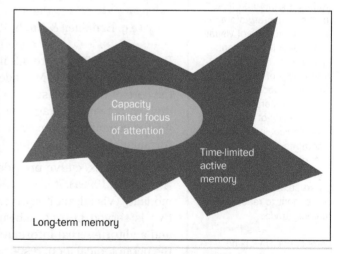

Figure 4.7 Cowan's embedded processes model. The embedded processes model presents WM as three components: temporarily activated information that is not yet accessible to conscious awareness; memory within the focus of attention; and information stored in LTM, which is currently inactive but could be retrieved/activated if relevant to the task.

Source: Reprinted from Cowan, N. (1998). Visual and auditory working memory capacity. *Trends in Cognitive Sciences, 2,* 77–78, with permission from Elsevier.

displaced from it, while the activated memory is time-limited, and information can decay if not rehearsed. In contrast to the multiple component model discussed below, in Cowan's model, the nature of the representation may vary in WM but it does so within a single structure that has fixed properties (see also Engle & Oransky, 1999), thus, 'the distinctness and non-interchangeability of phonetic and spatial information occurs because different types of features are being activated, not because of distinctly different storage modules' (Cowan, 1995a, p. 36).

Scan to watch a video on how WM makes sense of the world

On the other hand, multiple component models of WM propose that WM can be fractionated into component parts. This approach sees the principal function of WM as the coordination of resources and focuses on identifying and examining the nature of the structures that carry out this function (Baddeley, 1986; 1992a, b). WM consists of both storage and processing components (Baddeley, 1986) and might be defined as 'the simultaneous processing and storage of information' (Salthouse, 1990, p. 104). Towse and Hitch (2007, p. 110) see WM as a 'multicomponent, limited-capacity system responsible for retaining as well as transforming fragile representations'. For Baddeley (1992b), the term working memory 'refers to a brain system that provides temporary storage and manipulation of the information necessary for such complex tasks as language comprehension, learning and reasoning' (p. 556). Baddeley and Hitch's (1974) working memory model (and its subsequent versions) has been the most influential of such accounts, and it is to this model that we now turn.

Central executive is the component of working memory proposed to control and coordinate the activity of the other components including the phonological loop and the visuo-spatial sketchpad.
Visuo-spatial sketchpad is the component of working memory proposed for the temporary storage and manipulation of visual and spatial information.
Phonological loop is the component of working memory proposed for temporary storage and manipulation of sound or phonological information. It comprises a short-term phonological store for auditory memory traces and an articulatory rehearsal component to reactivate memory traces.
Episodic buffer is the component of working memory proposed for the temporary storage of information integrated from the phonological loop, the visuo-spatial sketchpad and long-term memory into single structures or episodes.

BADDELEY'S WORKING MEMORY MODEL

According to Baddeley (1986), 'the essence of the concept of working memory lies in its implication that memory processes play an important role in non-memory tasks' (p. 246). WM is not just a store for maintaining information in consciousness – it plays an integral role in ongoing or 'online' cognitive processing. Baddeley and colleagues' multi-component working memory model proposed three main components to working memory: the central executive, the visuo-spatial sketchpad and the phonological loop (e.g. Baddeley & Hitch, 1974; Baddeley, 1986). A further component, the episodic buffer, was added in more recent versions of the model (see Baddeley, 2000). Figure 4.8 illustrates the relationships between the main components of this WM model. Baddeley and Hitch (1974, p. 76) described the core of the WM system as 'a limited capacity "work space" which can be divided between storage and control processing demands'. This idea of a limited capacity system remains a basic assumption of the approach in later formulations (e.g. Baddeley, 1986).

The central executive provides the attentional control of working memory (Baddeley, 1996a). It is modality-free, in that it can deal with input from any modality (visual, auditory, etc.), and is similar to attention. The central executive is served by two sub-systems that are specialized for visual-spatial and auditory-verbal information; these are the visuo-spatial sketchpad and the phonological loop, respectively. These components hold and manipulate modality-specific information, the visuo-spatial sketchpad dealing with visual information and the phonological loop dealing with speech-based information. The case of KF, encountered above, suggests damage to the verbal aspect of working memory, while the other components remain unaffected by the brain injury, thus allowing access to long-term memory and effective long-term memory functioning.

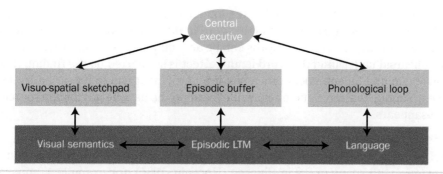

Figure 4.8   The working memory model showing the interaction with long-term memory structures and the episodic buffer. The three main components of working memory, the central executive, phonological loop and visuo-spatial sketchpad interact with structures in long-term memory.

Source: Adapted from Baddeley, A.D. (2000). The episodic buffer: A new component of working memory? *Trends in Cognitive Sciences*, 4, 417–423.

The phonological loop

The component of WM that has received the most scrutiny is the phonological loop. The phonological loop is specialized for speech-based information. This component of WM is closest to earlier notions of a short-term memory store (e.g. Atkinson and Shiffrin, 1968), and is implicated in tasks involving verbal materials, such as digit span and serial position tasks (see Figure 4.6). While Baddeley and Hitch (1974) called this component the 'articulatory loop', the term 'phonological loop' replaced it, to reflect the more central processing involved in sub-vocal articulation; the 'inner voice' does not rely on the speech musculature, and is retained in patients who have brain damage affecting overt articulation (conditions such as anarthria for example; see Baddeley & Wilson, 1985). Baddeley et al. (1975) proposed that the articulatory loop has a limited capacity restricted by temporal duration, and that it holds as many verbal items (words, letters etc.) as a person can say in about 2 seconds.

> Anarthria is a disorder affecting the motor function underlying speech.

The WM model proposes that the phonological loop has two sub-components: a phonological store, which holds speech-based information for a period of about 2 to 3 seconds (unless the information is rehearsed) and an articulatory control process, which allows the maintenance of information in the store and converts visual information (such as a written word) to a speech-based form. The articulatory control process uses sub-vocal rehearsal to fulfil these functions, a process that can be likened to 'inner speech' (Baddeley, 1986, 1992). Auditory presentation of phonological (speech-based) information gains direct access to the loop, while visually presented information gains access via sub-vocal articulation by the articulatory control process. Evidence for the phonological loop comes from a number of sources, which we will now examine.

> Inner speech refers to the subjective experience of hearing our thoughts, as if 'spoken' by an inner voice, when reading silently for example.

1. The word length effect

If participants can remember as many words as they can say in 2 seconds, then one might reason that the shorter the words are, the more of them that will be remembered. The word length effect refers to the advantage found for recall of lists of short words (e.g. car, lake, pen, tram, chair) compared to longer words (e.g. television, university, candlestick, hippopotamus, refrigerator). The duration it takes to articulate the word is the crucial factor, not the number of syllables. The words 'ticket' and 'harpoon' both contain two syllables, but 'harpoon' takes longer to say than 'ticket'. The longer the word, the more time it takes to refresh the word in the phonological store by sub-vocal articulation, therefore fewer long words can be accommodated in the store. This difference in rehearsal underlying the word length effect is supported by the finding that the effect is eliminated by sub-vocal rehearsal; if a participant has to repeat an irrelevant string (e.g. saying 'the' over and over) while learning the list, the advantage for shorter words disappears.

We might therefore predict cross-linguistic differences in memory span that reflect differences in word length in various languages. This has been demonstrated in a number of languages, with spans of 9.9 in Chinese (Hoosain, 1984), for example, compared to 5.7 in Arabic (Naveh-Benjamin & Ayres, 1986). The relatively larger digit span of Chinese speakers has been argued to reflect faster articulation rates for Chinese digits, a finding demonstrated both with Mandarin (Hoosain, 1984; Hoosain & Salili, 1988) and Cantonese (Stigler et al., 1986). Chen et al. (2009) found that the mean digit span of a sample of English speakers was equivalent to the lowest individual score of their Mandarin-speaking sample. Ellis and Hennelly (1980) found that digit span in Welsh was smaller than in English, reflecting longer articulation times for Welsh words and the smaller number of Welsh words that could be articulated in 2 seconds. Such data provide further evidence for a speech-based store with temporal limits. Again, it is the spoken duration rather than number of phonemes or syllables that is important; Da Costa Pinto (1991) reported faster articulation and higher digit span by Portuguese speakers despite more syllables and phonemes in the Portuguese digit words. This effect was explained by Da Costa Pinto in terms of a native language advantage, but this account has been challenged by data from Chincotta & Hoosain (1995); see also Chincotta & Underwood (1996). The cross-linguistic data concur with developmental data showing that span increases through childhood (from about the age of four years) as speech rate increases (e.g. Hulme et al., 1984).

2. The effects of articulatory suppression

As observed above, the ability to rehearse sub-vocally can be disrupted if we require a participant to rehearse a string that is irrelevant to the current task. For example, the person might be required to repeat the word 'the', or to count to three over and again, a process referred to as articulatory suppression (Murray, 1965). Articulatory suppression reduces memory span (Peterson & Johnson, 1971), and eliminates the word length effect. It also disrupts transfer of visually presented material to the phonological store, leading to poorer memory (Baddeley et al., 1984). The repetition of an irrelevant word or string uses the capacity of the articulatory control process, and prevents information in the phonological store from being refreshed, leading to a detriment in performance.

3. The irrelevant speech effect

Recall of visually presented verbal material is poorer when irrelevant speech is presented during learning. The effect is limited to speech sounds (non-speech sounds do not elicit the effect) and one does not need to understand what is being said in order for the speech to disrupt processing – even hearing irrelevant speech in an unfamiliar language produces the effect (Colle & Welsh, 1976). Any speech gains access to the phonological store and therefore irrelevant speech uses some of the available capacity, reducing performance on the target task. Box 4.2 examines a number of other ways in which extraneous sound can affect working memory.

Box 4.2 Practical Application: Reducing the cognitive ill-effects of office background noise

Many people find themselves having to work or study in open-plan office settings, relying on working memory to reduce the influence of distracting stimuli and to allow resources to be allocated to the task at hand. However, it is not always easy to dismiss the distracting influence of background noise. Banbury and Berry (2005) found that 99 per cent of workers in open-plan offices reported impaired concentration caused by various office noises; the sound of telephones ringing at unattended desks and background speech sounds were particularly distracting.

The irrelevant sound effect refers to the demonstrated impairment of verbal working memory by particular background sounds compared to silence. Some sounds gain obligatory access to memory, interfering with the verbal information being held in memory. Banbury et al. (2001) note that the distraction effect is rooted in the changing nature of the acoustic signal, which gains our attention; repetitive sounds or tones are not as disruptive and the sound level itself would also seem to be relatively unimportant. If reducing the sound level does not eradicate the ill-effects on cognition, how might workplace design compensate for the effect?

One way to reduce the effect on cognitive performance is to mask the office sounds by adding a continuous noise signal. It may seem paradoxical to address the problem by adding more sound, but the continuous signal is designed to reduce the perception of acoustic change, which is the basis of the distraction. A study by Schlittmeier and Hellbrück (2009) examined the use of background music compared to continuous noise for masking office sounds. Their participants completed a serial recall task while office noise was played at 55 dB, a typical sound level in open-plan offices. The office noise was presented alone, or was overlaid with legato music, staccato music or continuous noise. A silence condition was also included. While the participants reported preferring the music to the continuous sound, memory performance was better only in the continuous noise condition. That is, office noise affected serial recall performance negatively, in comparison to silence, whether it was presented alone or overlaid with music. Only the office noise with continuous noise produced similar performance to the silence condition. So, while the subjective ratings did not favour continuous noise, cognitive ill-effects were minimized only in that condition. Schlittmeier and Hellbrück suggest that, if continuous sounds are used in an office to offset the effects of background noise, giving office workers individual control over their presence may be conducive to an effective working environment.

4. The phonological similarity effect

Recall is poorer for an ordered list of verbal items when the items sound alike, relative to performance on lists of items that do not sound alike. Items that are similar in meaning (as opposed to sound) do not show this effect. For example, the sequence 'pit, day, cow, pen, rig' is easier to recall than the sequence 'man, cap, can, map, mad' (Baddeley, 1992b). The second list contains items that sound more alike than the first list. If we assume that the phonological store uses a speech-based or phonological code, then refreshing the items in the store makes use of phonological fragments within the items; confusion arises as the number of shared fragments increases. The phonological similarity effect disappears under conditions of articulatory suppression, supporting the use of a basic phonological code. However, when information from LTM comes into play, the phonological similarity effect may be diminished or absent. Nursery rhymes and song lyrics commonly utilize words with shared sounds, and memory for such sequences may well be improved (e.g. Copeland & Radvansky, 2001).

Given that the phonological loop holds and manipulates speech-based information, we could expect to see a substantial and obvious role for this WM structure in language and related cognitive processing. However, in adults, the role is not as obvious as one might expect. As Baddeley (1992b) notes, people who have a brain injury affecting phonological loop functioning show relatively few signs of general cognitive impairment. For example, PV, a patient described by Baddeley, Papagno and Vallar (1988), had a severely reduced digit span (of one or two items) following a left hemisphere stroke, yet her day-to-day life was relatively unaffected. She ran a shop without apparent difficulty and raised a family. Her intelligence and short-term *visual* memory were normal and her language function was relatively intact, with normal language comprehension for all but the most convoluted of embedded sentences (sentences that require you to hold the beginning of the sentence in mind until you get to the end, with a number of intervening clauses).

What then are the functions of the phonological loop? The phonological loop is known to play a key role in the acquisition of new vocabulary, not just in the person's native language but also in a second language (Service, 1992). Baddeley et al. (1988) found that PV, the patient with a phonological loop deficit who had intact long-term memory as measured by performance on a paired-associate task, showed a severely reduced ability to learn words in Russian, a language with which PV was not familiar. The loop's precise role in other aspects of adult language processing, such as complex speech comprehension, remains controversial (see Caplan & Waters, 1998; Engle & Conway, 1998; Was & Woltz, 2007). In children, poor performance on measures of phonological loop function is associated with poor vocabulary learning (e.g. Gathercole & Baddeley, 1989; Gathercole et al., 1997; Service, 1992), and very poor phonological loop skills are associated with developmental disorders such as specific language impairment (SLI; see Gathercole & Baddeley, 1990). There is evidence that the phonological loop is involved in the temporary storage of part solutions during mental arithmetic, while the central executive performs the more demanding manipulations. For example, Logie et al. (1994) found effects of both articulatory suppression and irrelevant speech on an addition task using a series of two-digit numbers (e.g. 12 + 43 + 18 + 26 + 35 = ?). Such data suggest a specific role for the phonological loop in mental arithmetic, although a more substantive role is performed by the central executive (Adams & Hitch, 1998). A role in action control is also likely (see Baddeley et al., 2001).

The visuo-spatial sketchpad

Suppose you are asked to say how many windows there are on the front of your house. To answer this question, you will most likely construct a mental image of your house and inspect that image in order to count the number of windows. Or suppose you are asked to describe the Sydney Opera House. Again, it is likely that you will try to visualize the building in your mind's eye, and try to describe what it looks like based on the visual image. The ability to manipulate visual images relies on visual short-term memory and Baddeley and Hitch's model proposes that this type of memory is provided by a separate component, the visuo-spatial sketchpad (VSSP).

While the phonological loop is specialized for speech-based information the VSSP is specialized for dealing with visual and spatial information. The VSSP, like the phonological loop, has a limited capacity, of about three or four objects according to Baddeley (e.g. 2003). Logie (1995) suggested two components comprise the VSSP. A

Visual cache is the component of the visuo-spatial sketchpad, within working memory, that stores visual information. **Inner scribe** is the component of the visuo-spatial sketchpad, within working memory, that allows spatial processing.

visual cache stores information relating to visual form and an inner scribe allows spatial processing. Evidence supports the notion of separate but strongly interconnected components for visual and spatial information. Logie (1995) proposed that the VSSP is analogous in structure to the phonological loop. By this account, the visual cache is similar to the phonological store, in that it is a passive store that holds information, while the inner scribe (similar to the articulatory control process) maintains information in the store through a type of rehearsal process. Logie's account (e.g. 1995) sees long-term memory involvement as central to VSSP functioning.

VSSP processing is evident in performance on the Brooks matrix task. Brooks (1967) devised a matrix task in which participants were presented with sentences to commit to memory; the sentences were either easy to visualize or could not be visualized (see Figure 4.9). In a 'spatial condition', the sentences were accompanied by a 4 × 4 matrix which could be used to aid memory. As the sentences could be visualized by use of the matrix, using the VSSP. Sentences such as 'in the starting square put a 1', 'in the

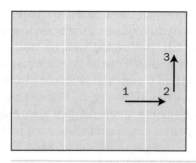

Visualizable/spatial instructions

in the starting square put a 1

in the next square to the right put a 2

in the next square up put a 3

Non-visualizable/nonsense instructions

in the starting square put a 1

in the next square to the quick put a 2

in the next square to the good put a 3

Figure 4.9   Depiction of the Brooks Matrix task. In the Brooks Matrix task, instructions are either easy to visualize using a 4 × 4 grid matrix or they cannot be visualized using the matrix. Memory for the sentences is then tested.

next square to the right put a 2', 'in the next square up put a 3', were used in the spatial condition. In a 'verbal condition', the adjectives 'up-down' and 'left-right' in the sentences were replaced with the non-spatial adjectives 'good-bad' and 'quick-slow'. This produced sentences that could not be readily visualized using the matrix (e.g. 'in the starting square put a 1', 'in the next square to the quick put a 2', 'in the next square to the good put a 3'). Memorizing these sentences required verbal coding, using the verbal component of WM, the phonological loop. Participants were required to recall the sentences. In the spatial condition, they typically recalled about 8 sentences compared to 6 in the verbal condition. Brooks then compared auditory and visual presentation of the sentences and found that for the spatial task auditory presentation was best, but for the verbal task visual presentation produced better performance. Auditory presentation in the spatial condition frees up the VSSP for the primary task, while visual presentation in the verbal task frees up the phonological loop for the primary task.

Baddeley et al. (1975) developed a task designed to interfere with performance on the Brooks task. In their pursuit rotor task, participants were required to track a moving target using a hand-held stylus (requiring visuo-spatial involvement) while sentences were presented auditorily. This dual-task requirement interfered with performance in the spatial condition, but not in the verbal condition (see Figure 4.10), providing further support for the involvement of the VSSP in the task. Baddeley and Lieberman (1980) later tried to separate out the effects of the visual and spatial components of this task using two secondary task conditions. In one condition, participants made brightness judgements, a task requiring visual but not spatial processing. In a second condition, blindfolded participants were required to track a moving pendulum with a torch. The pendulum contained a photosensitive cell which, when in contact with light from the torch, caused an auditory tone to be emitted. Sentences were again presented auditorily. They found greater disruption of performance in the spatial condition, relative to the brightness judgement condition. A practical example of a dual task issue is described in Box 4.3.

Data from dual-task performance shows selective interference of visual and spatial working memory tasks (e.g. Della Sala et al., 1999). Further evidence supporting the distinction between the visual cache and the inner scribe comes from neuropsychological

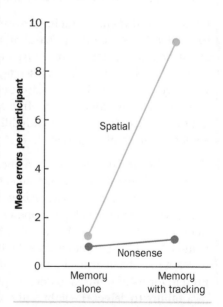

Figure 4.10   The effect of concurrent tracking on memory for visualizable (spatial) and non-visualizable (nonsense) sentences. Disruption of performance is seen in the spatial condition, compared to the verbal condition. Data from Baddeley et al. (1975).

Source: Gathercole, S. E. & Baddeley A. D. (1993) Working memory and language. Psychology Press.

case studies. Farah et al. (1988a) studied a patient, L.H., who sustained bilateral damage to the occipitotemporal regions of the brain in a traffic accident, while his parietal lobes were unharmed. L.H. performed well on tasks that involved manipulation of spatial imagery. He performed well on the Brook's task and on mental rotation tasks. He could point out locations on a map and he could also describe routes he was familiar with in the city where he lived. However, he showed impairments on visual tasks that required him to make judgements about relative size, colour and form. L.H.'s pattern of deficit suggested an impaired visual cache but an intact inner scribe, and his performance on spatial and visual imagery tasks supported Farah et al.'s distinction between visual mental imagery and spatial imagery.

A second patient, R.T., showed the reverse pattern (Farah & Hammond, 1988). Following a stroke, R.T. had lesions affecting the right parietal lobe and part of his right temporal lobe. He had impaired spatial manipulation abilities, with poor performance on mental rotation tasks, for example, but reading and object recognition were intact. A further case (M.G.) reported by Morton and Morris (1995) presents a similar profile of spared visual imagery despite impaired spatial imagery. Neuroimaging data support this dissociation, with separate brain areas for visual and spatial processing identified within the occipital, parietal and frontal lobes (e.g. Jonides et al., 1993).

Box 4.3 Practical Application: Is it safe to drive while using a mobile phone?

Little in our evolutionary history has prepared us for what is now an everyday task for many adults: driving. As Groeger (1999) put it, 'controlling one's own movements when travelling at 60 miles per hour, with half a ton of metal hurtling towards you at a speed that is difficult to determine is, quintessentially, a mid- to late-20th century problem' (p. 245).

Many of the difficulties facing drivers involve what are essentially dual-task demands: paying attention to, or being distracted by, features of the environment that may not be central to the primary task of safely navigating and controlling a motor vehicle. We can be distracted by factors external to the vehicle – a dog running onto the road, seeing a person we know – or by factors inside the vehicle – by the mind wandering (see Box 4.4), a radio commentary or a conversation with a passenger, for example. Recent research has investigated the effects of conversation on driver distraction and suggests that there are important differences between holding a conversation with a passenger in the car as opposed to with someone on a mobile phone.

The detrimental effect of mobile phone use is not explained by factors relating to physically operating the phone (handling the phone, selecting phone numbers, etc.); such actions take attention from driving but are not the most dangerous elements of mobile phone use. Strayer and Johnston (2001) used a dual task procedure in which participants performed a simulated driving task (pursuit tracking), while conducting a conversation by mobile phone or listening to the radio. The study compared the effects of using a hand-held or hands-free device. As participants performed the driving task, they were required to react to red and green lights, simulating responses to traffic lights. Reactions to the lights were measured in terms of failures to detect lights and delayed reactions. The results showed that the probability of a failure to detect the light and react appropriately doubled for participants using the mobile phone. It did not matter whether the phone was held or hands-free, suggesting that the performance detriment reflects attentional factors as opposed to peripheral factors relating to the physical manipulation of the phone. Passively listening to speech did not affect performance. In a condition in which participants listened to a book on tape, driving was not impaired.

However, it is not having a conversation per se that is the source of the problem; there is something particular about mobile phone conversations that affects performance. Speech evolved in a natural environment, in which people hold conversations face to face and share attention in the same environment while doing so. Telephone conversations lack that shared environment. What then are the differences between live (passenger–driver) and remote (other person–mobile phone–driver) conversations that can help or hinder driver behaviour? Drews et al. (2008) used a driving simulator to compare drivers conversing with a passenger, conversing on a (hands-free) mobile phone and driving without distraction. Driving performance was significantly worse when the driver conversed on the mobile phone, with lane adherence, vehicle distance and task completion (e.g. taking the correct exit) affected. The researchers also examined the transcripts of the mobile phone and driver-passenger conversations and noted important differences. Drivers conversing with a passenger heard more references to traffic compared to those conversing via mobile phone. As driving conditions became more demanding, speech was reduced in the 'passenger' condition, but not in the mobile phone condition.

Such data suggest that the passenger is sensitive to the current task demands and the conversation takes account of the traffic conditions, adapting to the cognitive demands of the situation. Mobile phone conversations, on the other hand, continue to place demands on the driver's attention when the demands of the driving task increase. Such demands even affect walkers who talk on their mobile phone: Hyman et al. (2010) found that 75 per cent of walkers who were on their mobile phone failed to notice a unicycling clown, wearing a vivid purple and yellow outfit, on their route.

Such findings are at odds with current road safety legislation, in some countries, which permits the use of hands-free mobile phones while prohibiting hand-held devices. This could lead drivers to assume that it is the physical handling of the phone that is dangerous and cause them to underestimate the detrimental effect of a mobile phone conversation on their driving.

The central executive

The central executive has been described as 'the workhorse and mastermind of human cognition' (Caplan & Waters, 1998, p. 77). It is the most important component of working memory – it is also the least well understood. Baddeley and Hitch's original model presented the central executive as a general processing mechanism that handled the more complex types of short-term memory task that were not delegated to the PL or the VSSP. It was presented as a supervisory system which played a key role in controlling and regulating working memory function. It coordinated the activities of the PL or the VSSP, and focused and switched attention. The central executive is generally seen as being involved in controlling active information, but not in storage per se (Logie & Baddeley, 1999), and it is useful to separate the storage and control functions of working memory. It is likely that the central executive consists of a number of subsystems, which have yet to be identified. Later versions of the model present the central executive as an attentional controller, similar to Norman and Shallice's (1986) concept of the supervisory activating system (SAS) in their model of attentional control of action, and Baddeley (1986) suggested that the SAS model provides a useful way of describing the functions of the central executive. For that reason the SAS model is examined here.

Norman and Shallice (1986) suggested two types of cognitive control reflecting the distinction between automatic and controlled processes (Schneider & Shiffrin, 1977). The automatic system of control allows us to perform routine and well-practised actions through the selection of learned habits and schemas without the need for deliberate cognitive control. We can perform quite complex sequences of actions through this mode of operation, using a system Norman and Shallice refer to as the contention scheduling system. Our actions are directed by relevant schemas, activated by triggers in the environment. For example, we can drive home along a familiar route without fully concentrating on the route; we may even make it all the way home without being fully aware of key stages along our route. A second type of process makes use of an attentional control mechanism (the supervisory activating system or SAS), which can interrupt automatic processing, select an alternative schema and allow attention to be directed towards a goal. Staying with the example of driving, if you go abroad and are required to drive on the opposite side of the road than you normally would, you have to exert more effort and deliberate control over what might otherwise be highly automated actions. It is important that routine actions do not dominate on such occasions. These two qualitatively distinct control systems allow three levels of functioning, according to the Norman and Shallice model:

1 a fully automatic mode for routine actions;

2 an intermediate, partially automatic mode which allows attentional control of actions; and

3 the deliberate control of action for non-habitual or novel tasks.

Scan to watch a demonstration of the Stroop effect

Thus, according to this approach 'contention scheduling – the system responsible for routine selection of action – was held to operate in the intact adult human modulated by a second system – the supervisory system – held to be responsible for the organization of non-routine (novel) behaviours' (Cooper & Shallice, 2000, p. 303).

Evidence for two separate control systems, one governing performance of routine actions and the other allowing control of non-routine action comes from studies of patients with frontal lobe damage. Patients with damage to the prefrontal cortex experience problems completing tasks that require SAS-type attentional control and their errors often reflect intact contention scheduling (Shallice, 2002). For example, 'capture errors' are associated with prefrontal damage. Capture errors involve a failure to override a routine set of actions; for example, we might leave the house on a Saturday and drive to work or college instead of to our intended destination. William James (1890) recounted an occasion when he went upstairs with the intention of changing his clothes, but instead went to bed. In the Stroop task (see Chapter 13) the automatic reading of a word when the task requires us to simply name the colour provides another example of a capture error.

Capture errors involve a failure to override a routine set of actions; a routine or well-practised action is performed when another action was intended.

Dysexecutive syndrome refers to a range of deficits reflecting problems with executive function and control, and often associated with injury to the frontal areas of the brain.

Baddeley and Wilson (1988) used the term dysexecutive syndrome to refer to the type of impairment that specifically involves deficits in executive function and that is often associated with dorsolateral prefrontal damage (see also Chapter 8). Affected individuals may demonstrate 'disturbed attention, increased distractibility, a difficulty in grasping the whole of a complicated state of affairs . . . [they are] well able to work along old routine lines. But they cannot learn to master new types of task' (Rylander, 1939, p. 20). Dysexecutive syndrome is characterized by an inability to exert control over one's behaviours and it may involve difficulties initiating, ceasing, suppressing or modifying actions as environmental cues change. For example, some patients demonstrate perseveration, the inappropriate repetition of an action. On the Wisconsin Card Sorting Test, a test of frontal lobe function, the patient is required to alter his or her card selection as a 'rule' supplied by the examiner changes (Milner, 1963). A number of trials follow one rule, then the rule changes. Patients often show perseveration in continuing to respond with the old rule even though the rule has now changed. Patients are aware that the

Perseveration is the inappropriate repetition of an action.

rule has changed and are often aware that they are making errors – despite this they continue to apply the inappropriate rule.

The central executive also allows us to maintain focus and to keep our attention on the task at hand, ignoring competing input from the environment; individual differences in working memory capacity, for example, predict the likelihood that one's mind will wander while engaged in a task requiring concentration (see Box 4.4 for further discussion of 'mind wandering'). A patient may show spontaneous and apparently uncontrollable imitation of a doctor, for example, or a compulsion to interact with objects (such as picking up and miming the use of an object, when not asked to do so), a tendency referred to as utilization behaviour. The ability to control responses to environmental cues is compromised: 'in the absence of control from the SAS, the patient simply responds to any cues of opportunities afforded by the environment (Baddeley, 2009, p. 54). The case of E.V.R. (Box 4.5) illustrates such a pattern of deficit.

> Utilization behaviour refers to dysfunctional automatic reaching for and use of objects in the environment.

The variety of executive deficits seen in such patients suggests that the central executive is further fractionated into subsystems or subprocesses, perhaps suggesting a 'series of parallel but equal processes, an executive "committee" perhaps' (Baddeley, 1996a, p. 13471). Shah and Miyake (1996) suggest visual and verbal subcomponents, but, as yet, the executive has not been refined into subcomponents in the way that the phonological loop and visuo-spatial sketchpad have.

Box 4.4 Research Close Up: Working memory and mind wandering

Source: Kane, M. J., Brown, L. H., McVay, J. C., Silvia, P. J., Myin-Germeys, I., & Kwapil, T. R. (2007). For whom the mind wanders, and when: An experience-sampling study of working memory and executive control in daily life. *Psychological Science*, *18*, 614–621.

INTRODUCTION

About a third of the thoughts we experience in our waking lives are 'off-task' and can be considered to constitute 'mind wandering' (Kane et al., 2007; Klinger & Cox, 1987). This type of spontaneous thought, far from being a cognitive weakness, may reflect fundamental properties of the architecture of the mind. Just as we spend a portion of our sleeping day dreaming, we spend a portion of our waking day mind wandering and daydreaming. These activities may have much in common and may fulfil similar, essential, cognitive functions, helping us to consolidate memory and to integrate and categorize experiences throughout the day (Christoff et al., 2008). Mind wandering might be considered to be 'a conscious manifestation of contrary unconscious processes created when we attempt to control the direction of consciousness' and therefore 'a natural product of the mechanism that allows consciousness to control itself' (Wegner, 1997, p. 296). If this is the case, we might expect to see an association between aspects of working memory and mind wandering. A study by Kane et al. (2007) examined the relationship between working memory capacity and the likelihood and context in which one's mind might wander.

METHOD

Kane et al. used an experience-sampling methodology, a technique in which participants are required, at various times during a day, to report on their current thoughts, and to categorize those thoughts as being 'on task' or 'off task'. Working memory span tasks were completed by 124 participants, who were prompted over the course of a day to report whether their mind had wandered from their current task and to detail the current task context.

RESULTS

The results, consistent with previous reports, showed that participants reported that their minds had indeed wandered off-task on almost one third of occasions. Considerable individual differences were noted, with one participant reporting no episodes of mind wandering while another reported being off-task on 92 per cent of probes (the average was 30 per cent). Participants' off-task thoughts generally involved thinking about everyday events and plans, while they were significantly less likely to report fantasizing or worrying. While the nature of the thoughts was broadly similar across participants, the frequency with which mind wandering was reported varied considerably.

Kane et al. also found that minds were more likely to wander in some contexts than others. Participants were less likely to find their minds wandering when they felt happy and competent, when they were concentrating, and when they were enjoying their current activity. The novelty or challenge provided by the current activity did not predict mind wandering, however. Participants with higher working memory capacity were less likely to report their minds wandering while engaged in tasks for which concentration was required. However, when engaged in tasks requiring little concentration, individuals with high working memory capacity were significantly *more* likely to mind-wander compared to participants with lower working memory capacity. Participants with lower working memory capacity reported more incidents of mind-wandering as the challenge and effort involved in their current task increased (see Figure 4.11).

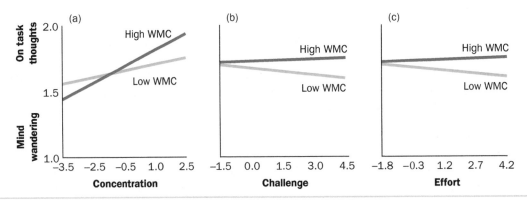

Figure 4.11 Differences in working memory capacity (WMC) reflect differences in mind wandering during a cognition task. The lines show the means for participants in two groups, the top and bottom quartiles of the working memory scores. The y-axis shows whether the participant was on task; a lower score indicates mind wandering. The x-axis shows self-ratings indicating whether the participants found the task to require concentration, whether they found it challenging and whether they rated it as requiring effort.

Source: Adapted from Kane, M. J., Brown, L. H., McVay, J. C., Silvia, P. J., Myin-Germeys, I., & Kwapil, T. R. (2007). For whom the mind wanders, and when: An experience-sampling study of working memory and executive control in daily life. *Psychological Science, 18*, 614–621.

DISCUSSION

Kane et al.'s study shows the importance of considering individual differences in factors such as working memory, but also the context of the task, and the cognitive demands posed by it. We might be inclined to think of mind wandering as the opposite of goal-directed thought, yet creative thought lies at their intersection (see also Chapter 9); it is in some ways goal-directed and in other ways spontaneous (see Christoff et al., 2008).

Box 4.5 When Things Go Wrong: Case E.V.R.

Executive function is crucial for effective planning and goal-directed behaviour. What happens when brain injury affects this function? Eslinger and Damasio (1985) described the case of E.V.R., an accountant, who at the age of 35 had a brain tumour removed leading to bilateral damage to the ventro-medial frontal areas. His intellectual abilities remained largely intact. He had above average intelligence scoring in the top 1–2 percentile, with a verbal IQ of 132 and a performance IQ of 135. Before his illness he was responsible, hard-working, and had been promoted at his job. He was sociable and active in his community. But after his surgery, E.V.R. could not keep a job, his planning of activities both immediate and into the future was severely impaired, and even minor decisions (what to wear, where to eat out) took an inordinate amount of consideration. He could no longer plan his finances and his business ventures ended in bankruptcy. His altered social behaviour and personality profile led Damasio (1994) to suggest that E.V.R. presented a case of 'acquired sociopathy' (see also Damasio et al., 1992). While E.V.R.'s intellectual capacity remained largely unaffected by his illness, he lacked the emotional or social intelligence to be able to flexibly alter his behaviour or predict the consequences of his actions. As Damasio put it, 'we might summarize [his] predicament as to know but not to feel' (1994, p. 45). This case illustrates the important role that emotion plays in cognition, an issue we will return to in Chapter 14.

Abnormal performance on everyday tasks despite apparently intact intellectual functioning is a commonly reported feature of frontal lobe damage. Shallice and Burgess (1991) had three patients with frontal damage attempt a real-world task called the multiple errands task. The test required the patients to complete a number of tasks within an unfamiliar shopping centre. The tasks varied in complexity (e.g. buy a postage stamp, or find out the Euro–Sterling exchange rate) and there were a number of rules the patient had to follow (e.g. 'do not go into a shop except to buy something that's on the list'). All three patients scored normally on tests of language and intellectual ability, yet all three performed poorly on the multiple errands task, having deviated from the rules (e.g. gone into shops when they were not supposed to) or failed to complete tasks. A number of socially inappropriate behaviours occurred (see Burgess et al., 2007). A patient left a shop without paying for the goods; another patient offered sexual favours in lieu of payment, an unusual, and generally unacceptable, offer! Such cases demonstrate the key role played by executive functioning in everyday planning and goal-directed behaviour.

The episodic buffer

The working memory model (e.g. Baddeley, 1996b) originally considered the role of the central executive in focusing, dividing and switching attention, and in linking WM to LTM, but it did not seem to have a storage component of its own. But some verbal learning tasks involve a larger storage capacity than is supported by data on the phonological loop, suggesting that working memory can make use of additional storage capacity. For example, when unrelated words are presented in a span task, a limit of about five or six items is typically found, but if the words are presented in a sentence, memory span increases to about 15 words (Brener, 1940). If the loop only holds seven or so items, where is the extra storage capacity coming from?

Furthermore, performance is facilitated when the sentences presented are grammatical; yet judgements of grammaticality require LTM involvement. LTM access has also been shown to affect VSSP function. For example, studies of boundary extension errors show that participants' visuo-spatial memory for a visual scene can be distorted (see Figure 4.12), such that the scene is often remembered as extending beyond the boundary originally presented (e.g. Intraub 1997; Intraub, Gottesman, & Bills, 1998; Intraub et al., 1996). Such errors occur after even very brief presentations and suggest 'a seamless integration of information physically presented in the picture and information that was inferred' (Intraub, 1997, p. 219). This would depend on information in the VSSP making contact with relevant information stored in LTM (Radvansky, 2006). The original WM model of Baddeley and Hitch did not suggest how this might occur, but other accounts speculated on the interaction of these memory systems. For example, Ericsson and

Figure 4.12   Viewers tend to remember seeing the area of a scene as extending beyond the boundary of the original photograph. Panels A and B shows similar scenes; Panel B had a wider broader frame than Panel A. When asked to draw what they had seen, participants tend to extend beyond the actual boundary. Panel C shows a participant's recall of seeing Panel A, and Panel D shows a participant's recall of seeing Panel B. The drawing in Panel D shows the roof of a house and an outline of a tree that were not in the original photograph (Panel B).

Source: Reprinted from Intraub, H. (1997). The representation of visual scenes. *Trends in Cognitive Sciences*, *1*, 217–221, with permission from Elsevier.

Kintsch (1995) proposed a 'long-term working memory', whereby information from long-term memory can be used to compensate for the limited capacity (short-term) working memory.

The need to explain how WM interacts with LTM and how WM can sometimes involve a larger storage capacity led to a proposed further component within WM. Baddeley's (2000) WM model differs in two ways from the earlier model. First, it shows that the WM modality-specific subsystems (phonological loop and visuo-spatial sketchpad) link to LTM, and second, the episodic buffer was introduced, which can be accessed by the central executive or by the slave systems, and which links to LTM (see Figure 4.8). The buffer is 'a crucial feature of the capacity of working memory to act as a global workspace that is accessed by conscious awareness' (Baddeley, 2003, p. 836). The episodic buffer is a temporary storage structure of limited capacity (it can hold about four chunks of information; Baddeley, 2009) that is controlled by the central executive and allows information from different sources (visuo-spatial sketchpad, phonological loop, LTM) to be integrated, essentially providing a means of interface between the modality-specific systems of WM and LTM. It can be considered to be the storage component of the central executive (Baddeley, 2003) and it 'is episodic in the sense that it holds episodes whereby information is integrated across space and potentially extended across time . . . it is assumed to be a temporary store . . . [and is] assumed to play an important role in feeding information into and retrieving information from episodic LTM' (Baddeley, 2000, p. 421).

Evaluation

Baddeley and Hitch's working memory model was proposed as a replacement for the concept of a unitary short-term store, and the concept of working memory has provided a useful description of a flexible, adaptable, yet capacity-limited system. It introduced a number of subsystems and showed how WM structures are involved not just in memory functions but in complex cognitive tasks more generally, such as learning and reasoning (Baddeley, 1996a, 2000). The model explained how, following brain injury, impaired STM (as measured by digit span) could accompany normal LTM. The model detailed a number of components, the activities of which can be tested, through dual task experiments for example. The addition of the episodic buffer went some way towards considering how LTM interacts with WM (although the model does not detail how interaction occurs) and provided a general multi-modal storage capacity to WM. The most successful component of the model is the phonological loop, although there remain some data that do not fit with the WM model (e.g. see Ward, 2001). The central executive, clearly a central component in the WM model, is as yet not well understood, and further research will be required in order to determine whether it is a single component of WM or actually consists of a number of high level processes, involving many interacting brain areas. Donald (1991) describes the central executive as presented in working memory models as 'a hypothetical entity that sits atop the mountain of working memory and attention like some gigantic Buddha, an inscrutable, immaterial, omnipresent homunculus, at whose busy desk the buck stops every time memory and attention theorists run out of alternatives' (p. 327). Alternative accounts of working memory share this weakness, and there is a need to specify the mechanisms that control working memory and the conditions under which they operate. The relationships between working memory, attention and consciousness are poorly understood, and it remains unclear as to whether working memory is the basis of conscious experience, or whether it arises from consciousness; WM is closely associated with conscious experience, but they are not one and the same (Baars, 1997). Research into implicit working memory is only beginning to emerge (e.g. Hassin et al., 2009), and neuroscientific research is beginning to unpack the complex relationship between memory and attention (e.g. Lewis-Peacock et al., 2012). Research looking at how to improve working memory, and the role of self-efficacy (see Box 4.6), is also providing new insights into memory functioning (see for example, Hoffman, 2010; Hoffman & Schraw, 2009; Kingston & Lyddy, 2013).

> Self-efficacy is a person's sense of their own competence to complete a certain task or achieve a goal.

Baddeley's WM model is arguably at its best when factors relating to LTM are minimized (Cowan, 1995b), and links to LTM are considered to a greater extent in other models of working memory (e.g. Cowan, 1995a; Ericsson and Kintsch, 1995; see also Oberauer, 2002). In practice, it is difficult to separate the processes of LTM and WM in everyday cognition, and research has begun to focus on the interactions between WM and LTM (e.g. see Burgess & Hitch, 2005, for an overview), as well as on individual differences. We turn to the structures and processes of LTM in the next chapter.

Box 4.6 Research Close Up: Self-efficacy and working memory

Source: Autin, F., & Croizet, J. (2012). Improving working memory efficiency by reframing metacognitive interpretation of task difficulty. *Journal of Experimental Psychology: General*, *141*(4), 610–618.

INTRODUCTION

We often think of working memory capacity as if it were fixed. But, in fact, the performance of our working memory can be affected by situational factors, by aspects of the task and by factors such as stress or emotion. But does self-efficacy affect working memory? Self-efficacy refers to a person's sense of their own competence to complete a certain task or achieve a particular goal. A study by Autin and Croizet (2012) examined this, across three experiments with 11-year-old children; their first two studies will be considered here.

METHOD AND RESULTS

Study 1

In their first study, Autin and Croizet randomly allocated children to three groups. Two groups of children completed an anagram task before their working memory task. The anagrams were so difficult that they could not be solved within the time allocated. One group of children, in the 'reframing' condition,

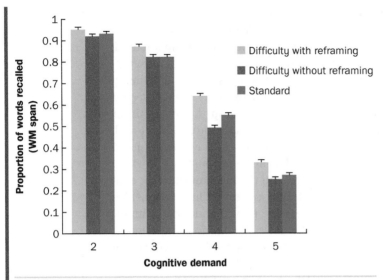

Figure 4.13   Working memory (WM) span as a function of the experimental condition in Study 1. Having a difficult task but reframing it; having a difficult task without the opportunity to reframe it; and the standard control condition. Cognitive demand of the WM test (2, 3, 4, or 5 words to remember) is shown along the x-axis. Error bars represent standard errors.

Source: Autin, F., & Croizet, J. (2012). Improving working memory efficiency by reframing metacognitive interpretation of task difficulty. *Journal of Experimental Psychology: General*, *141*, 610–618. APA; reprinted with permission.

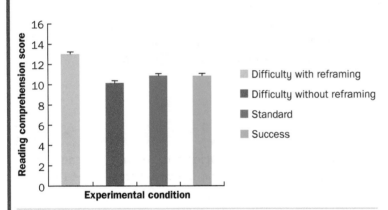

Figure 4.14   Reading comprehension score as a function of experimental condition. Having a difficult task but reframing it; having a difficult task without the opportunity to reframe it; and the standard control condition. The maximum score was 18. Error bars represent standard errors.

Source: Autin, F., & Croizet, J. (2012). Improving working memory efficiency by reframing metacognitive interpretation of task difficulty. *Journal of Experimental Psychology: General*, *141*, 610–618. APA; reprinted with permission.

were told that having difficulty with the task was normal and in fact showed that learning was occurring. The second group who did the anagrams did not get this reframing information. A third control group were not exposed to the anagram task, but went directly to the working memory task. All participants performed a listening span test. In the listening span task, participants listen to a series of sentences. After each sentence is presented the participant has to report whether the sentence makes sense or not, and also repeat back the last word in the sentence. At the end of the series, participants have to repeat back as many last words as possible, in the same order as they were presented. The series of sentences vary from two to five sentences, so participants have to remember up to five sentence-final words. The results showed that children allocated to the reframing condition had a greater working memory span than either of the two other groups (see Figure 4.13).

Study 2

In the second study, Autin and Croizet examined whether this effect would extend to higher level processing that relies on working memory span, in this case reading comprehension. The three conditions from the first study were replicated with a new sample of 11-year-olds, with one further condition added. In a 'success' condition, children did easier anagrams, and got them right. A difficult reading test followed, instead of the working memory test used in Experiment 1. The results were consistent with those of Experiment 1. Children in the reframing condition showed better reading comprehension than the other three groups, which did not differ significantly from each other (see Figure 4.14).

DISCUSSION

These data suggest that a brief psychological intervention that allows the child to re-interpret difficulty with a task in a positive light can support working memory performance both on a standard test of working memory and also on a higher level reading task that relies on working memory. The findings of Study 2 even suggest that this reframing of difficulty may be more beneficial than an experience of success on a prior task. The study relies on the fact that, in Western cultures at least, experiencing difficulty tends to be interpreted in terms of lower cognitive ability. However, as noted by the authors, some cultures would interpret an experience of difficulty on a task as a more temporary issue, reflecting a lack of mastery for example, and not as reflecting on a person's cognitive ability. In such cultures, a child's experience of difficulty on a task would not affect self-efficacy, potentially bringing an advantage on some cognitive tasks.

Summary

In this chapter we have considered how information is held and manipulated in memory. Early models of memory such as the Atkinson and Shiffrin model proposed three stores: sensory, short-term and long-term stores. We saw that the sensory memory stores are large capacity stores that hold information for a very short duration, serving to prolong rapidly presented input for processing in the short-term store. Sensory memory contains subsystems specialized for visual, auditory and other types of sensory input. The sensory stores hold information but do not code it in a form that allows categorization or processing of meaning. In order for the meaning of a stimulus to be appreciated the information must be transferred to short-term memory.

The short-term memory store as proposed by the multi-store account was a unitary store which had a limited capacity of about 7 ± 2 pieces of information. This, as it turns out, is an over-simplification of the short-term system, which must involve a number of relatively independent processes.

Working memory has been extolled as 'perhaps the most significant achievement of human mental evolution' (Goldman-Rakic, 1992, p. 111). The working memory model of Baddeley and colleagues was proposed in order to replace the model of short-term memory as a unitary store. The WM model suggested three components to WM: a central executive, like internal attention (see Chapter 3), which oversees the activities of two modality-specific systems; the visuo-spatial sketchpad for storing and manipulating visual and spatial information and the phonological loop for storing and manipulating speech-based information. Later, an additional component, the episodic buffer, was added to explain the additional storage capacity of the central executive and to link the components of WM and LTM. Other theories of WM (such as Cowan's account) focus on WM as embedded systems for attentional control with activation of stored knowledge from LTM playing a central role in WM processing. The central executive, a key concept in working memory, remains to be adequately specified, and while various models of working memory have been proposed no full explanation of executive functioning has as yet been forthcoming. Research has begun to address the relationship between long-term memory and working memory, examining whether they are structurally separate systems and the means by which they interact.

Review questions

1 What evidence is there supporting the main components of Baddeley's working memory model?
2 What are the functions of the phonological loop?
3 How has evidence from brain injury contributed to our understanding of normal memory?
4 What is the relationship between short-term and working memory?
5 How might we best measure the capacity of short-term memory?

FURTHER READING

Baddeley, A. D. (2003). Working memory: Looking back and looking forward. *Nature Reviews Neuroscience, 4*(10): 829–839.

Cowan, N. (2010). The magical mystery four: How is working memory capacity limited, and why? *Current Directions in Psychological Science, 19*, 51–57.

Della Sala, S. (Ed.) (2007). *Tall tales about the mind & brain: Separating fact from fiction.* Oxford, UK: Oxford University Press.

Miller, G. A. (1956). The magical number seven, plus or minus two: some limits on our capacity for processing information. *The Psychological Review, 63*, 81–97.

CHAPTER 5:
LONG-TERM MEMORY

Preview questions

1 How is the long-term memory system organized?
2 How does long-term memory differ from short-term memory?
3 What are declarative and non-declarative memories?
4 What is prospective memory?
5 What can we learn about normal memory from the study of memory disorders?

INTRODUCTION

In 1953, at the age of 27, a man who became known in the medical literature as H.M. underwent an experimental surgical procedure that aimed to alleviate his medically intractable epilepsy. H.M. had temporal-lobe surgery that involved removing the amygdala, the anterior two-thirds of the hippocampus, adjacent hippocampal gyrus and the parahippocampal gyrus (Squire, 2009). Following his operation, H.M.'s seizures were dramatically reduced. However, the reduction in seizure activity came at an enormous and unanticipated cost: H.M. was left with a profound and pervasive memory impairment, a pattern of memory deficit known as amnesia. H.M. retained his childhood memories, but he had a severe and lasting deficit affecting his memory for ongoing events. He did not remember people he had met; he could not retain his doctors' names; he could not recall activities he had just completed; he could not find his way around the hospital. However, his short-term memory was relatively intact – he could answer questions, for example, and repeat back a sequence of digits – but these experiences were not subsequently retained. His personality, intellect and ability to use language remained largely intact.

> Amnesia refers to a pattern of memory loss affecting elements of long-term memory, while short-term memory remains intact.

H.M.'s case, one of the most cited cases in neuropsychology, demonstrates three important aspects of long-term memory (LTM) processes (see Corkin, 2002). First, long-term memory processes are not distributed throughout the brain as had been previously thought; damage to particular areas within the temporal lobes will cause profound long-term memory loss. Before H.M., the standard view of long-term memory within psychology, influenced by Karl Lashley's work, was the idea that memory functions were widely distributed over the brain. Lashley performed experiments on rats, systematically removing particular areas of the cortex and examining the effects on the rats' learning. On the basis of his experiments, he could not locate any particular brain region that was necessary for memory, and so he concluded that it was the size of the cortical areas and not its location that was the important factor (the principle of mass action; Lashley, 1929). H.M.'s case (see Box 5.1) showed that particular brain regions are responsible for long-term memory function, and that disruption to these regions has devastating effects. Second, long-term memory encompasses a number of different abilities and some learning may be possible after damage to the system. H.M. was able to learn some new skills, but he could not remember new facts. Third, H.M.'s case showed that memory is separable from language, perceptual and other cognitive functions (Squire, 2009). These were relatively unaffected in H.M.'s case, despite his profound memory impairment.

In the last chapter, we looked at memory for currently active information. In this chapter, we consider long-term memory, the vast store of memories for events, facts and know-how, that we accumulate over a lifetime and make use of every waking moment. By examining what aspects of memory are preserved and what aspects are not in cases like H.M., much has been learned about the structure of long-term memory and its relationship to short-term memory. Before we consider long-term memory in normal cognition, we will look at memory function in amnesia and how the study of this condition has contributed to our understanding of long-term memory.

MEMORY AND AMNESIA

Amnesic syndrome refers to a pattern of memory loss characterized by impaired long-term memory and spared short-term memory. **Anterograde amnesia** is impairment of memory for events that occurred after the onset of amnesia. **Retrograde amnesia** is impairment of memory for events that occurred before the onset of amnesia.

The term 'amnesia' as used in cognitive psychology and neuropsychology generally refers to a condition known as the amnesic syndrome. This is a permanent and pervasive disorder of memory, affecting many memory functions. While individuals with amnesia differ considerably from one another, depending on the site, extent and cause of their brain damage, there are a number of general characteristics of amnesia, as outlined by Parkin (1997):

1 Short-term memory, as measured by digit span for example, is intact.

2 Memory for language, and concepts, is largely intact.

3 There is a severe and lasting anterograde amnesia – memory for events after the onset of the amnesia will be impaired.

4 There will be a retrograde amnesia, of variable extent – the patient will have loss of memory for events prior to the onset of amnesia.

5 Skill learning, conditioning and priming will be unaffected. The patient will also be able to engage in skills acquired prior to the onset of amnesia (e.g. play a musical instrument).

Scan to watch a video illustrating extreme memory loss

The brain areas involved in long-term memory are shown in Figure 5.1, and some of the implications for functioning with amnesic syndrome are outlined in Box 5.1, which considers the case that was introduced briefly at the opening of this chapter, that of H.M.

(a)

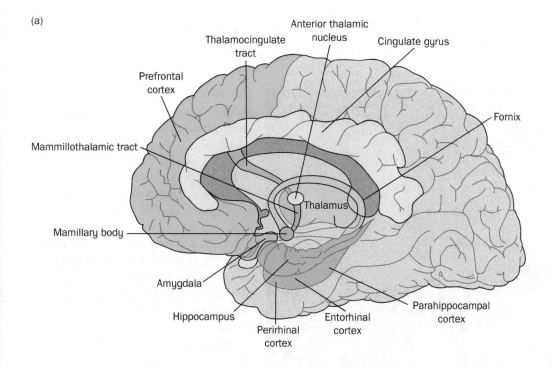

(b)

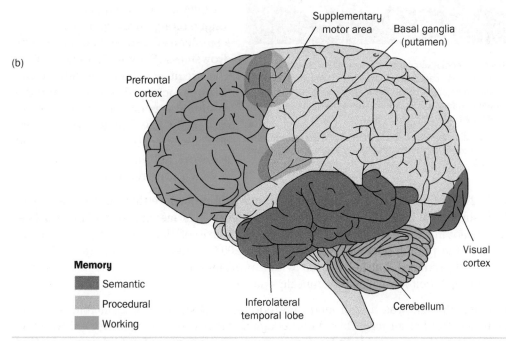

Figure 5.1   The brain areas involved in long-term memory. (A) A midline view of the areas involved in episodic memory, highlighting the medial temporal lobes including the hippocampus and parahippocampus. (B) A lateral view of the brain highlighting the areas involved in semantic, procedural and working memory.

Source: Adapted from Budson, A. E., & Price, B. H. (2005). Current concepts – memory dysfunction. *New England Journal of Medicine*, *352*(7), 692–699.

Box 5.1 When Things Go Wrong: The case of H.M.

'Every day is alone in itself, whatever enjoyment I've had, and whatever sorrow I've had' (H.M. in Milner et al., 1968, p. 217).

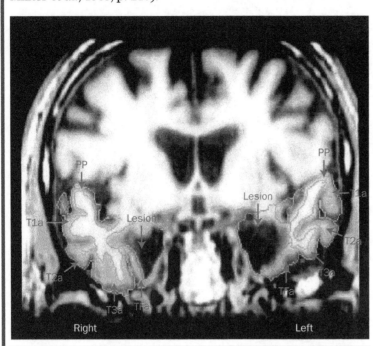

Figure 5.2   H.M.'s bilateral medial temporal lobe lesion. Left temporal-lobe white matter is more severely damaged than the right. (Coloured squares identify key sulci.) PP, planum polare; T1a, superior temporal gyrus, anterior; T2a, middle temporal gyrus, anterior; T3a, inferior temporal gyrus, anterior; Tfa, temporal fusiform, anterior.

Source: Kensinger, E. A., Ullman, M. T., & Corkin, S. (2001). Bilateral medial temporal lobe damage does not affect lexical or grammatical processing: Evidence from amnesic patient H.M. *Hippocampus, 11*, 347–360.

The severe memory impairment that H.M. developed following brain surgery changed the way that cognitive psychology approaches the subject of LTM. An only child, H.M. was born in Hartford, Connecticut in 1926. When he was seven years old, he was knocked down by a cyclist; the accident left him unconscious for several minutes (Scoville & Milner, 1957). By the age of 10 years, H.M. was experiencing minor seizures. Whether this was related to the accident is unclear; epilepsy was also noted in H.M.'s family history (Corkin, 2002). By the age of 16, H.M.'s condition had deteriorated. He experienced general convulsions, without warning and on a regular basis, with tongue-biting, urinary incontinence, loss of consciousness, and subsequent drowsiness (Scoville & Milner, 1957). The frequency and severity of the seizures increased over time and the condition was unresponsive to medication. By his twenties, H.M.'s condition was so severe that he could not work and his quality of life was severely compromised.

In 1953, at the age of 27, H.M. underwent an experimental surgical procedure that aimed to alleviate his symptoms. Neurosurgeon William Beecher Scoville resected H.M.'s medial temporal lobes (see Figure 5.1 and 5.2), removing the amygdala, the anterior two-thirds of the hippocampus, adjacent hippocampal gyrus and the parahippocampal gyrus (Squire, 2009). Following his operation, H.M.'s seizures were dramatically reduced, but he was left with a profound and pervasive memory impairment, a pattern of memory deficit known as the amnesic syndrome.

H.M.'s most striking impairment was a profound anterograde amnesia – he was unable to retain information encountered after his surgery. He did not recognize the researchers who worked with him regularly over five decades. He was unable to learn new words or the names of public figures he first encountered after the surgery. Half an hour after he ate lunch, he could not remember if, and what, he had eaten. It seemed that once the information left his consciousness, it was forgotten. However, as we will see, not all of his memory was affected; studies soon showed that he had some preserved function.

H.M. also showed some retrograde amnesia, that is loss of memory for information encountered before the onset of the amnesia. Scoville and Milner (1957) noted a retrograde loss spanning three years prior to the surgery. Later studies showed that H.M.'s retrograde amnesia extended to a period of 11 years prior to the onset of amnesia (Corkin, 2002). Retrograde amnesia tends to affect memory such that a temporal gradient is apparent: newer memories are more susceptible to disruption than are older memories, a pattern described by Ribot's Law. Consistent with this, H.M.'s memory of his childhood and adolescence was relatively spared. For example, he remembered that his first seizure had occurred on his sixteenth birthday (Hilts, 1995, p. 87). He did not, however, remember that a favourite uncle had died three years before his operation, nor did he recognize the medical staff he had met before his surgery (Shimamura, 1992).

H.M. had intact perception, intellect and language, and his personality was largely unchanged. He retained his sense of humour. When asked 'What do you do to try to remember?', he replied, 'Well, that I don't know 'cause I don't remember what I tried.' (Corkin, 2002, p. 158). This quote also illustrates H.M.'s insight into his own condition. H.M.'s IQ remained in the normal range, and even increased slightly after the surgery, presumably due to the reduction in seizure activity (Kalat, 2007). By comparison, his performance on the Wechsler Memory Scale was far lower than would be expected given his intellectual capacity (Scoville & Milner, 1957). His short-term memory was intact and his digit span (see Chapter 4) was normal – he could carry out a conversation and retain information as long as he could rehearse it in short-term memory. He showed good sustained attention – he could, for example, retain a three-digit number for up to 15 minutes if he was allowed to continually rehearse it. But as soon as his attention shifted from the task at hand, the information was lost.

> **Ribot's Law (1881)** of retrograde amnesia states that recently formed memories are more susceptible to impairment than are older memories.
>
> **Wechsler Memory Scale** is a widely used neurocognitive assessment that measures visual memory, auditory memory, and working memory.

Studies of H.M.'s memory showed that he retained some preserved learning. Milner et al. (1968) used a mirror drawing task to demonstrate this preserved ability. In the mirror drawing task (see Figure 5.3), the participant is presented with a star shaped pattern consisting of one star outline inside another. The task is to draw a line between the outer and inner stars – however, the participants can see their hand, the pencil and the stars only through a mirror (with left and right reversed). This is a tricky task, and participants generally require a few attempts before they can complete it. If H.M. could not form any new memories, then we would expect practice on the task to have no effect on his performance. But, as is evident on the graph shown in Figure 5.3, H.M.'s performance improved with practice. The time required to complete the task and the numbers of errors made decreased with practice. By the third day, H.M.'s performance was almost errorless.

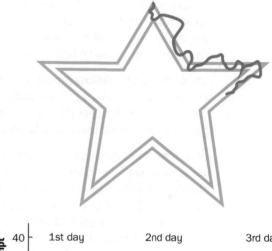

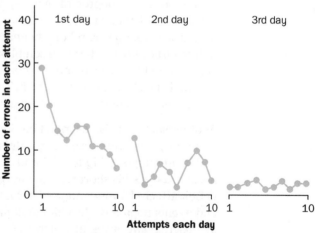

These data provided the first experimental demonstration of preserved learning in amnesia; other preserved domains of learning also became apparent (see Corkin, 2002, for an overview). For example, five years after his operation, H.M. moved with his

Figure 5.3 H.M.'s performance on the mirror-drawing task. The upper panel shows the double-star outline and a typical early attempt to remain with the boundaries of the two starts. By day 3, H.M.'s performance is close to error-free, showing that learning has occurred.

Source: Eichenbaum, H. (2011). *The cognitive neuroscience of memory: An introduction.* Oxford: Oxford University Press. Data from Milner et al. (1968).

parents to live in a bungalow near Hartford, Connecticut. Tested a few years later, he was able to draw an accurate floor plan of his house.

In December 2008, H.M. died at the nursing home where he had lived for 28 years, and his real name, Henry Gustav Molaison, was released. While he could not have fully appreciated his contribution to the scientific understanding of memory processes, he did seem to appreciate that the research would be of use. Speaking about his neurosurgeon, he once remarked, 'What he learned about me helped others, and I'm glad about that' (Corkin, 2002, p. 159).

Causes of amnesia include effects of brain surgery (as in H.M.'s case), infections such as herpes simplex encephalitis, head injuries or stroke, or conditions such as Korsakoff's syndrome (Parkin & Leng, 1993). Korsakoff's syndrome (or Wernicke-Korsakoff syndrome) describes a type of brain damage related to thiamine (vitamin B1) deficiency. It generally occurs following prolonged alcohol abuse in pre-disposed individuals, although it has been reported in other groups affected by inadequate nutrition. This reaction to thiamine deficiency often goes undiagnosed, and the opportunity to reduce some of its effects by administering thiamine is lost. Often, alcohol-misusing patients present with non-specific symptoms or with symptoms that mirror those of alcohol intoxication and therefore the illness can cause severe damage before it is diagnosed (Kopelman et al., 2009). Korsakoff's syndrome is associated with damage to thalamic, mammillary body and frontal brain areas (Colchester et al., 2001; Kopelman et al., 2001).

Amnesia can also follow injury, as in the case of N.A., a man who, at the age of 22 years, sustained a stab wound to the brain when a colleague accidentally thrust a miniature fencing foil up his nostril (Squire & Slater, 1978; Teuber et al., 1968), causing damage to the left dorsal thalamus and adjacent structures (Squire & Moore, 1979).

Infections such as herpes simplex encephalitis, a viral infection of the brain, can also cause amnesia. This illness can cause extensive brain damage to the temporal areas within a very short time from onset of symptoms. The case of Clive Wearing, a classical musician and scholar who developed herpes simplex encephalitis after a sudden illness demonstrates the degree of memory loss that can result. His retrograde memory loss extended back for many years, affecting both episodic and semantic memories. However, his musical ability was relatively unaffected; he retained the ability to sight read music (although he avoided the more complex scores) and he could still play the piano. Although Wearing could play the piano, he was not *aware* that he could do so – when asked whether he could play, he could not affirm it. This case demonstrates the intact skill performance that occurs in amnesia in the absence of conscious recollection (Sacks, 2007).

Another such case is described by Stefanacci et al. (2000). Patient E.P. developed profound amnesia after viral encephalitis damaged his medial temporal lobes extensively and bilaterally (see Figures 5.1 and 5.2 above). Like H.M., E.P.'s intellectual ability was normal, as was his short-term memory and memory for skills. However, E.P.'s memory deficit affected a wide range of verbal and nonverbal tests, with memory for both facts and events impaired. His childhood memories remained intact, however. Stefanacci et al. describe two ways in which E.P.'s behaviour adapted over time, suggesting some spared memory function, in the absence of conscious awareness. First, over time he became accustomed to a particular researcher coming to test him (the researcher visited on over 150 occasions). Although he always denied that he had met the researcher before, after many such encounters, when she arrived he would greet her and sit at the table where they usually carried out the testing. Second, one particular test that E.P. completed more than 90 times involved using the eraser tip on a pencil to point to objects on a computer screen. While E.P. had no conscious recollection of having performed the task before, after taking the test about 50 times he began to hold the pencil eraser end towards the computer without any prompting.

In patients with amnesia, language and concepts are generally intact – the person can answer a question and can understand what a particular object is, and what it does. However, most of our knowledge about the world and about language is laid down early in life. Is this kind of memory spared because it is different from our recollections of past events? Or is it spared because it is learned early on in life? What happens to new words that patients with amnesia will have encountered only recently? One of the problems with testing patients with amnesia is being sure that the information was stored in memory in the first place – 'we must never underestimate one of the most obvious reasons for forgetting, namely that the information was never stored in memory in the first place ' (Loftus, 1980, p. 74). Butters (1984) describes the case of P.Z., a college professor who developed amnesia as a result of Korsakoff's syndrome. He wrote an autobiography before his illness began, and so researchers had an accurate record both of personal events and concepts (e.g. new terms and theories in his field of expertise). He showed a similar retrograde amnesia for both life events and knowledge of scientific terms, whereby any terms encountered early in his career were intact but those acquired later were lost.

We turn to these different types of long-term memories in the next section. But first, in Box 5.2, we consider how popular depictions of, and misconceptions about, amnesia affect understanding of the symptoms, both in the public and in patients with a brain injury.

Box 5.2 Research Close Up: A new kind of amnesia?

Source: Smith, C. N. et al. (2010). Losing memories overnight: A unique form of human amnesia. *Neuropsychologia*, *48*, 2833–2840.

INTRODUCTION

Movies are an important source of information (or misinformation) about amnesia for many viewers and may influence people's understanding of memory loss. In the movie *50 First Dates* (directed by Peter Segal in 2004), a woman develops 'amnesia' following a head injury sustained in a car accident. In her case, memories gained each day are lost overnight while she sleeps. Each morning on waking she believes it is the morning of the day of the accident. As Baxendale (2004) noted, *50 First Dates* 'maintains a venerable movie tradition of portraying an amnesiac syndrome that bears no relation to any known neurological or psychiatric condition' (p. 1480). Such portrayals would seem to affect patients' expectations of memory loss after brain trauma. In 2010, Smith et al. reported an unusual case of functional (or psychogenic, that is of psychological origin) amnesia. As we will see, there are a number of problems with this assessment, however.

METHOD

The case is presented of a woman (F.L.) who reported suffering from amnesia after a car crash in which she lost consciousness for a short period. The woman claimed that her memory was normal during the day, but that she lost memories of the previous day when she slept at night. The woman's neurological examination was normal, and an fMRI scan revealed no abnormalities. She had no psychiatric history.

Three age-matched female volunteers acted as controls. A further two volunteers were asked to simulate the deficits F.L. reported. They were instructed to 'respond on the following tests as if you have no memory for material that was presented prior to today. That is, you should perform as you normally would and do your best when it comes to material that was given today. However, for any material that was not given today you should respond as if you have no memory for it' (p. 2834). A number of standard neuropsychological tests were used: Prose recall, paired-associate learning, recall of complex design, two-choice recognition memory for words and faces, and the Wechsler Memory Scale-Revised. The participants were also tested for recognition of photographs of scenes, mirror drawing, rotary pursuit, and retrograde memory tests such as the Autobiographical Memory Index, a test of news events/past public events, and a test of knowledge of cities. Testing took place over five days.

RESULTS

On the standard neuropsychological tests, F.L. showed impaired memory relative to the controls, while she had reasonably good, though not very good, memory for material learned within each day (Table 5.1). For recognition of scenes, F.L. could remember scenes studied earlier on the same day, but her performance was not as good as that of controls. She reported no memory for scenes seen the previous day, but when tested covertly in trials that mixed the previous day's scenes with the same-day scenes her performance was improved.

Table 5.1   F.L.'s performance on the neuropsychological tests, relative to controls and simulators

	Paragraph recall		Words		Faces	
	Immediate	Delay	Immediate	Delay	Immediate	Delay
F.L.	8	5	41	25	37	20
Controls	9.3	9.7	49.7	43.7	47.7	40.3
Simulators	7	6.5	49	27.5	43.5	22

Source: Adapted from Table 2, Smith, C. N. et al. (2010). Losing memories overnight: A unique form of human amnesia. *Neuropsychologia, 48,* 2833–2840.

F.L.'s performance on the motor skill tasks was poorer than both controls and simulators. On the retrograde memory tests, F.L. had no difficulty recalling autobiographical events from the time before the accident, but on the 'Recent Life' time period of the Autobiographical Memory Index she scored 19.5 out of 21 for personal semantic facts and 6 out of 9 for autobiographical events. These scores are not as low as might be expected given her complaints about her memory, but when questioned she said that many of the events were detailed in her journal, which she looks over each morning. Her memory for news events was poor and extended across the 30 previous years covered by the test. Her performance on the cities test was normal, with 84 per cent accuracy.

DISCUSSION

Smith et al. concluded that F.L. had a unique memory impairment, despite the obvious differences between F.L.'s impairment and the pattern seen in amnesia (e.g. her motor learning impairment). Because F.L.'s performance differed from that of the two 'simulators' who had been instructed to simulate her memory impairment, the authors conclude she was not malingering. But can we conclude that this is a case of a unique memory impairment? Merckelbach et al. (2011) outline three reasons why we should not accept that this is the case. First, they note the limited background information provided in the case study. For example, the case report notes a legal case, but does not say whether the individual was involved in litigation, which has been shown to affect scores on various tests of cognitive function. Second, Merckelbach et al. note that some of the neuropsychological test results suggest low effort or motivational issues. Third, they cite lack of connectivity with the scientific literature as a major cause for concern. Nowhere in the literature is a mechanism described whereby memories that are acquired during the day are 'wiped' while we sleep.

Further evidence would be required before we could safely conclude that Smith et al. have reported a new and unique memory impairment. But the case does show, however, that media portrayals affect the ways in which patients present with symptoms, and their role in patient beliefs about memory impairments. In this case, the patient's condition 'resolved' when she was restricted to sleeping for shorter periods, consistent with her belief that a longer period of sleep would destroy her memories. Smith et al.'s study demonstrates the profound influence that popular culture has on the public's understanding of complex conditions such as amnesia.

The cellular basis of long-term memory has been the subject of extensive study over recent decades. One of the most widely studied mechanisms by which memories may be maintained is long-term potentiation (LTP; see also Chapter 6), a mechanism that is inferred from animal models. LTP is a long-lasting increase in the strength of synapses that occurs with repeated stimulation. By contrast, long-term weakening of synapses can occur, a pattern referred to as long-term depression (LTD) or depotentiation. Originally observed in the hippocampus, activity that induces LTP has since been demonstrated in a number of brain areas (see Eichenbaum, 2010; Lynch, 2004, for a review).

THE STRUCTURE OF LTM

Is an apple bigger than a plum? What is 16×2? Who is the Prime Minister of the United Kingdom? What are the opening lyrics to your favourite song? How do you ride a bicycle? Providing answers to these questions requires access to long-term memory (LTM), but as is evident from the case of amnesia described in Box 5.1, there are different kinds of LTM.

William James (1890) made the distinction between primary memory and secondary memory. He described secondary memory, or long-term memory, as memory where 'an object which has been recollected is one which has been absent from consciousness altogether and now revives anew. It is brought back, recalled, fished up, so to speak, from a reservoir in which, with countless other objects, it lay buried and lost from view' (James, 1890, p. 648).

When we call something to mind, we are using short-term memory, but all of the memories that we have, whether we are currently thinking of them or not, are stored in LTM. If we use a computer analogy, all of the files you have stored on your hard drive is like LTM – you have files of different types, pictures, music, text documents and so on. If you want to use one of these files, you open it in a given application; the equivalent of calling it into short-term or working memory. When you see someone you know and call out their name, when you recognize a famous name in a news report, when you drive your car, when you remember to buy bread on your way home, all of these tasks rely on LTM.

MULTIPLE MEMORY SYSTEMS MODEL

As we saw in Chapter 4, short-term memory and working memory consist of a number of independent components. The Atkinson and Shiffrin (1968) model presented LTM as a single store. However, as is the case for short-term memory, there is general agreement that LTM consists of separate components; the precise number of components, their exact nature and the relationship between them continue to be debated.

The systematic investigation of memory began with Hermann Ebbinghaus's (1885) book *Über das Gedächtnis (On Memory)*. Ebbinghaus's studies focused on a particular aspect of memory, that required for rote verbal learning. Verbal learning involves the memorization and recall of word lists or other language-based stimuli such as nonsense syllables. Ebbinghaus used pronounceable consonant-vowel-consonant (CVC) trigrams (e.g. ROG, VAM, ZIG) as the basis for to-be-remembered lists. Ebbinghaus himself was the only subject in his experiments; he committed to memory long lists of nonsense syllables, measuring the time taken or the number of repetitions required until he could recite the list without error. His experiments are outlined in Chapter 6.

> Verbal learning refers to the area of experimental psychology concerned with how we learn and remember language-based items such as word lists.

Apart from James's distinction between primary and secondary memory (see Chapter 4), few early writers considered memory as consisting of different types. Research now addresses many sub-types of memory. In a tongue-in-cheek essay, Tulving (2007) lists 256 memory terms, including intentional memory, gist memory, olfactory memory, object-recognition memory, non-conscious memory, flashbulb memory, and generic memory. The use of so many terms for various kinds of memory reflects the breadth of tasks and skills that need to be considered. As Roediger, March and Lee (2002, p. 1) note, memory 'is a single term, but refers to a multitude of human capacities.' One way to approach this multitude of memory types is to group them according to whether they require conscious recollection.

Non-declarative or **implicit memory** refers to memory that is not accessed consciously and that we are not able to report verbally. It includes memory which benefits from previous experience but without our awareness of that experience.

Declarative or **explicit memory** involves conscious recollection of memories such as events, facts, people and places.

Free recall is when participants in a task recall the information in any order, without hints or clues to recall.

Cued recall is when a hint or cue is given to task participants to aid recall.

Recognition is when a task participant must verify if an item is a target.

It is generally agreed that there is a distinction in LTM between non-declarative (or implicit) memory and declarative (or explicit) memory. Ryle (1949) describes this distinction as 'knowing that' as opposed to 'knowing how'. We know that a bicycle has two wheels (declarative) and we know how to ride a bicycle (non-declarative). Declarative memory involves conscious recollection of information, whereas non-declarative memory is evident when performance that does not require conscious recollection is facilitated by prior learning – such as practising to ride a bicycle (Graf & Schacter, 1985, 1987; Schacter, 1987). For example, when an experienced driver drives a car, automatic processes guide behaviour; the driver does not have to consciously think about each step involved in driving and can often think about entirely unrelated matters while driving. However, past experience of driving is guiding current performance, even though the driver is not consciously dwelling on that past experience.

Some tests of memory rely on explicit recollection of information; others measure implicit memory. Methods such as free recall (e.g. what is the capital of France), cued recall (e.g. what word beginning with P is the capital of France?) and recognition (e.g. is Paris the capital of France?) require conscious recollection, whereas other methods, such as word association or word fragment completion (more on this below) do not.

The case of H.M., described at the beginning of this chapter, provides an example of this difference. H.M.'s amnesia led to a loss of declarative memory but non-declarative memory was relatively intact. H.M. could, for example, learn some new skills, such as mirror drawing. Cases of amnesia have provided clear evidence for a dissociation between declarative and non-declarative memory. Spiers et al. (2001) reviewed 147 cases of amnesia; in all cases, difficulties with declarative memory were noted, while non-declarative memory was intact.

An anecdotal account of intact non-declarative memory in amnesia was provided by the Swiss psychiatrist Edouard Claparede (1911). Claparede was treating a woman with amnesia who had been hospitalized for five years, but did not recognize the nurses and doctors who cared for her every day. The patient 'forgot from one minute to the next what she was told, or the events that took place' (p. 68). Claparede wondered whether she might be able to remember 'an intense impression involving affectivity' (p. 69). This 'intense impression' was to be conveyed by means of a pinprick! The next time Claparede greeted the woman (who did not remember him from previous occasions) he concealed a pin in his palm before shaking her hand – the pin pricked her, but 'the light pain was as quickly forgotten as indifferent perceptions: a few minutes later she no longer remembered it' (pp. 69–70). However, when a few more minutes had passed and Claparede again tried to shake her hand, the woman refused to extend her hand, even though she had no conscious recollection of the pinprick. She could not explain why she would not shake the doctor's hand. She said 'doesn't one have the right to withdraw her hand?' and, when pressed for an explanation, 'is there perhaps a pin hidden in your hand?' While she had no conscious recollection of the pin incident, she clearly retained some memory of the incident, at some level, that guided her behaviour. It has since become apparent that learning in amnesia can extend to a wide range of types of task; what these tasks have in common is that they do not require explicit memory, that is, they do not require retrieval of the original learning episode (Baddeley, 2004).

Endel Tulving (1972) proposed a tri-partite (three part) model of LTM. He made a distinction within declarative memory between episodic memory, memory for personally experienced events and episodes, including auto-biographical memory, and semantic memory, memory for facts about the world, including concepts and language. These different aspects of memory will be outlined in later sections of this chapter. Episodic memory relies on temporal context for recall; semantic memory does not. For example, let us say that you volunteer to take part in a memory experiment. On Day 1 you are pre-sented with a list of words, and on Day 2 you are given another list of words, some of which you saw on Day 1 and some of which you did not see. Your task is to identify the words that were presented on Day 1. This task is a test of your episodic memory – if you fail to remember one of the words, it is not the case that you have forgotten the word entirely, rather you have failed to recall that the word was presented in the context of the task on Day 1. Tulving (1972) makes the distinction between remembering and knowing; remembering that you saw the word is different from knowing the word (see Table 5.2).

> Episodic memory is memory for events, experiences and episodes. Semantic memory is memory for facts and knowledge about the world.

However, not everyone agrees that there is a clear-cut distinction between episodic and semantic memory. Cohen and Squire (1981) pointed out that not all information can be reliably classified as either episodic or semantic. For example, if you are asked if you are a good writer, and you agree that you are, are you recalling a specific event, say a good grade on a recent assignment (episodic memory), or are you using your knowledge about yourself and your own abilities (semantic memory) to answer the question? (See also Baddeley, 1984; Ratcliff & McKoon, 1986.) The distinction also blurs when we consider autobiographical memory (discussed later in this chapter). Squire (1986, 1993, 2004) proposed that LTM should be conceptualized as distinguishing between declarative (explicit) and non-declarative (implicit) memory, where declarative memory includes both episodic and semantic memory (see Figure 5.4).

Table 5.2 Some key differences between episodic and semantic memory (see Tulving, 1972).

Episodic	Semantic
Memory for events, experiences and situations	Memory for facts and language
Time-dependent	Not time dependent
Experiential	Symbolic
More vulnerable to interference	Less vulnerable to interference
Reflects questions such as When? Where?	Reflects questions such as What?
Reflects statements such as: 'I remember . . .' '"Dog" was in the word list presented during the experiment.' 'I had carrot soup for lunch.'	Reflects statements such as: 'I Know . . .' 'My teacher's name was Mr Brown.' 'Paris is the capital city of France.'

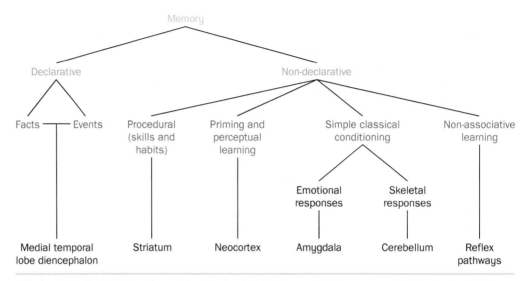

Figure 5.4   Squire's taxonomy of long-term memory. The types of memory and related brain structures involved in aspects of declarative and non-declarative memory.

Source: Reprinted from Squire, L. R. (2004) Memory systems of the brain: A brief history and current perspective. *Neurobiology of Learning and Memory, 82*, 171–177, with permission from Elsevier.

Whether semantic and episodic memory involve separate or interacting stores continues to be debated. The evidence supporting a dissociation between non-declarative and declarative memory is far clearer, however.

NON-DECLARATIVE MEMORY

When we think of remembering, we generally think of the conscious recall of an event, experience, or fact. However, much use of memory occurs without our conscious awareness. When you play a musical instrument, read a letter string, drive a car, memory is involved, though you may not be conscious of the role it is playing in guiding your actions. A whole range of other tasks involve this kind of non-conscious memory.

Non-declarative memory is demonstrated on a wide range of tasks, including classical conditioning, motor skill learning (see Chapter 8), and priming, which will be discussed later in this chapter (see Figure 5.4). While there are likely to be differences between these subcategories of non-declarative memory, it makes sense to group them as memories that do not require conscious recollection. Tulving (1985b, 1999) proposed that this type of memory, unlike declarative memory, is found in all animals and that it is, in evolutionary terms, the oldest of the LTM systems.

SKILL LEARNING

Procedural memory is a type of non-declarative memory involving memory for how to perform skills and actions.

One example of non-declarative memories is procedural memory, which includes knowledge of skills such as driving, tying your shoelaces, writing your signature, playing a musical instrument, or the motor skills involved in a sport. Procedural memory is closely associated with motor performance but cognitive skills (such as being able to subtract two numbers, for example) and some perceptual learning skills are also aspects of procedural memory. Such knowledge is generally acquired over time through practice and can become automatic; in fact, sometimes when we concentrate our thoughts on a skill we can disrupt the processes involved and performance can suffer, an effect sometimes referred to by sports psychologists as 'paralysis by analysis' (for an overview of how cognitive psychology has informed sports psychology see Moran, 2012; see also our discussion of 'choking' in Chapter 8).

Procedural memory is generally preserved in patients with amnesia, as we saw in H.M.'s case earlier. Clive Wearing, a musician who developed severe amnesia following a viral illness, also had intact procedural memory. His declarative memory was severely impaired, with a profound anterograde loss in addition to an extreme retrograde loss. However, his musical ability remained relatively unaffected by the illness; he retained the ability to sight read (although he avoided the more complex scores) and could still play the piano (see Sacks, 2007).

Scan to watch a video of Clive Wearing illustrating memory loss but retained musical skill

HABIT LEARNING

Habit learning refers to memory acquired over time through repeated associations between stimuli and responses. This type of memory has been studied extensively in experimental animals but it remains poorly understood in humans because of the difficulty in eliminating the influence of conscious (declarative) memory on the learning situation (Bayley et al., 2005; Knowlton et al., 1994). One set of tasks that has been used to investigate habit learning in the absence of input from declarative memory involves probabilistic classification learning. In such tasks, participants are required to learn a set of associations. The associations are not obvious, and they cannot be readily memorized, because of the probabilistic nature of the associations between stimulus and response. The participant has to use information gleaned across many trials to complete the task successfully (Knowlton et al., 1994). In one such study, Squire and Zola (1996) had participants complete a weather prediction task. On each trial, participants had to predict a weather outcome (rain or sunshine) based on one, two, or three cues (out of a total of four possible cues) that were presented (see Figure 5.5). Cues consisted of

> **Probabilistic classification learning** involves learning a set of associations that cannot be readily memorized, and information from across many trials must be used to complete the task.

In this learning game, you are the weather forecaster.
You will learn how to predict rain or shine using a deck of four cards:

Figure 5.5   The weather forecasting task. On each trial, participants have to predict which of two weather outcomes (sun or rain) will occur, given one, two or three of four cues. The two outcomes occur equally often and the weather outcome is determined by a probabilistic rule based on the individual cards – each of the cues is associated either 75 per cent, 57 per cent, 43 per cent or 25 per cent (approximately) with sunshine.

Source: Squire, L. R., & Zola, S. M. (1996). Structure and function of declarative and nondeclarative memory systems. *Proceedings of the National Academy of Sciences, USA, 93*, 13515–13522. © 1996 National Academy of Sciences, U.S.A.

cards featuring squares, triangles, circles and diamonds. Each cue was associated with a weather outcome with a fixed probability, with associations of 75 per cent, 57 per cent, 43 per cent or 25 per cent. When more than one cue was presented on a trial, outcome was predicted by conjoint probabilities. Participants responded by pressing a key to select a weather outcome, and they were given immediate feedback as to whether their response was correct or incorrect. Participants could not rely on memory for previous trials to learn the task, because the same configuration of cues had the potential to generate different outcomes, and so this ensured that declarative memory was not involved in the task. Typically on this task, participants' performance improves from guessing (50 per cent) to about 70 per cent correct. Patients with amnesia typically learn the task at about the same rate as controls, with similar response accuracy (about 65 per cent) after training over a 50 trial block (Squire, 2008; Squire & Zola, 1996). Patients with amnesia, while able to perform almost as well on controls on the task, remain unable to report factual details about the training episode, however (Squire & Zola, 1996).

REPETITION PRIMING

Priming refers to an implicit memory effect whereby exposure to a stimulus affects a subsequent response.

Category exemplar tasks are those where participants are given category names one by one and are asked to generate exemplars for each. Some categories will have been encountered during an earlier stage.

The term priming refers to the facilitatory effect of previous exposure to a stimulus on the subsequent processing of that stimulus or a related stimulus. For example, performance may be faster, accuracy may be improved, or there may be a bias towards a particular stimulus. In a typical repetition priming study, a set of stimuli are presented during a study phase; then, in the test stage, these (or related) stimuli are presented alongside new stimuli, and processing differences are examined. Priming can be conceptual or perceptual, depending on whether it is the stimulus form or the stimulus meaning that is salient (e.g. Roediger et al., 1989). Examples of perceptual priming tasks include word fragment completion, word stem completion, and identification of degraded stimuli or stimuli presented at the visible threshold. Conceptual priming tasks include category exemplar tasks and word association. Most repetition priming tasks do not require declarative memory processes and performance is unimpaired in patients with amnesia (Graf et al., 1984; Vaidya et al., 1995).

An example of a priming task is provided by Tulving et al. (1982). Their participants learned a list of low frequency words (e.g. toboggan, theorem, pendulum). The words were presented singly on a screen at a rate of one every 5 seconds. Participants were instructed to look at each word and they were told to 'Do the best you can to learn each of the words as they appear, as you will be tested later for your memory of them.' Participants were tested after one hour and again after one week. There were two types of test, a yes-no recognition test (declarative memory) and a fragment completion test (non-declarative memory). In the fragment completion test, participants were given incomplete word fragments, with dashes indicating the position of missing letters (e.g. _ob_gg_ _) and they were asked to complete the word by replacing the dashes with letters. Half were words from the target list, and half had not been seen during the learning phase. The results showed that performance was facilitated for fragments of words that had been presented during the learning phase. Tulving et al. also compared performance on the fragment completion task with that on the recognition task, thereby comparing implicit and explicit memory. They noted that recognition was not better for fragments that had been successfully identified compared to those that had not been identified, supporting the notion that fragment completion requires non-declarative, but not declarative, memory.

Squire (1987) used a similar task to demonstrate intact repetition priming in the absence of declarative memory in amnesic patients. A word stem completion task was used in this case. Participants studied a list of words. Then, in the test phase, the initial part of the word, the stem, was presented and the participants had to complete the word. For example, the word 'element' might have appeared in the study list. During testing, the stem ele___ would be presented. Note that there are several plausible responses to this stem; 'element' has been seen on the study list, but 'elephant' would also complete the stem. Squire used three test conditions. In the free recall task, participants had to report as many words from the list as they could. In a cued recall task, participants were presented with stems and were asked to recall words from the list that would complete the word. In the completion task, participants were asked to complete the stem – no mention was made of recalling words from the previous list. As is clear from Figure 5.6, patients with amnesia performed as well as controls on the fragment tasks, supporting the idea that the task relies on non-declarative, implicit memory. However, those with amnesia showed the usual deficit in performance on the declarative memory recall tasks, compared to controls.

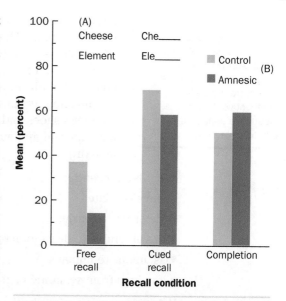

Figure 5.6   Word stem completion task from Graf et al. (1984). Patients with amnesia and controls saw common words and then had to recall them (free recall), or recall them given the first three letters (cued recall). (A) Two examples of study items. (B) Performance of the patients with amnesia and controls differs depending on the test used.

Source: Adapted from Squire, L. R. (1987). *Memory and brain*. New York: Oxford University Press.

Evaluation

These data support a dissociation between declarative and non-declarative memory, but it is important to appreciate that there is considerable interaction between the memory systems, and they are often bound together in terms of everyday experience. To use Squire's (2009) example, a frightening childhood event, such as being knocked over by a big dog, could provide a lasting conscious memory for the event, but it may also result in the person developing a fear of dogs.

The relationship between declarative and non-declarative memory may go even further. Some cognitive psychologists have argued that there is some procedural involvement in many tests of declarative or episodic memory (Kolers & Roediger, 1984). Similarly, studies examining memory consolidation have shown declarative and procedural memory processing to interact (e.g. Brown & Robertson, 2007). We turn to this, declarative, aspect of memory next.

DECLARATIVE MEMORY

EPISODIC MEMORY

Episodic memory is the system within LTM that allows us to remember our past experiences; it enables us to consciously re-experience past events (Tulving, 1983, 2002b). Tulving (e.g. 2002b) notes three key properties of episodic memory. First, it is associated with our subjective sense of time that allows use to engage in 'mental time travel' – we can, in the mind, 'travel back' to remember past events. The phrase 'that takes me back' reflects this property of episodic memory and is, Tulving argues, uniquely human. Second, there is a connection to the self. Self-reflection is a key aspect to this

Autonoetic ('self-knowing') consciousness allows humans to use memory to relive past events and imagine ourselves in the future, from a self-perspective. It is a distinctive aspect of episodic memory.

kind of memory; as Tulving (2002) puts it, 'mental time travel requires a traveller' (p. 2). Third, mental time travel is associated with a special kind of conscious awareness called autonoetic (self-knowing) consciousness. This type of consciousness allows us to imagine ourselves in the future, and to plan ahead and set goals. It allows us to recall a past incident and imagine how we might have behaved differently. It lets us put ourselves in another's shoes and answer hypothetical questions such as 'If you were the juror how might you have voted?' Tulving (2002, p. 5) proposes that episodic memory:

- evolved recently;
- develops late;
- deteriorates early;
- is vulnerable to disruption by brain damage;
- is unique to humans;
- evolved from semantic memory.

Episodic memory might be thought of as the pinnacle of human memory, and its loss in amnesia is devastating. But episodic memory is not simply a record of past experiences; memories are constructed anew when they are called to mind, and can differ from the original event, and with each recall of the event. In other words, memory is a constructive process.

Memory as a (re)constructive process

The concept of 'mental time travel' neatly describes the experience of remembering or of reminiscing. We have all experienced how vivid and well-defined past memories can be. However, it is important to appreciate that episodic memory is not an exact copy, it is not like watching a replay of an event or situation. Memory is constructive and when we recall our past experiences, we reconstruct the event in our minds, using information gained before, after and at the time of the event or episode itself.

Bartlett's (1932) pioneering research opposed the view that memory is based on 'unalterable traces', a notion typically identified with Freud's account of memory (e.g. 1900/1976). Bartlett showed that memory is reconstructive and not a passively recalled record of events. He wrote (1932, pp. 204–205):

> The first notion to get rid of is that memory is primarily or literally reduplicative, or reproductive. In a world of constantly changing environment, literal recall is extraordinarily unimportant. If we consider evidence rather than supposition, memory appears to be far more decisively an affair of construction rather than one of mere reproduction

That is not to suggest that recall is necessarily inaccurate, only that it is not an exact replica of past experience – it can be open to modification and error. It becomes important then to identify the conditions under which memory might be trusted as accurate and those that might lend themselves to inaccurate recollection.

Bartlett focused on the role of the schema (plural, schemata, or schemas) in remembering past events. He defined the schema as 'an active organization of past reactions, or of past experiences' (Bartlett, 1932, p. 201). Recall involved 'condensation, elaboration and invention . . . and these all very often involve the mingling of materials belonging originally to different "schemata" ' (p. 205). Schemas are organized memory structures that allow us to apply past experience to novel situations so as to guide behaviour. As such, they demonstrate the interaction between semantic and episodic memory.

Schemas produce expectations that reduce the ambiguity of new situations; however, these expectations can sometimes lead to erroneous judgements. For example, Brewer and Treyens (1981) found that participants in a memory task often reported items they had expected to see, based on context, but which had in fact not been present (see Box 5.3). The influence of schemas is also seen in boundary extension errors, whereby people remember more of a visual scene than was originally presented (see Chapter 4).

Box 5.3 Research Close Up: The role of schemas in memory

Source: Brewer, W. F., & Treyens, J. C. (1981). Role of schemata in memory for places. *Cognitive Psychology*, *13*, 207–230.

INTRODUCTION

As we encounter new information, schemas can guide our memories so that we are more likely to remember some objects or events than others (schema-consistent items) and we may even mistakenly 'remember' items that were not present. This schema-expectancy effect was demonstrated by Brewer and Treyens (1981). Their study set out to examine five hypotheses (p. 207):

(a) that schemas determine which objects are encoded into memory;

(b) that schemas act as frameworks for episodic information, so that schema-consistent information is more likely to be recalled;

(c) that information from schemas is integrated with episodic information, so that schema-consistent items might be recalled in error;

(d) that retrieval is guided by schemas; and

(e) that schemas influence what is communicated when retrieving information from memory.

METHOD

Brewer and Treyens set up a room so that it looked like the office of a graduate student. The objects within the room were carefully selected and had been coded for saliency and schema-expectancy. The saliency rating was essentially an index of how noticeable the object was within the room. The schema-expectancy rating was an index of how consistent an object was with the 'office schema'. The room contained a typewriter (it was the early 1980s after all) and typical desk items. There was a table with coffee-making facilities. Another table held a Skinner box (an essential piece of kit for the 1980s graduate student) as well as electronic parts and some tools. There was shelving on one wall, with box files, and the other walls contained a bulletin board and a calendar, among other items (see Figure 5.7). There were a few items that would not be expected: a skull and a toy top, for example. Some items that would be expected were missing; there were no books in the office, for example, nor was there a telephone.

Figure 5.7   The room used in Brewer and Treyens's study, showing the typical (e.g. chair) and less typical (e.g. skull) objects that might be recalled.

Source: Reprinted from Brewer, W. F., & Treyens, J. C. (1981). Role of schemata in memory for places. *Cognitive Psychology*, *13*, 207–230, with permission from Elsevier.

The participants ($n = 86$) were brought into this room, individually, and asked to wait there until they were called to take part in an experiment. After a delay of 35 seconds, the researcher returned and asked the participant to follow them to a nearby room. After a further minute, the participant was then told the real purpose of the experiment: to test their memory for the room they had just been in. Thirty participants completed a written recall task, 29 completed drawing recall (an outline drawing of the room was provided) and 27 were tested using verbal recognition only. Participants had a minimum of 15 minutes to complete the retrieval task, and could continue up to 30 minutes.

RESULTS

Objects reported by participants were classified as objects that were present, inferred objects that had not been present, or room frame objects (that is objects that were part of the room structure, such as the door, frame, doorknob, light switch, etc.). In total, 88 items were reported by one or more participants: seven were room frame objects, 62 objects had been present and 19 were inferred objects. The inferred objects tended to be schema-consistent items. For example, 30 per cent of participants reported that there were books in the office; in fact there had been none. For objects that had been present, recall was better for items that were consistent with the office schema.

In the verbal recognition condition, participants were presented with 131 object names; 61 of the named objects had been present in the office, 70 had not. Thirteen objects that had not been in the room, but that were consistent with the office schema, were mistakenly identified as having been present. Saliency was positively associated with memory performance in all three retrieval conditions: the more noticeable an object the more likely the participant would recall it and the less chance that an error would occur.

DISCUSSION

The Brewer and Treyens study made a number of important contributions to our understanding of schemas in memory. First, it brought a measure of ecological validity to a laboratory task, while at the same time controlling variables such as duration of exposure and testing time. Second, the study showed that information from schemas is integrated with episodic information, such that the resulting memory is a combination of schema and stimulus information. Third, the need to separate saliency from schema consistency is apparent. Salient objects, such as the skull, were likely to be recalled; they stand out as being distinctive. Some schema-consistent objects may be more salient than others. Furthermore, the participants, as students, would have been more familiar with a graduate student's office than they might have been with a novel location.

The study also showed how information from schemas affects retrieval, and that correct identification of objects, and erroneous recall of non-present objects could be predicted by schema consistency. More recent studies have found similar effects of schema influence during retrieval of eyewitness memories (e.g. Tuckey & Brewer, 2003), a topic addressed in Chapter 6.

Bartlett (e.g. 1932) was interested in the way in which participants recalled stories and the influence that memory biases, such as are provided by schemas, might have on retrieval. His method involved presenting participants with a story and testing their recall using a repeated reproduction method. They subsequently wrote down what they recalled of the story and their recollection of the details of the story was tested at various time intervals. Bartlett also used a serial reproduction technique, whereby one participant communicated the story to the next and so on, similar to the children's game. One story Bartlett used was a North American Indian folk tale called 'The War of the Ghosts'. This story, collected and translated by anthropologist Franz Boas, contains concepts that are quite unusual from a Western cultural tradition, with themes of supernatural entities, and imperviousness to harm. The story is reproduced in Figure 5.8.

One night two young men from Egulac went down to the river to hunt seals, and while they were there it became foggy and calm. Then they heard war cries, and they thought: "Maybe this is a war party." They escaped to the shore, and hid behind a log. Now canoes came up, and they heard the noise of paddles, and saw one canoe coming up to them. There were five men in the canoe, and they said: "What do you think? We wish to take you along. We are going up the river to make war on the people." One of the young men said: "I have no arrows." "Arrows are in the canoe," they said. "I will not go along. I might be killed. My relatives do not know where I have gone. But you," he said, turning to the other, "may go with them." So one of the young men went, but the other returned home. And the warriors went on up the river to a town on the other side of Kalama. The people came down to the water, and they began to fight, and many were killed. But presently the young man heard one of the warriors say: "Quick, let us go home: that Indian has been hit." Now he thought: "Oh, they are ghosts." He did not feel sick, but they said he had been shot. So the canoes went back to Egulac, and the young man went ashore to his house and made a fire. And he told everybody and said: "Behold, I accompanied the ghosts, and we went to a fight. Many of our fellows were killed, and many of those who attacked us were killed. They said I was hit and I did not feel sick." He told it all, and then he became quiet. When the sun rose he fell down. Something black came out of his mouth. His face became contorted. The people jumped up and cried. He was dead.

Figure 5.8 **'The War of the Ghosts' story illustrates how memory is influenced by prior knowledge.** Participants were told the story and had to re-tell it; they changed aspects of the story to fit their expectations.

Source: Bartlett, F. C. (1932). *Remembering: A study in experimental and social psychology*. Cambridge: Cambridge University Press (p. 65).

As participants recounted the tale, they shortened the details considerably, remembering the gist rather than the complete story. However, they also made considerable changes to the detail of their abbreviated versions, changes that Bartlett characterized as 'transformation in the direction of the familiar' (p. 178). For example, Bartlett noted that the phrase 'something black came out of his mouth' was replaced by one participant as the more familiar 'foamed at the mouth' (p. 72), while another participant stated that 'his soul passed out from his mouth' (p. 127). Similarly, participants made inferences based on the limited information provided in the story. For example, in the story, one of the young man declines the offer to join the group, saying 'I will not go along. I might be killed. My relatives do not know where I have gone. But you' he said, turning to the other, 'may go with them'. One participant recalled this as 'But you have no one to expect you' (p. 71) while another wrote 'You have no parents' (p. 20). In both cases, participants are making an inference that is plausible given the information in the story; but they are mistaken in thinking that the information was provided in the story. They are using information from memory schemas to adapt the story. Bartlett noted that the confidence with which the tale was recounted did not reflect its accuracy (p. 61), a problem that is discussed further in Chapter 14, when we look at the issue of eyewitness memory.

Bartlett was not himself immune to memory distortion. Brewer (1999) notes that Bartlett reported that one participant had replaced 'paddling' with 'rowing', but in fact the word 'paddling' does not appear in the story, which only mentions that the noise of paddles was heard.

Bartlett's study is often presented as demonstrating that memory is inherently inaccurate. However, this is an oversimplification of his findings. Bartlett was keen to use more ecologically valid tasks, but he himself noted that the types of story he used were likely to encourage abbreviation and transformation. He noted, for example, that the stories contained 'characters which would normally be expected to undergo much change in the course of transmission' (Bartlett, 1932, p. 119).

There are further issues that must be considered concerning Bartlett's methodology and his description of his results. It is also recognized that his quest for ecological validity was not entirely successful. As Roediger et al. (2000) point out, 'the War of the Ghosts' is 'about as similar to normal prose as . . . nonsense syllables are to words' (p. 117). That said, Bartlett's work was pivotal in showing that memory is a reconstructive process, a finding that has been confirmed many times since.

When we think of episodic memory, we tend to focus on the past, to think of it in terms of remembrance of past events. But the past cannot be changed, and so it makes sense for the cognitive system to focus resources on the past only insofar as it contributes to thinking about the future; the adaptive function of memory is to allow us to use past experiences in order to adapt our behaviour so as to deal more effectively with the present and future events. For example, you may remember a past examination, and perhaps regret choosing to answer a particular question. Perhaps you got overly anxious and this affected your performance. Or perhaps you look back with satisfaction and note a good performance. The focus on past performance only serves a purpose if it influences future behaviour, that is, if you can learn from the experience and apply it to a future examination or similar experience. The adaptive function of episodic memory lies in its potential for imagining of future events (Suddendorf & Corballis, 2008). Memory that allows us to keep track of plans and carry out intended actions is called prospective memory; it allows us to remember to remember (Winograd, 1988).

> **Prospective memory** allows us to remember to perform certain actions. It has been described as the ability to 'remember to remember'.

PROSPECTIVE MEMORY AND IMAGINING FUTURE EVENTS

Tulving (2004) proposed that a key role of the episodic memory system is to allow people to mentally 'travel forward in time'. This use of memory is an essential component of forward planning – it allows us to, for example, imagine the future, to think about what career path we might like to take after completing our degrees, it allows us to plan a summer holiday, and it allows us to remember to buy bread on the way home from work. This latter type of planning involves a type of memory called prospective memory, that is, memory for intended actions, actions that are to be performed at some future time (see Einstein et al., 2005). Individuals with amnesia lose their prospective memory, and find it difficult to conceptualize a personal future (Klein & Loftus, 2002). We use this kind of memory every day – remembering to take medication at a certain time, remembering what we intended to buy when we get to the store, remembering to submit an essay before the deadline, for example, all require prospective memory.

The most common prospective memory failure involves neglecting to carry out an action at the appointed time (Ellis & Cohen, 2008), forgetting that we intended to post a letter by 6p.m., for example. Prospective memory lapses often involve a failure to interrupt habitual routines (e.g. going straight home instead of taking a detour to the post office to mail the letter). They differ from action slips, errors within established or habitual routines, such as forgetting to brush your teeth before bed, or putting sugar into the teapot instead of into the cup (Morris, 1992, p. 199). Prospective memory is normally highly effective. March, Hicks and Landau (1998) found that while about a quarter of people's plans for the forthcoming week remained uncompleted, this was normally for reasons other than forgetting, which accounted for only 3 per cent of failures. However, when prospective memory fails the results can be embarrassing, or even catastrophic. Einstein and McDaniel (2005, p. 286) describe a distressing, and unfortunately not unique, example:

> **Action slips** involve an action being completed when it was not intended.

> After a change in his usual routine, an adoring father forgot to turn toward the daycare center and instead drove his usual route to work at the university. Several hours later, his infant son, who had been quietly asleep in the back seat, was dead.

In this case, a child was left to die in a hot car, because of a failure to interrupt the normal routine.

Unlike other kinds of memory, prospective memory is not necessarily triggered or cued by an obvious external event, rather retrieval in prospective memory is self-initiated (Craik, 1986). This aspect of the process 'defines one of the challenges to explanations of prospective memory: What happens to allow recall to take place?' (Morris, 1992, p. 202).

We can distinguish between event-based and time-based prospective memory tasks. Event-based memory may be triggered by a particular cue; for example, seeing my friend John reminds me to pass on a message to him, or passing by the computer reminds me to send an email to a friend. Tests of this kind of prospective memory are said to be event-based or event-cued tests (Graf & Grondin, 2008). When an intention is time-cued, a specific time prompts action, for example remembering to attend a meeting at 3p.m. or remembering to take a meal out of the oven in 30 minutes. Ellis (1988) makes the distinction between two kinds of intention, pulses and steps. Pulses are intentions that must be carried out at a particular time (e.g. I must remember to go to a dentist appointment at 4p.m.); steps are intentions that have a wider time frame (e.g. I must telephone John sometime this week). Ellis found that pulses are associated with better recall, and are more likely to be facilitated by means of a memory aid, such as making a note in a diary.

> Pulses involve intentions that are time-locked.
> Steps are intentions that have a wider time frame in which they can occur.

Wilkins and Baddeley (1978) carried out an early investigation of pulses or time-based prospective memory using a pill-taking analogue. This task simulates a real-life task; say, for example, you have to take antibiotics for a week, and you need to take a pill at specified times each day. Their participants (31 women) were required to push a button at 8.30a.m., 1p.m., 5.30p.m. and 10p.m., for one week, and the device recorded the times at which the button was pressed. While the majority of responses occurred within five minutes of the required time, 30 per cent of participants forgot to push the button on at least one occasion during the week and they were unaware of this omission for as many as 36 per cent of the errors. However, in no case did a participant forget that she had already pushed the button and repeat the action. Wilkins and Baddeley also found that those with poorer scores on a free recall task performed *better* on the time-based task. While there were a number of possible explanations in this case, Wilkins and Baddeley note that better free recall was associated with higher level of education, results which 'seem to support the myth that absent-minded persons tend to be those with higher educational level' (p. 33). However, Kvavilashvili (1987) found no correlation between participants' performance on retrospective and prospective memory tasks.

That is not to suggest that such results reflect the workings of two different components within memory; the task requirements are quite different in each case, and for a fair comparison to be made, more comparable tasks are needed. Such an example was provided by Hitch and Ferguson (1991). They had film goers recall films they had seen and report films they intended to see; they found a small but statistically significant correlation between retrieval of the seen and anticipated films. Furthermore, while memory for films already seen showed a recency effect, in that recall was better for those recently seen, retrieval of films to be seen in the future showed a proximity effect, with films to be seen sooner associated with better retrieval. Neuroscientific evidence also supports substantial overlap between brain areas engaged when thinking about the past and when imagining the future. Shared activity is evident in prefrontal cortex and medial temporal lobe regions, including the hippocampus and parahippocampal gyrus (see Schacter et al., 2007, for an overview).

It is only in the past two decades that prospective memory has begun to be studied systematically within cognitive psychology. For much of the history of memory research, the focus was on the past, on what was learned and remembered. Prospective memory is emerging as an interesting component of memory, and deficits in prospective memory have even been linked to clinical conditions such as compulsive behaviours, a topic we explore in Box 5.4.

Box 5.4 Research Close Up: Does a prospective memory deficit underlie checking compulsions?

Source: Cuttler, C., & Graf, P. (2007). Sub-clinical compulsive checkers' prospective memory is impaired. *Journal of Anxiety Disorders*, *21*, 338–352.

INTRODUCTION

Compulsive checking behaviours – repeatedly checking that a door is locked, for example, or that the oven has been switched off – are evident in over 50 per cent of patients with obsessive-compulsive disorder (OCD) and are found at a sub-clinical level (i.e. below the threshold for determining a clinical condition) in about 15 per cent of the general population (Stein et al., 1997). Compulsive checking can affect a wide range of behaviours and in OCD occurs as a rigid pattern of behaviour that causes distress and impairs functioning. One prominent theory of compulsive checking, the memory deficit theory, proposes that a deficit in prospective memory underlies the condition: the person knows, or believes, that they have a poor prospective memory and therefore thinks that they will make an error, this underlies the need to check than an intended action has been completed. This possibility of a link between memory and compulsive behaviours was explored in a study by Cuttler and Graf (2007).

METHOD

Cuttler and Graf (2007) recruited 126 undergraduate students (40 men and 86 women) and divided them into three groups on the basis of reported frequency of checking behaviours as reported on a standardized self-report inventory – three groups, high, low and medium checkers, were formed. Participants completed one event-cued and one time-cued prospective memory task, and they completed two questionnaires measuring subjective (self-reported) prospective memory. Event-cued episodic prospective memory was measured using a modified version of the standardized belonging task. In this task, a personal item (such as a watch, or a mobile phone) is taken from the participant at the start of the testing session and he or she is instructed to ask for its return at a later point, in this case when told later in the testing session 'we are now finished with all of the tests'. Participants rated how confident they were that they would remember to ask for the item back.

Time-cued episodic prospective memory was measured using the 'Phone-Call Reminder' task. Participants were told that the experimenter had to leave the room in exactly 30 minutes and that they should let the experimenter know when that 30 minutes had passed. Participants were allowed to check a stopwatch; they could look at it when and as often as they wished, but they were instructed to keep it facedown otherwise. Each stopwatch check was recorded, as was the time the participant gave the reminder.

RESULTS

The data showed that participants who reported more checking behaviours also reported more general prospective memory failures. Differences on the time-cued prospective memory task were not statistically significant, but those in the medium and high checking groups performed more poorly on the event-cued memory test (asking for their personal belonging back) compared to the low checkers: 56 per cent of the high checkers, 59 per cent of medium checkers and 80 per cent of low checkers requested the return of their belonging at the end of the task. There were also differences on the subjective measures of prospective memory, with reported frequency of prospective memory failure associated with checking behaviours, for example.

DISCUSSION

The Cuttler and Graf study supports the memory-deficit account of compulsive checking, that is the view that checking occurs in response to memory failure – the person cannot remember whether they locked the door and so they have to check it. Cuttler and Graf's study extended work in this area by considering prospective memory in addition to retrospective memory. However, the memory-deficit account of checking has produced conflicting results, particularly when patients with OCD are considered. Moritz et al. (2006) found no differences using source memory and meta-memory tasks comparing OCD patients with and without checking compulsions with controls and Jelinek et al. (2006) found no differences between patients with OCD and healthy controls on tests of verbal, nonverbal, and prospective memory. The relationship between memory failures and checking behaviours therefore remains to be established.

AUTOBIOGRAPHICAL MEMORY

Most of the day-to-day events that we will remember over a short period of time disappear from memory quickly. If you are asked what you ate for lunch today, you will probably be able to recall the details easily. If you are asked this question in a week's time, those details will likely have been lost. This makes sense, as it would not be useful for us to remember the banal details of everyday experience; we remember what is useful, salient or distinctive and other details are lost. As Conway (2009) notes, episodic memories provide a record of short-term goals and the degree to which they have been met. When certain episodic memories become embedded in the broader conceptual system, along with semantic memories, autobiographical memories are formed. These are our memories for both personal episodic information and personal semantic information. Personal episodic information includes personally experienced events, from everyday activities to once-in-a-lifetime experiences, for example remembering our tenth birthday or remembering when we first bought a car (see Brewer, 1996). Personal semantic information consists of facts about ourselves, such as where we were born, or where we went to school.

> Autobiographical memories are episodic memories for personally experienced events in a person's life.

Autobiographical memory involves personal experience (Linton, 1978) and it is closely associated with the self (Conway, 1992). Autobiographical memories might be thought of as our life histories, the facts and events that we can consciously recollect with some detail and that are time-marked as belonging to a particular phase in our lives. Even these highly personal memories are not free from bias, however. Memory is a reconstructive process, and when we recall life events, we reconstruct or interpret the memory 'record' rather than play it back passively.

Neisser (1981) provided an account of the potential susceptibility of autobiographical memory to bias and change. John Dean was the former counsel to US President Richard Nixon and a key witness during the Watergate hearings in the 1970s. Dean provided a detailed account of various conversations he took part in, including those with Nixon. His accounts were so detailed and expressed with such confidence as to be very convincing. However, conversations with the President conducted in the Oval Office had been recorded, as was standard practice, and when the transcripts of these recordings were released and compared with Dean's testimony, it became apparent that his memories were somewhat distorted. His recollection of particular conversations had been affected by subsequent events and by his beliefs about his own role in events. As Neisser remarked, Dean was basically correct as regards the existence of a 'cover-up' and the roles played by the particular individuals involved. But his account of the conversations was affected by memory distortions that involved, among other factors, confusion of single events with repeated episodes, and biases reflecting his own self-image and his perception of his role in the events. Dean's account of events might be characterized as 'systematic distortion at one level of analysis combined with basic accuracy at another' (Neisser, 1981, p. 102).

Dean's distortions that favoured his self-image mirror those reported in other contexts. For example, Bahrick et al. (1996) asked college students to recall their high school grades. The students accurately remembered A grades on 89 per cent of occasions, but D grades were remembered only 29 per cent of the time. In fact, 79 of the 99 participants inflated their grades and reported them as being higher than they actually were.

False memories are inaccurate recollections of events that did not occur, or distortions of events that did occur.

An experimental demonstration of such 'false memories' was provided by Loftus (1993, 1997). Her procedure was designed to increase the probability with which participants would report a fictional event as having occurred, in essence to plant a false memory that was 'at least mildly traumatic, had the experience actually happened' (Loftus, 1997, p. 71). Loftus had her participants recall childhood events that had been provided by close family members, who acted as confederates in the experiment. Three of the events had actually happened, one had not, but was a reasonably plausible childhood event – a shopping trip when the participant was five years old during which he/she had become separated from family members. The 'lost-in-the-mall' scenario contained elements that were plausible: the child was separated from family and lost for an extended period of time; he or she was upset and crying; an older woman helped the child; and he or she was subsequently reunited with the family (Loftus, 1997). Participants were invited to provide as much detail as they could about the four events.

Scan to watch Elizabeth Loftus talk about implanting false memories

Immediately after presentation of the scenarios, participants recalled, on average, 68 per cent of the true events. But close to a third of participants reported remembering the false event, and a quarter of participants continued to report recollection of the false event during two follow-up interviews.

Imagination inflation refers to strengthening of a false memory through repeated retrieval.
Demand characteristics are the aspects of a research study which convey the hypotheses or aims to the participants and may thereby shape performance.

Why would participants' false memories have persisted over time? Research has shown that imagining false events increases the likelihood that they will be 'recalled', an effect referred to as imagination inflation. Hyman and Pentland (1996), using a similar procedure as Loftus, had participants consider true and false events. In one condition, participants were instructed to imagine the event so as to aid their memory of it. The false event in this case was a scenario in which the participant, aged five, while playing with other children at a wedding, knocked over a punch bowl onto the parents of the bride. Those who imagined this scenario were more likely to report false memories of the event, although Hyman and Pentland note that demand characteristics may have played a role.

It remains a possibility that, unbeknownst to family members, the participant had experienced something like the false event described. Mazzoni and Mamon (2003) conducted an experiment using a false event which, while plausible, was not possible. They had their British participants consider two events; one was relatively common (having a dentist extract a tooth); the other described a medical test that is not conducted in the

United Kingdom (having a nurse remove a skin sample from the little finger). They found that imagining the false event increased the number of reported memories and belief that the event had taken place.

Anecdotal accounts of false memories for autobiographical episodes within families have been commonly reported. In such cases, a disputed memory arises between twins or siblings who are close in age, whereby the ownership of the memory is uncertain. Each member thinks that they are the protagonist in the event but the memory of one person has actually been appropriated by the other as their own. In such cases, visual imagery is often vivid, leading to confidence in the veracity of the memory. Sheen et al. (2001) found disputed memories to occur relatively frequently among twins, and that the content of disputed memories was not different to that of non-disputed memories, nor were disputed memories of more personal significance. In one case reported by Sheen et al., each of a pair of twins claimed that the other had been the protagonist in a 'running away from home' memory. Sheen et al. found that the details of the disputed memories were harder to recall, consistent with other unusual memory phenomena, such as *déjà vu* (see Box 5.5).

Scan to watch a clip detailing alternative theories of déjà vu

Déjà vu is a type of illusion of autobiographical memory; it might be described as the 'knowledge that a situation could not have been experienced, combined with the feeling that it has' (Thompson et al., 2004, p. 906). The term is applied to visual experience in particular. If you have visited a new place, a place you know you've never been before, and yet the scene looks familiar – the layout of the environment, the people present – then you are among the estimated two-thirds of the population that have experienced déjà vu (Brown, 2003, 2004a,b).

Brown and Marsh (2010) propose three possible mechanisms for déjà vu. The first is split perception; we get a brief glimpse of a visual scene before becoming fully aware of the scene. A second mechanism is implicit memory; we have already experienced the scene or part thereof but it has been stored such that only a feeling of familiarity is elicited when we re-encounter it. The third mechanism involves the notion of gestalt familiarity, that overall configuration of the present scene closely resembles a scene that we have encountered in the past, though the specifics are different. We therefore experience a sense of familiarity without being able to put our finger on why.

Research has established some consistent features of déjà vu (see Brown, 2003, 2004a,b). About two-thirds of people will experience déjà vu at some stage in their lives, and most will experience it more than once. Déjà vu is reported in equal frequency by men and women and it decreases with age. There is a positive relationship between déjà vu and both education and socioeconomic class, and frequency of travel is positively related to déjà vu experiences. Déjà vu is more likely to occur when the person is under stress or tired – it has, for example, been noted in increased frequency in soldiers on active duty (e.g. Linn, 1954). Déjà vu is most commonly reported for novel places or physical contexts, but something similar also occurs when new people are met and in novel conversations (Kusumi, 2006). The déjà vu experience typically lasts no longer than 30 seconds (Brown, 2004a), and it may be related to a number of other experiences including *déjà vecu* (the feeling that one has lived through a moment before), *jamais vu* (when something familiar momentarily seems unfamiliar), and *presque vu* (the feeling that we are about to experience a moment of insight). It is a normal aspect of memory but also occurs in pathological conditions, as Box 5.5 explores.

Box 5.5 Research Close Up: Mapping the déjà vu experience

Source: Brázdil, M., Marecek, R., Urbánek, T., Kašpárek, T., Mikl, M., Rektor, I., & Zeman, A. (2012). Unveiling the mystery of déjà vu: The structural anatomy of déjà vu. *Cortex*, *48*(9), 1240–1243.

INTRODUCTION

An estimated two-thirds of the normal population have experienced déjà vu, but it also occurs in a number of clinical contexts. It has been noted, for example, in some patients with temporal-lobe epilepsy, particularly as an aspect of the aura that may precede a seizure. The fact that the experience is similar in pathological and non-pathological contexts suggests a common underlying process, a suggestion that might predict structural differences in the brains of healthy participants who experience déjà vu compared to those who do not. Brázdil et al. (2012) set out to map any structural differences that might differentiate those who experience déjà vu from those who do not, within the normal population.

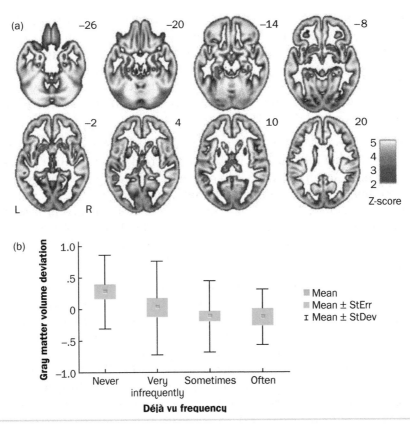

Figure 5.9 **(a) brain regions with grey matter volume in participants reporting déjà vu experiences; (b) the deviation from the mean volume is predicted by reported déjà vu frequency.** Figure 5.9 shows, in part (a), a set of regions with significantly less grey matter in participants who experienced déjà vu compared to those who do not. The areas include the bilateral mesiotemporal regions (with maximal effect within hippocampi and parahippocampal gyri), insular cortices, superior temporal sulci, basal ganglia and thalami. Part (b) shows the reduction in the mean deviation in grey matter volume, with participants who experience déjà vu showing significantly less grey matter in the relevant brain regions, with the deviation increasing with frequency of reported déjà vu.

Source: Reprinted from Brázdil, M., Marecek, R., Urbánek, T., Kašpárek, T., Mikl, M., Rektor, I., & Zeman, A. (2012). Unveiling the mystery of déjà vu: The structural anatomy of déjà vu. *Cortex*, *48*(9), 1240–1243, with permission from Elsevier.

METHOD AND RESULTS

Brázdil et al. (2012) had 113 healthy participants, with no psychiatric or neurological history, take a magnetic resonance imaging (MRI) scan of the brain. They completed a questionnaire on déjà vu experiences and were assigned to two groups: those who reported having experienced déjà vu and those that did not. A majority (77 per cent) reported having experienced déjà vu at some point. The imaging data were examined for differences in grey matter volume between the déjà vu and non-déjà vu groups, and a number of differences were noted (Figure 5.9), with a structural correlate for déjà vu in healthy participants (limbic-temporal network) identified that mirrored a pattern associated with temporal lobe epilepsy. The largest differences between the two groups were seen in the parahippocampal regions, in particular, an area associated with temporal lobe epilepsy. While there was no obvious lateralization, left hemisphere involvement seemed to be more extensive. No regions were found which showed significantly *more* grey matter in participants reporting déjà vu.

CONCLUSION

The data suggest a common physiology underlying normal and pathological déjà vu, and the authors' suggestion that 'small seizures' may underlie non-pathological déjà vu experiences is intriguing. However, as noted by Labate and Gambardella (2013), it is not clear how participants were screened for neurological status and a detailed neurological screening (to exclude the diagnosis of temporal lobe epilepsy) would be required before we could conclude that the mechanism is the same in healthy and pathological states.

As we have seen, autobiographical memory is mainly thought of as being about our experiences, recollections of events and episodes in our lives. But our knowledge of facts about ourselves (our names, where we were born, the name of our school) is an aspect of semantic memory, and it is to this aspect of declarative memory that we now turn.

SEMANTIC MEMORY

Semantic memory is our store of general knowledge about the world, the people in it, as well as facts about ourselves. It includes our knowledge of facts, language, and concepts (see Chapter 7). It contains all the knowledge we need in order to use language. It is a 'mental thesaurus, organized knowledge a person possesses about words and other verbal symbols, their meaning and referents, about relations among them, and about rules, formulas and algorithms for the manipulation of these symbols, concepts, and relations' (Tulving, 1972, p. 386). It contains knowledge we acquired at school and at university, as well as words we acquired as young children, and all the information that might be termed 'general knowledge'.

While episodic memory is personal and differs considerably from individual to individual (even people who have shared the same experience will have somewhat different memories of the event), people who share the same language and culture have much in common in terms of semantic memory. For example, people share common concepts and categorization structures. If you are asked to describe a dog, the description is likely to be similar to that provided by a friend. You might both mention features such as 'has a tail', 'barks', 'likes to chase a ball', and so on. Of course semantic memory also contains individual knowledge; a particular dog's name, for example, or the passcode for your bank card (see Box 5.6).

Box 5.6 Practical Application: Remembering passcodes

In the past few years, a number of high profile hacks have revealed prolific use of overly simplistic online passwords, with many computer users choosing names of family members, partners, or pets and with the sequences 'password', 'password1', and '123456' featuring amongst the most frequently used items (Burnett & Kleiman, 2005). Personal identification number (PIN) codes would seem to be no better. A survey by Bonneau et al. (2012) found that common PIN codes included birthdays, years of birth and the sequences 1234 and 1111. (Given that most people carry some form of identification along with their ATM card, a thief who acquires the ATM card will likely also have access to the birthday.) Bonneau et al. estimate that, based on reported passcodes, a thief could gain use of an ATM card once every 11 or so stolen wallets, using birthday information and other common codes. PIN codes based on words also showed limited variety, with 'love' and its corresponding PIN 5683, frequently used.

In selecting a passcode, there is a trade-off between security and memorability. While a complex, long and random passcode will be secure, it is only useful if you can remember it, along with the many other complex passcodes that you may be required to retain. The limitations of human memory typically require a compromise. What advice can cognitive psychology provide that will help you set up a secure, but memorable, passcode?

First, do not think that you have to use random passcodes, particularly if you have to remember multiple passcodes. Random passcodes are difficult to remember and are not necessarily more secure than passwords based on mnemonic phrases (e.g. see Yan & Blackwell, 2004). Passwords based on mnemonic phrases can be as readily remembered as simpler real word passwords, and can be as difficult to guess as randomly generated passwords; Yan et al. (2004) give as an example the phrase 'It's 12 noon I am hungry' as the basis for the password 'I's12&Iah', which uses upper and lower case, symbols and letters and at nine characters long will be difficult to break. The use of mental imagery to create the phrase may serve as a useful mnemonic.

Second, avoid dictionary words or word–number combinations ('password1' being one such frequently used password!). A passcode using mixed or special characters of 7–8 characters in length can be very effective, without being overly long. A misspelling or other variant of a dictionary word might form part of the password, or a variant from a little used language might be highly memorable, yet secure.

Third, self-generated strategies may be more effective than common mnemonics, for remembering four-digit sequences in particular. Derwinger et al. (2005) found that participants who generated and practised their own strategies performed better than a group using mnemonic instructions. They hypothesized that the use of a self-generated strategy may increase awareness of memory processes, increasing retention. In summary, using a personally known and meaningful self-generated code (that is not a name or a birthday!) and reflecting on its meaning, will aid memory. Nevertheless, humans remain the weak link in passcode security.

Metamemory is the ability to monitor and inspect the content of memory. It allows us to know whether we know something.

Semantic memory differs from episodic memory in a number of other ways. For example, metamemory, our ability to monitor and inspect the content of our memory (see Box 5.7 for an example), would seem to differ for semantic and episodic memory and the neural correlates of episodic and semantic metamemory would seem to differ in some respects (e.g. Reggev et al., 2011).

Metamemory is not memory per se, rather our knowledge about what we have stored in memory and how readily it might be accessed. Feeling-of-knowing judgements, for example, allow us to rate the likelihood that we know something that we cannot currently recall.

In Chapter 7, we will look at how concepts and knowledge are represented in semantic memory. Here, we focus on the durability of semantic memory and its relationship to other kinds of memory: how long-term is semantic memory?

Box 5.7 Research Close Up: Do we know what we don't know?

Source: Hampton J. A., Aina, B., Andersson, J. M. Mirza, H. Z., & Parmar, S. (2012). The Rumsfeld effect: The unknown unknown. *Journal of Experimental Psychology: Learning, Memory and Cognition, 38,* 340–355.

INTRODUCTION

[T]here are known knowns; there are things we know that we know. There are known unknowns; that is to say there are things that, we now know we don't know. But there are also unknown unknowns – there are things we do not know we don't know.

United States Secretary of Defence, Donald Rumsfeld 2002

The term metamemory refers to people's judgements about the contents of their own memories (Metcalfe & Dunlosky, 2008). There are things we know we know, and there are things we know we don't know. Hampton et al. (2012) examined whether these things we know we don't know, 'known unknowns', are restricted to particular types of memory, asking whether people are aware of the reliability of their judgements and whether this varies for different categories of knowledge. They examined the consistency of this knowledge over two time points. They predicted that the response options provided would affect performance depending on the kind of memory involved; a three-response condition (yes, no, unsure) should show more consistency than a two-response (true/ false) condition for general knowledge. They hypothesized that, if long-term memory contains a set of stable known facts, then better consistency over the two time points would be evident for the three-response condition, since participants have the option of saying that they are unsure.

METHOD AND RESULTS

Experiment 1 and 2

In Hampton et al.'s first experiment, 32 students saw 150 statements: 50 general knowledge, 50 category membership, and 50 autobiographical memory (see Table 5.3). Within each set, 15 statements were clearly true, 15 were clearly false, and 20 items were likely to create uncertainty.

The statements either appeared with a True/False response option or with three response options ('100 per cent sure it's true', 'Not 100 per cent sure either way', and '100 per cent sure it's false'). Participants were instructed to only use the sure options if they were 100 per cent certain either way. The statements were presented in random order, and presented again one week later. The results showed that the general knowledge statements showed more consistency over the two tests when the third response option (Don't know) was included, but there was no difference for the autobiographical or category statements. Participants were far more likely to be unsure about general knowledge statements than about the other types of statement. In Experiment 2, the categorization condition of Experiment 1 was replicated on a larger scale and confirmed the results.

Table 5.3 Examples of the types of statements used in each category

	Uncertainty	True	False
General knowledge	The internet was originally developed for military reasons.	Some boats have motors, others have sails.	The earth is flat.
Autobiographical	Growing up, I was often ill.	I have stayed in a hotel.	I am a certified pilot.
Category	Olive [fruit]	Apple [fruit]	Onion [fruit]
	Doormat [furniture]	Shelf [furniture]	Suitcase [furniture]

Experiment 3

In Experiment 3, information of a more personal nature was examined by including statements about beliefs and aspirations. Forty-four students saw 90 statements: 30 general knowledge statements (see Table 5.3), 30 belief statements (e.g. 'A father figure is important in a child's life') and 30 aspirations (e.g. 'It is my ambition to own a house one day'). Response options were as in Experiment 1. Consistency across tests was not greater for statements about personal aspirations or beliefs, but the pattern for general knowledge questions was as in Experiment 1, that is general knowledge statements showed more consistency over the two tests when the third response option (Don't know) was included. Participants were far more likely to be unsure about general knowledge statements than about the other categories.

Experiment 4

This experiment extended the procedure to consider another type of personally related information, hedonic statements, likes and dislikes. Forty students saw statements on general knowledge, categorization and likes and dislikes (e.g. 'I like pizza', 'I like watching tennis'). The previous results were again confirmed. For general knowledge alone, consistency was facilitated by the additional response option.

DISCUSSION

Across the four experiments, knowledge statements showed greater consistency when participants were allowed to use an 'unsure' response option, whereas for statements about personal beliefs and aspirations (Experiment 3) or likes and dislikes (Experiment 4), there was no such effect. These data illustrate an important difference in our metamemory for personal semantic information (such as aspirations, or what we like and don't like) and general knowledge. If we are unsure about a general knowledge statement, we are open to the possibility that it is accurate, or that we might have encountered the information but are unable to recall it; we are willing to use the 'unsure' response option. But, if we cannot recollect an autobiographical event, we are more likely to dismiss the event as not having ever occurred.

As Hampton et al. (p. 350) note '[f]ailure to find traces in autobiographical memory will be taken as evidence that a statement is false, whereas failure to find information about a general knowledge statement does not give any reason to believe that it is false'. In the same way, eyewitnesses can fail to recall an event that occurred, or be quite certain that they remember an event or recognize an individual, and yet confidence is not a good predictor of accuracy in the context of eyewitness testimony (see, for example, Wells & Loftus, 2003). This is an issue we will return to in Chapters 6 and 14.

We know from studies of amnesia that much of semantic memory remains intact and available even after a brain injury affecting memory. Our knowledge about language and concepts about the world tends to be formed early on in life and to be used throughout life. What about knowledge learned at school or at university? Does this remain? Despite popular belief that much of the information is lost, research shows that after a period of initial forgetting, much knowledge remains over a very long retention period.

Bahrick (1984) examined memory for Spanish learned at school in a large sample ($n = 773$) with up to a 50-year retention period. One hundred and forty-six participants were still at school or college and learning Spanish at the time of testing. Five hundred and eighty-seven participants had left school or college, and ceased formal language instruction, between 1 and 50 years previously. A group of 40 participants who had never learned Spanish was also included. This group was included as a baseline measure to establish how much Spanish one might pick up without ever having had formal instruction, incidentally, through popular media for example. Participants formed eight groups, depending on the time elapsed since their last course was taken in Spanish.

Participants were tested on measures of recall, recognition and comprehension. The data showed an initial sharp decline in retention over a six-year period, following which the remaining memories became stable and there was no further loss of knowledge until up to 25 years later. Some further forgetting occurred beyond the 30-year period (see Figure 5.10). Once knowledge has stabilized in semantic memory, it remains resistant to forgetting over potentially a very long period; this long-lasting store of knowledge was referred to by Bahrick (1984) as the permastore.

> Permastore involves the long-term retention of content that has been acquired and relearned over a period of time, even if rarely used thereafter.

Such findings have been repeated for other knowledge areas such as mathematics, cognitive psychology, or memory for novels (see Conway et al., 1992, for a review).

Similar findings pointing to very long-term retention have been noted for personal semantic memory. Bahrick et al. (1975) tested 392 high school graduates. The time since graduation varied from 2 weeks to 57 years across nine age cohorts. Tests were constructed using individual participants' high school year books, with a random selection of names and faces from the participants' graduating class included. Several measures were taken. In a free recall task, participants were asked to list as many names of people in their graduating class as they could. In the picture recognition test, participants were required to identify which of a set of pictures appeared in their year book, and which did not. In a name recognition test, participants were required to identify which of a list of names were graduates in their class. A matching test required participants to match pictures to names and names to pictures. In the picture cueing task, participants were shown pictures and their recall of the name was tested. Results for the tasks are shown in Figure 5.11.

Bahrick et al. found that their participants could identify approximately 90 per cent of the names and faces of those in their graduating classes. Visual memory was retained for at least 35 years while verbal memory was found to decline after 15 years. The ability to match names with faces is similarly long lasting. At graduation, participants could match 90 per cent of the names and pictures, and this level of retrieval showed little decline over the following 15 years. Performance on the free recall and picture cued recall tasks was poorer than on the matching and identification tasks (see Figure 5.11), and greater declines over time are evident on these tasks. After 48 years, free recall had decreased by about 60 per cent of initial performance, while cued recall declined by over 70 per cent.

As Bahrick et al. note, these data demonstrate far less decline in memory over time than is typically reported in laboratory investigations using material that lends itself less to real-life comparison.

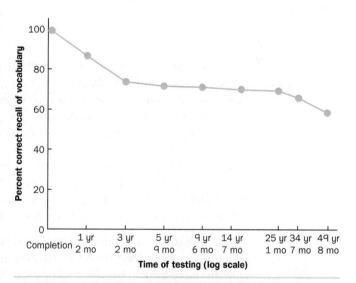

Figure 5.10 Memory for Spanish learned at high school. Memory for a foreign language learned at school undergoes some initial forgetting, but much knowledge of the language is retained even after a significant period of time has passed. The figure shows the average recall of Spanish vocabulary for participants up to 50 years out of school, by a sample of 773 participants.

Source: Bahrick, H. P. (1984). Fifty years of language attrition: Implications for programmatic research. *Modern Language Journal, 68*, 105–118.

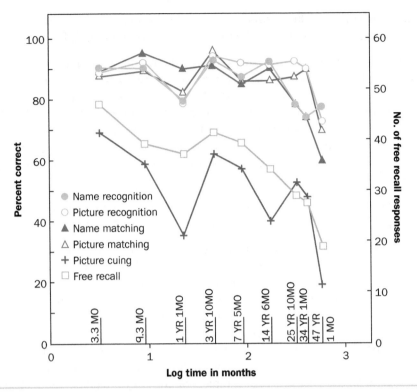

Figure 5.11 **The retrieval method affects memory for classmates.** Performance on the free recall and picture cued recall tasks was poorer than on the matching and identification tasks, and greater declines over time are evident on these tasks.

Source: Bahrick, H. P., Bahrick, P. O., & Wittlinger, R. P. (1975). Fifty years of memory for names and faces: A cross-sectional approach. *Journal of Experimental Psychology: General, 104*, 54–75. APA; reprinted with permission.

Evaluation

It is clear that we can draw a general distinction, within declarative and non-declarative memory and, within declarative memory, between semantic and episodic memory. However, the degree of separation or overlap between these systems continues to be explored and they may function more as a continuum, with a number of intermediate memory states that require study. Autobiographical memory – part episodic recollections and part semantic memory for the self – demonstrates the overlap of the two systems. This latter aspect of autobiographical memory, the area of personal semantics, is only beginning to be explored in depth. Personal semantics is highly personal but is not linked to any particular episode that can be recollected. It is in some ways like episodic memory and in other ways like semantic.

As Renoult et al. (2012) note, 'Although drawing a stark contrast between episodic and semantic memory has proved useful in spurring cognitive neuroscience research, these systems have largely been investigated in isolation, leading to an under-appreciation of their interactions and of potentially intermediate forms of memory' (p. 550). It would seem that existing models of declarative memory have some way to go before they can fully describe, and predict, capacities realized by semantic and episodic memory.

We close this section with an opportunity for you to assess your own memory. Box 5.8 looks at measuring everyday memory.

Box 5.8 Practical Application: Measuring everyday memory

Schacter (e.g. 1999) points out that there is a duality to memory – on the one hand, we are capable of remembering an immense number of facts about the world, about people we know, about childhood events, about things that happened last week, about our plans for the future. These pieces of information are generally called to mind readily, quickly, and effortlessly. On the other hand, there will be times when our memories fail us, and, assuming we notice that failure, such lapses hint at the complexity of the underlying processes. Schacter suggests seven categories of memory failure that he refers to as the 'seven sins of memory' – but rather than seeing these as design flaws, he suggests that they are 'more usefully conceptualized as by-products of otherwise desirable features of human memory' (p. 183). You have encountered many of these 'sins' already in this chapter:

1 Transience: a type of forgetting, decreasing accessibility of memories over time.

2 Absent-mindedness: a type of forgetting that reflects shallow processing, or attention failure.

3 Blocking: forgetting caused by a temporary access failure, as in the case of the tip of the tongue effect (see Chapter 12).

4 Misattribution: a source error, whereby we misattribute a memory to the wrong source.

5 Suggestibility: openness to false memory, as in the 'lost in the shopping mall' scenario, described earlier in the chapter.

6 Bias: distortions based on beliefs or prior knowledge, for example, re-interpreting the past in line with self-image.

7 Persistence: the tendency for some memories to be remembered even when we don't want to remember them, as occurs in obsessive thoughts or in some cases of memory following psychological trauma (post-traumatic stress).

You can get an idea of the extent of your own memory failures using the 'Everyday Memory Questionnaire' (EMQ), which was developed by Sunderland et al. (1983). The EMQ asks 28 questions about common lapses in memory. For each statement, you rate the frequency of each lapse using this scale from 1 to 9. Some of the types of lapse are more commonly experienced than others. See if you can identify how each lapse fits within Schacter's seven categories.

Scale

1 = Not at all in the last six months

2 = About once in the last six months

3 = More than once in the last six months

4 = About once a month

5 = More than once a month, but less than once a week

6 = About once a week

7 = More than once a week, but less than once a day

8 = About once a day

9 = More than once a day

1. Forgetting where you have put something. Losing things around your house.

2. Failing to recognize places that you are told you have often been to before.

3. Finding a television story difficult to follow.

4. Not remembering a change in your daily routine, such as a change in the place where something is kept, or a change in the time something happens. Following your old routine by mistake.

5. Having to go back and check whether you've done something that you meant to do.

6. Forgetting when something happened; for example, forgetting whether something had happened yesterday or last week.

7. Completely forgetting to take things with you, or leaving things behind, or having to go back and fetch them.

8. Forgetting that you were told something yesterday or a few days ago, and maybe having to be reminded about it.

9. Starting to read something (a book or a newspaper or magazine article) without realizing you have already read it before.

10. Letting yourself ramble on to speak about unimportant or irrelevant things.

11. Failing to recognize, by sight, close relatives or friends that you meet frequently.

12. Having difficulty picking up a new skill: for example, having difficulty in learning a new game or in working some new gadget after you have practised once or twice.

13. Finding that a word is 'on the tip of your tongue'. You know it, but cannot quite find the word.

14. Completely forgetting to do things you said you would do, and planned to do.

15. Forgetting important details of what you did or what happened to you yesterday.

16. When talking to someone, forgetting what you have just said.

17. When reading a newspaper or magazine being unable to follow the thread of a story; losing track of what it is about.

18. Forgetting to tell someone something important. Perhaps forgetting to pass on a message or remind someone of something.

19. Forgetting important details about yourself, e.g. your birthday or where you live.

20. Getting the details of what someone had told you mixed up and confused.

21. Telling someone a story or joke you have told them once already.

22. Forgetting details of things you do regularly, whether at home or at work. For example, forgetting details of what to do, or at what time to do it.

23. Finding that faces of famous people, seen on television or in photographs, look unfamiliar.

24. Forgetting where things are normally kept or looking for them in the wrong place.

25. Getting lost or turning in the wrong direction on a journey, a walk, or in a building where you have OFTEN been before.

26. Getting lost or turning in the wrong direction on a journey, a walk, or in a building where you have ONLY BEEN ONCE OR TWICE BEFORE.

27. Doing some routine thing twice by mistake. For example, going to brush/comb your hair, or putting two lots of tea in the pot, when you have just done so.

28. Repeating to someone what you have just told them or asking them the same question twice.

Scoring: A total score of between 28–57 is good; 58–116 is average; 117–252 is below average (Baddeley, 1999). However, as Baddeley (1999) notes having a 'below average' performance does not necessarily indicate that you have a poor memory – it could just mean that you lead a busy life and encounter more situations and opportunities for a lapse to occur in the first place!

Source: Sunderland, A., Harris, J. E., & Baddeley, A. D. (1983). Do laboratory tests predict everyday memory? *Journal of Verbal Learning and Verbal Behaviour*, *22*, 341–357.

Summary

This chapter examined long-term memory. Cases such as that of H.M. have shown that LTM processes are not distributed throughout the brain; damage to particular areas within the temporal lobes will cause profound LTM loss. H.M. and other cases with the characteristic deficits of amnesia show that memory consists of a number of different systems, some of which are unaffected by amnesia. Amnesia is associated with intact short-term memory, as measured by digit span, for example; memory for language, and concepts, is relatively unaffected; but there is severe amnesia for events that occur after the onset of the illness/injury. Skill learning, conditioning and priming will be unaffected. The patient will also be able to engage in skills acquired prior to the onset of amnesia (e.g. play a musical instrument).

It is generally agreed that there is a distinction in LTM between implicit or non-declarative memory and explicit or declarative memory, a distinction described as 'knowing that' as opposed to 'knowing how'. Explicit memory involves conscious recollection of information, whereas implicit memory is evident when performance that does not require conscious recollection is facilitated by prior learning. Some tests of memory rely on explicit recollection of information; others measure implicit memory. Methods such as free recall, cued recall and recognition require conscious recollection, whereas other methods, such as word association or word fragment completion do not.

Declarative memory includes episodic and semantic memory. Episodic memory is memory for events and episodes we have experienced. Memory is constructive and when we recall our past experiences we do not call to mind an exact copy of events as they occurred. When certain episodic memories become embedded in the broader conceptual system, autobiographical memories are formed.

Memory that allows us to keep track of and carry out intended actions is called prospective memory.

Semantic memory is our store of general knowledge about the world. It includes our knowledge of facts, language, and concepts, and, after a period of initial forgetting, much knowledge remains over a very long retention period.

Review questions

1 What is the difference between declarative and procedural memory?
2 How do episodic memories differ from semantic memories?
3 What can we learn about memory from amnesia?
4 What kinds of tasks require the use of prospective memory?
5 Based on the available evidence, is long-term memory best characterized as a two-part or three-part store?

FURTHER READING

Cohen, G., & Conway, M. A. (Ed.) (2008). *Memory in the real world* (3rd ed.). New York: Psychology Press.

Einstein, O., & McDaniel, M. (2005). Prospective memory: Multiple retrieval processes. *Current Directions in Psychological Science, 14,* 286–290.

Graf, P., & Schacter, D. L. (1985). Implicit and explicit memory for new associations in normal and amnesic subjects. *Journal of Experimental Psychology: Learning, Memory, and Cognition, 11,* 501–518.

Graf, P., Squire. L. R., & Mandler, G. (1984). The information that amnesic patients do not forget. *Journal of Experimental Psychology: Learning. Memory, and Cognition, 10,* 164–178.

Loftus, E. F. (1993). The reality of repressed memories. *American Psychologist, 48,* 518–537.

CHAPTER 6:
LEARNING AND FORGETTING

Preview questions

1 What is learning?

2 How do we learn?

3 Are there ways in which we can learn more effectively?

4 What causes forgetting?

5 Are memories for surprising, dramatic events (flashbulb memories) really accurate and complete , compared to memories for ordinary events?

6 Can we reduce or encourage loss of particular memories?

7 Is extraordinary memory an innate ability or a developed skill?

INTRODUCTION

As a student you are very much concerned with learning and with remembering learned information when required during examinations or in tutorials. If you have hastily read Chapter 1 you may have trouble remembering whether Wundt was a Gestalt psychologist, an introspectionist or a behaviourist; and was his first name Karl or Wilhelm? On the other hand, if you had gone over the chapter at intervals and tested yourself as you finished each study session you will most likely remember these details (see the final section of this chapter on effective study). In everyday life, we often struggle to remember some kinds of material (such as new computer passwords) but readily remember some other types of materials (such as where we first heard of the sudden death of a famous celebrity). As we shall see, there have been many suggested models for memory that try to explain its strengths and weaknesses. A popular idea is that memory is like a storeroom and this view was clearly put forward by the fictional detective, Sherlock Holmes:

'You see,' he explained, 'I consider that a man's brain originally is like a little empty attic, and you have to stock it with such furniture as you choose. A fool takes in all the lumber of every sort that he comes across, so that the knowledge which might be useful to him gets crowded out, or at best is jumbled up with a lot of other things so that he has a difficulty in laying his hands upon it. Now the skilful workman is very careful indeed as to what he takes into his brain-attic. He will have nothing but the tools which may help him in doing his work, but of these he has a large assortment, and all in the most perfect order. It is a mistake to think that that little room has elastic walls and can distend to any extent. Depend upon it there comes a time when for every addition of knowledge you forget something that you knew before. It is of the highest importance, therefore, not to have useless facts elbowing out the useful ones.'

From *A Study in Scarlet*, A. Conan Doyle (1887)

> **Learning** refers to processes of acquiring information for mental storage and later use.
> **Forgetting** refers to processes leading to a loss of ability to retrieve previously learned information.

In the course of this chapter we will present psychologists' ideas about learning and forgetting, some of which are similar and some different to Sherlock Holmes's view that memory is like an attic in the brain. As we will see as we progress through this chapter, the overall picture of memory, learning and forgetting that emerges from over 100 years of research is much more complex and intriguing than the simple 'attic' model suggests.

For the cognitive psychologist, learning is the process of acquiring knowledge which, if all goes well, can be retrieved later to help us meet our goals. Thus, we will review the factors that help or hinder learning and the factors that can lead to forgetting, that is failure to retrieve previously acquired knowledge when needed. We will look at the retention (or otherwise) of learned information over time periods of at least several minutes extending to weeks, months and years. We will focus on storage and retrieval from long-term memory (see Chapter 5) rather than short-term or working memory (see Chapter 4). Chapter 5 focused on the different kinds of information (e.g. semantic, episodic, procedural, prospective) stored in long-term memory; this chapter concentrates on the processes by which information becomes stored in (i.e. learned), and retrieved (i.e. remembered) from long-term memory and how information may fail to be retrieved (forgotten) when needed.

Cognitive analysis suggests that *encoding*, *storage* and *retrieval* (see Chapter 4 for an introduction to these topics) are the three main stages involved in learning and in remembering (or forgetting) and we will consider these stages in the following sections.

LEARNING: ENCODING, STORAGE AND RETRIEVAL

The first step in learning new information is to encode that information in an internal representation in working memory (see also Chapter 4). The initial representation then needs to be processed further to develop a memory trace or record in long-term memory (LTM). Processes, such as rehearsal in which the basic representation is repeated, are presumed to strengthen the trace. With meaningful materials, other processes of encoding can elaborate the traces and link the traces to already stored information.

> **Memory trace** is a mental representation of stored information.
> **Levels of processing** is a theory that better learning results from deeper semantic processing which produces stronger, more elaborated memory traces than superficial level processing.
> **Incidental learning** is learning that takes place without any intention to learn.

LEVELS OF PROCESSING

Craik and Lockhart (1972) stressed the importance of encoding in their levels of processing theory. On this view, 'shallow' or surface encoding of materials leads to poor retention but 'deep', more meaningful encoding leads to improved retention and remembering. Simple repetitive rehearsal on this account does not help memory but deeper processing does. Further, on this view, learning need not be intentional. Incidental learning in which learning is a by-product of attending to the material in some way could be strong if the material is processed deeply. An early test of the Levels of Processing theory (Craik & Tulving, 1975) is described in Box 6.1.

Box 6.1 Research Close Up: Levels of processing

Source: Craik, F. I. M. & Tulving, E. (1975). Depth of processing and the retention of words in episodic memory. *Journal of Experimental Psychology: General, 104*, 268–294.

INTRODUCTION

To test the idea of the levels of processing theory that more elaborate ('deeper') processing of the items to be learned would benefit learning and recall, Craik and Tulving (1975) ran the following study.

METHOD

Participants were presented with words printed in capitals or in lower case and for each word were asked to carry out one of three operations, which were as follows: (1) to say whether the word (e.g. *CHAIR*) was printed in capital letters or not; (2) to decide whether the word rhymed with another word (e.g. Does this word rhyme with mat? *DOG*) and (3) to decide if the word fitted a given sentence or not (e.g. Does the word field fit into this sentence? 'The horse lived in a —.'). Note that some items should be answered 'Yes' and some 'No'.

The three types of task vary in depth of processing required from shallow (1) to deep (3). It is worth noting that the participants were not instructed to learn the words; that is, the study was one of incidental learning. Thus, after the operations had been carried out on the words, participants were unexpectedly shown a mixture of words, 50 per cent of which had previously been used in the task and 50 per cent of which had not been previously used in the task. The participants were to say which words they had seen in the first part of the task and the percentage recognized correctly indicated how well the words were remembered.

RESULTS

From the results in Figure 6.1 it can be seen that as expected on the theory, a surprise memory test found that best recognition of the words occurred after the deeper, semantic processing required by the decision as to whether the word fitted a sentence and the poorest recognition was after the shallower surface processing of the print case reporting task, with the rhyme judging task being intermediate in its effects.

DISCUSSION

Although the results were in line with the levels of processing theory, this initial study was open to an alternative interpretation in that the times needed to make the three word judgements varied, with the semantic task taking longer than the other two, so that the semantically judged words were seen for longer and that might explain their better retention. However, when the exposure time factor was controlled, in subsequent studies in the same paper, the same results were found.

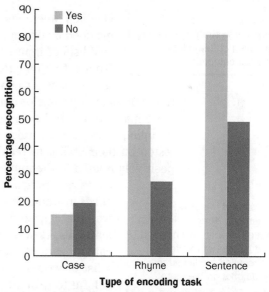

Figure 6.1   Effects of type of encoding task on recognition memory. This figure shows recognition memory separately for words that were judged 'Yes' and 'No' on the encoding decision.

Source: Adapted from Craik, F. I. M. & Tulving, E. (1975). Depth of processing and the retention of words in episodic memory. *Journal of Experimental Psychology: General, 104*, 268–294.

Similar levels-of-processing results to those reported by Craik and Tulving (1975) were also found when non-verbal items were to be learned. Bower and Karlin (1974) used faces as the stimuli and found that memory was better for faces that had been judged for 'honesty' rather than simply classed as 'male' or 'female'.

An incidental finding was that in semantic judgement tasks (is the word an 'animal'? is the word a 'plant'?), words that were responded to positively ('Yes') were better remembered than those given a negative response. Craik (2002) suggested this showed a role for elaboration of encoding as well as depth of coding. Positive trial encodings strengthen pre-existing links between the stimulus word ('Dog', say) and the category ('Animal') but this does not happen in the negative trials (e.g. 'Cat' does not have a pre-existing link to the test category 'Plant' to be strengthened).

Despite the strong empirical data showing effects in line with the levels-of-processing approach, the theory has been criticized as basically circular in that there is no independent measure of depth of processing. There is a risk of saying that processing was deeper because retention was better and that retention was better because processing was deeper (Baddeley, 1978; Eysenck, 1978).

MNEMONICS

Various strategies of encoding can enhance memory performance markedly. Such strategies to boost memory are known as mnemonics and many can be traced back to antiquity when orators had to rely on memory when making long speeches. (See Chapter 1 for more on mnemonics.)

Categorization is a mnemonic strategy involving grouping of items into familiar categories.

One key mnemonic principle is categorization. This principle is that items grouped or organized into categories will be better recalled than unorganized lists of items. Bousfield (1953) found that if lists of words were drawn from a few categories (such as animals, vegetables, professions, names) then even when 60 words were given in scrambled order, participants tended to recall them in groups or clusters by category. Mandler and Pearlstone (1966) asked participants to group 52 words into categories repeatedly until they produced reliable groupings. After this exercise in organizing the words, participants were unexpectedly tested on their ability to recall the words. Memory for the words was very strongly positively related to the number of categories (which ranged from 2–7) in the participants' groupings. It was also found that the basic result was not due to differences in study time during the organizing stage of the study. The key factor was the degree of organization that the participants had imposed on the materials. Bower et al. (1969) found further that hierarchically structured categorizations were particularly beneficial for retention. For example, if a list of words included specific animal words and car names it would be helpful to group the animals into say, domestic and wild animals and the cars into say, saloon cars, trucks, sports cars and so on. This is as Sherlock Holmes would have expected from his 'little attic' model of memory; material is best retrieved if it is stored in an organized way.

Method of loci is a mnemonic strategy in which a familiar route is imagined and images of the items to be recalled are linked to landmarks on the route. **Interacting images** is a mnemonic strategy in which vivid and bizarre images are formed of the items to be recalled, interacting in some way. **Pegword method** is a mnemonic strategy in which to be recalled items are linked by imagery to an already learned sequence list of imagable words.

In addition to organizing material into meaningful structures, use of images in encoding is an important aspect of many mnemonics, such as the method of loci, the method of interacting images and the pegword method.

In the method of loci, which some trace back to c. 500 BC (Paivio, 1971), a familiar sequence of places is imagined and in each place along the sequence is an object to be remembered. For example, if you needed to remember a shopping list (cheese, butter, milk, bread, tomatoes) using the method of loci you might imagine going around your home and imagining a giant cheese on the carpet in the first room, a pack of butter on a table in the second room, a bottle of milk in the third room and so on. To retrieve the items, you would re-imagine the tour of your home and if the method works you will 'see' the to-be-remembered items in your 'mind's eye'. Ross and Lawrence (1968) found that people trained in using the method of loci could recall 95 per cent of 40 item lists after a single presentation. The method works best when the images are seen as interacting. Bower (1970) found that recall of arbitrary pairs of nouns was greatly enhanced when participants were instructed to form images of the nouns interacting rather than just side by side. For example, imaging a dog driving a car rather than a dog beside a car would facilitate recall of the dog-car pair.

The pegword method is similar to the method of loci, but uses a sequence of highly imagable nouns linked by rhymes to the number sequence. The standard example is 'One is a bun, two is a shoe, three is a tree, four is a door, five is a hive, six is sticks, seven is heaven, eight is a gate, nine is wine and ten is a hen.' To recall up to 10 items in sequence, using the pegword method, you would image the first item interacting with a bun, the second interacting with a shoe, and so on. Bugelski et al. (1968) found near perfect one trial learning of lists of ten words using the 'One is a bun' pegword mnemonic with quite fast presentation rates of one new word per four seconds. A follow up study (Bugelski, 1968) found that people could readily learn many successive lists using the same 'One is a bun' system with little or no interference between lists. Thus, this mnemonic is a robust and easily learned method.

How might the benefits of these mnemonic methods be explained? Paivio (1969, 1971, 1983) and Yuille (1983) applied a dual-coding hypothesis according to which concrete words can be coded in two different ways, in a verbal code and in an imagery code. Abstract words can only easily be coded in one way, verbal. Thus, concrete words have two internal codes and so two ways of being remembered. Paivio (1965) found in a study using noun pairs representing the four possible combinations of abstract and concrete words that concreteness, especially of the first word of a pair, greatly facilitated recall of the pairs. The first word, it was argued, serves as a conceptual peg to which the second is linked.

> **Dual coding hypothesis** proposes that concrete words can be encoded both verbally and by means of images representing their meaning; in contrast, abstract words can only be coded verbally. Dual coding is one explanation of why concrete words are easier to remember.

Thus, mnemonics using imagery show the benefits predicted by the dual coding hypothesis.

Although specific mnemonics can be learned is it possible to improve our memory abilities by training? This question is addressed in Box 6.2 which discusses exceptional memory and whether it can be acquired.

Box 6.2 Practical Application: Exceptionally good memories – nature or nurture?

Memory failures are a common experience and most people would probably say that they wished their memory was better. This box concerns the practical question of whether we could improve our memory ability by training or whether good memory is essentially innate and not open to improvement by training. See Box 1.2 for a discussion on exactly how we train our memory.

Some rare individuals have the opposite complaint – that their memory is too good! The best known case of truly exceptional general memory ability is that of a Russian journalist, Solomon V. Shereshevskii. He was tested extensively by A. R. Luria (1968) and was found able to recall a huge variety of complex materials after very brief study periods, such as lists of more than 100 numbers, poems in foreign languages, technical diagrams and scientific formulae; moreover, he could recall such materials perfectly after gaps of many years and recall the materials in reverse order if asked.

The basis of Shereshevskii's remarkable ability was a strong capability to generate visual and other images which in turn seems to have built on synaesthesia (see Chapter 2). This is a tendency for stimuli from one sensory modality to evoke images in another modality. Thus, musical tones would elicit strong coloured images and taste images for Shereshevskii. He also had particular images for numbers, so that '1' was a well-built man and '2' a high spirited woman! Sometimes, he complained, the vivid and complex imagery evoked by the sound of the voice when someone spoke to him made it hard to focus on the meaning of what was said.

A more recent case of unusual memory has been reported by Parker, Cahill and McGaugh (2006) of a 41-year-old woman known as A.J., who can recall extraordinary details of every day of her life from her teens onwards. She reports that her remembering is automatic and effortless and is like a constantly running movie that never stops. A.J. likens the experience to having a split screen in awareness on which memories are constantly being replayed while she tries to attend to present tasks and interactions. At times she says that her condition is a burden and along with the Shereshevskii case, these real life examples suggest that having a normally forgetful memory is not so bad as we sometimes feel.

Most examples of exceptional memory ability, as are found in memory experts, or mnemonists, are unlike Shereshevskii or A.J., in that the exceptional memory ability is highly domain specific and has been acquired by extensive practice using suitable mnemonic methods, rather than being an effortless innate condition.

Practice effects in expanding short-term memory were demonstrated by Ericsson and Chase (1982). They repeatedly tested the digit span of one participant and his measured span grew from the typical seven items level to a span of around 80 digits after practising for an hour per day, 3–5 days a week, for 20 months. This remarkable result was achieved through the use of a special mnemonic based on the participant's strong interest and knowledge of running times for various distances. Thus, 3 4 9 2 would be recoded as '3 mins 49.2 secs, near record for mile'. Sequences not suitable as running times were recoded as dates or ages, so 1 9 4 4 becomes the year 1944, 'near end of WW2', 8 9 2 becomes 89.2 years, 'a good age'. Ericsson and Chase were able to teach the method to another participant with an interest in running and he also increased his digit span from 7 to 75 with extensive practice.

Some individuals deliberately practise memory skills for specific domains such as memorizing packs of playing cards, number sequences, faces and names in order to compete effectively in memory championships. Maguire et al. (2003) in a brain imaging study of competitors in the World Memory Championships found that during memorizing the mnemonists showed more activity than controls in brain areas used in navigation and spatial memory. This result is consistent with the high level of self-reports of using mnemonics of the method of loci type (discussed earlier in this chapter).

A striking case of superior acquired memory is provided by Rajan Mahadevan who shows a high level of ability to remember numbers. He held the world record for reciting the digits of *pi* to 31,811 places for a number of years. On being tested he was found to have a digit span of about 60 (Thompson et al., 2001). However, Ericsson et al. (2004) carried out further tests with Mahadevan and gathered evidence that his exceptional digit span was based on mnemonic methods that he had developed over the years as a mnemonist, rather than being due to an exceptional basic innate short-term or working memory capacity. His span for symbols such as !,*,&, @ and so on was in the normal range, as was his memory for word lists and stories. It was noted that he did expand his symbol span after a number of trials by recoding the symbols into digits to which he could apply his practised mnemonics.

Overall, it appears safe to conclude, that with a very few exceptions such as Shereshevskii and A.J., exceptional memory performance results from extensive practice with suitable mnemonics and is very specific to the domains in which practice has taken place.

ENCODING SPECIFICITY

The encoding specificity principle (Thomson & Tulving, 1970) looks forwards from the cues used at the encoding stage or study stage to the cues present during the test period. It will be helpful for retrieval at test, on this view, if the same cues are present at test as were available at the study period.

> Encoding specificity principle is that if the context at recall is similar to the context at encoding then memory will be enhanced.

Thomson and Tulving (1970) tested the principle in the following study. They had participants study pairs of words in which the to-be-remembered words, or 'targets', were printed in capitals. Alongside the 'targets' were words in lower case. These lower case words were either strong cues of the target (e.g. black-WHITE) or were weak cues, not related to the target words (e.g. table-WHITE). At recall, the participants were then shown cue words and had to recall the targets. Sometimes the cue words at recall were the same as at study (weak or strong) and sometimes the cue words were different (strong at recall if weak at study and vice versa). Recall was best if the same cues were present at study and at recall. The participants were greatly aided by the weak cues at recall if the cues had been present at study. This result showed that the presence of the same cues at test and at study was beneficial and indicated that people formed associations that encoded links between the weak cues and the target items during the study period. So, in the example above, it seems that people sought out associations of 'WHITE' to 'table', perhaps by imaging a white painted table, and so the cue 'table' became effective at retrieval.

The encoding specificity principle in essence says that recall will be best if the cues available at the time of testing match the context which was present in the study period.

CONTEXT DEPENDENT RETRIEVAL

It has also been found in a number of studies that reinstating the general context in which learning took place can assist later recall. A striking example of such context effects was provided by Godden and Baddeley's (1975) study of scuba divers who learned lists either under water or on dry land and were than tested either 20 feet under water or on land. It was found that lists learned under water were better recalled under water than on land and lists learned on dry land were better recalled on land than under water. Overall, recall in the same context as study was some 50 per cent better. It may be noted that recognition memory did not show the same context effects in later studies of divers (Godden & Baddeley, 1980) with high recognition irrespective of context. This difference between recall and recognition may well be due to the reduced need to encode cues for recognition tests in which the test itself supplies the needed cues. (See Chapter 5 for more on recognition versus recall.)

> Context effects occur if memory is better when the external environment at testing is the same as at learning.

Similar results have also been found for what we might call 'internal contexts' in the form of physiological states brought about by psychoactive agents (state-dependent learning) or in the form of moods (mood dependent memory effect). Eich (1980) found that materials learned while participants were in an altered physiological state due to alcohol or marijuana were recalled better when the state was recreated. As with the (external) context effect, the state-dependent learning effect was found for recall but not for recognition (Roediger & Guynn, 1996). Bower (1981) and Eich (1995) have reported mood manipulation studies in which happy/sad moods were induced at study and test and it was found that being in the same mood state at study

> State dependent memory effects occur if memory is better when internal physiological conditions at learning are reinstated at testing.
> Mood dependent memory means that memory is better when mood at learning is reinstated at testing.

and test was beneficial for recall. Mood-dependent effects are generally stronger for positive moods, perhaps because positive moods are more easily maintained (Ucros, 1989). As with other context effects, mood-dependent effects are generally stronger for tasks involving recall as against recognition (Kenealy, 1997). See Chapter 14 for more discussion of mood and emotion effects on memory.

SPACED VERSUS MASSED TRIALS

Spacing effect occurs when material studied on many separate occasions is better learned than material studied in one continuous session even if total study times are equal.

The spacing effect is that people remember material better when the material is studied on a number of different occasions (possibly briefly) over a long period of time ('spaced presentation'), rather than studied in one long period ('massed presentation'), even when the total study time is equated.

The spacing effect was first identified in experimental studies by Ebbinghaus and reported in his 1885 book *Memory: A Contribution to Experimental Psychology*. This phenomenon has been reported many times since, in a range of memory tasks such as free recall, recognition and cued-recall (Crowder, 1976; Greene, 1989). For example, Jost (1897) found that the recall of a list of nonsense syllables was three times better when 24 repetitions of the material were distributed across 12 days (two repetitions per day) as against when the same number of repetitions was spread over three days (eight repetitions per day). Similar results have been found for foreign vocabulary items (e.g. Bloom & Shuell, 1981) and on educational material such as spelling lists and multiplication facts (Rea & Modigliani, 1985) and even for lectures on statistics (Smith & Rothkopf, 1984). The practical benefits of distributed practice were also established by Baddeley and Longman (1978) in the setting of a post office where workers had to learn to use typing machines to add postcodes to letters for automatic sorting.

In practical terms, the spacing effect suggests that 'cramming' the night before an examination is not likely to be as effective as studying at intervals over a much longer span of time. Indeed, spacing is becoming formally applied in school learning situations (Willingham, 2002) so that physical activity breaks are inserted at frequent intervals during a class period and the same short lesson is repeated a number of times after each break.

Deficient processing view is that massed repetitions lead to deficient processing of the second presentation.
Encoding variability means that encoding varies with the context at the study period.

Several possible explanations of the spacing effect have been offered. According to the deficient processing view, massed presentation leads to deficient processing of the second presentation – we simply do not pay much attention to the later presentations (Hintzman et al., 1974). According to the encoding variability view, spaced repetition is likely to cause some variability in representation; under massed presentations, on the other hand, the corresponding memory representations are similar and relatively indiscriminable (Glenberg, 1977; Ross & Landauer, 1978). Thus, the spacing effect can be linked to encoding specificity in that some of the wide range of cues associated with items at study are more likely to recur at test with spaced as against massed learning conditions.

Evaluation

In this section we have been focusing on learning, particularly of verbal material. The role of encoding at time of study is important according to the main approaches reviewed here, the levels of processing and the encoding specificity theories. Levels of processing theory drew support from studies of encoding using imagery mnemonics, such as the one-is-a-bun, etc. method. Despite the strong empirical data showing effects in line with the levels-of-processing approach, the theory has been criticized as basically circular in that there is no independent measure of depth of processing. There is a risk of saying that processing was deeper because retention was better and that retention was better because processing was deeper (Baddeley, 1978; Eysenck, 1978).

The theory of encoding specificity received strong experimental support for its idea that reinstating cues present at study aids later retrieval. This approach explains the dependency of recall on context, whether external and environmental, or internal and involving moods or pharmaceutically induced states.

Further evidence in favour of encoding specificity arose from findings that study sessions spaced out over time are more effective than massed study sessions involving 'cramming' over a shorter period. This type of finding fits well with ideas of encoding specificity in that some of the wide range of cues associated with items at study are more likely to also be present at test with spaced as against massed learning.

The encoding specificity approach is not without its critics. In particular, Nairne (2002, 2010) has criticized the encoding specificity principle as in need of further refinement. He proposed that successful memory retrieval is brought about by cue distinctiveness rather than simple overlap. For example, on the distinctiveness view, a driver returning to a parking area would find it easier to recall where he or she had parked in an unfamiliar parking area than in a familiar one. Why? Because the familiar parking area is associated with many past parking memories but the new parking area is only associated with one. The two situations differ in distinctiveness of cues but not in overlap. Some experimental support has been found for Nairne's proposal (Goh & Lu, 2012) which is essentially a refinement of the encoding specificity principle rather than a completely distinct theory.

FORGETTING

Forgetting is said to occur when someone cannot retrieve information that had been previously available from memory. Forgetting has been a key topic from the earliest days of experimental psychology when Ebbinghaus (1885) undertook extensive studies of learning and forgetting with himself as the sole participant. He pioneered the use of lists of 'nonsense syllables' as the experimental materials to be learned and remembered. Nonsense syllables are three letter consonant-vowel-consonant strings that do not form words (e.g. CUV, LEL, ZIR). These materials were devised with the intention of ruling out any effects of meaning by making all the materials equally free of meaning. This proved difficult as nonsense syllables vary in resemblance to real words and can be scored for 'meaningfulness' in terms of number of associations they elicit (Glaze, 1928; Hull, 1933); however, in Ebbinghaus's studies, he discarded syllables that were too reminiscent of words in his judgement and otherwise learning materials were drawn at random so that meaningfulness differences between conditions can be taken to have had no effect on his basic findings. Later researchers moved away from the nonsense syllable technique to study meaningful learning but for many years, the nonsense syllable was the preferred type of item in the study of learning.

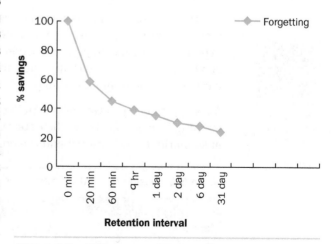

Figure 6.2 **Ebbinghaus's (1885) forgetting curve.** This curve plots amount retained (percentage savings on re-learning) against retention interval.

It is estimated that over a period of years, Ebbinghaus devoted some 830 hours to studying 6600 lists totalling 85,000 syllables. Among other results, these studies revealed the classic forgetting curve (see Figure 6.2). The graph in Figure 6.2 measures forgetting in terms of the savings in relearning a list after various amounts of time. So, with near immediate relearning a saving of close to 100 per cent is achieved compared to initial learning time; even after a delay of 31 days, some savings are still made (20 per cent) indicating that at least some memory of the list is retained even after a month's retention interval. In general, the typical forgetting curve shows steep forgetting at first followed by a gradual levelling off. The rate of forgetting is not constant but diminishes over time. Similar curves have been found repeatedly in experimental studies (Rubin & Wenzel, 1996) and with real life materials, as in Bahrick's (1983) studies of recall for street names, after retention intervals of up to 46 years.

> **Savings** is a way of assessing forgetting by comparing trials needed for relearning as against trials required for original learning. If fewer trials are needed for relearning then savings have been demonstrated. **Interference** occurs when remembering is disrupted by related memories.

Why does forgetting happen? As with short-term memory (see Chapter 4), decay of relevant traces is conceivable, but until recently most theorists proposed that interference from other related memories, rather than decay was the principal explanation of forgetting.

Accordingly, in the next section we will review the major findings regarding interference and its role in forgetting.

INTERFERENCE

> **Proactive interference** occurs when previous learning impairs later learning.
> **Retroactive interference** occurs when later learning impairs memory for earlier learning.

Two types of interference are typically distinguished and these are proactive and retroactive interference.

Proactive interference involves prior learning impairing later learning and retrieval; in retroactive interference, later learning interferes with retention and retrieval of earlier learning. This is the kind of interference that Sherlock Holmes proposed in his 'little attic' model when he said 'there comes a time when for every addition of knowledge you forget something that you knew before'.

The simplest experimental design to examine retroactive interference would be as laid out in Table 6.1.

The two groups learn the same material (A) to the same criterion of learning and both remember as much as they can of material A after different interpolated activities. The experimental group engage in a second learning task and the control group have some non-demanding filler activity, such as describing photographs or reading materials unrelated to the original learning task.

Scan to watch a video explaining proactive and retroactive interference

An early study by McGeoch and McDonald (1931) involved a number of groups initially learning lists of adjectives; the experimental groups then learned new lists that varied in similarity to the first list and the control groups read jokes as a filler activity. Both

Table 6.1 Design for study of retroactive interference.

	Experimental group	Control group
Time 1	Learn A	Learn A
Time 2	Learn B	Filler activity C
Time 3	Remember A	Remember A

Table 6.2 McGeoch and McDonald's (1931) results on retroactive interference

Interpolated activity	Adjectives recalled (%)
Reading jokes (control)	45
Learning 3-digit numbers	37
Learning nonsense syllables	26
Learning adjectives unrelated to originals	22
Learning adjectives of opposite meaning to originals	18
Learning adjectives of similar meaning to originals	12

types of group then recalled the initial training list of adjectives. Their results are outlined in Table 6.2.

It is clear from these results and from many subsequent studies, that the more similar the intervening learning, the greater the degree of forgetting of the original learning and this fits the view that interference of older learning by newer learning is a major factor in forgetting.

Recently, typical studies of interference in long-term remembering have used the paired associates learning paradigm which is often used in the study of learning. In this method, people are presented with lists made up of pairs of words (or nonsense syllables in early studies), on learning trials. On test trials, one word of each pair is presented (typically the first word of each pair) and participants attempt to recall the other word. The experimental designs for examining proactive and retroactive interference using paired associates are shown in Table 6.3.

> Paired associates learning is a memory task in which participants are presented with pairs of items (typically, words) at study and on test are given the first word and asked to recall the second word in each pair.

Underwood (1957) pooled data from 14 experiments using paired associates and the proactive design and found a marked effect, such that the more previous trials of the A-B type, the more proactive interference on tests of A-C learning. Similarly, retroactive interference has been regularly demonstrated (Postman & Stark, 1969) in laboratory studies of paired associates learning.

Anderson and Neely (1996) explained interference in terms of cues becoming associated to competing responses in the interference conditions but not in the control conditions.

Table 6.3 Experimental designs for testing for proactive and retroactive interference using paired associates

Stage	Experimental group	Control group
Proactive interference		
1	Learn List A-B	Unrelated activity
2	Learn List A-C	Learn List A-C
Test	List A-C	List A-C
Retroactive interference		
1	Learn List A-B	Learn List A-B
2	Learn List A-C	Unrelated activity
Test	List A-B	List A-B

They give the everyday example of people remembering where they have parked their cars in a supermarket parking area. The more times the same store has been visited the harder it becomes to remember where the car was parked, because the cue, asking oneself where the car is, becomes associated with many different locations (see also p. 187).

DECAY AND CONSOLIDATION

If interference could be eliminated, would forgetting still occur? If so, then trace decay, that is, weakening of memories due solely to the passage of time (see also Chapter 4) would be implicated as a possible cause of forgetting. However, it is impossible to examine the effects of pure passage of time without any possibility of interfering interpolated activity. Sleep has been explored as, at least, a state of reduced activity; given this we can compare the rate of forgetting following sleep with the rates measured following activity in an alert stage. An early study by Jenkins and Dallenbach (1924) had two student participants who underwent a wide range of tests involving learning and later recall of lists of ten nonsense syllables. In the waking conditions the list was learned in the morning to one perfect recall and then recalled after varied periods of normal awake activity. In the sleep conditions, the participants learned the lists at night just before going to bed and were then woken to recall the lists after different time periods. For both sleeping and awake conditions, the retention intervals were 1, 2, 4 and 8 hours. The results were as shown in Table 6.4.

Recall after varying retention intervals, when awake, showed the typical forgetting curve in that there was a steep early decline followed by a slower decline. After retention intervals filled with sleep, there was a small initial drop with no further loss after two hours. These results indicated that decay alone cannot explain the usual forgetting curve. However, interference could be the explanation, as interference would be much less during sleep as against when awake, hence the difference between the forgetting curves after waking and sleeping periods. The small drop in recall in the sleeping condition after 1–2 hours could be due to interfering effects of the small amounts of conscious activity before sleep and on waking before testing. Overall, Jenkins and Dallenbach (1924, p. 615) concluded that 'forgetting is not so much a matter of the decay of old impressions and associations as it is a matter of interference, inhibition, or obliteration of the old by the new'. This conclusion is rather similar to the memory theory of Sherlock Holmes, in which new memories displace old memories, with which we started this chapter!

Box 6.3 discusses an influential study using unusual participants (cockroaches) which provided further support for the consolidation theory of learning.

Table 6.4 Recall scores (max = 10) as a function of retention period and sleep versus waking in Jenkins and Dallenbach's (1924) study

	Number of hours since learning				
	0	1	2	4	8
After sleeping	10	7.0	5.4	5.5	5.6
After waking	10	4.6	3.1	2.2	0.9

Box 6.3 Research Close Up: Memory decay in cockroaches?

Source: Minami, H. & Dallenbach, K. M. (1946). The effects of activity upon learning and retention in the cockroach Periplaneta Americana. *American Journal of Psychology*, *59*, 1–58.

INTRODUCTION

Following on from their initial study of the effects of sleep compared with waking activity following learning, using student participants (Jenkins & Dallenbach, 1924) a further study was carried out which attempted to control more completely participants' activities and to reduce interpolated interfering activities to a minimum. This study by Minami and Dallenbach (1946) used cockroaches as participants. It had been found that these insects would spontaneously squeeze into narrow boxes lined ever more thickly with tissue paper until they were held fast and so immobilized. This tendency provided an opportunity to reduce post-learning activity to a minimum and thus reduce greatly the chance of interference.

METHOD

Minami and Dallenbach had cockroaches learn to avoid the dark path of a T maze in which an electric shock awaited and then had one group (controls) placed in their normal holding pens which allowed exploratory activity for varying times before returning to the T maze. Experimental group cockroaches were held immobilized in narrow cardboard boxes lined with tissue paper, for varying times after learning and before re-testing. Furthermore, the immobile insects were kept in dark conditions to minimize stimulation.

RESULTS

The results on re-testing showed considerable savings for the immobilized inactive cockroaches as against the normally active control cockroaches, over time periods from 15 minutes to 24 hours (see Figure 6.3).

A second study in the same paper found that increasing activity levels after learning, by making experimental groups use a cockroach sized treadmill, led to much more forgetting than control levels of normal post-learning activity.

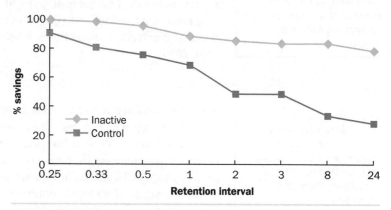

Figure 6.3   Savings scores. Savings scores on re-testing of cockroaches after retention periods of 0.25–24 hours for normally active control versus inactive experimental conditions.

Source: Based on data reported by Minami, H. & Dallenbach, K. M. (1946). The effects of activity upon learning and retention in the cockroach Periplaneta Americana. *American Journal of Psychology, 59*, 1–58.

DISCUSSION

The results of this study with cockroaches lends support to the consolidation view of forgetting (Wixted, 2004, 2010). On this view, memories when first formed are fragile and a period of consolidation is required to strengthen memory traces; retroactive interference interrupts the consolidation process and that is why forgetting occurs after interpolated learning activities. Sleep or inactivity allows consolidation to take place without interference from new memories.

The consolidation view, as tested in the cockroach study discussed in Box 6.3, incorporates the idea of decay – traces decay unless consolidated – and an idea of interference as operating by preventing consolidation. We will now consider the consolidation approach in more detail.

The approach to memory and forgetting in terms of consolidation is the dominant approach in neuroscience and neuropsychology but has been rather ignored until recently in cognitive psychology, where the interference based theories, largely deriving from laboratory studies of paired associate learning have been the norm. However, the two approaches are not incompatible and both might apply. A number of recent studies have addressed the effects of sleep on forgetting to test out ideas about the role of consolidation and we will now discuss highlights of this work.

Effects of sleep on memory

As we have seen from Jenkins and Dallenbach's (1924) classic study it has long been established that a list of words is better remembered if it is followed by a retention interval during which the learner sleeps than if the learning is followed by the same retention interval filled by normal daily activity . It is generally assumed that sleep protects memory from interference (e.g. Ellenbogen et al., 2006), and it has been suggested that this reflects active consolidation processes that occur during sleep (e.g. Born et al., 2006). In support of a consolidation view, sleep's protective benefits are particularly pronounced if it occurs right after study. For example, Ekstrand (1972) showed that retention after a 24-hour period that included eight hours of sleep was better if subjects slept right after study (81 per cent recall) than if they slept right before test (66 per cent). The beneficial effect of a period of sleep or inactivity is sometimes labelled retrograde facilitation (Wixted, 2004, 2010).

> **Retrograde facilitation** is the beneficial effect on memory of a period of sleep or inactivity following a study period.

Neuroscience accounts of sleep effects on consolidation

> **Long-term potentiation (LTP)** is the long-lasting improvement in signal transmission between two neurons that results from stimulating them at the same time.

We now consider neuroscience approaches to sleep effects on learning and forgetting, which stress the notion of long-term potentiation (LTP). In neuroscience, LTP is a long-lasting improvement in signal transmission between two neurons that results from stimulating them at the same time (Bear et al., 2007). As memories are thought to be encoded by modification of the strength of synaptic connections, LTP is widely considered one of the major neural mechanisms that underlies learning and memory (Cook & Bliss, 2006).

It seems that different phases of sleep may have different effects on memory . Sleep periods with rapid eye movements (REM) associated with dreaming, have different effects from non-REM sleep. It seems that non-REM sleep blocks the induction of hippocampal LTP (Jones Leonard et al., 1987) without disrupting the maintenance of previously induced LTP (Bramham & Srebo, 1989); these experiments, which were performed on sleeping rats, showed that while LTP can be induced during REM sleep (possibly accounting for the fact that we can sometimes remember our dreams), it cannot be induced during non-REM sleep (possibly accounting for the fact that we cannot remember any mental activity that takes place during that stage of sleep). As a result, it might be hypothesized that during non-REM sleep, recent memories that have begun to be consolidated through LTP are protected from interference that would occur if new memories began to be laid down by LTP.

© ia–64/iStock

Ekstrand and colleagues (1972; Yaroush et al., 1971) examined effects of non-REM and REM sleep on human verbal learning. These researchers used the fact that non-REM sleep typically precedes REM sleep Some participants in this experiment learned a word list, went to sleep immediately, and were awakened four hours later for a test of recall. Others slept for four hours, were awakened to learn the list, slept for another four hours, and then took a recall test. The control (i.e. awake) participants learned the list during the day and were tested for recall four hours later. The participants all learned the initial list to the same degree, but the results showed that four hours of mostly non-REM sleep facilitated delayed recall relative to the other two conditions, which did not differ from each other (i.e. REM sleep did not facilitate memory). These results have been replicated in studies by Plihal and Born (1997, 1999) and fit with the finding that many antidepressant drugs, which greatly reduce REM sleep, do not seem to cause memory problems (Vertes & Eastman, 2000).

Overall, it seems that consolidation processes are important in explaining the effects of of non-REM and REM sleep. It seems likely that consolidation problems also underlie patterns of forgetting in amnesia and we will now outline some recent research exploring this idea.

Retrograde amnesia

As discussed in Chapter 5, clinical findings over more than 100 years have indicated that brain damage leading to anterograde amnesia (i.e. to the inability to lay down new memory records) is also associated with temporally graded retrograde amnesia (Ribot, 1882) in which memories formed prior to brain damage are impaired, but the effect depends on the age of the memory trace at the time the damage occurs, with more recently formed memories suffering the most (Ribot's Law). In support of Ribot's Law, Brown (2002) reported a meta-analysis of 247 outcomes from 61 articles, which supported the view that the impairment gradually and continuously reduces as memories become increasingly temporally distant from the trauma.

It is accepted in neuroscience that the medial temporal lobes, which include the hippocampus and adjacent cortex, play a critical role in the formation of new memories. When patient H.M. (see also Chapter 5) had those areas removed to control his epileptic seizures, it soon became clear that his ability to form new memories was severely and permanently impaired (Scoville & Milner, 1957). Studies have found that temporally graded retrograde amnesia is very likely to be observed if the brain damage in question involves the hippocampal region (e.g. Manns et al., 2003). A review of 13 precisely controlled prospective animal studies, in which memory loss is examined over time following surgical lesions, supports the existence of temporally graded retrograde amnesia and its association with hippocampal lesions (Squire et al., 2001).

The temporal gradient of retrograde amnesia provides strong evidence that memories consolidate over time and that the hippocampal formation plays an important role in that process. On this view, if the hippocampal formation is damaged before the consolidation process is complete, recently formed memories that are still undergoing the consolidation process will be impaired. Older, consolidated memories will be retained, but more recent memories that have not completely consolidated will likely be lost.

Effects of alcohol and benzodiazepines

As indicated above, damage to the medial temporal lobes induces permanent anterograde amnesia. Temporary anterograde amnesia can be induced by certain drugs which, strange to say, can also produce *retrograde facilitation*. That is, recently formed memories are retained better than they otherwise would have been, even though new memories cannot easily be formed while in the drugged state. This phenomenon reinforces the view that memories consolidate over time and that much of what we forget is lost because of retroactive interference arising from ordinary mental activities. The argument is that certain agents (such as alcohol and benzodiazepines) close the hippocampus to new input, thereby inducing temporary anterograde amnesia, without affecting the ability of the hippocampus to consolidate previously formed memories (Bruce and Pihl, 1997). Because new input is prevented, recently formed (and, therefore, incompletely consolidated) memories are protected from the retroactive interference that they would otherwise encounter. As such, these drugs act in the same way that sleep does even though the individual remains conscious while intoxicated.

The anterograde amnesic effects of alcohol consumed prior to the learning of new material are well established (Lister et al., 1987). The extreme version of this effect is the alcoholic 'blackout', which involves a complete loss of memory for events occurring while the individual was conscious and (very) intoxicated with a blood alcohol concentration of around 0.20 per cent (White, 2004). It is generally accepted that blackouts are not the result of state-dependent learning but instead reflect a failure to encode or consolidate new information (Lisman, 1974). In spite of its effects on the formation of new memories, alcoholic intoxication generally does not affect retrieval of old memories after intoxication (Birnbaum et al., 1978). Whereas alcohol consumption induces a certain degree of anterograde amnesia for material studied under the influence of the drug, many studies have reported that it actually results in improved memory for material studied just prior to consumption (Bruce & Pihl, 1997; Lamberty et al., 1990; Mann et al., 1984; Parker et al., 1980, 1981). This phenomenon is referred to as retrograde facilitation or retrograde enhancement, and its existence makes alcohol-induced amnesia unlike the amnesia produced by damage to the medial temporal lobes.

How might the curious phenomenon of drug-induced retrograde facilitation be explained? Recent evidence suggests one very plausible explanation is that alcohol facilitates recently established memories because it prevents the formation of new memories that would otherwise cause retroactive interference (Mueller et al., 1983). Drinking alcohol does not protect memories that are years old (and fully consolidated). Instead, it is the recently formed memories that benefit most because, theoretically, those are the ones most vulnerable to the effects of retroactive interference.

Retrograde facilitation has also been observed with another class of amnesia-inducing drug, namely, benzodiazepines. The basic experimental paradigm is the same as that used with alcohol. Participants typically study one list of words before taking the drug and then study another list following drug administration. Memory for both lists is tested sometime later (usually while the participants are still under the influence of the drug), and performance is compared to that of a placebo control group. Typically, the drug group exhibits impaired recall for the list learned under the influence of the drug (thereby confirming its amnesia-inducing properties) and enhanced recall for the list learned prior to taking the drug (Coenen & Van Luijtelaar, 1997; Fillmore et al., 2001; Hinrichs et al., 1984; Weingartner et al., 1995). Coenen and Van Luijtelaar (1997) argued that the effects of benzodiazepines on memory were analogous to the beneficial effects of sleep. In both cases, information learned prior to being sedated is remembered better than it otherwise would have been, because retroactive interference is reduced due to the reduced rate of information uptake while sedated (or asleep).

This explanation is consistent with the idea that ordinary forgetting is a retroactive effect of subsequent memory formation that accompanies ordinary mental activity. If mental activity is reduced by sleep or if memory formation associated with mental activity is reduced by alcohol or a benzodiazepine drug, prior recently formed memories are protected from the effects of retroactive interference. To summarize, sleep, alcohol, and benzodiazepines all result in retrograde enhancement of memory, and the reason seems to be that a reduced rate of memory formation during the altered state protects recently formed memories from the interference that would otherwise take place.

It seems that in normal participants memory is adversely affected if consolidation is impaired by interfering later activities. Might people suffering from amnesia be especially liable to disruption of consolidation? This possibility is addressed in work reported in Box 6.4.

Box 6.4 When Things Go Wrong: Consolidation, retroactive interference and amnesia

Much of amnesic patients' difficulties in remembering new information (anterograde amnesia) may be due to extreme susceptibility to interference from incoming information disrupting consolidation of earlier acquired information. This theory draws support from observations such as those of Scoville and Milner (1957) who reported that all their patients with severe amnesia, including the famous amnesiac H.M. (see also Chapter 5), 'were able to retain a three-figure number or a pair of unrelated words for several minutes, if care was taken not to distract them in the interval. However, they forgot the instant attention was diverted to a new topic' (p. 15).

Cowan et al. (2004) examined the hypothesis that amnesia is often due to an extreme susceptibility to interference effects in a study inspired by Minami and Dallenbach's (1946) experiment with cockroaches (which we discussed earlier in Box 6.3). They sought to determine whether amnesic patients would retain material better if the training period was followed by an unfilled interval, resting alone in a quiet darkened room as against an interval filled with further cognitive tests. The material consisted of 15 words and patients and suitable control participants were tested immediately after presentation and again after 10 minutes, which were either filled or unfilled. The results are shown in Figure 6.4 and clearly indicate better retention after unfilled intervals than after filled intervals both for the patients and the controls.

Research on normal participants (Dudai, 2004) had found that new memory traces are relatively susceptible to interference and Dewar et al. (2009) examined this effect in amnesic patients by inserting the interfering activity at different points (early or late) in the retention interval. Amnesic and control participants were presented with 15 word lists and after immediate recall had a nine-minute retention interval before delayed recall. During the retention interval a three-minute picture naming task was inserted immediately after the first recall test or after three or six minutes; there was also an unfilled nine-minute retention interval. The results, shown in Figure 6.5 below, clearly indicate that the amnesic patients were particularly susceptible to early occurring interference.

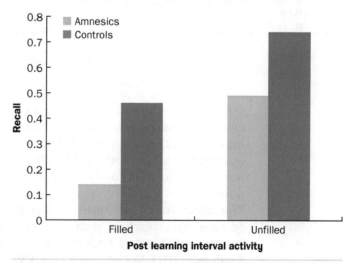

Figure 6.4 Proportion of list of words recalled. These data are after 10 minutes of filled or unfilled intervals for amnesic patients and healthy controls.

Source: Adapted from Cowan et al. (2004). Verbal recall in amnesiacs under conditions of diminished retroactive interference. *Brain*, 27, 825–834.

Dewar et al. interpret these results as showing that new memory traces can become consolidated in amnesic patients, but that post-learning interference disrupts this process substantially. As found in previous literature, this interruption is most detrimental when the interference occurs directly following new learning, that is, when the new memory trace has not yet had a chance to consolidate, but decreases with delay in interference.

In a follow up study by Dewar et al. (2010) it was shown that even when the interfering task (detecting notes in a piano recital) was quite dissimilar to the main memory task (memory for stories) strong retroactive interference was found for amnesic patients. See Figure 6.6.

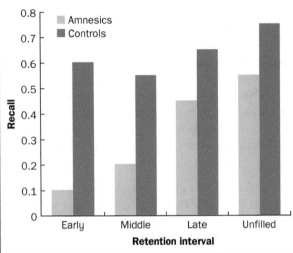

Figure 6.5 **Proportion of list of words recalled.** Data after nine-minute retention interval with interfering activity after varying time periods for amnesic patients and healthy controls.

Source: Adapted from Dewar et al. (2009). Delaying interference enhances memory consolidation in amnesic patients. *Neuropsychology, 23*, 627–634.

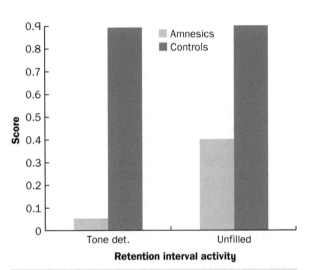

Figure 6.6 **Proportion of correct answers.** Data are correct answers for the story after a 10-minute retention interval with or without interfering activity (tone detection) for amnesic patients and healthy controls.

Source: Adapted from Dewar et al. (2010). Profound retroactive interference in anterograde amnesia. What interferes? *Neuropsychology, 24*, 357.

Evaluation

Overall, the studies outlined here strongly support the view that an important factor in anterograde amnesia is a heightened susceptibility to retroactive interference preventing consolidation. It appears that consolidation is hindered by any mentally demanding activity and not just activity involving materials similar to the to-be-remembered information. Dewar et al. (2007) distinguish similarity based retroactive interference which affects retrieval and diversionary retroactive interference which affects consolidation. This distinction of two types of interference was actually made by early researchers on interference such as Muller and Pilzecker (1900) and Skaggs (1925, 1933) but was subsequently ignored with emphasis being placed on similarity based interference (Anderson, 2003; McGeoch & Nolen, 1933).

FUNCTIONAL APPROACHES TO FORGETTING

Although forgetting is typically regarded in a negative light, as causing us problems in retrieving information when it is needed, there are times when we wish to forget things. When you change town it is useful to forget your old phone number and when a computer password has to be changed it is helpful if the old one is forgotten. In more dramatic cases, people are sometimes plagued with intrusive memories of traumatic events that they would rather not remember (Brewin, 2001).

> **Intrusive memories** are persistent unwanted memories, e.g., of traumatic events, that frequently come to mind.

How selective forgetting might be brought about has been investigated using three main paradigms: retrieval-induced forgetting (Anderson et al., 1994); directed forgetting, (Bjork et al., 1998) and the think/no-think method (Anderson & Green, 2001). We will now discuss these approaches to bringing about forgetting in turn.

Retrieval-induced forgetting (RIF)

The RIF paradigm was developed by Anderson et al. (1994; Anderson, 2005) and deals with the forgetting of memories apparently caused by retrieval of related memories. For example, if you focus on retrieving memories of what went well on a holiday that will likely reduce memory for what went wrong.

> **Retrieval induced forgetting (RIF)** is an impaired ability to recall some items caused by earlier retrieval of related items.

In the laboratory, RIF is generally studied by having participants learn category-item pairs such as 'fruit-apple', 'fruit-banana', 'furniture-chair', 'furniture-table'. After the learning phase, participants are given repeated retrieval trials with the same category and retrieval cue each time, such as 'fruit-a?'. In the example, participants repeatedly retrieve 'apple'. Finally, participants are asked to recall all the examples for each category. Typically, people are less likely to retrieve 'banana' than 'apple' or 'chair' or 'table' and this is known as the RIF effect whereby retrieval practice impairs recall of unpractised category members. It is explained on the assumption that the category cue 'fruit-a?' activates 'banana' to some extent and so successful retrieval of 'apple' requires inhibition of the competing response 'banana' (Bjork et al., 1998). The inhibition interpretation gains support from the finding that the effect persists even when novel cues are used, such as 'monkey-b?' which would cue 'banana' (Anderson & Bell, 2001; Saunders & MacLeod, 2006) and from impaired recognition memory (Hicks & Starns, 2004) and reduced lexical decision speed (Veling & van Knippenberg, 2004) for the unpractised target category member.

Scan to watch Robert Bjork talk about RIF

Directed forgetting (DF)

In the DF paradigm participants are instructed to forget some items but remember others. A real life example is provided by short order cooks who must try to forget previous orders and retain only the current order until it is in turn supplanted by the next order (Bjork, 1970).

> **Directed forgetting (DF)** is memory impairment brought about by instructions to forget some items.

There are two variants of DF which are the *item based* form of DF and the *list based* method of DF. In the item based method, participants are shown items to remember one at a time and after each item are told whether that item should be forgotten or retained. After the complete list, participants are tested on memory for all the items. Basden and Basden (1996) found markedly impaired recall for to-be-forgotten items than for to-be-remembered items, and the effect held for words and pictures. DF effects for the item based approach were also found on tests of recognition memory (Basden et al., 1993) in which participants only have to indicate whether each item was seen previously rather than recall items. It seems likely that participants carry out extra encoding of the to-be-remembered items when the 'remember' instruction is given and stop rehearsing the to-be-forgotten items when the instruction is received to 'forget'.

In the list method of DF, the participants are given two lists (both initially to be memorized) and are only told to forget the first list after it has been presented and before going on to memorize the second list. Finally, participants are asked to remember both lists. Typically, participants given the 'forget' instruction remember less of the first list than control participants and recall the second list *better than controls*. Thus, there is reduced proactive interference from the first list after instructions to forget it have been given. Unlike item based DF, recognition of the to-be-forgotten items seems to hold up (Bjork et al., 1998). List based DF seems to affect accessibility rather than availability. Accessibility refers to the ease with which a stored memory can be retrieved and is measured by ease of recall; availability refers to whether the trace is stored at all or not and is indicated by whether the item is recognized or not.

Think/no-think (TNT)

Think/no-think (TNT) is a memory manipulation in which participants are instructed not to retrieve a memory even when a strong cue is present.

The TNT paradigm is a relatively new type of task which reflects situations where a person wants to not retrieve a memory when confronted with a strong cue for that memory. For example, if you had been in a car crash at a set of traffic lights on your way to work or school, you might not want to remember the event every time you pass those lights. It has so far been explored using verbal materials rather than real life traumatic stimuli.

In the TNT method, participants study cue-target pairs, such as 'ordeal-roach' so that they can reliably recall the second word when given the first word as a cue. In the next stage, participants see the cue words and in most cases have to recall the target response word, but on some trials the cue words are printed in red and participants are instructed not to retrieve the response when the cue is red. The instructions are not only to not say the word, but also to keep the response from entering consciousness. After many trials with TNT instructions, there is a final test of people's ability to recall all the response words. Levy and Anderson (2008) found the expected effect with about 95 per cent of 'think' words recalled as against about 75 per cent of 'no think' words. A neuro-imaging study (Anderson et al., 2004) found that on no think trials people showed reduced activation in the hippocampal area relative to think trials. Hippocampal activation had been shown to be related to subjective reports of retrieval (Squire, 1992) and so the finding helps validate the method by indicating that no think trials probably did indeed involve absence of retrieval and also suggests that people can deliberately regulate hippocampal activation.

The TNT paradigm is still fairly new and failures to replicate the effect over three experiments closely following Anderson and Green's (2001) procedure have been reported by Bulevich et al. (2006). Hertel and Calcaterra (2005) found that the TNT effect depends on the participants' strategies; in their studies, the TNT effect was only found when participants used the strategy of thinking of a different word in the don't think conditions whether spontaneously or as a result of strategy instructions.

Evaluation

In this section we have been discussing forgetting; the loss of the ability to retrieve information that had been learned. Early studies used material intended to be meaningless, particularly nonsense syllables, in an attempt to get at pure learning without the complications of meaningful materials. However, nonsense syllables themselves proved to vary in their meaningfulness to participants and later studies used meaningful words, although often in lists rather than in meaningful text. The strong roles of interference from earlier learning on later learning (proactive interference) and of interference from later learning on remembering earlier learning (retroactive interference) was shown early in the study of memory. The importance of consolidation of memories was shown in studies of sleep versus waking activities following learning and from work with cockroaches that were immobilized or not after maze learning. Consolidation approaches furthermore explain the counter intuitive benefits on later recall of alcohol and some other drugs following a study period. These findings may explain the common student habit of study by day followed by drinking in the evenings! The symptoms of people suffering from anterograde amnesia after trauma can be explained quite well by difficulties with consolidation of new memories in that they seem especially badly affected by retroactive interference following study.

EVERYDAY/REAL WORLD MEMORY

The research on learning and forgetting that we have been discussing so far has largely been driven by theoretical concerns, such as, is forgetting due to decay, interference or consolidation problems? The resulting laboratory studies that use artificial materials with tightly controlled learning and recall conditions can seem far removed from everyday memory. In 1978, Ulric Neisser expressed some exasperation with laboratory based research in a keynote speech at an international conference on practical aspects of memory, when he said, 'If X is an interesting or socially significant aspect of memory, then psychologists have hardly ever studied X' (1978, p. 4).

These remarks provoked considerable controversy (e.g. Baddeley, 1993; Banaji & Crowder, 1989; Koriat & Goldsmith, 1996; Kvavilashvili & Ellis, 2004) and seem to have influenced many researchers towards studying memory phenomena drawn from everyday life (such as eyewitness testimony, face recognition, autobiographical memory and flashbulb memories) and to using more naturalistic methods and materials. The thrust of the everyday memory movement is often said to be a search for ecological validity in research. A study has ecological validity to the extent that its findings are applicable to everyday or real life settings. Two aspects of ecological validity have been distinguished by Kvavilashvili and Ellis (2004) in their thorough review of the history of the everyday memory movement and these are: representativeness and generalizability. Representativeness increases with the realism and naturalness of the study's materials and tasks. So, a study of different strategies employed by fast and slow learners of statistical computing methods (as in Green & Gilhooly, 1990) would be relatively high on representativeness of, in this case, classroom learning. Generalizability refers to the degree to which results are broadly applicable. Ebbinghaus's (1885) original studies of spaced versus massed learning using nonsense syllables may have been low in representativeness but the basic result has proven highly generalizable to many real world learning situations. Kvavilashvili and Ellis (2004) argued strongly that generalizability is the more important aspect of ecological validity since the more widely a finding can be applied the better.

> **Ecological validity** is the degree to which the results of a laboratory study can be applied to a real life situation.
> **Representativeness** increases with the realism and naturalness of the study's materials and tasks.
> **Generalizability** is the degree to which results are broadly applicable to a wide range of situations.

© 2Stockmedia/iStock

Over the years the heat has gone out of the controversy regarding the relative merits of everyday as against laboratory studies. Even by 1988, at the second International Conference on Practical Aspects of Memory, Neisser had modified his position and said: 'If X is an interesting or socially important memory phenomenon, the chances are good – though not 100 per cent – that quite a few people are trying to study it' (Neisser, 1988, p. 546). A concern with everyday aspects of memory has become mainstream and everyday memory research typically uses laboratory methods to reach generalizable conclusions and theory-driven researchers look for connections with everyday memory issues to show that their work has practical relevance. Thus, the two approaches are largely reconciled.

Some of the typical topics of everyday memory research, such as autobiographical memory and prospective memory have been discussed in Chapter 5, dealing with long-term memory. In this chapter, we will now turn to work on flashbulb memories as a good example of research that derives from a phenomenon in everyday life but which uses methods derived from laboratory studies.

FLASHBULB MEMORIES

Most people feel that they have exceptionally detailed and vivid memories for the circumstances in which they first learned of dramatic and highly significant events such as: the attacks on the World Trade Center on 11 September 2001; the London transport system attacks of 7 July 2005; the death of Princess Diana on 31 August 1997 and, for older readers, the assassination of John F. Kennedy, on 23 November 1963. Brown and Kulik (1977) examined memories for the Kennedy assassination and labelled such memories flashbulb memories. They proposed that dramatic, surprising events that were important for the individual, caused a special memory mechanism to activate and record in a permanent form information about the event and surrounding contextual information such as: who gave the information; where the news was learned; and what the individual did after learning the news.

Flashbulb memory is a vivid memory of a dramatic event and of the circumstances in which the event was experienced or heard about.

Scan to watch a video on flashbulb memory research related to 9/11

Neisser (1982) suggested that the apparent permanence of flashbulb memories was due to the well-established mechanism of rehearsal rather than to a special specifically 'flashbulb' mechanism. In this view, people are much more likely to discuss the news with others and that includes rehearsing the circumstances under which the news was heard. Important and dramatic public events are also repeated extensively in the news media not only on the initial occasion and for days afterwards, but also on anniversaries, and so memories of the flashbulb events are cued and retrieved relatively often as compared to other events. Consistent with the rehearsal explanation, Bonhannon (1988) in a study with 686 participants, found that memory for the Challenger space shuttle disaster after eight months was more detailed in participants who reported more re-tellings of the event during the retention period.

Although it was initially proposed that flashbulb memories were unusually accurate, it turns out that major inaccuracies are not uncommon in flashbulb memories. For example, Pezdek (2003) found that 73 per cent of respondents agreed that they had seen video records on television of the first plane striking the first tower of the World Trade Center on 11 September 2001. However, there were no such video records available. Presumably, participants were confused by the recordings of the second plane which were available. Perhaps more striking is the report by Ost et al. (2002), that a substantial number of UK respondents agreed that they had seen a film of Princess Diana's car crash; but this film does not exist. It seems then, that flashbulb memories are open to effects of leading questions as has also been demonstrated in studies of eye witness testimony based on normal memory situations (Loftus, 1975). See the next section of this chapter for more on effects of leading questions.

Weaver (1993) examined changes over time in recalls of ordinary memories (for a meeting with a friend or roommate) and of flashbulb memories (for the first President Bush announcing the beginning of the first Gulf War on television) over a total of one year.

Memories were elicited on three occasions: within two days, after three months and after 12 months. Weaver found that accuracy, as indicated by consistency, fell off quite markedly after three months but thereafter was stable, for both flashbulb and non-flashbulb memories. Both types of memories were equally accurate (consistent with first recall records). The main difference which emerged was that participants were more confident about the flashbulb memories but that did not translate into increased accuracy.

Overall, it appears that flashbulb memories are susceptible to similar forms of forgetting and distortion as normal memories. Advantages for memories of 'flashbulb' events may be attributed to their distinctiveness which reduces interference from similar memories (Cubelli & della Sala, 2008) and to rehearsal effects (Bonhannon, 1988). The possible role of emotion in flashbulb memories is considered later, in Chapter 14.

EYEWITNESS TESTIMONY

Scan to watch a clip on the reliability of eyewitness testimony

An important real life area in which considerable reliance is placed on memory is in the legal system, where witnesses are questioned on what they remember of events around a crime. The law tends to the common sense view that memory is rather like a videotape that witnesses can replay and report accurately. Jurors are no doubt influenced by how confident witnesses seem to be and by the volume of detail reported. However, a number of factors suggest that eyewitness testimony should be treated with caution. Some witnesses may not have attended very much to the events they are asked to report. For example, if you are walking down the street and a man steps briskly out of a bank as you are passing, jumps into a waiting car and is driven off, you may not attend much at the time, but later be asked to give a detailed report of the man's height, hair colour, clothes and the make, colour and registration plate of the car, if it turns out that you had witnessed a get away from a bank robbery. Witnesses inside the bank probably would realize that a robbery was happening but their recalls would likely be adversely affected by stress and anxiety. Indeed, Deffenbacher et al. (2004) in a meta-analytic review found clear impairing effects of stress and anxiety on recall of faces and of details in crime scenes compared with low anxiety and stress conditions. Further, if the crime involves a weapon, witnesses focus their attention on that, and are impaired in reporting non-weapon details (Tollestrup et al., 1994). See also Chapter 14 for more discussion of the role of emotion in memory.

A further factor is that witnesses in court are questioned in particular ways which may affect recall. In a classic study, Loftus and Zanni (1975) showed participants a film of a multi-car accident. For Group 'A', a broken headlight was seen in the film; for Group 'B', no broken headlight was seen in the film. Later, participants were asked either 'Did you see A broken headlight?' or 'Did you see THE broken headlight?'

It was found that Group A showed no difference from wording but in Group B, 15 per cent of those asked a question about 'THE' broken light responded 'yes' compared to 7 per cent who were asked about 'A' broken headlight. The small change from the word 'a' to the word 'the' doubled the false reporting of broken glass. See also Box 13.4 for a rather similar finding by Loftus and Palmer (1974).

Not just the words in questions, even small ones like 'the' and 'a', but also the gestures that accompany the questions can influence recall by eyewitnesses. Gurney et al. (2013) interviewed 90 people about the contents of a video they had watched. During the interviews, the researchers deliberately performed misleading hand gestures to suggest inaccurate information about the detail in the video. These hand gestures included chin stroking to suggest someone had a beard, although the man in the video did not have a beard. It was found that the witnesses were three times more likely to recall seeing a beard when one was gestured to them, than those interviewees who were not gestured to. Other hand gestures used in the research included touching a ring finger (to suggest a ring), grasping a wrist (to suggest a watch) and pretending to pull on gloves. All of these gestures implied details that did not actually appear in the video, and the results were similar to those with the misinformation about the beard.

From these and related studies, such as Loftus's study of implanting false autobiographical memories (discussed in Chapter 5) it seems that post-event questions and cues can change memory for the event. These effects can be seen as examples of *retroactive interference*, as we have discussed in earlier sections of this chapter, in which later information impairs and distorts recall of earlier learned material. These findings fit well with the view that memory is changeable and reconstructive rather than fixed and simply reproductive of what was initially perceived, as Bartlett (1932), Neisser (1967) and others have long proposed (see also Chapter 5).

As we have seen, memories appear to be liable to modification by misleading questions and later information that can affect earlier memories. A practical example of memory malleability is provided by the real life case of the Oklahoma bombing of 1995, which is discussed in Box 6.5.

Box 6.5 Practical Application: Eyewitness recall and the Oklahoma bombing – was there a third man?

On 19 April 1995 the Alfred P. Murrah Federal Building in Oklahoma City was destroyed by a huge truck bomb, which killed 168 and injured over 600 people. Forensic evidence quickly led to the arrests and later convictions of Timothy McVeigh and Terry Nichols. However, concerns quickly arose and persist that there was a third man involved. The main reason for this belief seems to lie in problems with eyewitness testimony (Memon & Wright, 1999).

McVeigh had rented the van used in the bombing and three staff at the rental shop had witnessed McVeigh signing papers (under a false name) and checking the vehicle before taking it away. The investigators quickly located the rental shop from which the bombers' truck had been rented and called the shop asking all staff to remain there until they could be questioned. The staff gathered what was at issue and discussed their memories of the truck rental events of the critical day before the FBI agents arrived to question them. One of the staff clearly remembered two men and gave a useful description of McVeigh but also of a second man with a black teeshirt, baseball cap and tattoo (not Terry Nichols, who had helped construct the bomb but not plant it). The other witnesses were less sure about their testimony and especially about the other man (code named John Doe2). But, as time went on, the unsure witnesses became more convinced of John Doe2's presence that day. However, there was surveillance camera evidence that McVeigh had been alone in a fast food outlet before getting a taxi to the rental shop; the taxi driver also testified that McVeigh was alone.

It emerged that there had been a second truck rental that afternoon, involving two men, one of whom indeed wore a black tee shirt and a baseball cap and had a visible tattoo. It appears that in reconstructing memories the two events had become merged (retroactive interference, again), particularly in the memory of the most confident witness and he had influenced the other witnesses when they discussed the events and so in turn affected their memories. Although assorted conspiracy theorists are sure there was a third man, and probably many more than three involved, insufficient evidence has been found to convince the investigating authorities that there was a third man. It seems most likely that this is a case of malleable memories providing somewhat unreliable witness accounts.

EFFECTIVE STUDYING

Student readers are faced with the major real life task of learning large volumes of information and then recalling and using it in examinations. Although most examiners do not want to see verbatim regurgitation of their lectures or of chunks of set text, nevertheless students must retain learned material and recall accurately what is important, in order to answer possibly challenging questions. Does the cognitive psychology of learning and forgetting offer any useful advice for student learning?

From earlier in this chapter, we have seen from laboratory studies that the deep processing of unconnected items (as in word lists) promotes memory as against superficial processing. Similar results have been found in real life learning of meaningful material at university level. Much of this work has involved comparing effects of learning styles. Three main styles of learning have been identified through questionnaire studies (Biggs et al., 2001) and these are:

- *Surface learning*: in which students try to learn texts by heart without seeking understanding.
- *Deep learning*: in which students make a determined effort to understand the material and make it meaningful to them.
- *Strategic learning*: in which students put effort into finding out what topics and types of questions are likely in their examinations and devise strategies to cover the minimum number of topics required.

It has been found that deep learning produces better examination results than surface learning (Entwhistle, 1987). In a study of medical students those combining deep and strategic learning did especially well in examinations (McManus et al., 1998). Thus, overall, as in the laboratory, deeper processing is more effective in real life than superficial processing; deeper processing focused on likely examination topics is especially effective, at least for medical students.

What might be involved at a more detailed level in deep learning? The survey, question, read, recite and review (SQ3R) approach devised in 1946 by Robinson offers specific suggestions for effective learning especially when reading textbook chapters. The method has been widely adopted and has been favourably tested in a laboratory setting (Morris, 1979) and in a real university context by Carlston (2011) who concluded that SQ3R offers specific suggestions for effective learning which improve examination performance. The SQ3R stages may be summarized as follows.

- *Survey*: get an overall view of what is in the chapter. Read the chapter summary and skim through the pages to get an idea of what topics are covered.
- *Question*: come up with relevant questions for each section, before you read the section.
- *Read*: read through a section with your questions in mind and try to relate it to what you have already read or know from elsewhere.
- *Recite*: at the end of a section, try to recall the main ideas of that section. If you are missing some, re-read the section.
- *Review*: after reading a whole chapter, recall the main ideas and try to interrelate them. If need be, go back to the beginning and start again.

This is a way to read for understanding which also promotes recall of important facts. Its effectiveness is probably also due to the realistic feedback it gives students about how well their learning is going. Simply reading texts can give one an illusion of knowing the material because it becomes familiar but it may not be well enough learned for recall. Testing requires recall as do examinations and so testing can indicate when more study is required.

A number of experiments have shown that testing in itself, even without feedback about the correct answers, can be effective. For example, Roediger and Karpicke (2006a) ran two experiments, in which students studied texts covering scientific topics. Some experimental groups took one or three immediate free-recall tests, without feedback, or restudied the material one or three times without the tests. Finally, all students then took a retention test five minutes, two days, or one week later. When the final test was given after five minutes, repeated studying improved recall as compared to repeated testing. However, on the delayed tests, more testing produced much greater retention than studying, even though repeated studying increased students' confidence in their ability to remember the material. It seems that testing is an effective means of improving learning, not just of assessing it.

Overall, Roediger and Karpicke argue that use of testing during learning may improve performance in educational settings at all levels from primary through to university level, at least in very factual subjects (Roediger & Karpicke, 2006b). Frequent testing leads students to space their study efforts (and spacing is known to boost learning, as discussed earlier in this chapter), and permits them and their instructors to assess their knowledge on an ongoing basis, so that re-studying can focus on problem areas.

Evaluation

Early studies with their focus on learning lists of nonsense syllables were very removed from real life learning and forgetting. More recent research has tried to remedy this gap between laboratory and everyday learning by studying more ecologically valid situations.

Flashbulb memories for dramatic and highly significant events such as the World Trade Center attacks have been compared with memory for more routine events; it appears that these memories can be explained in terms of features that usually benefit memories such as distinctiveness and frequency of rehearsal. A special kind of memory does not seem to be needed to explain flashbulb memories.

Eyewitness testimony is an important real world activity based on personal memories and recall processes. Lay ideas that memory is like a video recorder, and that eyewitness confidence and detail in testimony are cues to reliability, can lead all too readily to false convictions based on what is actually mistaken eyewitness identification. Research has shown how memories can be affected by misleading questions and by retroactive interference from events after the crucial incidents of the crime.

Finally, we discussed effective study methods to boost efficiency of learning and recall for meaningful material as found in university courses. This brought us round again to the importance of deep processing (for meaning) as against superficial processing (for rote recall without understanding). Frequent self-testing was also found to be useful to monitor the progress of learning and to avoid false confidence that one knows something merely because it has become familiar through reading over and over. In an examination, material needs to be recalled, not recognized, and so effective study will practise recall and assess progress in being able to recall what is needed when it is needed.

Summary

This chapter has covered the acquisition of knowledge (learning), its retrieval successes (remembering) and failures (forgetting).

What happens at encoding is important for later remembering. Levels of processing theory stresses the role of deep (meaning based) versus shallow (surface based) encoding. Tests of incidental memory support the approach in that 'deep' orienting tasks lead to better memory than 'shallow' tasks. The theory has been criticized for its possible circularity.

Mnemonic methods using interacting imagery at encoding (methods of loci and pegwords) have a long history and experiments support their value for memory.

A few very rare individuals display superior memory in general and seem to have underlying neural functioning differences from the normal. Shereshevskii, for example, had extremely strong synaesthesia which automatically generated vivid multisensory images. However, most people who display exceptional memory abilities do so in limited domains, such as number sequences, names and faces, the order of playing cards taken from a number of packs shuffled together, and extensive practice with suitable mnemonics can be shown to underlie their skills.

The encoding specificity theory points to the importance of having the same cues available at test as were present at encoding. Context dependent retrieval, whereby materials are best recalled in the same environmental (or internal) state as at learning, further supports the encoding specificity theory.

Spacing of learning trials is a way of boosting later memory and this too is linked to encoding specificity in that spaced trials give more encoding variability which gives more chance of some cues overlapping at test and learning.

Forgetting occurs when we cannot retrieve information that had been available from memory in the past. Early studies using nonsense syllables established the form of the forgetting curve (steep initial decline and then gradually reducing rate of decline) which has been found to hold over many types of materials.

The main theoretical ideas about forgetting are that it may be due to: decay of traces with time, proactive and retroactive interference with other memories, or lack of consolidation of memories (which are fragile initially, but strengthen with consolidation). Early studies minimizing activity during the retention (storage) stage, through sleep or other methods, found that rates of forgetting were markedly greater after retention periods filled with activity and attributed these results to greater retroactive interference from new memories formed during the active periods than during the inactive periods. Neuroscience based studies stress the role of consolidation as underlying benefits of sleep, inactivity and even of alcohol and tranquillizers, for recall of material learned shortly before sleep or ingesting alcohol or benzodiazapines. A marked susceptibility of amnesiacs to consolidation failure when any intervening activity occurs between acquisition and test has been found.

Functional approaches to forgetting stress the benefits of normal forgetting and have examined how selective forgetting may be brought about deliberately.

A movement to increase the real life relevance or ecological validity of memory research has been influential since Neisser deplored the artificiality of much laboratory research. As an example of real world memory, we discussed flashbulb memories for dramatic events. Overall, such memories seem explicable in terms of established memory phenomena (such as vividness, distinctiveness and rehearsal effects) and do not seem to require special processes. Research on eyewitness testimony uncovered problems in such testimony caused by misleading questions and post-event information as well as by anxiety and stress. Finally, effective study methods have been devised that stress deep processing and frequent testing to check progress. Simple re-studying without testing boosts confidence but is less effective than studying with repeated testing.

Review questions

1 What are the main factors that affect efficiency of learning?

2 To what extent is forgetting due to decay, to interference and to consolidation failures?

3 Are flashbulb memories special?

4 Is forgetting always a bad thing?

5 Can we deliberately forget information?

6 Could practice produce exceptional memory abilities?

7 How well does Sherlock Holmes's 'little attic' model for learning and forgetting hold up in the face of the evidence?

8 What study methods are especially effective and why?

FURTHER READING

Baddeley, A. D., Eysenck, M. W., & Anderson, M. C. (2009). *Memory*. Hove, UK: Psychology Press.

Ericsson, K. A. (2003). Exceptional memorizers: Made, not born. *Trends in Cognitive Sciences, 7*, 233–235.

Wixted, J. T. (2004). The psychology and neuroscience of forgetting. *Annual Review of Psychology, 55*, 235–269.

CHAPTER 7:
CONCEPTS AND KNOWLEDGE REPRESENTATION

Preview questions

1 What are concepts? And what are they for?
2 What advantages and disadvantages might there be to using concepts?
3 Can you clearly define Cake as against Biscuit?
4 Are some birds more 'bird-like' than others?
5 In what way is imagining a chair similar to seeing and using an actual chair?

INTRODUCTION

Although the world is full of unique objects and events, it is very useful to treat many distinct objects as if they were the same. So, new cups, tables and dogs are usually treated as if they are essentially the same as previously experienced cups, tables and dogs. When we treat distinct objects as the same as other distinct objects, we are using concepts to represent all the distinct objects that make up the categories concerned. Thus, concepts are mental representations of broad classes or categories of things, actions and relationships.

> Concepts are mental representations of classes of items such as 'cats', 'even numbers', and so on.

Dealing in concepts rather than in distinct individual objects is clearly an efficient way to work and emerges as an inevitable result of how the brain responds to stimulation, in that similar stimuli evoke similar activation patterns and by association will arouse similar memories and action tendencies. So, if something that looks like previously encountered tigers comes round the corner, this will activate thoughts of tigers and their properties, one of which being that they are dangerous to humans and the action tendency to flee will become very strong, very rapidly. Concepts allow us to organize information in long-term semantic memory very efficiently into hierarchical structures. Thus, if we have 'tiger' linked to the higher order concept 'mammal' we do not need to explicitly store the fact that tigers suckle their offspring; if required that can be deduced from the knowledge that 'all tigers are mammals' and that 'mammals suckle their offspring'.

Overall, our long-term knowledge about the world is based on concepts and relations among concepts. Also, representations of current situations are in terms of concepts. So for example, faced with the problem of a car that will not start we will draw on concepts of 'car batteries', 'ignition systems', 'electrical leads' to represent the situation and invoke rules such as , 'If the car battery is flat, then the car will not start' to help us towards a solution.

As we shall see, all higher-level mental activity, such as problem solving, reasoning and decision making, discussed in later chapters, involves imagining possible actions, choices and inferences, in terms of concepts. Clearly then, the study of concepts is a key area of cognitive psychology, essential to understanding how we represent knowledge and consequently has attracted a great deal of research interest over the years.

In the first main section of this chapter we will discuss theories about what concepts are and how they are used. The second main section will deal with the fact that when people work with concepts of concrete things such as 'cats', 'cups' or 'cars', they often experience images of the objects. Such images are like pictures but are purely mental. Visual images convey information as to what an object looks like and the image associated with a concept would seem likely to be important in using that concept. We will discuss whether images do play an important role and if so, how? For example, do images help people to solve problems and make good decisions? Thus, the second main section of this chapter will discuss what we know about images and imagery.

> Imagery is the mental representation of sensory properties of objects – experienced as like perceiving the object but with less vividness than in reality.

THEORIES OF CONCEPTUAL REPRESENTATION

Despite the pervasive role of concepts in cognition, there is no universal agreement on the best way to define concepts as a whole. It is more useful to think in terms of different types of concepts and in the following sections we will consider a number of alternative approaches to 'concepts' that have been put forward and we will explore the extent to which any of these approaches can cover all the data or if they apply to some but not all concepts. The approaches that we will consider are those in terms of definitions, prototypes, exemplars, theory, essentialism and grounded representations.

DEFINITIONAL APPROACH

Think of arm chairs and reading chairs and dining room chairs, and kitchen chairs, chairs that pass into benches, chairs that cross the boundary and become settees, dentist's chairs, thrones, opera stalls, seats of all sorts, those miraculous fungoid growths that cumber the floor of arts and crafts exhibitions, and you will perceive what a lax bundle in fact is this simple straightforward term. In cooperation with an intelligent joiner I would undertake to defeat any definition of chair or chairishness that you gave me.

(H.G. Wells, 1908)

Some concepts are well defined and clear black and white definitions can be given. Well-defined concepts are the essence of formal subjects such as mathematics and are sought throughout the sciences. So, for example, the well-defined concept of an 'even number' is of 'a number that is divisible by itself and by 2 without remainder'. An 'odd number' is simply 'any number that is not-even'. Some everyday concepts are similarly well defined, such as the concept of 'bachelor' as an adult, unmarried male. Note that concepts are typically formed from combinations of features that are themselves concepts. So, in the bachelor case, the definition uses concepts of 'adult', 'male' and 'unmarried'. Each of these requires its own definition and within a given legal system each would have its own clear criteria. So, to be adult, one would have to be above a certain age, currently 18 years in the UK; to be unmarried, one would have to have not entered into a legally binding state of wedlock; to be classed as male is normally unproblematic, but even this feature or concept has difficult cases, such as intersexed individuals – where a person has genital features characteristic of both sexes.

Many and perhaps most everyday concepts are not so well defined and exhibit a degree of fuzziness. So, for example, as pointed out in the quote above from H. G. Wells, there is no agreed formal definition of a chair (as against a stool, say) or of a cup (as against a mug). The lack of clear definitions can have important real life consequences. For example, a famous legal case in the UK hinged on the definitions of 'cake' versus 'biscuit' and you can see some of the details of this case and of a US case about whether burritos are sandwiches in Box 7.1.

Box 7.1 Practical Application: Cakes versus biscuits and burritos versus sandwiches

You might briefly consider what you feel are the defining features of cakes as against biscuits (or cookies in the USA)! This is not an easy matter. A food manufacturer in the UK produced a product which was sold as 'Jaffa Cakes' from 1927 onwards. These were orange flavoured, of a size typical of biscuits and covered in chocolate, but of a consistency typical of cakes (i.e. soft) rather than the consistency typical of biscuits (hard). Figure 7.1 shows a cross-section and both sides of a Jaffa Cake.

This product belatedly attracted the attention of the tax authorities in 1991 as chocolate coated biscuits, but not chocolate coated cakes, were liable to a purchase tax, known as Value Added Tax (VAT).

The tax authorities proclaimed that Jaffa Cakes were instances of the concept 'biscuit' and being chocolate coated should be taxed at 17.5 per cent per cent. The manufacturers fought the matter in court, asserting that Jaffa Cakes were actually instances of the concept 'cake' and so should be liable for 0 per cent tax. As a result of this dispute, many of the country's finest legal brains tussled over the issue, 'Was the so called Jaffa "cake" an example of the concept "cake" or of the concept "biscuit"?'

Eventually a ruling was reached that the product should indeed be classed as 'cake' because when it went stale it became harder (as did clear cut, agreed, examples of cakes) while clear cut, agreed, examples of biscuits went soft when stale.

A rather similar case in Worcester, Massachusetts, USA, 2006 (Commonwealth of Massachusetts, Superior Court Civil Action 2006-196313), ended in a ruling by Judge J. A. Locke that a burrito was *not* a sandwich! The case had been brought by a sandwich outlet in a shopping mall that had exclusive rights to sell sandwiches in the mall and feared competition from a pro- posed Mexican food outlet which would serve burritos. If burritos had

Figure 7.1 Outside and inside of a 'Jaffa Cake'.

Source: © gojak/iStock

been deemed to be examples of the concept 'sandwich', the Mexican food outlet would not have been allowed to open in the mall. The judge relied on a dictionary definition of 'sandwich' which stipulated that a sandwich is two thin slices of bread between which is a thin layer of meat, cheese or other savoury filling. As a burrito is made with a single tortilla, not two slices of bread, burritos were deemed not to be 'sandwiches'. It may be noted that the judge's preferred definition could be challenged, as it excludes 'open' sandwiches made with one slice of bread; it seems that the 'sandwich' concept may not be open to simple definition after all.

Although clear cut definitions of concepts are often desirable and can be found in formal subjects and sciences, such as mathematics, it appears that most everyday concepts are not well defined. McCloskey and Glucksberg (1978) showed this for a range of everyday categories in a study in which people were asked to put items such as 'chair' and 'bookends' into everyday categories, such as 'furniture' or 'ornaments'. Everyone put 'chair' into the 'furniture' category, but unusual items such as 'bookends' caused considerable disagreement between participants and inconsistency within participants over time. If the furniture concept was well defined such results would not be found because everyone would agree what was furniture and what was not, just as everyone would agree that '3' is an odd number and '4' is an even number.

Since most concepts that we work with in everyday life are not well defined, a major part of this area of study concerns alternative ways in which ill-defined concepts might be represented and used. This is the next topic that we will now go on to discuss.

PROTOTYPE APPROACHES

Consider for example the proceedings that we call 'games'. I mean board-games, card-games, ball-games, Olympic-games, and so on. What is common to them all? Don't say: 'There *must* be something common, or they would not be called "games" ' – but look and see whether there is anything common to all. For if you look at them you will not see something that is common to all, but similarities, relationships, and a whole series of them at that.

I can think of no better expression to characterize these similarities than 'family resemblances'; for the various resemblances between members of a family: build, features, colour of eyes, gait, temperament, etc. etc. overlap and criss-cross in the same way. – And I shall say 'games' form a family.

(Wittgenstein, 1953, pp. 66–67)

Introducing prototypes

One point which emerges from the Jaffa Cake saga is that everyday categories have members that vary markedly in how typical they are. The Jaffa Cake is not a typical cake being biscuit-like in shape and size, but it is not a typical biscuit either, and so lies in a border area. If all concepts were purely definitional and well defined then all examples would be equally representative and decisions about category membership would be clear cut. So, the number '7' and the number '13' are equally good examples of odd numbers. However, Rosch and colleagues (Rosch, 1973; Rosch & Mervis, 1975) found that over many everyday categories, people reliably judged some examples as more typical of the category than others. So, a robin is judged more typical of the 'Bird' category than is an emu. Both are agreed to be birds and on a simple definitional view should thus be equally typical, but they are clearly not seen as equally typical by most people.

A number of aspects of performance with concepts are affected by typicality. So, in sentence verification tasks (that is, judging whether a sentence is true or false), people were faster to respond 'True' to 'A robin is a bird' than to respond 'True' to 'A chicken is a bird' (McCloskey & Glucksberg, 1978; Rosch, 1973). In the study of semantic memory, as discussed in Chapter 5, an often used task is one of listing examples of category members (e.g. list as many birds as you can). As you would expect, in such tasks, highly typical instances are produced more often than non-typical instances (Mervis et al., 1976).

> **Typicality** is the extent to which an object is representative of a category.

People generally find it quite easy to make typicality judgements. The typicality rating task asks participants to rate on a seven-point scale how good an example is (e.g. a robin) of a given category (e.g. 'Bird') but the question arises of how are typicality judgements made? Rosch and Mervis (1975) obtained evidence on this question by asking participants to list all the attributes or properties that they could for 20 examples of 6 different categories (Furniture, Fruit, Vehicle, Vegetable, Weapons & Clothing). The examples varied widely in rated typicality – for example, in the Furniture category from the most typical, Chair, to the least typical, Telephone. It was found that very few properties were shared by all instances of a given category (contrary to the Definitional approach) but rather some properties were shared more or less widely among group members. Rosch and Mervis proposed that the members of a category shared a family resemblance to each other and that members could be given scores for how much they resembled other members of the group. So, if an item had say three attributes and the first attribute was also found in 16 other members, the second in 10 other members and the third in two other members, it was given a family resemblance score of $16 + 10 + 2 = 28$. It was found that the family resemblance scores for the items in the six categories correlated very highly with the ratings of the items' typicalities on a seven-point scale So, the more an item had a family resemblance to other items in the category, the more typical it was rated to be. From this it could be argued that typicality judgements could be based on how closely the item resembled all other category members. For example, a robin has more shared features with other birds than does a penguin, and is regarded as a more typical bird than is a penguin.

> **Family resemblance** is the tendency for members of a category to be similar to each other but without having any one characteristic in common to all of them.

The item in a category that has the highest overall family resemblance to the other category members could be said to be a prototype of that category. However, most prototype theories do not propose that the prototype needs to be an actual instance but rather that the prototype is a statistically average member of the category. Just as the average family with 2.2 children does not actually exist, so also the prototype may not actually exist. In support of this idea, it has been found that people can form a prototype without experiencing it directly. Studies of category learning have presented participants with examples derived by modifying an unseen prototype and after learning, participants correctly classified the now presented prototype more quickly and reliably than other new instances. This has been found with a wide range of stimuli, from dot patterns (Posner & Keele, 1970) to written character descriptions (Reed & Friedman, 1973) and schematic faces (Reed, 1972). The mental prototype seems to build up as an average picture of the category members even though the average is never actually experienced.

> **Prototype** is an ideal example that best represents a category.

Levels of categories and prototypes

Categories and concepts typically form into hierarchies, such as Animal, Dog, Pekinese, and so on (see Figure 7.2).

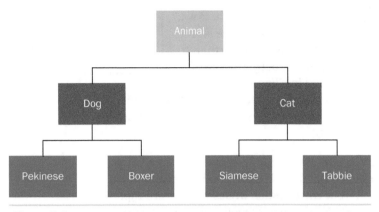

Figure 7.2   Example conceptual hierarchy of dogs and cats. Animals form natural hierarchies of species and breeds.

In a conceptual hierarchy, lower level categories are nested within higher-level categories.

When we deal with objects there is thus often a choice of level of categorization. For example, if we have to name a picture (of a particular saw) as quickly as possible, will we tend to give a high-level superordinate category label (e.g. Tool) a low-level subordinate category label (Cross-cutting handsaw) or an intermediate level label (Saw)? In practice the mid-level concepts seem to be most readily evoked and used. Rosch et al. (1976) argued that the mid-level is the fundamental one and called it the basic level of categorization. At this level the members of the categories are highly similar to each other but the category concepts are quite distinct. So Hammers and Saws are distinct from each other (few features in common) while types of saws are similar to each other, as are types of hammers. The superordinate category, Tools, consists of exemplars that have little in common. Another way of thinking about basic levels is to say that a basic level categorization is most informative for communication purposes. As Fodor (1998) commented, ' "It's a car" tells you a lot about a vehicle; but that it's a sports car doesn't add a lot to what "it's a car" already told you' (p. 91); and, we could add, that saying 'It's a vehicle', or worse, 'It's an artefact' is not as informative as 'It's a car'.

> Basic level categories are categories formed of items that are highly similar and at an intermediate level in a concept hierarchy.

Developmental studies of early language (Rosch et al., 1976) support the primacy of basic level concepts in that early acquired and early used words are labels for basic level concepts ('Dog' rather than the superordinate 'Animal' or the subordinate 'Alsatian').

Evaluation

Although the prototype approach has been usefully applied to a range of conceptual tasks such as category-exemplar generation and has led to fruitful theoretical ideas such as typicality, family-resemblance and basic level concepts, some limitations have been pointed out.

© krakozawr/iStock

First, can simple similarity to a prototype be the whole basis of categorization? It seems not. For example, a small dog, such as a Pekingese may be more similar to a cat than to other much larger dogs, due to its appearance (Komatsu, 1992) yet it is readily categorized as a dog.

This type of finding is difficult for the prototype approach which stresses similarity to prototypes as the sole basis of categorization. If that were the case, we would have more difficulty with separating small dogs from cats than we do.

Second, not all concepts have prototypes. For example, very abstract concepts such as 'rules', 'beliefs' and 'instincts', were found by Hampton (1981) to lack prototypes.

Third, the linkage between typicality and family resemblance scores seems to break down for goal-derived or ad hoc categories that are generated for specific goals. Examples of goal-derived categories would be 'things to rescue from a burning house', 'ways to escape from a hitman' and 'things to take to a picnic in the rain'. Barsalou (1985) found that the correlation of typicality and family resemblance score was near zero for members of goal-derived categories but was over +0.7 for established common categories of the type used by Rosch et al. The items that make up goal-derived categories have little in the way of common features although all in their own way contribute to the goal. (A practical application of the notion of ad hoc or goal derived categories to consumer behaviour is given in Box 7.2.)

> Ad hoc categories are categories formed of items that meet a given goal, e.g. the category of 'items to take on a picnic' is ad hoc.

Fourth, if a concept is represented only by a single prototype, then it is hard to account for people's knowledge of variability within the concept, for example that coins of a set value do not vary in size (low variability) while pizzas vary greatly in size (high variability). This aspect of knowledge is dealt with better by exemplar theories (Rips & Collins, 1993) which will be discussed in the next section.

Fifth, people bring to bear knowledge about likely relations between features and category membership (Malt & Smith, 1983). For example, in dealing with types of birds, seeing a single instance of a small blue bird on a tropical island being labelled a 'warrum' is enough to make people reliably judge subsequent small blue birds as 'warrums'. However, if a local heavily built tropical islander is labelled as a member of the 'klaatu' tribe, we are unlikely to class the next heavily built islander we see as a 'klaatu'. Knowledge about variability of features and their usefulness as cues affects judgements in ways not predicted by prototype approaches. Such knowledge allows rapid learning of some concepts, even from single examples, as in the case of the 'warrum' bird, which goes against the gradual build-up of prototypes over many examples. In addition, prior knowledge that some features 'go together', such as that small birds tend to sing and large birds tend to squawk, make it easier to learn concepts of new birds that match expectations as opposed to those that do not (Malt & Smith, 1984). Knowledge-based approaches to concepts, discussed in a later section, address these issues, which are not dealt with by the prototype approach.

Overall, prototype approaches have dealt well with some aspects of concept learning and the categorization of new examples, particularly when concrete concepts are involved. Limitations arise in dealing with abstract and ad hoc concepts, knowledge of concept boundaries, and of variability and relations among features. Problems with prototype approaches led to the development of exemplar and knowledge-based approaches, to which we now turn.

Box 7.2 Practical Application: Goal derived ad hoc categories and consumer goods

Ratneshwar et al. (2001) applied the ideas of goal derived or ad hoc categories to the concepts that people use to represent consumer goods.

We might initially imagine that people would represent say, nutritional goods as a hierarchy with Food and Drink at the top level. Drink might then be subdivided into Alcoholic versus NonAlcoholic and NonAlcoholic then subdivided further into Natural versus Artificial. Natural drinks could be further classified as Water versus Juice and so on. Food could similarly be subdivided into lower and lower level categories.

Ratneshwar et al. emphasized a more top-down perspective and examined categories that consumers might construct ad hoc depending on current goals. Specifically, they investigated how different goals affected category representations and participants' similarity judgements of food products.

© gmnicholas/iStock

The food products involved were: granola bars, chocolate bars, fruit yoghurt, frozen yogurt, ice cream, plain popcorn, an apple, an orange, a doughnut, a chicken sandwich, a turkey sandwich and a cheese pizza.

Participants rated the similarity of pairs of foods on a 10-point scale, either in a general context 'of things people might eat' or in a more specific context of 'things people might carry along to eat in their cars'. In the general context of 'things people might eat', apples and doughnuts were rated as quite dissimilar to each other (mean rating = 1.72) but in the specific context of 'things that people might carry along to eat in their cars', apples and doughnuts seemed much more similar (mean rating = 6.2).

In a separate manipulation, participants were divided into those for whom healthy eating was a prominent personal goal and those for whom this goal was of low importance. In the general eating context, people with a strong healthy eating goal, regarded granola bars and chocolate bars as quite dissimilar (mean similarity rating, 4.4) but those without a strong healthy eating regarded chocolate and granola bars as pretty similar (mean rating = 6.45). Presumably people with a low healthy eating interest see both bars as acceptable snacks, while people with a strong healthy eating goal see granola bars as healthy food (which is how they are marketed) and see chocolate bars as anything but healthy! Conversely, health conscious eaters saw frozen yogurt and plain popcorn as more similar (mean rating = 4.6) than did non-health-conscious eaters (mean similarity rating = 2.7).

Ratneshwar et al.'s study has a counterpart in the work of Wansink and colleagues (Wansink, 1994; Wansink & Ray, 1996). They investigated whether, and how, advertising might persuade consumers to consider using a target product in an atypical use situation instead of a normally preferred alternative. For instance, the target product might be soup, the atypical situation might be breakfast, and the preferred alternative might be hot cereal. Consumers' desire for a hot and nutritious breakfast could presumably be satisfied by soup, and yet soup is generally not considered a substitute for hot cereal at breakfast time. The two products are viewed as in different categories and have few surface similarities. Wansink and colleagues examined whether particular advertising strategies improved consumers' attitudes toward using the unfavoured target product in the new situation. Their findings are relevant to Ratneshwar et al.'s study because some of the advertisements in Wansink's (Wansink, 1994; Wansink & Ray, 1996) research encourage consumers to consider disparate products, such as soup and hot cereal, as alternatives. The most effective advertisements were those that increased the salience of goals that both products could meet. For example, in the case of hot cereal and soup, the most effective advertisements stressed hot temperature and nutrition as desirable goals. Wansink found that by making relevant goals salient, advertising improved consumers' attitudes toward use of the target product in the new situation. Thus, sales of soup could be boosted by promoting it as a suitable breakfast food delivering the warmth and nutrition desired at that time of day.

EXEMPLAR-BASED APPROACHES

Exemplar theories propose that categories are represented purely by stored examples or instances and each example is linked to the category name.

In view of the difficulties outlined above with prototype theory other approaches have been explored. A popular theoretical alternative to the prototype approach can be found in the form of exemplar approaches which we will now discuss. Exemplar theories assume that concepts are represented by stored examples alone; no prototype is assumed. How might this work? Suppose the task is to decide whether a new creature (a 'Wug') is a bird or not. The Wug's representation is compared with examples or instances of 'birds' already stored in long-term memory; if the Wug's similarity to previous birds is above a particular threshold, we decide it is also a 'bird'. The Wug would now be one of the examples available if the concept of 'bird' is considered in future. Different specific exemplar models propose that all examples (Reed, 1972) are stored and used, or that only selected, most typical examples are stored and used (Rosch, 1975). (Where typical examples are those that are highly similar to most other instances, e.g. a robin as against a penguin in the Bird category.)

Exemplar models were initially applied to data from experiments in which people learned artificial categories, such as categories of dot patterns or of schematic faces; while prototype models were mainly tested using natural pre-existing concepts and categories. Storms et al. (2000; also see Storms, 2004) sought to compare exemplar and prototype approaches in two studies that took four different measures of categorization performance (Category naming, Exemplar generalization, Typicality ratings and Speeded categorization) using natural categories. Eight everyday categories (fruit, vehicles, birds and so on) were used, with 25 exemplars and six non-exemplars for each category. The exemplars and non-exemplars were scored for similarity to each other exemplar (instance similarity) and to prototypes for each category derived by Rosch and Mervis's (1975) family resemblance method and by Hampton's (1979) method in which prototype properties are directly listed by participants. It was found that instance similarity measures were better predictors of categorization performance than either Rosch and Mervis's family resemblance or Hampton's similarity-to-prototype measure, thus supporting the exemplar approach.

Evaluation

An advantage of the exemplar approach is that it readily represents variability within a category which prototypes do not. For example, Rips and Collins (1993) invited participants to decide if an unseen object was a ruler or a pizza, based only on the information that the object was 19 inches. Pizza was the overwhelming choice even though prototypical rulers and pizzas are 12 inches, but pizzas are much more variable and so instances of 19 inch pizzas could be retrieved but instances of 19 inch rulers could not.

Although there are data supporting the exemplar approach, outstanding problems remain, such as how to deal with hierarchical structuring of concepts (Murphy, 2000), and how to incorporate the role of knowledge, and particularly the role of causal knowledge in forming categories. Shared causes are important for many concepts that cover very varied examples, such as concepts of 'drunken actions' or of 'tropical diseases'. The role of knowledge is considered explicitly in the theory and knowledge-based accounts that we will deal with in the next section.

THEORY/KNOWLEDGE-BASED APPROACHES

Prototype and exemplar approaches are based on notions of similarity or feature sharing between instances or between instances and prototypes. However, not all categories exhibit much superficial similarity or feature sharing. Goal-driven or ad hoc categories (Barsalou, 1983), as we have seen, generally consist of very disparate objects. So, the category of 'things you would rescue from a burning house' might include, babies, pets, money, jewellery, house deeds, insurance papers – all of which lack shared features and only belong in the category because they serve the purpose of the goal behind the category (which is to rescue things valuable to you).

Other categories may also have very diverse appearances, for example the category of 'drunken actions', or that of 'things you would keep in your backpack'.

In the case of 'drunken actions', Murphy and Medin (1985) argue that there is an underlying theory or knowledge that intoxication leads to unusual and reckless behaviour because of the effects of alcohol on the brain and this knowledge is important in classifying individuals as intoxicated from instances of their behaviour (such as jumping into a swimming pool while fully clothed, or throwing television sets out of hotel windows).

That categorization can be driven by knowledge rather than similarity was indicated by a study carried out by Rips (1989). He told participants to think of a pizza and a 25 cent coin (a quarter) and to estimate the largest and smallest size these might be. Then they were told that a third object was larger than the largest estimated quarter size and smaller than the smallest estimated pizza size. Two judgements were then asked for. First, was the new object more likely to be a pizza or a quarter? Answers favoured it being a pizza. The second question was whether the new object was more similar to a quarter than to a pizza. This time, the object was judged to be most similar to a quarter. In other words, category membership was assigned on grounds other than similarity, and was presumably based on knowledge of variability of pizzas versus quarters in size. Similar dissociations between categorization and similarity have also been found by Rips and Collins (1993) and Robertson et al. (1999). Such findings indicate that similarity to a prototype or to other instances is not the sole basis for deciding category membership.

The role of causal knowledge in forming concepts was demonstrated in a study by Ahn et al. (2000). A category was presented such that its members tended to have blurred vision, headaches and insomnia. Further, participants were told that blurred vision caused headaches and headaches caused insomnia. New items with missing pieces of information were presented and the items that were missing blurred vision were far less likely to be judged members of the group than were items in which insomnia was missing but the other features were present. Causal knowledge played a clear role in these judgements of category membership.

Evaluation

In the theory-based view, concepts are thought to include information about their relations to one another and about the relations (particularly, causal relations) among the features displayed by their examples. This approach helps deal with points which were difficult for the prototype view such as the role of knowledge of variability and how features typically relate to one another.

The theory-based view gives insights into how concepts can cover extremely varied examples, such as 'drunken behaviour' or 'healthy foods' on the basis of shared causation rather than shared surface features or characteristics. However, the approach leaves open the question of whether and how explanatory knowledge might affect judgements about similarity and typicality.

ESSENTIALISM

Essentialism is the view that all members of a given category share some key property.

As we have seen, most categories allow considerable variability among their members. So, the basic level category 'dog' includes examples from Pekingese to Great Danes. These vary markedly in appearance but do they share some essence of 'dogness'? An ability to cross-breed with each other might be a candidate 'essence' although it is not a simple feature. Many people seem to believe that objects do contain some 'essence' which may be hard to define but which makes them what they are, whether they are cats, dogs or toasters. Essentialism can be seen as a special case of the theory approach and is the view that people tend to believe that category members share some essential properties and that although appearances may be useful guides to category membership, it is the essential properties that are critical (Medin, 1989; Medin & Ortony, 1989). A bird with its feathers removed is still seen as a bird; the essential properties may be seen as residing in the creature's DNA. In a developmental study, Gellman and Wellman (1991) found that young children, of 4–5 years of age, believed that the insides of objects were more critical or essential than the outsides. Children felt that dogs would cease to be dogs if their insides were removed but would still be dogs if their outsides were removed.

Barton and Komatsu (1989) argued that there are different types of concepts which may have different forms of essential properties. They distinguished three broad types of concepts which can be labelled as *nominal, natural kind* and *artefact* concepts. Nominal concepts have clear definitions (e.g. 'Triangles are three-sided closed figures') and so fit the classic definitional approach. Natural kind concepts are those commonly identified as naturally occurring, such as cats, dogs, rainy days and so on. Artefact concepts relate to designed and human made objects that are generally defined in terms of their functions, such as television receivers, laptop computers, cars and so on.

Barton and Komatsu (1989) asked participants to consider different transformations of natural kind and artefact categories. Three types of transformation were compared. These were functional transformations (a she goat that did not produce milk; a television that did not show a picture), physical feature transformations (a striped goat or a pencil that was not cylindrical) and molecular transformations (water not composed of H_2O, a mirror not made of glass). It was found that natural kind concepts were most affected by molecular transformations but artefact concepts were most sensitive to functional changes. This indicates that the essential properties of artefacts are their functions; it does not matter what materials the television set is made from it remains a television as long as it functions as a television should. On the other hand, the essential properties of natural kind categories are their physical make up; so a goat made out of silicon ceases to be a goat even if it behaves like a goat.

Box 7.3 When Things Go Wrong: Category specific deficits and pathologies

From a variety of studies it seems that functional features or properties (what does the item do) are especially important in categorizing man-made objects and perceptual features (what does the item look, sound, smell like) are more important when categorizing living things.

This difference in the bases of concepts about living and non-living things is reflected in results of brain damage, in that many people with brain damage show category specific deficits; that is, they have difficulties with some categories of things but not with others. An early study by Warrington and McCarthy (1983) examined a global aphasic patient (known as V.E.R.) who had sustained a major left hemisphere infarction; such patients are aphasic because they have partially or totally lost the ability to articulate themselves either in written or spoken form as a result of an injury (see also Chapters 1 and 12 for more on aphasia). They found that V.E.R. showed a selective preservation of knowledge about foods, animals and flowers and a selective impairment of knowledge about non-living objects. Later Warrington and Shallice (1984) identified a case (known as J.B.R.) who was very poor at naming pictures of living things (6 per cent correct) as against non-living things (90 per cent correct). Thus, a double dissociation was identified suggesting that the neural basis of knowledge about categories of living things is separable from the neural basis of knowledge about non-living objects. The same double dissociation showed up in a more recent study by Laws et al. (2006) who found category specific deficits among a group of 55 individuals with schizophrenia, with some showing impairments in living thing categories and some in non-living thing categories.

Warrington and Shallice (1984) proposed the *sensory-functional distinction* meaning that for some categories perceptual features were critical and for others functional characteristics were critical. The most common pattern of deficit is for patients to have problems with living things but not with non-living things. Martin and Caramazza (2003) found this pattern to be four times more common than the reverse pattern of spared knowledge of living things and impaired knowledge of non-living things. Gainotti (2000) found that the common pattern was associated with temporal lobe damage and the less common pattern was associated with fronto-parietal damage. Interestingly, some yet more specific dissociations have been reported of patients with category specific impairments in their knowledge of fruit and vegetables but preserved knowledge of animals and man-made objects (Samson & Pillon, 2003).

On the essentialist view, experts in different domains (such as zoologists, botanists, chemists) identify the true essences of the concepts they deal with and lay people tend to defer to expert judgements. So, lay people accept that a platypus is a 'mammal', even if a highly untypical one, as that is the expert view. Malt (1990) gave participants objects that they were instructed were 'Halfway' between categories (such as a tree halfway between an oak and a maple, or a sea vessel halfway between a ship and a boat). The participants were given a choice between 'asking an expert', 'calling it whatever you want' and indicating that they could tell which it was if they thought long enough. If the pairs were natural categories, the expert option was strongly favoured; but, for artefacts the preference was strongly for 'calling it whichever one liked'. Thus, people seem to be more essentialist regarding natural categories than for artefact categories. Further evidence counter to the purely essentialist view was reported by Malt (1994). In this study it was found that although participants considered it essential that a liquid consist of H_2O molecules to be water, their judgements of what counted as water were influenced by other factors. So, pond water was judged to be water although its H_2O content was judged to be around 79 per cent; but tears were judged to be not water although believed to contain 89 per cent H_2O. Thus, source, location and function of a liquid also seemed to play a role in making judgements of whether a liquid counted as 'water' or not, as well as H_2O content.

GROUNDED REPRESENTATIONS VERSUS AMODAL REPRESENTATIONS

The approaches to concepts discussed so far have not specified the degree to which concepts are purely abstract as opposed to involving sensory or motor processes. In typical information processing approaches to knowledge it has been assumed that conceptual knowledge is represented by abstract symbols (e.g. Newell, 1980; Pylyshyn, 1984; Vera & Simon, 1993) and so the various models could be simulated in computer programs using abstract symbols to represent sensory and motor features such as 'red', 'graspable' or 'rough feeling'.

Grounded representations are representations that involve sensory-motor codes.
Amodal representations are representations that are abstract and do not involve any sensory codes.
Simulation is the extended re-enactment of a previous experience.
Re-enactment is the partial repetition of the internal processes involved in previous perceptions or actions.

Recently, however, a number of theorists, of whom Lawrence Barsalou (1999, 2003, 2008) is the most prominent, have argued for a more embodied view of concepts as grounded in modality specific systems for perception (e.g. vision, audition), action (e.g. movement, proprioception) and introspection (e.g. mental states, affect) with no need for amodal abstract symbols. Barsalou stresses the role of simulation in cognition, where simulation is the re-enactment of perceptual, motor and introspective states acquired during experience of the world. So, when we interact with a chair the brain takes on states representing what it looks like, the action of sitting on it, resulting feelings of relaxation and so on. When we encounter a new chair those states are re-activated to simulate the previous experience. Imagery is an example of mental simulation that can play a role in problem solving. For example, given the task of finding new uses for a brick, participants often imagine a brick and seem to read off properties from the image that can then support different uses (Gilhooly et al., 2007).

Evidence for a role for bodily states in conceptual processing has come from a number of studies. Klatzky et al. (1989) found that seeing an object, such as a car key, activates the appropriate hand shape, in this case, a precision grip for grasping and turning. Glenberg and Kaschak (2004) showed further evidence that object concepts activate arm movements. When participants were to indicate whether sentences made sense by a pulling movement, they were faster to verify 'Open the drawer' than when a pushing movement was to indicate acceptability of the sentence. In a recent study, by Wit et al. (2010), volunteers had to name tools or animals shown in pictures as fast as possible while squeezing a foam ball in one hand. Volunteers were slower and less accurate in naming tools when the tool's handle was on the same side as the squeezing hand than when the ball was in the other hand or when they were naming animal pictures. Squeezing the ball may have impaired tool naming by interfering with the motor simulation of grasping the tool with that hand, suggesting that motor simulation may play a functional role in tool identification.

Simulation also appears to play a role in the conceptual task of property verification. In this task, participants are given a word (say, horse) and then a property word which may or may not apply to the object (has mane or has horns, say). Solomon and Barsalou (2004) found that the larger the property mentioned the slower the verification responses and the more the errors. This mirrors findings from studies where the objects and properties were perceptually available (Morrison & Tversky, 1977) and supports the simulation view. In related studies, Solomon and Barsalou (2001) found a modality switching effect. So, that verifying *loud* for 'blender' was faster after verifying *rustling* for 'leaves' than after verifying *tart* for 'cranberries'. Switching from one modality to another slows verification and property sizes also affect verification. The abstract amodal view of concepts would not predict these findings.

Neuropsychological evidence has been invoked in favour of the grounded approach. For example, lesions to brain areas dealing with different modalities affect different types of conceptual knowledge. Damage to visual areas particularly increases likelihood of impaired performance with animal categories which are presumed to be processed visually; and damage to motor areas particularly affects tool concepts because motor processing is the main modality for such concepts (Barsalou, 2008; Simmons & Barsalou, 2003).

Neuroimaging evidence also indicates that when conceptual knowledge about objects is activated through object names being presented, brain areas that represent the object's properties in perception become active. So, processing artefacts stimulates motor areas while processing animals activates visual areas (Keither, 2005). Processing food terms causes activation of taste areas and processing names of smelly items stimulates smell areas (Gonzales et al., 2006). In the property verification task (Solomon & Barsalou, 2004) areas related to the properties being tested become active including brain areas for shape, sound, action and touch (Goldberg et al., 2006).

Scan to watch a video on neuroimaging and objects

Evaluation

Overall, a strong evidence base is emerging which supports the idea of embodied or grounded modality specific aspects of conceptual representation. However, whether abstract concepts such as 'truth' and 'justice' can be wholly explained in terms of simulated or re-enacted experience is highly controversial. Barsalou (2008) points to the widespread use of physical metaphors when dealing with abstract concepts, as indicating a role for grounded representations in dealing with abstract concepts. So, happiness is associated with 'up' and 'high' and sadness 'down' and 'low'; time is seen in Eastern culture as flowing from front to back with us facing forwards and so meetings that are brought forward are then closer than they had been, in our typical spatial model of time (Boroditsky & Ramscar, 2002). For more on physical metaphors and time concepts see Box 7.4 as well as discussion in Chapter 8. The area of abstract concepts as a whole has hitherto been little studied by either the traditional amodal approach or the grounded approach and as Barsalou observed (2008, p. 634) 'much more effort should be devoted to understanding them'.

Box 7.4 Research Close Up: Physical metaphors and concepts of time

Source: Boroditsky, L. (2010). Lost in translation, *Wall Street Journal*, 30 July 2010.

INTRODUCTION

Boroditsky (2010) and colleagues have carried out a number of studies to understand how different cultures use different physical metaphors for time concepts.

The Aboriginal Australian people known as the Pormpuraaw have a language in which they do not use the terms 'left' and 'right' but always refer to locations in terms of absolute directions 'north', 'south', 'east' and 'west' and intermediates, such as north-west. So they might say 'You have an ant on your north-west shoulder' rather than 'You have an ant on your left shoulder'.

Incidentally, about a third of the world's 7000 known languages use a similar system and speakers of such languages are especially adept at navigation and orientation tasks.

METHOD

Boroditsky and colleagues gave Pormpuraawans, English speakers and Hebrew speakers groups of pictures that showed events unfolding in time, such as a man at different ages, a banana being eaten or a crocodile growing. They were then asked to sort the shuffled pictures and arrange them on a flat surface so that the correct order in time was shown. Each person was tested twice, facing in a different main direction (north, south, east, west) each time.

RESULTS

The English speakers arranged the pictures from left to right and the Hebrew speakers from right to left, no matter which direction they were facing. The Pormpuraawans always arranged the pictures from east to west. So if they were facing south, the pictures were arranged left to right; if facing north, from right to left; if facing east, toward the body and if facing west, away from the body. Although the participants were not told which direction they were facing, the Pormpuraawans always knew the direction they were facing and arranged the pictures according to their preferred physical metaphor that time flows from east to west.

DISCUSSION

It emerged clearly that the speakers of different languages (English, Hebrew and Pormpuraawans) used different spatial metaphors to represent the flow of time. Other language groups show different metaphors. For example, in Mandarin Chinese, the future is seen as below and the past above and in the South American Aymara language, the future comes from behind and the past is in front.

In all cases the different language groups (Pormpuraawans, Mandarin, Hebrew, English and Aymara) all use concrete models to represent the flow of time, but vary in the exact model used (east to west flow; below to above flow and behind to front flow). These results lend further support to the embodied cognition view, that abstract concepts often involve physical metaphors rooted in sensory experience and motor actions.

IMAGERY AND CONCEPTS

When we think of a concept, such as 'cat', most of us will experience a visual image of a cat, possibly augmented by auditory imagery of purring or meowing. Visual images convey information as to what an object looks like and the image associated with a concept would seem likely to be important in using that concept. To what extent do such images convey useful information and how do we use images? Imagery associated with concepts would be expected to be important on embodied views of knowledge representation, such as that put forward by Barsalou, and introduced in an earlier section. Barsalou's simulation view of concepts proposes that knowledge of concepts is based on re-enactment of previous experiences with category members and so seeing the word 'chair' would evoke re-enactments of previous chair related experiences which would encompass visual experience and possibly motor and haptic (touch) experiences of sitting in chairs. These re-enactments or simulations could normally be reported as imagery. Imagery partially replicates actual experience, but can usually be distinguished as being less vivid and more under the person's control than actual perceptual experiences. It should be noted that there are rare pathological conditions such as Charles Bonnet syndrome (see Box 7.6 later) in which people have extremely vivid but uncontrollable hallucinatory images which are visually indistinguishable from perceptions of the external world (Plummer et al., 2007; Santhouse et al., 2000).

Scan for a discussion of what Charles Bonnet syndrome is

Although imagery can be found in all sensori-motor domains most research on imagery has focused on visual imagery as vision is for most of us the dominant perceptual channel and so we will focus on visual imagery. Images may be regarded as representing the appearance of objects and such knowledge of what members of common categories look like is an important part of our conceptual knowledge. We will now review findings on imagery including: the relationship between imaging and perceiving; scanning images; mental rotation; ambiguity in images and neuroscience approaches to imagery.

IMAGERY AND VISUO-SPATIAL PROCESSING: OVERLAPS?

We start with the question of the extent to which imagining an object uses the same processes as actually perceiving it. Regarding visual imagery, this is often discussed in the literature in terms of the degree to which imagery and visuo-spatial processing overlap. We all have the experience that closing our eyes helps when we try to imagine an object; this everyday observation is consistent with the idea that the same mental machinery is involved in seeing as in imagining. A number of experimental studies have reported interference between imagery tasks and simultaneous visuo-spatial processing, which supports the idea that imagery and perception draw on the same mental and neural resources. This type of result was first reported by Brooks (1968) in a series of studies which have now become classics in the field. (See also Chapter 4 for more on dual tasking, working memory and

Visuo-spatial processing is the mental manipulation of visual or spatial information.

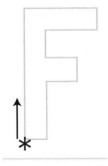

Figure 7.3 Brooks' imagery task.

the Brooks task.) Brooks asked participants to imagine a capital letter 'F' and then had them imagine going round the letter clockwise from a starting corner and indicate whether each corner was at the extreme top or bottom of the letter (see Figure 7.3).

Going round the figure F is each corner encountered at extreme top or bottom or neither? Beginning at the bottom left corner of the 'F', the answers should be 'yes, yes, yes, no, no, no, no, no, no, yes'. Participants were asked to either say their responses or point to a Y or N on a sheet of paper with Ys and Ns in rows in an irregular pattern. It was found that making a spatial response (pointing) slowed down performance compared to a verbal response. The reverse pattern was found when the main task was verbal, that is, remembering a sentence such as 'A bird in the hand is not in the bush' and indicating for each word whether it was a noun or not. These patterns of interference are consistent with the visual imagery task drawing on visuo-spatial resources.

A similar conclusion can be drawn from Baddeley and Andrade's (2000) study of reported vividness of imagery when imaging was combined with a range of dual tasks (see Figure 7.4). Participants were asked to imagine the appearance of various familiar objects while carrying out tapping in a pattern (visuo-spatial task) or counting aloud from 1–10 repeatedly (a verbal task). Participants were also asked to rate the vividness of their images on a 0–10 point scale where 0 meant 'No image at all' and 10 meant 'Image as clear and vivid as normal vision/hearing'. For visual images, self-reported vividness of the images was reduced by a tapping task but not by the counting task. When participants were given the task of generating auditory images of familiar sounds, such as the ringing of a telephone, reported vividness of auditory images was reduced by counting but not by spatial tapping. In terms of the Baddeley-Hitch model of working memory (see Chapter 4 for more details), this result indicates that visual imagery uses the visuo-spatial sketchpad part of working memory while auditory imagery involves the phonological loop component of working memory.

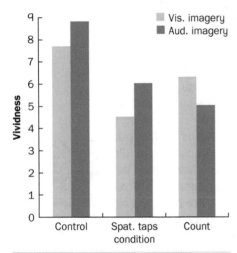

Figure 7.4 Baddeley and Andrade's (2000) result. Vividness of visual and auditory imagery as affected by Spatial (tapping) and Auditory (counting) dual tasks.

Source: Adapted from Baddeley, A. D. & Andrade, J. (2000). Working memory and the vividness of imagery. *Journal of Experimental Psychology: General, 129*, 126–145.

IMAGE SCANNING AND COMPARING

Images are usually generated for a practical purpose. For example, you might have to move a large wardrobe out of a room. Will it be too wide to go through the door? Using imagery you could try to compare the dimensions of the wardrobe with the height and width of the doorway to 'see' whether the wardrobe could go through. Or you may have bought a complicated electrical item that needs several electrical outlets to plug into. Are there enough outlets in your bedroom? Using imagery you might try to scan an image of your bedroom to find and count electrical outlets. A number of studies have examined such image scanning and comparing, focusing largely on the question of whether image scanning and comparing are like picture scanning and comparing.

In a typical experiment, Kosslyn (1973) asked participants to study pictures of objects such as a plane, a submarine and a clock-tower. The participants were then asked to form an image of one of the objects and to focus on one part such as the left or the top of the object in the image. Next, they were asked to look for a particular part such

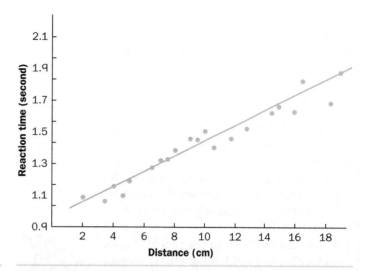

Figure 7.5 **Map for the scanning task.** Participants study the map before the scanning task.

Source: Kosslyn, S. M., Ball, T. M., & Reiser, B. J. (1978). Visual images preserve metric spatial information: Evidence from studies of image scanning. *Journal of Experimental Psychology: Human Perception and Performance, 4*, 56–60. APA; reprinted with permission.

Figure 7.6 **Scanning distance and reaction times.** The longer the distance to be mentally scanned the longer the time to scan between two points.

Source: Kosslyn, S. M., Ball, T. M., & Reiser, B. J. (1978). Visual images preserve metric spatial information: Evidence from studies of image scanning. *Journal of Experimental Psychology: Human Perception and Performance, 4*, 56–60. APA; reprinted with permission.

as the flag on the bell tower and indicate when they found that part. Times to report finding the target part of the image varied in accordance with how far the target was from the starting point in the image. So, parts of the pictures that were separated in space were also separated to a corresponding degree in the image. These results support the idea that images are like pictures in the mind.

Similar results emerged from a map scanning study (Kosslyn et al., 1978). Participants first studied a map of a fictitious island containing seven landmark objects (see Figure 7.5).

The participants first studied the map, then imagined the map and were asked to focus on one object and next to scan the map image to find a second named object. Time to report finding the second object showed a very strong linear correlation ($r = 0.97$) with the physical distance between the objects on the map (see Figure 7.6). These results again support the view that images encode relative distances with some accuracy.

Other studies have asked people to compare images. For example, Finke (1989) asked participants 'Which is larger a pineapple or a coconut?' and concluded that such comparisons were imagery based. Moyer (1973) found that such size questions were answered more rapidly the larger the difference between the objects in real life. Paivio (1975) had also found the same pattern when real objects were presented. So people are quicker to agree that a whale is larger than a cat, than that a cat is larger than a toaster, suggesting that the relevant images encode size in a picture-like way. The basic finding that difference judgements between symbolically presented items are made more easily for objects that are indeed widely different in reality is known as the *symbolic distance effect*. Again, the studies of image comparison tasks have been taken to support the view that images are picture-like representations that are examined by the mind's eye just as pictures are processed through the brain's eye. Similar conclusions can be drawn from studies of our ability to carry out mental rotation of images of three-dimensional objects as described in Box 7.5.

Box 7.5 Research Close Up: Mental rotation

Source: Shepard, R. N. & Metzler, J. (1971). Mental rotation of three-dimensional objects. *Science*, *171*, 701–703.

INTRODUCTION

In addition to being able to create, scan and compare images, people can also transform images, and in particular can undertake mental rotation. Is mentally rotating the representation of a three-dimensional object similar to physically rotating an actual object, in terms of time taken and accuracy with which it can be done? In a series of classic studies, Shepard and Metzler (1971) investigated this issue.

METHOD

Shepard and Metzler gave people pairs of pictures which were perspective drawings of three-dimensional objects (see Figure 7.7).

The pairs of drawings were either of the same object rotated in different ways or one object was the mirror image of the other and so not identical. Participants had to say whether the two drawings were of the same object.

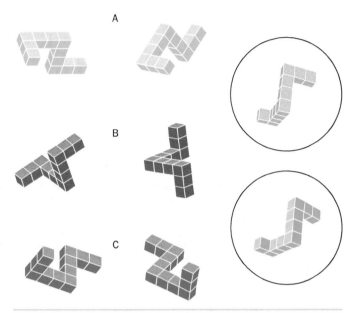

Figure 7.7   Mental rotation stimuli. Are the left and right figures, A, B, C same or different?

Source: Based on Shepard, R. N. & Metzler, J. (1971). Mental rotation of three-dimensional objects. *Science*, *171*, 701–703.

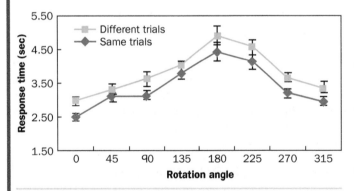

Figure 7.8   Time to make 'Same' and 'Different' judgements as function of angle between shapes.

Source: Based on Shepard, R. N. & Metzler, J. (1971). Mental rotation of three-dimensional objects. *Science*, *171*, 701–703. Reprinted with permission from AAAS.

RESULTS

Times to make correct 'Same' and 'Different' judgements showed a very strong relationship with the angle of rotation between the two pictured objects such that the more rotation needed to match, the longer the time taken to make a judgement. This results in an inverted U shaped curve plotting rotation angle against time taken with a peak at 180 degrees where the distance to be rotated is maximum (see Figure 7.8).

DISCUSSION

The results are consistent with the view that participants imaged one object and rotated the image until it either matched the other object or not. Other analyses indicated that participants would rotate either clockwise or anticlockwise depending on which direction would yield the smaller angular separation. Advance information on the object and the degree and direction of rotation given before the comparison stimulus was shown eliminated the angle size effect. This suggests that with advance information participants carried out the mental rotation before the comparison stimulus appeared. Overall, the results of the mental rotation studies indicated that visual images represented three dimensions and that mental rotation of three-dimensional images was similar in many respects to physical rotation of objects.

Critical views of imagery research and theory

Despite the results on scanning, comparing and rotating of images which are consistent with the idea that images operate like pictures in the head, some researchers, particularly Pylyshyn, have raised objections to that view and we will now discuss these criticisms.

Pylyshyn (1981) proposed that the image scanning results of Kosslyn et al. (1978) could reflect participants' beliefs or tacit knowledge about what should happen in such tasks. Participants would tend to know that it takes longer to scan a longer distance and respond accordingly by inserting a pause as suits the distance involved.

Pylyshyn (1981) tested participants using island materials similar to Kosslyn et al. (1978). He replicated the original results when the scanning task was given. However, when participants were asked to say what direction was one landmark from another (Northwest? Directly south?) the distance between the landmarks did not affect response time. So, if scanning was explicitly requested, participants produced scanning-like results. However, if the task does not explicitly request scanning, participants do not produce results consistent with image scanning. Further support for a possible role for task demand and experimenter effects came from a study by Intons-Peterson (1983) in which experimenters were given different expectations about how image scanning experiments might work out. In a map-scanning task based on Kosslyn et al. (1978) half the experimenters were told that scanning an image of the map would be faster than perceptually scanning the actual map and half were told the reverse. The results obtained reflected the experimenters' expectations. When perceptual scanning was expected to be faster, it was significantly faster than imagery scanning by 230 milliseconds. When imagery was expected to be faster, the gap between the imagery and perceptual conditions was reduced to a non-significant 41 milliseconds (and the imagery speed was increased by a significant 201 milliseconds over the condition with the opposite expectation). Presumably, the expectations were subtly picked up by participants from small unconscious cues given by the experimenters and affected how participants responded.

Pylyshyn (1973) criticized the image-as-picture metaphor on theoretical grounds. He pointed out that pictures can be arbitrarily damaged (e.g. cut in half or torn up into small pieces) but images can only be transformed in terms of meaningful components being added or removed. Also, we can perceive pictures without advance warning of their contents but images have to be intentionally constructed and are based on our knowledge of the objects being imaged. Thus, two people may form an image of the same chess position, but the expert player will 'see' relationships of attack and defence in the image that the non-player or the beginner will not 'see', because the expert has the requisite underlying knowledge.

Pylyshyn (1973, 1981, 2002) has consistently argued in favour of amodal propositional representations as underlying the experience of imagery and he argues that the experience of imagery has no real causal role in cognition, but is what is known as an 'epiphenomenon'. A concrete analogy is that the hum of a washing machine running is an epiphenomenon, that is, a by-product, of the machine's operation, but does not contribute to the machine's functioning. Similarly, Pylyshyn suggests that the imagery experience is a by-product of underlying cognitive processes, but has no actual functional role itself.

AMBIGUITY OF IMAGES

The well-known Necker cube and the Duck-Rabbit figure (Jastrow, 1899) are good examples of ambiguous reversible figures that typically generate alternative and indeed

Figure 7.9   Jastrow's Duck-Rabbit Ambiguous (reversible) figure.

Scan to see an animated version of the Necker cube

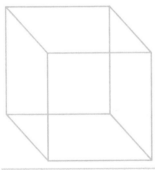

Figure 7.10   Necker cube: an ambiguous (reversible) figure.

alternating structures. In the Necker cube, perception alternates between a cube with the leading face to the right or left and in the Duck-Rabbit, perception alternates between a duck facing one way and a rabbit facing the other (see Figures 7.9 and 7.10). The Gestalt theory of perception proposed that ambiguous figures caused unstable representations that resolved themselves into alternating representations.

If images are like percepts, then images of figures like the duck-rabbit should also be ambiguous and reversible. To investigate this possibility, Chambers and Reisberg (1985) showed their participants a line drawing version of the duck-rabbit figure for 5 seconds and told them to image it for a later drawing task. Participants all indicated either seeing it as a duck or as a rabbit (but not both). They were then shown other ambiguous figures and shown how these reversed as one changed one's focus of attention. Participants were next asked to imagine the duck-rabbit figure and seek alternative interpretations of their image. Finally, they drew the duck-rabbit figure and reported their impressions of the drawing. It was found that although participants could easily re-interpret their drawings, that is come to see a rabbit they had *drawn* turning into a duck and vice versa, they could not reverse the mental image of either a duck (into a rabbit) or a rabbit (into a duck), that they had constructed at the beginning of the experiment. This supports the view that images are not exactly like pictures but rather always have some fixed interpretation on which they are based. Similar findings were also reported later by Chambers and Reisberg (1992). In this second study, participants were told the duck-rabbit figure was either a duck or a rabbit and then imaged the figure. On being tested with comparison figures that differed minutely from the original, participants who were told the figure was a duck were more sensitive to differences in the bill/ears part of the picture than to changes in the nose/back of duck head. The reverse pattern held for those participants who had been told the picture was of a rabbit. Chambers and Reisberg argued that in interpreting a picture and in forming an image of a creature people attend mainly to the face and for the duck interpretation the face is to the left (bill) and for the rabbit the face is to the right. Similar results showing difficulty in re-interpreting images have also been reported by Pylyshyn (2002). However, in some circumstances, when plentiful hints and cues were provided, Mast and Kosslyn (2002) did find image reversal with a stimulus that looked like a young woman in one orientation and an old woman if rotated 90 degrees. It seems then that image reversal is sometimes possible, but generally very difficult.

NEUROPSYCHOLOGY/NEUROSCIENCE OF IMAGERY

If imagery is a re-enactment of perception then it would be expected that brain areas known to be involved in perception would also be involved in imagery. A number of studies have examined this issue. Roland and Friberg (1985) found large activation effects in the occipital lobe (which is heavily involved in visual perception), as indexed by blood flow measures, when participants carried out visual imagery tasks as compared with tasks of similar difficulty levels that did not involve visual imagery (such as mental arithmetic). Farah et al. (1988b) found similar results for visual imaging with a range of neuroscience measures including event-related potentials. Zatorre et al. (1996) found similar effects with auditory imagery. Forming and using auditory images of songs had an activating effect in the secondary auditory cortex which was similar, but weaker than the activation obtained when listening to the songs.

In related studies, Kosslyn et al. (1995) had participants form images of varying size and not only found increased occipital activation but also that the specific occipital area activated depended on the size of the image being formed. Ganis et al. (2004) compared fMRI results when people imaged figures and actually perceived the figures. This fine grain comparison indicated that although similar brain areas were involved in the imagery and perceptual versions of the tasks, the areas most activated in imagery (occipital and temporal regions) were a reduced set of those activated during perception. This is consistent with the fact that people rarely confuse images with percepts, except in certain pathologies (see Box 7.6).

Overall, a large number of studies, reviewed by Kosslyn and Thompson (2003), have typically found involvement of the early visual cortex in imagery tasks, especially when finely detailed images and tasks involving object shape as against motion are involved.

Despite the wealth of neuroscience evidence that imagery and perception share brain mechanisms as re-enactment theory proposes, some neuropsychological studies have found cases of brain damaged individuals who have intact visual perception but imagery impairments and others who have intact imagery with visual perceptual deficits (Bartolomeo, 2002). These cases of double dissociation support the view that although brain areas for perception and imagery overlap they are not identical.

Box 7.6 When Things Go Wrong: Spontaneous vivid imagery – the Charles Bonnet syndrome

Being able to generate appropriate mental images when remembering or problem solving is a useful ability. However, in some clinical conditions very vivid spontaneous images can occur uncontrollably that are as detailed as real perceptions but frequently rather bizarre.

The first attempt to study and record such hallucinatory imagery began in 1760, when a Swiss naturalist, Charles Bonnet, became concerned when his grandfather Charles Lullin, who had severe cataracts, began to experience 'amusing and magical visions'. The 89-year-old Lullin had visions of people, birds, carriages and buildings, all of which were invisible to everyone but him. These vivid images appeared spontaneously and were superimposed upon such vision as he still had.

Bonnet recorded his grandfather's reports and the condition he described is now known as the *Charles Bonnet syndrome*. People with this syndrome see non-existent patterns such as brickwork or tiles, or phantom objects in great detail, including people, animals, and buildings. The images are very vivid and often fit in with the surroundings, for example a non-existent man in full Highland dress might be seen in the sufferer's favourite arm chair. These images last for a variable range of times from seconds to hours. The hallucinations are purely visual and are not accompanied by imaginary sounds or smells.

Floating, disembodied faces are often reported that appear at random times. These faces often have wide, unblinking eyes and prominent teeth, rather like gargoyles. The visions are sometimes life-sized, but often the hallucinations appear in miniature, an effect called 'Lilliput hallucinations', after the small Lilliputian people from *Gulliver's Travels*.

Charles Bonnet syndrome is most common in people at the early stages of sight loss, and the hallucinations usually begin while their vision is still present but slowly diminishing. The most common factor is *macular degeneration*, where cells in the retina malfunction and cause a slowly spreading blind spot in the centre of vision. Glaucoma and cataracts can also cause symptoms as well.

The cause of Charles Bonnet syndrome is not definitely known, but it seems likely that the brain is attempting to compensate for a shortage of visual stimuli.

Plummer et al. (2007) and Santhouse et al. (2000) suggest a specific mechanism. The most plausible hypothesis, they argue, is that neurons in the visual pathway going from the retina to the cortex become hyper-excitable, due to the loss of light receptors. It is as if the pattern-recognition regions of the cortex are trying to interpret the reduced light patterns that are coming into the eye, and are trying out hypotheses to explain the noisy input. The end result is a sequence of cortical guesses based on the degraded stream of incoming visual information. These guesses are experienced as vivid hallucinations, for example, of little men in top hats and tails dancing on the kitchen table.

Evaluation

Processing of images seems to involve the same mental and neural resources as processing the objects represented. Brooks showed this in visual image processing and similar results have been found with auditory images. Scanning and comparing images shows temporal characteristics similar to scanning and comparing objects. Similarly, mental rotation of images to compare images for identity shows similar characteristics to actual object rotation. A cautionary note in interpreting imagery results as supporting the 'picture-in-the-head' view has been sounded by Pylyshyn who has pointed to possible use of implicit knowledge and effects of demand characteristics to produce results that participants infer are wanted.

An area in which images show clear differences lies in the detection of ambiguity in images. This is relatively easy with real pictures such as the duck-rabbit, but much harder and rarely possible with images.

Finally, we note that neuropsychology and neuroscience studies tend to support the view that visual imagery involves a subset of the brain regions active in visual perception. These results are difficult to explain in terms of demand characteristics and implicit knowledge.

Summary

This chapter has concerned two important aspects of mental representation. First, how do we represent general ideas or concepts? And second, how do we represent information about sensory characteristics of objects in imagery?

We need concepts to deal with members of the same class or category as if they were identical. Although all cats are unique and even the same cat on two different occasions has changed even if slightly, it is not economical of mental resources to treat each unique object as if it were completely novel. Hence, we have developed everyday concepts of cats, dogs, tables, chairs and many other things.

A possible theory is that concepts are represented by clear cut rules stating necessary and sufficient features for an item to belong to the concept. What might be called formal or *nominal* concepts fit this view. So, 'triangles are three-sided two-dimensional closed figures' or bachelors are 'Never married, adult males'. However, few everyday concepts are so readily defined. It is not easy to provide hard and fast rules to decide what is a chair as against a stool, say, or what is a cake versus a biscuit.

An alternative view to the definitional approach is to say that concepts are defined by resemblance to a prototypical member of the category. So, a blackbird may be seen as the prototypical bird and new possible bird objects are compared with the prototype and those sufficiently similar to the prototype are accepted as birds. This view is associated with Rosch and her colleagues and has generated a range of studies showing that typicality is indeed a good predictor of various concept processing tasks such as making membership judgements and attribute listing. Some difficulties with this view are that similarity can be a poor guide to category judgements: for example, a small dog may resemble a cat more than a typical dog but still be readily categorized as a dog; not all concepts, particularly abstract concepts, have prototypes and goal-derived categories (e.g. things to take from a burning house) do not show the link between typicality and degree of resemblance (family resemblance) to other items in the category.

Exemplar approaches provide one alternative to prototype theories. On this view, concepts are represented by stored instances without any one prototype. Examplar models have generally been tested on data from studies in which participants learn new artificial categories such as dot patterns, and have shown good fits to such data. Recent studies have also shown that exemplar models can be applied to natural everyday categories. Difficulties for this approach include dealing with hierarchical structuring of concepts and how to account for the role of knowledge.

Knowledge-based approaches and essentialist approaches focus on relevance of prior beliefs about why categories have the characteristics they do. So, for example, the category of 'drunken behaviours' includes reckless behaviours in pursuit of immediate goals and ignoring of more important distant goals. The category 'makes sense' through some understanding of the effects of alcohol on the brain and especially on the frontal lobes, which are the neural basis of executive functions such as inhibition. Essentialism argues that people tend to assume there is a hidden 'essence' that scientists may uncover that makes, for example, a cat a 'cat', or water 'water'. Children do show strong beliefs that the 'insides' of animals are what make them the animals they are. However, source, location and function of liquids seemed to influence judgements of whether a liquid was water more than the percentage of H_2O – which is presumably the essence of water.

Finally, we considered the grounded (or embodied) approach to concepts. On this view, associated with Barsalou and colleagues, when someone thinks of the concept 'chair', previous experiences with chairs are re-enacted or simulated and guide suitable naming and using actions. A number of studies have found evidence of a role for bodily states in conceptual processing. Seeing tools has been shown to activate appropriate anticipatory finger and hand movements. Neuropsychological and neuroscience studies also support the notion that conceptual processing involves the same brain regions as processing the objects themselves; for example, thinking of smelly objects activates olfactory regions. How this approach can deal with abstract concepts is less clear, although studies have indicated frequent use of physical metaphors in dealing with abstract concepts, such as regarding time as flowing from one's front to one's back.

In regard to imagery, scanning, rotating and comparing images shows temporal characteristics similar to scanning and comparing objects which supports interpretations of images as 'pictures-in-the-head'. However, implicit knowledge and effects of demand characteristics might also be involved in producing such results. An area in which images show clear differences from pictures lies in the detection of ambiguity in images. This is found to be easy with real pictures such as the duck-rabbit, but much harder with images.

Finally, we noted that neuropsychology and neuroscience studies support the view that visual imagery involves a subset of the brain regions active in visual perception.

Review questions

1 What is wrong with the 'definitional' approach to conceptual knowledge?

2 What are the strengths and weaknesses of the prototype and exemplar approaches?

3 How promising do you find the embodied, grounded, approach of Barsalou and colleagues?

4 Are images just like pictures?

5 What do you think neuropsychological and neuroscience studies have added to our understanding of concepts and images?

FURTHER READING

Barsalou, L. W. (2008). Grounded cognition. *Annual Review of Psychology, 59,* 617–645.

Kosslyn, S. M. (2005). Mental images and the brain. *Cognitive Neuropsychology, 22,* 333–347.

Murphy, G. L. (2004). *The big book of concepts.* Cambridge, MA: MIT Press.

CHAPTER 8:
MOTOR CONTROL AND ACTION

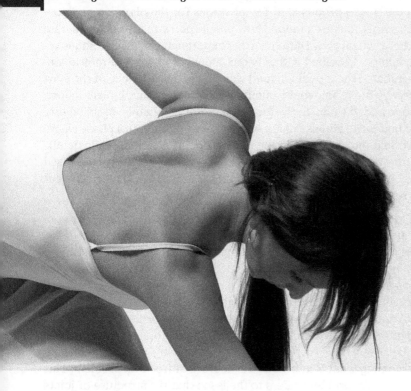

© AYakovlev/iStock

INTRODUCTION

The topics of motor control and action cover how we move our body to achieve our goals. In its entirety this includes a vast range of activities such as kissing, blinking, singing, walking, hammering a nail, focusing your eye on a target and any other human activity that requires a body part to move. You can appreciate that since all these actions are planned in the brain and performed by the body they must share something in common, but certainly the precise mechanisms for kissing are different from hammering a nail. The goal of this chapter is to step away from detailed mechanisms for individual movements and provide insight into what is common to how we move our body and form plans of action. To achieve this we break description of the topics of motor control and action into three parts. The first part describes how we use our motor system to produce movements. No matter what the motor activity, it is being coordinated by the nervous system and implemented by muscles. By adopting a common framework for describing how movements are planned and performed we enable a means to talk about general properties of movement control. However, such a framework is difficult to generalize

Motor system includes the components of the central and peripheral nervous systems along with the muscles, joints and bones that enable movement.

for description of how we achieve complex action sequences. Thus, we move to a higher level of description that takes for granted that details of movement generation will be achieved and strives to understand how units of motor behaviour can be strung together. In the final section we discuss how the motor system interconnects with other psychological functions such as cognition and perception. This discussion includes the topics of embodied cognition and representations of action that relate perception to action.

MOTOR CONTROL

Motor control is the study of how body movements are planned by the brain and performed by the body. The modern study of motor control goes back for over a century to the studies of Woodworth (1899) who proposed different stages for the planning and control of movement. In a classic study he examined how people perform the task of sliding a pencil back and forth between targets. Data from this experiment revealed that movement between targets could be described with a two-component process of motor control. The impulse phase initiated the movement and was planned in advance of the start of the movement. In essence the brain would calculate in advance what limbs to move and how they should move and this plan in the form of a motor command would be sent from the brain out to the body. The impulse phase was followed by a control phase where vision was key to controlling the accuracy of the final endpoint position. While details such as the estimate of time needed to incorporate visual information have been revised (Elliott et al., 2001), the basic question of how to produce a movement that is efficient and incorporates sensory information in a timely manner remains relevant today.

Following Woodworth, studies in the early twentieth century explored the motor control problem from primarily a physiological perspective (Latash & Zatsiorsky, 2001). A basic formulation of the problem was simply how to get the body from one posture to another and research over the past century has revealed many fundamental problems the brain and body must solve to get from one point to another. One of the early pioneers of the twentieth century in studying motor control was the Russian scientist Nikolai Bernstein (1967). Like Woodward he also emphasized that the coordination of motor structures with sensory information was key to understanding motor control. However, a key contribution of Bernstein was to recognize that producing a movement plan requires overcoming what is known as the degrees of freedom problem. This

Degrees of freedom of a joint are the number of ways it can move. For example, the shoulder has three (up-down, forward-backward, rotate along axis of bone).

degrees of freedom problem refers to the issue that the structure of joints and muscles in the body provide a redundant system. This means that when performing a task the joints do not need to all move in all possible ways. A demonstration of redundancy comes from when we get injured and even though we cannot perform a particular joint motion, we can still achieve many of the same tasks we did before the injury. This redundancy clearly provides us with great versatility in performing actions in changing situations. However, for a motor control system trying to formulate a movement plan this redundancy poses a serious computational problem that we will discuss in the following paragraph.

This computational problem of how to plan a movement out of the multitude of alternatives is reminiscent to what we encountered in vision (see Chapter 2) with the so-called

Inverse problem in vision is where there are more than one interpretation of the 3D world given the 2D image information.

'inverse problem' where out of the multitude of possible interpretations of a visual scene, a unique one is perceived. To illustrate the situation faced by our motor planning system, consider standing in front of a lift, with your hand in front of you, having the goal of pressing the call button so you can ride the lift. You could move your hand along any number of paths, and for any particular path your speed along the path could vary (e.g. start fast and finish slow or start slow and finish fast). In addition, the joints you recruit to do the movement could differ (e.g. both the shoulder and elbow move and their contribution could vary), and your muscle activations could change (e.g. muscles relaxed or tense while achieving the same path). Given all the possible factors for achieving this simple goal we can see that the motor planning system is confronted with a difficult task to plan what body parts will move with what motion. However, we don't stand on the ground floor frozen with confusion about how to press the call button. We simply act on achieving our goal and the effortless way in which this occurs, shows that our brain has worked out an efficient strategy for producing movements. (While a more impressive example of motor expertise might be how an Olympic gymnast dismounts from the uneven bars, even the simplest movement reveals tremendous sophistication.) In the following we will review some of the proposals that have been put forth to describe how movements are planned and produced. However, before proceeding we will illustrate how developments in understanding motor control are being used to create new devices that provide help for those requiring assistance with their movement.

Box 8.1 Practical Application: Designing machines to help us move

Developments in mobility assistance are being advanced by the study of motor control and action production. Up to now, systems to assist with mobility required the user to learn and adapt to the device. Moving away from this scenario, to one where the device adapts to the user, requires an understanding of the ways humans plan and control their own movements.

An example of systems that conform to the user to provide mobility assistance is the robotic exoskeleton. These systems can take on many different forms, but typically include a set of mechanical linkages with motors at the joints that strap to the body and provide assistance for an individual to move. After years of development, exoskeletons have evolved into sophisticated medical products such as *CYBERDYNE's Robot Suit HAL (Hybrid Assistive Limb)*, which has recently been released for applications involving well-being in Japan (Figure 8.1); moreover it has started to be used in the improvement of functional mobility and regeneration in Europe. Similar whole-body systems resembling a movie character Iron Man (Favreau, 2008) have been demonstrated to enable individuals to lift massive weights. The key feature for any such system is that it is the human who must be in control. To achieve robot devices that assist walking has required advancements in many areas. One of these is development of an extremely detailed understanding of how individuals control their own walking movements. This has informed the design of sophisticated control software and associated mechanical design. Another development that is still in its infancy is the ability to reliably sense the bio-electric signals that appear on the skin when the person tries to move and use this to inform the intentions of the wearer. This window into the intentions of the wearer is crucial since otherwise disagreement between the wearer and the robot exoskeleton could lead to catastrophic results.

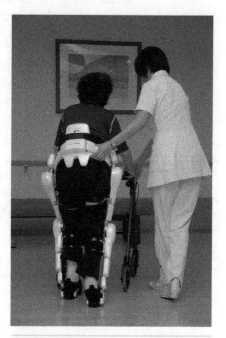

Figure 8.1 Robot assistive device to aid walking. CYBERDYNE's Robot Suit HAL (Hybrid Assistive Limb) is connected to the body and has sophisticated electronics to sense intended motor activity as well as algorithms to compute robot movement. Thus, it provides an assistive force to help those too weak to walk unaided.

Source: Prof. Sankai, CYBERDYNE, Inc./University of Tsukuba.

THEORIES OF MOVEMENT PLANNING

How the brain plans and executes movements is still a hotly debated topic. The three approaches we will explain were developed independently and each emphasizes a different aspect of how movements are planned and controlled.

Equilibrium point hypothesis is a theory of motor control that emphasizes how the problem of control can be simplified by taking into account muscle properties.

The first theoretical approach, known as equilibrium point hypothesis, emphasizes the special relationship between the brain and the muscles (Feldman, 1966, 1986; Feldman & Latash, 2005). This approach is sometimes termed a mass-spring model since it reflects an important intuition that our muscles, like springs, exert different forces depending on how much they are stretched. The model can effectively explain how we can begin a movement with our body in one stable posture and end in another stable posture. The crucial observation of the equilibrium point hypothesis is that any stable posture requires the setting of various control parameters for muscle activation to achieve stability. Thus, moving from one posture to another can be achieved by simply resetting these parameters so that the spring-like properties of the muscle move you into the next posture. This planning exploits the spring-like properties of the muscles to simplify what the brain must control to move the body. The problem of planning is simplified since one needs only to have a stable starting posture and know the parameters that are necessary to stabilize the body in the desired end posture. From this plan the movement can emerge from the inherent muscle properties. While this is an attractive theory in showing how incorporating knowledge of muscle properties can simplify motor planning there have been some criticisms. For example, it has been argued that it would only be a successful strategy for certain ranges of movements and muscle properties (Katayama & Kawato, 1993; Kawato, 1999; Kawato & Gomi, 1992). Outside of this range it was argued that planning using principles of the equilibrium point hypothesis became much more complex. However, there is debate over this point and arguments for the general utility of the approach (Ostry & Feldman, 2003).

Dynamical systems approach to motor control emphasizes interaction between the body and the environment and uses special mathematics that describe how a system's behaviour changes over time.

The second theoretical approach, known as dynamical systems theory, is related to ecological theories of psychology (Gibson, 1979) and emphasizes motor control as a process of self-organization between an animal and its environment. In simplest terms, dynamical systems is a branch of mathematics that includes rules which describe the evolution of the state of a system over time. For example, it can explain how the swinging motion of a pendulum will evolve over time. Of course, the human body and human movement are more complex than a pendulum but dynamical systems are effective in explaining complex systems interacting with the environment (Kelso, 1995; Turvey, 1990). Models of behaviour that use dynamical systems have provided elegant descriptions of motor behaviours. For example, in locomotion, walking and running are distinct motor patterns and there isn't an in-between state. This situation can be modelled as a dynamical system with walking and running as different stable states and a transition occurring between them determined by speed. Another example of a state transition arises from the observation that when we move two limbs together there is a tendency for them to exhibit mirror symmetric movements (Schmidt et al., 1990; Swinnen, 2002), meaning that if we held a mirror between the limbs then the reflection of one of the limbs would match what the other limb was doing. Even if we try to move our fingers in an antisymmetric manner, we will spontaneously change to a symmetric manner at a particular frequency (Haken et al., 1985; Kelso, 1984). This result is illustrated in Figure 8.2 and you can perform this experiment for yourself right now. Place your two hands in front of your body with palms facing each other. Now begin slowly with moving your fingers back and forth in an antisymmetric manner – one finger moving

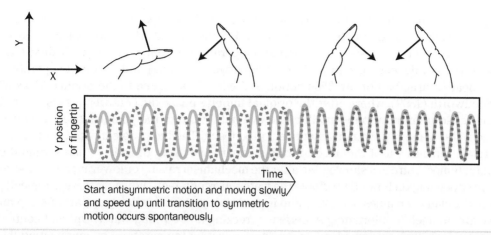

Figure 8.2 **Example of dynamical systems theory.** Start with your two fingers moving in alternate directions – one moving towards the body and the other away and steadily increase the frequency of these movements. At some point when the fingers begin to move more rapidly there is a transition from the original antisymmetric motion to a symmetric pattern. This transition is predicted by dynamical systems theory.

Source: Adapted from Haken, H. et al. (1985). A theoretical model of phase transitions in human hand movements. *Biological Cybernetics*, 51(5), 347–356.

towards the body while the other is moving away in an alternating fashion. Once you have achieved a stable pattern of movement then start slowly increasing the frequency of these back-and-forth finger motions. At some point as you increase the frequency you will find that both fingers are moving in a symmetric manner – both are moving towards and away from the body at the same time. This transition from antisymmetric to symmetric is neatly described in dynamical systems by a state transition of the motor system that is controlling the finger movements. Strengths of the dynamical systems approach have been to draw upon parallels with the behaviour of physical objects and to offer a rigorous theory that enables detailed modelling and prediction of rhythmic behaviour. However, it is an open area how to apply this approach to discrete movements.

The strengths of these first two approaches are to make clear that the brain can simplify its planning by knowledge of the body and has likely been driven to particular solutions by its interactions with the environment. The next approach we will consider is known as optimal control theory (Diedrichsen et al., 2010; Scott, 2004; Wolpert & Ghahramani, 2000; Wolpert & Kawato, 1998). Optimal control does not focus on constraints of the body, but instead views motor control as the evolutionary or developmental result of a nervous system that tries to optimize organizational principles (Schaal et al., 2007). Optimal control has been influential in the field of robotics. In optimal control, the problem of planning a movement is solved by using an optimization principle to define the best movement. Optimization principles which have been explored include planning a movement to be the smoothest motion between two points (Flash & Hogan, 1985), planning the least amount of torque-change at the joints (Uno et al., 1989) or planning the least amount of spatial errors in task achievement (Harris & Wolpert, 1998). The characteristics of coordination are therefore determined by the movement structure imposed by the optimization principle used. Optimal control theory arose from early engineering models for control of robots and has been actively used in recent developments in cognitive robotics where engineers were faced with the difficult process of designing robot controllers that could mimic human actions (Atkeson et al., 2000).

Optimal control theory of motor control provides a framework for implementing principles that produce movements that optimally satisfy some criterion.
Torque is a measure from physics that measures rotational force such as when muscles apply a force for a limb to rotate about a joint centre.

Scan to watch a fun clip on robotic controls

Optimal control theory is an advanced form of simple feedback mechanisms. The classic example of simple feedback is a heating thermostat where you set the desired temperature. In this system the existing temperature is compared to the desired temperature and depending on the difference between existing and desired temperature the heat is turned on or off. This notion of feedback is related to the original ideas of Woodworth (1899), where after the original impulse phase the control phase is entered and sensory information is available to evaluate whether the goal has been achieved and suitably modify the movement using feedback. The big problem with simple feedback is reminiscent of the uncomfortable experience many of us have had setting the water temperature in a shower. We alter the mechanism raising or lowering the temperature depending on how comfortable the water currently feels, however there is typically a time delay in changes occurring and if we do not predict this delay as part of our plan we are doomed to alternately experience freezing and burning water. Optimal control theory deals with this problem, as we do in adjusting temperature, by augmenting the

Forward models are used to predict the relationship between actions and their consequences. Given a motor command the forward model predicts the resulting behaviour of the body and the world.

available sensory information with predictions of the sensory information obtained from a forward model (Jordan & Rumelhart, 1992; Kawato, 1999). The forward model obtains these predictions from simulating the effects of our commands. Mental access to the prediction of a motor command is necessary because we need to be able to move quickly in complex ways and predictions of the sensory consequences of our motor commands are available faster than the sensory feedback resulting from the motor commands. Early studies of typing on a keyboard showed that there does not seem to be time enough for feedback to be involved in highly skilled performance

(Rumelhart & Norman, 1982). Think about how quickly you can move your hands and fingers in a single second to achieve a complex interaction with the world and consider further that visual information takes time to process and planning movements will also take some fixed amount of time. The challenge for the motor system is to deal with the world as it is *now* based on sensory information that is a tenth of a second old and with motor commands that will take effect in muscles a tenth of a second in the future.

A diagram illustrating optimal control theory is shown in Figure 8.3. As can be seen in Figure 8.3 the process of optimal control theory is cyclical, with motor commands being sent out of a control policy and the result of the motor command coming back to the control policy in the form of an estimate of the state that reflects how the motor command has changed things. To better understand the process we will describe this cycle starting with the control policy and going clockwise.

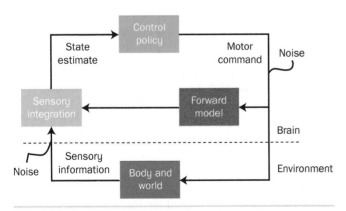

Figure 8.3 Optimal control theory. A motor command is sent from the control policy to the body and this results in a change in the world that is sensed. This sensed change in the world, along with the prediction of the change provided by a forward model are combined to estimate the current state of the body in the world. Consideration that physiological noise in transmitting motor commands and sensing the world is incorporated into the model.

- *Control policy*: the control policy takes as input the current state estimate and outputs a motor command. The control policy is the most complex aspect of optimal control theory. It provides a set of rules that determine what to do given a particular goal and state estimate. The control policy can take into account the importance of the goal to be achieved, the confidence in both the incoming sensory information and the outgoing motor commands as well as other factors.

- *Motor command*: the motor command is output from the control policy and contains the information about how the body is supposed to move.
- *Noise*: physiological noise is introduced into the motor command due to imperfect neural transmission along the pathway from brain to body.
- *Forward model*: the forward model takes as input the motor command and outputs a prediction of the sensory consequences of the motor command.
- *Body and the world*: the body takes as input the motor command that has been degraded by noise and produces an action that changes the state of the body and typically also the world; this creates new sensory information.
- *Sensory information*: the changes to the body and world create sensory information (e.g. visual information of an object being moved, auditory information of an impact sound, proprioceptive information of the limbs changing position).
- *Noise*: just like the motor command, the sensory information is also corrupted by physiological noise arising from imperfect sensing and neural transmission. This noise will lead to uncertainty in estimating the state of the body and the world.
- *Sensory integration*: sensory integration takes as input all the sensory information as well as the prediction of the forward model and outputs an estimate of the current state of the system.
- *State estimate*: the state estimate provides an internal representation of what is the current state of the body and world and this is input to the control policy.

Optimal control theory is applicable to a broad range of topics and in Box 8.2 we explain how it can account for errors we make in judging the force of our actions.

What makes optimal control theory attractive for cognitive modelling is that it describes aspects of motor control that are not fixed by physiology or the relationship between organism and environment. Instead, the state estimate upon which a movement is planned is heavily influenced by the forward model and the reliability of sensory information. Ways to cope with noisy and unreliable information were discussed in Chapter 2 in the context of Bayesian Decision Theory. In a Bayesian approach one applies an estimate of prior information about the world and the likelihood of the particular situation to best interpret the noisy, unreliable data. This approach has been used to treat the uncertainty arising from the noise and unreliability of our motor system (Gepshtein et al., 2007; Kording, 2007; Kording & Wolpert, 2006; Trommershauser et al., 2006). These studies show that when creating a plan for movement we incorporate our knowledge of the uncertainty of the visual information and the motor apparatus to plan movements that will gain us the highest reward. For example, in playing darts, regions of the highest point reward are surrounded by regions of the lowest point reward and so it is only optimal to go for the highest reward if we are confident of our sensorimotor system achieving high accuracy. Another feature of optimal control theory is that one can take the different 'boxes' in the optimal control model and map these functions onto the known functions of different brain areas involved with motor control. For example, aspects of the forward model appear to be based in the cerebellum, aspects of sensory integration appear to be based in parietal cortex, and aspects of the control policy appear to be based in the basal ganglia (Shadmehr & Krakauer, 2008).

> Basal ganglia are a group of neurons in the base of the forebrain that are connected to cortex and involved in action selection. Disorders of the basal ganglia are related to movement disorders such as Parkinson's disease.

Evaluation

We have briefly reviewed three theories of motor control and these ideas provide us insight into the fundamental building blocks of how movements are produced. Each theory highlighted an important consideration of how to solve this complex problem. The equilibrium point hypothesis showed that the complexity of forming a plan can be simplified by cleverly exploiting the properties of how muscles operate. Dynamical systems illustrated that theories of how a system evolves over time can, for repetitive rhythmic movements, successfully explain transitions between different action states. Finally, optimal control theory provided a framework to implement optimal organizational principles within the loop of planning, producing and sensing our actions. Resolving debate as to which is the most appropriate theory to explain what happens in the human brain has proven daunting. At issue is that each theory has a compelling description of some aspect of behaviour and theory; development past the 'sweet spot' of any one theory has led to more complicated versions, which by their complexity lose some of the compelling simplicity and parsimony of the original theory. An example of this is elegant work by Sternad and colleagues (2000) exploring dynamical systems that showed, for a special case of movement, how control of rhythmic movements (the 'sweet spot' for dynamical theory) could be tuned to produce single discrete movements.

Box 8.2 Research Close Up: Tit-for-tat and force escalation

Source: Wolpert, D. M., Shergill, S. S., Bays, P. M., & Frith, C. D. (2003). Two eyes for an eye: The neuroscience of force escalation. *Science, 301*(5630), 187.

INTRODUCTION

This research, conducted by Daniel Wolpert and colleagues began with the observation that whenever two children play tit-for-tat it quickly ends in tears with one complaining they had unfairly been hit very, very hard (Wolpert et al., 2003). Since the goal of a game of tit-for-tat is to hit the other person as hard as you have been hit it should not inevitably end with claims of unreasonable force escalation. However, since it is known that forces can be mis-estimated Wolpert hypothesized that we reliably underestimate the forces we produce and thus, we would always hit harder than we thought we did. To test this hypothesis Wolpert and colleagues explored how forces were exchanged under different experimental conditions.

METHOD

Three different experimental conditions were explored using specially designed equipment that included force transducers to measure the forces being applied and computer controlled torque motors that allowed specific forces to be applied. In the first experimental condition six pairs of individuals participated. A session began when the torque motor applied a small force to the left index finger of one of the participants. Participants then took turns using their right index finger to press on their partner's left index finger. Both partners were instructed to exert the same force on their partner that they had just experienced, but they were unaware of the instructions given to the other.

In the second and third experimental conditions 12 participants were tested individually in their ability to match a range of forces generated by the computer-controlled torque motor. In the second condition the computer-controlled torque motor provided forces to an individual's left index finger that they then matched by pressing their right index finger upon their left index finger. The third condition was like the second, except that instead of matching the force by pressing with their right index finger they manipulated a joystick that controlled the amount of force applied to the left index finger.

RESULTS

The results of the first experimental condition (Figure 8.4a) showed that when trading touches partners quickly escalated forces by approximately 38 per cent per turn. If individuals had been accurate then there would have been a flat line showing no increase in forces as the original small force would have been obtained for all turns of force exchange. The results of the additional conditions are shown in Figure 8.4b, which plots the matched force against the presented force. When individuals matched the

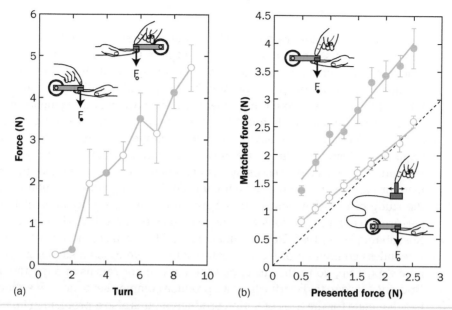

Figure 8.4   We underestimate the application of our own force. (a) In a tit-for-tat game of exchanging touches there is a consistent escalation of force between partners as the number of turns increase. (b) When we match a computer-generated force with a force directly generated by our finger then we consistently overestimate forces (filled-in circles). However, when we match a presented force by using a joystick we are more accurate (open circles).

Source: Shergill, S. S., Bays, P. M., Frith, C. D., & Wolpert, D. M. (2003). Two eyes for an eye: The neuroscience of force escalation. *Science*, *301*(5630), 187. Reprinted with permission from AAAS.

presented force by using finger presses then they consistently produced more force than had originally been applied to them by the computer-controlled torque motor. To appreciate the amount of force over-estimation one should compare the experimental results to the dashed 45-degree diagonal line that represents correct performance (matched force equals presented force). In the third condition when individuals matched force by use of the joystick then performance was much more accurate, with the matched forces nearly overlapping the diagonal line of correct performance.

DISCUSSION

The results of this series of experiments demonstrate that although we can accurately match forces when mediated by an external device like a joystick we are greatly inaccurate when we match forces generated by our own body. When asked to create a force that matches a received touch we greatly overestimate the force applied to others and even to ourselves. While this suggests that next time we want to touch someone gently we should touch them very, very lightly it also provides an opportunity to see how optimal control theory can be used to explain why this happens. The forces we generate ourselves also inform a forward model and the predictions of this forward model will be combined with the perceived sensory consequences of our self-generated actions. A consequence of this combination seems to be that perception of our own actions has a special status that leads to substantial underestimation of force. One possible reason for this is that for interactions with the environment, it is useful to attenuate the effect of the forces we generate ourselves, as a means to become more sensitive to forces we receive from external sources.

The question of why internally generated forces might be mis-estimated was explored in a follow-up experiment that investigated schizophrenia (Shergill et al., 2005). Because schizophrenics can report self-generated actions as being of alien origin it was hypothesized they would have less of a tendency to create excessive matching forces when using finger presses. Experimental results confirmed this hypothesis with schizophrenics being more accurate than controls in generating matching forces. This illustrates the significance of mechanisms that treat our own actions as special. Moreover, interpretation of the results highlight that one important function of the forward model could be to diminish the effects of our own actions as a means to aid our sensory system in separating the effects of ourselves from the effects of the world.

PRODUCING COMPLEX ACTIONS

In the previous section we discussed how the motor system produced movements of the body. This discussion included concepts of how the brain, body and environment act together to produce movements. However, the goals of these movements were kept simple to emphasize the processes involved in planning individual body movements. In this section we move from the problem of how individual movements are produced to focus on movement goals and how these lead to complex sequences of actions. In switching focus from achieving individual movements to achieving goals through sequences of movements we are moving into an area that is more tightly interwoven with other cognitive processes. It has been observed that cognitive theories of movement production are scarce (Rosenbaum, 2005). Though one exception to this has been the study of grasp, which is not surprising given the significance of hand actions in performing complex actions to achieve goals (Jeannerod, 1984; Jeannerod et al., 1995; Rosenbaum et al., 1995; Rosenbaum et al., 2001). Even so, these models do not provide a seamless continuum of explanation from how we grasp a single raisin on a table to how we get up, go to the store, buy the package of raisins and get them back home. Bridging this gap to describe how we produce complex sequences of actions is an ongoing challenge for theories of action production. It is also a problem in how to get robots to perform useful action sequences that we describe in Box 8.3.

Scan to watch a clip of a robot producing complex actions

Box 8.3 Practical Application: Producing complex actions in robots

Increasingly, robotic systems are being developed for use in applications such as surveillance and performing actions in environments that are inhospitable to humans (Voyles & Adams, 2011) as well as in the field of social robotics (Breazeal, 2004; Kennedy et al., 2009). For such robotic systems to function productively it is essential that they can effectively execute sequences of actions. One way for this to be accomplished is for the robot to be entirely autonomous – to plan and execute all functions independently of human input. This is a difficult problem but tremendous progress has been made to produce robots that can walk, crawl and otherwise locomote. Examples include the many impressive robots from Boston Dynamics (www.youtube.com/user/BostonDynamics) that can move under their own power over complicated terrain and obstacles. However, these robots are generally unable to be totally autonomous, and to achieve complex actions they are under the control of a human who will direct the sequential ordering of their actions. This link between man and machine is known as tele-operation and is perhaps well known from the way that mission control on earth directs actions in space vehicles and planetary rovers.

The design of tele-operation for human-robot systems require appreciation of how individuals and teams execute plans, and how to effectively incorporate robot behaviours into human-mediated action plans. One growing application for such systems is social robots that can aid humans in day-to-day activities. These robots could be placed in the homes of aged or vulnerable individuals to assist in their care and be monitored from a central location. One question that has arisen is how many social robots can a single operator effectively control (Zheng et al., 2011). To address this question these researchers put robots in a mall scenario where the robots acted as mobile information kiosks. When any one robot was occupying the time of a human controller with a human-robot interaction the other robots needed to either act autonomously or enter a waiting state. To optimize performance the repertoire of autonomous robot behaviour was designed, along with the human-robot interface to minimize the time any human in the mall would spend waiting for a robot response. Experimental results showed that human performance peaked with the control of 3 robots by a single human controller and that this was consistent with a cognitive model of multiple robot control.

ACTION SEQUENCES

Lashley (1951) observed in his seminal work that humans are continually active and this activity has a complex temporal structure that appears only in animals with a highly developed brain. Lashley went on to criticize the predominant explanation of the day – associative chain theory – as inadequate to completely explain how we produce a sequence of actions. Associative chain theory states that the end of one particular action is associated with stimulating the start of the next action in the sequence. This can be an effective method for simple and limited sequences but it has difficulty with general sequences such as when an element of the sequence repeats. For example, if the actions comprising the sequence are run-jump-spin-walk-turn then we can take the end of jumping to signal the start of spinning. However, if we are given the additional sequence of run-jump-spin-jump-turn then 'jump' becomes problematic since the end of jump now has to signal the beginning of both spinning and turning.

> Associative chain theory is a behaviourist theory that explains how sequences of action arise from linking together associations between individual action components.

There are, of course, ways to fix this problem with associative models by creating new basic elements that include the preceding and following action (Wickelgren, 1969). Thus when jump is preceded by run and followed by spin we can code this as the triple: run-jump-spin. Likewise when jump is preceded by spin and followed by turn we can use the triple: spin-jump-turn. Though this solution is effective it generates the issue that the movement triples obscure the elemental nature of the individual movements; it would seem that a jump is a jump, regardless of the movements surrounding it. This example of a sequence of actions (run, jump, spin, walk, turn) is somewhat contrived, and the full force of Lashley's arguments was directed at language where behaviourist models of language production held that the words in a sentence were chained together by associative links. There is extensive coverage of language in Chapters 12 and 13 and Lashley's own words are persuasive in relating language to general behaviour (1951, p. 121):

> the problems raised by the organization of language seem to me to be characteristic of almost all other cerebral activity. There is a series of hierarchies of organization; the order of vocal movements in pronouncing the word, the order of words in the sentence, the order of sentences in the paragraph, the rational order of paragraphs in a discourse. Not only speech, but all skilled acts seem to involve the same problems of serial ordering, even down to the temporal coordination of muscular contractions in such a movement as reaching and grasping.

There were two key ideas from speech production that were used to advance cognitive models of serial planning. These two ideas are the pattern of errors we make when we speak and how the production of different speech sounds are coordinated to produce fluent speech. A simple error that everybody makes at one time is a slip of the tongue where words are switched about in a sentence. For example, Lashley points out the example 'Let us always remember that waste makes haste' where the words waste and haste are switched. These errors suggest that rather than a sentence being produced sequentially one word after another, it seems as if before the sentence begins all the words are somehow available and ready to take a particular grammatical structure. Errors occur by misplacing words in the structure rather than in purely sequential errors of what goes after what. Lashley also pointed out that the production of speech involves several inter-related but somewhat independent neurological systems. Moreover, different articulators of the vocal tract (e.g. lip, tongue) are critical at some times of an utterance and not critical at other times. When an articulator is not critical it is able to prepare for upcoming sounds to be produced as long as it does not interfere with intelligibility of the current sound being produced. This leads to a phenomenon known as coarticulation where the target sound is being articulated at the same time that future sounds are being prepared (see Chapter 13). From these results, Lashley concluded that control of speech articulators are best modelled as arising from the interaction of separate mechanisms governed within a hierarchy of constraints. The question then becomes what mechanisms and what overarching constraints? Our discussion of motor control provides many choices of what mechanisms might be involved in producing movement. What we lack is description of what form the overarching constraints might take, and this is covered in the next section.

HIERARCHICAL MODELS OF ACTION PRODUCTION

What Lashley encouraged was a study of action sequences that was not dominated by the way one element related to its direct neighbours. Since different mechanisms could work simultaneously in parallel to create sequences it was important to consider how these mechanisms could be organized to produce sequences of actions. A first attempt at such a model of sequence production was provided by Miller et al. (1960) who developed what they called a test-operate-test-exit (TOTE) unit. Once selected a TOTE unit would continuously test whether a condition was met and then exit once the condition was satisfied. For example, if we had one sock in our hand and a pile of socks on the floor and we wanted a matching pair then we would first 'test' to confirm we only had one sock. Next we would 'operate' to pick up a sock and 'test' to see if it matched. If it didn't we would 'operate' to pick up and check another until we found a match and could 'exit'. This architecture also allowed TOTE units to call other TOTE units, thus permitting a hierarchical structure to be used to produce a sequence of actions. For example, the TOTE unit to find matching socks could be embedded within a larger structure to get dressed that contained additional TOTE units for finding your pants, finding your shoes and finding your shirt.

> **Parallel processing** is the ability to divide the process of solving a problem into multiple parts and to work simultaneously on each part.

These ideas were further advanced by Estes (1972) who proposed hierarchies of control elements which activated other control elements at the levels below. An example of such a hierarchy is shown in Figure 8.5 for accomplishing the action of locking money in a safe. As can be seen in Figure 8.5 each node of the hierarchy corresponds to a particular action schema. In this example the action schemas and their position in the hierarchy map directly onto the sequence of actions that need to take place for the action to be achieved. This way of representing the action hierarchy is straightforward and has an intuitive appeal to representing how accomplishing a goal can be achieved by a hierarchical arrangement of schema. However, it is not the only way to represent an action and recently it has been shown that another possible structure is to represent the correlational relationship of the different actions within the hierarchy (Botvinick, 2008; Botvinick & Plaut, 2002). For instance, picking up the key is more likely to occur with both locking and unlocking the door and thus forms a stronger correlational relationship than does picking up the key with picking up the money.

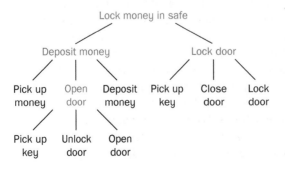

Figure 8.5 Hierarchical representation of an action sequence for locking money in a safe. The action sequence is divided into the two main nodes of 'deposit money' and 'lock door'; however, a sub-node occurs on 'open door', which is the branch point for a further hierarchy.

Source: Reprinted from Botvinick, M. M. (2008). Hierarchical models of behavior and prefrontal function. *Trends in Cognitive Sciences, 12*(5), 201–208, with permission from Elsevier.

The example presented for locking money in a safe illustrates much of the essence of a hierarchical structure of an action sequence. However, what is not seen in this static figure is a sense of how the temporal structure of an action is achieved. To produce an action sequence it must be possible to traverse the hierarchy in a manner that activates currently desired units while suppressing currently undesired units. Models of how hierarchical structures can be used to produce sequences have developed from theories of recurrent networks (Elman, 1990; Jordan, 1986, 1997). Recurrent networks are a type of artificial neural that can be designed to control the timing of operations. They have been used to demonstrate sequential behaviour resembling that of humans in a variety of domains. For example, Cooper and Shallice (2000) designed a network to produce a sequence of actions and used it to inform a theoretical understanding of how errors occurred when producing sequences. An example of the network demonstrating the making of instant coffee is shown in Figure 8.6a. Within this hierarchy, patterns of activation and inhibition work in a manner of interactive activation (McClelland & Rumelhart, 1981; Rumelhart & McClelland, 1982) to produce a sequence. One operating characteristic of interactive activation is that when one unit of a hierarchy is selected for activation, other units at the same level of hierarchy are inhibited. This facilitates the selected action schema to complete. For example, when the schema for putting milk into coffee was activated the units for putting sugar and grinds into the coffee were suppressed. The temporal ordering of the activations of nodes in the schema is shown in Figure 8.6b for the hierarchy producing a proper sequence for making a cup of coffee.

Recurrent networks are a type of artificial neural network with connections between units arranged so to obtain a cycle of activation. This design allows a temporal context to be designed into the computation.

Interactive activation is a term used to describe the pattern of network activity generated by excitatory and inhibitory interactions of feature detectors and object representations.

In Box 8.4 we examine the case where even experts go wrong with producing complex actions and use what we have learned so far in the chapter to try and explain how this might happen.

Box 8.4 When Things Go Wrong: Choking – when actions let us down

We've all seen it before, the tennis player who repeatedly double faults their service in the finals, the footballer who kicks a penalty kick 10 metres wide in a penalty shoot-out, or the golfer who misses the putt that would win a championship. Probably some of us have experienced a similar situation ourselves. The psychological definition for choking is the occurrence of inferior performance despite striving and incentives for superior performance (Baumeister, 1984; Baumeister & Showers, 1986). This definition does little to convey the gut-wrenching experience when, despite years of training and sometimes overwhelming odds in favour of a winning performance, this inferior performance leads to

© pioia666/iStock

a crushing defeat. Psychological studies of choking cover everything from how students fail exams to how elite athletes miss shots. There are similarities, but we concentrate on how failure follows from our inability to produce actions. We discuss choking in three parts. First, we define the unique factors that are stirred up by pressure situations. Second, we consider models that explain mechanisms of why performance changes under pressure. Finally, we discuss these different factors and models in the context of motor control and production of action sequences.

Producing movement to a high standard requires multiple mental processes to go right. Various studies, including interviews with elite athletes who had catastrophic performance failures (Edwards et al., 2002), reveal that the factors of self-confidence, control, anxiety, arousal, and effort relate to reductions of performance. The effects of self-confidence and control become evident following an athlete making an initial error that leads to a rapid decrease in self-confidence and feelings of control. This occurs even if self-confidence and feelings of control had been high at the start of the performance. Anxiety and arousal are useful to discuss together since anxiety can be divided into a cognitive component and a somatic component that is similar to physiological arousal. Cognitive anxiety is demonstrated by expressing an upcoming event as difficult and that one feels nervous. Somatic anxiety and arousal are demonstrated by physical symptoms of feeling tension in the body and other bodily feelings and autonomic body responses such as speeding up of the heart. Finally, effort is the response of an athlete to address the level of challenge. If an action is challenging then increasing effort can work to compensate for difficulty. This large number of factors contributing to performance and an assortment of ways to measure them has spawned a large literature to explain how performing an action under pressure can lead to failure.

Theories to explain the fall of performance under pressure include cue utilization theory (Easterbrook, 1959), cognitive interference theory (Sarason, 1984), Wegner's ironic process theory (Wegner, 1994, 1997) and processing efficiency theory (PET) by Eysenck and Calvo (1992), attentional control theory (Eysenck et al., 2007) and the conscious processing hypothesis (CPH) by Masters (1992). We will compare CPH and PET since they illustrate many of the relevant properties and have been the subject of much experimental scrutiny. In CPH, performance is modelled to decrease because increasing anxiety leads to a disruption of automatic processing. To compensate for the disruption to automatic processing skilled performers are hypothesized to switch to a style of performance that, like novices, involves conscious awareness of individual components of an action. Thus, instead of performing actions automatically as a whole they begin to analyze their actions part by part and this results in less fluency and effectiveness. Similar decreases in performance can be accomplished simply by asking experts to focus on a particular part of their performance. In PET, performance is modelled to decrease because other activities such as cognitive anxiety begin to consume resources and this leaves less resources available for performing actions (Beilock, 2010). Importantly, in distinction to CPH, PET allows increasing the effort for a task as a means to compensate for the loss of cognitive resources due to anxiety. This capability to allocate more effort allows normal performance to be obtained under low anxiety conditions and such a compensatory mechanism is not available with CPH. Comparisons of CPH to PET have provided mixed results. For example, a study comparing CPH to PET found that aspects of both theories were required to explain performance on how average golfers failed at a putting task (Wilson et al., 2007).

Although many models have been proposed there is yet no definitive model to describe why we sometimes perform worse under psychological pressure. It is thus interesting to speculate how the different factors and models of choking might relate to the theories of motor control and sequential action production we have discussed. For instance, the breakdown of smooth continuous performance could be modelled within hierarchical models of action production such as the one we presented for making instant coffee. The process described in CPH of breaking down a fluid action sequence to focus on particular components can be described as focusing on subnodes of a hierarchy and this is consistent with reducing top-down control, which leads to action production becoming disorganized. Considering the effect of arousal and somatic anxiety we can see that they have an effect on the general motor activity as reflected in the tension reported by athletes preceding their choking. Relating this to the model of optimal control theory (Figure 8.3) we can see that if this general arousal was not accurately accounted for in the forward model or if it contributed to internal noise in the nervous system then the predicted consequences of the motor command would not be accurate and this would lead to disrupted movement. Similarly, if the control policy didn't accurately reflect confidence in the probability that a particular movement could be achieved then movements would be attempted that were not optimal. These considerations illustrate how the theories presented in this chapter can be applied to explain how even highly trained movements can go wrong under pressure.

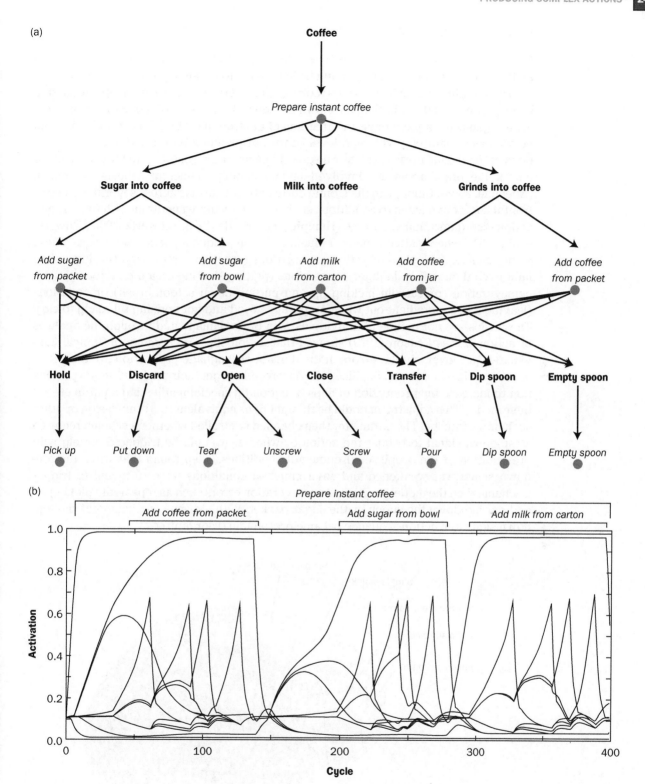

Figure 8.6 Cooper and Shallice's recurrent network (2000) for making instant coffee. The hierarchical structure reflected in part (a) contains all the action elements necessary to make the coffee with the three main divisions of the sequence 'sugar into coffee', 'milk into coffee' and 'grinds into coffee'. To make the coffee in the proper sequence, it is necessary to properly activate the different nodes. The timecourse of activation of nodes for successful coffee-making is illustrated in part (b).

Source: Cooper, R. & Shallice, T. (2000). Contention scheduling and the control of routine activities. *Cognitive Neuropsychology, 17*(4), 297–338. Taylor and Francis (http://www.informaworld.com)

BRAIN DAMAGE AND ACTION PRODUCTION

Not only was the model of Cooper and Shallice (2000) able to produce meaningful action sequences but the model could be 'damaged' to obtain the type of errors associated with brain damage in the frontal cortex. The frontal cortex is responsible for action planning and it is thought that, as shown in Figure 8.7, the coordination of action is set in an organized manner across the anatomy of the frontal cortex. This organization can be seen as a hierarchy with high level control of planning performed in anterior portions of the frontal cortex, and as one goes from anterior frontal cortex towards motor cortex the brain areas are involved in increasingly elemental aspects of control (Koechlin, 2008). Damage to the frontal cortex is often diffuse across several regions of frontal cortex and leads to conditions such as dysexecutive syndrome (Chapter 4) and action disorganization syndrome (Humphreys & Forde, 1998; Schwartz, 2006; Schwartz et al., 1991), where patients make frequent errors in producing action sequences. These errors include such slips of action as insertions (entering a room and turning on the light even though it is daylight), confusions (putting shaving cream on a toothbrush), perseveration (repeatedly picking up and putting down a toothbrush) or omissions (leaving a key ingredient out when preparing a food and not noticing till ready to eat). These slips are not unique to individuals with brain damage and through the analysis of action diaries Reason (1979) showed that action slips are common in typical individuals. Moreover, similar errors in the domain of language production are described in Chapter 12. Cooper and Shallice (2000) were able to get their model of action production to increase the production of slips of action by specially adjusting a parameter of their model. This adjustment could be thought of as equivalent to a brain lesion or other such brain damage. The parameter they changed controlled whether a schema required a top-down signal to trigger the action or whether it could be triggered merely with presentation of the proper environmental conditions. They found that when the top-down signal was weakened and environmental conditions were sufficient to trigger a schema then the model performed perseveration errors such as repeatedly picking up and putting down the spoon or the sugar packet. With extreme weakening of the top-down signal the action sequence became profoundly disorganized.

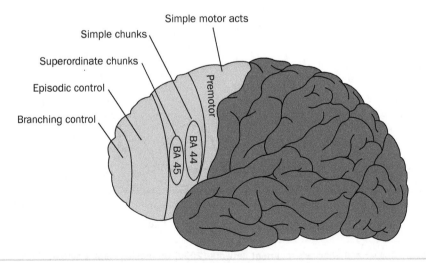

Figure 8.7   Brain imaging studies have shown that the anatomy of the frontal cortex reflects a hierarchical structure of action planning. If we consider a tree diagram then the final nodes of the tree are represented in premotor cortex which would contain the motor primitives for simple motor acts. As one moves towards the tip of the frontal cortex, known as the prefrontal cortex, one encounters regions that are higher nodes in the planning hierarchy.

Action disorganization syndrome fits into a broader family of movement disorders known by the general term apraxia that can arise from patterns of brain damage to the frontal and parietal cortex, basal ganglia and the nerve fibres connecting these regions (Cooper et al., 2005; Gross & Grossman, 2008; Wheaton & Hallett, 2007). The distinguishing characteristic of apraxia is the inability to successfully carry out skilled motor acts despite preserved sensory and motor systems as well as an ability to comprehend and cooperate. The most widely recognized type of apraxia is ideomotor apraxia and it is demonstrated by an inability to pantomime tool use and gesture when verbally instructed to do so. While there is a tendency that the same actions can be performed naturally during daily living, they can become slow, deliberate and error-prone (e.g. holding a comb upside down) when asked to perform the same action. However, this striking difference of capabilities between verbal instruction and natural performance cannot be attributed to a language deficit as patients with ideomotor apraxia can demonstrate that they know what they have been instructed to do. A typical cause of apraxia is stroke where the blood supply to the brain malfunctions resulting in damage to brain tissue. Given the unfortunately common occurrence of stroke there is motivation to better understand specifically what brain damage leads to apraxia and how to rehabilitate individuals to best recover function. In Box 8.5 we discuss how technology and cognitive science are combining to tackle this problem of rehabilitation.

> Apraxia is a neurological condition typically resulting from brain damage where a person loses the ability to perform activities that they are physically able and willing to do.

Scan to watch a clip illustrating apraxia in a patient

Box 8.5 Practical Application: Smart technology for rehabilitation

Brain damage can lead to a variety of deficits in the execution of multi-step actions that are associated with action disorganization syndrome and apraxia. A common feature of both patients with apraxia and action disorganization syndrome is that they are impaired in performing tasks of daily living, ranging from making a hot drink, preparing a meal, or self-care tasks like washing and dressing. These deficits reflect cognitive difficulties and are not attributable to weakness, which is also often associated with brain injuries resulting from stroke.

Research has shown that patients with apraxia and action disorganization syndrome do respond to therapy if visual or verbal prompts (cues) are given to guide the patient through successive steps in the required sequence of actions. However, this is labour intensive for the therapist and it is not clear whether short-term gains are maintained when the cueing is withdrawn. As a result patients with apraxia and action disorganization syndrome often suffer a loss of independent living.

In a new research project called Cogwatch (http://cogwatch.eu/) engineers, computer scientists and psychologists are using principles of cognitive neuroscience to develop novel rehabilitation methods to ultimately help people suffering from apraxia and action disorganization syndrome. After injury, various mechanisms operate to improve brain function ranging from some restoration of brain function in areas surrounding the primary damage, to relearning of the skill by intact brain regions. Rehabilitation involves a multifaceted approach including assessment and supported practice, where the support may be literal, but also informational, motivational and emotional. It is embedded in learning contexts designed to facilitate how new experiences mediate the functional reorganization of the brain.

The CogWatch approach to rehabilitation involves an automated smart environment. The smart environment senses the state of the inhabitant

© http://cogwatch.eu/

and evaluates their actions in terms of how the environment can react to improve action outcomes, thus improving quality of life. Components of the smart environment include physical sensors (e.g. cameras, microphones, force sensors) and smart devices to pick up information about the activities of the inhabitant. These components are linked to computers and software to determine how to assist and rehabilitate the inhabitant to perform everyday tasks.

As an example of the Cogwatch concept, consider a fictional inhabitant, Anna, making a cup of tea assisted by Cogwatch. Anna starts by taking a tea cup from the cupboard and places it on the countertop and then stops uncertain what to do next. [*CogWatch infers that Anna wants to make a cup of tea and activates the virtual tutor to guide her through the task. It displays a mirror representation of the items that are on the countertop including the cup, kettle, and tea caddy. Virtual hands appear at mirror positions corresponding to Anna's hands and then start moving towards the virtual tea caddy.*] Anna, cued by the virtual hands, moves her own hands towards the real tea caddy. She opens the caddy and takes a teabag out and puts the bag in the cup. [*The virtual tutor synchronizes its hand movements with Anna's hand movements.*] After a pause Anna then moves her hand towards the kettle [*cued by the virtual tutor*] but instead of turning the kettle on to boil the water, she starts to pick it up as though to pour the water into the cup. [*CogWatch detects the approaching omission error and displays an error message at the same time as providing vibration on the wristband display – the CogWatch – of the potential error. The virtual hands indicate the recovery by moving the virtual kettle back to its base and turns it on to boil the water. Meanwhile, CogWatch monitors Anna's movements. If she does not return the kettle to its base, the virtual tutor provides further cues.*] However, Anna has been made aware of the error and corrects it. She boils the water and successfully completes making her tea without further CogWatch prompts.

ACTION REPRESENTATION AND PERCEPTION

THEORIES OF ACTION REPRESENTATION

Cognitive sandwich describes the view that perception and action are like slices of bread that surround cognition as the filling of a sandwich.

The term cognitive sandwich is used to describe the view that cognition is like the filling of a sandwich: surrounded on one side by a slice of perception and on the other by a slice of action. Our discussions of motor control and sequence planning were largely consistent with such a sandwich model since it emphasized motor processes in isolation. In this section we place the sandwich in a blender by taking the view that cognitive representations of action intermingle with representations of both perception and action. These theories of action representation are becoming increasingly important to guide investigation in domains where the body plays a central role such as sport, dance and rehabilitation.

Historical perspectives

Ideomotor theory relates how thinking about the results of an action can give rise to producing the action.

There is a long tradition known as ideomotor theory that intimately connects perception to action. Ideomotor theory arose from the philosophical question of how could the mind, which apparently has no direct access to (neuro)physiological mechanisms, control the body to achieve its goals. The answer proposed was that human actions can arise from ideas of the sensory consequences they produce. For instance, a particular action is associated with the sensory outcomes of that action, and by thinking about these sensory outcomes one can produce the action. This effectively equates action planning with thoughts of what the sensory consequences of that movement would be. The history of ideomotor theories has been extensively reviewed (Shin et al., 2010; Stock & Stock, 2004). Ideomotor theory developed in the nineteenth century in Germany with the scholars

Hebart, Lotze and Harless, and in Britain with the scholars Laycock and Carpenter; it was later incorporated by William James (1890) in his influential *The Principles of Psychology*. Ideomotor theory was largely ignored in the behaviourist approach to psychology since it was difficult to empirically verify. A factor contributing to this was that technical limitations of the early twentieth century made it difficult to measure the physical properties of movements with much precision and this held back the study of how motor intentions could be related to producing action. In contrast, during the same period research into perception advanced since it was possible to relate measures of physical stimuli to both their subjective experience and neural mechanisms (Haggard, 2001). However, this situation has changed dramatically in recent years as the means to precisely measure human actions has greatly advanced and sophisticated models of action representation have developed.

Common codes for action perception and production

Concepts associated with ideomotor theory came to the fore again in the 1990s within the framework of common coding (Hommel et al., 2001; Prinz, 1997). Common coding addressed the problem of how sensory codes can be internally related to motor codes. For example, if we are told that we have to press a button with our left hand when we see a green light and press a button with our right hand when we see a red light, then we need somehow to relate the colour seen to the hand used to press the button. To obtain this

> Common coding is a theory of perception and action production which holds that both production and perception share certain representations of actions in the world.

relationship the cognitive sandwich approach holds that sensory codes are translated to motor codes by cognitive mechanisms. Common coding holds that instead of a translation mechanism between sensory and motor codes there is a layer of representation that includes event codes and action codes (Figure 8.8). In this extra layer, aspects of event coding overlap with those of action coding. One intuitive way to think of the situation is to imagine that the sensory codes are in Spanish and the motor codes are in English and the problem is to get the two to work together. One way to achieve this would be to obtain formal translations to send between sensory and motor codes, and this is the cognitive sandwich approach. Another way would be to add an event/action

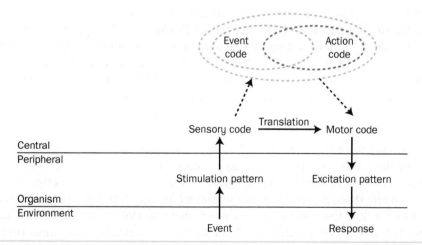

Figure 8.8   Common coding and the relationship between perception and action. Events in the world are transformed into sensory codes which must activate motor codes to form a response. Common coding, shown in dashed lines, allow late representations of event codes and early representations of response codes to share the same codes.

Source: Prinz, W. (1997). Perception and action planning. *European Journal of Cognitive Psychology*, 9(2), 129–154. Taylor and Francis (http://www.informaworld.com)

manager that spoke Spanglish to mediate communication and this is the common coding approach.

One predicted consequence of common coding is that because the common code is a resource for both perceiving and producing actions there would be interference between perception and production when they both tried to access the same resource at the same time. Evidence for interference was shown in a number of studies using reaction times, which showed both that perception impaired action planning and that action planning impaired perception (for a review see Heyes, 2011; Vogt & Thomaschke, 2007). Another predicted consequence of common coding is that there will be properties of action that are common to both perception and production. One example is the 1/3 power law of drawing, which influences not only how we draw a motion but also how we visually perceive the drawing movement (Viviani & Stucchi, 1992). From the perspective of action production this law describes how, when drawing a shape on a flat surface the hand will slow down for the highly curved parts and speed up for the straight parts in a way that follows a precise mathematical formulation (Lacquaniti et al., 1983; Viviani & Cenzato, 1985). From the perspective of visual perception the law describes how the speed along a curved path must vary to produce the perception of uniform motion. Thus, the same regularity between speed and geometry captures both motor and visual processes (Flash & Handzel, 2007; Handzel & Flash, 1999; Pollick & Sapiro, 1997). Brain imaging investigations of the 1/3 power law by Dayan and colleagues (2007) have shown results consistent with common coding. This fMRI study compared brain activity when viewing motion of targets that did and did not conform to a 1/3 power law. Results showed that when viewing a target that obeyed the power law there was extensive brain activation not only in visual areas, but also areas related to motor production.

A final result from common coding comes from the hypothesis that if the observed action of another is similar to how an observer would perform the action themselves, then there will be greater overlap of the common codes. Thus viewing your own performance of an action would lead to a more effective activation of a common code and this would lead to individuals excelling at identifying their own actions. This prediction has been tested successfully in several experiments where people viewed recordings of their own and others' actions. For example, from viewing point-light displays of themselves and their best friend dancing, boxing or jumping people can identify themselves better than they can identify their friend (Beardsworth & Buckner, 1981; Loula et al., 2005; Prasad et al., 2005). Visual familiarity cannot explain this effect since people have greater visual familiarity viewing their friends than themselves. Similarly, it has been shown that people can identify their own handwriting from a single moving dot (Knoblich & Flach, 2003) and can also identify their own clapping movements (Flach et al., 2004).

Evaluation

Common coding can explain how performance changes when perception and action compete for the same resources. It can also explain how regularities between perception and action would exist and why we can recognize our own actions better than those of another. While these are significant theoretical accomplishments on their own, it is important to consider the wider implications of such a model for the cognitive sandwich approach. The pervasive separation of perception from action that exists under the cognitive sandwich approach has often created a research context where the motor system appears to simply serve perceptual and cognitive processes. Common coding can be seen to raise the status of motor processes in cognition. One aspect of common coding not discussed so far was what neural mechanism might support this function. In the next section we describe mirror neurons, which provide evidence of single neurons that represent both perception and action.

Mirror mechanisms and action observation

A neural mechanism to unite perception and action was provided by the discovery of so-called mirror neurons in the macaque monkey in a region of the frontal lobe known as the premotor cortex (Dipellegrino et al., 1992; Gallese et al., 1996). These neurons displayed the remarkable property of being sensitive to an action being performed, say picking up a raisin, whether the monkey itself or the experimenter performed the act (Figure 8.9). Such neurons thus appear to represent both performing an action and viewing the same action performed by another. This representation unites perception and action in a single neuron and, it has been argued, provides a basis for understanding the goals of others (Rizzolatti & Sinigaglia, 2010). What is new in this mirror mechanism is that understanding actions is not gained by mapping viewed actions onto abstract concepts built up from visual representations but instead mapping them directly onto representations of action production (Rizzolatti et al., 2001).

> Mirror neurons are neurons with the special property that they represent both the sensory aspects of perceiving actions as well as motor aspects of how to produce the action.

From the discovery of mirror neurons in the premotor cortex of the macaque monkey in the early 1990s neuroscience research proceeded in two directions. The first direction was to further explore the monkey brain for other evidence of mirror neurons. This resulted in mirror neurons being found in the parietal cortex that responded to both doing and seeing an action (Fogassi et al., 2005) as well as in the premotor cortex that responded to both doing and hearing an action such as cracking open a nut (Kohler et al., 2002). These results support the existence of a fronto-parietal mirror network in the monkey. The significance of this is twofold. First, the monkey data involves measuring from single neurons and thus provide direct evidence that a single neuron is encoding information relevant to perception and production. Second, the fact that mirror neurons were found in two regions of the brain and involved in the coding of two forms of sensory information (sight and sound) suggest that this is a general information processing strategy, rather than a mechanism with limited scope. The other major research direction was to explore whether mirror neurons would be found in the human brain. Given the ethical difficulties in measuring properties of individual neurons in the human brain (Mukamel et al., 2010) this research focused on using brain imaging to find brain areas that demonstrated mirror properties consistent with dual representations of perception and action. A diversity of tasks and types of analyses were performed to explore mirroring mechanisms in humans, and a variety of brain regions were put forward. However, agreement on a common definition of mirror areas in humans has proven elusive. One consequence of this is the proposal that the core human mirror neuron system (MNS) contains only the inferior frontal gyrus and the inferior parietal lobule, which are homologous to regions found in the monkey (Rizzolatti & Sinigaglia, 2010).

> Homologous in biology means to have the corresponding position, structure and possibly function. It is common to consider across species what anatomical parts are homologous. For brain regions this is important for using data obtained in say monkeys to predict relations in human brain.

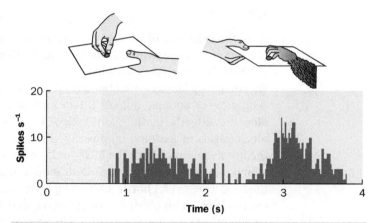

Figure 8.9 Example of the activity of a mirror neuron in monkey premotor cortex. Mirror neurons found in area F5 of monkey cortex have the special property that they become active whether the monkey is observing the experimenter grasping a piece of food or if they grasp the food themselves.

Source: Reprinted from Rizzolatti, G., Fadiga, L., Fogassi, L., & Gallese, V. (1996). Premotor cortex and the recognition of motor actions. *Cognitive Brain Research, 3*, 131–141, with permission from Elsevier.

Central to debate over the anatomical extent of a human MNS, and interpretation of brain imaging experiments in humans, is a theoretical understanding of what functional capabilities mirror neurons provide for the interpretation of a movement. If we look at any movement there is the interpretation on the surface of a complex sequence of limb movements, but underlying this complex motion pattern there is frequently a simple goal that the movement is trying to achieve (Byrne & Russon, 1998). It is argued that the crucial function mirror neurons provide is access to the goal of the movement (Cattaneo et al., 2010). Thus, when we view somebody performing an action, mirror neurons act to simulate the viewed action in a way that gives us access to the goal of the viewed action. However, much intense debate remains about the role of the MNS regarding its role in action recognition and conceptual processing (Gallese et al., 2011; Hickok & Hauser, 2010; Kalenine et al., 2010; Kilner, 2011; Mahon & Caramazza, 2008).

One proposed function of the human MNS is imitation and learning motor actions from visual models (Caspers et al., 2010; Heiser et al., 2003). Most likely, the function of the MNS in imitation learning is not limited to representing the goal of the observed action,

Motor primitives are the basis set of elemental movements that serve as building blocks for an animal's repertoire of movements.

but also to represent the motor primitives (Flash & Hochner, 2005). The most impressive evidence for the involvement of the human MNS in imitation learning comes from a series of fMRI studies where participants were asked to imitate guitar chords in the scanner (Buccino et al., 2004; Vogt et al., 2007). The beauty of this task is that participants are not restricted to action observation, but they can also perform the to-be-learned actions in the scanner. Vogt and colleagues (2007) found that the MNS was activated more strongly during observation of non-practised actions compared to practised actions, and that passive observation induced weaker activations than observation in order to imitate (Buccino et al., 2004). Unlike most other studies on imitation, in addition to the MNS, the prefrontal cortex was also activated during action observation and motor preparation (Buccino et al., 2004; Vogt et al., 2007). This implies that a (mirroring) mechanism of automatic perception-action matching alone is insufficient to account for imitation learning, instead higher-order supervisory operations associated with the prefrontal cortex are involved which most likely engage in the manipulation and restructuring of the elementary motor representations provided by the MNS.

Evaluation

Does the existence of mirroring mechanisms mean that we can learn novel motor skills also by pure observation, from the couch? Certainly, a number of behavioural studies indicate the effectiveness of learning by observing and the likely involvement of motor encoding (e.g. Mattar & Gribble, 2005; Vogt, 1995). However, behavioural work on learning sequences of actions indicate limitations of observational practice (Shea et al., 2011). Most recently, the guitar chord task of Vogt and colleagues was used to study the brain mechanisms of learning by observing (Higuchi et al., 2011). They found evidence for the involvement of both the MNS and prefrontal cortex in pure learning by observing, which indicates the validity of their model of imitation learning also for observational practice. However, chords learned by observation were executed less proficiently than chords learned by observation-imitation, and this was reflected in weaker neural efficiency effects for the observationally practised chords in cortical as well as subcortical regions, particularly the basal ganglia. These fascinating results caution against the all-too-simple idea that, since motor structures are involved during action observation, we can lean back and learn novel actions just by watching others doing the work. See Box 8.6 for more on the topic of action observation in a research focus on watching dance.

Box 8.6 Research Close Up: Using dance to study action representation

Source: Calvo-Merino, B., Grezes, J., Glaser, D. E., Passingham, R. E., & Haggard, P. (2006). Seeing or doing? Influence of visual and motor familiarity in action observation. *Current Biology, 16*(19), 1905–1910.

INTRODUCTION

Although psychologists and neuroscientists have long studied the production and perception of human movement there is not a rich tradition of studies on dance. This is somewhat surprising since dance offers movements that are intrinsically interesting for how they are produced by an experienced dancer, conceived of by a choreographer and appreciated aesthetically, socially and emotionally by an audience (Blasing et al., 2012; Reynolds et al., 2011). One recent exception to this has been a study by Calvo-Merino and colleagues (2006) that used dance to study how the neural basis of action representation changes with expertise. The existence of mirror neuron systems in humans leads to a prediction that differences could be found between novices and expert dancers in viewing dance movements. This is because expert dancers have these sophisticated movements in their personal movement repertoire and this knowledge should make itself evident in their brain activity.

METHOD

The study used fMRI to examine brain activity of male and female ballet dancers when viewing gender-specific ballet movements (see also http://shar.es/pfNU6). Because some ballet moves are performed by only males and others only by females (Figure 8.10) the motor expertise to perform these gender-specific movements would be found only in that gender. However, since male and female dancers train together they have equal visual familiarity with all moves. This design allows one to isolate motor from visual expertise. This is important because an explanation based on mirror neurons would be considerably strengthened if brain activity differences could arise only from differences in motor experience.

RESULTS

Results showed different brain activity in premotor, parietal, and cerebellar brain regions when dancers viewed moves from their own motor repertoire, compared to opposite-gender moves that they frequently saw but did not perform. These results show evidence for mirror regions, which suggest that we understand actions not only by visual recognition but also motorically.

DISCUSSION

The results of this study confirmed similar findings of a previous study by Calvo-Merino and colleagues (2005) that compared ballet dancers to capoeira practitioners where the visual familiarity of the groups wasn't as

Figure 8.10   Male and female specific ballet moves used in the study by Calvo-Merino et al. (2006).

Source: Reprinted from Calvo-Merino, B., Grèzes, J., Glaser, D. E., Passingham, R. E., & Haggard, P. (2006). Seeing or doing? Influence of visual and motor familiarity in action observation. *Current Biology, 16*(19), 1905–1910, with permission from Elsevier.

closely matched. Further evidence for the role of motor expertise in perceiving dance movements has been provided by Cross and colleagues in a study exploring how learning a dance is reflected in changes in brain activation (Cross et al., 2006) and by Jang and Pollick (2011) comparing expert ballet dancers with experienced ballet observers. Besides its use in the study of expertise, dance is increasing as both a subject of research on its own to explore memory (Wachowicz et al., 2011), spatial representation and timing (Himberg & Thompson, 2011; May et al., 2011) as well as a tool in rehabilitation (Houston, 2011; Worthen-Chaudhari, 2011). It also has entered into the domain of neuroaesthetics (Zeki, 2001, 2003) to study the neural basis of how movement in the performing arts is appreciated aesthetically (Calvo-Merino et al., 2008).

EMBODIED COGNITION

We already discussed embodied cognition in Chapter 2 in the context of perception and in Chapter 7 for the embodiment of concepts, so it is useful now to return to this topic to discuss how embodied cognition relates to motor control and action representation. In the embodied view of cognition, perception and action are intimately connected. In fact, in the most radical views of embodiment, the connection between perception and action is so tight and connected with the environment, there is little need for the kinds of abstract symbolic representations often used to explain cognition (Barsalou, 1999). Less radical views of embodiment hold that for simple actions, motor information is incorporated directly into representations; however, for complex actions both perceptual and motor information are combined in a flexible manner (Borghi, 2005).

Connections between perception and action that demonstrate embodiment are present in common coding and mirror neurons. Both illustrate that perceptual representations of the world are connected to representations of action. While mirror neurons, by definition, are restricted to observing other living beings, the theory of common coding has been shown by Tucker and Ellis (1998) to extend to interactions with inanimate objects. These experiments by Tucker and Ellis had participants view photographs of objects and judge whether the objects were upright or inverted. The objects included such items as frying pans, teapots and knives that afforded grasps by their handles. The photos were arranged so that some showed the object graspable with the left hand and some with the right. Response times were measured with both the right and left hands. What was found was that response times were quicker when the upright/inverted decision was produced with the hand that could produce the grasp. Further evidence that visual representation is not independent of the action response comes from experiments on categorizing objects (Borghi, 2005) as well as human brain imaging experiments which showed that just viewing tools activated brain regions involved in producing actions with the tools (Beauchamp & Martin, 2007; Grafton et al., 1997).

There are several consequences of recent work on embodied cognition (Shapiro, 2007). One of these has been to elevate our appreciation of the importance of the body in cognition, and to include it as an important component to understanding cognitive performance. For example, the importance of brain and body relations can be seen in the equilibrium point hypothesis that was described earlier in this chapter. In this theory the unique structure of the body – and in this case the spring-like properties of the limbs – are essential to how the brain comes about its control strategy. Further examples of the importance of the body are described by Chiel and Beer (1997) who argue that it is the structure of the body that provides both constraints and opportunities for neural control. Another consequence of work on embodied cognition has been to recognize the importance of the environment in cognition. Although it is debatable about whether it should truly be considered cognition, it has been pointed out by Clark (1997) that we organize our environment to reduce cognitive load. From placing our TV remote control always at the same place to buying distinctive luggage that is easily recognizable at the baggage carousel we actively put structure into the world that gives us advantage in solving everyday problems.

The final consequence of embodied cognition we will discuss is how the body plays a central role in metaphor. Metaphor provides us with a scaffolding upon which we can understand one thing in terms of another. When told that 'you are a star', you don't think that you are being called a luminous ball of hot burning gases, instead metaphorical reasoning provides you with the understanding that you are bright and high up above others. Lakoff and Johnson (1980) propose that basic spatial relations like up, down, front, back, etc. form the basis of this scaffolding and are interpreted in relation to our body. In this way 'up' is understood intrinsically as it relates to my body with my head corresponding to 'up' and my feet to 'down'. Thus, the communication of complex information relies on an embodied representation of the concepts we wish to express.

Gesture

An important topic that illustrates how the body and action are related to cognitive processes is gesture. It is a broad topic that crosses the boundaries of perception, action and cognition (Kendon, 2004; McNeill, 1992, 2005). Theories of gesture typically incorporate description of how gesture relates to the linguistic component of speech (de Ruiter, 2000; Goldin-Meadow, 2003; Kita & Ozyurek, 2003; Krauss et al., 2000; McNeill, 1992, 2005; McNeill & Duncan, 2000) as well as to speech prosody (Esposito et al., 2007; Esposito & Marinaro, 2007) (see Chapters 12 and 13). However, it is clear that even alone, gesture can convey clear messages. In this section we will focus on how gestures make cognition visible and reveal embodied processes.

There are a variety of different types of gestures. Deictic gestures are pointing movements done in order to draw attention to a location or thing in the world. Beat gestures are baton-like movements that do not appear to have a direct meaning, but instead are used in tight synchrony with speech to accent important aspects of the information being conveyed. Metaphoric gestures (Cienki & Müller, 2008; Littlemore, 2009) exploit the structure of a metaphor to understand one thing in terms of another by using the spatial structure and timing of a movement to relate to concepts being communicated. Iconic gestures depict physical properties of the object of reference. For example, making the motion of putting on a hat to complement the words 'I put on a hat' or drawing a circle when saying 'doughnut'. These definitions of gestures are not exclusive since a single gesture might have a component of several different types of gesture. For example, in a study of academic lectures (Sweetser, 1998) one prevalent gesture was to use the index finger of the dominant gesture hand to point successively to fingers of the other hand. Here the individual fingers of the other hand could be considered to be icons representing various ideas represented as objects and the motion of the index finger can be a metaphor for the succession of ideas. Another example of a gesture was rotating the hand in circles starting outward from the body as would be accompanied by the words *and so on* or *etcetera*. Iconically this gesture represents ideas travelling outward from the speaker and metaphorically it can be seen as representing reasoning as motion through space.

Hostetter and Alibali (2008) have emphasized the embodied nature of gesture by considering gesture as simulated action. They theorize that gestures result because ideas are being simulated in terms of perceptual and motor properties, regardless of whether the idea is about something physically spatial or only metaphorically spatial.

For example, when experimental participants describe a viewed cartoon where they saw a cat climb a drainpipe they will form the iconic gesture of moving hand over hand as if climbing since the action being discussed is activating a motor simulation that is part of the embodied representation. Similarly, it is argued that metaphoric gestures arise from the spatial representations upon which the metaphor is based. For example, describing fairness with the two palms facing up and arms moving up and down in alternating fashion represents the act of balancing two separate entities and this leads to the use of gesture to present this simulated action. Hostetter and Alibali (2008) acknowledge that we do not always gesture, even when possible, and explain that context and other influences interact to form a dynamic threshold that controls the likelihood of a gesture. An example of the importance of context in setting a threshold can be seen in an experiment where people were told that their videotaped explanations of how to use survival items would be viewed by either first-year college students in a dormitory bonding exercise or by campers actively preparing for a winter excursion (Kelly et al., 2011). Results showed that the explanations to the campers where the stakes were high produced three times as many gestures containing semantic information; and three times as much time was spent gesturing.

A possible objection to the idea that our ideas are embodied in physical actions such as gestures can be offered by the proposition that ideas like those in the physical sciences and mathematics are abstract and have little connection to physical experience. However, at least for teaching physical sciences and mathematics there is evidence that gesture can play a role. For example, Roth (2000) found that students who lack adequate domain knowledge to talk about a science topic can still use gestures to correctly explain these topics. Similarly, Núñez (2004) describes how professors of mathematics use gesture to explain concepts such as oscillation of a mathematical sequence by horizontal back and forth motion of the hand. Moreover, it has been shown that inhibiting gesture when explaining a math task requires cognitive resources (Goldin-Meadow et al., 2001). While these examples do not eliminate a role of purely symbolic processing in scientific and mathematical reasoning, they add to an increasing literature of embodied views which hold that depicting (Tversky, 2011) and processing abstract information (Landy & Goldstone, 2007) is effectively grounded in physical relations that can be depicted by gesture.

Summary

We divided the problem of motor control and action into three topics: (1) motor control, (2) producing complex actions and (3) action representations and perception. Although each of these three topics has an independent research tradition there are increasing efforts to investigate phenomena that span these traditional boundaries. The need to span the boundaries is prompted by applications such as robotics where aspects of all three topics need to be integrated to realize a working system and rehabilitation where recovering motor function is intertwined with cognitive abilities.

The first section on motor control strived to provide an explanation of how we control our body to perform an action. Understanding this process provides us with mechanisms that can be used as building blocks for constructing ever more complex actions. There is, however, no theoretically defined motor primitive that has yet achieved universal acceptance as the essential building block. The three theories of motor control introduced – equilibrium point hypothesis, dynamic systems theory and optimal control theory – each have their relative strengths for explaining certain phenomena and future research is certain to see efforts to come up with a theory of motor planning that provides a broadly confirmed motor primitive.

In the second section on producing complex actions we essentially assumed that the problem of producing elements of a complex action was solved. With this assumption it was possible to make progress on understanding how extended sequences of action could be achieved. This led to the primary claim that complex action sequences are the result of hierarchical plans. Whether producing language or making a cup of instant coffee we can construct action hierarchies that enable goals to be achieved by the interactions amongst the nodes of the hierarchy. Confirmation of this hierarchy came from models that could both produce action sequences in typical individuals as well as reproduce the types of errors in action planning found in individuals with brain damage to their frontal cortex.

In the final section we considered evidence that representations of action production are related to perceptual representations. While this conceptual duality of shared representations for perception and action has a long history in ideomotor theories, recent evidence from neuroscience has brought it back to the fore. The neuroscientific evidence includes the discovery of mirror neurons that have been shown to be active both when an action is performed and when the same action is perceived. Although the specific function of mirror neurons still remains controversial it has helped to inspire embodied theories of perception that tightly link our sensory perception of the world with the actions we produce. An example we explored of embodiment was gesture where we explored how these actions make our thoughts visible.

Review questions

1 Describe different models of human motor control and how they relate to the body.

2 How do hierarchical representations account for the production of action sequences?

3 How do action slips inform our understanding of action planning in healthy and damaged brains?

4 How do theoretical models and data from neuroscience support the idea that representations of action and perception are shared?

5 How does gesture make thought visible?

6 What advantages are provided by embodied theories of cognition?

FURTHER READING

Goldin-Meadow, S. (2003). *Hearing gesture: How our hands help us think.* Cambridge, MA: Belknap Press of Harvard University Press.

Haggard, P., Rossetti, Y., & Kawato, M. (2008). *Attention and performance XXII: Sensorimotor foundations of higher cognition.* Oxford: Oxford University Press.

Jeannerod, M. (2006). *Motor cognition: What actions tell the self.* Oxford: Oxford University Press.

Jordan, M. I. (1997). Chapter 25 Serial order: A parallel distributed processing approach. In J. W. Donahoe & V. Packard Dorsel (Eds.), *Neural-network models of cognition* (pp. 471–495). Amsterdam: Elsevier Science.

Lashley, K. S. (1951). The problem of serial order in behavior. In L. A. Jeffress (Ed.), *Cerebral mechanisms in behavior.* New York: Wiley.

Scott, S. H. (2004). Optimal feedback control and the neural basis of volitional motor control. *Nature Reviews Neuroscience, 5*(7), 534–546.

CHAPTER 9:
PROBLEM SOLVING

INTRODUCTION

Cognition involves the acquisition, storage, retrieval and use of information. In previous chapters the focus has been on acquisition of information in perception, its storage and retrieval in learning and memory. In this chapter we examine how we use information in problem solving and then go on to discuss using information in decision making and reasoning in later chapters. First, what do we mean when we say we have a problem?

Whenever we want something, but do not have an immediate way to get what we desire, there is a problem. For example, suppose you are studying at university far from home when a family emergency breaks out. You want to go home to help but there are vital exams that week and there are many possible ways to get home, varying in costs and speed. When can you leave campus and how should you travel? By train, bus, plane or by a mixture? This is a difficult problem which calls for extensive thinking. Thinking involves exploring possibilities mentally, in imagination, so that good solutions can be reached in advance of physical action. In our example, by thinking you

Problem is a situation in which you have a goal but do not know how to achieve it.
Thinking is a process of mental exploration of possible actions and states of the world.

Preview questions

1 We cannot observe thinking directly in others, so how can it be studied scientifically?
2 Problems come in all shapes and sizes. Can we sort them into types?
3 Can we explain how some problems are solved with a sudden flash of inspiration or 'insight'?
4 What factors help and hinder insight?
5 What can analogies with computer problem solving tell us about human problem solving?
6 How do experts differ from beginners in solving problems in their area of skill?
7 What is involved in creative problem solving?
8 Does putting a problem aside really help creativity? And if so, how?
9 Can creativity be increased by training?

might remember that there is a cheap coach home which would meet your needs, and so avoid impulsively buying an expensive plane ticket.

This chapter focuses on the kinds of thinking involved in problem solving. We begin by defining and explaining key terms, such as 'thinking' and 'problem' more fully and then briefly set the historical context of current research. We will discuss ideas about problem solving as a sort of search and then go on to current studies of 'insight' problem solving in which the solver has a strong 'Aha!' experience as a solution comes suddenly and surprisingly. The role of knowledge or expertise in problem solving will be discussed and finally we will look at solving 'divergent' or 'creative' problems where many new solutions are sought rather than just a single solution. Problem solving is clearly an important cognitive process and is the basis for progress in every area of human activity. Technology provides many cases of effective problem solving, as in developing mobile phones, computers, space vehicles and so on. The arts and sciences, as we shall see when discussing creativity, also involve extensive problem solving, as in developing better theories of the structure of matter or devising new styles of music or genres of literature, for instance.

PROBLEMS AND PROBLEM TYPES

Although thinking may often be relatively free-floating and undirected as in daydreaming, much thinking is directed towards achieving particular goals such as solving a problem, making a difficult decision (see Chapter 10 for decision making), drawing a logical conclusion (see Chapter 11 for reasoning) or producing a creative product.

Research on thinking has generally focused on goal directed thinking in problem solving. This raises the question of what do we mean by a 'problem'? Problems can be said to arise when a person or animal has a goal but does not have an immediately available way of reaching the goal. All problems have a goal, a starting situation in which the goal is not yet achieved and a set of actions that can be selected from and combined to bring about the goal state. Problems come in a great many shapes and sizes but can be classified in terms of a few broad characteristics, such as: degree of definition; whether an adversary is involved or not; whether extensive knowledge is needed or not; and whether the time scale of the problem is long or short.

Well-defined problem is a problem in which starting conditions, actions available and goals are all completely specified.
Ill-defined problem is a problem in which starting conditions, or actions available or goals are not completely specified.
Knowledge-rich problems are problems that require extensive specialist knowledge.
Knowledge-lean problems are problems such as puzzles that do not require specialist knowledge.
Non-adversary problems are problems in which the solver is dealing with inert problem materials with no rational opponent.
Adversary problems are problems in which the solver has to deal with a rational opponent as in board games.

There are a number of ways we classify problems based on these characteristics which help us to group different types of problems together for understanding and research. In general, we tend to refer to problems as either well-defined or ill-defined depending on the amount of information provided initially. We then determine whether specialized knowledge is required to solve a problem, making them either knowledge rich or knowledge lean. Finally, we consider whether the type of problem involves a rational opponent. All of these components help us to understand a problem more fully so that we can consider the different problem solving techniques and strategies involved or required in each. It also means that research can be conducted on the same types of problems.

As indicated, some problems are well defined and this means that the nature of the initial state, goal state, and possible methods to be used to solve are clearly laid out. In contrast many problems are ill defined in that one or more of the key components are not fully specified. Some examples are given in Table 9.1.

Problems may be classified as non-adversary or adversary problems. In adversary problems the solver is dealing with a thinking opponent who

Table 9.1 Examples of well- and ill-defined problems

Well defined	Ill defined
Anagrams	Improve quality of life
Chess	Devise a fair tax system
Rubik cube	Invent a best-selling toy

seeks to defeat the solver's goals (e.g. noughts-and-crosses (or tic-tac-toe), chess, poker, bridge). On the other hand in non-adversary problem solving the problem material is inert and is not behaving with a view to frustrating the solver (e.g. anagram puzzle solving, computer programing.)

A further difference is that between knowledge-rich problems which require a high degree of specialist knowledge (e.g. medical diagnosis, high-level chess) and knowledge-lean problems that can be tackled by anyone without specialist knowledge (e.g. anagrams, simple logic tasks). Finally, some problems are *large scale* and require months or years of effort (e.g. designing power stations, writing epic novels) and some are *small scale* and can be tackled within minutes (e.g. as crosswords, simple decision tasks).

All these have been studied by psychologists although research has generally been carried out using non-adversary, well-defined, small-scale, knowledge-lean puzzles. Such materials are good starting points for research as non-adversary problems avoid the complexity of anticipating a competitor's actions, well-defined problems are likely to be interpreted similarly by all participants, small-scale problems fit into the usual time available in a laboratory study and knowledge-lean problems can be tackled by most participants with a normal educational background.

BRIEF HISTORY AND BACKGROUND

Although the main historical approaches to cognitive psychology, as outlined in Chapter 1, have addressed the study of thinking and problem solving, only the *Gestalt* and *information processing* approaches are still influential in this area. We will now explain these two approaches which have focused on different aspects of thinking and problem solving and differ in methods of data gathering, as much recent research is based upon these approaches and the early research conducted.

GESTALT APPROACH

The Gestalt psychologists saw problem solving as much like perceiving a new pattern in an ambiguous drawing (e.g. seeing first the duck then the rabbit in the duck-rabbit figure discussed in Chapter 7). The key process, they argued, was one of changing the way the problem was seen, or in other words of restructuring the way the problem was represented.

A frequently cited example of restructuring (Wertheimer, 1945) comes from a true story regarding the ninetheenth-century mathematician Gauss (Hall, 1970). When Gauss was a six-year-old schoolboy his class were given the task of adding all the numbers from 1 to 100. Within a very short time Gauss announced the answer: 5050. How had he done it? Not by super-fast addition of $1 + 2 + 3 + 4 + \ldots + 98 + 99 + 100$, but by noticing a structure in the number sequence. The numbers form into pairs (1, 100), (2, 99), (3, 98) all of which have the same sum (101)

> **Gestalt approach** to thinking likens problem solving to seeing new patterns; it stresses the role of insight and understanding in problem solving.
> **Restructuring** is changing how one represents a problem.

Insight is a restructuring of a problem that makes the solution obvious and understandable.

and there are 50 such pairs so answer is $101 \times 50 = 5050$. A restructuring that leads to a rapid solution is known as an insight.

Box 9.1 gives a real life example of insight problem solving in which a Gestalt-style restructuring was life-saving.

Box 9.1 Practical Application: Life-or-death problem solving with insight

On 5 August 1949, a group of 15 firefighters in Montana, USA, set out to tackle a forest fire in a steep sided gulch, known as Mann Gulch (Lehrer, 2008). The side of the gulch which was alight was mainly pine trees and the side from which the men began their advance largely contained tall dry grass. At first the wind was blowing the flames away from the men. Suddenly the wind reversed and sparks soon started a fire in the tall grass on the men's side of the gulch and was soon spreading extremely rapidly toward the men. The leading firefighter, 'Wag' Dodge, ordered the men to drop their gear and run up the side of the gulch to the ridge. Very soon it became clear that the fire could not be outrun. What to do?

Dodge stopped and with the flames less than 50 yards away did a surprising thing: he lit a match and started another fire in the grass in front of him! Why?

The flames of the fire he had started quickly moved up the slope leaving a large patch of burned ground in front. He then went into the middle of the burned out patch and lay down. The main fire then burned fiercely around the patch where he was lying before sweeping on up the hill. When it had passed, Dodge emerged alive and well. Thirteen of his colleagues died because they did not have the crucial insight at the critical time that the fire could be deprived of fuel by burning the grass ahead of the flames and so creating a fire-break. Dodge's method of creating an escape fire is now standard practice but had never been used previously by the US forest service firefighters.

Interestingly, much of the early Gestalt work on problem solving was carried out with animals, particularly with apes (Kohler, 1925). If insight could be demonstrated with animals then its existence in humans would be hard to doubt. Kohler set apes manipulation problems in which they had to build towers from boxes to reach high-hanging fruit or use a short stick to retrieve an out of reach long stick which could then be used to retrieve otherwise unreachable fruit. Kohler reported that the apes frequently solved such problems with little or no overt trial and error but quite suddenly after a period of apparently examining the problem situation.

Duncker (1945) sought to demonstrate insight and to find out how it is achieved in human participants by using a think aloud method to make the normally covert thought processes more observable. In this method participants simply report as much as they can in normal language. This think aloud method is widely used in the study of thinking (see Ericsson & Simon, 1993, for more details) and we will come across other examples later. In Duncker's (1945) study, participants with no specialist knowledge were shown a figure similar to that in Figure 9.1, representing a body with a tumour in the middle, and the goal was to find a way of destroying the tumour by radiation without destroying the healthy tissue around the tumour. Participants' think aloud records indicated that they restructured the goal into subgoals which if achieved would solve the problem, such as 'try avoiding contact between the rays and healthy tissue'. In turn, this subgoal could lead to a further subgoal of 'try to use the throat as a route for the rays to the tumour'. The key subgoal was 'to reduce the intensity of the rays on their way through healthy tissue'

Figure 9.1   Duncker's x-ray problem. Find a way to destroy a tumour in the centre of the body without destroying healthy tissue. Participants are told that someone has envisaged the problem as in the diagram.

which in turn led to the insightful solution 'use a lens to focus a weak bundle of rays on the tumour' (see Figure 9.2). The insight was that the large effect desired could be achieved by adding together small effects at the target site. The kind of restructuring seen here, of the overall problem into sub-problems is also addressed in the information processing approach, discussed later in this chapter.

Barriers to insight

The Gestalt psychologists identified two important barriers to insight which were labelled set and functional fixity.

> Set is a tendency to persist with one approach to a problem.
> Functional fixity is a difficulty in thinking of a novel use for a familiar object.

Set effects arise from a tendency to solve problems in one particular way, using a single approach, or being stuck in a rut in your thinking. A famous example is the nine dot problem: i.e. connect the nine dots below with four connected straight lines without lifting your pencil from the page as you draw. See if you can solve it!

• • •

• • •

• • •

Most people confine their efforts to the lines that stay within the square shape. The layout induces a strong set effect and the problem cannot be solved until the self-imposed restriction of solutions to the square shape is overcome and the person 'thinks outside the box'. (The solution is given at the end of the chapter.)

Sets can also arise from extensive experience or training with particular types of problems. So, given a run of water jar problems in which three jars of different sizes have to be used to get target amounts of water, people will be greatly slowed down or fail altogether when a problem comes along in which only two out of the three jars must be used (Luchins, 1942) even when the 'set breaking' problem is very simple for people not exposed to the set inducing training.

Scan to see a solution to the Duncker candle problem

Another block to insight is functional fixity (Maier, 1931), which refers to a tendency to use objects and concepts only in their customary way. An example problem which demonstrates fixity effects is Duncker's (1945) candle problem in which the task is to support a candle on a door using an assortment of materials such as a box of tacks and some matches (see Figure 9.3). The problem requires using the box in an unusual way. The box is emptied and the tray of the box is attached to the door by a tack. The tray can then serve as a platform on which the candle can be secured by lighting the candle and setting it in some molten wax dripped onto the tray. When the wax hardens the candle stands securely fixed to the door. Duncker found that this task became significantly easier if the box was presented empty with the tacks out already. Duncker argued that when the box was presented full, its container role was salient, making it harder to restructure the way participants represented its function.

ONE SOLUTION. . . . . .

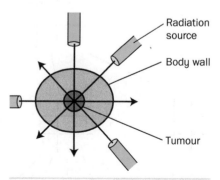

Figure 9.2   **Solution to Duncker's x-ray problem.** The solution is reached by crossing weak rays so that the total effect adds up to enough strength at the site of the tumour.

Adults often find it difficult to think of novel uses for familiar objects, as in the candle problem. However, young children (of about five) suffered less from functional fixity in tasks requiring unusual uses of familiar objects, presumably because they had less

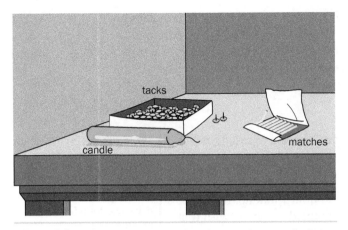

Figure 9.3   Duncker's candle problem. The task is to use the items in the picture to fix a candle to the door so that it will burn securely.

strongly fixed associations of how objects are used (Defeyter & German, 2003). Similarly, Amazonian Indians, unfamiliar with the tools to be used in a task, showed less functional fixity than Westerners for tasks requiring the tools to be used in unusual ways *until* the typical use was shown to them (German & Barrett, 2005) whereupon they also showed functional fixity at similar levels to Western participants.

Evaluation

The Gestalt approach stressed organization, insight and restructuring, showed how these processes could be investigated and highlighted the roles of set and functional fixity as barriers to solving problems. These were major contributions. Many of the issues raised by the Gestaltists are still under active investigation (e.g. insight processes, which will be discussed again later in this chapter). However a major drawback with the approach was a lack of clarity in its explanations. How restructuring actually came about was always unclear. Also, the approach did not address how we solve problems that do not require restructuring or insight. The information processing approach, to be discussed next, offers a route to greater clarity of explanation and is more widely applicable to a range of problem types, while preserving some of the strengths of the Gestalt approach.

INFORMATION PROCESSING APPROACH

The information processing approach was inspired by the development of programable digital computers which began in the mid-1940s. As explained in Chapter 1, it was quickly realized that computers could be programmed to tackle many complex tasks such as playing chess, suggesting medical diagnoses given the symptoms and (still not perfectly) automatic translation between natural languages. Computer programs to solve problems could be seen as comparable to *strategies* that humans might use to solve the same problems. A program which sought to mimic human thinking would be labelled a simulation program and should be distinguished from an artificial intelligence program which seeks to solve the problem as effectively as possible without any attempt at mimicking human strategies. So, for example, an artificial intelligence program to play chess would explore millions of possible move sequences in seconds, which a human cannot do. A simulation program might build up a memory bank of opening move patterns through exposure to many games, which is a more human-like approach. Despite this distinction, many ideas developed in artificial intelligence research have been

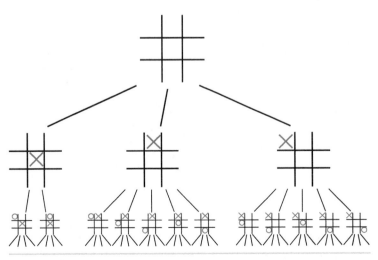

Figure 9.4   Part of a tree diagram for noughts-and-crosses.

adopted in the information processing approach to human problem solving and modified as possible descriptions of human approaches.

Some key ideas of the information processing approach to problem solving will now be considered.

Problem space

A very important idea in the information processing approach to problem solving is that of problem space which is a way of representing a problem as a graph, with points representing states of the problem and with lines connecting the points representing possible actions that lead from one state of the problem to other states. Problem spaces may be defined further into two sub-types: state-action spaces and goal-subgoal spaces, which we will now outline.

State-action spaces

In state-action space representations problems may be solved by searching through a series of operations which will transform the starting state into

Problem space is an abstract representation of possible states of a problem. State-action space is a representation of how problems can be transformed from starting state through intermediate states to the goal. Goal-subgoal space is a representation of how an overall problem goal can be broken down into subgoals and sub-subgoals.

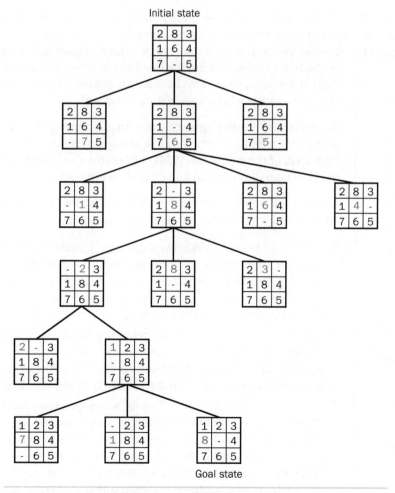

Figure 9.5   State-action tree for the eight-puzzle task. Move one tile at a time into empty space on tray until the numbers are in order 1–8 starting at the top left.

Source: http://www.aspgod.com/project/ai/8-puzzle.html

intermediate states which in turn are transformed into further intermediate states until ultimately the goal state is reached.

These operations may be represented in diagrams such as tree graphs which resemble an upside-down tree with the starting state at the top. A partial tree diagram is shown in Figure 9.4 for the familiar game of noughts-and-crosses (or tic-tac-toe). This is an adversary problem in which each player takes turns entering their symbol, an X or an O, and the first to get a row, column or diagonal in the grid filled with their symbol is the winner.

At the start of the noughts-and-crosses game the grid is empty. The first player puts an X in one of the empty cells. There are nine possible first moves. For reasons of space Figure 9.4 shows only three of the possible first moves. To each possible first move there are eight places for the second player to put a circle. To show the whole tree just for the first and second moves we would need a diagram with 73 grids (i.e. 9×8 plus the starting empty grid). The whole tree representing all possible games, where the game stops when someone wins or a draw occurs, would have 10 levels and a total of 255,168 grids or states. So, even this fairly simple game generates a very large tree of possible states. Analysis of the whole tree confirms what you may have found from experience of playing, that if both players adopt a strategy of blocking their opponent from getting a line, then a draw will always result.

Consider also the eight-puzzle task shown in Figure 9.5. In this task you are presented with a square tray containing eight tiles numbered 1–8 and a space. The task is to rearrange the tiles moving one at a time into the empty space until a target arrangement is reached (usually having the numbers in order 1–8 as you read from left to right in the usual way). This is, in a way, simpler than the noughts and crosses situation, as there is no opponent to deal with.

As can be seen from Figure 9.5, as with noughts and crosses, the state-action tree grows rapidly. Even with just four possible moves at each state, by the fifth level of the tree some 1024 ($= 4^5$) states would be generated. How might the goal state be found in large problem spaces?

Analysis of possible strategies indicates three main methods by which a state-action tree can be searched systematically:

1 **Depth first search**: This involves a light load on memory in that only one possible move at a time is considered. An example of depth first search would be to take the rightmost move at each choice point in the eight-puzzle tree. However, this may or may not find the goal and would not generally be guaranteed to find the best solution even if it did eventually solve.

2 **Breadth first search**: This generally involves a very heavy working memory load in that it generates the whole tree by considering each possible move at each level and storing the resulting tree. However, this method is an algorithm in the sense of *always* reaching the goal.

3 **Progressive deepening**: This is a compromise method that involves 'depth first' to a limited number of moves, backs up, and then searches down alternative branches depth first again to a limited depth, backs up and continues until all branches have been searched to this limited depth. If the goal has not been found, the method extends the depth limit to a deeper level and begins the search again . . . and so on until a solution is reached. This method is algorithmic (like breadth first), as it will execute a complete search if necessary, but also may be lucky and find the solution early (as may depth first).

Depth first search is searching a state-action space by generating one state only from each intermediate state.

Breadth first search is searching a state-action space by generating all possible states from each intermediate state.

Algorithm is a problem solving method that is guaranteed to solve but may do so only with high mental load.

Progressive deepening is searching a state-action space by using depth first search to a limited depth, When depth limit is reached, search backs up to start and repeats, avoiding previously explored branches and so on until the whole space has been searched up to the initial depth limit. If a solution is not found, increase depth limit, and repeat until the goal is reached.

The above basic search methods involve a 'blind' search in that they only classify states as 'goal' (in which case stop) or 'not goal' (in which case continue the search). If intermediate states can be evaluated for promise, that is, likely to be a step towards the solution then such states can be selected as the basis for further exploration. A simple method of using intermediate evaluations is known as 'hill climbing'. The name comes from a way of climbing a hill in a thick fog. If one could only see one step ahead, then by testing out each of four steps (north, south, east, west) one could find which possible step would lead to the highest ground and take it. Repeating this process would lead to a peak, that is a state from which all possible steps lead to lower ground. This method can be described as a heuristic method, in that it will often be helpful, but is not guaranteed to find the best solution. For example, it may find a foothill rather than the highest point in the space that could have been reached from the starting point. If the person could look (or think) ahead more than one step such a method would be improved and in general the further ahead one can look or imagine and the more accurate the evaluation method the better performance will be. In the case of the eight puzzle a possible evaluation procedure might be to count the number of tiles in their target positions or one might try counting the number of tiles that are in sequence. The development of more accurate evaluation functions has been one important factor in improvements in chess playing programs over the years.

> **Heuristic** is a problem solving method that often finds a low effort solution but is not guaranteed to solve.

Scan to watch animated solution to a state-action problem

Box 9.2 Research Close Up: Experimental study of state-action problem solving

Source: Thomas, J. C. Jr. (1974). An analysis of behavior in the Hobbits-Orcs problem. *Cognitive Psychology, 6*, 257–269.

INTRODUCTION

A number of studies have examined human search in problems that lend themselves to a state-action representation. An early example is Thomas's (1974) experiment on the Hobbits and Orcs task.

METHOD

The task was based on the Hobbits and Orcs characters in *Lord of the Rings* (Tolkien, 1966) and the goal is to get three Hobbits and three Orcs across a river. The only way to cross is by a boat and the boat can carry only one or two passengers at most. There must be at least one passenger in the boat for it to cross and you have to avoid Orcs outnumbering Hobbits on the same side of river or the Hobbits will be eaten! The task was presented on a computer and participants could only see one state at a time.

The entire state-action space for the Hobbits and Orcs problem is set out in Figure 9.6.

RESULTS

Although the problem could be solved in a minimum of 11 moves, participants typically required over 20 moves. Thomas (1974) found that states 5 and 8 presented most difficulty in terms of errors and times to make moves.

DISCUSSION

The difficulty at state 5 may be because there are a larger number of possible moves than usual at this state. The difficulty at state 8 may well be because people are engaging in a hill-climbing form of search, feel that they are making progress at that point (four creatures are on the target bank) and are reluctant to backtrack, which is necessary at this point in order to progress – the correct move involves

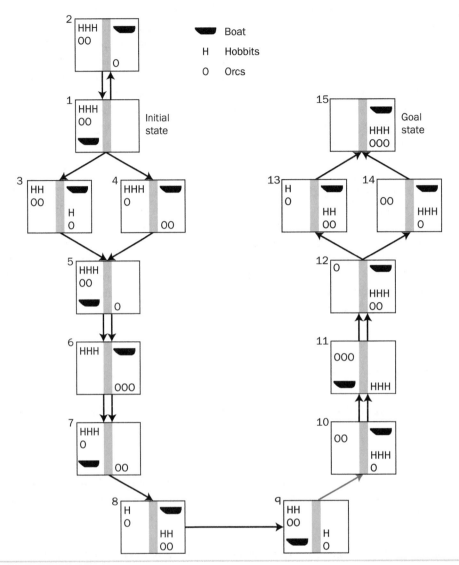

Figure 9.6   Hobbits and Orcs problem space. All possible moves and states of the problem are shown in this diagram.

Source: Adapted from Thomas, J. C. Jr. (1974). An analysis of behavior in the Hobbits-Orcs problem. *Cognitive Psychology*, 6, 257–269.

going to a state with only two creatures on the target bank. Problems such as this, which require a detour, are typically difficult (Wickelgren, 1974), presumably because of the prevalence of simple hill-climbing strategies.

Similar results favouring the use of simple hill climbing with a look (or think) ahead of only one step were found in detailed analyses of possible models for human search patterns in a range of water jar tasks and variants of the Hobbits and Orcs task (Atwood & Polson, 1976; Jeffries et al., 1977; Atwood et al., 1980). Hill-climbing has also been found in some insight problems such as the nine-dot problem which require back-tracking (MacGregor et al., 2001.) and we will discuss these later in this chapter.

Goal-subgoal spaces

In addition to the state-action form of problem space, an alternative type of problem space involves a goal-subgoal space. In this representation the problem is divided into goals and subgoals and each subgoal can be tackled by splitting it into subsubgoals and so on. An everyday example is that of a travel problem. To go from London to Edinburgh (goal) could be achieved by flying (subgoal), or taking a train (subgoal), or taking a bus (subgoal), or taking a car (subgoal). The flying subgoal can be reached by contacting British Airways (subsubgoal), or easyJet (subsubgoal). These subsubgoals can yield alternative subsubsubgoals (e.g. contact airline by use of internet or use of telephone or go to a travel agent) and so on. Thus the top level goal of the travel problem yields a tree of alternative subgoals at each level and the subgoal generation process eventually reaches low level goals that can be achieved by an action (e.g. dial the travel agent's phone number). Problems with a large number of possible alternative actions seem to lend themselves to this form of hierarchical goal = subgoal analysis which is often referred to as *problem reduction* or as *means-ends analysis*.

A number of laboratory studies have investigated problem reduction using the Tower of Hanoi task. In this task the participant is presented with three pegs on one of which are stacked n discs in descending order of size (largest on bottom). The goal is to move all the discs from the starting peg to a target peg, moving one disc at a time and never placing a larger disc on top of a smaller disc. The non-target peg can be used as a temporary holding place. The minimum number of moves increases rapidly with n according to the formula $2^n - 1$. A three-disc example is shown in Figure 9.7 and requires a minimum of seven moves. A four-disc version would need 15 moves, a five-disc version 31 moves and so on.

Scan to watch a video solution of an eight-disc problem

Anzai and Simon (1979) found that the strategies used in this task tended toward problem reduction as more experience was built up with the task. At first participants tried a state-action representation with forward search from the starting state, trying to work from the start to the end in a linear process. It was only with more experience that they came to the problem reduction strategy which works back from the overall goal to generate subgoals and subsubgoals until action can be taken.

Evaluation

The information processing approach provides a clear account of solving well defined problems that can be represented as involving searches through problem spaces. In

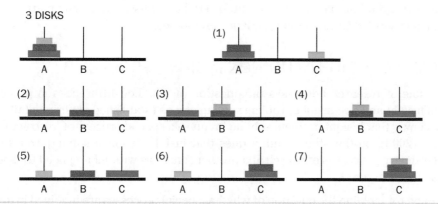

Figure 9.7   Tower of Hanoi. The task is to move discs from the left peg to the right peg; never place a larger ring on top of a smaller ring. The solution path of this three-disc problem is through states marked 1–7.

such tasks the initial way of representing the problem allows a solution and search within that representation can be successful. Search is limited by working memory to considering just a few possible moves ahead. Often looking ahead is limited to one step. Choice of moves is guided by evaluations of promise – does a move look to bring the solution closer? Although this is often a useful heuristic, it can lead to difficulties with detour problems in which the goal must be moved away from before it can be reached (such as with the Hobbits and Orcs task.)

> **Detour problems** are problems in which the hill climbing method does not work well, as the solver has to move away from the goal at some stage.

However, not all tasks fall into the pattern of well-defined problems in which the initial formulation is adequate for the solution. How information processing approaches might handle tasks that require a change in representation brings us back to insight tasks, which are the focus of the next section.

INSIGHT REVISITED

The information processing approach outlined above has provided convincing analyses of processes involved in solving problems that can be tackled by searching within a particular representation, either by using state-action space search methods or goal-subgoal strategies. However, the understanding of how we solve problems which need a change in the way they are represented (i.e. insight problems), has lagged behind. However, recently there has been a resurgence of interest in explaining insight problems, first introduced, as we saw earlier in this chapter, by the Gestalt school, as a challenge for the information processing approach. We will now look at some of this recent work.

With non-insight problems, search progresses within the initial representation; in contrast, insight problems require change in the initial representation before a solution is possible. We previously introduced the x-ray problem and the nine-dot task as investigated by the Gestalt school; two further examples of insight problems are as follows:

1 The matchstick problem: how would you arrange six matches to form four equilateral triangles?

2 A man married 20 different women in one month. All the women are still alive and not divorced. No anti-polygamy law was broken. How can this be?

In both these examples the initial representation needs to be restructured. In Problem 1, there is a strong tendency to work in two dimensions but solution requires the use of three dimensions to build a small pyramid so that the base is one triangle and the sides form three more triangles. In Problem 2, the word 'married' is usually interpreted as 'became married to' but needs to be re-interpreted as 'causes to become married', that is, the man is entitled to carry out marriage ceremonies.

COMPARING INSIGHT AND NON-INSIGHT PROBLEMS

A major line of research addresses the question of whether differences in processes between insight and non-insight problem solving can be established experimentally. The Gestalt view is that insight problem solving involves a special process of 'restructuring'. Weisberg (2006), on the other hand, argues that insight problem solving arises from normal ordinary processes of search and problem analysis without any need for special or unusual processes.

One method for tackling the question of whether special processes are involved in insight tasks as against non-insight tasks uses ratings of feelings, specifically on how close the solver is to the solution and on how confident they feel about solving the problem when they first hear it (Metcalfe and Weibe, 1987). Metcalfe and Weibe compared insight versus non-insight tasks and found that 'Feeling of knowing one could solve' taken at the start was a better predictor (correlation with solution = 0.4) for non-insight than for insight tasks (correlation = 0.08). 'Feeling of warmth' (i.e. how close one felt to solution) per 15 seconds during solving, shown in Figure 9.8 indicated a steady increase in feeling that one is near solution with non-insight tasks but no increase in warmth with insight tasks until solution was reported. This result supports the idea of sudden restructuring in insight tasks.

> Feeling of warmth rating is a rating of how close the solver feels to problem solution, taken at intervals during the solving process.

Neuroscience approach to insight versus non-insight tasks

A 2004 study used functional magnetic resonance imaging (fMRI) and electro-encephalogram (EEG) methods to determine whether differences in brain activation patterns between insight and non-insight problem solving were visible (Jung-Beeman et al., 2004). The study used 124 Remote Associate Test (RAT) items. In this task people have to find a word that is an associate of three test words: e.g. 'What word links 'boot', 'summer' and 'ground'?

To compare insight versus non-insight solving the researchers had participants give self-reports after each item as to whether the solution arose from insight or not. A self-reported insight solution was one in which participants reported an 'Aha' feeling coupled with certainty that the solution was correct. Non-insight solutions could arise from a systematic process of trying out one association after another on each item until an association was found that fitted all three items. The results indicated that fMRI showed increased activity in one particular brain area, the right anterior superior temporal gyrus, for insight solutions compared to non-insight solutions. EEG records also showed increases in activity in the same area shortly before

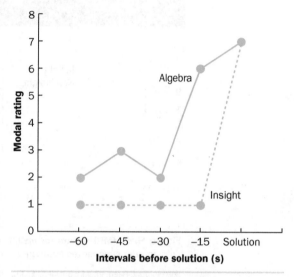

Figure 9.8 Warmth ratings for insight versus non-insight problems. Indicates steady growth of 'warmth' for algebra but sudden leap in warmth for insight problem just before solution.

Source: Metcalfe, J., & Weibe, D. (1987). Intuitions in insight and non-insight problem solving. *Memory and Cognition, 15*, 238–46.

solution. These findings suggest differences in neural processes between insight versus non-insight solving. The findings are consistent with a previous study (Bowden & Jung-Beeman, 2003) which found that priming words sent to the right hemisphere produced more insight solutions in RAT tasks than primes sent to the left hemisphere.

Think aloud effects on insight versus non-insight problems

A further analysis of differences between insight and non-insight problem solving has examined possible differential effects of thinking aloud on insight versus non-insight tasks. Schooler et al. (1993) had participants think aloud or not while tackling three insight problems and four non-insight tasks. Results indicated that thinking aloud impaired insight but not non-insight tasks. This was interpreted as supporting the view that insight tasks involve (special) unconscious processes that cannot be readily verbalized. However, the status of this result has been questioned as failures to replicate have been reported (Fleck & Weisberg, 2004; Gilhooly et al., 2010). Gilhooly et al. suggested that there was a confounding in the Schooler et al. study between insight tasks and spatial tasks since the insight problems were mainly spatial, and that the apparent negative effect of thinking aloud on insight tasks was because thinking aloud interferes with spatial tasks. This interference arises because thinking aloud requires the spatial

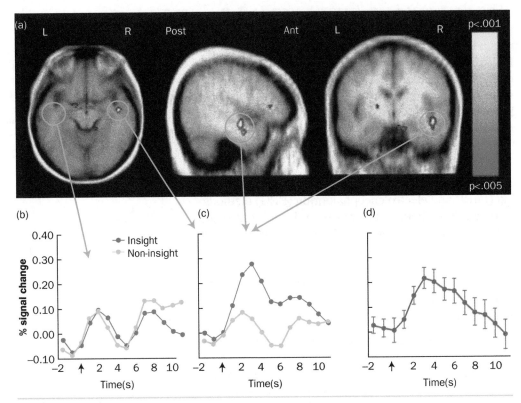

Figure 9.9   fMRI results for insight versus non-insight problem solving. Indicates increased activity in right anterior superior temporal gyrus just before solution reports in insight task.

Source: Jung-Beeman, M., Bowden, E. M., Haberman, J., Frymiare, J. L., Arambel-Liu, S., Greenblatt, R., Reber, P. J., & Kounios (2004). Neural activity when people solve verbal problems with insight. *PLoS Biology, 2*, 0500–0510.

thoughts to be re-coded into a verbal form for reporting. Overall, the evidence from think aloud studies for special unconscious processes in insight solving is quite weak.

RECENT THEORIES OF INSIGHT

From the results reviewed above, the empirical distinction between insight and non-insight problem solving seems to be well established. However, *how* to explain insight solving theoretically is still an active area. Two main approaches have recently been developed: *representational change* (Ohlsson, 1992); and *progress monitoring* (MacGregor et al., 2001) – sometimes labelled 'the criterion for satisfactory progress theory'.

Representational change

As we mentioned earlier, the Gestalt accounts of insight processes such as restructuring were vague. In his representational change theory, Ohlsson (1992) has developed a more specified account of insight in information processing terms.

The main stages and processes in representational change theory may be described as follows:

* *Problem perception*. Person encodes the problem.
* *Problem solving*. Heuristic search processes based on initial representation. These processes draw on possible actions or operators from long-term memory which change the current state of the problem into new states.

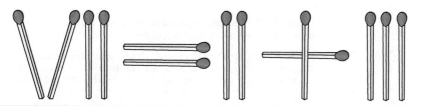

Figure 9.10   Matchstick algebra problem. Reposition one match to make this equation correct.

- *Impasse.* With insight tasks, the initial representation is misleading and does not permit a solution. Hence, impasses arise in which the person experiences a blank mind and can think of no more actions to try.

- *Restructuring.* A new encoding is derived through elaboration, re-encoding, or constraint relaxation. Elaboration involves adding information to the initial representation by noticing previously ignored features. Re-encoding involves completely changing the encoding rather than just adding new features. For example, changing the interpretation of 'married' in the marrying man problem leads to a re-encoding of the problem. Constraint relaxation involves loosening constraints on what is required in the goal or what actions are permitted. Removing the constraint to work within the square shape in the nine-dot problem is an example of this process. Ohlsson proposes that these restructuring processes take place outside consciousness and involve automatic processes such as spreading activation.

- *Partial insight.* Retrieval of possible actions following restructuring breaks the impasse and leads to a sequence of steps that achieve solution.

- *Full insight.* Retrieval of possible actions following restructuring leads immediately to a solution state or to a state close enough to the solution so that the solution can be anticipated within a limited mental look-ahead.

The representational change theory has been investigated using matchstick algebra problems (Knoblich et al., 1999). In these tasks an incorrect equation involving Roman numerals is presented and the participant's task is to reposition one match to make the equation correct (see Figure 9.10).

Our usual experience of equations often involves changing numerical values but not changing operators (+, −, =). These problems require re-encoding in which groups of matches forming conceptual units or 'chunks' need to be broken up and reconfigured. More difficult problems also require relaxation of constraints on the form of equations (see Figure 9.11).

Knoblich et al. found that re-encoding chunks, e.g. changing VII to VI and II to III by moving one match in the first problem, was easier than relaxing the constraint on the typical form of equations, e.g. from IV = IV + IV to IV = IV = IV, in the second problem.

Figure 9.11   Matchstick algebra problem requiring constraint relaxation. Reposition one match to make this equation correct.

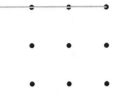

Figure 9.12 **Modified nine-dot problem (version A).** A version of the nine-dot problem with a hint to go out of the box.

Source: Adapted from MacGregor et al. (2001). Information processing and insight: A process model of performance on the nine-dot and related problems. *Journal of Experimental Psychology: Learning, Memory and Cognition, 27,* 176–201.

Overall, the matchstick algebra problem solving studies lent support to the representational change theory, but how well the theory would extend to a wide range of other problem areas remains to be determined by further research. So far, the theory has been extended to apply to the car parking problems discussed in Box 9.3.

Progress monitoring

MacGregor et al. (2001) have developed an alternative to representational change theory which is known as 'progress monitoring theory'. According to this approach the main source of difficulty in insight tasks is the use of inappropriate heuristics (particularly hill-climbing methods). They propose that, as people search for actions that would help them to reach a solution, they monitor their progress against some criterion. Failure to meet a progress criterion triggers restructuring, rather than impasses. The theory can be explained through the example of the nine-dot problem to which MacGregor et al. (2001) applied their approach.

Traditional explanations for the difficulty of the nine-dot task propose a fixation (set) on the square shape, so that other solutions are not considered. However, instructions to search outside the square were not found to be helpful (Weisberg & Alba, 1981). Lung and Dominowski (1985) suggested other inappropriate constraints, for example assuming all lines begin and end with dots.

Progress monitoring theory proposed an alternative explanation involving two main points. These are (1) use of a *maximization heuristic* in which each move or decision is an attempt to make as much headway as possible towards the goal and (2) use of *progress monitoring* in which the rate of progress is assessed constantly, and if it is deemed to be too slow and inefficient, then *criterion failure* occurs. An alternative strategy may then be sought.

Progress monitoring theory as applied to the nine-dot task suggests (1) the maximization heuristic would be for each move to cover as many new dots as possible and (2) that progress monitoring would involve the rate of progress being assessed against the number of dots required to be covered per line to solve, and if no move meets the criterion, *criterion failure* occurs. An alternative strategy may then be sought (e.g. extending lines).

MacGregor et al. explored the progress monitoring theory explanation of the nine-dot task by testing participants with two variants of the problem labelled version A and version B, shown in Figure 9.12.

If 'constraint relaxation' is all that is required to think 'outside the box', then participants should do better on version A than B since A shows a line going out of the box.

Figure 9.13 **Further modified nine-dot problem (version B).** This includes a hint to use the diagonal.

Source: Adapted from MacGregor et al. (2001). Information processing and insight: A process model of performance on the nine-dot and related problems. *Journal of Experimental Psychology: Learning, Memory and Cognition, 27,* 176–201.

However, if criterion failure is necessary then participants will do better on version B, because they can cover fewer dots in the next two moves, and so will realize they are on the wrong path sooner. MacGregor et al. found that only 31 per cent of those given version A were successful but 53 per cent of those given B solved.

Further experiments on progress monitoring theory used coin manipulation problems such as the eight-coin problem shown in Figure 9.14 in which people have to move only two coins so that each coin is left touching exactly three others.

If the strategy employed simply seeks to achieve a short-term goal of bringing *one* particular coin to rest in contact with three others, then there is 'no move available' in the upper version of the problem, but 20 moves are available in the lower version. Thus, criterion failure will be reached much sooner in the upper version and so more solutions should result. In the lower version a lot of effort would be wasted exploring what look to be promising moves which would not lead to solution. As predicted by the theory, 92 per cent solved the problem in the upper version compared with 67 per cent in the lower version. (The solution is shown in Figure 9.15.)

Overall, the central claim of progress monitoring theory is that insight is most likely to occur when constraint relaxation follows criterion failure. There is good evidence for this from the above studies. So, the theory deals well with the motivation for changing strategy but it is less clear about how new strategies are actually reached.

Figure 9.14 Two versions of the eight-coin problem. Move only two coins to leave each coin touching three others.

Source: Adapted from: Ormerod et al. (2002). Dynamics and constraints in insight problem solving. *Journal of Experimental Psychology: Learning, Memory and Cognition, 28,* 791–799.

Figure 9.15   Solution to the eight-coin problem.

Source: Adapted from Ormerod et al. (2002). Dynamics and constraints in insight problem solving. *Journal of Experimental Psychology: Learning, Memory and Cognition, 28,* 791–799.

Box 9.3 Research Close Up: Testing and evaluating two insight theories

Source: Jones, G. (2003). Testing two theories of insight. *Journal of Experimental Psychology: Learning, Memory and Cognition, 29,* 1017–1027.

INTRODUCTION

Jones (2003) sought to compare the representational change and progress monitoring theories and to do so used car parking problems in which toy cars in a parking lot must be moved around to let a toy black taxi out of the parking lot. The problems varied so that some were simple and would not induce impasses, restructuring or insight, while others were more difficult and did tend to produce impasses and insight. The main difficulty in the insight inducing problem is to consider moving the taxi before the exit path has been cleared. Example problems are shown in Figures 9.16 and 9.17.

METHOD AND RESULTS

Jones's (2003) experiment involved three conditions: in the normal condition, four progressively harder problems that required ever more moves (but in which the taxi always moved last) were followed by an insight task in which the black taxi had to be moved as an intermediate step as well as at the end to get out. The rotated condition was the same as the normal condition except that for the insight task, the display was rotated 90 degrees so the exit was to one side rather than at the foot of the picture; and in the

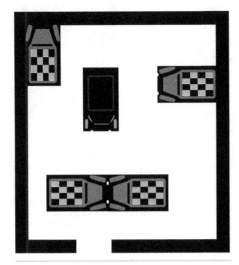

Figure 9.16 Taxi problem. Move cars to let the black taxi out of the parking area.

Source: Jones, G. (2003). Testing two theories of insight. *Journal of Experimental Psychology: Learning, Memory and Cognition, 29,* 1017–1027. APA; reprinted with permission.

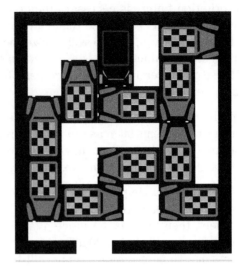

Figure 9.17 More complex problem. Move cars to let the black taxi out.

Source: Jones, G. (2003). Testing two theories of insight. *Journal of Experimental Psychology: Learning, Memory and Cognition, 29,* 1017–1027. APA; reprinted with permission.

easy condition, four easy problems were followed by an insight problem. A number of dependent variables were examined: moves; times per move; eye movement fixations and durations. The representational change theory predicted that impasses would occur before the taxi was moved and that the rotated and easy conditions would lead to better performance on the insight problem than the normal condition. Progressive monitoring theory predicted that there would be no difference between rotated and easy conditions and that early impasses would be associated with better performance (because looking ahead further would lead to the solver seeing the impasse before actually reaching it). Results indicated that impasses did tend to precede moving the taxi and that rotated and easy conditions did involve earlier impasses and showed better performance than the normal condition.

DISCUSSION

It was concluded that both representational change and progress monitoring received some support. The results suggested that progress monitoring applies to the first stage of solving, leading to impasse, and that representational change applies to breaking of the impasse and subsequent insight. Thus, it seems that both theories have support and we can conclude that the two theories can be seen as dealing with different stages of insight solving and so are complementary rather than contradictory. The study has limitations in that only one type of problem was explored so safe generalization awaits replication with a broader range of tasks.

KNOWLEDGE-RICH (OR EXPERT) PROBLEM SOLVING

Expertise is the accumulated high level knowledge that allows outstanding performance in complex problem areas.

So far, we have been considering largely knowledge-lean problems in which no specialized knowledge is required. Recent years have seen a growth of interest in the study of knowledge-rich problems in which domain expertise is required. We will now look at how expertise is acquired, what expert knowledge involves and how it affects problem solving.

EXPERTISE ACQUISITION

Acquisition of domain expertise in many areas seems to require approximately 10 years of intensive study. Chess is a clear case in which we have objective performance ratings and good records of starting ages and lengths of time playing. From these data 10 years is the typical time of intensive study before reaching grandmaster level (highest level) (Holding, 1985). Clearly, strong motivation is required to maintain study over many years. Furthermore, Ericsson (1999) has shown that deliberate practice of skill components, guided by a training schedule and by coaching, is needed for the best results – not sheer unguided practice. For example, Ericsson and Krampe (1993) found large differences in total hours of deliberate practice between professional and amateur musicians and these differences began to show from early ages.

NATURE OF EXPERTISE

Expertise typically seems to involve extensive memory for familiar patterns which cue appropriate actions. This is shown in chess via the chess memory task, in which it has been found repeatedly that experts remember realistic board patterns well after brief exposure but not random patterns while novices are equally poor on both (Chase & Simon, 1973; De Groot, 1965). Further, this advantage is domain specific in that chess experts are no better than novices in non-chess memory tasks. The explanation for this domain specific memory advantage is that experts have built up extensive long-term memory of familiar patterns which helps them encode or chunk new (realistic) positions into familiar sub-patterns. Similar findings have been reported in numerous other domains, such as the Japanese game of GO-Moku (Reitman, 1976), bridge (Charness, 1979) and programming (Adelson, 1981).

Experts represent or 'see' problem situations differently from novices as they draw on a more elaborate set of schemata. For example, in physics Chi et al. (1982) used sorting tasks in which participants grouped problems into categories and the groupings indicated that experts would put together problems that required similar physical laws while novices tended to group together problems that involved similar concrete objects. Thus, the experts 'saw' the problems in terms of underlying principles (e.g. laws of motion) while the novices 'saw' the problems in terms of more superficial characteristics such as the objects involved (e.g. slopes, pulleys, weights).

In terms of problem solving, Larkin (1978) found that experts in physics problem solving tend to spend more time analysing problems to fit them into familiar schemas before trying actions than do novices who lack ready-made schemas. Experts then tend to work forward from the starting state to the goal using approaches which they recognize as promising while novices tend to work backwards in a more effortful search as they lack pre-existing schemas that can be readily applied. This pattern probably arises because experts have a large repertoire of familiar types of problem that they can classify new problems with and reapply old solutions, whereas novices have to work out problems from basic principles.

Although De Groot (1965) found few differences between more and less expert chess players in depth or breadth of search in deciding moves in chess, his study was small scale with only five experts and five novices. Later studies using larger groups of participants and wider ranges of skill did find steady increases in depth, breadth and speed of search as skill level increased (Charness, 1989; Holding & Reynolds, 1982). So, it seems that experts can carry out wider, deeper and faster searches through possible sequences of chess moves than can novices. Holding (1979) also found that experts were better able to evaluate possible moves in terms of how likely they were to lead to a winning position. Thus, experts in chess have developed more appropriate search processes as well as more useful representations of the tasks.

Evaluation

Overall, expertise research has extended the information processing approach to problems which require extensive background knowledge to tackle. In the case of expert problem solving, the emphasis is mainly on recognition of familiar problem patterns and application of previously acquired solutions as against extensive searching through possible action sequences. Thus, chess masters and expert diagnosticians in medicine can recognize many thousands of patterns (of board positions or of symptoms) and apply previously learned solutions or diagnoses. Acquisition of expertise requires extensive practice over roughly 10 years, a time which has been found to apply in many different areas.

CREATIVE PROBLEM SOLVING

So far, we have been looking at problems, whether insight or non-insight, knowledge-rich or knowledge-lean, that have one correct answer and these are often labelled 'convergent' problems. Problems that have many possible answers are labelled 'divergent' and it is often said that these require creative thinking because of the variety of solutions that could be considered. We will now review research on creative thinking from early studies to more recent work on unconscious processes in creativity.

> **Creative** in relation to a product is generally defined as novel to the producer of the product and valuable in some way; alternatively, that the product is novel and meets a goal.

First, some definitional points should be addressed. What do we mean by 'creative'? When is a solution creative? An often given definition of what makes a solution creative is that it is novel and valued or useful in some way.

Regarding novelty, Boden (2002) distinguishes the personally creative (novel for the individual) versus the historically creative (i.e. novel in the history of world). From the point of view of psychology, personal creativity is critical. Even if a particular solution has been found before, if it is new to the solver, it may be creative.

Weisberg (2006) disagrees with the inclusion of 'value' in the usual definition and suggests instead that a creative product is novel, and is also intentional, that is, designed to meet a goal. This is a useful proposal since it removes possible changes in the 'creative' status of a product whenever value judgements shift, as can happen, particularly in the arts. For example, Van Gogh's work was little valued in his lifetime but is now very highly regarded.

The main approaches that have been followed in the study of creative thinking and problem solving are those drawing on personal accounts and those based on theories and laboratory studies and we will now review these approaches.

PERSONAL ACCOUNTS

Many famous scientists and artists have given personal accounts of their experiences of creative problem solving – often long after the events described. Such accounts have been used as the bases of some models of creative problem solving and so a small selection will be given here.

Henri Poincaré

Poincaré (1908) was an important French mathematician in the nineteenth century and took a strong interest in the psychology of creative thinking. He provided the following report of his own experience in solving some difficult problems in mathematics:

> For 15 days I strove to prove that there could not be any functions like those I have since called the Fuchsian Functions. Every day I seated myself at my work table – stayed an hour or two, tried a great number of combinations and reached no results.

> One evening, contrary to my custom, I drank black coffee and could not sleep.

> Ideas rose in crowds; I felt them collide until pairs interlocked, so to speak, making stable combination. By the next morning I had established the existence of a class of Fuchsian Functions; I had only to write out the results, which took but a few hours.

Herman Helmholtz

Helmholtz (1898) was a major figure in nineteenth-century physiology and made important contributions to the study of colour vision among other topics. At a dinner in his honour he made the following remarks about his views on creative work:

> So far as my experience goes, happy thoughts never came to a fatigued brain and never at the writing desk. It was always necessary, first of all, that I should have turned my problem over on all sides to such an extent that I had all its angles and complexities in my head and could run through them freely without writing.

> To bring the matter to that point is usually impossible without long preliminary labour.

> Then after the fatigue resulting from that labour has passed away, there must come an hour of complete physical freshness and quiet well being, before the good ideas arrived. Often they would come in the morning as I awoke, but they especially liked to make their appearance while I was taking an easy walk over wooded hills in sunny weather.

Tchaikovsky

Tchaikovsky (from Vernon, 1970, pp. 57–60), the famous composer, made the following observations:

> Generally speaking, the germ of a future composition comes suddenly and unexpectedly.

> If the soil is ready – that it to say, if the disposition for work is there – it takes root with extraordinary force and rapidity, shoots up through the earth, puts forth branches, leaves, and finally blossoms.

WALLAS'S FOUR-STAGE ANALYSIS

On the basis of reports such as those by Poincaré, Helmholtz, Tchaikovsky (given above) among many others, Wallas (1926) proposed an influential four-stage analysis of creative problem solving. The four stages proposed were:

1 Preparation
   - Person familiarizes themselves with problem
   - Involves conscious work
   - Rarely leads to solution
   - However – this stage is essential – without initial work no further progress would come about.

2 Incubation

  - Problem 'set aside'
  - No conscious work.

3 Illumination (or inspiration or insight)

  - Doesn't always lead to solution of problem
  - 'Great idea' might come to mind, but must be developed and verified.

4 Verification

  - Conscious work must be done on ideas generated through illumination
  - Solutions can be tested and developed.

Although the above order was intended to be typical, Wallas also suggested that not every problem goes through stages from 1 to 4 in strict order and stated that: 'The four stages constantly overlap each other as we explore different problems' and 'Even when exploring the same problem the mind may be unconsciously incubating on one aspect of it, while it is consciously employed in preparing for or verifying another aspect' (1926).

INCUBATION RESEARCH

Incubation is a period in which a problem is set aside; it may be 'immediate', directly after presentation, or 'delayed', after a period of conscious work.

As indicated above, Wallas (1926) proposed as beneficial an 'incubation' stage in problem solving, during which the problem is set aside and not consciously addressed. In an extensive review, Dodds et al. (2003) identified 39 relevant experiments since the 1930s of which 29 (i.e. 75 per cent) reported significant beneficial effects of incubation. Such studies have generally used a method in which participants in the incubation condition work for a pre-set time followed by a different (interpolated) activity for a fixed time (incubation period) and finally return to the target problem for a post-incubation period. A variation involves having participants work until an impasse is experienced (Ohlsson, 1992), following which an incubation period is provided. Performance of the incubation groups is contrasted with control data from groups working continuously.

How might incubation work?

The six main hypotheses regarding incubation effects can be summarized as follows.

1 *Conscious work*: This suggests that although incubation is intended to be a period without conscious work on the target task participants may nevertheless carry out intermittent conscious work (Seifert et al., 1995, p. 82). Any conscious work during the supposed incubation period would reduce the time required when the target problem was re-addressed – but would impair performance on the interpolated task. As a check against this possibility, performance on the interpolated task during the incubation period should be compared with performance of a control group working on the same interpolated task without being in an incubation condition. A deficit in the interpolated task on the part of the incubation group would be consistent with the hypothesis of some conscious work on the target task during incubation. Although this seems a rather basic methodological check, surprisingly it had not been routinely carried out in previous research (Dodds et al., 2003) until Gilhooly et al.'s (2012) study which found no evidence of intermittent conscious work during incubation on a divergent task.

2 *Unconscious work*: This approach argues that incubation effects occur through active but unconscious processing of the problem materials. Poincaré (1929) suggested that the 'subliminal self' unconsciously combined and recombined ideas until an interesting relevant combination was formed whereupon the valuable idea would become conscious (i.e. Wallas's inspiration stage). More recently, Dijksterhuis and Meurs (2006) have applied a theory of unconscious thought to incubation. On this view, unconscious thought, compared to conscious thought, has a large capacity, proceeds relatively slowly, tends to be bottom up, is good at integrating many sources of information, is relatively poor at following rules and tends to divergent rather than convergent thinking. Dijksterhuis and Nordgren (2006) report a number of studies in which better decisions and better creative thinking was found when the tasks were not worked on consciously. However, their studies did not follow the classical method of incubation research in which the problem is set aside after an extended period of conscious work. Rather, Dijksterhuis and Meurs had the participants immediately put aside the problem for a period after the task was presented, and before any conscious work could be carried out. This manipulation made explanations of incubation in terms of reductions in set less likely as participants had not had time to develop misleading sets. They interpreted their results as favouring an explanation in terms of unconscious work. Box 9.4 presents an example of this line of research.

3 *Fatigue dissipation*: Helmholtz (1896, see Woodworth & Schlosberg, 1954, p. 838) suggested that a break is simply an opportunity to rest and return with more energy to the problem. This suggests that more demanding interpolated tasks should be less beneficial than less demanding interpolated tasks.

4 *Selective forgetting*: This view proposes an important role for automatic reduction in idea strength or activation. The proposal is that misleading strategies, mistaken assumptions and related 'mental sets' weaken through forgetting and thus a fresh start or 'set shifting' is facilitated when the problem is resumed. Simon (1966) specified this hypothesis further in terms of decay of irrelevant or misleading material in working memory (see Chapter 4 for more on working memory) when attention was shifted away from the problem while useful information accumulated in long-term memory over repeated attempts.

Box 9.4 Research Close Up: Unconscious work in incubation?

Source: Dijksterhuis, A., & Meurs, T. (2006). Where creativity resides: The generative power of unconscious thought. *Consciousness and Cognition, 15,* 135–146.

INTRODUCTION

Does the unconscious work hypothesis apply to a divergent task with many solutions such as the classic laboratory creativity task to come up with as many new uses as one can for a brick? Dijsterhuis and Meurs investigated this possibility in a study using immediate incubation in order to rule out beneficial forgetting and attentional shifting explanations, thus leaving unconscious work as an explanation.

METHOD

Participants were asked to write down uses for a brick in one minute, under one of three conditions: immediate generation; after three minutes of unconscious thinking, in which a three-minute visuo-spatial interpolated task was given immediately after the problem statement and then one minute was allowed to report uses; and after a three-minute conscious thinking condition in which participants had three minutes to think of uses without reporting uses, followed by a one-minute period to report uses.

RESULTS

Results indicated that the three-minute unconscious thinking condition produced better results in terms of the rated creativity of the uses written down in the one-minute generation period than did the two conditions without incubation periods. Dijksterhuis and Meurs argued that as the participants had not worked consciously on the task in the unconscious thinking (i.e. incubation) condition no sets could have been established before the incubation period and so the benefits of incubation in this study could not be explained by set shifting.

DISCUSSION

The results in favour of the immediate incubation group are striking in that the time available for conscious work is much less (one minute, i.e. the response generation period) in the incubation condition than in the conscious work condition (four minutes total, i.e. three minutes conscious work without writing down responses plus one minute written response generation). This contrasts with standard incubation studies in which the amount of conscious work time is equal for incubation and continuous work conditions. Dijksterhuis and Meurs's basic result appears to be robust and we have recently replicated the main findings of a benefit from an incubation period immediately after the task instructions for divergent thinking in studies in our laboratory (Gilhooly et al., 2012). The notion of unconscious work seems to be supported for divergent tasks such as the brick uses problem.

INFORMATION PROCESSING THEORY OF CREATIVE PROCESSES

We have previously seen that information processing ideas of search through spaces of possible actions and working with goals and subgoals can explain much routine problem solving. Can such concepts be usefully applied to creative problem solving? Two example attempts addressing creative problem solving in information processing terms are those of Herbert Simon (1966) and the Geneplore model (Finke et al., 1992).

Simon model

Simon (1966) applied standard information processing approaches to creative problem solving. He pointed out that 'Creative advances are rare events' and any theory should be consistent with this rarity of occurrence. The information processing approach to problem solving proposes considerable search through vast numbers of alternative hypotheses. In this model, search is slowed by limited capacity of working memory (see Chapter 4) and by the slow rate of transfer of information into long-term memory. On the other hand, search is aided by improved representation methods and by good heuristics; consistent with this view are the many scientific advances Simon noted that followed improvements in instruments that give better representations of very small objects (microscopes) or of very distant objects (telescopes). In this approach, incubation is analysed as familiarization with repeated attempts and selective forgetting in between attempts, allowing fresh approaches to be taken.

Geneplore is a model for creative thinking which stresses the role of a generative and exploratory phase.

Geneplore model

Finke et al. (1992) developed the Geneplore model whose name is derived from 'generate' and 'explore'. The proposal is that creative work involves an initial stage in which 'pre-inventive structures' are generated and are then interpreted during an exploratory phase.

The Geneplore model has been investigated using the creative synthesis task in which participants were given three shapes to combine to make 'interesting objects'. See Figure 9.18 for sample constructions in the creative synthesis task.

> Creative synthesis task is a task in which participants have to combine presented shapes to make novel interesting combinations.

Finke et al. examined the effects of (a) giving broad target categories first (e.g. make a mode of transport, or a piece of furniture) or (b) giving target categories *after* the object produced, and found that more highly rated 'creative' responses (33 per cent vs. 22 per cent) were produced when the category was given second. This result is thought to arise because the initial pre-inventive forms would be less constrained by preconceptions if no goal was given in advance and hence more unusual solutions would be forthcoming.

INCREASING IDEA PRODUCTION

Setting a problem aside or incubation, as discussed above, is a possible way of boosting creativity but can we take deliberate steps to increase the flow of creative ideas? A large number of suggestions have been made over the years. It may be that some external cues can make a difference and we look at some ideas about this next.

Cues for creativity

Social psychologists have often found that small cues can have large unconscious effects. For example, participants provided with cold drinks rated people they met in the study as less pleasant and friendly than when they were given warm drinks. Further, after holding a warm pad (versus a cold pad) people were more likely to pick a gift for a friend instead of for themselves (Williams & Bargh, 2008).

In the area of thinking, Forster et al. (2005), found that participants who were asked to think for a few minutes about the characteristics of 'punks' as against 'engineers' produced many more original and creative uses for everyday objects in a typical divergent thinking task. The interpretation was that the perceived unconventionality and rule breaking tendencies of punks cued or 'primed' unconventional approaches to the divergent uses task.

Forster et al. (2005) also found that the kind of art used for office decoration could cue creative behaviour even when attention was not explicitly directed toward the artwork. They found that posters on the laboratory wall, in which a regular pattern had a deviation, such as a picture of 12 crosses, 11 of which were green and one of which was red, produced more creative responses on the uses test than a picture of 12 green crosses. The deviant item it is suggested, cues or primes unconventional thinking.

Slepian et al. (2010) looked at whether being exposed to a light bulb might affect insight. Why? Slepian et al. reasoned that because the light bulb is a conventional symbol of insight it could cue or prime insight processes. The researchers first checked that the link between light bulbs and concepts relating to creativity could be established experimentally. Using lexical decision tasks it was found that participants exposed to a bare light bulb (as against fluorescent lighting) were faster at recognizing

PRESENTED SYMBOLS

"Rectangle, triangle, rectangle, letter V, number 8"

EXAMPLES OF LEGITIMATE PATTERNS

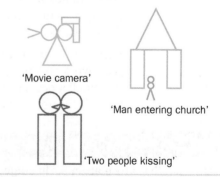

'Movie camera'

'Man entering church'

'Two people kissing'

Figure 9.18 Example creative synthesis responses.
The task is to make interesting combinations of presented shapes.

Source: Finke, R. A., Ward, T. B., & Smith, S. M. (1992). Creative cognition: Theory, research, applications. Examples of presented symbols and legitimate patterns. © 1992 Massachusetts Institute of Technology, by permission of The MIT Press.

words associated with insight such as *create, conceive, envision.* In a second study, participants working on creativity and insight problems solved faster after a light bulb was turned on in the room as against a fluorescent light of equal brightness!

In addition to manipulating environmental cues, another approach is to train particular procedures. One of these that you are very likely to hear about is brainstorming and we will now outline this method and the main research findings about it.

Brainstorming

Brainstorming is stimulating the production of unusual ideas, by stressing quantity as against quality and deferment of evaluation of ideas.

A practical businessman who worked in the advertising industry, Alex Osborn, became dissatisfied with conventional means of developing new ideas – which were constantly needed in advertising. In response to this need, Osborn (1958) developed the brainstorming method described in his book *Applied Imagination.* The method has been subsequently taken up very widely by a broad range of organizations. It was originally proposed as a method for problem solving groups but can be readily adapted for individual use.

Brainstorming aimed to assist in the idea generating stage of problem solving and involves two main principles:

1 Deferment of judgment
2 Quantity breeds quality

and four rules:

1 Criticism is ruled out
2 Free-wheeling is welcomed
3 Quantity is wanted
4 Combination and improvement sought.

The deferment of judgement principle meant that evaluation of ideas was to be postponed until after a fixed period of idea production. This counters the normal tendency to evaluate ideas as they are produced. This could be inhibiting developments from earlier ideas that could lead to useful later ideas. The quantity breeds quality principle stresses that the more ideas produced the more likely at least one good idea will be produced. The rules suggest ways of generating ideas without evaluation and by freely associating to and modifying previously generated ideas.

Early studies indicated that brainstorming did result in more ideas and more high-quality ideas than were obtained with conventional methods for tasks that required novel ideas (Meadow et al., 1959; Parnes & Meadow, 1963; see also, Kerr & Murphy, 2004).

A practical issue that arises, however, is when we have a number of people, say 12, who could work on a brainstorming problem. Is it better to have one large group, or three or four smaller groups or even have people work individually? This question has provoked a lot of research and is discussed in Box 9.5.

Box 9.5 Practical Application: Are more heads better than one in brainstorming?

An issue that arose at an early stage in assessing brainstorming as a practical tool was whether real groups outperformed an equivalent number of individuals. Osborn's (1958) original motive was to assist production of novel ideas in commercial settings such as advertising agencies, and he saw the group interaction element as an important part of the process. But is it? The answer has clear practical implications. For example, if 16 people are available to work on a task is it better to have them work as real groups of four or eight people interacting with each other to produce ideas or have them work as 16 individuals? Taylor et al. (1958) examined this issue in a study in which the results from 12 groups of four people were compared with the pooled results from 48 individuals where all the participants had followed brainstorming instructions on suitable problems that required original thinking. The real groups followed standard brainstorming instructions and those working individually followed brainstorming instructions modified for individual use. After idea production, the 48 individuals' ideas were put into 12 sets of four representing nominal groups of four and these nominal groups were then scored as if they were real groups, i.e. duplicated ideas were only counted once. From these data emerged what is known as the 'nominal group superiority effect'. In other words, the nominal groups outperformed the real groups. This effect has been found over a range of tasks and indeed has been shown to increase with group sizes (Dunnette et al., 1963; Bouchard & Hare, 1970; Dillon et al., 1972) so that the bigger the groups the bigger was the nominal groups' advantage. In practical terms, it seems then that use of nominal groups can be a good way of using a number of people to generate many possible solutions.

Why were nominal groups better for brainstorming than real groups? One suggestion was that being in a real group inhibited the free flow of ideas. Perhaps people feared implicit evaluation by other group members even if overt evaluation was allowed by the rules of brainstorming?

Another type of explanation of the nominal group superiority effect stresses the notion of 'production blocking' resulting from people in the group having to wait their turn to contribute an idea. This may result in forgetting of ideas and distraction by others' suggestions (Nijstad et al., 2003). Interestingly, better performance has been found with electronic real groups as against electronic nominal groups as with electronic groups there is no need to wait for a turn and so there is no response blocking (Kerr & Murthy, 2004; Vallacich et al., 1994). Moreover, even large electronic groups ($N > 9$) outperform nominal groups – in contrast to the general finding that greater group size leads to greater nominal group superiority in face to face groups (Vallacich et al., 1994). Overall, it does seem that brainstorming with real groups can be useful if production blocking can be overcome with the use of electronic groups.

Evaluation

There is some evidence that environmental cues in the form of suitable pictures (asymmetric) or reminders of unconventional groups (punks, say) can boost creative performance. Working in face-to-face brainstorming groups with an emphasis on generating ideas as against evaluating ideas has some benefits compared to conventional working. However, merging the results of individuals (nominal groups) has been found to give better results than face-to-face group work. There are problems with real groups in the form of anxiety about implicit evaluation by group members and production blocking due to waiting for turn taking. Electronic versions of brainstorming overcome these problems and seem promising.

Box 9.6 When Things Go Wrong: Psychopathology and creativity

Is there any truth in the popular idea that creative genius and madness are linked? There is some evidence that *manic-depression* is especially frequent among writers and poets (Jamison, 1993). Manic states are characterized by a rapid flow of ideas and extreme confidence and so may promote the development and expression of unusual ideas. Mood cycles would also provide contrasting perspectives which could feed in to creative work.

Weisberg (1994) analysed the work of composer Robert Schumann who suffered bouts of mania and depression throughout his career. It turned out that Schumann was definitely more productive in the years when he was manic as against the years when he was depressed. However, when the quality of the compositions was examined, by noting how many recordings were available for each piece, it was clear that there was no link between quality of the work and whether Schumann was manic or depressed.

Note that the connections reported between mania and creativity are basically correlational and it may be that being productive and creative leads to manic states (of euphoria) and not being productive leads to depression; the causal direction may not be from psychopathology to creativity but may be the reverse (Weisberg, 2006).

Summary

This chapter concerns the kinds of thinking involved in problem solving and creative thinking.

'Thinking' was defined as involving changes in mental representations, usually in the service of goals. Although problems vary widely in content and in the degree to which they are well or ill defined, it can be said that problems, in general, arise when a person does not know how to reach a goal and must think through alternative possible actions and ways of representing the problem before solving.

The key approaches that were important historically and still inform the questions addressed in current research were outlined. These were the Gestalt and the currently, still dominant, information processing approaches. The key notions of problem structuring and restructuring, insight, fixity, problem space, heuristics and problem reduction are set out.

Recent research on insight problem solving within the information processing approach is discussed. In particular, two main theories (representational change and progress monitoring) are presented and evaluated. Progress monitoring seems to account well for the initial stages of insight problem solving that lead to impasses that are then resolved through representational change. Recent evidence from neuroscientific studies is also discussed. A special role for right hemisphere representations in creativity tasks emerged from these studies.

The role of expert knowledge is considered in the light of research on skill in problem solving in chess and other areas which require extensive knowledge for effective performance. Expertise generally requires extensive study (10-year rule) to develop and much expertise involves recognizing patterns which are not evident to the novice.

Creative problem solving is considered with a discussion of evidence from self-reports by famous creative artists and scientists. The influential four-stage model (preparation, incubation, insight and verification) is explained and recent research on incubation effects and why they might occur is discussed. Incubation seems to arise from a number of distinct processes including beneficial forgetting and unconscious work.

Recent information processing theories regarding creative thinking are presented. Simon's model illuminates large historical trends, such as the relative rarity of creative advances in science due to large problem spaces and the importance of technological developments such as microscopes in improving problem representations.

The brainstorming technique is outlined. The emphasis is on separating generation and evaluation. Working in real face to face groups proves inhibiting compared to nominal groups which combine individuals' work. However, electronic groups do show some benefits.

ANSWER TO CHAPTER PROBLEM

1 Solution to the nine-dot problem.

Review questions

1 In the light of work presented in this chapter, can human thinking be studied scientifically?
2 Evaluate the main historical approaches and their contemporary influence.
3 To what extent does research explain problem solving with insight?
4 How do experts differ from novices in problem solving?
5 Why might putting a problem aside for a while be helpful?
6 Is brainstorming worthwhile?
7 Are creativity and madness really linked?

FURTHER READING

Feltovich, P. J., Prietula, M. J., & Ericsson, K. A. (2006). Studies of expertise from psychological perspectives. In K. A. Ericsson, N. Charness, P. J. Feltovich & R. R. Hoffman (Eds.), *The Cambridge handbook of expertise and expert performance*. Cambridge: Cambridge University Press.

Novick, L. R., & Bassok, M. (2005). Problem solving. In K. J. Holyoak and R. G. Morrison (Eds.), *The Cambridge handbook of thinking and reasoning*. Cambridge: Cambridge University Press.

Weisberg, R. W. (2006). *Creativity: Understanding innovation in problem solving, science, invention and the arts*. New York: John Wiley & Sons.

CHAPTER 10:
DECISION MAKING

INTRODUCTION

In everyday life we face an endless stream of decisions ranging from the not very important, such as which socks to wear today, to the moderately important, such as where to go on holiday, to the very important, such as which university's offer of a study place to accept. We could say that decisions are a type of problem in which the alternatives are set out and the problem is to choose the best of the options available. This may be easy, for example if the choice is between different amounts of money, most people most of the time would readily choose the larger amount. However, if the alternatives are complicated and have uncertain consequences, for example deciding between job offers, the decision may be very difficult and have no clear correct solution. Typically, difficult decisions require a lot of thinking to figure out the possible results of different choices and so decision making is a major cognitive activity, which will draw on long-term knowledge, working memory and mental simulations to anticipate events.

Decision making is the cognitive process of choosing between alternative possible actions.

Scan to watch a video of Dan Ariely about our rationality

© PIKSEL/iStock

Normative approaches attempt to establish ideal ways of deciding that will give the best decision possible. Economists have tended to develop normative models.
Descriptive approaches aim to describe how decisions are actually taken as against how they should be made. Psychologists focus on the descriptive approach.
Risk A decision involves risk if there is a probability that one of the options could lead to negative outcomes for the decision maker.
Riskless decisions involve choices where the outcomes of the choices are known with certainty.
Single-attribute decision problems involve alternatives that vary in only one dimension.
Multi-attribute decision problem is a decision task in which the alternatives vary in many dimensions or aspects.
Expected value is the long-term average value of a repeated decision which is determined by the probability and size of the outcome. So if the chance of winning £100 in a gamble is 0.5, then the expected value is £50.

How then do we make decisions, both great and small? Are there ideal ways to decide that would always deliver the best answer? For centuries, these questions have been of great interest to a wide range of researchers in different disciplines, including economists, philosophers and mathematicians as well as more recently to psychologists. Economists, philosophers and mathematicians have focused on proposals for ideal ways to make decisions and, as we shall see, have come up with ways of making the best choices in small-scale, well-defined decision tasks, such as simple gambles. The search for good ways to make decisions is sometimes labelled the normative approach. Psychologists, in contrast, follow a descriptive approach of trying to understand what people actually do as against what they should, ideally, do. As we will see, normative approaches have supplied ideas that have been then used in descriptive theories. Economists are beginning to develop theories of behavioural economics that make more realistic assumptions about human thinking based on descriptive theories. So, there has been a lot of interaction between descriptive and normative approaches.

Although all decision problems are similar in that they all involve choosing between alternatives, decision problems differ in a number of ways. One major difference is between problems that involve risk as against those that are riskless. If you decide to bet that a particular horse will win a race that is clearly a risky decision. The result of the bet is unknown when you make the decision. You may lose the money you bet or you may win a great deal. On the other hand, deciding between pairs of socks to wear is riskless. If you choose the red socks that is what you will be wearing.

The objects which you are choosing between may vary in only one way, for example, the socks may be identical except for colour, or for type of material. Such choices are among single-attribute alternatives. In real life, multi-attribute alternatives are surely more common. For example, deciding between mobile phones which differ in functions, in sizes, weights, charging schemes and many other aspects represents a multi-attribute decision problem.

In the rest of this chapter we will explain in more detail about normative and descriptive approaches built on normative theories; discuss risky and riskless choices; heuristic (short-cut) decision methods; naturalistic decision making out of the laboratory; and neuroscience approaches that are leading to the new field of neuroeconomics.

We will first consider normative approaches which were developed early in the study of decision making and built on the idea of expected value which will be explained in the next section.

EXPECTED VALUE THEORY

The earliest normative approach to risky decision making goes back to the seventeenth century mathematicians Blaise Pascal (1623–62) and Pierre de Fermat (1601–65) who both had a strong interest in gambling and in the practical question of which gambles were good and which ones should be avoided (Hacking, 1975). They proposed that people should act to *maximize* the expected value of choices. What does this mean? The expected value of a risky choice is the average result you would get if you repeated the action many times over. For example, if a lottery ticket had an 85 per cent chance of winning £100, its expected value would be 0.85 × £100, that is £85 (an average). If you can continually take the same risk (i.e. your lottery ticket is valid every week with the same chance of winning), you would get nothing sometimes (15 per cent of the time) and you would get £100 the rest of the time (85 per cent of the time). So a long-term average over all the purchases is £85. Looking at this example using the expected value model, you should be willing to buy the lottery ticket for any price under £85 as it would mean you would profit overall (even if it is only a small profit). Even buying the ticket for £84.99 would be considered rational because you would make something, even if it is only 1p.

The expected value approach is an optimal way to deal with risky decisions in which we can put a money value on the possible outcomes and can say exactly what the probabilities of the possible outcomes are. Both of these conditions are met in many gambling situations in which the outcomes are monetary and the events have known properties of randomness (e.g. dice, coins, roulette wheels, lottery tickets).

Does the expected value model fit people's behaviour in real life? Research suggests not. With similar decisions to the lottery ticket case, Kahneman and Tversky (1984) found that people's choices showed marked departures from the expected value model predictions. For example, nearly all their participants would not bet $10 on a fair coin coming up heads if they would lose $10 for tails. The expected value of such a bet is zero (because you would win $10 as often as you would lose $10). As the experimenters increased the gain for heads while keeping the loss for tails constant, most people would not take the gamble until the gain for heads was $30 with the loss for tails fixed at $10. In this latter case, the expected value is

© Sean Gladwell/Dreamstime.com

(0.5 × $30 − 0.5 × $10) = $10. This means that many people passed up the opportunity of smaller but positive expected gains of up to $9.99. From the expected value point of view, people are acting against their own interests in not accepting bets with positive expected values, even if the expected values are quite small. To put it bluntly, the participants made choices that left most of them poorer; if they had all followed the expected value approach, most would have been richer at the end of the experiment than when they started.

Real life throws up other striking departures from what the expected value model would predict. For example, why do most of us take out insurance? The insurance companies, to stay in business, must give in claim payments less than they take through charges to customers. Thus, overall the average customer must lose, that is pay in more than he or she gets back. So, from the expected value point of view people should not take out insurance. Why people take out insurance will be considered further when we discuss more recent theory.

Why do so many people engage in gambling at casinos, racetracks, street bookmakers and so on? Casinos set the odds on their games so that overall customers as a whole will lose. The expected value for the gambler of any casino bet is negative and so on the expected value model should not be taken.

Tens of millions of people buy national lottery tickets every week in many countries around the world. In such lotteries, typically there is a very large prize for correctly predicting which six out of 49 numbers will be drawn plus a range of smaller prizes for getting five, four or three correct. Usually, about half the total money staked on the lottery is returned to the players. This means that the expected value of a lottery ticket is around 50 per cent of its purchase price. On average you pay a pound and get back on average 50p. So, the expected return from buying a single ticket for £1 in the UK's weekly draw is *minus* 50p. In other words, when you buy a single £1 lottery ticket, an expected value theorist would say that you are basically throwing away 50p!

Overall, from all the examples we have just looked at, it seems very clear that the simple expected value model does not fit actual behaviour very well. (However, you might like to note that, if you sincerely want to be rich, it is certainly a defensible view that you should follow the expected value model whenever the outcomes are monetary and the probabilities can be accurately known. It's your decision!)

The departures in actual behaviour from expected value theory are intriguing and subsequent theories stressing subjective probabilities and subjective measures of value (utility) have been developed to provide better explanations. We will consider these alternative ideas in the following sections.

Further difficulties for the expected value model as a descriptive model come from other experiments by Kahneman and Tversky (1984). They gave participants the following questions. Try to decide your answers as you read the questions.

1 'Would you prefer $800 for certain, or an 85 per cent chance to win $1000 (and so, a 15 per cent chance of winning nothing)?'
What would you answer?

2 'Would you prefer an 85 per cent chance of losing $1000 (with a 15 per cent chance of losing nothing) or a sure loss of $800?'
What would you prefer?

For Question 1, Kahneman and Tversky found that most people preferred the certain option of $800 for sure. This finding is counter to the prediction of the expected value model. If we do the expected value calculation as follows then the gamble is worth $(0.85 \times \$1000 + 0.15 \times 0) = \$850$.

So, on the expected value model, since the gamble is worth $850 and the sure thing is only worth $800, the gamble should be preferred; but, as we have seen the sure thing is generally preferred to the gamble, despite the gamble having a greater expected value. This preference may be said to reflect risk aversion.

Risk aversion is avoiding risky choices even when a higher expected value than riskless alternatives.
Risk seeking is a preference for risky choices even when riskless alternatives of higher value are available.
Utility is the subjective value of an option.
Subjective probability is how likely a person believes an outcome to be irrespective of the objective probability.

In a similar study Kahneman and Tversky (1984) asked participants Question 2 above and found that most people preferred to take the gamble. However, once again the expected value model would predict the opposite pattern of choices to that found. This time the expected value calculation would be that the gamble was worth $(0.85 \times -\$1000) = -\$850$ while the sure loss would be worth $-\$800$. So, on the expected value analysis the sure loss is less bad than the gamble and thus the sure loss should be preferred. This preference can be labelled risk seeking.

The departures of results from those predicted by the expected value model may be due to people dealing not with objective money values or indeed with objective probabilities but rather with subjective value (or utility) and subjective probabilities.

UTILITY AND PROSPECT THEORY

The idea of utility as against objective value has a long history and goes back at least to the eighteenth-century mathematician, Bernoulli (1738). In the case of money, utility theory proposes that the subjective value or utility of a given additional amount of money decreases the more money you already have. Theoretically, a plot of utility against money will be a plot showing diminishing returns. This graph shown in Figure 10.1 captures our intuition that an extra £1 is worth more to a penniless person than it is to a billionaire. The poor person would cross a busy road to pick up a pound coin while a rich person probably would not, because the utilities of the coin are very different for the two individuals.

Kahneman and Tversky (1979, 1984; Kahneman, 2003; Tversky & Kahneman, 1992) developed prospect theory to overcome problems with the expected value approach. The theory deals with how people choose amongst gambles (or 'prospects') and importantly extended the utility plot into the area of losses. Kahneman and Tversky proposed that decisions about monetary gambles are about *gains and losses relative to one's current wealth*. A key insight of prospect theory is that losses are felt more keenly than corresponding gains. That is, a loss of £10 has greater negative utility than the gain of £10 has positive utility. The general finding that losses of any kind are weighted disproportionately to gains of the same amount is often labelled loss aversion. The resulting S-shaped utility function is shown in Figure 10.2. The S-shaped utility function with a steeper slope for losses than for gains explains risk aversion in the area of gains and risk seeking in the area of losses.

> **Prospect theory** is a decision theory stressing relative gains and losses.
> **Loss aversion** is a key idea of prospect theory that there is a greater dislike of losing utility than liking for gaining the same degree of utility.
> **Endowment effect** is a tendency to over-value a possessed object and to require more money to sell it than to buy it in the first place.
> **Status quo bias** is a tendency to prefer the current state of affairs.

The notion of loss aversion is a key idea of prospect theory and its reality is supported by the real world phenomena of the endowment effect and status quo bias, which prospect theory explains quite readily.

The endowment effect (Thaler, 1980) involves an unwillingness to give up some good, say a coffee mug, even for a sum greater than what one would pay for it in the first place. A classic demonstration of the endowment effect was provided in a study by Kahneman et al. (1990) in which they gave some participants coffee mugs worth about $5. The participants were then asked for how much they would be willing to sell the mugs. A similar group of participants were shown the same mugs and asked how much they would pay for the mugs. The sellers tended to want about $7 to sell the mugs but the prospective buyers on average would only offer about $3. The sellers require more to compensate for the pain of losing something they already have, the mug, than the

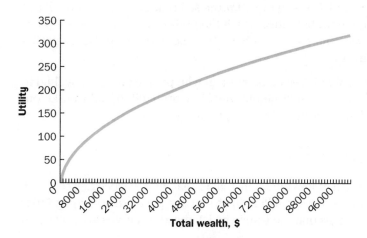

Figure 10.1 Plot of utility versus money. This figure shows diminishing growth of utility of extra wealth as wealth grows.

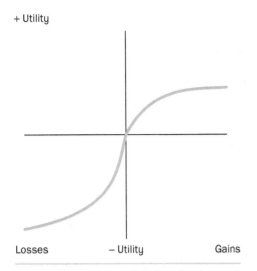

Figure 10.2 Schematic plot of gains and losses versus utility according to prospect theory. The S-shaped curve shows a steep fall with losses and more gradual growth with gains.

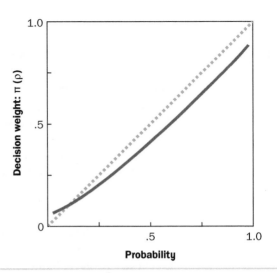

Figure 10.3   Decision weights versus probability. This figure shows that decision weights (the solid line) overweight low probabilities and underweight high probabilities. The dotted line shows what would happen if the decision weights equalled the objective probabilities.

buyers are willing to pay for the pleasure of gaining the same mugs that they do not yet have.

In the status quo bias, people have a strong preference for the current state of affairs and are reluctant to change, presumably because of the risk of losses which are more aversive and are more salient than gains. Samuelson and Zeckhauser (1988) demonstrated such an effect in a study in which some participants were told that they had inherited a set of investments and were offered a set of alternative investments that could be switched into. Compared to a control group who were to imagine having the cash equivalent of the inherited investments and the same alternatives to select, the experimental group were very unlikely to move away from the original inherited investments.

SUBJECTIVE PROBABILITY AND PROSPECT THEORY

Prospect theory also addresses the issue of probability. The expected value model assumed both objective values and known objective probabilities. Prospect theory, as we have seen, replaces objective values with subjective values or utilities. It also proposes that people's perceptions of probability systematically depart from objective values. In particular, Kahneman and Tversky (1979) proposed that objective probabilities are transformed into subjective probabilities which they refer to as 'decision weights'. In general, people tend to *overweight* small probabilities and *underweight* large probabilities, as indicated in Figure 10.3.

The overweighting of small probabilities could explain why people are fairly willing to gamble on lotteries where the prize is large but very low probability and to take out insurance where the potential loss is large but very unlikely.

FRAMING AND PROSPECT THEORY

Prospect theory includes the idea of loss aversion, that is, that we are especially sensitive to losses. The pain of losing £10 is more repellent to us than the pleasure of gaining £10 is attractive. This leads to predictions that the way in which the alternatives are presented (or framed) in a decision problem, in terms of gains or losses, will strongly influence the choices made. From a rational point of view, framing should not have any effect. The alternatives are the same whether described in terms of gains or losses. If people are not affected by framing then their choices are said to show invariance. Invariance requires that a person's choice between two options should not be affected by the way in which the options are described.

> Framing effects arise when irrelevant features of a situation affect the decisions that are made. Invariance is the principle that choices between alternatives should not be affected by how the options are described.

Tversky and Kahneman (1981) examined the degree to which participants showed a constant view or were swayed by framing (alternative presentation) when given a pair of problems (the Asian disease problems), shown in Box 10.1, that could be presented in terms of lives lost or lives saved.

Box 10.1 Research Close Up: The Asian disease problems

Source: Tversky, A., & Kahneman, D. (1981). The framing of decisions and the psychology of choice. *Science, 211*, 453–458.

INTRODUCTION

Tversky and Kahneman explored their ideas about the different impacts of framing decisions in terms of potential losses as against potential gains, in studies using problems of how to deal with an imaginary Asian disease. The options for treating the disease could be presented ('framed') in terms of gains (lives saved) or losses (lives lost). It was predicted from prospect theory that these different ways of presenting the alternatives would sway the choices made, so that a risky option would be preferred when the choices were among losses and a sure option would be preferred when the choices were among gains.

METHOD

Problem 1: Imagine that the USA is preparing for the outbreak of an unusual Asian disease, which is expected to kill 600 people. Two alternative programmes to combat the disease have been proposed. Assume that the exact scientific estimates of the consequences of the programmes are as follows:

- If Programme A is adopted, 200 people will be saved.
- If Programme B is adopted, there is a one-third probability that 600 people will be saved and a two-thirds probability that no people will be saved.

Which programme, A or B, would you choose?

Now consider *Problem 2*. The same introduction is followed by a choice between two programmes C and D.

- If Programme C is adopted, 400 people will die.
- If Programme D is adopted, there is a one-third probability that nobody will die and a two-thirds probability that 600 people will die.

Which of programmes C and D would you choose?

RESULTS

It was found that there was a strong preference for Programme A over Programme B (72 per cent vs. 28 per cent in a study with 152 participants). In a separate similarly large group of participants ($n = 155$) there was a strong preference for Programme D over Programme C (78 per cent vs. 22 per cent). The intriguing point of these results is that Programme A is completely equivalent to Programme C (in both, 200 live and 400 die) and Programmes B and D are also completely equivalent to each other (in both, there is a one-third chance that 600 will live and a two-third chance that 600 will die).

DISCUSSION

Tversky and Kahneman explain the pattern of results in these problems by saying that participants 'frame' or construe the problems in different ways.

In Problem 1, participants are working in a positive 'gains' frame, i.e. in terms of lives saved. The majority choice of the sure option is typical of risk aversion in the domain of gains.

On the other hand, in Problem 2, participants are working in a 'losses' frame, i.e. in terms of lives lost. The majority choice of the risky option reflects typical risk seeking behaviour in the domain of losses as discussed earlier in the text.

Thus, Tversky and Kahneman induced participants to show a striking departure from one of the major assumptions of normative decision theory. Participants did not show invariance and were clearly affected by the way the problem was described.

Similar effects of framing have been demonstrated within individuals as well as between individuals and over many areas of decision making (Maule & Villejoubert, 2007), such as business, finance, politics, management and medicine. In the case of medicine, Edwards et al. (2001) found that patients were much more likely to accept a surgical treatment when it was presented as having a 90 per cent survival rate as against a 10 per cent death rate. Thus as in many areas of problem solving, how a decision problem is presented and, so, internally represented, is extremely important.

MAKING PROBABILITY JUDGEMENTS

Availability heuristic involves judging frequency or probability of events by how easy it is to bring the events to mind.
Representativeness heuristic involves judging frequency or probability of an event or object by how representative or typical it is of its category.

In order to choose effectively between options the decision maker often has to reach judgements about the probability of certain outcomes. For instance, a business traveller in Britain might have to decide whether to fly to Paris or take the Eurostar train. What outcomes might be considered and the subjective probabilities ascribed to those outcomes will be critical in what decision is made. If a plane bound for Paris had recently crashed this possible outcome will be salient and may deter the executive from the plane choice. Since the perceived probability of outcomes (as against the objective probability) is critical in decision making, much research has been aimed at unravelling some of the processes involved in probability judgements. Tversky and Kahneman have been particularly influential in this area and have proposed two major heuristics, availability and representativeness, which they argue are often used in making probability judgements.

AVAILABILITY

Consider the following question.

> If a word of three letters or more is sampled at random from an English text, is it more likely that the word starts with 'r' or has 'r' as its third letter?

What do you think? Using the Word problem, Tversky and Kahneman (1974) found a very strong tendency for people to report that a word beginning with 'r' was more likely to be picked out by random sampling than a word with 'r' in the third position. However, in fact the reverse is true. Tversky and Kahneman suggest that people tackle this question by comparing how easy they find it to think of words beginning with 'r' as against words with 'r' as the third letter. Since starting letters usually provide the best cues for word retrieval, people are able to think of more words that start with 'r' than they do having 'r' in third place. That is, words beginning with 'r' come to mind more readily, are more available than words with 'r' as the third letter. Differences in availability thus lead people to misjudge the relative frequency of the two types of words.

Reliance on availability of examples to judge frequency is actually a reasonable thing to do, since frequency does affect availability. However, since availability can also be affected by recency and emotional impact, among other factors, availability is not always a valid guide to objective frequency or probability. Thus a single, recent, vivid accident can deter possible travellers from flying across the Atlantic, say, because a recent well-publicized accident makes the highly unlikely outcome of another accident very available when the person contemplates travelling. Consistent with this view, Lichtenstein et al. (1978) showed that causes of death that have more publicity (e.g. murder) are judged more likely than causes that have less publicity (e.g. suicide), contrary to the true state of affairs.

The availability heuristic can lead to contradictions of basic laws of probability as well as to the simple inaccuracies indicated above. Tversky and Kahneman (1983) report that when subjects were given 60 seconds to list seven-letter words of the form '- - - -ing' more words were reported than when subjects were given the same time to list seven-letter words of the form '- - - - - n -'. This result reflects a difference in availability since of course, the set of '- - - - - n -' words includes the set of '- - - - ing' words, and so is considerably larger. Interestingly, Tversky and Kahneman also found that when subjects were asked to rate the frequencies (in a sample of 2000 words from a novel) with which they would expect '- - - - ing' and '- - - - - n -' words to occur, they rated the former much more frequent than the latter. Comparable results were found in a comparison of frequency judgements for words of the forms '- - - - - ly' and '- - - - - l -'. Those judgements, based on availability, violate a fundamental law of probability, known as the 'extension rule'. If the extension of a set, A, includes the extension of a set, B, then the probability of A must be greater than or equal to the probability of B. For example, if I have a bag of mixed fruits (say some apples, bananas, pears), the probability of pulling a fruit out of the bag must be bigger than the probability of pulling out an apple.

So, use of the availability heuristic can lead to rather gross errors which decision makers should strive to avoid.

REPRESENTATIVENESS

A second heuristic which Tversky and Kahneman (1983) identified is that of representativeness. Representativeness is an assessment of the degree to which an example fits our idea of a typical member of the category (for more on representativeness see Chapter 7). It is well established (Rosch, 1978) that judgements of the representativeness of examples of categories can be made reliably and with high agreement among participants (e.g. that 'robins' are representative or highly typical instances of 'birds' but 'penguins' are not). You might like to think how representative is a particular individual (say 'George Clooney' or 'Johnny Depp') of the category 'Hollywood actors' or how representative is a particular act (e.g. 'murder') of the behaviour of a category of people (e.g. 'police officers')? Tversky and Kahneman propose that representative or typical instances tend to be judged more likely to occur than unrepresentative instances and that such judgements can lead to error.

Scan to watch an illustrated version of the Linda problem

A particular form of error attributed to the representativeness heuristic is that known as the conjunction fallacy. A classic task used by Tversky and Kahneman to demonstrate the conjunction fallacy is given in Box 10.2.

Conjunction fallacy is the mistaken belief that the conjunction of two events (A and B) is more likely than either one of A or B.

Box 10.2 Research Close Up: The Linda problem

Source: Tversky, A., & Kahneman, D. (1983). Extensional vs. intuitive reasoning: The conjunction fallacy in probability judgment. *Psychological Review, 90*, 293–315.

INTRODUCTION

Tversky and Kahneman devised a study of the effects of representativeness on making probability judgements and on the conjunction fallacy. They presented people first with information about an imaginary person (Linda) such that the information evoked the stereotype of a feminist. As Linda was very representative of the class of feminists would that skew people's judgements about the likelihood of other possible characteristics of Linda? And in particular would the conjunction fallacy be strengthened by the stereotypical information?

METHOD

The description of Linda in the problem was intended to be representative of a feminist (F) and unrepresentative of a bank teller (T). In Tversky and Kahneman's study, a group of 88 undergraduates then ranked eight further statements about Linda by 'the degree to which Linda resembles the typical member of that class'. The description given and the eight statements were as follows:

> Linda is 31 years old, single, outspoken and very bright. She majored in philosophy. As a student, she was deeply concerned with issues of discrimination and social justice, and also participated in anti-nuclear demonstrations.

Now rank the following statements according to how likely you think they are to be true of Linda.

- Linda is a teacher in elementary school
- Linda works in a bookstore and takes Yoga classes
- Linda is active in the feminist movement (F)
- Linda is a psychiatric social worker
- Linda is a member of the League of Women Voters
- Linda is a bank teller (T)
- Linda is an insurance salesperson
- Linda is a bank teller and active in the feminist movement (T and F)

RESULTS

The overwhelmingly chosen order of *typicalities* for the key statements ('Feminist', 'Teller' and 'Teller and Feminist') was, 'Feminist' most typical, then 'Teller and Feminist', then 'Teller'. Thus Linda was seen as highly typical of the class 'Feminist', moderately typical of the class 'Feminist bank tellers' and untypical of the class 'Bank tellers'. More surprising, and in violation of the extension law of probability, was that nearly all participants also ranked the conjunction 'Teller and Feminist' as *more probable* than either 'Teller' or 'Feminist' alone.

DISCUSSION

Since the set of Tellers includes the set 'Tellers and Feminists', the probability of Teller must be greater than the probability of 'Teller and Feminist', similarly, the probability of Feminist must be greater than the probability of 'Teller and Feminist'. Thus, it seems that the representativeness heuristic has led to an error (violation of the extension law), just as did the availability heuristic when participants judged the probabilities of words ending 'ing' or '_n_'.

The conjunction fallacy has proved to be a very robust phenomenon and has been replicated under many variations of the task, described by Tversky and Kahneman (1983). Even medically trained participants were affected by the fallacy when given a brief case history and asked then to say whether the patient was more likely to develop one particular (unusual) symptom (B) or a combination of the unusual symptom (B) and a typical symptom (A). The experts overwhelmingly judged the conjunction A and B to be more likely than the single symptom B. Again, this judgement violates the extension law of probability.

Interestingly, if the task was stated in terms of frequencies rather than probabilities, this manipulation greatly reduced the fallacy. Consider the following:

> A health survey was conducted on a sample of 100 adult males in British Columbia, of all ages and occupations. Please give your best estimate of the following values.
>
> * How many of the 100 participants have had one or more heart attacks?
> * How many of the 100 participants both are over 55 years old and have had one or more heart attacks?

Only 25 per cent of 117 statistically naive participants gave a higher estimate for the conjunction question (Tversky & Kahneman, 1983). When 147 similar participants were given the same problem but asked to estimate percentages rather than absolute numbers a clear majority gave higher estimates for the conjunction. Fiedler (1988) found the same facilitating effect in a frequency version of the Linda problem in which it was stated after the standard Linda description that 100 people fitted her description. Participants were asked to say how many of the 100 people fitting Linda's description are bank tellers and how many are bank tellers and active feminists. Fiedler found that the rate of conjunction violations fell from 91 per cent in the original version to 22 per cent in the frequency version. Hertwig and Gigerenzer (1999) replicated this result almost exactly.

Overall, it seems that using frequencies rather than percentages facilitates correct thinking in conjunction tasks, probably by inducing a more concrete representation of the task.

BASE RATES

In considering the extent to which evidence affects the probability of a hypothesis being true one should generally take into account the probability that the hypothesis is true when the evidence is not taken into account (i.e. the base rate). A number of studies have found a tendency to ignore base rates. However, as we shall see, whether base rates are used varies with task conditions. A striking example study is that of Casscells et al. (1978) using the Harvard Medical Problem presented below:

> Base rate of an event is the overall probability of the event in a population; so, the base rate of 'engineers' in the UK is the probability that a randomly selected person in the UK will be an engineer.

> If a test to detect a disease whose prevalence is 1/1000 has a false positive rate of 5 per cent, what is the chance that a person found to have a positive result actually has the disease, assuming you know nothing about the person's symptoms or signs?

If you are inclined to say '95 per cent' to the Harvard Medical Problem, then you are in agreement with most of the medically trained participants in Casscells et al.'s study. However, the correct answer is 2 per cent. Most participants answer on the basis of the *false positive* rate and the inferred *true positive* rate of 95 per cent. However the base rate of the disease is very low and must be taken into account. The rationale of the correct approach is perhaps most clearly conveyed for the non-mathematically inclined by considering frequencies as follows. Of 1000 patients only 1 will have the disease and 999 will not. Of the 999 healthy patients the test will report that c. 50 have the disease. So even assuming the test correctly diagnoses the one sufferer, it will misdiagnose 50 as ill who are not. Thus, of the 51 who are diagnosed ill only one will actually be ill, giving the probability that a person with a positive result is ill as 1/51 = 2 per cent. Of course this is an increase over the base rate of 0.01 per cent, but still quite a low probability in absolute terms.

Tversky and Kahneman (1980) also found a tendency to ignore base rates in the following problem:

> A taxi-cab was involved in a hit-and-run accident one night. Two cab companies, the Green and the Blue, operate in the city. You are given the following data:
>
> **(i)** 85 per cent of the cabs in the city are Green, and 15 per cent are Blue.
>
> **(ii)** in court, a witness identified the cab as a Blue cab.
>
> The Court tested his ability to identify cabs under appropriate visibility conditions. When presented with a series of cabs, half of which were Blue and half of which were Green, the witness made correct identifications in 80 per cent of the cases, and was wrong in 20 per cent of cases.
>
> What was the probability in percentage terms that the cab involved in the accident was Blue rather than Green?

Tversky and Kahneman found a median response of 80 per cent which indicates that the base rate information was ignored and the response based only on the probability of the witness saying Blue if the cab was Blue. Taking account of the low base rate of Blue cabs (15 per cent) the correct answer should be 41 per cent; a marked increase over the base rate certainly, but well short of the typical answer. The correct answer may perhaps be more understandable if one imagines the accident being staged and witnessed repeatedly, using all the cabs in the city. Out of the 85 Green cabs the witness would wrongly report 17 (20 per cent) as Blue and would correctly report 12 of the 15 Blue cabs as Blue (80 per cent). Thus of the 29 reported to be Blue 12 would actually be Blue; hence, the probability that a cab was Blue given that it was reported to be Blue is 12/29 = 0.41 = 41 per cent.

As with the conjunction fallacy, a manipulation which reduces or even removes the base rate fallacy is to state the problems in terms of frequencies. For example, Cosmides and Tooby (1996) developed a frequency version of the Harvard Medical School problem which reads as follows:

> One out of 1000 Americans has disease X. A test has been developed to detect when a person has disease X. Every time the test is given to a person who has the disease, the test comes out positive. But sometimes the test also comes out positive when it is given to a person who is completely healthy. Specifically, out of every 1000 people who are perfectly healthy, 50 of them test positive for the disease. Imagine that we have assembled a random sample of 1000 Americans. They were selected by a lottery. Those who conducted the lottery had no information about the health status of any of these people. How many people who test positive for the disease will actually have the disease? ___out of___.

With this version the proportion of correct answers rises from 12 per cent with the original Casscells et al. (1978) wording to 76 per cent with the frequency wording. Thus, expressing base rate problems in frequency terms helps considerably (as was the case also with conjunction effect problems). The reader may also have noticed that the explanations of the cab problem and of the original Harvard Medical problem were in frequency terms for ease of understanding. Gigerenzer (1993, 2007) suggests that thinking in frequencies is developmentally (and evolutionarily) prior to thinking in probabilities or percentages, which requires specific training. Posing problems in terms of frequencies may evoke quite concrete representations of the situations described and hence provide guidance for inferences and checks on erroneous inferences.

Box 10.3 Practical Application: Removing 'availability bias'

In making decisions individuals often use biased samples of information because they remember information that is easily available in memory, for example, because it is especially vivid or recent. The problem is that individuals typically assume that the information that is available is also most frequent, probable and causally important (Tversky & Kahneman, 1974). This assumption is often wrong. People typically overestimate the likelihood of vivid causes of death like accidents or murders and they underestimate the likelihood of less vivid causes like disease or strokes. Individuals also give too much weight to recent readily recalled information. For example, the purchase of earthquake insurance 'increases sharply after a quake and then decreases steadily as memories fade' (Slovic et al., p. 465).

Heath et al. (1998) found in a survey that many successful organizations tried to deal with staff's tendency to rely on biased, available information by bringing in processes to collect information more systematically. At a Motorola division that developed equipment for mobile phones, one group realized that an availability bias was causing it to overlook some customers when it evaluated new products. The group had account managers only for large accounts, so when managers evaluated new products, they mainly considered only the needs and requirements of large customers. However, the group also had smaller customers who did not have their own account manager. Together, these small customers accounted for a large percentage of revenues. Motorola overcame the availability bias by surveying customers up to four times a year and then weighted all of the customer responses based on customer numbers and importance in sales terms. This way the smaller customers' needs were also considered as well as the more available requirements of the larger customers.

Heath et al. (1998) also found that hospitals had a range of procedures to ensure that individuals systematically collected information more broadly than was their natural tendency. Accident and emergency doctors are often confronted by vivid but potentially misleading information. One doctor states that, contrary to what one might expect, stabbings and bullet wounds are 'relatively straightforward affairs' because they leave 'clear tracks on the body'. Other injuries are more difficult to treat because they leave no visible cues. 'It would be all too human to focus on a lacerated scalp – a gory but basically insignificant injury – and miss a fractured thighbone that had invisibly severed a major artery' (Rosenthal, 1994, p. 48). To counter reliance on highly available information the medical profession has developed a series of strict procedures for information gathering in accident and emergency situations so that less salient possibilities are not overlooked.

If people focus mainly on information that is highly available, it is not surprising that they are frequently unaware of missing information. Heath et al. found that some professions and organizations have learned to counter the tendency to ignore missing information. Murder squad detectives learn to notice the absence of items at murder scenes, since many murderers take back something that belonged to them after committing the crime. 'You look at what's been taken and you find out who it belonged to originally' (Fletcher, 1990, p. 75).

A particularly important form of missing information is the absence of experience with highly unusual events. Nuclear technicians rarely see a meltdown and airline personnel rarely witness a crash. Many organizations have procedures that encourage individuals to pay attention to such rare possibilities despite the fact that such events are unlikely to be available in their own experience. For example, at the US Federal Reserve Bank, which certifies the security of banks, senior bank examiners deliberately recount stories of failed banks to keep junior examiners aware that they should be vigilant. By forcing staff to rehearse such information, organizations help individuals learn from the experiences of others that are rare but highly informative.

Overall, from Heath et al.'s survey, it seems that 'availability bias' can be dealt with, once it is recognized as an issue.

THE AFFECT HEURISTIC

Affect heuristic involves substituting feelings (positive or negative) for target attributes in decision problems.

In real life, an affect heuristic by which readily available *feelings* or affective assessments (such as, like, attractive, positive versus dislike, repellent, negative) are substituted for target attributes seems to be a common way of quickly making decisions (Slovic et al., 2002; Finucane et al., 2003). In an example study, Finucane et al. (2000) found that if people were told about the risks of nuclear power (i.e. possible negative effects such as radiation leakage) then their assessment of its possible benefits such as cheapness, reliability, low carbon emissions, etc., went down; conversely, if they were told of the possible benefits of nuclear power first their assessment of the risks of nuclear power were reduced. Similar results were also found with scenarios involving use of natural gas and food preservatives. These results support the idea of affect-based decision making. Normatively, judgements of risks and of benefits should be independent of each other but Finucane et al. argued that people tended to form emotional responses to the initial component to which they were exposed (risks or benefits) and the emotional responses affected the second presented component. In a separate study, Finucane et al. found that the rated benefits and risks over some 23 technologies (e.g. water fluoridation, mobile phones, microwave ovens) and activities (e.g. surfing, smoking cigarettes, eating beef) were strongly negatively correlated, especially when judgements were made under time-pressure versus no time pressure. That is to say, if the risks were rated highly harmful, the benefits were rated low in attractiveness and *vice versa*. Very similar findings also emerged from a study of judgements by toxicologists regarding exposures to very small (non-hazardous) quantities of chemicals (Slovic et al., 2002). These findings are consistent with a general tendency to use an overall affective response to each item to guide assessment of risks and benefits such that a positive affective response leads to a low assessment of risk and a high assessment of benefits and the opposite for negative affective responses.

© Kuzma/iStock

Affective responses to alternatives can be useful in real life and have the benefit of avoiding extended thinking to make decisions. Just going with the one that feels right is a low effort way of deciding. This is probably most useful in situations where learning what choices are good and what are bad is important. Bechara et al. (1997) presented people with four decks of cards on a table. They were then asked to choose cards over many trials and depending what the card said they either won or lost money. Gradually it would emerge that two decks were usually good and two usually bad. It took people about 25 trials to consciously report this. However, skin conductance recordings showed electrical spikes associated with fear responses when people reached for a bad deck after about 13 trials. Participants' choices of the good decks rose after the 13th trial even though they could not consciously report which decks were good and which bad until many more trials had elapsed. Damasio (1994) labels emotional responses such as feelings of fear, 'somatic markers'. Interestingly, inability to use affective cues or somatic markers in decision making appears to have a marked negative effect on quality of decisions (Damasio, 1994); this is explored in Box 10.4.

Box 10.4 When Things Go Wrong: Brain damage and decision making – the role of 'somatic markers'

The importance of affect in decision making was underlined in studies by Damasio (1994) of patients with damage to the ventro-medial frontal cortices of the brain. Such patients can undertake abstract reasoning tasks as well as normals but have impaired emotional reactions coupled with poor ability in making risky decisions. Damasio proposed that normally, risky decision options evoke 'somatic markers', i.e. affective responses that warn people of danger and so deter risky decisions; however, these cues are not available to patients with damage to the ventro-medial frontal cortices. In a gambling situation, participants could select cards from any one of four decks. On the back of each card was a statement of whether the card had won or cost the participants money. Normal people and patients with brain damage outside the prefrontal cortices soon learned to avoid decks with attractive payoffs but also with catastrophic losses. However, patients with prefrontal cortical damage did not come to learn appropriate anticipatory responses and did not avoid the high risk decks, even after extensive learning opportunities. The normals and control patients showed learned skin conductance responses indicating fear reactions to the 'bad' decks after about 13 trials. However, the patients with prefrontal cortical damage did not show skin conductance responses and without the affective 'warning signals' learned much more slowly and even continued to make bad choices even after consciously reporting which decks were good and which bad. It seems that lack of 'somatic markers' or affective responses in the prefrontal cortex brain damaged group led to impaired decision making under conditions of risk that would normally evoke an affective heuristic. See also Chapter 14 for more detailed case studies of decision making in individuals with impaired emotional responses due to brain damage.

DECISION PROCESSES FOR MULTI-ATTRIBUTE ALTERNATIVES

Most real life choices involve selecting amongst complex alternatives that vary in many ways. For example, in buying a new mobile phone, there are many functions a phone may have that differ in quality and ease of use. How good is the camera? How easy would it be to watch video on the screen? Or to read extended documents? How compact is the phone? How long does a battery charge last? What is the payment scheme? How long are you locked into the contract? And so on. This is an example of deciding between alternatives that vary on many attributes. How can one balance out advantages on costs say with disadvantages in terms of battery life or photo quality? The general problem is said to be one of deciding between multi-attribute alternatives.

How should such decisions be made? And how do they actually seem to be made? We consider these questions in the following sections.

MULTI-ATTRIBUTE UTILITY THEORY

Even when no risk is involved, making a choice among items that differ on many attributes can be demanding. A normative approach, known as multi-attribute utility theory (MAUT), suggests that the decision maker should (1) identify the relevant dimensions or attributes, (2) decide on weights to be assigned to the attributes, (3) obtain a total utility for each object by summing the weighted attribute values and (4) choose the object with the highest weighted total (Wright, 1984). For example, if the decision maker has to choose between a number of houses, he or she might identify buying price, and distance from work, number of rooms, garden size, privacy, distance from services (shops, schools, etc.) as relevant attributes. Then the relative importance of the attributes would have to be considered. Is price a more important consideration than distance from services? Each alternative must then be scored on the attribute dimensions. The same scale length should be used for all attributes (e.g. from 0 to 100). So a given house may be assessed at '50' in terms of cost and '90' in terms of garden space, but '10' on distance from work. Clearly all the scales have to be used in such a way that a higher score is 'more desirable' than a lower score. Having obtained the scores on each house for each attribute, overall utilities for each house can be obtained and the 'best' chosen. Needless to say, there are difficulties with this approach in practice. The decision maker may not be certain what the relevant dimensions are, and the attribute weightings and scorings may suffer from unreliability over time.

MAUT is one possible model for how decisions might be made between complex alternatives. Some alternative possible strategies will now be outlined and then we will review relevant empirical studies to see which seem most useful.

ELIMINATION BY ASPECTS

A less demanding procedure than MAUT was described by Tversky (1972) as a possible strategy that individuals might use in order to reduce cognitive effort or processing load. This procedure is known as elimination by aspects (EBA). In an EBA process, the chooser would first select an attribute and eliminate all options that did not meet some criterion level on that attribute. In the example of house purchasing for instance, 'price' is usually a critical attribute. The chooser will often have determined a ceiling price and so all houses over that ceiling price could be eliminated from consideration (irrespective of their other desirable qualities). Then, 'distance from work' might be taken as the next important consideration and all houses more than a certain journey time from work could be eliminated. If the chooser continues in this way to eliminate alternatives, sooner or later, only one option will be left and so the decision will effectively be made. EBA is clearly a less demanding procedure than that proposed by MAUT. Very different choices can arise depending on the order in which aspects are used to eliminate alternatives. Tversky suggests that the importance or weighting of attributes will influence the order of elimination.

SATISFICING

A further simplifying technique which might be used in decision making, known as 'satisficing' has been described by Simon (1956, 1978). The fundamental idea is that rather than expend time and effort in a bid to maximize utility, people are generally content to set a minimum acceptable level which will satisfy them but be short of the maximum. This may apply especially in the case of sequential decisions. For example, in buying a house, houses come onto the market continually and it would be difficult to establish that a given house was actually the optimum choice, since a better one might appear the next day. Thus, buyers may set acceptable levels, either for a total utility or on key aspects of the properties, and choose the first property that meets all their minimum requirements. Should the initial minimum requirements prove too ambitious, Simon (1978) suggests that the satisficing level is gradually adjusted in the light of the average values present in the market, so that the decision maker may become more realistic about his or her criteria in the light of experience.

TESTING MULTI-ATTRIBUTE CHOICE MODELS

In order to determine which (if any) of the main models for multi-attribute choice are reasonably descriptive of behaviour one needs to be able to infer how people process information during decision making. Payne (1976) pioneered a technique which has proven useful in the study of choice processes. In Payne's study participants were presented with information, on cards, about aspects of a number of properties. Each card was face down and gave information about one aspect of one property (e.g. House B is in the suburbs). The cards were arranged in a property × attribute array so that participants could easily either obtain information property by property (i.e. examine all the attributes of Property A then all the attributes of Property B and so on) or obtain information attribute by attribute (e.g. check properties first for 'number of rooms', then check for 'cost', etc.). Figure 10.4 shows an example display of the type Payne used as modified into a computerized version (Payne et al., 1993). Participants were free to examine the cards in any order they wished. Payne distinguished two classes of strategies. One class was labelled 'compensatory' and the other 'non-compensatory'. The MAUT approach, described above, is an example of a compensatory strategy in which an overall assessment is arrived at for each alternative by summing over all attribute values (a good rating on one attribute can compensate for a poor rating on another attribute). On this approach people would tend to scan all the attributes of a property before going on to the next property. EBA and satisficing are non-compensatory strategies and would lead to people going through each property in relation to a key attribute such as cost, before scanning properties for say, location. On the basis of the information search patterns shown by his participants, Payne reported a variety of different compensatory and non-compensatory strategies. Interestingly, decision makers often used both within the same task, for example by using non-compensatory strategies to reduce the number of choices to a small number and then using a compensatory strategy to make the final choice. Payne also observed that non-compensatory strategies increased in frequency as task complexity was increased by manipulating the number of alternative apartments and the number of attributes per alternative.

Time pressure has also been found to shift preferred decision strategies. For example, Zakay (1985) reported that use of lexicographic strategies increased with time pressure. Payne et al. (1988) found that processing accelerated, focused on a narrower subset of information and became more attribute based (i.e. more non-compensatory) under severe time pressure. In a related study, Fasolo et al. (2005) examined the effects of conflicts among the attributes of the alternatives on choice strategies. They pointed out that difficult decisions arise when alternatives which are attractive on one aspect (say, price) are less attractive on another (say, convenience) and vice versa.

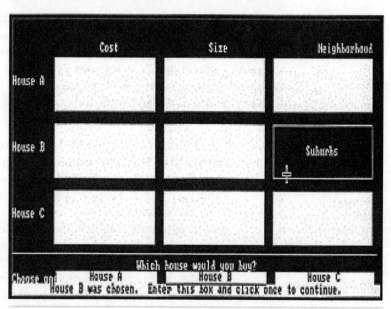

Figure 10.4   Information board of the type used by Payne (1976). Participant chooses a card to reveal information about the property's standing on the attribute of interest. In this case, that house B is in the suburbs.

Source: Payne, J. (1976). Task complexity and contingent processing in decision making: An information search and protocol analysis. *Organizational Behavior and Human Performance*, 16, 366–387.

Participants were asked to recommend a digital camera to a friend, making a selection from five models described along eight features (zoom, resolution, image capacity and so on). Information about alternatives was displayed on a board, similar to the kind used by Payne et al. (1988), containing an 8×5 grid of boxes where the rows were attributes and the columns cameras. Fasolo et al. varied the amount of conflict among attributes and found that when conflict was high participants tended to use compensatory strategies (getting an overall evaluation of each alternative) before choosing and when conflict was low participants preferred a non-compensatory strategy (e.g. eliminating all alternatives above a certain price) to simplify the problem. The results indicate that when choices are difficult people adopt a more demanding strategy to help ensure a good decision; with easier tasks less effortful strategies are seen to suffice and tend to be used.

Overall then, studies indicate that no single decision strategy is always used in choosing between multi-attribute alternatives. Rather, it seems strategies are adopted that tend to compromise between minimizing cognitive load and maximizing the utility of the outcome chosen. Generally, cognitive load in decision making could be minimized by simply choosing at random but the resulting decisions would tend to be very poor. Quality of decision making would be maximized by assessing all alternatives on all relevant dimensions, integrating the resulting information for all alternatives and selecting the best, but the information processing required would be very demanding. Participants generally compromise between effort and quality of decisions and may change method during a task; for example, in Payne's (1976) study people used simple (non-compensatory) techniques to reduce the number of choices and then analysed the remaining few options more exhaustively using compensatory methods such as MAUT.

TWO-SYSTEM APPROACHES TO DECISION MAKING

Intuitively, you will probably feel that some of your decisions are made almost immediately with little or no conscious work while other decisions are only reached after extensive thought. Deciding between complex alternatives, such as job offers, say by using MAUT surely involves extensive conscious work, whereas decisions about less weighty matters, such as choices between posters for a bedroom wall, seem less effortful and more intuitive. Can psychology cast any light on these very different modes of decision making?

Two-system view is that there are two modes of thought, System 1 and System 2.
System 1 is a hypothetical system that carries out rapid intuitive thinking.
System 2 is a hypothetical system that carries out slow deliberate thinking

The differences between the intuitive and more reflective forms of decision making have been highlighted recently in what are known as two-system approaches to thinking, and decision making, for example Evans (2003, 2008), Kahneman (2003), Sloman (1996), Stanovich and West (2000), and others. In these accounts two distinct cognitive systems are proposed. System 1 is seen as automatic, implicit, fast, effortless and emotional, and as generating intuitive, immediate responses. This system is assumed to be relatively old in evolutionary terms and is very similar between humans and other animals. Only the final product of such processes is available to consciousness, that is the person cannot explain why they made their decision. System 2, on the other hand, is seen as evolutionarily recent and is special to humans. It permits abstract reasoning and hypothetical thinking, operates relatively slowly and sequentially, is unemotional, is limited by working memory capacity and is highly correlated with general fluid intelligence and with performance on sequentially solvable problems. People can explain the bases of such decisions. The two systems are seen as interacting and an important role for System 2 is to inhibit and over-ride System 1 when appropriate, for example when the costs of errors are high an immediate gut-reaction probably is not a wise basis for action and should be checked. In the other direction, automatic System 1 processes markedly influence what information the person attends to and focuses on, and so what information System 2 works with (Evans, 2008) in reaching a decision.

In decision making both intuitive System 1 and reflective System 2 routes are possible. Overall, System 2 will be more involved in careful analytical decision making that seeks to combine many types of information in a rule-governed procedure. Normative procedures such as proposed by MAUT would be expected to require System 2 processing. System 1 will be more involved in decision making based on heuristics and biases (Tversky & Kahneman, 1974) and on 'gut feelings' (Gigerenzer, 2007).

Although when dealing with formal probability problems heuristics (such as availability) often lead to errors (as in the Linda problem, Box 10.2), Gigerenzer has proposed that heuristics often have validity in the real world. In the next section, we will look further at this idea that heuristics are adaptive and useful (and not just sources of error).

FAST AND FRUGAL HEURISTICS: THE ADAPTIVE TOOLBOX

As we have seen, a number of heuristic methods have been proposed as ways of simplifying decision making and a number of studies have supported the descriptive value of heuristics such as satisficing, EBA and so on. Gigerenzer and colleagues (Gigerenzer et al., 1999; Gigerenzer, 2007) have developed the idea that as well as saving cognitive effort, many simple heuristics have considerable real world validity and can do as well or even better than more complex methods that take into account more information. Gigerenzer and colleagues refer to these heuristics as fast and frugal, as they are simple and fast to execute as they require little effort; thus their use would involve System 1 rather than System 2. Together, Gigerenzer et al. argue that the heuristics form an 'adaptive toolbox' as the heuristics are generally valid for the real life situations in which they have developed.

In an example study of fast and frugal heuristics, Goldstein and Gigerenzer (2002) asked American and German students 'Which city has the larger population, Detroit or Milwaukee?' Although the German students had far less knowledge of American geography than the American students, they were nearly 100 per cent correct (Detroit) but the American students scored only 60 per cent correct. The German students used the *recognition heuristic* in which the option recognized is chosen as having the target attribute (largest). Many German students had not heard of Milwaukee and so only recognized Detroit while all the American students recognized both and so could not apply the recognition heuristic as it would not distinguish between the two options for them. Ayton and Onkal (2005) found the same advantages of the recognition heuristic in a study comparing predictions by English and Turkish students of the outcomes of English Football association matches in which famous football teams often play against less well-known teams (e.g. Manchester United vs. Shrewsbury Town). The Turkish students outperformed the English students by using the recognition heuristic. Again, Ortmann et al. (2008) found that selections of stocks and shares by laypeople which were based on whether a company was recognized or not, outperformed selections made by financial experts. Thus, the recognition heuristic is often a good way to make decisions where recognizability is correlated with the criterion attribute for the

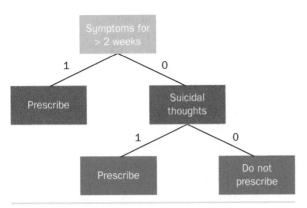

Figure 10.5   Example of a two-cue fast-and-frugal tree for prescribing anti-depressants: 1 = YES, 0 = No.

Source: Smith, L., & Gilhooly, K. (2006). Regression versus fast and frugal models of decision making: The case of prescribing for depression. *Applied Cognitive Psychology*, 20, 265–274.

groups of people being tested. Too much knowledge of the domain can make the heuristic unworkable. So knowledge of some US cities, some companies and some English football teams enables the recognition heuristic to be effective in the studies just outlined since larger cities, more successful companies and richer (more successful) football teams will be better known worldwide.

Gigerenzer and colleagues have also identified simple decision trees (fast-and-frugal trees) in areas such as medicine and law where one might expect a great deal of information to be integrated in reaching treatment decisions or sentencing decisions. Only a few key attributes are considered in a priority order so that if the first attribute has the critical value a decision is made otherwise the next most important value is considered. For example, around 19 medical measurements could be used to measure severity of a suspected heart attack. However, Breiman et al. (1993) found that very effective decisions can be made using just three cues, in order of priority (blood pressure >91, age >62.5, sinus tachycardia present). Smith and Gilhooly (2006) found similar use of fast-and-frugal decision trees used by general practitioners making decisions about whether to prescribe anti-depressants or not (see a decision tree for anti-depressant prescription in Figure 10.5). In the judicial area, Dhami and Ayton (2001; Dhami, 2003) found that magistrates in the English court system very clearly tended to make decisions about whether to grant defendants bail or not on the basis of a small decision tree involving again just three cues which were checked in priority order (Did prosecution oppose bail? Had a previous court opposed bail? Did the police hold the accused in custody?). If any of these cues were positive, bail was refused.

Evaluation

Overall, the heuristics identified and explored by Gigerenzer and colleagues generally work well because the bases of the decisions reflect some underlying reality in the environment which permits effective shortcut solutions. The use of shortcut, rules-of-thumb heuristics are experienced as intuitions or 'gut feelings' and can be assigned to the operations of System 1. The main difference between Gigerenzer's approach and that of Kahneman and Tversky's heuristics-and-biases approach is that Gigerenzer stresses the validity and adaptive value of real-life heuristics while Kahneman and Tversky were more inclined to point out the errors that heuristics (such as availability) can lead to. As a broad generalization, heuristics seem to be most useful when dealing with common situations but tend to mislead when dealing with abstract problems that are best dealt with by explicit calculations following logical and mathematical rules.

HEURISTICS AND CONSEQUENTIALISM

So far, we have largely been assuming that decisions are made on the basis of the *consequences* expected to follow from each of the choices available, a view known as *consequentialism*. Baron (1994) argued that the best decisions are those that yield the best consequences for the achievement of the decision maker's goals. Although such a proposal would surely be widely accepted, Baron points to numerous examples of non-consequentialist decision making, particularly concerning ethical and policy decisions and a selection of these are outlined in the following sections. Baron (1994) argues that the breaches of consequentialism reflect people's use of less demanding heuristics which often do work well (i.e. match consequentialist recommendations) but fail in certain circumstances. Example heuristics would be: 'Do no harm', 'Avoid unfairness', 'Don't breach people's rights'. Such heuristics can be seen as further examples of fast-and-frugal heuristics of the type identified by Gigerenzer and colleagues.

Omission bias

Ritov and Baron (1990) asked people to make decisions about vaccinations where omission (not giving vaccine) and commission (giving vaccine) were options. In one study, people were to imagine that their child had 10 chances in 10,000 of dying from flu in an epidemic if the child was not vaccinated. The vaccine would prevent flu but would itself kill a certain number of children. Participants were asked to state the maximum death rate due to the vaccine at which they would still give their child the vaccine. From the consequentialist point of view, a rate of vaccine-caused deaths up to nine out of 10,000 should be acceptable as it is an improvement over the unvaccinated rate of 10 out of 10,000. The mean acceptable risk reported was considerably lower at five deaths per 10,000. People tended to state that they would feel more responsible for deaths caused by their action (of vaccinating) than by their omission (not vaccinating). Other studies have also found a tendency to judge consequences less bad when the consequences are due to omissions rather than commissions. For example, Spranca et al. (1991) gave people scenarios in which one tennis player knowingly allows his rival to eat an allergy-producing substance before a match (omitting to warn him) or deliberately causes the rival to eat the allergen (commission). In terms of consequences, the omission and commission have the same effect; yet, people tend to judge the commission worse. Thus, there seems to be a bias to downplaying the negative consequences of omissions as against commissions which have the same effects.

Punishment

From the consequentialist point of view, punishment is only valuable if it has a deterrent effect and prevents the undesired acts being repeated by the perpetrator or others. However, it seems that many people feel that retribution is the main function of punishment and are little swayed by the consequences of punishment. Baron and Ritov (1993) had people assess penalties for makers of vaccines and birth-control pills which had caused harm. In one scenario, participants were told that a high penalty would make the company try harder to make a safer product. In a contrasting case, people were told that a high penalty would make the company stop making the drug leaving only more dangerous products on the market. Most participants, including a group of judges, gave the same penalties in both cases despite the very different consequences of the penalties in the two situations. These results suggest a bias toward retribution in making decisions about punishment.

Resistance to coerced reform

Although people will often endorse certain reforms as having desirable consequences for society or even the planet, the same people will often say that they would not vote for the consequentially desirable reforms. For example, most of Baron and Jurney's (1993) participants in the USA agreed that a 100 per cent tax on gasoline (i.e. petrol in UK) would be a good measure on the whole (to reduce global warming) yet many of the same people would not vote for such a tax. The main reasons given for this inconsistency were (1) that the tax would be unfair and harm some more than others, (2) that harm would be caused to some and (3) that the tax would impair a right of people to choose for themselves. Similar results were found when the proposed reforms involved abolition of television advertising during political campaigns, compulsory vaccination for a dangerous flu virus, compulsory treatment for a highly contagious disease and elimination of law-suits against obstetricians. In all cases, consequentialism was breached as a result of the application of simple heuristic rules.

NATURALISTIC DECISION MAKING

Naturalistic decision making refers to making real life decisions in the field.

Critical incident analysis is gaining information about naturalistic decision making by analysing detailed recalls of recent important decisions.

Recognition primed decision is expert knowledge based decision making in which cues in the situation are recognized as indicating particular actions.

Klein (1998), Lipshitz et al. (2001) and Phillips et al. (2004) studied decision making by firemen, nurses, the police and military in real-life emergency settings. This work goes out of the laboratory settings typical of Kahneman and Tversky and even of Gigerenzer and his group, to analyse what happens in real situations. In such situations the decision maker may not be explicitly presented with options to decide amongst but rather has to generate one or more possible actions. The method followed by Klein et al. is that of critical incident analysis in which participants are asked to recall in as much detail as possible a recent case in which they had to make an important decision.

In a range of such enquiries it was found that recognition primed decision making was most common. For example, during a critical incident analysis a fire officer reported that recently he had been in a burning building and noticed a pattern of cracks developing in the walls (Klein, 1999). From the crack pattern he recognized that this was a situation of imminent collapse of the building and the associated response of exiting as soon as possible came immediately to mind.

Typically, it was found that in many critical situations only a single action was mentally generated and it was then chosen to be executed. The basic finding that initially produced possible actions are often very appropriate was replicated in a study of expert chess players (Klein et al., 1995). The players were asked to think aloud while deciding their moves to sample positions and it was found that the very first moves that came to mind were rated as high quality and much better than chance by independent expert judges.

NATURALISTIC DECISION MAKING AND IMPORTANT REAL-LIFE CHOICES

The relevance to real life of laboratory based theories of decision making such as multi-attribute utility theory (MAUT) may seem questionable compared to the more field based naturalistic decision making model. But is naturalistic decision making a better fit to real life when important choices must be made and people are acting without extreme time pressures? Results from five studies of real-life decision making were compared with laboratory and naturalistic decision making models by Galotti (2007). In these studies, participants reported on their experiences of tackling real-life decision problems covering areas such as choosing a college, choosing a major subject, choosing a birth attendant/helper and choosing a kindergarten. Participants consistently limited the amount of information they considered to relatively few options and to a somewhat larger set of criteria. Over time, the number of options considered shrank as the problem was pondered, but the number of criteria used did not. Participants gave subjective ratings for the importance of their criteria and for the value of each option on each criterion and finally for the overall attractiveness of each option. Using these data the fit of people's intuitive choices with the predictions of normative models (such as MAUT) was surprisingly good. In these non-expert decisions people did indeed consider a number of options in contrast to the 'one-option' decisions often seen in time pressured expert naturalistic decision making which is generally based on recognition primed decision mechanisms (Klein, 1998).

Evaluation

Overall, it seems that many real-life 'decisions' by experts do not actually involve conscious decision making between alternatives. From Klein and colleagues' interviews, it seems that a heuristic identified by Gigerenzer (2007) as take-the-first-option can be, and is, usefully applied by experts in time-critical situations. The naturalistic decision making approach then strongly supports the use of fast-and-frugal heuristics, particularly those based on expert recognition, in real-life situations where immediate responses are required. Again, System 1 intuitive processes are strongly implicated in such time pressured situations. However, when decisions are important and time pressure is low, people do tend to approximate to the more reflective, effortful decision processes indicated by MAUT and these processes call on System 2.

NEUROECONOMICS: NEUROSCIENCE APPROACHES TO DECISION MAKING

Two key ideas from studies of human decision making are the notions of utility and the role of dual systems in reaching decisions. Recently, researchers have begun to apply tools of neuroscience such as brain imaging and neuropsychological analyses of effects of lesions to decision making to uncover neural bases of deciding and so build up a new hybrid discipline of neuroeconomics (see Camerer et al., 2005; Sanfey et al., 2006).

> **Neuroeconomics** is the study of neural processes underlying economic decisions.

When alternatives differ widely it seems natural to suppose that decisions between such alternatives must be made by assessing the alternatives on a common scale of subjective value or utility. Is there a neural basis for a common utility scale? A number of early animal studies indicated the existence of brain reward systems (Olds, 1977) localized in brain areas such that animals would take electric shocks, exert large effort and forego food to have those areas stimulated electrically. Activity in such areas could serve to represent a common scale of pleasure or utility for a range of desirable inputs. An option that activated reward systems strongly (indicating a more desirable, higher utility option) would be preferred to one that activated reward systems more weakly. So, decisions would favour options that activate reward systems most strongly.

Scan to watch a video on neuroeconomics

Recordings from dopamine neurons (Tobler et al., 2005), in the orbitofrontal cortex (Roesch & Olson, 2004; Tremblay & Schulz, 1999), and posterior cingulate cortex (McCoy et al., 2003) have shown neural responses that relate directly with reward size in primates and similar results have also been reported in human studies, for example with monetary rewards (Elliot et al., 2003). Thus activity in dopamine neurons is linked to reward size and so such activity is linked to choices as choices follow reward. An interesting FMRI study by McClure et al. (2003) found that people's stated preferences for Pepsi versus Coke were matched by responses in the ventromedial prefrontal cortex on tasting these drinks.

Neuroscientific studies have also supported the dual systems approaches to decision making discussed previously. For example, when people are asked to decide between say £10 today or £11 in one month many people choose £10 today. However, if the choice is between £10 in a year and £11 in a year and one month, the delayed alternative is often preferred, even although the time gap between the two alternatives is still one month, just as it was when £10 was available immediately. It was hypothesized that short-run impatience is driven by the limbic system which reflects System 1 activity and responds impulsively to immediate rewards. Choices of the delayed rewards are governed by the lateral prefrontal cortex, which reflects System 2 activity. In an fMRI study McClure et al. (2004) found indeed that there was relatively greater fronto-parietal activity (associated with deliberative processing) when participants chose delayed options and relatively greater activation of the limbic system (associated with emotional processing) when participants made choices of immediate options.

Similar results emerged from studies of the intriguing Ultimatum Game (Sanfey et al., 2003). In this game, the participant is told that a certain sum of money, say £10, is available and that the other unseen player can decide how the £10 should be split. However, if the participant does not agree with the split then neither player will receive any money. Typically, the game is to be played once and once only on a completely anonymous basis and no bargaining or discussion is allowed. From expected value or expected utility points of view, the participant should accept any split in which he or she gets something greater than zero, no matter how small. Typically, however, people will reject splits in which they would only receive small amounts. Low offers (say around £2 in our example) have about a 50 per cent chance of being rejected (see Roth, 1995) even although it is clearly better to have £2 than nothing. The rejection of low offers seems to be based on an emotional (System 1) response of anger to what is seen as an unfair offer (Pillutla & Murningham, 1996). A cooler System 2-based judgement would accept the low offer. Consistent with this view, Sanfey et al. (2003) in an fMRI study found that rejection of unfair offers was associated with relatively greater activation in the right anterior insula (related to negative emotions such as disgust) and acceptance of unfair offers was associated with relatively greater activation in the dorsolateral prefrontal cortex (related to controlled cognitive processing). See Figure 10.6.

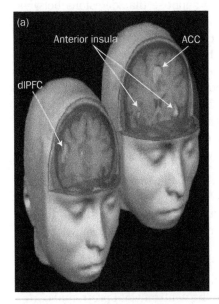
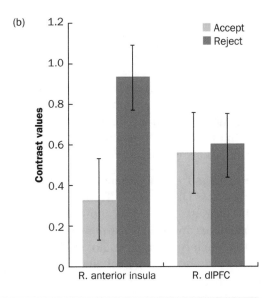

Figure 10.6 Deciding and fMRI. Rejection of unfair offers was associated with relatively greater activation in the right anterior insula (related to negative emotions such as disgust) and acceptance of unfair offers was associated with relatively greater activation in the dorsolateral prefrontal cortex (related to controlled cognitive processing).

Source: Sanfey, A. G., Rilling, J. K., Aronson, J. A., Nystrom, L. E. & Cohen, J. D. (2003). The neural basis of economic decision-making in the ultimatum game. *Science, 300*, 1755–1758. Reprinted with permission from AAAS.

Overall, results from the new area of neuroeconomics are encouragingly consistent with concepts previously developed through behavioural studies (e.g. utility and System 1 vs. System 2 based decision making).

THE AGEING BRAIN AND FINANCIAL DECISION MAKING

Recent studies in neuroeconomics help explain why, despite having more experience, older people often make poor financial choices. Tempting offers are often mailed out to retired people offering investment seminars and opportunities. At the seminars people are told 'there's a high rate of return', and 'only a few opportunities are left'.

Despite their years of experience older people are more likely to err in their financial decisions by overemphasizing potential benefits and downplaying potential risks. It seems that older people are less upset by possible financial losses than young people are.

Sumit et al. (2009) studied how ageing impacts real-life financial behaviour in a variety of choices people make about loans and credit cards. They found that younger and older people made more mistakes – that is, decisions that cost them money – than did middle-aged people. For mortgage loans, for instance, 25-year-olds and 80-year-olds had loans with annual percentage rates of about 6 per cent; 50-year-olds had rates of 5.5 per cent. On average, across the different types of choices, people made the fewest mistakes at age 53.

Good financial choices require an understanding of how financial systems work, and the mental acuity to find and choose the best option. Sumit et al. (2009) noted that 'Experience brings improvement but after a point, the accumulation of experience starts to get overwhelmed by decline of cognitive function.'

This fits with knowledge of cognitive ageing in which it is generally found that a wide variety of skills, including memory, analytical reasoning and processing speed, decrease as we age. The one thing that stays constant or even increases is *crystallized* intelligence, a person's accumulated knowledge about the world.

Affective processes are also involved in decision making and it has been found that older people generally feel more optimistic than young people do, and are more likely to focus on the potential upsides of a situation. This tendency to focus on the positive changes the decisions older people make.

Samanaez-Larkin et al. (2007, 2010) examined brain function differences between older and younger participants in response to anticipated gains and losses. In the 2007 study, participants inside a functional magnetic resonance imaging (fMRI) machine watched as a screen showed an amount of money they could gain or lose, such as '+$5' or '−$1'. Then, after a short delay, they had to hit a button very quickly to get a favourable outcome, such as gaining the $5 or avoiding the $1 loss. After doing this 180 times with various amounts of money at stake, each person ranked how anticipating each gain or loss amount made them feel – from 'very negative' to 'very positive'. The researchers also analysed the fMRI images to see which areas of the participants' brains were most active as they anticipated a gain or loss.

The researchers found that younger and older adults felt equally good when expecting a gain, and they showed the same increase in activity in the nucleus accumbens, a part of the brain that plays an important role in anticipating rewards.

When expecting a loss, however, younger and older adults responded differently. Younger adults reported being more upset and showed higher blood flow in the insula, a part of the brain implicated in negative emotions. As the amount of money at stake increased, so did negative feelings and insula activation. The older adults, on the other hand, did not feel as bad as younger adults did, and showed less activation in the insula.

Whereas looking on the bright side is emotionally beneficial, it has drawbacks in financial decision making, when it is important to consider possible losses. Think of the 'high rate of return' promised at the investment seminar. If they are not worrying about those risks, the older people at the seminar might be more likely to sign up, even if the investment is not a good one overall.

In Samanez-Larkin et al.'s (2010) study younger and older adults took part in an investment game. When choosing between the good and bad stocks, older people were significantly more likely to choose the bad one than younger people were. Before making a risky decision, all participants showed increased activation in the nucleus accumbens, the same region that was activated by expecting a gain in the previous study. Now they were expecting the reward of a risky, but ultimately profitable, choice. But, in older adults this pre-risk activity in the nucleus accumbens was much noisier, with more variability in its strength and timing. This variability in nucleus accumbens activity could be linked to difficulty in picking the right stock, due to fuzzier signals in the nucleus accumbens not clearly differentiating the risky stock from the safe. People who invest in the stock market take on some risk, but they generally do it expecting to make a profit. This study suggests it can be particularly hard for older people to differentiate profitable risks from unprofitable ones.

A practical implication of this work is that if older people know they are prone to focus on the benefits or 'upsides' of their financial decisions, then taking the time to think carefully about possible losses might help them avoid costly choices.

The next section goes beyond cognitive problems for investors brought on by ageing and looks more broadly at psychological factors involved in financial crises and suggests remedies.

THE PSYCHOLOGY OF FINANCIAL DECISION MAKING AND ECONOMIC CRISES

Might psychological factors have been involved in causing the financial crisis that started in 2008? While blame has been cast on reckless banks, mortgage loan policies, and lax credit card practices, these are not the only contributors to the economic downturn. Garling et al. (2010) examined the psychology of financial decision making, including the role of risk in making economic choices, how individuals behave in stock and credit markets, and how financial crises impact people's well-being.

Risk taking is a very important component of financial decision making. If we take out a big loan, will we be able to pay it back? Should we buy shares of a company that is unknown but has potential for great success? Garling et al. (2010) noted that when it came to making decisions under uncertainty, people tend to be more influenced by *perceived risk* than by objective risk. People who are extraverted and high in sensation seeking are likelier to take more and higher financial risks than are people high in conscientiousness and anxiety. As Garling et al. put it: 'The general implication is that financial crises may have more serious consequences for people who are more likely to take financial risks.' Overall, extraverts and sensation-seekers are likely to suffer more and the anxious and conscientious are likely to suffer less when financial crises strike as they will generally have taken fewer risks.

Normative theories of decision making state that stocks and shares should always be traded based on their real objective value. However, Garling et al. noted that behaviour on the Stock Exchange reveals a different reality: stock investors *overreact* to news (especially of events that threaten the world economy), selling winning stocks too soon while hanging on to losing stocks too long, and following other traders' leads in buying and selling stocks. According to Garling et al., stock market investors are prone to cognitive biases (such as overconfidence), which are reinforced by affective and social influences and these may contribute to several phenomena observed in stock markets (e.g. volatility of stock prices, due to excessive trading).

Many people rely on credit, not through using credit cards, but also in the form of car loans and hire purchase agreements. Credit use involves many different stages of decision making, including deciding whether or not to purchase something using credit and working out how to pay the loan back. As Garling et al. noted, credit users face a complex task when they decide to take up credit and they often fall prey to cognitive errors, such as over-confidence.

Are financial crises inevitable? Garling et al. argue that bringing about change in financial institutions may not be easy, but they offer suggestions for improving economic decision making. For example, educating consumers – by offering economics courses to children in school and teaching consumers how to appropriately handle credit – and by making financial institutions more responsible (e.g. banks offering web-based programs to assist with budgeting and so help mental accounting).

The above analysis suggests that consumers would benefit from greater awareness of how even important choices about taking out loans may be swayed by presentational factors which are strictly speaking irrelevant to making good decisions. Box 10.5 takes up this theme and reports a field study carried out by credit providers on how consumers' credit choices can be manipulated. Let the buyer beware!

Box 10.5 Practical Application: A field study in consumer credit decision making

Normative models of choice by consumers assume individual rationality: that is, consumers make important decisions by weighing costs, benefits and preferences. Psychology, in contrast, emphasizes the importance of context and cognitive limitations. Preferences are considered to be highly changeable, and limited rationality makes problem solving and deciding error prone. Evidence from laboratory psychology experiments supports this view of consumer choice (Kahneman, 2011). It suggests that choices can be manipulated by framing the context, presenting visual cues, and other factors that change the presentation of the choice but not its content or actual value.

Bertrand et al. (2005) designed a set of marketing treatments for consumer banking in order to explore the real-world role of 'cues' and 'frames' that have been shown to influence consumer choice in the laboratory. With the aid of a South African bank, they devised a field experiment involving over 53,000 customers to test various psychological factors that might influence borrowing behaviour. For example, they varied whether the lender's rate was compared to a competitor's (thus establishing a reference level), and whether this comparison was presented as a loss or a gain. They also experimented with suggested loan uses and with the addition of photographs to the loan offer letter, because visual cues can be used to arouse positive emotions that are conducive to consumption (Slovic et al., 2002). None of the marketing treatments changed the economic terms of the loan offer; they only varied the way in which the loan offers were presented or 'framed'. Consumers in this study were experienced borrowers, who had on average taken out three loans previously.

It was found that firms can exploit consumers' psychological biases, to increase purchase of credit without lowering costs to the customer. The key features of their findings were as follows. Take up of loan offers was greatest when the number of options was low, when the options were presented in a loss frame (i.e. choosing a rival offer would lead to customer losing out), when the text included an attractive photograph and when there was no promotional lottery (such promotions reduced sales). It was noticeable that the magnitude of the psychological effects was large, with each statistically significant intervention equivalent in effect on choice to drops in the monthly interest rate ranging from one percentage point (most often) to sometimes as much as four percentage points.

The authors note that by using these psychological factors, firms could raise demand while reducing the numbers of customers considering competing options from rival banks. While the implications of these findings were directly relevant to the marketing of consumer goods and services in the private sector, they may also be relevant for the design of social programmes, such as health care or retirement savings plans. The authors point out that through increased focus on the marketing of their programmes, governmental agencies may achieve broader participation without having to rely on greater financial incentives. Since the framing of any initiative, programme or product can be just as important as the actual terms of the offer, attention should be paid to understanding these effects in the formation of public policies.

Summary

In this chapter we have reviewed some of the major concepts and research findings in the area of decision making.

Decision problems were characterized in terms of whether they were risky versus riskless or single attribute versus multi-attribute. Approaches in decision making were divided into normative and process approaches. Normative models seek to characterize the behaviour of an ideally rational decision maker. The simplest normative model, the expected value maximization model, clearly does not fit individual behaviour. This is partly because the subjective value (utility) of money, say, is not a simple linear function of money amounts and people tend to over-weight very small probabilities and under-weight high probabilities. The prospect theory approach fits much of the data including the effects of framing which lead to violations of basic principles of rationality such as invariance (Tversky & Kahneman, 1981).

In the case of multi-attribute decision making, the load of processing differing attributes into an overall value measure leads to suboptimal but simple strategies such as elimination-by-aspects and satisficing. Use of elimination-by-aspects, at least as an initial stage in multi-attribute decision problems, has been shown by Payne (1976; Payne et al., 1993).

Since risky decisions require that decision makers take account of probabilities, the question of how people handle probability information has been tackled in a number of studies. Tversky and Kahneman (1974, 1983) have provided many demonstrations of how inappropriate usage of heuristics such as availability, representativeness and ignoring of base rates can lead to misjudgements of likelihood and to violations of laws of probability, such as the extension rule. However, it seems that if problems are posed in terms of frequencies rather than probabilities most responses are quite accurate.

Gigerenzer (1993, 2007) has stressed the generally beneficial aspects of real-life heuristics such as the recognition heuristic which allow effective decision making with little effort (fast-and-frugal heuristics). Studies of real-life decision making using the naturalistic decision making approach also support the real life prevalence of fast-and-frugal heuristics, such as take-the-first option thought of in a given situation.

Studies of the neural bases of decision making indicate the frequent use of emotion-based heuristics and the involvement of System 2, deliberative processes, in over-riding impulsive, impatient and emotion-based choices.

Review questions

1 To what extent are people rational decision makers?

2 What are the relative roles of System 1 and System 2 processes in decision making?

3 Compare and contrast Tversky and Kahneman's heuristics and biases approach with Gigerenzer and colleagues' fast-and-frugal heuristics approach.

4 What problems do people have when dealing with probabilities?

5 Why does converting probability questions into frequency questions help people get the right answers?

6 What role do 'gut-feelings' play in decision making?

7 Do neuroscience approaches increase our understanding of decision making?

FURTHER READING

Gigerenzer, G. (2007). *Gut feelings.* London: Allen Lane.

Herbert, W. (2011). *On second thought: Outsmarting your mind's hardwired habits.* New York: Random House.

Kahneman, D. (2011). *Thinking, fast and slow.* New York: Allen Lane.

Newell, B. R., Lagnado, D. A., & Shanks, D. R. (2007). *Straight choices: The psychology of decision making.* Hove: Psychology Press.

CHAPTER 11:
REASONING

Preview questions

1. Are people rational thinkers?
2. Why do we often leap to conclusions?
3. Why do apparently simple reasoning tasks lead to so many errors?
4. Has evolution programmed us to be very good at reasoning about social contracts and cheating?
5. Why is it hard to seek out and deal with evidence against our beliefs?
6. Do scientists show biases in their thinking in the same way as lay people?

INTRODUCTION

Reasoning processes extract new information from already established pieces of knowledge and so are very useful in many areas of life. Reasoning is one of the ways in which information is used and so its study has become an important part of cognitive psychology. We will start introducing the topic with some examples of reasoning in action, before going on to more general points about reasoning and its study. First, a famous example of reasoning, featuring Sherlock Holmes:

> Reasoning is the cognitive process of deriving new information from old information.

> *'Is there any point to which you would wish to draw my attention?'*
>
> *'To the curious incident of the dog in the night-time.'*
>
> *'The dog did nothing in the night-time.'*
>
> *'That was the curious incident,'* remarked Sherlock Holmes.
>
> (A. C. Doyle, *Silver Blaze*, 1892)

In the *Silver Blaze* story, a racehorse of that name disappears from its Dartmoor stable one dark night, despite a guard dog being in the stable. Moreover, the horse's trainer is found dead not far away, on the moor. As a crucial step in solving the mystery, Holmes engages in reasoning, which we may reconstruct as follows:

Someone entered the stable and led Silver Blaze away.

If a stranger enters a place guarded by a guard dog, then the guard dog will bark.

The guard dog in the stable did not bark.

Therefore, whoever entered the stable and led Silver Blaze away was not a stranger.

This piece of reasoning reduced the number of suspects to one and the case was solved.

We do not have to be Sherlock Holmes to reason and, in fact, reasoning is pervasive in our thinking although in simple cases it may be so automatic as not to be recognized as such.

For example, suppose you are waiting for a friend who is arriving by train and has agreed to call you on arriving at the station. At the expected time she does not call. You conclude she has not yet arrived. The reasoning pattern would be similar to that of Holmes in the case of Silver Blaze:

If my friend has arrived she will call.

She has not called.

Therefore, she has not arrived.

Scan to watch animation on inductive and deductive reasoning

During the rest of this chapter we will be reviewing research and theory on how people derive new information from old information through reasoning. Why is this of interest? One reason is that people who can correctly derive new information by reasoning do well on tests of general ability or intelligence and in turn do better in education and in the occupational world (Stanovich, 1999). So, understanding reasoning will help us understand an important individual difference. Secondly, reasoning processes, which serve to produce new knowledge from existing knowledge, are crucially involved in many real-world occupations, such as law and science (see Boxes 11.3 and 11.6) and detection (as in the Sherlock Holmes example above). So, the study of reasoning is relevant to many real-world occupations and activities.

Deductive reasoning is drawing logically necessary conclusions from given information.
Inductive reasoning is the process of inferring probable conclusions from given information.
Premises are statements assumed to be true from which conclusions are drawn.
Valid arguments are those in which the conclusions must be true if the premises are true.
Propositional reasoning is reasoning about statements connected by logical relations such as 'and' 'or', 'not', 'if'.

DEDUCTIVE REASONING

The reasoning problems discussed in this chapter can be broadly classed as deductive and inductive tasks respectively. Inductive reasoning is concerned with establishing the likely truth or falsity of statements in the light of evidence. We will initially consider deductive tasks and explain inductive reasoning in later sections.

In deductive tasks, people are required to determine what conclusions, if any, *must* follow when they are given statements that are *assumed* to be true. For example, if we take it as true that 'All statistics lectures are extremely interesting' and that 'Today's 9 am lecture is a statistics lecture', it *must* be true that 'Today's 9 am lecture is extremely interesting'. The conclusion is true only if the assumptions (known as premises) are themselves true and the argument is valid. Deductive reasoning is of two types. The first is propositional reasoning, which deals with simple statements linked by logical relationships such as *if, and, not, or*. For example, 'If it's Tuesday then there's a psychology tutorial' and 'There is not a psychology tutorial today' leads with certainty to the conclusion 'Today is not Tuesday'. (Note that the pattern of reasoning here is the same as used by Sherlock Holmes in the story of the dog that did not bark in the night.) The second type of deductive reasoning is *syllogistic reasoning* which deals with statements about groups related by terms such as *all* and *some*. For example, 'All apples are red things' and 'Some apples are sweet' leads to a conclusion through syllogistic reasoning that 'Some red things are sweet'.

> **Syllogistic reasoning** is reasoning about groups/sets using statements connected by logical relations of 'some', 'none', 'all' and 'some not'.

The topics of deductive and inductive reasoning are very closely related and both have been extensively studied in recent years. In the case of both deductive and inductive reasoning, clear normative theories of how these tasks should be tackled have been developed by logicians over the centuries and human performance can then be compared to these ideal benchmarks. As we shall see there are frequent departures from the normative benchmarks when people tackle reasoning tasks, which leads to questions about the extent to which people are completely logical or rational in their thinking.

In the remainder of this chapter we will look both at research involving formal reasoning tasks and real-life reasoning as found in science, law and medicine. We start with deductive reasoning dealing with propositions, move on to syllogisms and then discuss inductive reasoning involving testing and generating hypotheses.

PROPOSITIONAL REASONING

Propositional logic is a set of rules devised by logicians which enable valid arguments to be developed. This form of logic concerns arguments consisting of sequences of simple statements linked by logical relations such as *and, or, not* and *if . . . then* (also known as the *conditional rule*). For example, given 'If it's Wednesday, then I eat fish', and 'It's Wednesday', what follows? For most people it is obvious that 'I eat fish' follows. But if the second statement is 'I am not eating fish today', many people find the conclusion ('It's not Wednesday') harder to draw. A considerable research effort, which we review later in this chapter, has gone into looking at how people handle propositional reasoning tasks and the extent to which human reasoning matches propositional logic or not.

Logicians have developed *inference rules* that can be used to derive correct conclusions from patterns of propositions, such that different patterns trigger different inference rules. Three examples of inference rules are as follows:

> **Inference rules** are rules for reaching a conclusion given a particular pattern of propositions, e.g. *modus ponens* which states that given 'If p then q' and 'not q' we can infer 'not p'.

1 *Modus ponens* (from the Latin for 'mode of affirming') states that given 'If p then q' and given p is true, it follows that q is true. For example, 'If it's Saturday then I go to the cinema'; 'It's Saturday'; 'Therefore, I go to the cinema'.

2 *Modus tollens* (from the Latin for 'Mode of denying'): given 'If p then q' and given 'not-q'; therefore, not-p follows. For example, 'If it's Saturday then I go to the cinema'; 'I am not going to the cinema today'; 'Therefore, today is not Saturday'.

3 *Double negation*: not (not p); therefore, p. For example, 'It is not not Saturday'; 'Therefore, it's Saturday'.

The conditional ('if . . . then') rule has attracted much research in the psychological study of reasoning. As we have seen above, there are two valid inference patterns involving such rules (viz., *modus ponens* and *modus tollens*). On the other side of the coin, there are two main mistakes or fallacies when arguing from conditionals and these are:

1 *Affirming the consequent*: arguing from 'If p then q' and 'q' that 'p' is true. For example, 'If it's Saturday then Sue goes to the cinema'; 'Sue is going to the cinema'; 'Therefore, it's Saturday'. This is an invalid inference because the rule does not mean Sue only goes to the cinema on a Saturday.

2 *Denying the antecedent*: arguing from 'If p then q' and 'not p' that 'not q' is true. For example, 'If it's Saturday then Sue goes to the cinema'; 'It's not Saturday'; 'Therefore, Sue is not going to the cinema today.' This is an invalid inference because the rule does not mean Sue only goes to the cinema on a Saturday.

Before going on to discuss results from studies of human reasoning, we should mention that the type of 'if . . . then' conditional discussed so far is known as *material implication* and that there is a different form of conditional, that is, the 'if and only if' rule of *equivalence* (also known as the *biconditional*). For example, 'A closed figure is a triangle if and only if it has exactly three sides' is an equivalence rule. In the case of equivalence, from 'q if and only if p', one can validly assert 'p' given 'q' (affirming the consequent) and 'not-q' given 'not-p' (denying the antecedent). That is, in the example, if a closed figure is a triangle, then it has three sides and if it does not have three sides it is not a triangle. Thus, affirming the consequent and denying the antecedent are valid arguments if the rule is one of equivalence but not if the rule is one of material implication. Misinterpretation of material implication as equivalence is a possible source of error in conditional reasoning.

Basic results

A number of studies have examined performance with conditionals involving both abstract materials (e.g. 'If there is an A then there is a 7') and concrete materials (e.g. 'If it is Wednesday then Mr Jones eats fish at 3 am'). Participants have been asked to say whether each of the four possible arguments *modus tollens, modus ponens*, affirming the consequent and denying the antecedent are valid for such arguments. We can summarize results from a wide range of studies (e.g. Evans, 1977; Marcus and Rips, 1979; Markovits, 1988; Schroyens, 2010; Taplin, 1971), by saying that people typically perform with near 100 per cent accuracy in the case of *modus ponens*, and about 60 per cent accuracy on *modus tollens*. About a quarter of the time people correctly reject the two fallacies, affirming the consequent and denying the antecedent. Typical results are shown in Figure 11.1.

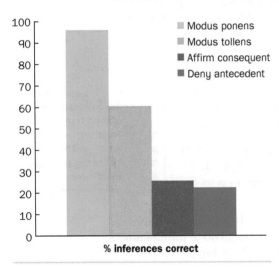

Figure 11.1 Typical percentage correct responses for the four main conditional arguments. Good performance on *modus ponens*, fair performance on *modus tollens* and high error rates on affirming consequent and denying antecedent.

Source: Adapted from Marcus, S. L. and Rips, L. J. (1979). Conditional reasoning. *Journal of Verbal Learning and Verbal Behaviour, 18*, 199–233.

Suppression effects

It has been suggested that what are usually classed as fallacies in conditional reasoning could result from misinterpretations of the premises (Rumain et al., 1983). For example, given the premise, 'If there is a dog in the box, then there is an orange in the box', participants may assume this also means 'If there is not a dog in the box then there is not an orange in the box'. Interpreting the 'if . . . then' relationship as equivalence, conclusions that would be fallacies under the intended conditional interpretation now follow validly; so, 'there is not a dog' implies 'there is not an orange' and 'there is an orange' implies 'there is a dog', on the equivalence interpretation. However, Rumain et al. found that giving participants additional antecedents, such as 'If there is a tiger in the box then there is an orange in the box', makes it clear that dogs are not required for there to be an orange in the box and so block equivalence interpretations and thus *suppress* the fallacies of affirming the consequent and denying the antecedent.

Later studies have found that some kinds of additional antecedents also block valid inferences on the bases of *modus ponens* and *modus tollens* (Byrne, 1989). In these studies, Byrne used pairs of conditional statements such that the second statement was an additional condition, for example:

* If she meets her friend then she will go to a play.
* If she has enough money then she will go to a play.

When participants were given the above dual premises and were told that 'She meets her friend', they were unsure whether she had gone to the play and the rate of correct *modus ponens* conclusions was far lower than with the single conditional premise (i.e. 'If she meets her friend then she will go to a play'). Similarly, when given as true that 'She did not go to the play' the rate of valid *modus tollens* conclusions also dropped sharply. It seems that they are now unsure why she did not go to the play. It is as if the extra premises are interpreted as forming a conjunctive condition with the first premise (e.g. to make 'If she meets her friend *and* she has enough money, then she will go to the play'). These studies indicate the importance of premise interpretation and how surrounding context can affect interpretations and so influence reasoning.

Mental logic approaches

David Braine proposed that people have mental logic rules that they can apply to solving reasoning problems. Braine et al. (1984) argued that people generally have available a set of mental inference rules (or *schemas* in their terminology) that permit direct inferences when the schema conditions are met. The schemas typically match some rules of logic (such as *modus ponens*) but may not include others (such as *modus tollens*). The mental rules/schemas may also include fallacious inferences, such as denying the antecedent. Thus, the schemas may or may not match the formal inference rules discussed earlier. The schemas take the form of 'Premises → Conclusion'. For example, one schema ('disjunctive syllogism') may be represented as:

* Premises: p *or* q; *not* p
* Conclusion: *therefore*, q.

Thus, given any two statements whatsoever, represented by p and q, if it is true that either p or q or both are true and not p is also true, it follows that q must be true. For example, 'It's Saturday or Sue goes to the cinema'; 'It's not Saturday'; 'Therefore, Sue goes to the cinema'.

Braine et al. (1984) proposed some 16 simple inference schemas on which people make few errors. When given problems that should directly evoke particular individual schemas they generally rate these schemas as being unproblematic. The proposal is that given information such as 'Either I will go out or I will study' and 'I will not go out' the appropriate schema (disjunctive syllogism) is evoked and by applying it, the conclusion 'I will study' is reached.

In an experiment carried out to test and explore Braine et al.'s (1984) mental logic theory that people reason by applying rules in the form of schemas, participants were presented with premises on a computer monitor, one line at a time at a speed they determined and finally they were shown a proposed possible conclusion which they had to judge as true or false. An example problem is as follows:

1 There is an L or a W.

2 If there is an L then there's not an E.

3 If there is a W then there's not an E.

4 There is an E or an O.

Is there is an O?

(Answer is 'Yes, there is an O'.)

As you can see, the tasks required application of more than one schema. From the first three lines above, it can be concluded that there is not an E. Using that conclusion, we can infer from line 4 that there is an O.

Braine et al. argued that participants' ratings of problem difficulty would depend on the length of the problem in words and on the difficulty of the schemas used in solving the problem. As expected, they found that problem length and rated schema difficulty did contribute separately to rated problem difficulty. Overall, Braine et al.'s mental logic theory, that people reason using a limited number of schemas, met with a good measure of support from their experiments.

Mental models

Mental models approach is the view that people tackle logical reasoning problems by forming mental representations of possible states of the world and draw inferences from those representations.

In the mental models approach (Johnson-Laird, 2008; Johnson-Laird and Byrne, 1991; Johnson-Laird et al., 1992), the basic notion is that the meaning of connectives (*and, or, if,* etc.) can be represented by mental representations of possible states of the world, known as mental models. What is meant by mental models should become clearer by considering a participant's report on how he had thought about the premise 'All the artists are beekeepers' (*note: this is equivalent to 'if people are artists, then they are beekeepers'*). The participant reported, 'I thought of all the little artists in the room and imagined that they all had beekeepers' hats on' (Johnson-Laird and Steedman, 1978, p. 77). This self-report suggested to Johnson-Laird the hypothesis that a class of things (e.g. 'artists') can be represented by thinking of a few examples. So, to represent the above premise, the reasoner imagines a small number of artists (e.g. people with paintbrushes) and tags each of them as a beekeeper by adding a beekeeper's hat to each image of them. Since the sets of artists and beekeepers are not identical the reasoner should add a few beekeepers without paintbrushes who are therefore not linked to artists in the representation.

Deductive propositional reasoning then begins with the construction of one or more mental models which represent the first premise. One source of variation lies in how completely the models are developed to take all possibilities into account. For instance, '*if* a person is an artist *then* that person is a beekeeper' may be initially represented just as:

a Artist – beekeeper.

So, if we are now told that 'Smith is an artist', the conclusion 'Smith is a beekeeper' can be drawn (*modus ponens*). However, the simple one-model representation will mean we cannot draw a conclusion if told there is someone who is not a beekeeper. To draw a conclusion from 'denial of the consequent', the representation must include two models and would look like the version below:

a Artist – beekeeper

b Not beekeeper – not artist.

As an argument is built up, premises are added and the set of models is modified until a conclusion is drawn from the final set of models. Mental models, it is argued, offer economical forms of representation that appear psychologically plausible. Johnson-Laird (1999, p. 116) proposed that models are built in accordance with the principle of truth, and wrote: 'Individuals minimise the load on working memory by tending to construct mental models that represent explicitly only what is true and not what is false.' Thus, mental model representations tend to be incomplete from the strictly logical point of view (since they tend not to represent what the logic of the premises rules out as not true) and this incompleteness is a source of error in dealing with reasoning tasks.

Incomplete mental models can explain the striking phenomenon of 'illusory inferences' which are seemingly compelling, but invalid inferences. Consider the following situation:

> Either Jane is kneeling by the fire and she is looking at the TV or else Mark is standing at the window and he is peering into the garden.
>
> Jane is kneeling by the fire.

Does it follow that Jane is looking at the TV?

Did you say 'yes'? Most people do say 'yes' to this question (Johnson-Laird, 2006: Legrenzi et al., 2003).

However, the inference is not valid; it is an example of an illusory inference. Simply because Jane is kneeling by the fire, it does not follow that she is looking at the TV; she may be, but it is not *necessarily* the case.

Johnson-Laird argues that the principle of truth leads people to form models in which the possibility of it being false that she is both kneeling and watching TV is not represented and this principle explains the illusory inference.

Johnson-Laird et al. (1992) applied his mental models theory to over 60 problems used by Braine et al. (1984) and found that the number of mental models needed per problem correlated highly ($r = 0.73$) with rated problem difficulty reported by Braine et al. (1984). Thus, the results are consistent with the notion that the more models required for a correct deduction the harder the task will be.

Other tests of the theory have concerned the basic phenomena of '*if . . . then*' reasoning. The theory is consistent with the usual finding that *modus ponens* is easier than *modus tollens* for conditionals because modus ponens requires only one model while *modus tollens* requires three models.

Further data reported by Johnson-Laird et al. (1992), found that as predicted on the basis of the number of models involved, exclusive disjunctions (i.e. '*p or q, but not both*') were harder than conditionals and that *modus tollens* was easier with biconditionals (or equivalences) than with conditionals.

Evaluation of mental models versus mental logic

Johnson-Laird et al. (1992) stated that the mental models theory has the virtue of being falsifiable which is a desirable property of any scientific theory. The mental models approach 'is in principle simple to refute: an easy deduction that depends on many models violates its principal prediction' (p. 436). In response, mental logic theorists, O'Brien et al. (1994) presented results from tasks that would appear to require many models, but which participants handled well. For example, consider the following problem:

If O or K or R or C then X

If E or F or G or H then Y

K

F.

What follows?

In O'Brien et al.'s study 100 per cent of participants answered correctly, 'X and Y', although the problem involves 58 mental models. In response, Johnson-Laird et al. (1994) argued that participants would not blindly generate models unnecessarily but would realize that only a small part of the premises needs to be represented, which could be done with a manageable number of models. However, this means adding procedures to the model to enable participants to know when models are unnecessary and makes the approach less straightforward than initially seemed.

Although both mental logic and mental models approaches have had reasonable success in dealing with propositional reasoning, the mental models approach, as we shall see, also applies readily to the next type of reasoning, syllogistic reasoning, which we now consider in the following section.

Box 11.1 When Things Go Wrong: The case of mental illness and reasoning

Obsessive-compulsive disorder, anxiety and depression are three common forms of mental illness and are examples of neuroses which are disorders of behaviour and feeling. One view of neuroses is that they are due to faulty reasoning either from invalid inferences or from false beliefs and this is the basis of Beck's (1976, 1991) influential cognitive-behavioural therapy. (See also Box 14.7.) An example of a typical invalid inference (affirming the consequent) that a depressed person might make without realizing that it is invalid, is: 'If you're worthless then you fail at everything'; 'I failed my exam'; 'So, I am worthless'.

In contrast to the cognitive-behavioural approach, Johnson-Laird et al. (2006) proposed that neuroses originated in overemotional reactions to situations (the hyper-emotion theory) and that reasoning errors were not a key factor in such mental illnesses. They argued that if anything, neurotic patients should reason better about material related to their disorder than controls, because the patients tended to be very preoccupied with their condition and mulled over material related to their condition very often.

To test this idea, Johnson-Laird et al. (2006) tested three groups – controls, obsessive-compulsives and depressives – with materials relating to guilt or sadness or neutral topics. The tasks presented participants with a short background story followed by a proposition for which they were to list all possible states of affairs consistent with the proposition. An example would be the proposition:

The alarm rings or I feel tired or both.

Participants were to list possible combinations of being tired and the alarm ringing or not, given the proposition was true. The correct listing would be:

The alarm rings and I don't feel tired. The alarm does not ring and I feel tired. The alarm rings and I feel tired.

Participants were also asked to list what was impossible. In this case, that 'The alarm does not ring and I do not feel tired'.

The obsessive-compulsives, the depressives and the controls performed equally well with this neutral material.

Participants were also given the following short story:

> Suppose I am at my house with some friends. We decide to join some other friends in a bar. We leave the house joking among ourselves, but I forget to close the bathroom window.

Then, they were asked to list possibilities and impossibilities for either:

> The burglar alarm rings and I feel guilty.
>
> *or*
>
> The burglar alarm rings and I feel depressed.

The results (see Figure 11.2) showed that the obsessive-compulsives did better (63 per cent correct) than depressives or controls on the 'guilt' test sentence (21 and 23 per cent respectively) but the depressives did better (66 per cent) than obsessive-compulsives (7 per cent) or controls (27 per cent) on the 'depression' test sentence. So it seems that, contrary to common sense and to Beck's theory (1991) a tendency to a particular mental illness can enhance reasoning about matters related to that specific mental illness.

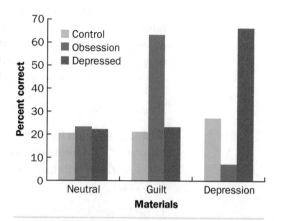

Figure 11.2   Pattern of per cent correct results in reasoning about neutral, guilt and depression related materials by normal controls, obsessive-compulsive and depressed patients. Depressives have advantage in reasoning about depression related material and obsessive compulsives have advantage in reasoning about guilt related material.

Source: Adapted from Johnson-Laird, P. N., Mancini, J. L., & Gangemi, A. (2006). A hyper-emotion theory of psychological illnesses. *Psychological Review, 113,* 822–841.

SYLLOGISTIC REASONING

A fairly common type of deductive problem, even in everyday thinking, is to determine what conclusion, if any, follows from assumptions about category membership. Such problems are known as categorical syllogisms and represent the other main type of deductive reasoning, after propositional reasoning, which we discussed in the previous sections. Syllogisms have been frequently used in laboratory studies of reasoning and their main features may be conveyed by a few examples. Consider the following:

> All dogs have whiskers
>
> All terriers are dogs
>
> Therefore, all terriers have whiskers.

In this problem we have to determine what conclusion, if any, follows from assumptions about categories of things, 'terriers', 'dogs', and properties such as 'having whiskers'. In this example about dogs, since the third statement (the conclusion) definitely follows necessarily from the first two (the premises) this is a *valid* syllogistic argument that leads to a true conclusion and may be compared with:

> All cats are mammals
>
> All dogs are mammals
>
> Therefore, all dogs are cats.

In this case the conclusion plainly does not follow from the (true) premises and the form of the argument is *invalid*.

In addition to validity, syllogisms can be varied in many ways for experimental purposes. For example, they may be varied by changing the quantifiers ('some', 'all') used in the argument; the terms may be abstract or concrete; the premises and conclusion may be negative or affirmative; the propositions in the argument may be empirically true or false, and so on. Clearly, many features of the task can be readily manipulated. A number of variations are also possible in the response requirements. Participants can be asked to generate valid inferences from given premises; to judge a possible conclusion as valid or not; or to select a valid conclusion from a list of alternatives.

Basic findings from syllogistic reasoning studies

Some of the main factors associated with the difficulty of syllogisms, such as beneficial effects of concrete material as against abstract material, were established in very early studies (Wilkins, 1928). Consider the following argument about abstract letters. Is it valid?

> All Cs are Ms
>
> All Ds are Ms
>
> Therefore, all Ds are Cs.

This abstract argument may well be accepted, even though it follows the same invalid pattern as a previous concrete example, that led from true premises to the conclusion that 'all dogs are cats'. Try substituting 'Cats' for Cs, 'Dogs' for Ds and 'Mammals' for Ms and the invalidity should be clear.

Atmosphere effect is a tendency to draw conclusions in syllogisms that are over influenced by the form of the premises rather than the logic of the argument.

Wilkins found that although concrete premises led to better performance, even in the case of concrete syllogisms, participants accepted many invalid conclusions. Why might this be so? A controversial proposal is that there is an atmosphere effect which leads participants to accept invalid conclusions that are similar to the premises. For example, if both premises are of the form 'All . . . are . . .' people are inclined to accept a conclusion of the form 'All . . . are . . .'. We will now discuss the atmosphere effect.

The atmosphere effect

To account for common errors in syllogistic reasoning, Woodworth and Sells (1935) hypothesized an 'atmosphere' effect which predicted that the form of the premises would influence people's expectations about the form of the conclusion. In particular, they proposed that if *both* premises involve 'all', people are disposed to accepting an 'all' conclusion. If any *one* premise involves 'some', people will be disposed to a 'some' conclusion. If any *one* premise involves 'not', people are disposed to accept a 'not' conclusion. The argument below is often accepted by participants as valid as the atmosphere hypothesis would predict.

> All Cs are Ms
>
> All Ds are Ms
>
> Therefore, all Ds are Cs.

The above argument is invalid (substitute cats for Cs, dogs for Ds and mammals for Ms to make invalidity clear). However, the abstract version is often accepted as valid by participants and so are many other invalid arguments (Sells, 1935; Sells & Koob, 1937).

Atmosphere versus conversion errors (illicit conversion) and probabilistic inference

An alternative to the atmosphere hypothesis was put forward by Chapman and Chapman (1959) who proposed that people applied heuristics which were not appropriate (known as 'conversion' and 'probabilistic inference'). These terms will be explained below, but first let us look at the Chapmans' results from giving participants a number of syllogisms that did not have any valid conclusions, e.g.:

Some Ls are Ks

Some Ks are Ms

Therefore, (1) No Ms are Ls, (2) Some Ms are Ls, (3) Some Ms are not Ls, (4) None of these, (5) All Ms are Ls. (The correct conclusion is (4) 'None of these'.)

Participants tended to be wrong on these items and the kind of error that they made depended on the form of syllogism. The study used different types of syllogism and the atmosphere effect predicted the preferred errors on many of these; but it failed on syllogisms that involved premises of the following type:

(A)

Some X are Y

No Y are Z

and

(B)

Some X are not Y

No Y are Z.

The predicted response for both (on atmosphere) is 'Some Z are not X' but in fact participants tended to choose 'No Z are X', especially on (A), but split fairly evenly between the universal and the particular conclusions on (B). The Chapmans proposed that their results could be better explained by the operation of two reasoning errors called 'conversion' and 'probabilistic inference'. There are two conversion errors. These are to assume (1) from 'All X are Y' that 'All Y are X' and (2) that 'Some As are not Bs' implies 'Some Bs are not As'. Using concrete versions makes the errors clear. 'All women are human' does not imply that 'All humans are women'. Again, 'Some humans are not politicians' does not imply that 'Some politicians are not humans'. The Chapmans argued that participants tend to make conversions unless they have information to the contrary (which they do not have with abstract material). Probabilistic inference involved 'plausible reasoning' that is not valid in deductive logic, so people will tend to argue that 'Some cloudy days are wet', 'Some wet days are unpleasant', and so 'Some cloudy days are unpleasant'. The conclusion could be true but it does not necessarily follow even if the premises are true. The Chapmans reported that these two errors accounted better for their data than did the atmosphere hypothesis.

In 1969, Begg and Denny re-examined the atmosphere versus illicit conversion issue with new experimental results and reported that atmosphere predicted the data very well. They also re-analysed the data from earlier studies (Sells, 1936; Chapman & Chapman, 1959) and found that there was considerable consistency among the various data sets and that, overall, the atmosphere predictions were more often upheld than the conversion and probabilistic inference predictions. Begg and Denny emphasized that although their results do support the use of the atmosphere 'formula' as a convenient predictor of error patterns their study was not decisive about the underlying processes that lead people into error.

Wason and Johnson-Laird (1972) made other observations which suggested that the atmosphere hypothesis cannot be the complete explanation of syllogistic reasoning. For example, from Sells's data, when participants are given:

All B are A

All C are B

they accept the correct conclusion 'All C are A', *twice* as often as the incorrect conclusion 'All A are C' although both are equally predicted by the atmosphere hypothesis. Again, Wilkins's (1928) data shows that the atmosphere effect is weaker with familiar as opposed to abstract or unfamiliar material and the atmosphere hypothesis does not explain this difference. Another attack on the atmosphere hypothesis that has been influential was developed by Henle (1962) and this will be discussed next.

Henle on 'rationality'

How rational are people in their reasoning? The atmosphere hypothesis and the ideas of probabilistic inference and illicit conversion suggest major shortfalls from rationality. A contrary view was put forward by Mary Henle (1962) who argued for the essential rationality of everyday thinking. Henle proposed that many apparent instances of illogical thinking involve the implicit introduction of additional premises, the ignoring of some of the given premises and the misinterpretation of still other premises – but she claimed, the inferences people make are generally rational, given how they have interpreted the premises. Henle illustrated her points with responses given by a sample of graduate students to syllogisms that might be encountered in everyday life, e.g.:

> It's important to talk about things that are in our minds.
>
> We spend so much of our time in the kitchen that household problems are in our minds.
>
> Therefore, it's important to talk about household problems.

Participants were asked to assess the validity of the argument, and give their reasons. Henle found that some participants *did not accept the task* as an exercise in pure logic, and did not distinguish logical validity from factual truth: for example, 'No, it's not important to talk about things in our minds unless they worry us'.

Interestingly, this type of response, in which the task is not accepted as a purely logical exercise, is actually fairly typical of people from cultures with little formal education. A number of participants interpreted the premises or the conclusion so that the intended meaning was changed. Participants sometimes ignored entire premises: for example, 'I don't think of household problems so it's not important for me to talk about them'.

Occasionally participants introduced premises that had not been given: for example, 'It's only important to talk about things that really worry us a lot and household problems don't; so it's not important to talk about them.'

Henle (1962) concluded:

> that when subjects arrive at apparently invalid conclusions, or when they fail to spot a fallacy, they often do so because they have worked with materials different from those intended or because they have undertaken a task different from the one intended. In such cases, if we consider the materials and task as they were actually understood by individual subjects, we fail to find evidence of faulty reasoning. It must be concluded that the presence of error does not constitute evidence that the laws of logic are irrelevant to actual thinking. The data tend, rather, to support the older conception that these laws are widely discernible in the thinking process.

Henle made a useful point in stressing the effects of the different ways in which participants can interpret task materials and goals. It is easy to assume that people interpret a task exactly as the experimenter intends, but then go on to make extraordinary errors in reasoning. Taking account of possible interpretations may well make people's behaviour more understandable, and may indicate that they have followed logical steps, but based on interpretations different from those intended by the experimenter. Later studies (Ceraso & Provitera, 1971; Begg & Harris, 1982; Newstead & Griggs, 1983) found that many participants misinterpreted traditional premises, but went on to make valid inferences based on the premises as they had understood them. Ceraso and Provitera (1971) examined the role of interpretation by using syllogisms in which the premises were given very clear interpretations. So, instead of simply being told, 'Some As are Bs', participants were told 'Some of the As (but not all) are Bs, but all of the Bs are As'. Another group were given the traditional syllogism statements. People given the clarified premises performed much better than did a traditionally instructed group.

Culture and logic

> In the far North all bears are white.
>
> Novaya Zembla is in the far North.
>
> What colour are the bears there?

You may readily deduce that the bears are white in Novaya Zembla. In contrast, Luria (1971) in a study of non-literate peasants in Soviet Central Asia found that many participants simply did not accept the task as an exercise in decontextualized logic but insisted on tackling it as a real request for solid contextualized real-world information. A typical response was as follows:

> But I don't know what kind of bears are there. I have not been there and I don't know. Look, why don't you ask old man X, he was there and he knows. He will tell you.

Similarly Cole (1971) gave the following deductive task to non-literate Kpelle adults in rural Liberia:

> At one time Spider went to a feast. He was told to answer this question before he could eat any of the food. The question is: Spider and black deer always eat together. Spider is eating. Is black deer eating?

For schooled participants this is an easy question of conjunctive logic. For the non-literate Kpelle it was a question of fact with no obvious answer and a typical Kpelle respondent handled it as follows (Cole, 1971, p. 187):

> Participant: 'Were they in the bush?'
>
> Experimenter: 'Yes.'
>
> Participant: 'They were eating together?'
>
> Experimenter: 'Spider and black deer always eat together. Spider is eating. Is black deer eating?'
>
> Participant: 'But I was not there. How can I answer such a question?'
>
> Eventually the participant stated that the black deer was eating – but gave the following non-logic based reason:
>
> 'The reason is that black deer always walks about all day eating green leaves in the bush. When it rests for a while it gets up again and goes to eat.'

Among other things, this answer indicates that just because someone gives the correct answer to a reasoning problem, that does not mean the answer was reached by applying rules of logic.

Greenfield (2005) explains such findings by Cole and Luria in terms of a *collectivistic* versus an *individualistic* cultural mindset. The collectivistic mindset is typical of preindustrial societies which are largely rural and lack formal education. This mindset stresses practical and contextualized knowledge to be used in real social settings against theoretical abstract knowledge to be used in artificial classroom settings. Formal education tends to induce an individualistic mindset in which the existence of different points of view is recognized and formal abstract knowledge of rules and principles (as found in science and mathematics for example) is valued. The individualistic mindset is typical of industrialized, largely urban and formally educated populations. Although by some counts, roughly 70 per cent of the world's population are collectivist (Triandis, 1989), Greenfield (2005) points out that both tendencies are present with varying strength in many people, for example, those who have been born into a strongly collectivist group but migrated when young to a big city and received some schooling. Even in highly individualistic societies such as in North America or the United Kingdom, religions generally stress communitarian collectivist values and both tendencies will be present in many people. By using suitable priming methods the less dominant mindset can be evoked, that is individualism in the case of Asians and collectivism in North Americans (Gardner et al., 1999).

Mental-model approaches to syllogisms

Four figures of syllogism are the four possible layouts of terms which give four syllogistic figures, i.e. A-B, B-C; B-A, B-C; A-B, C-B; B-A, C-B.

A series of studies by Johnson-Laird and his colleagues (Johnson-Laird, 1975; Johnson-Laird & Steedman, 1978) revealed an interesting effect due to the figure of the syllogism. (The figure of a syllogism refers to the way the three terms A, B and C are laid out. There are four possible figures i.e. A-B, B-C; B-A, B-C; A-B, C-B; B-A, C-B, and these layouts affect what valid conclusions are preferred.)

In the experiments, participants had to draw conclusions from syllogistic premises dealing with concrete but uncontroversial matters, for example, 'Some of the parents are scientists; all of the scientists are drivers; therefore . . . ?' This particular syllogism in which the topic-term has not been specified (is it about parents or about drivers?) tended to elicit the conclusion 'Some of the parents are drivers' rather than the equally valid 'Some of the drivers are parents'. While, on the other hand, the premises 'Some of the scientists are parents; all of the drivers are scientists' would tend to elicit the conclusion 'Some of the drivers are parents' rather than the also valid 'Some of the parents are

Figural bias is the effect of figure on preferred conclusions.

drivers'. Indeed, throughout their experiments, premises of the form 'A-B; B-C' produced a bias towards conclusions of the form 'A-C' (even if 'C-A' conclusions were also valid). This strong effect was dubbed the figural bias effect.

The atmosphere hypothesis, and the conversion and probabilistic inference hypothesis, do not predict the figural bias effect. In view of this and other problems with the earlier approaches, Johnson-Laird and Steedman (1978) put forward the mental-models theory. As we have outlined this approach above in the discussion of propositional reasoning, only a brief recap will be given at this point.

The broad stages proposed by the theory are (1) interpretation of premises; (2) initial heuristic combination of the representations of the two premises; (3) formulation of a conclusion corresponding to the combination of premises; and (4) a logical test (or series of tests) of the initial heuristic combination, which may lead to the conclusion being modified or abandoned. In terms of broad stages, the main novelty over previous approaches is the provision of a final testing stage that can lead back to a changed combination of information in the premises which in turn may be tested again.

In the mental models approach, the premise representations are assumed to take the form of examples of the items in the premises. So, to represent the premise that 'All the drivers are scientists', participants imagine a few drivers and tag each of them as a scientist, by adding a white laboratory coat to each of them. Since the sets of drivers and scientists are not identical, participants should add a few scientists who are not driving to the representation.

Having representations of the individual premises, the next step is to combine them in some way. Johnson-Laird proposes that there is a heuristic bias towards forming connections that link up all the classes if possible. So, given:

All A are B

Some B are C

these would be combined to yield the invalid conclusion 'Some As are Cs' (and this conclusion is often made).

The mental models theory proposes a combination of premises to yield a tentative conclusion, followed by a logical testing process. Differences in persistence of testing preliminary conclusions would lead to differences in the conclusions finally drawn by different individuals to the same premises. The theory was expressed in the form of a computer program and its performance compared to that of human participants on a set of 64 problems. With some syllogisms the process of testing does not lead to any modifications (hence thoroughness of testing does not matter). Such syllogisms were predicted to be easier than those to which the model would produce a modified conclusion after testing. This prediction was upheld (80.4 per cent correct on predicted 'easy' problems vs. 46.5 per cent correct on others).

An explanation for figural bias is that it arises from the processes of combining premise representations in working memory. That is, with a syllogism of the form A-B, B-C, people encode the first premise and then add on to it a representation of the second premise (A-B, B-C) with a resulting bias toward a conclusion of the form A-C. In the case of B-A, C-B premises, since the middle terms are not adjacent, it would be necessary to store the second premise in working memory first, then encode the first premise to make the combination (C-B, B-A) giving a bias toward C-A conclusions.

Johnson-Laird and Bara (1984) obtained relevant data from an experiment concerning conclusions given to syllogisms that were presented for brief exposures (10 seconds). Even with this short exposure there were clear figural effects; more significantly, however, there were unpredicted effects, due to figure, on the frequency of responses indicating 'no valid conclusion'. The A-B, B-C figure yielded the fewest such responses and the B-A, B-C figure produced the most. With short presentations participants experience difficulty in making combinations of premises in certain figures (such as B-A, B-C, in which reordering of terms in one of the premises is needed to effect premise integration) and thus have a high rate of (incorrect) conclusions that 'no conclusion can be drawn'. It has also been pointed out (Johnson-Laird, 1983; Johnson-Laird & Bara, 1984) that for certain syllogisms two or three different combined models of the premises are possible and that all the possible models must be considered before a correct conclusion can be drawn. Johnson-Laird (1983, p. 104) reports data from studies which found that the rate of drawing correct conclusions declined sharply as the number of possible combined models increased from one to three. Johnson-Laird (1983) proposed that these results were due to the load on working memory (see Chapter 4 on short-term memory) occasioned when more than one model must be constructed and evaluated. Using dual task methods, Gilhooly et al. (1993, 1999, 2002) found support for the general notion that syllogisms load working memory, particularly the central executive and phonological loop components of the Baddeley-Hitch working memory model (Baddeley, 2000; also see Chapter 4). A broad range of studies, reviewed by Gilhooly (2005), also supported the view that difficult syllogisms heavily load working memory.

Box 11.2 Research Close Up: Believability, validity effects and dual process theory

Source: Evans, J. St. B. T., Barston, J. L. & Pollard, P. (1983). On the conflict between logic and belief in syllogistic reasoning. *Memory & Cognition, 11*, 295–306.

INTRODUCTION

Evans et al. (1983) investigated how the believability of a conclusion and argument validity might interact in affecting the acceptability of arguments as valid or not. In Evans et al.'s studies four type of argument, representing all combinations of valid versus invalid and believable versus unbelievable conclusions, were presented and participants had to say whether the conclusion necessarily followed *if the premises were accepted as true.*

METHOD

Participants were given examples of four types of argument as follows:

Valid argument, believable conclusion (no conflict)

No police dogs are vicious

Some highly trained dogs are vicious

Therefore some highly trained dogs are not police dogs

Valid argument, unbelievable conclusion (conflict)

No nutritional things are inexpensive

Some vitamin tablets are inexpensive

Therefore, some vitamin tablets are not nutritional

Invalid argument, believable conclusion (conflict)

No addictive things are inexpensive

Some cigarettes are inexpensive

Therefore, some addictive things are not cigarettes

Invalid argument, unbelievable conclusion (no conflict)

No millionaires are hard workers

Some rich people are hard workers

Therefore, some millionaires are not rich people

Participants indicated whether they accepted the conclusions or not.

RESULTS

The results shown in Figure 11.3 indicated that both the validity of the arguments and the believability of conclusions affected how likely people were to accept the conclusion as following from the premises. In addition, the two factors showed an interaction in that the effect of believability was stronger for invalid arguments as against valid arguments.

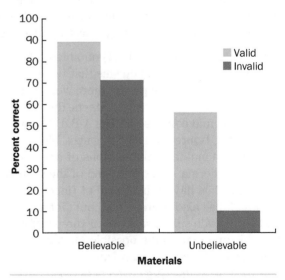

Figure 11.3   Percentage of arguments accepted as function of conclusion's believability and the logical validity of the argument.

Source: Adapted from data in Evans, J. St. B. T., Barston, J. L. & Pollard, P. (1983). On the conflict between logic and belief in syllogistic reasoning. *Memory & Cognition, 11*, 295–306.

DISCUSSION

From the results reported by Evans et al. (1983) presented in Figure 11.3, believability affects both valid and invalid syllogisms, but has a much larger effect on invalid syllogisms such that unbelievable conclusions are much more likely to be correctly rejected for invalid syllogisms than is the case with valid syllogisms. These results support the existence of belief bias in dealing with syllogisms. That is to say, invalid syllogisms with believable conclusions are likely to be accepted as valid, but valid syllogisms with unbelievable conclusions are likely to be rejected as invalid. This indicates that people tend to deal with syllogisms not as purely logical problems for which the believability of conclusions is irrelevant.

The belief bias effect has been interpreted in terms of the dual systems or processes approach to thinking (also discussed in relation to decision making in Chapter 10). In this approach (Evans, 2003, 2008), it is proposed that true reasoning is the province of System 2 which involves controlled sequential rule-following processes that heavily load working memory. Such processes would enable correct resolution of syllogisms which show belief–validity conflicts. System 1 thinking processes are rapid, parallel, automatic and reflect prior learning (and so beliefs). This system would produce automatic acceptance of believable conclusions irrespective of the validity of the argument. It is suggested that both systems are activated in syllogism tasks but in varying degrees for different individuals and task conditions.

Instructions that emphasize the logical nature of the task can reduce belief bias and opposite instructions can increase the effect (Evans, 2003). Thus, System 2 can over-ride System 1 when the goal requires exact and careful reasoning (Stanovich, 1999). Time pressure (Evans & Curtis-Holmes, 2005) and concurrent working memory load (De Neys, 2006) have both been found to increase belief bias and these findings can be explained as due to reduced time and resources limiting the use of System 2 as against System 1.

Neuroscience studies by Goel and colleagues (Goel, 2005; Goel & Dolan, 2003; Goel et al., 2000) using fMRI have found that different brain areas were active when dealing with syllogisms with real life content (and so prone to belief bias) as against abstract syllogisms of identical logic. Content based reasoning evoked activity in the left hemisphere temporal system whereas abstract tasks were associated with activity in the parietal cortex. In syllogism tasks involving belief-validity conflicts, similar to the syllogisms used by Evans (1983), Goel and colleagues found that logically correct judgements involved activity in the right inferior prefrontal cortex which they suggest is critical in detecting and resolving conflict (System 2), while incorrect judgements were associated with activity in the ventral medial prefrontal cortex, which they argue is associated with intuitive (System 1) responses. These results support the idea of two systems and also suggest a neural basis for the distinction.

Evaluation

Mental models theory is continually evolving and has been extended to a wide range of reasoning tasks (Johnson-Laird and Byrne, 1991, 1993a; Johnson-Laird, 2006, 2008). Although it is an impressive exercise in model-building some possible problems have been pointed out. For example, Wetherick and Gilhooly (1990) and Ford (1995) have indicated other possible explanations of figural bias and of the number-of-models effect on difficulty.

Wetherick and Gilhooly argued that figural bias may simply be due to people picking as the topic of the argument the first term which is the topic of its premise. So, if we are told 'All the scientists are drivers' and 'All the drivers are golfers' it is natural to take 'Scientists' to be the topic here and to draw a conclusion about scientists, 'All the scientists are golfers'. If the premises were 'Some drivers are golfers' and 'All the scientists are golfers' a conclusion in which 'drivers' was the topic ('Some drivers are scientists') would be more natural. Thus, the figural effect may arise from assumptions made about which term is the topic (scientists or drivers?).

The mental models approach to syllogisms assumes that all participants approach the task in the same way and no explicit mechanisms of change or improvement are provided. However, in any large sample of participants, some will get most syllogisms correct, a few will be at guessing level and the remainder will show the typical variations in item difficulty discussed here and addressed by the mental models approach. Galotti et al. (1986) found that people classed on a pre-test as 'good reasoners' (but who had no training in formal logic) either used or quickly developed short-cut rules which would make laborious explorations of multiple model possibilities unnecessary. For example, better reasoners used the rules that two 'some' premises could only yield no valid conclusion and similarly that two negative premises must give no valid conclusion. Ford (1995) in a very detailed study, using concurrent verbal think aloud and written protocols, found that her participants split into a group who mainly used verbal rules and representations and a group who used spatial representations like Venn diagrams. Both groups solved at about the same level as each other and showed patterns of difficulty over syllogisms similar to those found by Johnson-Laird and Bara (1984). However, Ford's participants showed no signs of using mental model representations.

Belief bias and dual system theory

As mentioned above, arguments can vary independently in validity and in the truth or believability of the conclusions. Many studies have used abstract materials and so believability is not an issue for those situations. Essentially no participant has prior beliefs about whether or not 'All As are Cs'. However, with real-life materials prior beliefs would be expected to influence judgements of how valid an argument is.

For example, suppose you are given the following syllogism (Kahneman, 2011).

> All roses are flowers
>
> Some flowers fade quickly
>
> Therefore, some roses fade quickly.

Belief bias is a tendency to accept invalid but believable conclusions and to reject valid but unbelievable conclusions to arguments.

There is a strong tendency to conclude that this is a valid argument since the conclusion is true. However, if we work just with the premises given, the conclusion does not follow because it may be that there are no roses in the set of flowers that fade quickly. This is an example of belief bias and more can be found on this topic and on its theoretical implications in Box 11.2.

Box 11.3 Practical Application: Psychological model of legal reasoning

The law involves reasoning by jurors and judges to reach definite conclusions, either 'guilty', or 'not guilty' (or additionally 'not proven', if in Scotland). Such reasoning may occasionally be a straightforward application of *modus ponens*. For example, in most jurisdictions there is a law to the effect that if a shop sells alcohol to people below some critical age (18 in UK) then the law has been broken. So, if the owner of the Allnite Corner Shop has definitely sold alcohol to Darren Smith (17 years and 11 months old) then it is simple for jurors or a magistrate to apply the if-then rule and conclude that the shopkeeper is guilty.

Such simple cases are rare. More commonly there are many pieces of relevant information of uncertain reliability, some pointing to guilt and some to innocence. How do jurors or appeal court judges reason with such complex material to reach a definite verdict? In legal thinking on this question (Ellsworth, 2005) two schools of thought are:

a the *rationalist* approach according to which logical reasoning, using rules of deduction, induction and reasoning by analogy leads to conclusions in a one directional process from evidence to verdict;

b the *realist* approach according to which conclusions emerge from unconscious biases, prejudices and attitudes and then the conclusions are justified afterwards by selective picking and weighting of evidence (e.g. dismissing all the defence witnesses as unreliable).

Simon (2004) has developed an alternative cognitive model which proposes that jurors seek to form a coherent mental model of the facts in the case such that one verdict is strongly supported and the other possible verdict is only weakly supported. Using a connectionist approach the idea is that the pieces of evidence are given different weights and are each linked initially more or less strongly to each possible verdict. As evidence comes in and is reflected on, one verdict begins to become more strongly activated and feeds back activation to the pieces of evidence that support it and so an early tendency to one verdict becomes ever stronger. Thus, reasoning here is not seen as a one way process from presented information to conclusion but an *interactive process* where the emerging favoured verdict affects the weights of the pieces of evidence which in turn strengthen the favoured verdict.

In studies (Simon et al., 2001), participants were shown a story about an investor who had a dispute with a software company. Each statement was initially rated as supporting or not supporting a conclusion that the investor had libelled the company on an electronic forum. The statements were usually rated initially as roughly equally supporting the libel conclusion and the no libel conclusion. However, when participants were asked to make a definite decision about guilt or not, and after the decision rated the statements again, the ratings polarized so that those who voted guilty rated the statements on the second occasion as strongly supporting the guilty verdict. Those who voted not guilty showed the opposite pattern. Interestingly, when asked to recall how they had originally rated the statements, the participants reported their post-judgement extreme ratings rather than the original middling ratings.

Simon (2004) proposed that in view of the polarizing effect that takes place, advice on legal aspects of cases (e.g. exactly how burglary is defined) should be given before the evidence is heard rather than after, as is the norm. It seems from Simon's results that giving legal advice after the evidence is too late to affect conclusions that have been reached in such a way as to form coherent mental models of the case. Other empirical studies of jurors have also supported the benefits of giving legal advice before the evidence, e.g. Lee and Horowitz (1997) found improved recall of relevant information and reduced recall of irrelevant information when jurors were given prior instruction in legal aspects of the case.

INDUCTIVE REASONING: TESTING AND GENERATING HYPOTHESES

In the last two major sections we have considered studies of deductive inference from statements (premises) that were to be taken as true. Related tasks arise in inductive reasoning when there is a need to test statements (hypotheses) for truth against external data. Detectives and scientists, for instance, constantly face the inductive problems of generating hypotheses and deciding whether their hypotheses are true or false.

> **Hypothesis testing** is assessing hypotheses for truth/falsity against data.
> **Hypothesis generation** is deriving possible hypotheses from data for later testing.

Two types of inductive task can be distinguished and these are generally labelled hypothesis testing and hypothesis generation.

In hypothesis testing, people are required to determine the implications, if any, of some particular observation(s) for the truth of possible generalizations (hypotheses). For example, if we hypothesized that 'All guard dogs in Scotland weigh over 30 kgs', then observations of guard dogs, their weights and geographical locations would bear on the hypothesis just given about guard dogs in Scotland. Note that in this form of reasoning we cannot conclusively prove the hypothesis true, as no matter how many guard dogs are examined in Scotland, a new one might come along that is under 30 kgs. On the other hand the hypothesis could be shown to be false if a single guard dog weighing less than 30 kgs was discovered.

In hypothesis generation, the person can obtain observations (e.g. weights, colour, barking volume, colour, geographical location) on the objects of interest (e.g. guard dogs) and seeks to make a generalization supported by the evidence. Such hypotheses may need further testing and again cannot be conclusively proved but could be disproved.

Hypothetico-deductive reasoning is a form of inductive reasoning in which a hypothesis is tested by deducing necessary consequences of the hypothesis and determining whether the consequences are true (supporting the hypothesis) or false (disconfirming or falsifying the hypothesis).

A possible general approach in hypothesis testing is to follow the hypothetico-deductive method. In this technique, implications are deduced from the hypothesis and the implications are then checked against data for truth or falsity. If the implications of the hypothesis turn out to be true, then the hypothesis is supported, otherwise it can be rejected on the grounds that if validly drawn inferences from the hypothesis lead to empirically false conclusions then the hypothesis must be false. Whether the apparently simple prescription embodied in the hypothetico-deductive method is descriptive of behaviour in the face of inductive problems has been the topic of numerous studies, a selection of which will be considered in this chapter. Our review will start with tasks in which people do not have to generate hypotheses, but rather are given some particular hypothesis to test and sources of potentially relevant data. Next, we will discuss a range of more complicated tasks in which people are required to both generate and test their own hypotheses. The hypothesis generating and testing behaviour of scientists in real life will then be considered.

Box 11.4 Practical Application: Training in reasoning – Lipman's *Philosophy for Children* programme

An oft stated goal of education is to develop thinking skills, including reasoning. Can reasoning be trained even at primary school level? A philosopher, Lipman (1974) decided that the best way to teach children to think was through stories and classroom discussions. He therefore wrote a short children's book called *Harry Stottlemeier's Discovery* (the title is a play on the name Aristotle). The book features Harry and his classmates. Adults occasionally enter in, but the primary philosophical work is the children's. Harry and his friends discover several basic concepts and rules of Aristotelean logic; and they puzzle over questions about the nature of thought, mind, causality, reality, knowledge and belief, right and wrong, and fairness and unfairness.

The story begins with Harry, a thoughtful boy, making a mistake in class one day. He hears his teacher explain that all planets revolve around the sun. Then, lost in a daydream, he misses the explanation about comets which also revolve around the sun. The teacher asks him, 'What has a long tail, and revolves about the sun once every seventy seven years?' The correct answer is Halley's comet but since Harry has not been listening he doesn't know this. Remembering that all planets revolve round the sun, Harry concludes that this too must be a planet. The class laughs when he gives the wrong answer, for they have heard their teacher explain that comets travel round the sun but are not planets.

Harry is saved by the school bell and when walking home wonders to himself why his answer was wrong. He thinks to himself, 'All planets revolve about the sun, but not everything that revolves about the sun is a planet'. Suddenly Harry has an idea: a sentence can't be reversed. 'If you put the last part of a sentence first, it'll no longer be true.' He tries a few examples, 'All oaks are trees, but not all trees are oaks', 'All cucumbers are vegetables, but not all vegetables are cucumbers'. It's true that 'All planets revolve about the sun' but if you turn it round and say that 'All things that revolve about the sun are planets' then it's no longer true. Harry has discovered that 'All X are Y' universal statements cannot necessarily be reversed. In other words he has discovered the 'conversion error' discussed earlier in connection with syllogistic reasoning.

Harry then he meets his friend Lisa. In talking about his discovery she points out that Harry's rule does not always work. The sentence 'No eagles are lions', she says, can be reversed and still be true, 'No lions are eagles'. Logic is more complicated than Harry thinks. However, he and Lisa soon discover a new rule, 'If a true sentence begins with the word *no*, then its reverse is also true. But if it begins with *all*, then its reverse is false'.

In the *Philosophy for Children* programme, children as young as six or seven years of age work with the *Harry Stottlemeier* book and similar materials coupled with extensive classroom discussions of what they are learning.

Evaluations of the *Philosophy for Children* approach in educational practice have been positive. For example, children who undertook the programme were shown to perform significantly better on follow up studies than controls not only in reasoning, but also in maths, reading, and creative production (Nickerson et al., 1985). A meta-analysis by Trickey and Topping (2004) synthesized the results from some 10 studies that involved good research practice in the area as follows: measuring outcomes with norm-referenced tests of reading, reasoning and cognitive ability, curriculum measures, measures of self-esteem, and pupil behaviour. All ten studies showed positive outcomes with a mean effect size of 0.43 (about half a standard deviation). Trickey and Topping concluded that *Philosophy for Children* has 'a consistent moderate positive effect . . . on a wide range of outcome measures'.

TESTING HYPOTHESES: THE FOUR-CARD SELECTION TASK

Wason (1966, 1968) devised a deceptively simple looking task to explore hypothetico-deductive reasoning. Because this task involves a mixture of deduction and induction it is often presented within the context of deductive reasoning. However, as Wason saw this task as investigating falsification in assessing hypotheses, it is discussed here with 'induction' which is concerned with establishing the truth or falsity of empirical hypotheses.

Scan to have an interactive attempt at a four-card selection task yourself

Suppose you are given four cards showing:

Each card has a letter on one side and a number on the other. Your task is to name the cards which need to be turned over to test the following statement: 'If a card has a vowel on one side, then it has an even number on the other side.' You may find it instructive to pause here and decide on your answer before reading on.

Let us now consider a number of task variants. In each variant, try to decide which of the four cards need to be turned over to test the given rule.

Abstract version: each card has the letter A or B on one side and the number 1 or 2 on the other side. Rule: If a card has a '1' on one side it has an 'A' on the other side.

Concrete version: each card represents a journey and has a destination on one side and a means of transport on the other side. Rule: If a card has a 'Manchester' on one side it has a 'Train' on the other side.

Drinking rule: each card represents a person in a bar and has the person's age on one side and what he or she is drinking on the other side. Rule: If someone is drinking alcohol they must be 18 or over.

Negative abstract version: each card has the letter A or B on one side and the number 1 or 2 on the other side. Rule: If a card has a '1' on one side it does not have a 'B' on the other side. Cards show:

In all the above cases, the first and fourth card should chosen. Why? See below.

On the 'official' intended interpretation of the rule as one of material implication (see discussion of conditional reasoning above), the most common answers are wrong. To see why they are wrong, and what the correct answer is, let us look at a concrete example. Take the proposed rule or hypothesis, 'Paper burns at 250 degrees C'. If we had a furnace set at 250 degrees C we could test this proposed rule by inserting samples of paper and noting whether they burn or not. A difficulty arises, in that no matter how many different samples of paper conform to the rule there could always be as yet untried papers that would not. Thus, no matter how many 'positives' are recorded, the rule can never be absolutely verified; but, it would be falsified if just one sample failed to burn at 250 degrees C. This is a general characteristic of universal hypotheses and the example should cue us to the need to consider potentially falsifying data as well as potentially supporting data in testing rules.

Suppose now that a study was conducted on what sorts of things burn at 250 degrees C and that four cards are available representing four individual experiments. On one side of each card is listed the type of material put into the furnace and on the other side, whether it burned or not. Which of the four cards below would have to be turned over to test the hypothesis, 'If it is paper, it will burn at 250 degrees C?'

Clearly we must look at the 'Paper' card to see if it burned or not. The 'Plastic' card can be ignored as irrelevant. Surprisingly, perhaps, the 'Burned' card does not need to be turned over. Once we know that the material burned, whether the material was paper or not does not affect the truth of the hypothesis. No information regarding the truth of the hypothesis would be gained by turning over the 'Burned' card and so it should be left untouched. (Paper or Plastic on the other side would both be consistent with the proposed rule.) The 'Did not burn' card should definitely be turned over, since it would be falsifying if 'Paper' were on the other side.

Similarly, in the abstract version: i.e. 'If vowel on one side, then even number on the other side', the cards showing 'E' and '7' should be examined because they could falsify the rule. The '4' and the 'K' cards may be left unturned since whatever is on their other sides would be consistent with proposed rule. The logic of seeking falsifying evidence was stressed by the influential philosopher of science, Karl Popper (1959). Popper's views were the underlying inspiration behind Wason's four-card task – which can seem rather an arbitrary and highly artificial exercise in logic but is actually rooted in thinking about the very practical question of how science should be done (Wason, 1995).

Basic results

In testing a rule of the form 'if p then q', there are four possible cases that we might find, and these are *p and q, p and not q, not p and q* and *not p and not q*. In logic, only the second case (*p and not q*) is inconsistent with the rule while the remainder are consistent.

When participants are given a conditional rule to test and the opportunity to observe what is paired with cases of p, q, not p and not q in the four-card task, they almost always select the cards showing p and q, rather than the logically correct cards showing p and not q.

One way to describe these results is to say that people are biased towards verification or conformation and so choose the potentially confirming cards (p, q) and ignore the potentially falsifying case (not q). (Note: the p card is potentially falsifying as it might have not q on the reverse side as well as potentially confirming if it has q on the reverse side.) Participants will generally recognize that the not q card falsifies the rule if the not q card is turned over to reveal p, but rarely spontaneously examine it.

Procedural variations

Wason and others examined a number of procedural variables in an attempt to locate the sources of difficulty in this task. For example, in one study (Wason, 1969), the task materials were made strictly binary with only two possible letters and numbers, but this had no effect. Thus the source of the difficulty was not confusion induced by the sheer number of possibilities in the 'Vowel-even number' cards.

It was suggested that participants might have been confused by the expression 'the other side of the card' and might have misinterpreted this to mean 'the side face downward'. Wason and Johnson-Laird (1970) therefore presented participants with cards that had all the information on one side and used masks to hide the appropriate part of the card. Again, no facilitation occurred.

Perhaps the apparent 'set' for verification could be broken by instructions which emphasize falsification? However, Wason (1968) found that instructions to pick cards which 'could break the rule' did not enhance performance.

Performance on other reasoning tasks is often improved by concrete material. Wason and Shapiro (1971) found marked improvement when the task was presented in terms of four journeys. The four cards were said to represent journeys, with names of towns (destinations) on one side and modes of transport on the other. Participants were given cards marked, face up, as follows and were told that the cards represented journeys made by the experimenter.

Manchester   Car   Train   Leeds

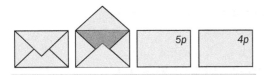

Figure 11.4   Envelopes version of selection task.

The proposed rule to be tested was 'Every time I go to Manchester, I go by train'. (Answer: turn over 'Manchester' and 'Car' cards.) The facilitating effect was replicated by Gilhooly and Falconer (1974).

Further improvement in performance was found when the task was made very lifelike and concrete by Johnson-Laird et al. (1972). Participants were asked to imagine that they worked in the Post Office, sorting letters, as shown in Figure 11.4.

Their task was to discover whether the following rule had been broken. (This rule was in effect at that time in the UK.)

If a letter is sealed, then it has a 5 penny stamp on it.

Envelopes were provided either sealed or not and bearing either a 4 penny stamp or a 5 penny stamp on their showing side. A parallel abstract condition had the following rule:

If an envelope has a D on one side, then it has a 5 on the other side.

Again, suitable envelopes were provided to test the rule. And 22 out of 24 people tested were correct in the concrete condition, but only 2 out of 24 were correct in the abstract condition.

In sum, it appeared from these early studies that the main facilitating effects on selection task performance were those of using realistic material. Subsequent research reviewed below suggested a range of reasons why concrete materials were helpful in this task.

Interpretation factors

A number of investigators have pointed to ambiguities in the standard four-card task. Typical patterns of performance on the task might be explained in terms of people making interpretations different from that intended, but then going on to reason correctly on their interpretations.

Smalley (1974) distinguished three sources of ambiguity:

1 Is the rule 'reversible' or not? i.e. does $p - q$ also mean $q - p$ or not?

2 Does the rule refer to both sides of the card or just to the showing side?

3 Is the task one of verification, falsification or both?

Putting together these ambiguities leads to $(2 \times 2 \times 3) = 12$ possible interpretations of the task. These 12 interpretations logically require certain patterns of card selection. Smalley showed that such interpretations occurred and that his participants' choices were consistent with their interpretations.

Further evidence for the interpretation approach to the four-card task was provided by Bracewell (1974) who gave one group a greatly 'clarified' statement of the task (cf. Ceraso and Provitera's syllogism experiment discussed earlier in this chapter). The rule was given as follows:

If either the showing face or the underside face of the card has a J on it then 2 is on the remaining face. This hypothesis should not be interpreted to mean that 2 only occurs with J.

Please indicate the card or cards it is necessary to examine in order to see if the above hypothesis is false.

The success rate with clarified instructions was much higher than that obtained with standard instructions.

The beneficial effects of realistic material could be explained on the 'interpretation' view, to reductions in ambiguity with realistic material. A rule, such as 'If I go to London, I go by car', is unlikely to be interpreted as reversible (i.e. as implying 'If I go by car, I go to London') because the reversed version is implausible. No such plausibility checks would prevent reversal of an abstract rule. In the 'Post Office' variant, the nature of the task – to seek potentially falsifying information – fits the thematic structure and so makes the task less ambiguous.

Matching bias

Evans (1984; Evans & Lynch, 1973; Wason & Evans, 1975) put forward the view that, in the abstract version of the selection task, most people exhibit a matching bias in that they simply select the cards showing the symbols mentioned in the rule, that is, the responses match the input and no 'deeper' processing is involved. One main source of evidence for this view is the finding that with a negative form of the rule ('If B on one side, there will not be 3 on the other') the success rate is very high. Most participants select the 'B' card and the '3' card which is the correct potentially falsifying choice pattern. This arises simply through 'matching'; the participants do not show any special insight into the logic of the task and when re-tested with positive versions of the rule, make the usual errors, as the matching hypothesis predicts.

> Matching bias, in the four-card task, is choosing the cards mentioned in the rule.

Memory-cueing (availability) accounts

The rule that Johnson-Laird et al. (1972) used in their 'postal' study was a real-life rule and was well known to their participants at the time of the experiment. However, the rule stopped being used in the United Kingdom many years ago and later studies, using young adults, failed to find facilitating effects of the postal rule condition compared to the abstract condition (Griggs & Cox, 1982). Thus, it is possible that prior experience of specific counter-examples helped performance. People for whom the rule was a real everyday rule would be more likely to think of possible counter-examples from memory, than would people for whom the rule was an arbitrary laboratory invention; in other words, falsifying possibilities would be more available to people familiar with the rule in real life.

Griggs and Cox (1982) found a similar effect to that of Johnson-Laird et al.'s 'postal study' in an experiment involving the rule governing the legal drinking age in Florida (where the experiment was conducted). Participants were asked to imagine that they were police officers and they were to ensure that the regulation ('If a person is drinking beer, then the person must be over 19') was being followed. Participants were given four cards that contained information about four people: on one side of each card was the person's age and on the other side, what they were drinking. Face-up, the participants saw cards showing '16 years of age', '22 years of age', 'Drinking beer', 'Drinking coke'. The task was to turn over the cards that definitely needed to be turned over to determine whether the rule was being violated. This turned out to be a very easy version of the task and correct choices were made by nearly 75 per cent of participants. As with the postal task, a memory-cueing explanation was suggested.

Pragmatic reasoning schemas

It is a reasonable conclusion from the low levels of performance typical with abstract versions of the conditional-rule testing task, that people do not use formal 'syntactic' rules of logical implication in these tasks. Data outlined in the preceding section raised the possibility of specific memory cueing. A third possibility was developed in Cheng and Holyoak's (1985) notion of pragmatic reasoning schemas. Such schemas are quite abstract rule systems, in that they apply to a wide range of contents, but are not so wide and abstract as syntactic, logical rules. A relevant schema in the context of the four-card problem is the 'permission schema'. The core content of the permission schema is, 'If one is to do X , then one must satisfy precondition Y'.

Cheng and Holyoak examined the possible rule of the permission schema in the following study. Participants in Hong Kong and Michigan were instructed in a problem about checking passengers' forms at an airport. The rule to be checked was 'If the form says "ENTERING" on one side, then the other side includes Cholera among the list of diseases'. Four cases corresponding to p, q, not-p, and not-q were available for examination. Half the participants were given a reason for the 'cholera' rule by being told that the form listed diseases for which the passenger had been inoculated and that a cholera inoculation was needed to protect the entering passengers from the disease. It was expected that this explanation would invoke the 'permission schema' (which matches closely the logic of the conditional). The expectation was justified in that both Hong Kong and Michigan participants showed a marked increase in correct performance when given the rationale for the rule. This result is not consistent with the memory-cueing explanation since participants did not have relevant memories; nor is it consistent with the syntactic rule view, since the logical structure of the task is not affected by the rationale. The result is, however, consistent with the pragmatic reasoning schema approach.

Social contract theory

Cosmides (1989; Tooby and Cosmides, 2009) argued that as a result of evolutionary pressures, people have a number of innate special purpose mechanisms to handle problems that have been critical to survival over many millennia. Specifically, she proposed that special purpose cognitive mechanisms have evolved to detect cheaters. In a social contract, individuals agree to take a benefit (e.g. eating deer meat) only if they have paid an agreed cost (e.g. gathered sufficient branches for a cooking fire). Cheats are those who eat the deer meat without having gathered the wood. Thus, possible cheats might be among those who eat the deer meat (they may not have gathered wood) or those who have not gathered wood (they may illicitly eat the meat). Cosmides proposed that humans have evolved so that they possess a 'cheat detecting algorithm' which will focus in on possible cases of cheating.

> Social contract theory proposes that rules expressing payment of costs for privileges will be easily solved in 4 card tasks as the correct choices would uncover cheating.

The relevance of these evolutionary arguments for the four-card task is that versions of the task which fit the social contract pattern produce high rates of correct (falsifying) answers. The Drinking Age problem of Griggs and Cox (1982) and the Postal problem of Johnson-Laird et al. (1972) are good examples of facilitating problems where a cost has to be paid (in waiting to be old enough or in money) before a benefit can be taken (drinking beer or sending a sealed letter). Cosmides argues that the only reliable facilitations of the four-card task with thematic materials occur when the rule used is a social contract and is understood as such by the participants.

In a series of experiments, Cosmides (1989) set out to test the rival claims of social contract theory, availability and pragmatic schema approaches. We will first outline the studies comparing social contract and availability explanations.

Problems were devised which concerned unfamiliar social contracts, unfamiliar descriptive rules, familiar descriptive rules and abstract rules. An example unfamiliar social contract is 'If a man eats cassava root, then he must have a tattoo on his face'. This rule was framed as a social contract by means of a background story according to which the rule holds among certain Pacific islanders; the cassava root is described as a powerful aphrodisiac only available to married men and only married men are tattooed. In the social contract condition participants are to take on the role of an enforcer of the rule. The four cards indicate on one side whether a man is tattooed or not and on the other side whether he is eating cassava root or molo nuts. The task is to decide whether to turn over cards showing 'Tattooed', 'Not-tattooed', 'Cassava root' or 'Molo nuts'. In the unfamiliar descriptive version the participants are to take on the role of an anthropologist trying to decide whether a proposed descriptive rule that eating cassava roots always goes with being tattooed is being broken. The familiar descriptive problem was a transport and towns problem using places and means of transport familiar to the participants. The abstract version was similar to Wason's original problem. In all cases a 'detective' type of set was induced to encourage participants to look for violations of the rules.

The results of these studies were that participants made a high rate of falsifying (p and not q) choices in the unfamiliar social contract condition (c. 70 per cent), a low rate with unfamiliar descriptive problems (c. 23 per cent) and a medium rate with familiar descriptive problems (c. 42 per cent). The unfamiliar abstract baseline condition yielded c. 27 per cent falsifying responses. Availability of relevant memories cannot explain the high correct rate with the unfamiliar social contract task (although there does seem to be an advantage for familiar descriptive tasks over baseline). Thus, social contracts produced a strong facilitation even when the material was unfamiliar and could not have cued relevant memories.

Further studies by Cosmides (1989) produced more support for social contract theory. In particular, experiments involving so-called 'switched' social contracts produce unusual choices predicted by social contract theory. Consider the cassava root rule. In its normal form this is 'If a man eats cassava root then he must have a tattoo on his face'. In the switched version it is 'If a man has a tattoo on his face then he eats cassava root'. Simply taking the surface logic of the switched rule, a falsifying approach would predict choices of 'Tattoo' and 'Molo nuts'; however, on the social contract interpretation, participants would choose 'Not-tattooed' and 'Cassava root' (more abstractly, the not-p and q cards). This prediction arises because it is among the 'Non-tattooed' and the 'Cassava root' eaters that cheats may be found. Participants were tested with the switched social contract, unfamiliar descriptive rules, familiar descriptive rules and abstract descriptive rules. The results indicated a high rate of the not-p and q choices for the switched social contract (c. 70 per cent) with a near zero rate of such responses in the other conditions. Thus, the social contract theory was again upheld and the data from these experiments cannot be explained in any obvious way by the availability or memory-cuing approach.

An alternative explanation for the ease of processing social contract rules might be found in the pragmatic permission schema approach of Cheng and Holyoak (1985). Cosmides pointed out that although all social contracts are 'permissions' not all permissions are social contracts, since social contracts always involve costs and benefits while permissions as a class do not always do so. Cosmides argued that permission rules have only been facilitating when they have incorporated costs and benefits and hence have been social contracts. To test this notion, experiments were carried out in which the same rules were framed by means of background stories as either social contracts (in which the actions were taking benefits and the preconditions were costs to be met) or as permissions where the same actions and preconditions were without costs or benefits to the individuals. For example, the Cassava root rule was framed as a social contract as previously, or as a permission in which there was no individual advantage to eating Cassava roots or Molo nuts and being tattooed was not painful. The permission rule was justified as balancing out the frequency with which the two foods were eaten to conserve food supplies for the group. The outcome was that falsifying choices (p and not-q) were more frequent for the social contract version than for the permission version (80 per cent vs. 45 per cent). Switching the rules to 'If a man has a tattoo on his face then he eats cassava root' produced a high rate of not-p and q choices in the social contract version compared with the permission version (65 per cent vs. 0 per cent), as predicted by social contract theory.

Overall, Cosmides's evolutionary approach has led to identification of rules which will reliably produce response patterns matching falsification choices (p and not-q) or if switched will produce choices unlikely to occur in the standard abstract version (not-p and q). These findings were replicated by Gigerenzer and Hug (1992).

> Deontic rules are rules regarding obligations and typically involve terms such as 'should', 'must', 'ought, 'may' and so on.

The research reviewed above on the social contract approach and on the pragmatic reasoning schemas approach has highlighted the facilitating effect of deontic rules, on four-card selection tasks, that is, use of rules regarding what may or must be done. The research suggests that people do generally have a good grasp of basic deontic rules expressing simple social contracts since their selection task choices are in line with such understanding. This high level of understanding may reflect some evolutionary pressure leading to special purpose mechanisms becoming hard-wired into human brains (Cosmides's proposal) or it may reflect the importance of such practical social knowledge which might be acquired through general purpose learning mechanisms during normal development.

The work discussed in the next section (Oaksford & Chater, 1994, 2003) re-addresses the basic issues of inductive reasoning in the four-card selection task and pursues an interpretation of data which leads to a more optimistic conclusion about human rationality than is sometimes drawn (e.g. Cohen, 1981).

The selection task as optimal data selection

Wason's initial studies of the selection task (1966, 1968) were inspired by Popper's (1959) notion that seeking falsification was the rational way to test scientific hypotheses and by extension any causal or indicative hypothesis. As we have seen repeatedly, few people spontaneously adopt a falsifying approach to the standard abstract selection task and this aversion to falsification has been seen as a sign of imperfect rationality. However, Oaksford and Chater (1994; and Chater & Oaksford, 2001, 2003) have proposed an alternative normatively based approach. This is an approach in terms of comparative testing of hypotheses to reduce the tester's uncertainty between them and involves the use of a statistical rule known as *Bayes's theorem.*

In the selection task, a hypothesis is proposed, for example, that 'if a card has p on one side then it has q on the other side'. Among other things, this hypothesis implies that the probability of a card having not-q on it given it has a p on it is zero and so the probability of q's must be at least as great as the probability of p's. The alternative hypothesis is the hypothesis that p and q are unrelated (i.e. the null hypothesis), so the probability of not-q given p could be greater than zero and the probability of q could be less than the probability of p. Bayes's theorem allows the investigator to revise the probabilities of hypotheses in the light of data which are more or less likely if the hypotheses are true.

Oaksford and Chater show that if the proposed rule and the alternative null hypothesis are viewed as equally likely initially, and the probabilities of p's and q's are seen as fairly low, then the best choices on Bayes's theorem to discriminate between the two hypotheses are the p card, the q card and the not-q card in that order. The not-p card would yield no discriminating information. The predicted preference order of card choices then is p > q > not-q > not-p, and this is the order found in a review of 13 papers reporting a total of 34 abstract selection tasks (Oaksford & Chater, 1994).

The optimal data selection model argues that people will home in on rare events as being most informative and the predictions are based on that assumption. However, in a direct test, Oberauer et al. (2004), gave participants extensive experience of stimuli involving frequent and rare combinations of features, and followed this experience with suitable four-card tasks involving rare and common features. No evidence emerged to show that choices in the four-card task were related to the experienced frequencies so there are results counter to the optimal data selection model as well as supporting results. A further criticism is that the mechanisms by which selections are made are not specified.

GENERATING AND TESTING HYPOTHESES

In studies of conditional rule testing, such as those discussed above, people are given a rule and possible evidence which may or may not support or disconfirm the rule. Usually, in real-life situations we are not given rules to test but must generate possible rules (hypotheses) first which can then be tested.

The processes of generating and testing self-produced hypotheses have been examined in a number of ways. We will discuss two of the main approaches that have involved the study of (1) Wason's reversed 20 questions task, and (2) performance in simulated research environments.

Wason's reversed 20 questions task

Wason (1960) devised a special task in which people generate over-restrictive hypotheses. Participants were given three numbers, 2, 4, 6, and told that these conformed to a rule which they had to discover. The means of discovery was to be by generating other three-number series that might match the rule or not. The experimenter gave feedback on each triple produced by the participants who were asked to announce their rule when they were highly confident that it was the correct answer. The correct rule was simply 'numbers in increasing order of magnitude'. As you might expect, people stuck to much more restrictive hypotheses, for example, 'intervals of 2 between increasing numbers', 'arithmetic series'. However, the main interest lay in how the hypotheses were tested. The overwhelming tendency (Wason, 1960) was for people simply to generate series consistent with their particular hypothesis and to keep on doing so until they felt sufficiently confident to announce their hypothesis as correct. Few participants either tried out series that went against their own hypotheses or spontaneously varied their hypotheses. Very little evidence was found for a falsification strategy.

A number of task variations were attempted – with little effect. Even imposing a charge of 12.5 pence for each incorrect rule announcement, although it made participants more cautious about claiming to know the answer, did not affect the bias toward verification.

Tukey (1986) argued that participants in this task do in fact behave in ways that are rational in terms of various alternative philosophies of science. The stress on falsification in many studies of inductive reasoning is derived from Popper's (1959) analysis of scientific method. Tukey points to alternative accounts of scientific inquiry by, for example, Mill (1875/1967), Lakatos (1970) Kuhn (1970) and Bayesian theorists (Hesse, 1975). In Tukey's study it emerged that participants were not always testing particular hypotheses on each trial, but would quite often be examining instances 'at random' or just because they were 'different' in order to gather information that could lead to useful hypotheses. Certainly, people very rarely reported attempting to 'disconfirm' their hypotheses. Attempts to confirm and to simply explore accounted for over half the trials according to the participants' reports. Overall, Tukey's study suggests that an overly narrow view, based on Popperian philosophy of science (Popper, 1959), was initially applied to this task. When alternative approaches to scientific testing were considered, much of the participants' behaviour could be regarded as rational and intelligible rather than irrational and biased.

Box 11.5 Research Close Up: Role of external representations in rule discovery

Source: Vallée-Tourangeau, F. & Krüsi Penney, A. (2005). The impact of external representation in a rule discovery task. *European Journal of Cognitive Psychology*, *17*, 820–834.

INTRODUCTION

The reversed 20 questions task, or 2-4-6 task, is intended to represent real-world hypothesis testing. However, in its standard version, the task is not like real-life situations since the hypothesis testing is carried out mainly in the head, that is, the task involves purely internal representations of triples and possible hypotheses. On the other hand real-world hypothesis testing usually involves using apparatus and instruments which help the person arrive at and test hypotheses. Test results are often represented as graphs and some representations may be more likely than others to help productive hypothesis generation testing (Cheng, 1996; Reinmann, 1999). Vallée-Tourangeau and Krüsi Penney (2005) examined the impact on hypothesis-testing behaviour of a richer external representation of the problem space in a variant of the 2-4-6 task in which sequences involved the digits from 1 to 6.

METHOD

In this study, triples were generated by working with three dice each of which had six sides as usual. Participants rotated the dice or changed the order of the dice to produce new triples. Control participants carried out the 2-4-6 type of task without dice, but with numbers 1 to 6.

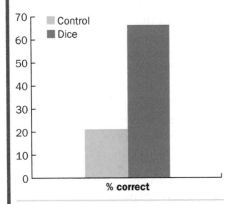

Figure 11.5 Percentage correct in Vallee-Tourangeau and Penney's (2005) study of the 2-4-6 task using dice versus controls.

Source: Adapted from Vallée-Tourangeau, F. & Krüsi Penney, A. (2005). The impact of external representation in a rule discovery task. *European Journal of Cognitive Psychology*, *17*, 820–834.

RESULTS

The results in Figure 11.5 indicated that the task was made considerably easier when dice were used to generate the triples for testing as compared with standard paper and pencil methods (control group).

DISCUSSION

As can be seen from Figure 11.5 only 21 per cent of the control participants announced the correct rule, which is similar to the performance observed in the original Wason study (1960). In contrast, 66 per cent of the participants with the dice version solved correctly.

As the authors put it: 'Participants appeared less complacent and more creative by testing a larger more heterogeneous sample of triples, reflecting a broader exploration of the triple space than in either control condition, which led to a greater incidence of announcing the correct rule.'

In other words, the experimental participants produced more triples, which were of a more varied kind, before announcing their guess than did control participants. It appeared that providing an external, easy to manipulate representation of the space of possible triples made the possible test items salient and easier for participants to generate.

In a follow-up study, participants were given a different way of representing the choice of digits. Instead of dice, which may have cued ideas of randomness and thus have prompted consideration of more possible sequences, participants had to make up their number sequences by choosing from three sets of six-sided counters (hexagons.). In each set were six hexagons, one having one dot, one having two dots, one having three dots and so on up to one having six dots. By choosing hexagons the participants could thus make up sets of numbers to be tested for conformity to the rule or not.

This version of the test produced equally beneficial results to the 'dice' version. Thus, it was concluded that it was the ability to manipulate the possibilities externally that was crucial rather than the use of dice themselves.

It seems that the external environment in this study helped promote wide testing. It is easier to manipulate possibilities externally in many and varied ways and then observe the results than to manipulate possibilities internally, within working memory. Internal manipulation is probably more liable to effects of habits and 'sets' (see Chapter 10, problem solving). And leads to less varied possibilities being generated and tested.

Simulated research environments

Although philosophers of science tend to stress the importance of falsification (Popper, 1959) and of considering more than one hypothesis at a time (Platt, 1964), the results of Wason and others, discussed above, suggest that naive participants tend neither to consider alternative hypotheses nor to seek out potentially falsifying data. Studies by Mynatt et al. (1977, 1978) sought to investigate such tendencies in complex environments that were intended to simulate real-life research.

In the 1977 study, people saw computer generated displays on a screen showing various shapes (circles, squares, triangles) of varying degrees of brightness (dim or bright). A particle could be fired across the screen (from a fixed position) in any direction, and it would be stopped when it approached some objects but not others. The overall task was to produce a hypothesis that would account for the behaviour of the particle. The correct answer was that the particle stopped on approaching dim shapes.

Scan to watch a video on confirmation bias

At first, participants were allowed to formulate a hypothesis on the basis of the particle's behaviour with one particular configuration of objects (a configuration that favoured adoption of a wrong hypothesis in terms of object shape). They then chose between pairs of environments; in one they could make observations which would probably confirm the typical wrong hypothesis and in the other they would test alternative hypotheses. Evidence for a confirmation bias, involving failure to choose environments allowing tests of alternative hypotheses, was found. However, if participants did obtain explicit falsifying information, they generally used this information to reject incorrect hypotheses. Behaviour in this task was not affected by instructions stressing confirmation or disconfirmation.

> Confirmation bias, in hypothesis testing, is a tendency to seek out and attend only to information consistent with the hypothesis while ignoring falsifying information.

In the 1978 study, participants were allowed 10 hours to explore a very complex environment of 27 objects, varying in shape, size and brightness, in which particles were deflected on approaching objects. The angles of deflection were governed by a formula involving parameters whose values were determined by the shape, size and brightness of the objects. No one solved and Mynatt et al. inferred a 'confirmation bias'. It was clear from the thinking aloud records that deliberate attempts to falsify hypotheses almost never occurred.

Similar results also emerged from Dunbar's (1993) study of participants attempting to solve a problem in genetics through simulated experiments. The problem was such that there was a typically drawn dominant hypothesis, which most participants started with. Seeking data consistent with the dominant hypothesis led to poor performance while focusing on discrepancies and difficulties with the initial hypothesis led to more solutions.

Box 11.6 Practical Application: Real scientific research environments

Studies of real-life hypothesis testing in the sciences (Chalmers, 1978; Dunbar & Fugelsang, 2005; Mitroff, 1974) are consistent with laboratory studies in that scientists do not seem overly disposed to seek falsifying data or to accept that favoured theories require revision or abandonment in the face of apparently falsifying results.

For example, Galileo ignored much data that was apparently inconsistent with Copernican theory and protagonists of Newton's theory of gravity did not abandon it in view of the 'misbehaviour' of certain planets. The typical reaction to observations inconsistent with a favoured theory is to seek an explanation that preserves the theory. In the case of the planet Uranus's orbit that was not as predicted, a new undiscovered planet was postulated and in due course the theory received spectacular support from the discovery of Neptune in the predicted place. Other anomalies in Newton's theory were never resolved, but the theory was not abandoned.

Mitroff (1974) closely surveyed the attitudes and beliefs about scientific practice of a group of 43 geologists engaged in the study of lunar geology under the auspices of the Apollo space research programme. These well-established scientists saw their aim as (mainly) confirming rather than falsifying hypotheses. The only hypotheses that they were interested in falsifying were the hypotheses of rival scientists! As Mitroff puts it, these scientists differed markedly from the 'story book scientist' who is supposed to be completely disinterested and uncommitted to any particular hypothesis. The real scientists tended to be strongly committed to particular points of view and would only reluctantly abandon their views in the face of contrary evidence – rather than immediately, as a simple falsificationist position would suppose. Perhaps then, the laboratory participants in the Mynatt study discussed above are not untypical, in seeking confirmation rather than falsification. Indeed, the relatively high rate of appropriate reactions to falsifying data reported by Mynatt may reflect the artificiality of the environment: e.g. participants would probably not doubt their 'instruments' in the way that real scientists might.

Indeed, Fugelsang et al. (2004), in a study of real biological scientists at work found that unexpected results were nearly always attributed to problems with methods; only if the unexpected results held up on replication did scientists tend to accept them and revise their views accordingly. Similarly, Gorman (1986), has shown in a laboratory task that the possibility of error in feedback 'insulates' hypotheses from rejection.

Mitroff's moon scientists pointed out that 'commitment' was valuable from the point of view of motivating individual scientists. Also, since there would always be scientists with opposing commitments, the 'scientific community' would not be biased as a whole and the rivalry of competing factions would ensure that opposing views would be thoroughly tested by the opposition. Okada and Simon (1997) found that participants who worked in pairs on Dunbar's (1993) genetics problem performed better than single participants presumably because of mutual critiquing of each other's hypotheses and interpretations of data. Even a few cases of extreme commitment or outright bias could be useful, because those biased individuals would keep alive ideas that might prove useful again at a later date, after having been abandoned by most researchers in a given area.

Summary

This chapter concerned how people go beyond information they have been given to derive new knowledge through reasoning.

Reasoning divides into deductive and inductive reasoning. In deductive reasoning conclusions can be drawn that must be true from given statements. Inductive reasoning is concerned with establishing the likely truth or falsity of statements in the light of evidence.

Deductive reasoning splits into propositional reasoning, in which conclusions are drawn from statements involving logical relations such as 'if . . . then', 'and', 'or', and syllogistic reasoning in which conclusions are drawn from statements involving relationships between categories such as 'all', 'some', 'none' and 'some . . . not'.

Conditional inferences (using 'if . . . then' statements) have been found to be prone to the errors of affirming the consequent and denying the antecedent. The *modus ponens* inference is made correctly most of the time but the *modus tollens* inference often proves difficult.

Mental logic approaches explain propositional reasoning in terms of intuitive mental rules that correspond to some of the rules of logic, such as *modus ponens*, but lack others, such as *modus tollens*. Errors are attributed to a lack of appropriate rules or to misinterpretation of task materials, for example, interpreting a conditional as if it was an equivalence. The mental models approach assumes that people tackle reasoning problems by forming mental representations of possible states of the world and drawing inferences from those representations.

Many theories have been put forward for syllogistic reasoning. The atmosphere hypothesis proposes syllogisms are handled by a non-logical process. An alternative proposal for syllogisms is that various 'illogical' processes which have some plausibility may jointly produce many errors. In particular, illicit conversion of premises and probabilistic inference have been proposed. Henle (1962) developed the influential view that people do reason logically, but often misinterpret the premises or the task demands, thus producing errors.

In the mental models approach differences in syllogism difficulty were explained in terms of the number of models required to represent premises and their combinations. Figural bias effects were explained in terms of preferred ways of combining premise representations.

Belief bias effects, as demonstrated in syllogisms, and backed up by neuroscience studies, suggest a role for rapid intuitive thinking drawing on System 1 processes which could be modified and overridden by executively controlled slower System 2 processes to overcome biases.

Studies of inductive reasoning have focused on the four-card selection task which requires hypothetico-deductive reasoning. Typically participants ignore the important potentially falsifying information. Concrete rule-content emerged as an important factor in the four-card task with particularly substantial facilitation for rules in terms of social contracts. Currently, the most likely explanation for such 'content' effects seems to lie in the evocation of reasoning schemas regarding social contracts.

Wason's reversed 20 questions task requires participants to generate their own hypotheses about number sequences and test their hypotheses by making up fresh examples. As in the four-card task, participants tend to ignore potentially falsifying information. However, performance can be improved by allowing participants external aids (such as dice) which make it easier to generate new sequences.

Studies of simulated and real life scientific discovery indicated that ignoring potentially falsifying information is widespread in real settings as well as in laboratory studies.

Review questions

1 To what extent are people logical thinkers?

2 What are the roles of System 1 and System 2 processes in reasoning?

3 If we can put men on the moon, how come we can't solve the four-card selection task?

4 How does mental illness affect reasoning?

5 Why are syllogisms difficult?

6 Why might reasoning about social contracts and cheating be relatively easy?

7 Are we biased towards confirming our beliefs?

8 Do scientists really follow Popper's ideas about how to do science?

FURTHER READING

Evans, J. St. B. T., & Frankish, K. (Eds.) (2009). *In two minds*. Oxford: Oxford University Press.

Johnson-Laird, P. N. (2008). *How we reason*. Oxford: Oxford University Press.

Oaksford, M., & Chater, N. (Eds.) (2010). *Cognition and conditionals*. Oxford: Oxford University Press.

Shafir, E., & LeBoeuf, R. A. (2002). Rationality. *Annual Review of Psychology, 53*, 491–517.

CHAPTER 12:
LANGUAGE PRODUCTION

INTRODUCTION

In 1970 in California, a case of child neglect was discovered that was to have a profound impact on our understanding of language development. A girl, named in the literature as 'Genie', had been isolated from the age of 20 months until she came to the attention of social services at the age of 13 years and 7 months. When found, Genie was undersized and severely malnourished. She had painful calluses from being phys-ically restrained over long periods. Throughout her years of isolation, Genie had not been spoken to and she had been beaten when she made a noise. She had not been exposed to language – she had spent many years locked in a room at the back of the family home where she was not able to overhear her family's conversations, and where she was not exposed to language sounds from radio, television or other sources (Curtiss, 1977).

When Genie was found, she did not speak and seemed to understand no more than a few words (Rymer, 1992). Once Genie was taken into care and was exposed to language, in some ways her language development seemed to proceed as it would for a younger child who had typical exposure to language (Curtiss, 1977). She progressed from single words, to two-word and then three-word combinations, and she rapidly acquired vocabulary. However, her language development showed some significant deviations from the normal pattern. Genie had a vocabulary of more than 200 words before she began to combine them, whereas children typically combine words earlier. The word types evident in her early vocabulary also differed from the normal pattern. For example, while most children's early vocabulary consists of basic class words (e.g. 'dog', 'cat'), Genie's vocabulary development showed an emphasis on colours and numbers, shape and size terms, and basic (e.g. 'dog'), superordinate (e.g. 'animal') and subordinate (e.g. 'Labrador') category words (Curtiss, 1981; Fromkin et al., 1974). Genie seemed to seek out words that would allow her to differentiate between similar objects (e.g. pen versus pencil) rather than acquiring labels for a category of object. By contrast, a typically developing child might initially use 'pen' for pens, pencils, crayons and other objects of similar shape, a pattern referred to as over-extension.

Syntax refers to the rules governing the ways words can be combined to create meaningful sentences.
Content words are words that provide meaning to the sentence; these contrast with function words which do the grammatical work of the sentence.
Language production refers to a number of processes by which we convert a thought into language output, in the form of speech, sign language or writing.
Social cognition refers to the ways in which people make sense of themselves and of others in order to function effectively in a social world.

The most striking feature of Genie's language reflects her problems developing syntax or grammar (see Table 12.1), evident in the ways she combined words. Curtiss (1981) described Genie's sentences as '. . . the stringing together of content words, often with rich and clear meaning but with little grammatical structure' (p. 21). Some examples of Genie's utterances illustrate this feature of her language: 'I like hear music ice cream truck'; 'Think about Mama love Genie'; 'Dentist say drink water'; 'Applesauce buy store' (Curtiss, 1977). Genie's case reflects three key issues in language acquisition. First, her failure to fully acquire language suggests that there may be a critical or sensitive period for language acquisition, and particularly for grammar development; if the child is not exposed to language in a social context within this period, normal development is constrained (see Lenneberg, 1967). Second, her language reflects the dissociation between the acquisition of vocabulary and the flexible use of this vocabulary to form novel sentences. Third, her case suggests that language acquisition, like many cognitive functions, relies on interplay between input from the environment (nurture) and biological makeup (nature).

This chapter examines the nature of language and the cognitive processes involved in language production, with a focus on speech. Language is a quintessentially human ability and the ability to communicate our thoughts to others through language is fundamental for social cognition. Language also shapes mental representation and thinking (e.g. Crystal, 1997). Once acquired, language is 'fundamental to all distinctly human thought and consciousness' (Donald, 1999, p. 139). It is therefore important for cognitive psychology to study the processes involved in speech production and to try to understand how a thought is turned into spoken words.

Two basic stages in speech production have long been recognized: the formulation of a thought and its conversion into speech (e.g. James, 1890). However, cognitive psychology

Table 12.1 Levels of linguistic analysis

Level	Refers to:
Semantics	The level of meaning in language
Syntax	The rules by which words are combined to make meaningful sentences
Morphology	The rules by which words are constructed and modified
Phonology	The sound units within a language

remains relatively poorly informed as to the precise nature of the processes underlying language production. As we will see in the next chapter, greater progress has been made towards understanding language comprehension, while less research has addressed the processes underlying production (MacNeilage, 1999). Methodological constraints provide one reason for this bias: it is difficult to control experimental stimuli in order to study language production. When examining language comprehension, we can manipulate the words, sentences or other stimuli that are presented to research participants and measure the effect on comprehension. Comprehension follows on the presentation of the stimuli. But production proceeds from cognition to motor output, and it is a far more difficult task to control or inspect the content of someone's thoughts. Speech production proceeds in a top-down manner, that is, it is conceptually driven (see Chapter 2).

> Conceptually driven or top-down processes reflect the influence of higher order cognitive processes such as thoughts, beliefs and expectations.

In spite of the methodological challenges posed by the topic, our understanding of speech production has seen substantial development in recent years. Knowledge of speech production derives from a number of sources, involving, for example, experimental methods, computational modelling, neuroscientific methods and neuropsychological case studies. In the present chapter we focus on learning about language production by examining what happens when the system fails. Two types of system failure are considered. First, we consider speech errors; slips of the tongue and other speech errors reveal much about the processes underlying speech. Errors can be induced experimentally or recorded from spontaneous speech. Second, the effects of physical damage to the areas of the brain responsible for language production will be examined.

Let's start by considering what language is: How might we define 'language'?

LANGUAGE AND COMMUNICATION

Language is our principal means of communication and forms the basis of the majority of social interactions. Communication can be fairly readily defined as any means by which information is shared (e.g. Field, 2003) or as a process whereby 'a source encodes and transmits a signal, which is detected

> Communication refers to any means by which information is shared.

by a receiver and decoded into meaningful terms' (MacFarland, 1999, p. 387). Many definitions of language would include its use in communication as a core feature, but clearly language goes beyond communication. The information sharing function of language may be a relatively minor role; Aitchison (1996, p. 25) suggests that language has been particularly important for human evolution because it promotes social bonds and social interaction and because it provides an effective means of persuading others.

There are two ways in which we can use language to communicate. One way is through writing. Written language is a new (and arguably humankind's greatest) invention; the earliest evidence of writing dates to about 5000 years ago. Writing developed from a number of distinct systems originating in different parts of the world and this is reflected in the considerable cross-language variation in scripts today (see Chapter 13). Writing involves converting thoughts or speech to print. In contemporary society, reading and writing are essential skills and anyone who fails to acquire them, for whatever reason, is at a considerable disadvantage. Writing also plays a vital role in language survival, by allowing a record of the language to be retained across generations: a language without writing is unlikely to survive.

The principal way we use language is through speech (or a related mode of output such as sign language). This aspect of language has been a feature of human cognition for tens of thousands of years, and is without parallel in the animal kingdom. Spoken language is found in all human groups and would seem to be qualitatively different from the communication systems of other species.

People also communicate non-verbally. Non-language vocalizations (e.g. grunts, groans) can convey information, and gestures can supplement or substitute for spoken language (see Jacobs & Garnham, 2007; McNeil, 1992). There are many speculative accounts of the origins of human speech. Some accounts highlight the interaction between spoken language and gesture use (e.g. Corballis, 2003). Gesture is so closely tied to human language that we continue to gesture even when we cannot be seen; it is common for people to gesture as they communicate over the telephone, for example (Bavelas et al., 2008; see Chapter 8 for more on gesture and embodied cognition). Subtler non-verbal signals such as body language and tone of voice (see Chapter 2) also communicate to others, whether we are aware of this or not.

Languages vary on a number of dimensions, but also have features in common, an issue we explore next.

LANGUAGE UNIVERSALS

Estimates regarding the number of languages in use worldwide vary considerably, depending on the criteria used to count speech systems as distinct languages. There are about 6000 languages (e.g. Comrie 1989; Crystal, 1998; Krauss 1992; Moseley, 2007) in use worldwide, and this figure is decreasing. Many of these languages are close to extinction, with a very small number of speakers and few or no child speakers. For example, Krauss (1992) noted 187 indigenous languages in North America, only 20 per cent of which were still being learned by children. In fact, just 4 per cent of the world's languages is spoken by 96 per cent of the world's population, placing many languages on the 'endangered' list (Crystal, 2000). Krauss (1992, p. 7) estimated that as few as 10 per cent of the world's languages will remain in a hundred years, with minority languages facing increasing pressure from the dominant, majority languages (see also Crystal, 2000).

Languages vary in the number and type of sounds used, in basic word order, in the size of their vocabularies (reflecting the number of items in the lexicon) and in their rules for sentence construction. However, all are capable of expressing complex and new ideas: there are no 'primitive' languages. Though the precise way in which concepts are expressed may differ across languages (e.g. Boroditsky, 2001; see Chapter 13), the expression of complex ideas is evident in all languages and in all human groups.

Mental lexicon is our store of knowledge about words and their uses.
Linguistic universals are linguistic features said to be found in all languages.

Languages have some key features in common, though it proves to be a difficult task to identify a set of linguistic universals, that is, features that are shared by all languages. Aitchison (1996, p. 177) lists the following features as 'absolute universals' and acknowledges that even these are problematic. According to Aitchison, all languages:

- have consonants and vowels;
- combine basic sounds into larger units;
- have nouns (words for people, places and objects, e.g. book);
- have verbs (words that represent actions or 'doing', e.g. to read);
- can combine words in meaningful ways;
- can express who did what to whom;
- can express sentences as negatives;
- can express sentences as questions;
- are structure-dependent, that is, involve a syntactic structure or grammar;
- allow recursion (the use of a rule within itself, allowing, for example, embedded sentences).

There are, as Aitchison points out, immediate problems with this listing. Sign languages are language, though they do not use a system of vowels and consonants. Some languages do not reliably distinguish between classes of nouns and verbs. Some nouns can represent actions (e.g. 'destruction') and nouns can be used as verbs ('to text'). Table 12.2 provides a summary of the parts of speech, such as nouns and verbs. While all spoken languages are based on combinations of vowel and consonants sounds, the precise set of sounds varies considerably across languages (see the section on phonology to follow). MacNeilage (1999) identifies the syllable, that is a vowel and consonant combination, as a universal unit of speech. Some languages use other sounds in addition to vowels and consonants. For example, in tonal languages,

> Tonal languages use changes in tone to alter the meaning of the word.

Table 12.2 The lexical categories (word classes or 'parts of speech') of English. See *The Cambridge Grammar of the English Language* (Huddleston and Pullum, 2002).

Category	Description
Verb	A very large class of words among which are many denoting actions (*run, jump, swim*) or states or experiences (*feel, see, think*). Auxiliary verbs mark tense, aspect and modality (*has eaten, is eating, may eat*). Verbs that take a direct object (as in *The dog ate the bone*) are called transitive verbs. Others are intransitive (*The dog slept*).
Noun	An extremely large class of words including the words denoting people, places, things, or abstract ideas in the broadest sense. The nouns include not only *desk, book, football, house*, etc., but also *absence, thought, possibility, failure*, etc. Proper nouns begin with a capital letter and name particular people, places, or things: *Barack Obama, London, Disneyland*. The pronouns are a special subclass of the nouns, used for referring to things without naming them (often because they are named elsewhere in the context): *he, she, I, you, they, it*.
Determinative	The fairly small class of determinatives includes words usually used with nouns to specify definiteness or quantity: *the, a, some, all, every, many, much, several, this*, etc. Sometimes they occur without nouns (*Some may disagree; I like this*), or in other uses (*So much the better*).
Adjective	The adjectives are a large class of words that typically modify or qualify the meaning of nouns, as *brown* does in *the brown dog* or *Our dog is brown*: words like *happy, cloudy, intelligent, mysterious, cool*, and many others.
Adverb	The great majority of the adverbs are formed from adjectives by adding *ly*: *nice* is an adjective and *nicely* is an adverb. They very commonly modify words other than nouns, providing information about where, when, how, or to what extent things happen: *locally, recently, awkwardly, extremely*, Adverbs unrelated to adjectives include *soon, quite, too, always, seldom*.
Preposition	Prepositions often precede noun phrases to indicate spatial or temporal relationships, as in *the book is on the shelf*. The prepositions include *after, at, before, by, despite, during, except, for, in, into, of, on, over, since, through, to, under, with, without*. some occur before clauses (*after we met*), and some occur without anything following (*Go right in*).
Subordinator	There is a very small class of words called subordinators that function to mark clauses embedded in other clauses: *that* as in *that nobody loves me*; *whether* as in *whether anybody loves me*; *for* as in *for someone to love me*.
Coordinator	There is a very small class of words called coordinators, used to link clauses or phrases together: *and, or, but, nor*, and a very few others. (The subordinators and coordinators are traditionally classed together and called 'conjunctions'.)
Interjection	An interjection is a word that interrupts a sentence with an immediate expression of emotion or sentiment: *yikes, oops, shush, ouch*, etc.

altering the tone of expression communicates meaning. In English, and non-tonal languages generally, we can change the tone of the utterance for emphasis, or to convey emotion, but doing so does not alter the meaning of the word. In a tonal language, the tone carries meaning. In Mandarin, for example, a language with a relatively small number of syllables, 'ma' can mean 'mother', 'horse' or 'scold', if the tone is even, falls then rises, or falls, respectively (Ladefoged, 1993, p. 255).

Some languages use unusual classes of consonant sounds. There are about 30 languages in Southern Africa (e.g. the Xhosa, Khoikhoi and Sosotho languages) which use a 'click' sound (like the 'tut tut'/ 'tsk' sound in English). These clicks may originally have aided communication while hunting, as they mimic natural environmental sounds and therefore would not have startled prey (Knight et al., 2003). Sounds that qualify as meaningful differ substantially across languages. Even in languages with many features in common (e.g. German and English) the precise set of speech sounds varies. Given this diversity, an approach to defining language based on broad design features may prove more fruitful.

Hockett's design features for human language

Scan to watch a
video about animals
learning language

Charles Hockett's (1960) set of 16 design features for human language was formulated with the aim of identifying properties that are unique to human languages and differentiate them from other animal communication systems. While animal communication systems share some of the following features, only human language demonstrates the full set. The design features treat speech as the standard mode of expression.

1 *Vocal–auditory communication channel*: Languages normally transmit information via spoken sound with the sender speaking and the receiver hearing the spoken signal (sign systems use the tactile-visual medium to similar effect). Many animal systems use vocalizations as the means of communicating while other animals use non-vocal means to communicate. For example, a honeybee uses a 'figure of eight' shaped dance to signal information about the location, distance and quality of a food source (Von Frisch, 1962).

2 *Broadcast transmission and directional reception*: The speech signal is transmitted out from the source (the speaker's mouth) and is localized in space by the receiver.

3 *Rapid fading*: The spoken message fades after production, unlike, for example, written language, which can be inspected over time.

4 *Interchangeability*: The sender can also be a receiver and vice versa. The speaker role is interchangeable and not fixed.

5 *Feedback*: The speaker has access to the message and can monitor its content. This allows us to monitor and correct errors or slips in spoken language and, as Hockett pointed out (1960, p. 6), this kind of cognitive access forms the basis for the internalization of language as verbal thought.

6 *Specialization*: The energy expended in producing the message does not alter the meaning of the message. Whether we whisper or shout the utterance, the meaning of the words remains the same, although we can change the emphasis by altering the vocal energy, or indeed communicate non-literal meaning using a change in tone (e.g. sarcasm).

7 *Semanticity*: Sounds within speech refer to objects and entities in the world: words have meaning. There is an element of semanticity in some animal calls. For example, vervet monkeys use a system of predator alarm calls with distinct calls for snakes,

eagles and leopards (Seyfarth et al., 1980). The calls are more likely to be made in the presence of other monkeys and, in particular, in the presence of kin (Cheney & Seyfarth, 2005). This use of specific calls by animals is referred to as *functional reference* and the information contained in the signal allows the signaller's conspecifics (members of same species) to react appropriately. However, there is little flexibility in their use.

> **Functional reference** refers to the use by animals of a specific call to stand for a specific object or threat.

8 *Arbitrariness*: The relationship between the spoken word and its referent in the world is arbitrary. Apart from a small number of onomatopoeic words (e.g. *hiss, buzz, cuckoo* and *murmur*), the form of the signal (the way it sounds) does not relate to its meaning directly.

9 *Discreteness*: The speech signal is composed of discrete units. Vocabulary is built up from smaller meaning units and the meaning units in turn are built from the basic sounds of the language. These sounds are perceived categorically. Change the /p/ sound in 'pin' to a /b/ sound and you have a different word with its own meaning, 'bin' (we follow the convention here of representing sounds by a letter between forward slashes, e.g. /p/).

10 *Displacement*: We can use language to refer to things that are displaced from the present situation, either in time or space. By contrast, animal systems tend to be tied to the current context. In the vervet monkeys' signalling system mentioned above, the issuing of an alarm call is triggered by the presence of a perceived threat but the calls cannot be used flexibly outside of that context. There is no way to communicate 'I saw that eagle earlier' or 'Bob says he saw a leopard' (see Harley, 2010).

11 *Productivity*: Language allows us to create novel utterances. This aspect of language is a fundamental distinguishing feature of human language and its basis lies in syntax (Chomsky, 1986). Productivity is also referred to as openness or generativity. From the earliest stages of language development, speech is characterized by novelty. We do not just repeat back speech we have heard; we say things in new ways. Likewise, we can understand novel sentences that we will not have encountered before.

12 *Cultural transmission*: A language is learned through interaction with more experienced users of the language within a verbal community.

13 *Duality (of patterning)*: Meaningful elements are created by combining a small set of meaningless units. For example, the 40 or so sounds of the English language are as and of themselves meaningless; however, they combine in meaningful ways to allow us to utter all the words in the English language.

14 *Prevarication*: Language can be used to deceive and lie. Furthermore, the messages we create may lack an obvious meaning.

15 *Reflexiveness*: We can use language to communicate about language. The sentences you are currently reading are an example of this property of language. Animal systems lack this feature; as Harley (2008) comments, 'bees will never dance a book about the psychology of the bee dance' (p. 57).

16 *Learnability*: A language can be learned by a speaker of another language.

These features are not independent, as Hockett noted. For example, semanticity and arbitrariness are related: words have meaning, they refer to something in the world (semanticity) and the relationship between the sound of the word and the thing it refers to is not physically direct (arbitrariness).

The design features apply to spoken language and do not apply fully to sign languages (which it is generally agreed show similar linguistic properties to spoken language) or to written language. However, they provide a useful general way of differentiating animal communication systems from language. While animal systems have some of Hockett's properties for language, the full set of design features is only found in language.

COMPONENTS OF LANGUAGE

Language is a structured system which uses a finite set of sounds to construct words, sentences and ultimately conversations. The components of language, from the smallest to the largest parts, are phonemes, morphemes, syntax and discourse. In order to understand language, it is useful to consider these components independently; we start with the sounds of language, phonemes.

Phonemes

Phonemes are the basic sounds that make up speech within a language and the term phonology refers to the system of sounds in a language. There are about 100 basic sound units or phones (as listed in the International Phonetic Alphabet) that can be used to make up words. This represents the full set of available sounds; the study of these raw sounds is called phonetics. No one language uses all these sounds; instead, languages use a subset of phones, and languages vary considerably in the number of sounds used. The sounds within a language are called phonemes. These are the smallest meaningful sound units in a language. The number of phonemes within a language varies – there are 44 in (British) English, while some Polynesian languages (e.g. Hawaiian) have as few as 12, and there are over 140 in the African language Khoisan (Chierchia, 2001). Table 12.3 shows the number of phonemes in a selection of European languages.

> Phones are the basic speech sounds.
> Phonetics is the study of speech sounds.
> Phoneme is the smallest meaningful sound unit within a language.
> Allophones are phonetic variants of the same phoneme.

Some basic vowel sounds occur in all languages, but consonants can be used differently and are perceived differently. For example, in English, there is no perceived difference between the aspirated (i.e. said with a puff of air) /p/ sound in *pin* and the unaspirated /p/ in *spin*, but in Thai these are two distinct phonemes. Similarly, in English the /t/ sounds in *tea* and in *trip* are different phones, but these are treated as one phoneme; if you substitute the *t* sounds, the pronunciation may sound a little odd, but it is still the same word. Phonemes also change as a function of the surrounding sounds in words and in sentences, an effect referred to as co-articulation. Different phones that are treated as the same phoneme within a language are called allophones. Phonemes therefore do not correspond directly to physical sounds; rather they are 'abstract representations of the phonological units of a language, the units used to represent the forms of word in our mental lexicons' (Fromkin et al., 2003, p. 285). A phoneme is a rather subjective category that is recognized as meaningful by the speakers of a language, but is not necessarily constant as objectively measured (see Chapter 13).

Table 12.3 The number of phonemes in a selection of European languages (from Tambovtsev & Martindale, 2007).

Language	Number of phonemes
Finnish	56
German	51
Italian	49
English (British)	44
Swedish	41
Dutch	39
French	36
Norwegian	36
Greek	25
Portuguese	25
Spanish	24

Source: SKASE Journal of Theoretical Linguistics

The tendency to perceive the difference between two allophones decreases with age (e.g. Iverson et al., 2003), suggesting a critical period beyond which the adult is 'tuned' to the sounds of his or her native language. While a child can discriminate between the full set of phones, an adult generally cannot; a child who is exposed to a second language can acquire native-like ability and accent, while the parents, coming late to the language, may struggle to acquire it and never acquire a native-like accent (see Bongaerts et al. 1995; Dewaele, 2009; Singleton, 2001). For example, the difference between /l/ and /r/ sounds in English is not readily discriminated by Japanese adults, for whom /l/ and /r/ are treated as allophones (Ingram, 2007). While young children can appreciate the difference, by adulthood this ability is reduced. This reduction in discrimination with linguistic experience may serve to reduce the ambiguity in the incoming speech signal, facilitating language comprehension, an issue we return to in Chapter 13.

Phonological and phonotactic rules describe which sounds can go together in a given language. For example, in English, a /t/ sound does not follow a /b/ sound and [ng] can occur at the end of the word (as in 'king') but not at the beginning. These rules differ across languages so that sounds that are 'natural' and easy to produce and discriminate in one language may not be so easy for adult speakers of another language. Speech segmentation relies on knowledge of word boundaries using information about phonotactic probabilities in a language (see Chapter 13).

> **Phonotactic rules** stipulate which combinations of sounds are 'permitted' in a language.

Changing a phoneme within a word will change the meaning of that word, for example *bat* and *pat*. This is an example of a minimal pair, so called because the words differ by just one phoneme. All spoken languages use vowels and consonants, but, as outlined above, the exact set used varies across languages. Maddieson (1984) examined a 300 language sample and found that the number of consonants varied from 6–95 sounds, with a mean of 23, while vowel sounds varied from 3–47, with a mean of 9.

Morphemes

Morphemes are the meaning units of a language. They are the building blocks of words. A single word may consist of several morphemes. The term morphology refers to the study of the rules in a language according to which words can be constructed. Morphology can be considered as a special case of syntax (see below).

> **Morphemes** are the meaning units of language.
> **Morphology** is the level of linguistic analysis concerned with morphemes and their role within words.
> **Free morpheme** is a morpheme that can stand alone as a word.
> **Bound morpheme** is a morpheme that cannot form a word on its own, but forms a word when attached to a free morpheme.

In English, regular plural nouns are created by adding –s to the end of a word, for example, *one car* but *two cars*; *one horse, two horses*, etc. In these examples, there is one morpheme in the singular forms (*car*) but two in the plural (*cars*), the stem or root word (car) and the plural suffix inflection (-s). The noun *car* is an example of a free morpheme, as it can occur on its own, whereas the plural form –s is a bound morpheme, because it does not carry meaning unless it is attached to a free morpheme. Here, the –s is an example of an inflectional morpheme; it serves a grammatical function but does not change the syntactic category of the word to which it is attached (*car* is still a noun when the –s is added to make *cars*). Similarly, the verb endings –ed and –ing are inflectional morphemes. Some bound morphemes, like –ify, –ish, –able and –ment, are derivational morphemes, as they create new words with new meaning when added to a stem. They can change the grammatical category of the word. For example, the verb *develop* becomes a noun when you add –ment to give *development*. Words can be altered by adding a morpheme to the start of the word (a prefix) or to the end (a suffix) and language-specific rules govern the ways in which words can be altered. The verb *depend* becomes *dependence* when we add the suffix –ence, meaning 'condition' or 'state'; adding the prefix –in, meaning 'not', yields *independence*, and so on.

Such alterations apply only to content words (e.g. nouns, adjectives and verbs); these are open class words which can be altered or invented as usage changes. In some languages inflections on content words can be particularly informative. In Hungarian, for example, the morpheme at the end of the word indicates the word's role in the sentence, and codes whether it is a direct or indirect object. For example, consider these sentences in English and in Hungarian (example from Hoff, 2005):

The boy gave a book to the girl.

A fiú egy könyvet adott a lánynak. (The boy a book gave the girl.)

Here, 'book' is the direct object in the sentence (it is given), while girl is the indirect object (the book is given to the girl). While in English we tend to rely on word order, in most cases, to understand the role of the word in the sentence, in the Hungarian sentence above the morphemes *et* at the end of 'könyvet' and *nak* at the end of 'lánynak' give the role of the word. In this example, content words are altered to indicate the word's role in the sentence; in grammatical terms the inflections are accusative and dative case markers, respectively.

> **Function words** provide grammatical structure that shows how content words relate to each other within a sentence.

Function words, the words that do the grammatical work of a sentence do not change (prepositions, for example; see Table 12.2) – they are a closed class of morphemes. As we will see, content words and function words are to some extent treated differently in language processing.

Semantics and the lexicon

Morphemes make up words, which in turn make up our vocabulary. Our knowledge of words and their meanings are stored in a kind of mental dictionary called the mental lexicon. The lexicon is a part of the semantic memory system (see Chapter 5). It holds our store of words and associated knowledge and links words with our general knowledge about concepts and the world. As adults, we have a store of tens of thousands of words, from which we normally have immediate access to target words as we construct a sentence. Only occasionally will we experience difficulty in calling a target word to mind, a temporary failure referred to as the tip-of-the-tongue effect (more on this later in this chapter).

It is difficult to estimate the size of an adult's vocabulary; some studies suggest that adults know about 70,000 words (e.g. Bock & Garnsey, 1998; Nagy & Anderson, 1984). Miller (1977) estimated that the average English speaking college student had a vocabulary of about 150,000 words; subsequent estimates put the figure closer to 20,000 word families, where a word family consists of a base word, and inflected and derived forms (e.g. Goulden, Nation & Read, 1990). The range of estimates reflects the difficulty in accurately measuring vocabulary and the importance of defining the unit of measurement.

Words are symbols; they are meaningful sounds and generally have a particular referent. A word might be defined as 'the smallest unit of grammar that can stand on its own as a complete utterance' (Crystal 1997, p. 440); in writing, words are generally separated by spaces. People also use other meaningful sounds, though not all are words. For example, we might use a groan to signal disagreement or a yawn to signal boredom, but these are not words. A few words are not referential, that is they have no clear referent – greetings and social conventions (e.g. saying *hello*) for example.

> **Word** is the smallest unit of grammar that can be meaningfully produced on its own; it can consist of one or more morphemes. **Semantics** is the study of meaning.

The question of what words mean and how they relate to each other raises some complex issues. Semantics refers to the meaning of words and morphemes and the relationship between the words we use and the objects they refer to in the world.

Syntax

We construct novel sentences when we speak; we do not generally repeat back or 'parrot' previous productions. Imagine you are telling a story to a friend when another friend joins the group and you have to start your story over. The chances are, though the meaning or gist of your story will not change, the exact sentences you use will differ. This reflects the productivity of human language; we do not rely on rote or stock phrases, or on memory for practised utterances. Instead we create new sentences as and when we need them. This is evident from the earliest stages of syntactic development in young children.

> **Productivity of language** refers to the ability to generate novel utterances.
> **Phrase** is a group of words referring to a particular idea.
> **Slang** describes an informal pattern of speech that is considered to be 'non-standard'.

Two aspects of the language system allow us to use language productively: syntax and morphology. The term syntax describes the rules that determine the construction of phrases and sentences in a language. It relates to grammar but the term syntax is used more often than grammar, to differentiate it from the notion of 'prescriptive' grammar. Prescriptive grammar reflects conventions for sentence construction and is based on tradition and language prestige rather than actual language use. For example, split infinitives ('*to boldly go* where no-one has gone before') and prepositions at the end of sentences ('prepositions are not good words to end a sentence *with*') violate conventions of prescriptive grammar, but are often found in everyday speech.

Similarly, slang may not always meet with approval, but could nevertheless be syntactically correct: the ambiguous 'I don't know nothing' might not be considered 'good form', but the same sentence would never be uttered as 'know I nothing don't'. The study of syntax reflects descriptive grammar, that is, it reflects how language is used.

Sentences follow a hierarchical structure and are made up of two parts: a noun phrase (NP) which contains a noun, often the subject of the sentence, and a verb phrase (VP) which contains the verb and conveys the 'action' of the sentence. For example, in the sentence 'Sarah drank the coffee', Sarah (the subject of the sentence) is the NP and 'drank the coffee' is the VP. English, French, German and related languages use a subject-verb-object or SVO word order, that is, in a declarative (active voice) sentence the subject (or agent of the sentence) comes first, followed by the verb and then the object of the sentence. The order in which the words occur determines the meaning of the sentence; to use Pinker's (1994) example, 'dog bites man' is not news-worthy, but 'man bites dog' is (p. 83). The most common word orders are SOV and SVO (Greenberg, 1963) and although there are examples of the six possible types (SOV, SVO, VSO, VOS, OVS, OSV), OVS and OSV are extremely rare (Dryer, 2005; Song, 2001). Some languages have more flexible words orders; for example, Japanese is mainly SOV and Russian is SVO but both languages can use other word orders because of their use of case markings. This agent-first bias in world languages is not restricted to spoken languages. It is also found in the 'homesign' produced by deaf signers with hearing parents (Goldin et al., 1990). It also appears in second languages acquired without explicit instruction (Klein & Perdue, 1997).

> **Subject** of a sentence is the word or words that gives what the sentence is about or performs the action.
> **Object** of a sentence is the word or words that receives the action, or is acted on, by the subject of the sentence.

One key property of syntax underlies the productivity of sentence construction. Recursion refers to the repeated application of a rule and, using recursion, the same rule can be applied again and again to create a novel

> **Recursion** refers to the ability to extend sentences infinitely by embedding phrases within sentences.

utterance. Recursion has been argued to be an essential property of human language (e.g. Chomsky, 1986). Embedded sentences make use of this property, and sentences can in principle (though not generally in practice) be extended indefinitely. For example, the English language nursery rhyme 'The house that Jack built' is an example of a cumulative rhyme using recursion:

This is the house that Jack built.

This is the malt that lay in the house that Jack built.

This is the rat that ate the malt that lay in the house that Jack built.

This is the cat that killed the rat that ate the malt that lay in the house that Jack built.

This is the dog that worried the cat that killed the rat that ate the malt that lay in the house that Jack built . . .

Recursion would seem to be a resilient property of human language as even young children who have been deprived of language input retain the ability to use recursion (Goldin-Meadow, 1982). The extent to which recursion is uniquely human has been challenged, however. For example, songbirds have been shown to be sensitive to recursion and can classify novel patterns accordingly and reliably reject 'ungrammatical' patterns (Gentner et al., 2006).

Discourse

Discourse refers to multi-sentence speech and includes dialogue, conversation and narrative. Pragmatics refers to the understanding of the communicative functions of language and the conventions that govern language use.

Discourse refers to multi-sentence speech and includes dialogue, conversation and narrative. At this 'higher' level of language function, the social conventions that affect language processing become increasingly relevant and people rely on schemas (see Chapters 5 and 7) in order to process language. Pragmatics refers to the understanding of the communicative functions of language and the conventions that govern language use. At the level of discourse, the function of language in communicating directly and indirectly comes to the fore. A distinction is made between linguistic competence, which refers to our ability to construct sentences, and communicative competence, which refers to our ability to communicate a message effectively (Hymes, 1972). Language can be perfectly well formed, but if we fail to appreciate the social conventions governing its use, we may not communicate as we intended.

Effective discourse is based on a shared understanding between those engaging in a conversation. For example, if two people are conversing and one asks the other a question, there is an implicit agreement that the response will be related to the question. Similarly, participants in a conversation are expected to adhere to the topic of the conversation. If someone wishes to deviate from the topic or to change the subject, it is customary to signal this change of focus, by prefacing the utterance with 'by the way . . .', for example.

Conversations require turn-taking and cooperation and participants follow a set of implicit social conventions. A variety of verbal and non-verbal signals serve to regulate the conversation by indicating who speaks when and for how long. These turn-taking cues act to minimize overlap between speakers and reduce gaps or silences in conversation. Conversational turn-taking has several features (Sachs et al., 1974). One party speaks at a time; the person speaking changes. The duration of a turn is not predefined; the order of turns also varies. Transitions between turns are coordinated; overlap is minimized. These patterns hold in the absence of face-to-face information, for example, in telephone conversations (De Ruiter et al., 2006). Despite the differences in linguistic features across languages, there are striking universals in turn-taking patterns, as is explored in Box 12.1.

Box 12.1 Research Close Up: Cross language universals in conversational turn-taking

Source: Stivers, T. et al. (2009). Universals and cultural variation in turn-taking in conversation. *Proceedings of the National Academy of Sciences of the United States of America, 106*, 10587–10592.

INTRODUCTION

Stivers et al. set out to examine the extent to which there are cultural differences in turn-taking in everyday conversations. They tested two opposing hypotheses. The 'universal system' hypothesis predicts little cross-linguistic variability and predicts that most languages will use a 'minimal-gap minimal-overlap' convention, as in found in English. On the other hand, the 'cultural variability' hypothesis, based on anthropological accounts, holds that turn-taking practices differ considerably across languages and cultures.

METHOD

Stivers et al. (2009) analysed video recordings of informal conversations in 10 languages from five continents. The languages varied in structural properties (e.g. word order, grammar) and were drawn from different cultures, ranging from hunter–gatherer groups to large-scale industrialized societies. All conversations were spontaneous, informal conversations, with 2–6 participants. Questions and responses were timed, coded for their form and function, and coders judged whether the responses were delayed.

RESULTS

Striking similarities emerged across the languages supporting a 'minimal-gap minimal-overlap' norm. While there was some variation across languages, the mean response time for a turn transition was very similar across languages (see Figure 12.1). Of the languages examined, Danish had the slowest response time on average (+469 milliseconds), while Japanese had the fastest (+7 milliseconds). Italian (309 milliseconds), English (236 milliseconds) and Dutch (109 milliseconds) fell between these extremes. The mean response time across languages was +208 milliseconds, and each language's mean was within 250 milliseconds of the cross-language mean: as Stivers et al. note, this is about the time it takes to say a single syllable in English. In other words, responses tended neither to overlap nor be delayed by more than half a second.

Furthermore, the factors that predicted the speed of a response were

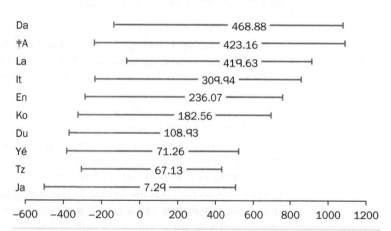

Figure 12.1 **Mean time (in milliseconds, shown on the x axis) of turn transitions for 10 languages.** Speakers of all languages have an average offset time within 500 milliseconds, while averages vary considerable across the languages. Languages shown along the y axis are: Da, Danish; ǂĀ, ǂĀkhoe Haillom; La, Lao; It, Italian; En, English; Ko, Korean; Du, Dutch; Yé, Yélî-Dnye; Tz, Tzeltal; Ja, Japanese.

Source: Stivers, T. et al. (2009). Universals and cultural variation in turn-taking in conversation. *PNAS, 106*, 10587–10592.

identical across the languages. When visible responses were made (e.g. a headshake, a nod), they occurred faster than speech in all the languages. Confirmation responses were faster than disconfirmation responses. Questions accompanied by a gaze received faster responses than those without, and answer responses (e.g. 'yes') were significantly faster than non-answer responses (e.g., 'I don't recall').

DISCUSSION

These data support strong universals in turn-taking patterns across languages, and suggest a common pattern whereby the gaps between turns, and overlaps, are minimized. While there were some differences between languages, in real terms these differences are very small. The 'long silences' associated with Nordic languages, for example, evident in the Danish response times, amount to a delay equivalent to about one syllable. The data were limited to question–response sequences, however; it would be interesting to see if similar findings apply to other types of interactions.

Grice (1957, 1975) identified a set of four conversation rules or maxims that describe effective conversations and reflect the expectations of listeners. Grice's four maxims are:

1 *Maxim of quantity*: The speaker should provide enough information in order to be understood but not too much information.

2 *Maxim of quality*: The speaker should provide accurate information.

3 *Maxim of relevance*: The speaker should provide information that is relevant to the current topic of conversation.

4 *Maxim of manner*: Ambiguity and vagueness should be avoided.

If the maxims are violated, more cognitive processing is required to determine the response, or the participants may have to backtrack or repair the conversation. Of course, violation of these rules can also form the basis of humour – hyperbole, sarcasm and irony violate the maxim of quality.

Thus far, when we consider the meaning of words we have treated this as what the word *denotes*, that is its literal meaning; a word denotes its referent. We are also able to communicate indirectly, however. If you were sitting next to an open window and someone said to you 'It is cold', the utterance might be taken as meaning 'Can you close the window?' We must also consider the connotations that words evoke. Connotation refers to the non-literal aspects of word meaning and reflects social and cultural factors that affect the literal processing of word meaning. Words can be perceived as having a positive or negative connotation (see Jay & Danks, 1977). If you hear someone say, 'Bob eats like a pig', it is of course literally true, in that the manner of eating (the movements of the jaw, and so on) is similar in many animals; however, it is likely that something else is meant. It is likely that Bob is being insulted and the connotation created by the phrase could mean that Bob is a messy eater or that he is greedy. Similarly, words can attract a positive value through use and this affects understanding of their literal meaning. The word 'natural' is much used in advertising, for example, and its use relies on the fact that people perceive 'natural' as having a value: 'natural' is equated with 'good'. The many entirely natural but life threatening infections that assail humanity do not seem to be evoked by the term, nor do 'natural disasters' spring to mind.

Having considered the constituents of language we now move on to examine how language is put together so that phonemes, morphemes and syntax become discourse. Much of what we know about this process is derived from the study of speech errors.

SPEECH ERRORS

Speech is produced at a rate of about 15 speech sounds and 2–4 words per second (Levelt, 1989) and for the most part is fluent and well formed. Slips and errors in spontaneous speech are quite rare, with some studies finding errors less than once per 500 uttered sentences (Dell et al., 1997; Garnham et al., 1981; see also Levelt, 2001). Error rates are low despite the rapid rate at which sounds must be selected from a production vocabulary of about 20,000 words (Groome et al., 1999). Hesitations and pauses in spontaneous speech are common, however.

Many of the theories of speech production outlined later in this chapter originate from analyses of speech errors. Data about errors come from several sources. The first source involves examining temporary breakdowns in the system's functioning, which occur from time to time, under normal conditions. Speech errors such as slips of the tongue and tip-of-the-tongue effects (when we cannot fully access a target word from the lexicon) are examples of this type of 'malfunction'. Second, errors can be induced in the laboratory, by having people articulate very quickly, for example. Third, the study of acquired brain injury has shown how damage to certain brain areas affects speech and language processing. Aphasia is the term used for acquired disorders of language, a topic we return to shortly. First, we look at hesitation and pauses in normal speech.

> Aphasia is the term given to a group of speech disorders that occur following brain injury.

HESITATIONS AND PAUSES

Disfluencies such as pauses are more common than actual errors and vary with the situation and the individual. They are a natural characteristic of fluent speech. Estimates suggest that about six in 100 words are affected by disfluency (Fox Tree, 1995). These pauses can be silent or filled (common fillers include *um*, *ah* or *er*; see Maclay & Osgood, 1959, for an early account of their use). Filled pauses occur with less frequency than silent pauses (O'Connell & Kowal, 2004) and may serve to announce a delay in speech (Clark & Fox Tree, 2002). During pauses, the speaker plans the articulation of their next words (Butterworth, 1980). Goldman-Eisler (1968) found that when participants were instructed to speak about a given topic, pause duration accounted for as much as half of the total time (although the method used to arrive at this estimate has been questioned; O'Connell & Kowal, 2004). The use of pauses varies with context, task demands and from individual to individual. Schacter et al. (1991) found that pauses in academic lectures varied with academic discipline, with science lecturers producing fewer pauses than humanities lecturers. This may reflect the more precise terminology employed by scientists; if there are fewer words to choose from, word choice is facilitated. Pauses within clauses and sentences would seem to reflect formulation of ideas and word selection (Velmans, 2009).

> Disfluency is a hesitation or disruption to the normal fluency of speech. By contrast, the term 'dysfluency' is used to refer to an abnormal disruption to fluency, such as following brain damage. The use of the prefix 'dys-' signals 'abnormal'.
> Clause is a part of a sentence containing a subject and verb.

Some disfluencies may facilitate comprehension. For example, Fox Tree (2001) found that hearing an 'uh' aided listeners' recognition of subsequent words, suggesting that some disfluencies may act as cues that direct listeners' attention towards a particular word (see Box 13.1 in the next chapter). Hesitations have also been studied as potential cues to deception, as is explored in Box 12.2.

Box 12.2 Practical Application: Using verbal cues to detect a liar

There is a widespread misconception that it is easy to tell a liar from his or her demeanour, that certain behavioural cues reliably indicate when someone is lying. In fact, the average person cannot detect lies reliably and attends to the wrong cues when attempting to do so. Even people who might be expected to have had considerable exposure to deception are not necessarily effective at lie detection. Ekman and O'Sullivan (1991) examined lie detection by a sample of 509 people, including members of the US Secret Service, CIA, police and judges, as well as college students and other adults. They showed participants a videotape of 10 people who had been instructed to lie or tell the truth. Only the Secret Service personnel could detect lies at an above chance level, with average accuracy in this group of 64 per cent.

What can psychology tell us about how to detect lying? Vrij et al. (2001) note that someone who is lying, compared to someone telling the truth, tends to have a higher voice pitch, produces more hesitations and speech errors, speaks more slowly and uses fewer illustrators (e.g. hand gestures), and shows decreased hand, leg and foot movements. Furthermore, the liar's account of events produces fewer details than a true account (Vrij, 2004). These features are associated with the increased cognitive load involved in lying and are also observed when people engage in a cognitively complex or challenging task. People *perceive* lying to be associated with the following features: higher voice pitch, slow speech, more hesitations and errors, delayed responses to questions, averting eye gaze, smiling more often, and increased movements (Vrij, 2000). We therefore seem to attend to the wrong cues when attempting to detect lying, while people who attend to speech-related factors rather than behavioural cues would seem to be more effective at lie detection (Mann et al., 2004; Vrij & Mann, 2001).

Many studies of lie detection involve laboratory manipulations, with 'liars' instructed to deceive under various conditions. In real-life, lying may present differently, particularly when the stakes are high and the consequences of getting caught out in a lie are serious. Vrij and Mann (2001) examined the behaviour of a murderer who had been interviewed by the police on several occasions. The series of interviews had been videotaped. While the man initially denied that he was involved in the victim's death, the evidence suggested otherwise. He subsequently confessed to the crime and was convicted of murder. The videotaped interviews therefore allowed the researchers to examine the man's behaviour while lying (pre-confession) and telling the truth (during his confession).

While lying, the man produced longer pauses, slower speech and had more speech disturbances than when telling the truth, features that are consistent with lying carrying a heavier cognitive load. In a second part to Vrij and Mann's study, 65 police officers watched video fragments that had been selected from the interviews. The overall accuracy rate in the experiment was 64 per cent, which was significantly above chance; however, this resulted from good detection of truth rather than accurate detection of lies. In fact, accuracy of lie detection (at 57 per cent) was not above chance. The individual differences in lie detection were striking, and may reflect differences in selection of cues. Mann et al. (2004) found that police officers' accuracy was negatively correlated with reliance on stereotypical but non-diagnostic cues such as gaze aversion and fidgeting.

Such knowledge is now being applied to improve interview techniques. Vrij et al. (2010) support an 'information gathering' approach to interviewing that contrasts with the 'accusatory' approach often adopted. They note the advantages of the information gathering approach over an accusatory style: it increases the amount of detail provided by a suspect and is associated with more non-verbal and verbal cues to deceit being produced; it is less likely to elicit false confessions; and it is associated with lower interviewer confidence, which safeguards against bias. In addition, Vrij and colleagues suggest asking unanticipated questions to reduce the effects of preparation on the part of the suspect and asking questions about the precise time of events if a suspect appears to be using a scripted answer. Finally, because lying is more cognitively demanding than telling the truth, increasing the cognitive load may serve to differentiate liars from truths tellers. For example, having suspects give their account of events in reverse order increases cognitive load, as does asking event-irrelevant questions.

While speech does not provide us with a linguistic version of the 'Pinocchio's nose' with which to identify a liar, it does provide some relatively diagnostic cues that might be attended to. Such an approach would seem to be more effective than relying on stereotypical body language cues.

SLIPS OF THE TONGUE

In *The Psychopathology of Everyday Life* (1924/1938/1975), Freud treated speech errors as a particular class of parapraxes (action slips). While his emphasis was on supposed underlying repressed thoughts, he recognized that errors could be informative as regards language processing, asking 'whether the mechanisms of this disturbance cannot also suggest the probable laws of the formation of speech' (p. 71). So-called 'Freudian slips' are errors based on a substitution of a semantically or phonologically similar word (see Table 12.4), and, most researchers would now acknowledge, they reflect the cognitive processes underlying sentence formulation, rather than unconscious motivations or conflicts (e.g. see Norman, 1981; Reason, 1990, 2000).

> **Parapraxes** are slips of the tongue or other actions originally thought to reflect unconscious motives.

Fromkin's (1971) analysis provided the first systematic account of error types. Fromkin showed that when errors occur they are not random; in fact they are systematic and are highly informative as to the nature of the underlying processing. The majority of speech errors are sound based errors (Fromkin, 1971, 2004) and errors tend to occur at one linguistic level (e.g. affecting phonemes or morphemes). Types of error are summarized in Table 12.4.

Table 12.4   Examples of types of speech error

Type	Description	Example(s)
Anticipation	Substitutions of a sound in anticipation of a sound that occurs later in the phrase. A full word can also be produced too early within a sentence	Cuff of coffee [cup of coffee]
Perseveration	The repetition of a sound from a previous part of the utterance	proliperation [proliferation]
Transposition/Exchange errors (also called metatheses or spoonerisms)	Transposition of two segments. Exchange errors can also affect words, where two words swap places in the sentence	You hissed all my mystery lectures [missed all my history lectures] You have tasted a whole worm [wasted a whole term]
Blend	A non-word is made based on two semantically related words	Mownly [mainly/mostly] Swinged [switched/changes]
Additions	A sound is added in	Similarily [similarly]
Deletions/omissions	A sound is omitted	Slit second [split second]
Semantic substitutions including Freudian slips	Retrieval of an incorrect but semantically related target	This room is too hot [cold]
Phonological substitutions or malapropisms including Freudian slips	A phonologically similar word is selected in error. Mixed errors, in which the target word and error share both semantic and phonological features, can also occur.	Projects [products] There's a pest in every class [pet] (this could be a deletion)

Lexical bias refers to tendency for phonological speech errors to result in real words.

Analysis of speech errors points to the importance of the phrase as a unit of production, as errors rarely jump across phrase boundaries. The vast majority of morpheme exchanges occur within clauses (Garrett, 1975). Errors preserve the consonant-vowel distinction and phonological errors are in keeping with the phonological constraints of a given language (Fromkin, 1971). Exchange errors show a lexical bias in that they are more likely to result in a word than a non-word (Rapp & Goldrick, 2000) – for example 'barn door' becoming 'darn bore' (Nooteboom & Quene, 2008). The frequency of lexical bias has been disputed; some researchers have argued that lexical bias is not common in spontaneous speech and is more likely to be induced experimentally (e.g. Garrett, 1980), but others argue that it also applies to natural speech (Dell & Reich, 1981). It would seem that the lexical bias effect reflects both immediate feedback between speech sounds and word forms (Dell, 1986) and monitoring of inner speech producing a real word bias (Levelt et al., 1999). In other words, non-word errors are more readily detected and repaired, while real word errors can 'slip through the net' and remain undetected before being uttered (Nooteboom, 2010).

Content words tend to exchange with content words and function words with other function words. Harley (2008) found no instances of content words and function words exchanging in his corpus of several thousand speech errors. Function words and bound morphemes (such as inflections) are generally left in place when a content word or morpheme moves, a pattern referred to as morpheme stranding. The following examples from Fromkin (1971) illustrate:

* nerve of a vergious breakdown [verge of a nervous breakdown];
* a weekend for maniacs [maniac for weekends].

Boomer and Laver (1968) found that stressed and unstressed syllables did not exchange with each other; errors were consistent with the stress pattern in the utterance. Furthermore, transpositions generally stay within the same syntactic or morphological class (Fromkin et al., 2010). These patterns of error suggest a systematic process whereby a sentence is constructed such that 'the word's skeleton or frame and its segmental content are independently generated' (Levelt, 1992, p. 10) and shows that speech production is highly rule governed (Fromkin et al., 2010).

Transposition errors, or metatheses, have been noted for centuries, and have become associated, perhaps unfairly, with the Reverend William Archibald Spooner, who was warden of New College, Oxford in the early 1900s. Many transposition errors were attributed to Spooner and this class of error has therefore become known as 'Spoonerisms'. Among the errors attributed to the Reverend Spooner (see also Table 12.4) are the following:

* you were fighting a liar in the quadrangle/lighting a fire;
* work is the curse of the drinking class/drink is the curse of the working class;
* the queer old dean/the dear old queen.

Many of these are apocryphal or exaggerated; if they were as frequently produced as some commentators have supposed it would suggest an underlying pathology (Potter, 1980).

Speech errors are generally collected from spontaneous speech, either by recording speech or having participants note their own errors in diaries, and large collections of speech errors can be accumulated in this way (e.g. Fromkin, 1971; Harley, 2008). An early example of such a corpus is provided by Meringer and Meyer's (1895) analysis based on a collection of an estimated 8,800 errors in German. Errors can also be induced experimentally, with various techniques developed to elicit errors. For example, the SLIP (Spoonerisms of Laboratory-Induced Predisposition) technique introduced by Baars and Motley (1974) aims to force transposition errors in research participants within a controlled setting. Another type of speech production error that has been induced experimentally with some success is the tip-of-the-tongue (TOT) state.

THE TIP OF THE TONGUE STATE

The tip of the tongue (TOT) state is a temporary inability to access a word from memory; when we experience a TOT, we generally can say whether we know the word and we may have access to some information about the word, such as its initial letter, what it sounds like, or whether it is a long or short word. In languages in which the noun has gender, that information can be available in the TOT state, showing that access to syntactic category information is preserved, although access to the specific phonological word form is unavailable (e.g. Vigliocco et al., 1997). This has implications for models of speech production, as is discussed below.

> Tip-of-the-tongue (TOT) state refers to a temporary inability to access a known word.
> Feeling-of-knowing is a subjective sense of knowing that we know a word, and is an example of meta-memory – our knowledge about the contents of our memories.

In the TOT state the target word is known to us, but we cannot access it; we have a feeling-of-knowing about the target, that is, we are aware that we know the word, yet we cannot produce it. In a review of research on the TOT state, Brown (1991) notes that it:

* is universal;
* occurs about once a week;
* increases in frequency with age;
* frequently affects recall of proper names;
* often involves an available initial letter;
* is often accompanied by other words;
* is resolved on almost half of occasions.

Brown and McNeill (1966) were the first to induce the TOT state experimentally. They read participants' definitions of rare words and asked them to produce the word to which they were referring. For example, they read the definition 'a navigational instrument used in measuring angular distances, especially the altitude of sun, moon and stars at sea'. The target word in this case was 'sextant'. The inability to access low frequency targets induced a TOT state in some participants (nine of 56 participants for this particular definition). Some of the incorrect words produced by participants show that some information is available and that lexical retrieval can involve partial activation. For example, in the case of the target *sextant*, some of the errors included *sexton, sextet, compass* and *protractor*; these are phonologically or semantically related targets. Bilinguals would seem to be more prone to the TOT experience (e.g. Gollan & Acenas, 2004), suggesting that competing lexical activations increase the likelihood of a TOT state occurring. However, the small differences in reaction times observed in the laboratory do not carry profound implications for everyday functioning of bilinguals (Baker, 2006) and should not detract from bilinguals' advantages in other domains (see Box 12.3).

Box 12.3 Research Close Up: Bilingual lexical access

Source: Sandoval, T. C., Gollan, T. H., Ferreira, V. S., & Salmon, D. P. (2010). What causes the bilingual disadvantage in verbal fluency? The dual-task analogy. *Bilingualism: Language and Cognition, 13,* 231–252.

INTRODUCTION

The cognitive effects of bilingualism have been studied for many years and a number of processing costs have been identified. Bilinguals would seem to be at a disadvantage compared to monolinguals on tasks involving the rapid retrieval of words from memory, though ability to access semantic information about those words is not impaired (Bialystok et al., 2009). For example, there is a bilingual disadvantage on the verbal fluency task, in which participants must name in one minute as many words as they can beginning with a given letter (e.g. name words beginning with the letter 's') or belonging to a given category (e.g. names of animals).

METHOD

Sandoval et al. (2010) examined the verbal fluency of 30 monolinguals and 30 bilinguals when naming 15 semantic categories (e.g. 'types of clothing' 'supermarket items', 'spices') and 24 double-letter categories (e.g. words beginning with 'fa'), with order of block presentation counterbalanced. The bilingual participants were English dominant English-Spanish bilinguals. Participants were instructed to name as many examples as they could think of that belonged to each category, with each trial allowing one minute for responses. In Experiment 1 responses were given in English; in a second experiment, responses were made in both languages.

RESULTS

The bilingual participants produced significantly fewer correct responses compared to the monolinguals in both the semantic and letter categories. While both groups of speakers performed better in the semantic category compared to the letter category, the bilingual disadvantage was equal for both types of stimuli. Furthermore, in the semantic task, the monolinguals produced responses of higher word frequency. Bilinguals were also slower than monolinguals to produce their first response at the beginning of a trial. Sandoval et al. suggest that interference between languages accounts for these differences. In a second experiment, responses were made in both languages. The bilinguals produced fewer responses in Spanish (the non-dominant language) than in English, and they were slower to produce their first response for a category in Spanish compared to English. Comparing performance in the two languages, Sandoval et al. found that bilinguals produced more cross-language intrusion errors when using their non-dominant language, while very few intrusions occurred when they spoke in the dominant language.

DISCUSSION

These data suggest that between-language interference in bilinguals creates processing costs that negatively affect verbal fluency, at least in the context of such experimental tasks. Does that mean that bilingualism is disadvantageous in terms of cognitive performance? The balance of evidence would suggest that the advantages of bilingualism far outweigh any potential disadvantages. In addition to the cultural, social and communicative advantages associated with bilingualism and multilingualism, cognitive advantages include greater flexibility and creativity in thinking (Baker & Prys Jones, 1998) and better executive function (Bialystok et al., 2008).

Several of the most influential theories of speech production have been based on analysis of speech errors. Here, we look at three models of speech production: Garrett's
and Dell's accounts, which are based on speech error data and Levelt's account which
takes a different approach.

THEORIES OF SPEECH PRODUCTION

It is generally agreed that there are a number of stages to speech production (e.g.
Levelt, 1989). The first, conceptualization, is a poorly understood process by which a
thought forms and is prepared to be conveyed through language. The processes by
which an abstract thought or idea becomes a verbal thought remain elusive (think, for
example, of the stages before you say to yourself 'I wonder if I turned the oven off
before leaving the house'). The second stage involves the formulation of a linguistic
plan. The concept or proposition must be translated so that the thought becomes language and the sentence that we want to output is planned. This process of translating
from concept to language also remains a mysterious process, and if the goal of such
theories is, as Clark and Clark (1977, p. 10) suggested, 'to discover how speakers turn
ideas into words' we are arguably no closer to the holy grail. Levelt (e.g. 1989) considers the formulation stage as comprising two sub-stages. During the lexicalization
sub-stage, the words are selected from the mental lexicon. In order for this to occur the
concept must connect with the abstract word form or lemma. The lemma contains
semantic and syntactic information about the target word but does not yet
specify its phonological form. Formulation also involves syntactic planning;
during this sub-stage the order in which the selected words will be output is
decided. The third stage involves articulation of the plan. During this stage
the sounds for the word are accessed, the lexeme is specified giving the full
phonological form of the word, and the motor program for speech output is
planned and articulated. In a final fourth stage, the output is monitored so
that corrections can be made if necessary.

> Lemma is an abstract word
> form that contains syntactic
> and semantic information
> about the word.
> Lexeme is the basic lexical
> unit that gives the word's
> morpho-phonological
> properties.

The theoretical approaches to understanding speech production have much in common.
It is recognized that clauses seem to be an important structure for speech planning
and that processing proceeds from the abstract concept to syntactical processing, to
precise phonological patterns. The various models of speech production differ in terms
of the emphasis placed on these various components and in the extent to which they
consider the processing stages to involve serial, parallel or interactive processing, that
is, whether they favour a modular or interactive view of speech processing. Modular
or serial theories posit a series of non-interacting stages, with different types of
processing being completed at each stage (e.g. Fromkin, 1973; Garrett, 1980, 1982;
Levelt et al., 1991a). On the other hand, interactive or parallel theories (e.g. Dell, 1986;
MacKay, 1987) propose a less constrained account, with multiple sources of information
operating to influence speech output. The debate over which type of theory provides
the more accurate account continues.

MODULAR THEORIES OF SPEECH PRODUCTION

Garrett's model

Serial or modular theories propose that speech production progresses through a series
of stages or levels, with different types of processing being completed at each level.
According to Garrett's hierarchical model (e.g. 1980, 1982, 1992), speech is produced via
a series of stages, proceeding in a top-down manner (see Chapter 2) so that processing

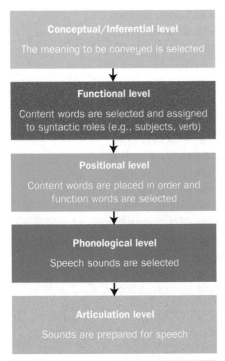

Figure 12.2 **The stages of speech production proposed by Garrett (e.g. 1975).** At the inferential level, we conceptualize the message that we want to express. At the functional level, the syntactic and semantic framework of the sentence is constructed. At the phonological level the sounds for the content words are acquired.

at lower levels does not influence that at higher levels (see Figure 12.2). Garrett developed his model to address patterns of errors in speech production (see also Dell, 1986, described below).

Figure 12.2 shows the various levels proposed by Garrett. At the inferential level, we conceptualize the message that we want to express. As noted previously, little is known about processing at this level or how the initial leap from thought to language-like representation might occur, particularly given that there may be a number of ways to express a thought. At the functional level, the syntactic and semantic framework of the sentence is constructed. At this stage, word exchanges would be predicted because the structure is present but the selected words, while activated, have not yet been allocated to their places within that structure or framework. Because the syntactic category of the word has already been determined, this model predicts that errors will not cross syntactic category (e.g. that nouns will swap with nouns but not nouns with verbs; verbs may swap with other verbs, though in reality verb exchanges are relatively rare). At the positional level, the words are allocated to positions within the syntactic frame. The function words are in place at this stage and so, where errors occur, bound morphemes tend to remain in their correct place (e.g. verb endings such as –ed and –ing). At the phonological level the sounds for the content words are acquired and sound errors can occur at this stage. In this model, the lexical bias effect described earlier in this chapter occurs during a later monitoring or editing stage where non-word errors are detected – word errors are more likely to 'slip through' undetected. The interactive models provide a rather different account of lexical bias, as we will see.

Evaluation

Garrett's model suggests that content and function words are treated differently and this is supported by the data on errors. One might argue that the relative sparing of function words reflects their higher frequency in language use (e.g. see Stemberger, 1985); however, bound morphemes have a lower frequency of use and yet are treated like function words in that they are retained in the syntactic frame of the sentence.

Garrett's model provides a good account of the speech error data. However, Garrett's stages operate independently of each other and therefore this model does not predict errors that occur 'across levels'. For example, a type of error called a **non-plan internal error** occurs when concepts from the message level intrude when articulating the sentence, specifying the words at the phonological level. For example, someone intending to say 'let's get a coffee' while standing outside the library might say 'let's get a book'. Some 'Freudian slips' fall into this category, as a suppressed thought might interfere with current output; by Freud's account this was always the case: 'A suppression of a previous intention to say something is the indispensable condition for the occurrence of a slip of the tongue' (Freud, 1922, p. 52). Such errors have led to more interactive accounts of the stages of processing, such as that of Dell and colleagues outlined below. Before we look at interactive models, however, another influential modular account is considered, Levelt's model.

Non-plan internal errors occur when the intrusion is external to the planned content of the utterance.

Levelt's model

Levelt and colleagues (e.g. Levelt, 1989; Bock & Levelt, 1994; Levelt et al., 1999) have presented a number of computational models of speech production leading to the sequential system called Weaver++ (Weaver stands for Word-form Encoding by Activation and Verification). This model focuses on the production of single words rather than the construction and output of whole sentences – it considers, for example, how we access (and say) the word 'cat' when we see a picture of a cat. A series of stages follow sequentially, from conceptualization to articulation (see Figure 12.3). Levelt's theory is based mainly on latency data (e.g. reaction times to picture naming) rather than error patterns, in contrast to Dell's and Garrett's models.

The theory focuses on the lexical access aspects of speech production. In Weaver++, the first two stages of processing involve lexical selection. Three stages of form encoding follow, before articulation occurs. These two systems, for lexical selection and for form encoding, would seem to involve quite different processes and involve different areas of the brain (Levelt, 2001).

The first stage is conceptual preparation, which Levelt et al. (1999) define as 'the process leading up to the activation of a lexical concept' (p. 3). The second stage involves lexical selection: a lemma or abstract word is retrieved from the mental lexicon and its syntactic category is activated. A number of words might be primed based on meaning, with selection dependent on relative activation so that the more appropriate selection occurs. For example, if I am shown a picture of a horse and asked to name it, the concepts *horse* and *animal* might be activated. These concepts activate the corresponding lexical items in the lexicon. This is an abstract word or lemma, which is 'essentially the lexical item's syntactic description' (Levelt, 2001, p. 13464).

Levelt et al.'s third stage involves morphological encoding. Once the lemma is selected, processing proceeds from the conceptual/syntactic domain to the phonological/articulatory domain; Levelt et al. recognize this as a crucial change. At this point, a TOT state can be produced – a lemma has been activated but the specific phonological form (lexeme) is not yet available. Because the lemma is a syntactic word, information about syntax is available, while the sound of the word is not yet accessed. This predicts the finding that in a TOT state a speaker has access to syntactic information, although they cannot produce the word. In many languages nouns have grammatical gender; this is unrelated to word meaning, that is, grammatical gender is a linguistic property unrelated to the conceptual properties of the referent. For example, in French *mouton* (sheep) is a masculine noun while *chèvre* (goat) is feminine. The word for 'milk' is masculine in French and Italian, and feminine in German, Dutch and Spanish. In languages with grammatical gender, information relating to noun gender can be activated in the TOT state, when the word

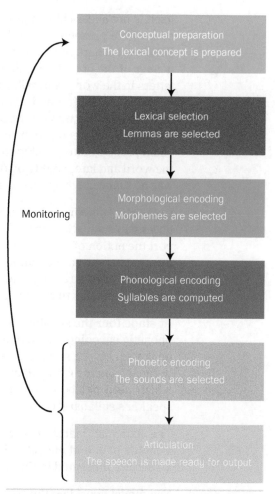

Figure 12.3 Levelt's model of speech production. In parallel to the processing stages, output monitoring allows the speaker to detect and correct errors.

Source: Adapted from Levelt, W. J. M., Roelofs, A. P. A., & Meyer, A. S. (1999). A theory of lexical access in speech production. *Behavioral and Brain Sciences*, 22(1), 1–37.

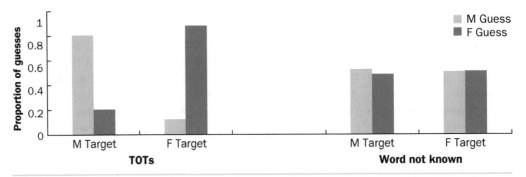

Figure 12.4   Responses to masculine and feminine target words for TOT words and words that could not be retrieved. Distribution of masculine (M guess) and feminine (F guess) responses for masculine (M target) and feminine (F Target) words, for TOTs compared to words that were not retrieved (here labelled 'word not known'), show access to knowledge of word gender for TOT words.

Source: Data from Vigliocco et al. (1997). Grammatical gender is on the tip of Italian tongues. *Psychological Science, 8,* 314–317.

itself is not accessible. Vigliocco et al. (1997) demonstrated this in Italian. Their participants were presented with definitions and asked to provide the corresponding word. Whenever a participant was unable to provide the word, they were asked to guess the gender of the noun (masculine/feminine), guess the number of syllables, give as many letters in the word as possible and state their position in the word, and report any other word that came to mind. Participants were subsequently shown the target word and asked whether it was the word they were thinking of. Vigliocco et al. found that noun gender was correctly reported 84 per cent of the time when participants were experiencing a TOT state (see Figure 12.4). By contrast, when participants could not produce the word and later could not affirm that the provided word was the target, performance was at chance level (53 per cent).

However, sometimes Italian speakers can access phonological information without accessing syntactic information (e.g. Miozzo & Caramazza, 1997), which does not support the notion of two separate stages for syntactic and phonological information – the distinction between semantic and phonological information remains. Processing at this stage involves three types of information; the word's morphology, its stress patterns, and the segments that make up the word are activated.

At stage four the syllables that make up the word are computed. Stage five performs phonetic encoding: the actual speech sounds activate at this stage. Levelt et al. (1999) posit the use of a syllabary, with phonological information allowing word articulation derived from the retrieval of syllables. These are 'highly overlearned gestural patterns, which need not be recomputed time and again. Rather they are ready made in the speaker's syllabary' (p. 5).

The sixth and final stage is articulation. The phonological information is transferred to a motor plan and executed by the articulatory system and speech musculature. The stages are presented in Figure 12.3.

The model considers the role of self-monitoring at multiple levels throughout the processing stages (Figure 12.3). This provides a mechanism for the detection of errors that allows us to repair speech and involves the cognitive mechanisms involved in speech comprehension (see Chapter 13). The precise means by which the mechanism operates and the attentional systems governing it are not elaborated.

Evaluation

Levelt's account shows how a series of specialized modules contribute to the process of speech production. It accounts for much data on speech production, including some patterns in bilingual speech. It also shows how speech might be monitored so that errors can be corrected. However, as a modular account, feedback between levels is limited. The retrieval of the word form occurs only after the lemma has been selected; there is no feedback from word form to lemma levels. However, some types of speech errors suggest that feedback does occur. Sometimes, the target word and the error share both form and meaning information, for example, saying 'rat' when you meant 'cat' (Treiman et al., 2003). This suggests that there is interference from lower to higher levels; Levelt et al. explain such errors as resulting from a failure in the monitoring processes. However, interactive models account for these and some other types of speech errors more successfully. We now turn to one influential account of an interactive type.

INTERACTIVE THEORIES OF SPEECH PRODUCTION

Dell's model

The final model of speech production that we will consider is Dell's cascaded or spreading activation account (Dell, 1986, 1995; Dell & O'Seaghdha, 1991; Dell et al., 1997), which is based on connectionist principles (see Chapter 1). This model uses the concept of spreading activation in a lexical network to show how competing activation across different levels might predict speech errors. In this model, activation from one level can affect processing at other levels, that is, processing is interactive. Processing is also parallel such that information can be processed at the different levels at the same time. These features, interactive and parallel processing, differ from the features of the serial models such as Levelt's.

There are four levels in Dell's model with processes corresponding to those described for Garrett's model above: that is, a semantic level, a syntactic level, a morphological (word) level and a phonological (sound) level. The semantic level is where we conceptualize what it is we want to say; at the syntactic level the structure of the sentence is devised; at the morphological level the morphemes that make up the target words are selected and at the phonological level the sounds that make up those words are activated.

Figure 12.5 illustrates the levels and connections. The connections between the layers allow bidirectional spreading of activation. That is, a word unit can activate the phonological units at the layer below (top-down spreading) and the semantic units at the layer above (bottom-up spreading; Dell & O'Seaghdha, 1991). According to this model, lexical access involves six steps:

1 The semantic units are activated by an external source (e.g. information from vision in a picture naming task, when you see a picture of the concept to be lexicalized or translated into words).

2 Activation spreads through the network.

3 The word unit with the highest level of activation is selected and linked to the syntactic frame for the sentence, in the appropriate slot. Once the word has been placed in the frame, its activation reduces to zero.

4 When the time is right, based on the slot in the syntactic frame the word is assigned to, the phonological information activates. If a single word is to be produced (e.g. in a picture naming task), selection of the word triggers the phonological information.

5 Activation continues to spread, but phonological units linked to the selected word become more highly activated.

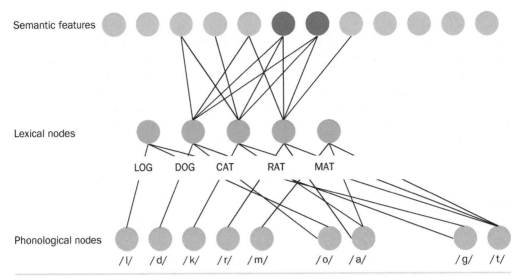

Figure 12.5   Dell's spreading activation model. The nodes in the top layer of Figure 12.5 represent the semantic features of the words. The words cat, rat and dog share semantic features and shared nodes are highlighted in red. The nodes in the middle layer represent lemmas or words. The nodes in the bottom layer represent the sounds that make up the start of the word, the vowel in the middle of the word, and the sound at the end of the word. Activation spreads throughout the network and the word that receives the most activation is the one that is selected (see also Levelt, 1999).

Source: Adapted from Dell, G. S., & O'Seaghdha, P. G. (1991) Mediated and convergent lexical priming in language production: A comment on Levelt et al. *Psychological Review*, 98, 604–614.

6 The most active phonological units are selected, and these are linked to slots in a phonological frame for the word; this allows the correct phoneme to drop into the correct 'slot' in the word so that the sounds are output in the correct order (see Dell & O'Seaghdha, 1991, pp. 605–606).

During the planning stage, the various words selected for the sentence become active; activation drops off once the word is placed in the sentence. This is an interactive rather than sequential account and feedback can occur from later to earlier levels such that phonological level activation can inform processing at earlier stages. Like Levelt's model, Dell includes a monitoring process to account for self-corrections and repairs. Errors occur when activation for a non-target overrides that of the target morpheme, phoneme or word. So word substitutions occur because a semantically related, but incorrect, choice achieves a higher activation than the target word. The lexical bias effect is accounted for by a backward activation process. Because words have lexical entries, they are represented by nodes in the network; non-words do not have associated nodes, but may have activation associated with phonotactic regularities. Words should therefore attain stronger activation and be more likely to be produced in error.

Similarly, the model accounts well for exchange errors (see Table 12.2 above). Exchanges of whole words (e.g. 'the sky in the sun') occur when a word of the same category – in this example, a noun – is dropped into the wrong slot in the syntactic frame. Once it has been output, its activation drops to zero, leaving the remaining noun to take the remaining noun slot in the sentence frame, because it has high activation and has not been selected.

Evaluation

This model accounts well for many patterns of speech error and some errors produced by people with aphasia are more in keeping with a parallel model than a serial model.

For example, Blanken et al. (2002) reported a mixing of word selection and word form access, in a German patient with aphasia, that supports an interactive account. Similarly, mixed errors (see above), in which the target word and the error share both form and meaning information, suggest that feedback does occur.

The spreading activation model deals with data from speech errors rather well. It also contributed to our understanding of sentence production rather than focusing on single word production alone, as is the case in Levelt's model. However, the model does not address the semantic level in any detail, focusing instead on the construction of syntactic, morphological, and phonological representations (Dell, 1986).

As yet there is no resolution to the debate between modular and interactive accounts of speech production, and a complete model may need to consider both modular and interactive aspects of the system. Dell and O'Seaghdha (1991) suggested that Levelt et al.'s (1991) data might be reconciled with spreading activation accounts by a 'characterization of the language production system as globally modular but locally interactive' (p. 604). The degree of informational encapsulation and interaction between components remains to be established in future research.

NEUROSCIENCE OF LANGUAGE PRODUCTION

Language involves a number of interacting brain areas, with many of the key language areas located within the left cerebral hemisphere in the majority of people. Language involves a number of cognitive processes, interacting with systems for attention, memory, perception and motor function. Sociocultural knowledge informs the ways in which we use language with others. Therefore many areas of the brain must contribute to language processing. Neurolinguistics is the study of the relationship between brain areas and language functioning.

> Neurolinguistics is the study of the relationship of brain function to language processing.

LATERALIZATION OF FUNCTION

Sensory information coming into one side of the body is processed on the contralateral (opposite) side of the brain. Similarly, fine motor movements such as hand movements are controlled by the contralateral cortical hemisphere. Information presented to the left visual field is processed in the right hemisphere, while information presented to the right visual field goes to the left hemisphere. The right side of the brain controls the left hand, and the left side of the brain controls the right hand. Information presented to each ear is processed in both hemispheres, but precedence is given to the contralateral side; stimuli presented to the right ear are processed in the left hemisphere.

Scan to watch a video on split brain experiments

Different functions are associated with the left and right cortical hemispheres. Language is largely a left hemisphere function while the right hemisphere is specialized for functions related to spatial/holistic processing (e.g. see Springer & Deutsch, 1981). When a cognitive function is *lateralized*, one cortical hemisphere is dominant for that function; for example, in most people the left hemisphere is dominant for language and the right hemisphere is dominant for face recognition. This lateralization of function is particularly apparent when we consider the effects on cognitive processing of a set of conditions that gives rise to the split-brain phenomenon. When the band of fibres connecting the two hemispheres, the corpus callosum, is severed, we can isolate the functions of the two hemispheres. In rare cases, these fibres may be severed surgically, to treat epilepsy for example. The corpus callosum may have failed to develop due to a developmental

> Lateralization of function refers to the asymmetric representation of cognitive function in the cerebral hemispheres of humans and higher primates.

condition. In such cases, the difference in the hemispheres' functions becomes more visible. As Sperry (a pioneering researcher in this field, and Nobel prize winner in 1981) (1974) noted (p. 7):

> Each hemisphere . . . has its own . . . private sensations, perceptions, thoughts and ideas all of which are cut off from the corresponding experiences in the opposite hemisphere. . . . In many respects each disconnected hemisphere appears to have a separate 'mind of its own'.

The split brain is explored further in Box 12.4.

Box 12.4 When Things Go Wrong: The split brain

We are unaware of the division of labour between the left and right hemispheres because the two hemispheres of our brains communicate so effectively via a number of connecting bands of fibres between the hemispheres, called commissures. The largest of these is the corpus callosum. This band of over 200 million fibres is surgically severed in a *commissurotomy*, a rare surgical procedure which is performed in order to reduce the effects of a type of intractable epilepsy that is unresponsive to drug therapy.

After the procedure the 'split-brain patient' behaves surprisingly normally, considering such a radical operation has been performed. However, on careful testing, it is apparent that the left and right hemispheres no longer communicate and are effectively working independently. The left hemisphere is dominant for language, in most people. If an object is placed in the right hand of a (blindfolded) split brain patient, he or she can name the object, as the information is relayed to the left hemisphere and it can make contact with the speech centre. However, if the object is placed in the left hand, the patient cannot name it. The patient can, however, pick a matching object from an array of objects, using the same hand. A picture that is presented to the right visual field can be named; a picture presented to the left visual field cannot, although, again, the object can be matched given an array of choices. Interestingly, when information is presented to the right hemisphere and cannot be named, the person reports not seeing it, suggesting a close alliance between language and subjective experience and consciousness (e.g. Cooney & Gazzaniga, 2003 ; Sperry & Gazzaniga, 1967). However, the patient can select a related picture, using the left hand, but, unaware of what the right brain saw, he or she will often invent a reason for the selection (see Figure 12.6).

Figure 12.6 Demonstration of cognition in the split brain. A picture of a chicken claw is presented briefly to the right visual field, and goes to the (speaking) left hemisphere, while a snow scene is shown to the (non-speaking) right hemisphere. Asked to point out what he saw from a set of pictures, the patient's left hand points to a snow shovel while his right hand points to a chicken. When asked why he picked those particular pictures, the patient said 'Oh, that's simple. The chicken claw goes with the chicken, and you need a shovel to clean out the chicken shed.'

Source: Gazzaniga, M. S. et al. (Eds.) (1998). *Cognitive Neuroscience: The Biology of the Mind*. W.W. Norton & Co.

THE LEFT HEMISPHERE AND LANGUAGE

In the majority of people, speech is lateralized in the left hemisphere of the brain, and the left hemisphere is dominant for the majority of language functions. Rasmussen and Milner (1977), using the Wada test (a pre-surgical test of hemispheric dominance involving the selective anaesthesizing of the left and right hemispheres), found that 96 per cent of their patients who were right handed and over 70 per cent of those who were left handed had language lateralized in the left hemisphere (see also Kemp et al., 2008). Of the right handers, 4 per cent were right hemisphere dominant. Of the left handers, 15 per cent had bilateral representation of language, while 15 per cent were right hemisphere dominant. This dominance of the left hemisphere for language is evident in data from a number of sources: from studies of functional asymmetries in the typical population, from testing of split brain patients, and from the patterns of deficit seen in acquired language disorders such as aphasia. However, the degree of lateralization can vary in the typical population; there would seem to be, for example, differences in laterality between men and women (e.g. Shaywitz et al., 1995). Further consideration of differences in men's and women's language use is provided in Box 12.5.

Box 12.5 Research Close Up: Do men and women use language differently?

Sources: Hyde, J. S. (2005). The gender similarities hypothesis. *American Psychologist, 60*, 581–592; Leaper, C. & Ayres, M. (2007). A meta-analytic review of moderators of gender differences in adults' talkativeness, affiliative, and assertive speech. *Personality and Social Psychology Review, 11*, 328–363.

INTRODUCTION

An extremely lucrative section of the self-help industry has sprung up around the notion that men and women communicate in radically different ways, one bestselling book even relying on the metaphor that men and women 'come from different planets'. This focus on differences supports stereotypes of gender differences and ignores evidence to the contrary.

Differences in language and communication, when they are found, are surprisingly small, and the distribution of men and women on such measures mostly overlap, as two meta-analytic studies demonstrate.

METHOD AND RESULTS

Meta-analysis is a statistical technique that allows comparisons to be made across independent studies that can be combined on the basis that they address similar research questions: the effectiveness of a meta-analysis depends to a large degree on the criteria used to include studies in the analysis. Hyde (2005) reported a set of meta-analyses of research studies reporting gender differences across six categories, assessing cognitive variables such as abilities, verbal or non-verbal communication, personality variables, measures of psychological wellbeing, motor behaviours, and miscellaneous constructs such as moral reasoning. Hyde found that 78 per cent of the studies reporting gender differences showed small effect sizes (Cohen's d (a measure of the difference between two means) range of 0.00 to 0.35), with a median effect size of 0.21 (Fiske, 2010). Strong gender differences were supported only for motor skills such as throwing speed and distance, on some measures of sexuality (such as reported incidence of masturbation and attitude to sex outside of a committed relationship) and physical aggression. Measures of vocabulary, reading and speech production showed small or negligible effects, and any stronger effects are likely to be context dependent. For example, one of the stronger (though still small) effects among the communication variables suggested that men are more likely than women to interrupt a conversation (d = 0.33). An effect like this is likely to be influenced by other factors such as personality, topic of conversation and factors concerning the other interlocutors. Yet, the stereotype that men interrupt and women don't prevails.

Leaper and Ayres (2007) conducted meta-analyses of studies examining gender differences in adults' talkativeness, affiliative speech, and assertive speech. While there were statistically significant effects for all three language constructs, the average effect sizes were negligible. Contrary to the stereotype, men were found to be more talkative than women (d = 0.14) across the studies examined. Consistent with the stereotype, men used more assertive speech (d = 0.09), while women used more affiliative speech (d = 0.12). However, in all cases the effect seizes are so small that it would not be prudent to conclude that there are differences, particularly when there is inconsistency across studies examining these constructs. Studies of these language constructs in children have also produced very small effects (e.g. Leaper & Smith, 2004: talkativeness, d = 0.11 in favour of girls; assertive speech, d = 0.11 in favour of boys; affiliative speech, d = 0.26, in favour of girls).

DISCUSSION

To conclude that there are robust sex differences in speech production, we would expect to see repeated demonstrations of the difference across a variety of studies and contexts and always in the same direction. We would also expect to see consistent strong effect sizes, as occurs when we measure throwing distance, for example. This is quite simply not the case, and it would seem that gender differences in language ability have been greatly exaggerated. Wallentin's (2009) comprehensive review of sex differences in verbal abilities and language cortex concluded that there are no sex differences in language proficiency and highlighted the inconsistent findings relating to differences in language-related cortical areas. Wallentin also notes the problem of publication bias – studies that have found statistically significant differences are more likely to be published than those showing null findings. We therefore do not know how many unreported studies finding no gender differences may be out there.

EVIDENCE FROM THE TYPICAL POPULATION

Dichotic listening task is one where different stimuli are presented to each ear.

The dichotic listening task (see also the section on attention in Chapter 3) involves the simultaneous presentation of stimuli to the left and right ear. While auditory processing involves both contralateral (opposite side) and ipsilateral (same side) connections from ear to brain, contralateral connections are dominant; that is, while stimuli presented to the right ear are received by the auditory cortex of both cerebral hemispheres, the dominant connections are contralateral and therefore verbal stimuli presented to the right ear are predominantly processed by the left hemisphere (Kimura, 1967). Tests using the dichotic listening task have shown that there is a right-ear advantage for verbal stimuli (see Chapter 13). Participants report more words (or speech sounds) that have been presented to the right ear compared to the left (Springer & Deutsch, 1981). This left hemisphere specialization seems to be in place at quite a young age, as children as young as two years of age show a right-ear advantage for speech sounds (Hiscock, 1988) and infants under 10 months show greater left hemisphere activity when brain waves are measured during presentation of speech (Molfese & Betz, 1988). Studies suggest that the right-ear advantage may be restricted to consonant sounds (Best, 1988). Consonants and vowels may be treated differently; many non-speech vocalizations, and even the calls of apes, are vowel-like. On the other hand, the rapid changes in consonant sounds evident in human speech are complex auditory patterns and require high level sequential processing (some would argue that language is a special case of sequential processing).

Different areas within the left hemisphere process information relating to meaning and to syntax. Another way in which we can examine language in the normal brain is through measuring event-related potentials (ERPs; see Chapter 1). ERPs provide high temporal resolution (meaning that very quick changes in brain activity, with time scales of milliseconds, can be detected) and are tied to a particular event, such as a stimulus presented to a research participant. Electrodes are placed on the scalp to measure changes in electrical activity in the cortex as stimuli are presented. The changes in the brain waveform are informative as regards the nature of language processing. For example, Kutas and Hillyard (1980) compared brain waves as normal, semantically anomalous and physically anomalous sentences were presented (as written stimuli) to participants. Brain activity in response to semantically incongruous sentences differed from that seen when physically incongruous sentences were presented (see Chapter 13), supporting the notion that syntactic and semantic information are treated differently and processed in different areas of the brain (see also Hagoort & Brown, 2000; Osterhout & Holcomb, 1992).

Language has also been studied in the normal brain using a method called transcranial magnetic stimulation (TMS). TMS is a non-invasive way of stimulating particular cortical areas such that their functions are facilitated or inhibited. While the stimulation is short-lived and effects are largely temporary, in some circumstances TMS has been shown to alter the functioning of the brain beyond the initial period of stimulation, and therefore the method has implications in terms of therapeutic interventions. For example, Wirth et al. (2011) used TMS to enhance participants' performance on an overt picture naming task, and de Vries et al. (2010) used TMS to enhance grammar learning, or specifically the ability to detect syntactic violations. De Vries et al. showed that Broca's area plays a crucial role in grammar processing. Such studies suggest potential applications to remedial intervention in cases of language disorder after brain injury.

> **Transcranial magnetic stimulation** is a non-invasive method of temporarily exciting or inhibiting cortical areas.

So far we have considered the left hemisphere as the site of language processing, but the right hemisphere also has a role to play, albeit a supporting role. The right hemisphere is involved in emotional aspects of speech, prosody and aspects of non-literal speech. People who have damage to the right side of the brain have difficulty in appreciating the emotional tone of an utterance (Caplan, 1987), and they have difficulty in understanding non-literal speech such as sarcasm, figurative language and indirect requests (Weylman et al., 1988), suggesting a role for the right hemisphere in processing the pragmatic aspects of an utterance. Similarly, studies of individuals with split-brain syndrome show that the right hemisphere is very limited when it comes to syntactic and phonological processing but it may be capable of other language functions, albeit not in the specialized way of the left hemisphere (e.g. Gazzaniga, 1983). While the right hemisphere is involved in the processing of tone in non-tonal languages (such as English), it is the left hemisphere that processes tone in tonal languages (such as Chinese) in which tone carries meaning (Gandour et al., 1992).

EVIDENCE FROM APHASIA

Speech production results from the processing that occurs in a number of language areas located around the Sylvian fissure of the left hemisphere, an area referred to as the peri-Sylvian language region. Damage to any of these areas can impair the ability to produce speech or writing. We can learn much about speech processing in normal cognition by examining the ways in which language is affected by brain injury.

Some of the key left-hemisphere language areas are shown in Figure 12.8; the figure does not reflect the considerable individual variability in the functional localization of

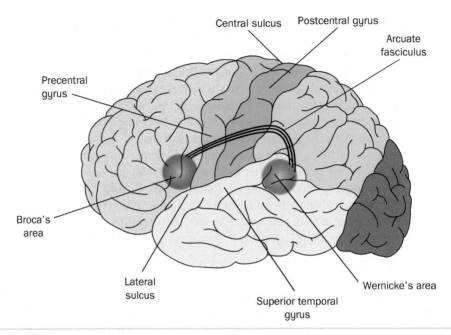

Central sulcus Postcentral gyrus

Arcuate fasciculus

Precentral gyrus

Broca's area

Lateral sulcus

Superior temporal gyrus

Wernicke's area

Figure 12.7 **Key left hemisphere language areas described by the Wernicke–Geschwind model.** In fact, the precise location, and role, of the language areas continue to be debated, not least because of the considerable individual variability that is evident in the functional localization of language.

Electrocortical stimulation of the surface of the cortex allows a surgeon to locate, and avoid damage to, brain regions associated with a particular cognitive function. Wernicke-Geschwind model is a simplified model of language function used as the basis for classifying aphasia disorders.

language, however. In patients undergoing surgery to these areas, electrocortical stimulation while the patient is awake allows the surgeons to locate individual language areas and to reduce the risk of post-operative neurological deficits.

The Wernicke-Geschwind model, proposed by Karl Wernicke (1874), and later Norman Geschwind, notes a number of key areas for language (see Figure 12.7) and presents a simplified account of their role in language processing. The model proposes that we repeat a heard word by processing of the following sequence of brain areas. Following processing of the word in the auditory cortex, information about word meaning is processed in Wernicke's area and the output is sent to Broca's area via a band of connecting fibres called the arcuate fasciculus (see Figure 12.7). Broca's area prepares the speech output and a motor program for output is then articulated via the motor cortex. When we read a word out loud, a similar sequence is involved, with processing starting at the back of the brain in the primary visual cortex and continuing into Wernicke's area via the connections of the angular gyrus. While this model represents a simplification of the processing involved, it does provide a useful overview of the principal cortical brain areas for language and their functions.

Aphasia (or dysphasia as it is sometimes called) is the term used to describe a deficit in language following brain injury. It generally refers to spoken language, with the terms agraphia and alexia used specifically for deficits in writing and reading, respectively.

Crossed aphasia refers to language dysfunction following right hemisphere damage in a right-handed individual.

In aphasia, the internal processing of language has broken down; it is not that the person's muscles or motor control for producing language have been damaged (as may occur in conditions such as apraxia and anarthria, for example). In a small percentage of people, damage to the right side can produce aphasia; aphasia following right hemisphere damage is called crossed aphasia.

Aphasic disorders can be classified according to whether they are of fluent, non-fluent or pure type. In the pure disorders a particular facet of language (e.g. the ability to repeat back sentences) is affected, while other language functions remain intact. The fluent disorders are characterized by fluent but empty speech, that is, the person produces fluent sentences, but the content of the utterances is not as they intended. The non-fluent disorders are characterized by reduced speech output, slow or effortful speech. Generally, damage to the anterior regions (near the region marked as Broca's area in Figure 12.7) creates a non-fluent type of disorder while more posterior damage (near Wernicke's) can cause a fluent type of aphasia. However, the site of damage can vary considerably from patient to patient, even with similar deficits, and younger people tend to show a non-fluent pattern of deficit regardless of the site of damage; fluent disorders are very rarely found in children, for example (e.g. Murdoch, 2009). In what follows, we will describe in a general way the main deficits associated with each category of aphasia; in fact, people with aphasia show quite a range of individual differences in performance on language tasks, and in terms of recovery of function.

Broca's aphasia

One of the first cortical areas involved in language production to be identified occupies the left inferior frontal gyrus and is known as Broca's area (see Figure 12.7). In 1861, a French doctor, Paul Broca, localized language to the left hemisphere, and attributed the production of speech to the area now named after him. (A paper by Marc Dax, dated to 1836, is now acknowledged as the first to identify the left hemisphere as the seat of language.) Broca's account was based on the aphasic disorder of a patient he encountered at the Bicêtre hospital in Paris. The man, called Leborgne, presented in his twenties with a severe reduction in speech output; over the subsequent years he gradually lost the use of his right arm and leg, an impairment confirming left hemisphere damage, as limb movement is largely controlled by the contralateral cortical hemisphere. Broca wrote of Leborgne (1861a):

> **Broca's aphasia** is an acquired language disorder characterized by non-fluent speech, reduced speech output and problems with grammar processing.

Scan to see a patient exhibiting Broca's aphasia

> He could no longer produce but a single syllable, which he usually repeated twice in succession; regardless of the question asked him, he always responded: tan, tan, combined with varied expressive gestures. This is why, throughout the hospital, he is known only by the name Tan.

Broca called this disorder 'aphemia' (meaning 'without speech'), as he believed that the patient could understand language and therefore that the speech deficit was independent of language function itself; that it was a specific problem with voluntary speech. The similar term 'aphasia' was subsequently coined by Trousseau (Broca, 1864; cited in Dronkers et al., 2007). It is now recognized that there are some comprehension problems associated with Broca's aphasia, and these problems are particularly apparent when test sentences move beyond simple syntax (e.g. passive voice constructions). It is also now clear that it is the abstract representation of speech that is impaired in Broca's aphasia; in deaf signers with aphasia, the linguistic components of sign language are similarly affected (LeBrun & Leleux, 1986; Poizner et al., 1984).

After Leborgne's death at the age of 51 years, the area now known as Broca's area was discovered on autopsy to have been damaged by infection, which left a large abscess in that region. Broca concluded that this area of the brain was responsible for speech production. Leborgne's deficit was severe, leading some modern commentators to question whether he had a more global aphasia.

> **Global aphasia** is an acquired language disorder involving extreme impairment of language function.

Non-fluent aphasia is when the patient's speech output is reduced, laboured, or absent.

Broca did not dissect the brain but preserved it and so his analysis of the damage was restricted to a surface inspection. Dronkers and colleagues (2007) were able to access Tan's preserved brain, and subject it to high resolution MRI scanning. They found substantial lesions extending into medial regions of the brain, in addition to the surface lesions that Broca reported, suggesting that global aphasia may be the more likely diagnosis.

Patients with Broca's aphasia show deficits ranging from severe mutism to dysfluency or laboured speech. Broca's aphasia is one of a number of disorders that are categorized as non-fluent, expressive or productive aphasia. Speech output is reduced and non-fluent, but word selections tend to be meaningful. Function words (those that do the grammatical work in a sentence) rather than content words tend to be compromised. People with non-fluent aphasia are aware of their speech problems, which has implications for testing, as motivation may be an issue.

Figure 12.8   The cookie theft picture from the Boston Diagnostic Aphasia Examination. The picture shows a number of characters and actions within a familiar scene (a stereotypical kitchen scene) and elicits predictable spoken descriptions involving nouns (boy, girl, cookie, stool, silk, water), and verbs (looking, taking, spilling, falling) as well as discourse around intentions (such as to take without being seen).

Source: Cookie Theft picture. (Adapted) From the Boston Diagnostic Aphasia Examination – Third Edition, by Howard Goodglass in collaboration with E. Kaplan and B. Barresi, #11880, Austin, TX: PRO-ED. Copyright 2001 by PRO-ED, Inc. Reprinted (Adapted) with permission.

The following excerpt from Buckingham (1981) illustrates the marked dysfluency and reduced output associated with non-fluent aphasia. In this excerpt, B.L., a patient with Broca's aphasia, is trying to describe a picture from the Boston Diagnostic Aphasia Examination, called the cookie theft picture (see Figure 12.8).

The description is as follows:

> B.L.: Wife is dry dishes. Water down! Oh boy! Okay Awright. Okay . . . Cookie is down . . . fall, and girl, okay, girl . . . boy . . . um . . .
>
> Examiner: What is the boy doing?
>
> B.L.: Cookie is . . . um . . . catch
>
> Examiner: Who is getting the cookies?
>
> B.L.: Girl, girl
>
> Examiner: Who is about to fall down?
>
> B.L.: Boy . . . fall down!

A number of features of Broca's aphasia are apparent from this excerpt. First, reduced output is apparent. This type of speech output is sometimes known as telegraphic speech, because the sentences are reduced to the most basic units required to convey meaning – the content words such as nouns and verbs. The selection of content words is correct, showing that the patient can access the words from the lexicon. The function words are by comparison relatively sparse – inflections such as verb endings, conjunctions (e.g. and, but) and prepositions (to, under) are absent.

Goodglass and Geschwind (1976) defined Broca's aphasia as a condition 'marked by effortful, distorted articulation, reduced speech output, and agrammatic syntax but sparing of auditory comprehension' (p. 237). However, as mentioned above, while comprehension of everyday conversation may be relatively intact, people with Broca's aphasia have difficulties in understanding complex syntax. When comprehension depends on processing and understanding the syntactic structure of the sentence, it fails (Cornell et al., 1993).

Broca's area is just one part of the left inferior frontal cortex; a number of areas have been identified, within that region, that contribute to various aspects of language function. For example, separate areas for semantic and phonological processing have been identified within the left inferior frontal cortex (e.g. see Gough et al., 2005). Grodzinsky and Santi (2008) provide a useful overview of the state of current knowledge around the functions of Broca's area and reiterate a key role in syntactic processing (see also de Vries et al., 2010).

Wernicke's aphasia

A few years after Broca's discovery, Carl Wernicke reported a contrasting pattern in two patients who, after brain injury, showed normal pace and intonation but jargon-like speech. Wernicke's aphasia is associated with damage further back in the brain than the region associated with Broca's aphasia, in the upper part of the left temporal lobe (and extending to the angular gyrus, and the supramarginal gyrus; this region is the inferior parietal lobule). Wernicke's aphasia is classified as a fluent aphasia. While speech output is fluent, it is empty, that is, it is not meaningful. This condition was sometimes referred to as neologistic jargonaphasia, the word neologism referring to the patients' tendency to produce non-words, which may reflect partial activation of phonological information (Ellis et al., 1983). These patients are generally unaware of the problem with their speech output. An example from Goodglass (1983) illustrates some of the characteristic speech patterns of the disorder, again using the cookie theft picture (see Figure 12.8):

> **Wernicke's aphasia** is a fluent aphasia, characterized by fluent but meaningless output and repetition errors.
> **Fluent aphasia** is when the patient's speech is fluent, but not meaningful.

Scan to view a patient exhibiting Wernicke's aphasia

> Well this is . . . mother is away here working her work out o'here to get her better, but when she's looking, the two boys looking in other part. One their small tile into her time here. She's working another time because she's getting, too.

Another excerpt from Goodglass (1993, p. 86) shows similar features. In this case, the patient was responding to being asked 'How are you today?': 'I feel very well. My hearing, writing been doing well. Things that I couldn't hear from. In other words, I used to be able to work cigarettes I didn't know how . . . Chesterfeela, for twenty years I can write it.'

People with Wernicke's aphasia are likely to produce phonemic paraphasias, that is substitution errors in which a similar sounding word (or non-word) is produced instead of the target word (e.g. 'why' for 'wine'). There are made-up words or neologisms and overall there is a striking contrast to the pattern seen in Broca's aphasia. The function words and the grammatical structures of the sentences produced are relatively intact; the problem concerns the content words. Wernicke (1874) speculated that while Broca's area was involved in motor programs for speech output, the area now known as Wernicke's was involved in processing sounds for meaning. He also speculated as to what would happen if the connections between the two areas were severed: the patient would have difficulty repeating back what was said.

Table 12.5 Summary of language deficits in aphasia and site of damage

Type	Lesion site	Effect on speech output	Other deficits
Broca's aphasia	Anterior	Non-fluent output, reduced effortful speech	Repetition Naming
Wernicke's aphasia	Posterior	Fluent but 'empty' or meaningless speech	Comprehension Repetition Naming
Conduction aphasia	Arcuate fasciculus	Fluent	Repetition Naming
Anomic aphasia	Can be anywhere in language region	Fluent but with word finding difficulty	Naming
Global aphasia	Large area of damage	Extremely limited language function	Comprehension Repetition Naming

Conduction aphasia is when the patient has a specific difficulty affecting the repetition of speech.

The arcuate fasciculus was identified as the band of fibres that connects Broca's and Wernicke's areas (in fact, it is now known to link Wernicke's and the motor/premotor frontal areas) and 'disconnection' of this band of fibres is associated with a specific deficit in repetition, a disorder known as conduction aphasia. Bartha and Benke (2003) outline the main characteristics of conduction aphasia: severely impaired repetition, frequent phonemic paraphasias (saying unintended syllables or words, e.g. saying 'whine' instead of 'while'), repetitive self-corrections and word-finding difficulties. Repetition deficits are a key feature; spontaneous speech is generally fluent, although paraphasic, and comprehension is close to normal. Neuroimaging studies have revealed that the neurological bases of conduction aphasia are more complex than originally thought. As Ardila (2010) notes, relatively few cases of conduction aphasia have a lesion limited to the arcuate fasciculus, and, furthermore, conduction aphasia can occur when damage is limited to the cortex, without subcortical lesions. The main symptoms of the different categories of aphasia are summarized in Table 12.5.

Anomic aphasia

Anomic aphasia is when the patient has a specific difficulty with word retrieval.

Anomia is a word finding disorder that has been likened to the TOT effect in normal speech. Relatively small lesions within the language areas can produce anomia, as can transient conditions that reduce blood supply to these areas (Obler & Gjerlow, 1999). For the individual with anomia, access to the word that he or she is searching for is denied, but the patient has not lost knowledge of the word or of its meaning. Allport and Funnell (1981, p. 405) illustrate one patient's word finding problem with the following excerpt, again using the cookie theft picture in Figure 12.8 (the square brackets shows their guess as to what the patient was trying to say):

> Well it's a . . . [kitchen] it's a place and it's a girl and a boy and they've got obviously something which is made . . . some . . . [biscuits], some . . . made . . . well . . . [the stool] it's just beginning to . . . [fall] go and be rather unpleasant . . . and . . . this is the [mother?] the woman, and she is [pouring?] putting some . . . [water] stuff. . . .

The same patient could select the correct name for an object when shown a picture and two written object names as long as the two words were not related in meaning. Therefore it is not that knowledge of words is impaired; rather the patient's ability to access the words is deficient. Allport (1983) suggests that this reflects a problem with translation between word forms and their conceptual representations. A similar pattern has been observed in developmental disorders of language such as specific language impairment (SLI). Constable et al. (1994, p. 1) reproduced the speech of a seven-year-old boy with SLI as he tried to name a set of handcuffs presented in a picture naming task:

> Key . . . oh what do you call them . . . oh yeah . . . you put . . . you put . . . with your . . . with your . . . oh . . . with your . . . when you . . . when someone's stole something . . . and . . . what do you call them . . . necklace? . . . no . . . I just don't know the word.

Evaluation

Neuropsychological cases have contributed valuable data towards cognitive accounts of speech and language production. However, we must be cautious in interpreting data from such cases. As mentioned above, there is considerable variation between patients; people with the same pattern of deficit can have damage to different areas and those with similar damage can have differing language deficits. Lesions to Broca's area can occur without Broca's aphasia (Dronkers, 1996) and a Broca's-type aphasia can follow damage to areas outside Broca's area (Caplan & Hildebrandt, 1988). Furthermore, particular types of aphasia are generally associated with a reduction in a particular behaviour (use of function words, for example) rather than a complete absence of such features (Kolk, 2007). These factors must be taken into account when considering aphasia syndromes as applied to models of normal language use.

Box 12.6 Practical Application: Supporting language expression in 'locked-in syndrome'

In the book *The Diving Bell and the Butterfly* (1997), French journalist Jean-Dominique Bauby described his life after a stroke affecting the brain stem left him with a condition known as 'locked-in syndrome'. Patients with the condition are described as 'locked in' because, although they are awake, they cannot move; they are essentially locked inside their paralysed bodies. A particularly distressing aspect of the condition is the inability to communicate with others. As Gosseries et al. (2009) note, 'testimonies from victims relate that the worst aspect of the experience was the anxious desire to move or speak while being unable to do so' (p. 192).

In 'classic' locked-in syndrome, eye blinks and up-down eye movements remain intact, allowing some patients to communicate by means of an eye blink or eye movement system. Patients with total locked-in syndrome are unable to produce any voluntary movements (Gosseries et al., 2009; Kübler et al., 2001). The ingenuity of patients in such situations is remarkable; in one case, a patient used eye blinks to communicate via Morse code (Feldman, 1971).

Jean-Dominique Bauby painstakingly dictated his 136-page memoir using eye blinks. A frequency-ordered alphabet (e.g. in English: E-T-A-O-I-N-S-R-H-L-D-C-U-M-F-P-G-W-Y-B-V-K-X-J-Q-Z) was read aloud to him – he selected the target letter by blinking his left eyelid as the letter was read. The system relies on an effective partnership between the patient and an interlocutor, who notes the letters and may become adept at predicting the patient's intended word. With practice, the system can allow the patient to communicate immediate concerns, though it does not lend itself to conversation and the patient has to rely on the interlocutor to convey his or her meaning.

Advances in augmentative and alternative communication technologies have facilitated communication for those with locked-in syndrome. Eye-controlled computer-based technology reacts to patients' eye movements, allowing them to navigate a computer system with eye movement fixations functioning much as a mouse is used to move a cursor. The computer screen can show a keyboard, from which patients select letters by eye fixation. A speech synthesizer can then allow their completed sentence to be read out loud. Menu keys also allow the user to control the environment, for example, the patient could call for assistance, browse the internet or send an email (Gosseries et al., 2009). The advantage of this system is the control and independence it affords the patient. Recent developments in brain–computer interfaces (BCI) hold further promise. BCI systems make use of brain activity, via electroencephalogram (EEG) oscillations or event-related brain potentials (ERPs), or blood flow based measures, for example, to drive external devices in real-time, essentially allowing the impaired motor system to be bypassed (Birbaumer et al., 2008). While such systems are still in their infancy and remain to be fully tested in patient populations, the results so far are promising.

WRITING

Having looked at the processes involved in the production of speech, this chapter ends with a brief overview of another form of language production: writing. The processes involved in writing are similar to those involved in speech production, but writing requires access to the orthographic (written) form of a word rather than its phonological form. Writing processes will therefore differ to some extent according to the orthographic properties of the language used (see also the section on reading in Chapter 13). Writing also differs from speaking in that when we write we have more time to think about what it is we want to express and to 'translate' it into a written form. We can take our time over the construction of sentences, whereas speaking is time pressured. We can also monitor the output more easily; we can read the sentence we have written and inspect it, and correct it if necessary. Unlike speech, writing is often a solitary activity; while a writer will have a reader in mind when writing, he or she lacks the immediate feedback that occurs during a spoken conversation. Another difference between discourse and writing is that writing makes fewer demands on memory and therefore more complex ideas can develop through writing. The act of writing ideas down can facilitate thinking and bring about deeper understanding of the subject matter (Pijlaarsdam et al., 1996).

Research examining writing focuses on the later stages of the process, including composition and revision processes, as the earlier processes such as lexical retrieval and structuring a sentence have much in common with speech processes. Writing a textbook or an essay involves a number of higher cognitive processes collectively referred to as composition. Composition is a process by which ideas are turned into symbols (Kellogg, 1999). Like speech production, composition involves the various components of language, with smaller units contributing to the overall goal of discourse-level output. As is the case for speech production, writing involves a number of stages.

THE HAYES AND FLOWER MODEL OF WRITING

Hayes and Flower (1980) proposed a cognitive model of writing that focuses on three main domains affecting the writing process. These are the task environment, long-term memory and the immediate cognitive aspects of the writing process. The task environment includes the topic of focus, the intended readership and the purpose of the writing task. The writer must have an accurate understanding of these factors in order to progress the writing task. For example, if you are writing an essay on the psychology of language, you must identify the topic and the main points, write with a reader in mind (in this case an examiner who will be grading the essay) and consider the factors that will lead to the essay receiving a good grade.

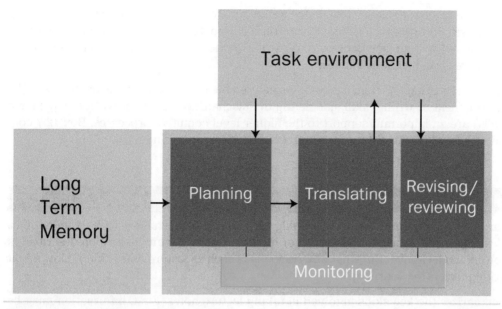

Figure 12.9   The Hayes and Flower model of writing. The model aimed to identify the key cognitive aspects of the writing process.

Source: Adapted from Hayes J. R., & Flower L. S. (1980). *Identifying the organization of writing processes.* Hillsdale, NJ: Lawrence Erlbaum Associates.

The second component of the Hayes and Flower model concerns the writer's long-term memory. The availability and accessibility of relevant information in long-term memory supports the writing process. In addition to knowledge about the subject matter, the long-term memory system stores schematic information that will shape the writer's view of readers' expectations. The third component concerns the writing process itself and the immediate cognitive demands it brings. Working memory demands (see Chapter 4) are relevant to this component.

Hayes and Flower discuss three general stages of writing: planning, translating and reviewing (see Figure 12.9). Planning includes the sub-operations of generating, organizing and goal setting. Translating converts ideas from memory into sentences on paper. Reviewing involves reading and editing. Revision is a key stage in the writing process; good writers revise more, and focus on the meaning of the text rather than the more superficial qualities of the writing (Flower et al., 1986). This model considers writing as a metacognitive act, with an executive process monitoring the key processes of planning, translating and revising (Peverly, 2006). The goal of writing is to create 'reader-based prose', as opposed to 'writer-based prose' (Peverly, 2006). Hayes's (1996) revised model of writing acknowledges the central role of working memory capacity in skilled writing.

Evaluation

The Hayes and Flower model brings together three key aspects of writing: the writing task itself, the cognitive processes involved in writing, and the writer's knowledge and long-term memory. The model moved away the previous sequential models and placed an emphasis on multiple cognitive sub-processes that allow writers to plan, revise and re-draft text. Later versions of the model also considered the role of working memory in writing. But a number of questions remain. What aspects of long-term and working memory function predict writing quality? How might memory processes support the developing writer? How does cognition differ in expert and novice writers? What role does oral language fluency play in the writing process? What role do reading skills play in the writing process? The element of time is also absent in this and other cognitive accounts of writing (see Becker, 2006): when do the various cognitive activities occur, when are certain actions initiated?

Models of writing typically have not considered the role of lower level processes in the development of writing skill, yet clearly the mechanical aspects of writing (e.g. motor skills) are an important support to the higher level cognitive processes. Box 12.7 considers how physical writing speed affects cognitive processing.

Box 12.7 Practical Application: Taking lecture notes – speed predicts quality

As a student, your writing skills are tested thoroughly throughout your studies, with examinations, essays and practical reports all demanding the type of high-level planning and execution described in the Hayes and Flowers model above. But what of writing tasks such as lecture note taking? How might aspects of that writing task affect learning?

Peverly (2006) summarizes the key skills involved in taking lecture notes. First, information must be held in verbal working memory and this is subject to capacity restrictions (see Chapter 5). Second, the key points must be selected from the information held in working memory, and third, those key points must be transcribed before they are forgotten; this requires efficient writing. All of this must take place while attention is maintained on the ongoing lecture. Although many individual differences come into play here (including working memory capacity, verbal ability, etc.), Peverly (2006) was most interested in writing speed itself. If you can write the key points down quickly, will later test performance be facilitated?

Peverly and colleagues had students listen to a lecture on problem solving and take notes. Measures of transcription speed, working memory, spelling, and identification of salient information were also taken. Their data showed that faster handwriting speed was associated with higher quality lecture notes. By practising the basic processes that allow us to take notes, we increase note-taking speed, and this frees up working memory for attending to the higher level processes involved in selecting salient information, following the argument being made in the lecture, integrating the current information with previous points made, and so on. As Peverly summarizes, 'the best way to enhance the efficiency of a limited-capacity processing system is through instruction and practice, especially of basic skills, so that the capacity of working memory can be devoted to the higher order skills necessary to achieve academic goals' (2006, p. 209).

These data suggest that interventions designed to improve transcription fluency may lead to improved lecture note taking and thereby improved test performance.

Summary

In this chapter we have considered the nature and components of language and the cognitive processes involved in the production of speech. Language is our principal means of communication and seems to be uniquely human. While language shares properties with other animal communication systems, no animal system has all its features. The special features of language are productivity, displacement and duality of patterning.

The components of language are phonemes, morphemes, syntax and discourse. The basic sound units of a language are phonemes; its meaning units are morphemes. Sentences are composed of morphemes and are structured using syntax.

Speech production involves four main stages. Stage 1, conceptualization, prepares a thought for conversion into language. The second stage involves the formulation of a linguistic plan. Formulation also involves syntactic planning; during this sub-stage the order in which the selected words will be output is decided. The third stage involves the articulation of the plan. During this stage the sounds for the word are accessed and articulated. In a final fourth stage, the output is monitored so that corrections can be made if errors occur. Models of speech production differ in terms of the degree of modularity and interaction said to occur between processing levels.

This chapter examined speech errors and their contribution to our understanding of speech production. Speech errors occur in a number of types and are not random. They support the idea that the production of speech involves a number of distinct stages.

This chapter also examined the language deficits that follow brain injury in adults. The patterns of deficit in Broca's aphasia, Wernicke's aphasia and anomia suggest a dissociation between syntactic/output and semantic/comprehension processes in language processing.

Finally, we considered language production in the form of writing, and the three stages of the writing (as composition) process: planning, translating and reviewing.

Review questions

1 What are the main features of human language?

2 What do the acquired disorders of language contribute to our understanding of normal speech production?

3 How does the analysis of speech errors contribute to our understanding of normal speech production?

4 What are the key differences between modular and interactive accounts of speech production?

5 How do the processes of writing differ from those of speech production?

FURTHER READING

Brown, R., & McNeill, D. (1966). The 'tip of the tongue phenomenon'. *Journal of Verbal Learning and Verbal Behavior*, *5*, 325–337.

Clark, H. H., & Fox Tree, J. E. (2002). Using uh and um in spontaneous speaking. *Cognition, 84*, 73–111.

Dronkers, N. F., Plaisant, O., Iba-Zizen, M. T., & Cabanis, E. A. (2007). Paul Broca's historic cases: High resolution MR imaging of the brains of Leborgne and Lelong. *Brain, 130*(5), 1432–1441.

Harley, T. A. (2010). *Talking the talk: Language, psychology and science*. Hove: Psychology Press.

Hockett, C. F. (1960). The origin of speech. *Scientific American, 203*, 88–96.

CHAPTER 13:

LANGUAGE COMPREHENSION

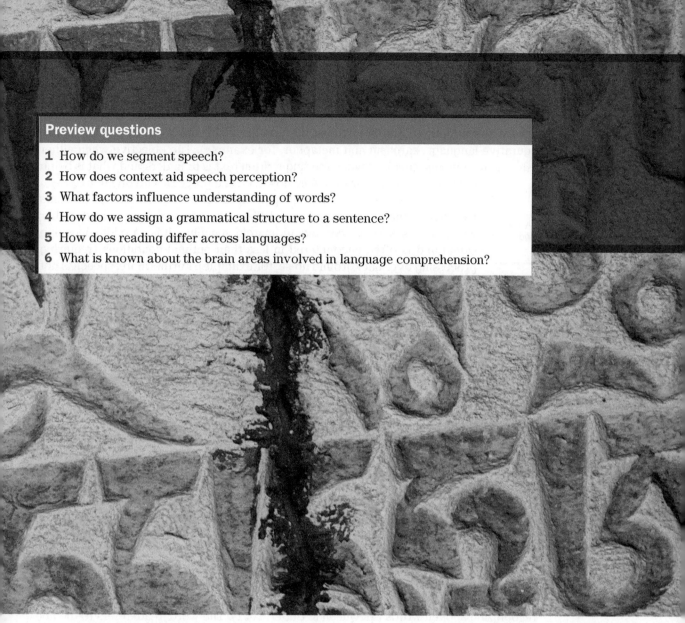

Preview questions

1 How do we segment speech?
2 How does context aid speech perception?
3 What factors influence understanding of words?
4 How do we assign a grammatical structure to a sentence?
5 How does reading differ across languages?
6 What is known about the brain areas involved in language comprehension?

INTRODUCTION

Imagine you are a passenger in a car on a cold day. Your friend is driving; the driver's window is open. You say 'It is chilly today.' Your friend closes the window. This example illustrates some of the complexities involved in language comprehension. Your friend must detect speech sounds over background noise and decipher words within a string of sounds (itischillytoday) that correspond to 'It is chilly today.' The meaning of these words and the grammatical structure of the sentence must be analysed. And then, the intention of the utterance must be considered. Here, you are not merely commenting on the fact that it is cold; a request is implied – that your friend closes the window.

The goal of language comprehension is understanding – to extract meaning from the language that we hear or read. It is estimated that an adult knows between 50,000 and 100,000 words (Clark, 2003); when we encounter a word, either by hearing it or reading it, the goal is to recognize it. This is achieved quickly, accurately and automatically; it is only when the system breaks down that we become aware of its complexity (see, for example, Box 13.1).

In this chapter we will focus on how we understand speech and written language. The higher level cognitive processes involved in these two comprehension tasks have much in common; whether we are listening to speech or reading text, understanding requires accessing semantic information and appreciating the meaning of the words, the intention of the utterance, and sometimes the non-literal meaning (when we encounter figurative language, sarcasm and metaphor, for example). The objective when either listening to someone speak or when reading written text is to understand what is being communicated. At lower levels, however, the processes involved in speech perception and visual word recognition differ markedly. Speech presents us with a virtually continuous signal of sounds from which we must decipher words, phrases, sentences and, ultimately, meaning. It is a rapidly decaying signal and is often encountered in less than optimal conditions (requiring processing over background noise, for example). Furthermore, speech is not simply a string of precise phonemes (speech sounds; see Chapter 12). Sounds blend into each other and are affected by previous and subsequent sounds within utterances, as well as factors specific to the speaker. In other words, speech perception is not a simple matter of categorizing incoming sounds into classes of sounds used within a language. It is a far more complex process. Although the result of speech perception may well be to assign sounds to categories, it is not achieved via a serial bottom-up sound-by-sound process (see Chapter 2 on bottom-up processes in perception).

> **Speech perception** is the process by which we convert a stream of speech into individual words and sentences.

In addition to considering speech, the current chapter also examines comprehension of written language. When we read, we are presented with written text, a visual string of words, with boundaries indicated by spaces (between words) and punctuation marks (between phrases and sentences). In many scripts this written signal can be decoded into corresponding speech sounds; some of the challenges involved in extracting meaning from text reflect related cross-linguistic differences in the representation of sounds in scripts.

We will begin by considering speech. Speech processing is a fast, accurate and automatic process – once we have acquired language, we readily understand a spoken utterance. The speed with which the task is achieved does not reflect the complexity of the process. We take speech perception for granted and underestimate the challenge posed by the speech signal. In English, we do not have a specific word for the act of recognizing spoken words (McQueen & Cutler, 2001). The word 'read' refers to the act of recognizing written words, but there is no one word for the process of word recognition in speech (some languages, McQueen and Cutler point out, do have words for this purpose – such as 'verstaan' in Dutch and 'kikitoru' in Japanese).

Word recognition is the starting point for language comprehension and understanding language is the key to much of higher cognition. As Pinker (1994, p. 15) remarks, 'simply by making noises with our mouths, we can reliably cause precise new combinations of ideas to arise in each other's minds'. This ability to convert 'noises' into thoughts begins with understanding speech.

UNDERSTANDING SPEECH

In Chapter 12, we looked at the sounds that make up speech within a language, phonemes. As we hear someone speak, we hear the sounds that make up words, and we gain other prosodic information from the sound signal, such as the rhythm and stress patterns of the language, intonation, speech rate, placement of pauses and emotional tone. Prosody might be defined as 'aspects of an utterance's sound that are not specific to the words themselves' (Ferreira, 2003a, p. 762).

> **Prosody** refers to the rhythm, intonation and stress patterns in speech.

While we perceive a sequence of words within the stream of speech, the speech signal itself is not produced as discrete units; there are few clear boundaries between words in spontaneous speech and sounds blend together as they are produced so that phonemes differ as a function of the other sounds used. Words in speech are not presented as distinct units as occurs when we read. Some commentators have questioned the importance of the word as a unit in early speech analysis; for example, Grosjean and Gee (1987) suggest that an over-reliance on the concept of a 'written dictionary' word is misapplied to speech perception. A key issue for those conducting research in the area of speech perception is: given the variation in incoming sounds, how does the system come to treat them as a small number of discrete phonemes making up particular words within a given language?

The speech sounds produced by a single speaker vary with context. There are further variations when we consider individual differences, differences in accent and indeed changes over time. Factors such as speech rate, the speaker's age and sex, as well as the amount and type of background noise affect the acoustic form of a spoken word. The sounds we produce change as we age (e.g., Hodge et al., 2001; Russell et al., 1995) and they change as societies change; archaic sound patterns are evident in old radio or television recordings. Harrington et al. (2000a, 2000b) analysed the Queen of England's annual Christmas broadcasts recorded over a period of 40 years, and noted considerable change in the Queen's pronunciation of vowel sounds from the 1950s to the 1980s. The changes in vowel sounds mirrored the changes in vowels within Standard Southern British English during the same period, while the distance between the Queen's language and the average speaker's vowels remained about the same.

A speaker may produce as many as 150 words per minute, with each word spoken in, on average, 400 milliseconds. When someone is speaking quickly, this rate can double to one word per 200 milliseconds (Levelt, 1989). Speech occurs at a rate of 10–15 phonemes per second, and can be understood at rates as fast as 50 phonemes per second for artificially speeded speech (Pinker, 1994). Syllables are produced every 200–400 milliseconds (Buonomano & Karmarkar, 2002). Recognition precedes completion of the heard word; some studies suggest that people can recognize a word on average just 275 milliseconds after the start of the word (Marslen-Wilson & Tyler, 1980). Speech perception requires rapid segmentation of this continuous signal. The problem of deciphering speech becomes apparent when we hear a foreign language that we do not understand. It is initially very difficult to work out where one word ends and the next begins, without knowledge of the structure of the language. As we will see, speech perception utilizes a number of cues in order to make sense of the stream of sounds that is heard.

Massaro defines speech perception as the 'process of imposing a meaningful perceptual experience on an otherwise meaningless speech input', a process whereby a 'continuous input is transformed into more or less a meaningful sequence of discrete events' (2001, p. 14870). Speech provides a continuous signal extended in time, where each segment cannot be taken on its own but instead depends on what went before and what follows. Blended sounds can occur at boundaries between words so that there is no 'gap' in the signal that would reliably indicate a word boundary. A spectrogram (see Figure 13.1) provides a visual representation of a speech waveform, by mapping the frequencies of sounds within an electrical signal generated from a recorded sound. It shows that the speech signal is continuous without clear boundaries between words. Low amplitude gaps in the signal are not reliable indicators of word boundaries, but may simply reflect a closure of the airway during the production of a word; for example, in the word 'spoken', the airway closes as you purse your lips to produce the /p/ sound. (As noted in

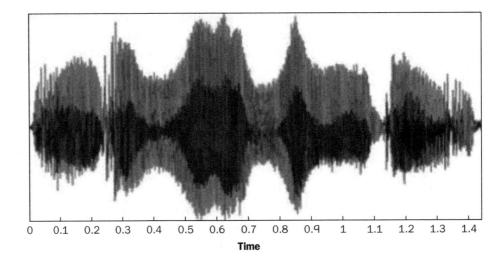

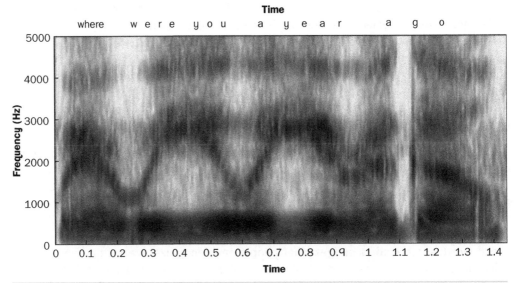

Figure 13.1   A waveform (top panel) and spectrogram (bottom panel) for the sentence 'Where were you a year ago?' Note that there is not a straightforward correspondence between word boundaries and points of low acoustic energy.

Source: Byrd, D., & Mintz, T. H. (2010). *Discovering speech, words, and mind*. Wiley.

Chapter 12, following convention, we will use a letter between forward slashes, e.g. /p/, to denote a speech sound.) When we read text, gaps between words and punctuation marks denote word boundaries; there is no equivalent in the speech waveform. Furthermore, the same phoneme can vary depending on the other sounds being produced. For example, consonants are affected by the following vowel sound. Miller and Jusczyk (1989) summarized the two major issues of speech perception as the segmentation and invariance problems.

Invariance problem
reflects the variation in the production of speech sounds across speech contexts.

THE INVARIANCE PROBLEM

The invariance problem refers to the lack of invariance in speech sounds. A particular phoneme is not uttered in exactly the same way on each occasion, even by the same speaker; its form is affected by other phonemes that precede or follow it. Co-articulation is one contributor to this problem; the position of the vocal apparatus from a previous sound, or its required position to produce the next sound, will affect the production of a given phoneme. Sounds blend together so that a continuous, fluent output of speech is produced. Therefore a one-to-one correspondence between acoustic cues in the speech signal and our perception of the speech sounds that make up words is not provided, and the same word can be produced with slight variations as a function of surrounding words.

> Co-articulation is the tendency for a speech sound to be influenced by sounds preceding or following it.

THE SEGMENTATION PROBLEM

If spoken language forms a continuous signal, and if there are few reliable gaps in the signal that reflect word boundaries, how then do we segment speech so that we perceive discrete words? It is not as if each sound can be taken and analysed in and of itself. If we extract words from a sentence in spontaneous speech, and present them in isolation, recognition is greatly reduced. Pollack and Pickett (1964) recorded participants' conversations and spliced out individual words from their sentences. The participants were later presented with individual words produced in the course of their conversation, which were played back to them out of context. Recognition of individual words was reduced to between 35 per cent and 62 per cent accuracy. For four-word segments played back to participants, recognition improved to between 70–100 per cent accuracy, depending on the speaker. This demonstrates the role of the surrounding context in the recognition of individual words.

> Segmentation problem refers to detection of distinct words in what is a continuous string of speech sounds.

One important source of information that aids segmentation is provided by the sound patterns within a language. Cutler and Norris (1988) proposed a metrical segmentation strategy, suggesting that speakers of English use the rhythmical patterns of the language in order to segment speech. In English, stresses within the speech stream differentiate strong from weak syllables. Strong syllables tend to contain a full vowel, while weak syllables have a reduced vowel, usually schwa, that is, the /ə/ sound in about or paper (McQueen et al., 1994). In English, strong syllables tend to be word initial, therefore this provides an effective cue to guide segmentation; most content words in English will begin on a strong syllable.

In their analysis of 33,000 English words, Cutler and Carter (1987) found that 12 per cent were monosyllabic, 50 per cent were polysyllabic with the stress on the first syllable (e.g., 'cycle'), 11 per cent were polysyllabic with secondary stress on the first syllable (e.g., 'psychological'), and 27 per cent were polysyllabic with a weak initial syllable (e.g. 'illogical'). So 73 per cent of the words in their list had word initial strong syllables. In the same study, an analysis of spontaneous speech showed that words with strong initial syllables accounted for over 90 per cent of the words used (a total of 190,000 words were sampled). Therefore while it is not always the case that a strong syllable marks a word boundary in English, on a majority of occasions, particularly considering content words, this applies. Other languages are fixed stress languages, that is the stress always falls on a given position; for example, in Finnish, stress always falls on the first syllable, while in Polish the stress falls on the penultimate syllable (Cutler et al., 1997).

Stress patterns, as well as factors such as prosody, provide an important cue to a speaker's accent, as is explored in Box 13.1.

Box 13.1   When Things Go Wrong: Listener perceptions of foreign accent syndrome

In September of 1941, a young Norwegian woman, referred to as Astrid L., was injured by shrapnel, damaging the left frontal area of her brain. The brain injury led to a Broca's type aphasia (see Chapter 12) with an initially marked agrammatism, which became less pronounced over time. However, the young woman was left with an odd manner of speech affecting prosody (the pitch, stress and intonation of the language), which was perceived by others as a foreign accent – in many cases, she was mistaken for a German, and a threat, considering that Norway was under German occupation at that time. Monrad-Krohn (1947, p. 410) described the patient two years post-injury:

> [S]he spoke quite fluently but with such a decided foreign accent that I took her for German or French. She complained bitterly of constantly being taken for a German in the shops, where consequently the assistants would sell her nothing . . . She had never been outside of Norway and never had anything to do with foreigners.

This is one of the early descriptions of a disorder (or set of disorders) which has become known as 'foreign accent syndrome'. Whitaker (1982, pp. 196–198) identifies four characteristics to this disorder:

1 the accent sounds foreign to listeners and to the patient;

2 the accent differs from the patient's speech before injury;

3 the disorder results from brain damage (as opposed to a psychiatric condition for example);

4 there is no history of the foreign language in the patient's background.

Why are such patients perceived as having a foreign accent? The perceiver may be as important as the speaker in determining the interpretation (Miller et al., 2006). In the case of Astrid L., her deviant prosody no longer distinguished between two pitch accents of the East Norwegian dialect; the grammatical errors associated with her Broca's type disorder would have added to the impression that she was foreign (Moen, 1991). Based on her community's experiences of other languages, guessing that she was German might have been the likeliest possibility, based on the dysfluency.

Miller et al. (2006) described the case of E.J.C., a retired shop assistant from Tyneside in the north of England. She had lived in the same Tyneside locality for most of her life. Apart from short holidays, she had not spent much time abroad, and she had never learned a foreign language. Her friends, family and acquaintances all spoke English with a British English accent consistent with their locale. But, following a brain haemorrhage, E.J.C. was perceived as speaking with a foreign accent, which most listeners identified as Italian. In E.J.C.'s case, vowel and stress changes formed the main basis for the altered speech. Comparing a detailed analysis of E.J.C.'s speech to a native Italian speaker, Miller et al. conclude that 'E.J.C. did exhibit a number of changes typically associated with Italian speakers' (p. 402). E.J.C. also exhibited grammatical errors, which would have contributed to the perception of foreignness in her speech.

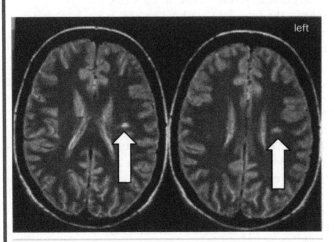

Figure 13.2   MRI scans of E.M., showing the location of her lesion in the white matter ventral to the primary motor cortex. The lesion location is indicated with arrows. Note that the left side of the brain is shown in the right side of the picture.

Source: Reprinted from Scott, S. K., Clegg, F., Rudge, P., & Burgess, P. (2006) Foreign accent syndrome, speech rhythm and the functional neuroanatomy of speech production. *Journal of Neurolinguistics, 19*(5), 370–384 with permission from Elsevier.

Scott et al. (2006) describe the case of E.M., who, following a stroke, developed an accent described as sounding German, Polish or South African, and quite unlike her original Scottish accent. E.M. had a small left hemisphere lesion in the white matter underneath the precentral sulcus, dorsal and medial to the anterior insula, and ventral to primary motor cortex (see Figure 13.2). This pattern of damage is found in several other cases of foreign accent syndrome in the literature and suggests that the disorder reflects a disconnection between motor control and planning of articulation (Scott et al., 2006).

Listeners use their extant knowledge of the sounds of other languages to make a judgement about heard speech. They 'focus on salient elements in speech, and these are interpreted through their experiential and attitudinal filters' (Miller et al., 2006, p. 404). The various patterns of altered speech grouped together as foreign accent syndrome may tell us as much about listener perceptions than the speaker's underlying pathology.

CUES TO WORD BOUNDARIES

Infants exposed to English as their native language learn to use this stress-based strategy to segment speech. By the age of about 7½ months, English-learning infants can segment English words that conform to the dominant stress patterns of the language, treating strong syllables as markers of word onsets, while errors are made when the dominant stress pattern is violated (Jusczyk et al., 1999). This has been established using a method called the head turn preference procedure. The infant sits on the parent's lap, facing forward. The parent wears headphones playing background noise, so that no subtle signals are unintentionally communicated to the child. There is a light in front of, to the left of, and to the right of, the infant, and each light has a loudspeaker next to it. The speakers and lights are controlled by the researcher who is watching the infant in an adjacent room through a one-way mirror. At the start of the experiment, the light in front begins to blink on and off. When the infant focuses on that light, the light stops blinking, but a light to the left or to the right then begins to blink. When the child looks at the blinking light, a speech sample is played over the speakers. The speech sample continues to play as long as the child looks at the light. When the child looks away for more than two seconds, the sound stops, and the light in front blinks again to direct the child's attention back before the next trial begins. Because the length of time for which the speech sample plays is dependent on the child's attention, this tells us something about the child's interest. For example, infants tend to show a preference for their native language over an unfamiliar language, or for familiar over unfamiliar voices; this is reflected in longer eye fixations and playing durations.

Jusczyk and Aslin (1995) used this method to examine segmentation abilities in young infants. They familiarized infants for 30 seconds to word pairs such as feet and bike, or cup and dog. These words were subsequently embedded in fluent speech passages, which were played to the infants. If the infant recognizes the familiar word from among the embedded speech, that is, successfully segments the speech, this should be associated with longer gaze time. Such studies show that by around 7½ months, English-learning infants are able to segment words that conform to the predominant stress patterns of English words (Jusczyk, 1999). Initially, infants rely heavily on stress patterns, but they subsequently begin to appreciate other cues (such as those described next) so that by the age of 24 months the perception of word boundaries is at a level similar to that of native speaking adults (Jusczyk, 1999).

The development of word recognition requires the extraction of the regularities in a language that can be reliably used to distinguish word boundaries. Phonotactic constraints, 'permissible' patterns of sounds within a language, also serve as effective cues to segmentation. In English, for example, a word can end in 'rk' (e.g. 'work', 'dark') but words do not start with 'rk'. This is an example of an onset pattern; the onset of a word is the initial phoneme or

Phonotactic constraints describe the language-specific sound groupings that occur in a language. **Onset** of a word is the initial phoneme or phonemes. The rime follows the onset.

phonemes, while the rime follows the onset. In the word 'train' for example, /tr/ is the onset and the /ein/ sound is the rime. Cross-linguistic surveys of sound patterns (e.g., Greenberg, 1978) show clear preferences for some onset patterns over others. Onsets like the 'bl' in 'blip' are commonly used, while the onsets in 'bnip', 'bdip' and particularly 'lbip' are less so. English tolerates onsets like 'blip' only, while 'lbip' tends to be avoided in many languages, and is misperceived by speakers of English (as 'lebip'; see Berent et al., 2007). Through early exposure to our native language, we develop tacit knowledge about how sounds go together in a language. This knowledge then guides speech perception. Knowledge about sentence structure, provided by syntax, may also play a role in speech segmentation (Mattys et al., 2007).

SLIPS OF THE EAR

Slips of the ear occur when we misperceive a word or phrase in speech.

In Chapter 12, we saw how slips of the tongue contribute to our understanding of the processes underlying speech production. In the same way, 'slips of the ear' are revealing with respect to the processes of speech perception. Slips of the ear occur when there is a misperception of a word boundary and the error reveals language-specific patterns affecting the segmentation process.

These kinds of slips are sometimes referred to as mondegreens after a mishearing of a line in the seventeenth-century Scottish ballad 'The Earl of Murray'. One line of the ballad is 'They had slain the Earl of Murray and laid him on the green'. The latter part of the sentence was misheard as recounting the fate of the unfortunate 'Lady Mondegreen' ('They had slain the Earl of Murray and Lady Mondegreen'; Wright, 1954; see also Pinker, 1994). Such errors are relatively common when we listen to poems and songs, because the prosodic information that might guide segmentation may be reduced, context may not cue word selection, or archaic or unfamiliar language might be used. Many such errors have been noted in song lyrics, including Bob Dylan's '*The ants are my friends/They're* blowin' in the wind' (Target: 'The answer my friend/Is blowing in the wind') and Jimi Hendrix's 'Excuse me while I kiss *this guy*' (target: 'kiss the sky'), a mondegreen used by Hendrix in at least one performance. These errors are typically word boundary errors and are consistent with the types of spontaneous errors reported in the research literature. For example, Bond and Garnes (1980) examined multiple word slips and found that 70 per cent involved errors in identifying the word boundary. They identified word boundary shifts ('an ice bucket' – 'a nice bucket'), word boundary deletions ('ten year party' – 'tenure party') and word boundary additions ('descriptive linguistics' – 'the script of linguistics').

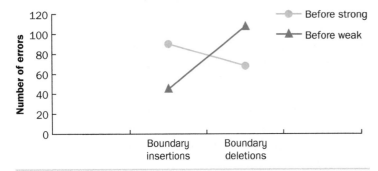

Figure 13.3 The number of word boundary insertions and deletions before strong and weak syllables in spontaneous slips of the ear. In English, more boundary insertion errors occur before strong syllables, while boundary deletions tend to be more frequent before weak syllables.

Source: Data from Table 2 in Cutler and Butterfield (1992). Rhythmic cues to speech segmentation: Evidence from juncture misperception. *Journal of Memory and Language*, 31, 218–236.

Cutler and Butterfield (1992) collected examples of such slips from spontaneous speech (see Table 13.1). They describe four categories of slip: deletion of a boundary before a weak or strong syllable and insertion of a boundary before a weak or strong syllable. They reported errors of all four types among the 246 errors they collected. Based on the stress patterns of English described above, they predicted more insertion errors before strong syllables and more deletion errors before weak syllables. The data confirmed this hypothesis (see Figure 13.3), supporting the role of strong syllables in segmentation in

Table 13.1 Examples of 'slips of the ear' from Cutler and Butterfield (1992)

Input	Error
She's a must to avoid	She's a muscular boy
How big is it?	How bigoted?
Into opposing camps	Into a posing camp
I can't fit any more on	I can't fit any moron
The effective firing rate	The effect of firing rate
She'll officially	Sheila Fishley
The parade was illegal	The parade was an eagle
For an occasion	Fornication

English; people hear strong syllables in English as marking the onsets of lexical words (content words).

Such cues are language-specific, and just as the structure of a native language will affect accent in a second language, segmentation of incoming speech is also biased towards the dominant patterns of the native language. Listeners use knowledge of the rhythmic structure in their native language in order to segment speech, leading to language-specific differences in segmentation (see Cutler et al., 1986, 1992; McQueen et al., 2001) and errors in segmentation when listening to a non-native language with a different rhythm (see Cutler et al., 1997, for a review).

In Chapter 12 we saw how disfluencies and errors in speech production reflect processing stages and occur at predictable junctures in sentence production. The effect such disfluencies might have on speech comprehension is explored in Box 13.2.

Box 13.2 Research Close Up: Is speech comprehension affected by disfluency?

Source: Corley, M., MacGregor, L. J., & Donaldson, D. I. (2007). It's the way you, er, say it: hesitations in speech affect language comprehension. *Cognition*, *105*, 658–668.

INTRODUCTION

It is estimated that about 6 per 100 words uttered contain a disfluency (a normal interruption in speech) such as a pause, correction or a filler such as 'um' or 'er' (Fox Tree, 1995). Corley et al. (2007) used event related potentials (ERPs; see Chapter 1) along with a memory task to examine the effect of such fillers on comprehension. They focused on an ERP component called the N400; this component is associated with the processing of meaning in language (Kutas & Hillyard, 1984). Corley et al. hypothesized that, because disfluencies tend to occur before less predictable words, listeners may be able to use the speaker's hesitation as a cue to infer that a less predictable word is about to be uttered. If this is the case, Corley and colleagues predicted that the N400 component, which is associated with effort of processing of semantic information and peaks following a semantic anomaly, will differ following a hesitation, with a reduction in the difference in the N400 for predictable and less predictable words.

METHOD

Corley et al. presented twelve native British English speakers with sentence frames containing target words. The target words were either predictable or not predictable from context. For example:

- Everyone's got bad habits and mine is biting my   [er]   nails
- Everyone's got bad habits and mine is biting my   [er]   tongue
- That drink's too hot; I just burnt my   [er]   tongue
- That drink's too hot; I just burnt my   [er]   nails

The sentences were either fluent or disfluent (containing the filler 'er' as the point indicated in the sentences above). During the ERP part of the study, participants simply listened to the sentences while brain activity was recorded. In a memory test conducted 55 minutes later, some of the words were presented visually, along with words that had not been presented previously, and participants had to indicate whether they recognized the words from the earlier part of the study. This allowed memory for sentences presented with and without disfluencies to be tested.

RESULTS

The results showed the typical N400 effect when unpredictable words were presented relative to more predictable words, but this effect was reduced for the disfluent sentences, suggesting that disfluency aids comprehension. The mean voltage difference showed that the N400 effect for fluent items [3.14ìV] was reduced for disfluent items [1.19ìV]. Longer-term effects of disfluency were also evident. While overall, 62 per cent of the presented words were correctly recognized on testing 55 minutes later (with a false alarm rate of 24 per cent), recognition was slightly, but significantly, better for words that followed a hesitation (66 per cent vs. 62 per cent, $p < 0.05$).

DISCUSSION

One interpretation of these findings is that the hesitation facilitated processing, such that the unpredictable word was easier to process than if it had occurred without the hesitation. Furthermore, words that followed the 'er' hesitation were slightly more likely to be recognized in a subsequent memory test. These findings suggest that processing of sentences differs for disfluent and fluent speech and that the occasional hesitation might serve to facilitate comprehension for the listener.

CATEGORICAL PERCEPTION

While there is much variation in the way sounds are produced, we are rarely aware of this and we generally find speech perception to be unambiguous. This is because the cognitive system tends to treat speech sounds as falling within discrete categories rather than as falling along a continuum. This tendency, called categorical perception, helps counteract the invariance problem. Categorical perception means we are more sensitive to differences in speech sounds *across* phonetic categories than *within* (Osterhout et al., 1997), although we are still able to detect differences and discriminate between speech sounds within a category (Massaro & Cohen, 1983). Categorical perception applies in particular to consonant sounds; vowel sounds are treated as continuous (see Studdert-Kennedy, 1974). Vowel sounds are produced by unobstructed air leaving the larynx and seem to be treated quite differently by the system. They carry information about stress, rhythm and prosody (see Studdert-Kennedy, 1975) and show no right ear advantage (see below).

Categorical perception is the perception of stimuli on a sensory continuum as falling into distinct categories.

Categorical perception was first demonstrated by Liberman et al. (1957). Using a speech synthesizer, they created an artificial continuum of sounds to test the perception of phonemes. Their study showed that, while the physical presentation of sounds may be continuous, perception is categorical, that is, a distinct phoneme will be perceived even for ambiguous points on the continuum. For example, the /b/ sound in 'bit' and the /p/

sound in 'pit' differ in just one feature – voicing. The /b/ sound is voiced, that is, the sound is produced while the vocal cords are vibrating; this is said to give a voice onset time of zero. Unvoiced sounds, such as /p/, are made without vibration of the vocal cords; there is a short delay between the closing of the vocal tract and the beginning of the vibration of the vocal cords (the difference actually reflects the duration before the voicing of the subsequent vowel sound; see Field, 2003). This delay may be as little as 80 milliseconds but this small difference allows us to make a /p/ sound or a /b/ sound. By artificially altering the voice onset time using synthesized sounds, a continuum from /b/ to /p/ can be created. While the mid-points along that continuum are objectively ambiguous, people will perceive a /p/ or /b/. For example, using a voice onset time of zero, participants will clearly perceive a /ba/ sound; at a voice onset time of 80 milliseconds, the sound will be a clear /pa/. The boundary at which a /p/ becomes a /b/ is determined by a number of factors, including the rate of speech and context, and can be altered through selective adaptation – by repeatedly presenting a /ba/ sound, we can move the boundary towards the /p/ end of the continuum (Eimas & Corbit, 1973).

> **Voicing** is when speech sounds are produced while the vocal cords are vibrating.

Scan to watch a clip of the vocal tract in action via MRI

Eimas et al. (1971) devised the high amplitude sucking paradigm to test categorical perception in young infants. This technique relies on the fact that babies tend to suck on a soother at a fairly regular rate and this rate increases when the child's attention is drawn to a new stimulus, such as an unusual noise or other change in the environment. Eimas and colleagues played a sound to babies aged four months. The same sound was played repeatedly until the infants' sucking rate had settled into a steady rhythm. The sound was then changed. The assumption was that if the sucking rate increased, the child had detected a change in sound. The infants were played sounds along the /ba/–/pa/ continuum, and showed categorical perception by the age of four months. However, this ability is not restricted to humans; for example, chinchillas show a similar pattern (Kuhl & Miller, 1978).

Babies can distinguish between the speech sounds of many languages at a young age (Kuhl, 1993) but this ability disappears as they acquire experience of the sounds of their native language. Phonemes come to sound like a prototype as categorical perception develops and distinctions not made in the native language are treated as belonging to the same category. For example, in Japanese the /l/ and /r/ sounds are assigned to the same category, but they are perceived as absolutely distinct by a native English speaker (see Massaro, 1994).

THE RIGHT EAR ADVANTAGE FOR SPEECH SOUNDS

Connections between the ears and auditory cortex are mainly contralateral, such that the left hemisphere language areas are accessed more efficiently by stimuli presented to the right ear. Consistent with this, adults show a right ear advantage for speech sounds over non-speech sounds (Lieberman et al., 1967). Along with data from categorical perception, the right ear advantage has been taken as evidence for the special treatment of language by the brain. The advantage was initially demonstrated using dichotic listening tasks, in which different words are presented to the right and left ears simultaneously. Participants in such experiments report more verbal items presented to the right ear, an advantage that holds for both words and nonsense syllables. The advantage applies to consonant sounds in particular; Shankweiler and Studdert-Kennedy (1967) found no advantage for vowels but a large right ear advantage for stop consonants (such as /pa/, /ga/, /ba/). This right ear advantage reflects superior left hemisphere processing of language stimuli. However, as is the case with categorical perception, the

> **Right ear advantage** for speech sounds refers to the finding that language sounds are processed more efficiently when presented to the right ear compared to the left.

right ear advantage is not restricted to humans and therefore may not be language specific. Sea lions, for example, show a right ear advantage for recognition of calls of conspecifics, that is members of their own species (see Böye et al., 2005) and macaque monkeys show a similar advantage (Petersen et al., 1978).

TOP-DOWN INFLUENCES: MORE ON CONTEXT

Thus far, we have seen that a number of factors affect the perception of speech and that context, such as is provided by surrounding sounds, influences recognition. The effect of context can lead to the perception of absent speech sounds, so that perception is consistent with the sentence context. This may be an important property of the system controlling speech recognition, as much speech perception takes place against a backdrop of background noise which might well obscure some phonemes. It is important that we can still understand what is being said, when some of the sounds within the speech stream become inaudible. The phoneme restoration effect demonstrates this property of the cognitive system. Warren and Warren (1970) presented participants with recordings of spoken sentences in which a phoneme had been deleted and replaced with a non-speech sound (e.g. a cough). The deleted phoneme is indicated by the asterisk in the following sentences, with the critical sounds (*eel) produced in exactly the same way in each one:

> **Phoneme restoration effect** describes the tendency to hear a complete word even when a phoneme has been removed from the input.

- It was found that the *eel was on the axle
- It was found that the *eel was on the shoe
- It was found that the *eel was on the table
- It was found that the *eel was on the orange

Participants were unaware of the missing phoneme and instead reported a sentence that was consistent with the overall context; that is, for the above sentences, they reported the words 'wheel', 'heel', 'meal', and 'peel' respectively. Since the actual sound was always the same, perception was guided by top-down processing such that the sentence context dictated the meaning. In a similar study, Warren and Obusek (1971) placed a coughing sound in the middle of the sentence 'The state governors met with the respective legislatures convening in the capital city', replacing the last letter 's' in legislatures. Their participants restored the 's' to its correct location and estimated that the cough occurred at a boundary, and not in the middle of the word. Thus, phonemes that are absent can be restored in speech perception; however, whether the effect is a true top-down effect on perception or occurs after perception is debated (Samuel, 1997).

This ability of the cognitive system to restore distortions in speech suggests that a detailed auditory analysis is not always necessary for effective speech perception and it explains our ability to hear speech in poor conditions (such as over a poor telephone connection) and above background noise. Saberi and Perrott (1999) partitioned a recorded sentence into short segments of about 50 milliseconds and then time-reversed each segment, before splicing them back together into their original order; the sentence was therefore 'globally contiguous but locally time-reversed' (p. 760). They found that participants had accurate comprehension of the sentences using segments of up to 5 milliseconds in length. Longer segments (100 milliseconds) were partially intelligible. Such data reflect the many sources of information operating to allow accurate speech perception.

VISUAL CUES: THE MCGURK EFFECT

We think of speech perception as a task of auditory perception but cues from other modalities, notably vision, also play a role in accurate comprehension (see also the discussion of multisensory perception in Chapter 2). Face processing involves analyses conducted specifically to facilitate speech recognition, lip-reading being the most obvious example of a visual cue to speech content. Particularly in a noisy environment, we can use facial cues to aid understanding of speech. This is well demonstrated by a phenomenon known as the McGurk effect. McGurk and MacDonald (1976) presented participants with conflicting visual and auditory cues. They heard a recording of the sound /ba/, but at the same time viewed a video recording of a person mouthing /ga/. They found that participants reported a blending of the visual and auditory cues, perceiving the sound as /da/. The McGurk effect has proven to be a robust effect; it even holds across genders,

> **McGurk effect** is a perceptual illusion that illustrates the interplay of visual and auditory processing in speech perception.

where a male voice might be paired with a recording of a female face (Green et al., 1991). The boundary between sounds created by categorical perception can be manipulated via a conflicting visual stimulus. For example, Massaro and Cohen (1983) used a speech synthesizer to create a set of sounds along a continuum from /ba/ to /da/. As participants listened to these recordings, they saw a video of a person mouthing either /ba/ or /da/. When an ambiguous marginal version of a sound was played – for example a marginal version of /da/ – participants were more likely to interpret it as /ba/ when the face seen in the video was saying /ba/. The effect demonstrates the role of visual cues in disambiguating speech and facilitating speech perception.

Scan to watch a demonstration of the McGurk effect

MODELS OF SPEECH PERCEPTION

Models of speech perception attempt to explain how information coming in from the continuous stream of speech that we hear makes contact with our stored knowledge about words. These models fall into two broad categories: those that consider the processes of speech perception to be modular and those that argue that interactive processing underlies speech perception. Modular theories propose a series of independently functioning modules that process information without being influenced by context; that is, at the lower level of speech processing, knowledge about words does not influence processing (e.g., Cutler & Norris, 1979). While the influence of top-down knowledge on initial processing continues to be debated, it is clear that our store of knowledge about words affects speech perception in some key ways (Treiman et al., 2003).

The degree of interactivity between top-down and bottom-up processes is explored in the second class of models. Interactive models propose that multiple sources of influence affect speech processing, and that top-down influences play a major role. Two influential models will be discussed here, both of which take an interactive approach, but consider interactivity of top-down and bottom-up processes to different extents: the Cohort model proposed by Marslen-Wilson and Tyler (1980; see also the Distributed Cohort Model, Gaskell & Marslen-Wilson, 1997) and the TRACE model of McClelland and Elman (1986).

THE COHORT MODEL

We do not have to wait until the whole word is uttered before it is processed; some words can be recognized based on partial information (although that is not to say that all words can be recognized before their acoustic offset; see Grosjean & Gee, 1987). Marslen-Wilson and Tyler's (1980) cohort model of speech recognition reflects the sequential nature of speech perception and assumes that incoming speech sounds have direct and parallel access to the store of words in the mental lexicon. The model proposes that we establish expectations regarding likely target words once we have heard the initial phonemes of a spoken word. The set of words that are consistent with the initial sounds

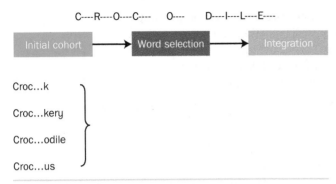

Figure 13.4   The cohort model of spoken word recognition. Initially a large set of words forms the cohort based on the initial phonemes heard. As the speech input progresses the options decrease until only the target word is left. Here, the word 'crocodile' is recognized at 'od' as no other words in English compete thereafter.

Source: Adapted from Marslen-Wilson, W. D., & Tyler, L. K. (1980). The temporal structure of spoken language understanding. *Cognition*, 8, 1–11.

is the 'word initial cohort'. As more phonemes follow as input, and therefore more information about the target word is provided, the set of available candidate words reduces, such that those which no longer fit the incoming pattern lower in activation and are dropped from the set while those remaining in the cohort become fewer, until only the target remains (see Figure 13.4). This is the *uniqueness point*, although of course the target may be recognized before this point, if few words share the acoustic sequence, for example.

The original model assumed that candidate items dropped out from the set once any inconsistent information was input. The auto-complete function of predictive texting and of some Internet search engines follows a similar logic: candidate words are suggested, and the set alters as you continue to type. The original cohort model considered sentence context as a strong cue to word identity; the cohort can reduce down based on information such as context, so that unlikely selections will attract lower activation and drop from the set of candidate words. The original version of the cohort model proposed that the bottom-up processing of the acoustic signal and the top-down influence of sentence context would operate simultaneously. However, the revised model (e.g. Marslen-Wilson, 1990) has moved the role of context to a late point in processing; instead of affecting word selection early on, context only plays a role at the integration stage, at the point at which sentence meaning is decided. The revised model therefore places more emphasis on bottom-up processes. The revised theory has also re-appraised the notion of activation of cohort words so that activation of items is a matter of degree rather than all-or-none. For example, words which are acoustically similar but not entirely consistent with the target can have some degree of activation associated with them. Similarly, there is more flexibility in the degree of match required from the first phoneme of the word. This revision has addressed some findings that were inconsistent with the original model (e.g., Frauenfelder et al., 2001).

The gating paradigm (Grosjean, 1980) has been used to identify a word's uniqueness point. A spoken word is presented as a 'left to right' sequence of sounds, in segments of increasing duration. For example, initially 40 milliseconds of the word might be presented; then 80 milliseconds, and so on until the word is presented in full. The participants must guess the word in each case and may also supply a confidence rating as to how sure they are that they have identified the correct target word (see Grosjean, 2008). This method allows one to determine how much of a word needs to be heard before it can be correctly isolated – the word's isolation point is the point at which the listener has a definite candidate word in mind and this point occurs close to Marslen-Wilson and Tyler's uniqueness point. Grosjean (1985) uses the term total acceptance point for the moment, beyond the isolation point, when the selected word comes to be used in sentence interpretation; this is effectively the point of word recognition.

Lexical decision task is a task where participants are presented with a letter string and they must decide whether or not it is a word.

Electrophysiological evidence for the model was provided by an event related potential (ERP) study by O'Rourke and Holcomb (2002). They had participants perform a lexical decision task (that is, to decide whether a letter string is a word) while ERPs were measured. The stimuli were selected such that they differed in their recognition points, that is, for some words, the point at which no other words matched the acoustic sequence occurred early, for some it occurred late. For example, the word 'crocodile' has a recognition point at the second syllable (see Figure 13.4), since no other English words will complete the segment 'crocod . . .' (Taft & Hambly, 1986). O'Rourke and Holcomb found that the N400 ERP component (a wave linked to processes involved in word recognition; see Bentin et al., 1985; Holcomb, 1988) occurred sooner for words that had early recognition points, consistent with a faster response time in the lexical decision task.

Electrophysiological evidence also supports the facilitatory effect of context, and suggests that it plays an early role, consistent with the original cohort model but not the revised version. For example, Van Petten et al. (1999) recorded ERPs as participants heard consistent or incongruous words as the end of spoken sentences. They found that the N400 started 200 milliseconds before the words' isolation points, which supports the idea that word recognition can occur before the point at which the provided acoustic input is sufficient to be able to *uniquely* identify the word. Such a process is efficient as access to meaning can occur before the word is complete and multiple meanings are briefly activated within the cohort words (Marslen-Wilson, 1987).

Evaluation

Generally, tests of the cohort model have treated words as isolated within the speech stream. The cohort model itself proposed that the starting sounds of a word form the initial word cohort. However, the model does not address precisely how the start of a word is identified within a fluent and continuous stream of speech. The size of the cohort generated would also seem to be important, yet the model does not directly address the effect of cohort size on the speed of word recognition. Furthermore, some studies have shown that the recognition of a word within fluent speech can occur after subsequent words have been presented (e.g., Bard et al., 1988; see Dahan, 2010) – the cohort model suggests that a word is identified once other candidate words have been ruled out, and so it is not clear why such a delay in word recognition is sometimes experienced.

TRACE

The TRACE model of speech perception (McClelland & Elman, 1986; see also Elman & McClelland, 1988) presents an alternative to the modular view than lower level phonemic processes are unaffected by processing that occurs at higher levels in the system. TRACE considers top-down effects as playing a key role in speech perception. TRACE is a connectionist model, the 'trace' referring to the entire network of units and the particular pattern of activation associated with it: 'the pattern of activation left by a spoken input is a trace of the analysis of the input at each of the three processing levels' (McClelland & Elman, 1986, pp. 66–67). The model has some similarities with the cohort model of Marslen-Wilson and Tyler (1980). The concepts of activation and competition are central, for example, but TRACE claimed to improve on the cohort model by considering top-down processes and the processing of sub-optimal (noisy) input. Like the revised cohort model, TRACE takes a gradated approach to activation levels, in that words can acquire a level of activation as a function of shared features with other candidate words.

McClelland and Elman (1986) use as an example the sentence 'she received a valuable gift' – what contributes to the perception of the phoneme /g/ in 'gift'? A number of factors, including acoustic information, cues from other phonemes in the same word, as well as the syntactic and semantic context contribute to speech perception. They recognized that a model must capture these multiple sources of information influencing speech perception. The model therefore addresses the fact that 'the perceptual system uses information from the context in which an utterance occurs to alter connections dynamically, thereby effectively allowing the context to retune the perceptual mechanism in the course of processing' (McClelland & Elman, 1986, p. 62). When conditions degrade (such as when encountering speech against a noisy background), more top-down processing comes into play and semantic and syntactic cues may become more influential. The model's architecture is based on that of earlier models (e.g., HEARSAY; see Erman & Lesser, 1980) but it uses a dynamic, self-updating processing system in order to reflect the online and interactive nature of speech processing.

> **Localist representation** is where a single unit represents a particular concept.

Processing units form three levels; dealing with features, phonemes and words. The three levels of units follow a *localist representation*; that is, particular units represent particular features, words etc., rather than activation being distributed across a set of units to represent features, as is typically the case in connectionist models. At the feature level, feature detectors process information about several sound properties, (sub-phoneme features, such as voicing and manner of articulation, for example). Phoneme detectors respond to each phoneme and at the word level detectors represent each word. Processing occurs in time slices to simulate the gradual build-up of information from the incoming speech stream (and to account for effects such as co-articulation). TRACE does not make a word-by-word sequentiality assumption, however, unlike the cohort model (see also Grosjean & Gee, 1987). Activation can be bidirectional with bottom-up connections from feature to phoneme to word and top-down activation from word to phoneme to feature. Excitatory and inhibitory links within levels create a set of possible responses such that activation of a unit represents the 'combined evidence' for the presence of the particular linguistic unit (McClelland et al., 2006). Figure 13.5 shows the architecture of the TRACE model,

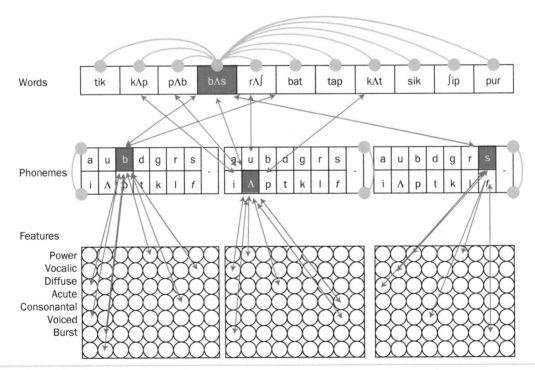

Figure 13.5 Architecture of the TRACE model. Red lines indicate excitatory links and blue lines inhibitory links. Units within a layer compete through inhibitory connections – note that the full set is shown here for the lexical layer only, for clarity only a schematic connection is shown at the phoneme level.

Source: Reprinted from McClelland, J. L., Mirman, D., & Holt, L. L. (2006). Are there interactive processes in speech perception? *Trends in Cognitive Sciences, 10*(8), 363–369 with permission from Elsevier.

with processing units at the feature level, phoneme level and word levels. As shown in Figure 13.5, excitation is bidirectional, that is there are both bottom-up (features to phonemes to words) and top-down (words to phonemes to features) influences. Inhibitory connections within a level allow units to compete for activation; for example, units at the phoneme level represent different possible interpretations of the speech input at that moment, and so activation of one unit inhibits other units at that level, reducing ambiguity.

Evaluation

This interactive account of the processes involved in speech perception shows how a number of factors contribute to the perception of a particular phoneme and accounts for categorical perception, co-articulation and lexicality effects. McClelland and Elman (1986) summarized TRACE's successes as:

1 successfully identifying successive phonemes from overlapping speech input;

2 accounting for how word level information is used to supplement speech information in identifying phonemes;

3 accounting for phonotactic effects without explicit phonotactic rules being represented while also accounting for irregulars.

But TRACE arguably overestimates the role of top-down effects; given the acoustic information provided in the speech signal under normal conditions, will top-down processing always have a great deal of involvement, from the earliest stages, in speech perception? Given the information available in the speech signal it may be that the role of top-down processes is overplayed. Norris et al. (2000) suggest that such models 'run the risk of hallucinating' (p. 302); in the case of a mispronunciation, for example, empirical evidence suggests that such errors are noticed, and do affect performance. While the balance of evidence arguably leans towards the interactive accounts, the precise extent of top-down influence on early perceptual processes continues to be debated.

UNDERSTANDING WORDS AND SENTENCES

Words do not occur in isolation; language comprehension generally involves understanding sequences of words and sentences. Levy (2008) suggests that any realistic theory of sentence comprehension must be able to account for:

1 processing of input that is not perfectly formed;

2 how we resolve ambiguity;

3 how we make inferences on the basis of incomplete input; and

4 how we overcome points of difficulty within a sentence; some grammatical structures, as we will see, pose difficulty for the system.

The ambiguity that we noted in the speech signal (see above) continues at the level of sentences. Words may have multiple meanings and there may be more than one way to interpret the grammatical properties of words as used in a sentence.

LEXICAL ACCESS

Word recognition is a process of lexical access. This is the process by which we retrieve information about word meaning from the store of words called the lexicon, a component of semantic memory, so as to understand what is

> **Lexical access** is the process by which we access stored knowledge about words.

being communicated. There are two main types of models of lexical access. Serial search models or autonomous search models (Forster, 1979, 1989) propose a series of stages to word recognition, with orthographical access, phonological access, and semantic/ syntactic access occurring at three separate stages, only one of which is accessed at a given time. When a word is initially encountered, either by reading it or by hearing it, a perceptual analysis is carried out and the pattern is then analysed. Entries in each lexicon are arranged by frequency and are retrieved via a search process. Direct access models, such as Morton's (1970, 1979; Morton & Patterson, 1980) logogen model, propose parallel word access. Each word or morpheme within the lexicon is represented by a logogen (a unit that specifies the word's phonological, semantic, orthographic features) and retrieval occurs through activation rather than a search process. Information from orthographic, phonological and semantic representations can be processed in parallel. Similarities between stimuli will lead to activation and this, combined with thresholds on words, accounts for effects such as semantic priming. This model has influenced subsequent models of word recognition, particularly connectionist accounts.

Word naming tasks require participants to name a word, while response time is measured.
Sentence verification tasks present a sentence frame with a target word, and the participant must decide if the word fits in the frame.

Lexical access has been investigated using a number of methodologies, experimental and neuroscientific. Lexical decision tasks present strings of letters to participants; some of these strings are words (e.g. clip) and some are non-words (e.g., plic). Participants must decide if the string is a word; accuracy and response time are measured. The assumption is that the duration it takes to respond reflects the amount of processing involved in the decision. Word naming tasks require participants to name a word, while response time is measured. Speed of access is inferred from speed of response. Sentence verification tasks present a sentence frame and a target word; the participant must decide if the word fits in the frame (e.g., 'The carrot grew in the . . .' LAKE). This requires access to word meaning. By manipulating the stimuli used in such tasks, we can investigate how the process of lexical access is achieved, and the different stages involved. A number of important factors affecting lexical access have been identified; here we will look at the effects of frequency, semantic priming, syntactic context and lexical ambiguity.

Frequency effects

Although we have a large vocabulary (estimated at between 50,000 and 100,000 words), a large set of these words will be used rarely (low frequency words), while a smaller number of words will be used very often (high frequency words). The frequency with which a word is used in a language affects cognitive processing; the higher the frequency, the easier the word is to process, generally. Frequency effects apply to open-class words such as nouns, verbs and adjectives, while closed-class words (such as articles, conjunctions, prepositions) do not tend to produce such effects. Frequency is a particularly important factor in lexical decision (deciding whether a letter string is a word; Whaley, 1978). The magnitude of the effect of frequency differs depending on the task used (e.g., Balota & Chumbley, 1984) which has led researchers to try to develop a method which can capture performance *during* lexical access, as response time to experimental tasks may reflect lexical access or post-access decision making. Eye tracking provides one such method. Studies of eye movements when reading show that people fixate on low frequency words for about 40 milliseconds longer (Rayner et al., 2003). Because frequency has such an effect on performance, it is important that it is controlled in experiments using words as stimuli. Several lists of word frequency counts are available

Open-class words are content words such as nouns, verbs and adjectives. New words can be added to this class of words.
Closed-class words, such as articles, conjunctions, prepositions, remain stable over time and are not added to.
Eye tracking involves the measurement of people's eye movements while reading or inspecting a visual scene.

for that purpose, for example the Kucera-Francis (1967) written frequency norms, CELEX (Baayen et al., 1995), the Brown verbal frequencies (Brown, 1984) and the Thorndike-Lorge counts (Thorndike & Lorge, 1944).

Priming effects

Priming (see also Chapter 5) refers to a methodology used to examine the influence of task context on performance. The methods used to study priming effects measure responses to a target stimulus as a function of its relationship with a preceding stimulus, the prime, which provides a context for the target. When semantically related words are used in a lexical decision task, response time decreases, an effect known as semantic priming. This effect was first described by Cattell (1888). For example, if the target word NURSE is preceded by the prime HOSPITAL, lexical decision is faster than when preceded by a neutral word (SCHOOL). The word HOSPITAL primes responses to NURSE; through spreading activation, the related word becomes more likely to be selected (Meyer & Schvaneveldt, 1971). The closer the words are in meaning, the greater the semantic priming effect. Semantic priming speeds processing and allows context to be used in speech and visual word recognition. The priming stimuli that are studied generally have a facilitatory effect but an inhibitory effect can also be observed.

Another type of priming effect, related to frequency (see above) is repetition priming. Response times in a lexical decision task decrease with repeated exposure to a word (Scarborough et al., 1977). The effect of repetition on low frequency words is stronger than that on high frequency words, a finding known as the frequency attenuation effect (Forster & Davis, 1984).

> **Repetition priming** refers to the finding that repeated exposure to a word leads to faster responses in a lexical decision task.

Syntactic context

The syntactic category of the word and sentence context have also been shown to affect lexical decision time. For example, Wright and Garrett (1984) presented participants with sentences such as:

a If your bicycle is stolen you must   FORMULATE
b If your bicycle is stolen you must   BATTERIES
c For now, the happy families live with   FORMULATE
d For now, the happy families live with   BATTERIES.

The target word in each case is the last word, shown in capitals above. Target words were matched for frequency and were semantically incongruous with the preceding sentence. In sentences (a) and (d), the nonsensical final word is of the correct syntactic category (a main verb to follow the modal verb 'must'). Participants are significantly faster in recognizing words when they occurred in sentences that provided the appropriate grammatical context than when not. For example, in the sentences above, the word 'batteries' is recognized faster when it occurs in sentence (d) compared to sentence (b). Targets belonging to the syntactic category appropriate to the context produce faster response times, an example of syntactic priming of the target word.

Mostly, research has considered syntactic priming in the context of speech production, and it is well documented that exposure to certain syntactic constructions increases the likelihood that they will subsequently be used (e.g., Bock, 1986). However, emerging data suggests a similar effect for comprehension. For example, Thothathiri and Snedeker (2008), using an eye movement paradigm, noted reliable effects of syntactic structure on ambiguity resolution in sentence processing.

Lexical ambiguity

Many words have multiple meanings. The word 'bank', for example, has more than one meaning. Its most frequent meaning refers to a financial institution, but it could also mean 'side' (as in 'riverbank'), or 'lean' or 'rely' (to bank on something). In the case of 'bank', the various meanings are associated with the same pronunciation, while homographs share spelling but have more than one pronunciation (e.g., tear, row, lead). Dominant meaning and context play key roles in resolving lexical ambiguity.

> Homographs are words with the same spelling, but more than one meaning and pronunciation.

Ambiguous words will have multiple representations in memory and therefore may be treated differently than unambiguous words. Foss (1969, 1970) demonstrated this difference using a phoneme monitoring task in which participants listened to sentences and responded when they detected a particular phoneme, e.g. /r/. Foss found that response times were slower when the phoneme followed an ambiguous word in a sentence compared to when it followed an unambiguous word. This is consistent with the view that when an ambiguous word is encountered, more than one meaning is initially activated, rather than just the one appropriate to the current context. Context subsequently influences processing, but initially multiple meanings are active.

To explore this effect, Swinney (1979) used a cross modal priming technique in which participants performed a visual lexical decision task while at the same time listening to related sentences, such as:

> The government building had been plagued with problems. The man was not surprised when he found several [spiders, roaches and other] bugs in the corner of his room.

The disambiguating phrase [spiders, roaches and other] was included in some cases. The ambiguous word 'bug' has two meanings: a surveillance device and an insect. Presence of the phrase [spiders, roaches and other] suggests the latter meaning, 'insect'. A concurrent lexical decision task presented words visually; words such as 'ant', 'spy' or the neutral word 'sew' were presented visually and the time taken by participants to decide if the stimulus was a word was measured. If the context provided by the auditory phrase [spiders, roaches and other] primes the meaning of 'ant' but not 'spy', we could conclude that only one meaning of the word 'bug' was active. However, Swinney found that both meanings were initially active as facilitation occurred for both 'ant' and 'spy' for target words presented closely following the ambiguous word. These and subsequent data suggest that, in general, context does not affect initial access to multiple meanings, although the nature of the task, the context and the word (meaning) frequency play important roles in activation of meanings (see Harley, 2008, for an overview).

Ambiguous words have also been used extensively in studies of bilingual lexical access. The use of cross-language or interlingual homographs has contributed to research in this area, as many languages share lexical items which have different meanings and pronunciations in the two languages. Words such as the French and English PAIN, or COIN, the German and English, GIFT or WAS, or the Dutch and English ANGEL or STEM. Evidence from such studies suggests that both languages are activated in bilinguals, that is, that initial access is language non-selective (e.g., Dijkstra, 2005; Kroll & Dussias, 2004).

Ambiguity at the sentence level has also been studied extensively in human factors research and particularly in relation to human error as is explored in Box 13.3.

Box 13.3 Practical Application: Language ambiguity and accident prevention

On 27 March 1977, two Boeing 747 passenger aircraft collided at Tenerife's Los Rodeos airport, in the Canary Islands, killing 583 people. A number of factors contributed to the disaster, not least the fog engulfing the airport that day, diverted flights due to airport closures, and technical issues affecting radio communication between the control tower and the two planes. One key element that contributed to the disaster was miscommunication between the pilot of one of the aircraft and air traffic control.

Cushing (1994) analysed the voice-recorder data from the accident and identified several points at which miscommunication contributed to the unfolding of events. One miscommunication stemmed from ambiguity in the pilot's phrase 'we are now at take-off'. The pilot meant 'we are now taking off', while the tower controllers interpreted the phrase as 'we are now at the take-off point'. The dialogue from the tower recording illustrates (from Cushing, 1994):

1705:53.41 Tower: KLM eight seven zero five you are cleared to the Papa Beacon, climb to and maintain flight level nine zero, right turn after takeoff, proceed with heading four zero until inter-cepting the three two five radial from Las Palmas VOR (1706:08.09).

1706:09.61 KLM 4805: Ah- roger sir, we are cleared to the Papa Beacon, flight level nine zero until intercepting the three two five. We are now at takeoff (1706:17.79)

1706:18.19 Tower: OK . . . Stand by for takeoff, I will call you. (1706:21.79).

As Cushing notes, part of the confusion here comes from line 1705:53.41, because an instruction is given to the pilot concerning actions after take-off. This does not necessarily imply permission to take-off. The pilot interpreted the instruction as permission to take-off, however. The air traffic controller expected the pilot to be standing-by for take-off and went on to direct the other airplane onto the run-way and directly into the path of the KLM which had begun its take-off run (1706:50: Collision occurs.) The pilot should have been alerted by the phrase 'Stand by for take-off'. However, a squeal is heard at 1706:19.39, ending at 1706:22.06, and may have compromised that communication. The phrase 'We are now at take-off' should not be ambiguous: it should be clear to each side what was meant, and yet the tower controller thought that the pilot was awaiting further instruction.

Note the timeline here; like any conversation, the dialogue moves on quickly; the ambiguity goes unde-tected, with devastating consequences. The pilot began to take off, without having being cleared to do so; the plane collided with an airplane already on the runway. All 248 people on board the fully fuelled airplane that was taking off were killed. There were 335 fatalities and 61 survivors from the airplane that had been on the ground. As a result of the subsequent investigation, changes were introduced to standardize communication in the aviation sector, which has improved passenger safety. However, while the meaning of phrases can be agreed, ambiguity at the sound level remains a significant prob-lem, particularly in the presence of background noise.

The study of the contribution of language comprehension to accidents has a long his-tory. Benjamin Whorf (1956) used the following example, based on his work assessing insurance risk. There is a storage area in a factory where gasoline drums are placed when they are no longer in use. If this area is referred to as containing 'gasoline drums', we might predict cautious behaviour. However, if they are described in the factory as 'empty' drums, workers' behaviour might be risky, due to, he argued, the use of the word 'empty'. For example, workers might be careless with cigarettes, underestimating the risk posed. Of course, even 'empty' drums would contain gas vapour and therefore are potentially hazardous. Whorf argued that the language used affects our perception of the situation; other effects on cognition are explored further in Box 13.4.

Box 13.4 Research Close Up: Does language influence cognition?

Source: Loftus, E. F., & Palmer, J. C. (1974). Reconstruction of auto-mobile destruction: An example of the interaction between language and memory. *Journal of Verbal Learning and Verbal Behaviour, 13,* 585–589.

INTRODUCTION

Does language affect the way we think? This question has been debated for many years, the debate being particularly influenced by the linguistic determinism hypothesis, associated with the work of Benjamin Whorf (1956), which proposed that the way in which we use language determines the way we think and, therefore, people who speak different languages think differently. In its strong form, the hypothesis has been discredited. However, a weaker version of the hypothesis remains; the idea of linguistic relativity suggests that language use can shape or influence thought, to some degree. We know that the way in which language is used can affect cognition. A study by Loftus and Palmer (1974) examined how the words used when a witness is questioned might influence his or her memory for events.

METHOD

In Experiment 1, 45 students saw one of seven films depicting a traffic accident, with films varying from 5–30 seconds. Participants then completed a set of questions about the film. The critical question involved a judgement of the speed of the vehicles at the time of the collision. The verb used varied in the questions, so that participants were asked one of the following questions:

1 About how fast were the cars going when they hit each other?
2 About how fast were the cars going when they smashed into each other?
3 About how fast were the cars going when they collided with each other?
4 About how fast were the cars going when they bumped into each other?
5 About how fast were the cars going when they contacted with each other?

In a second experiment, 150 participants saw a one-minute film of a multiple car accident. Fifty of the participants were asked 'About how fast were the cars going when they smashed into each other?' Fifty other participants were asked, 'About how fast were the cars going when they hit each other?' The final 50 participants were not questioned about the speed of the vehicles. A week later, all participants were asked 'Did you see any broken glass?' No broken glass was evident from the film, but Loftus and Palmer hypothesized that, if the language used affects the reconstructive process of memory (see Chapter 5), the participants who heard the verb 'smash' would be more likely to report having seen broken glass, since that would be consistent with the schema of a car 'smash'.

RESULTS

Loftus and Palmer found that, in Experiment 1, the participants' estimates of the cars' speed varied depending on the verb used during questioning, even though the cars' speed was always the same in the film. Speed estimates varied from 40.5 mph when the verb 'smashed' was used to 31.8 mph when the verb 'contacted' was used (see Table 13.2).

In a second experiment, those who were questioned using the verb 'smash' estimated the vehicle speed as being significantly faster than those who heard 'hit'. Table 13.3 shows the distribution of responses to the question 'Did you see any broken glass?' The use of the verb 'smashed' was associated with more 'yes' responses to the presence of broken glass, as well as the higher speed estimates.

Table 13.2 Verbs used in Loftus and Palmer (1974) Experiment 1 and mean speed estimates in miles-per-hour reported by participants.

Verbs	Mean speed estimate (mph)
Smashed	40.5
Collided	39.3
Bumped	38.1
Hit	34.0
Contacted	31.8

Table 13.3 Distribution of responses to the question 'Did you see any broken glass?' in Loftus and Palmer (1974) Experiment 2

	Verb used in questioning		
Response	Smashed	Hit	Control (no question about speed)
Yes	16	7	6
No	34	43	44

DISCUSSION

The findings of Experiment 1, taken alone, could be due to a response bias; the participants are uncertain as to the actual speed of the vehicles and so they estimate in line with the expectation that seems to be suggested by the wording of the question. The findings from Experiment 2, however, support a 'reconstructive hypothesis', that is that memory has been distorted by the verbal label. A week after the participants had viewed the film, those who were questioned using a biasing verb ('smash'), reported aspects of the event that had not occurred (seeing glass). These data suggest an influence of language on cognition – here, memory – that persists over time. Some further effects of language on cognition are discussed in Chapters 6 and 7.

SYNTAX AND SEMANTICS

The term syntax refers to the rules that govern language use; for example, most languages favour a particular word order, such as subject-verb-object in English (see Chapter 12). Several species can respond to 'words' or verbal labels (see Box 13.5) but only humans can use complex syntax. When we hear or read a sentence we generally readily assign structure and meaning to it, although many sentences can be ambiguous, at least temporarily. The adage 'Time flies like an arrow' has almost 100 grammatically possible interpretations (Altmann, 1998), among them the interpretation attributed to Groucho Marx: 'Time flies like an arrow; fruit flies like a banana'. Despite this ambiguity, on hearing the sentence, we show a preference for one structure and interpretation; it is only when we realize a mistake may have been made that we go back and look for other alternatives. The process by which we establish a mental representation of the syntactic structure of a sentence is called parsing. The psychological study of parsing has been heavily influenced by ideas from the field of linguistics. In fact, the study of the psychology of language is sometimes referred to as psycholinguistics, reflecting the influence of linguistics on psychological models of language generally. The influence of linguistics reflects a recognition that 'human minds feed on linguistic symbols' (Miller, 1968, p. 29).

Parsing is the process by which we assign a syntactic structure to a sentence. Psycholinguistics is the branch of study concerned with the mental processes underlying language comprehension and production.

Box 13.5 Practical Application: Communication with working animals – training dogs to recognize words

Dogs are not only our best friends. They contribute in important ways to a number of service roles, including search and rescue. Their success in such roles is due partly to their bond with people and partly to their ability to understand not only word labels but also, to some extent, intentions – they can engage in cooperative communication. For example, a dog can respond to a verbal command such as 'fetch' or 'find', and can be trained to locate a missing person using reward-based searching and air scenting. But research shows that dogs' skills extend considerably beyond this; they can also respond to hand signals and gestures, and even photographs of objects or people. This flexibility is unique among (non-human) animal species. Just how much can a dog understand and how might such skills be honed by training?

Kaminski et al. (2004) showed that a Border Collie, Rico, could 'fast-map', that is infer the referent of a new word by exclusion learning. Rico knew the labels of over 200 objects. When presented with a new spoken word, and a novel item amongst a set of familiar items, Rico could reliably infer that the new word must belong with the novel item. On hearing the verbal label, he would fetch the novel object. Furthermore, he could hold that information in memory; tested 4 weeks after the original training session, he could reliably retrieve the object given its name.

In a subsequent study, Kaminski et al. (2009) tested Rico and four other dogs using a task in which the dogs had to infer an intended referent given only an iconic sign instead of a verbal command. Five Border Collies (three males, two females; all were family dogs that lived with their owners) were tested at their homes. Three of the dogs, including Rico, were experienced in the 'fetching' communicative frame and were used to fetching objects by their labels. The experiment took place over two adjacent rooms in the owner's home. Eight familiar items were placed in one room, while the dog and owner were in the other room. The researcher then joined the dog and owner, and the owner was instructed to request the target object by giving one of three visual cues to the dog. An identical replica, a miniature replica, or a photograph of the object was presented and the dog was instructed to 'fetch' the target. Several of the distractor objects were made from the same material as the target (e.g. rubber), so that smell could not be used to identify the target.

The dogs were presented with the identical replica first, then with the miniature replica, and then with the photograph. On each trial, the dog went to the other room to locate the object; this is important, as if the owner or researcher were in the same room as the dog they might influence the response by providing subtle cues as to the target object. If the dog retrieved the correct object, he or she was rewarded vocally or with a treat. If the wrong object was retrieved, the trial was repeated up to three times.

All of the dogs could use the replicas. The three experienced dogs could do so immediately, while the two inexperienced dogs required only a few trials before they could respond appropriately to them. Two of the dogs could use the photographs at above chance levels. Why are dogs so successful in this task when even great apes could not complete this task? Kaminski et al. suggest that dogs have a special understanding of human cooperative communication, and can respond to cues like gaze, gestures and vocalizations due to a long shared evolutionary history.

Search and rescue dogs often have to work at a considerable distance from their handlers and communicating a 'find' may require a series of interactions between dog and handler. Understanding how dogs learn to identify referred-to objects, and how we can better communicate with them, has important practical implications that are only beginning to be appreciated.

Cognitive psychology has been greatly influenced by the linguist Noam Chomsky (1957, 1965, 1980). Chomsky aimed to establish a set of rules, a grammar, that would describe the well-formed grammatical sentences in a language, but produce none that are ungrammatical. Chomsky made the distinction between a sentence's deep and surface structure (or, to avoid connotations raised by the terms 'deep' and 'surface', d-structure and s-structure). This influential idea suggests that superficially different sentences can have the same underlying structure and meaning, and that sentence components can maintain their role in a sentence even though their position in a sentence changes. Chomsky's work also provided a framework that could be tested empirically.

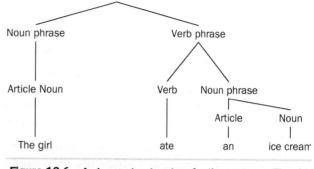

Figure 13.6 A phrase structure tree for the sentence 'The girl ate an ice cream'

For example, active and passive voice sentences have different surface structures but essentially have the same deep structure:

- Active voice: The boy ate the cake.
- Passive voice: The cake was eaten by the boy.

There may be a change in emphasis (the focus of the first sentence is on the boy while in the second it is on the cake), but in each case the boy is doing the eating and the cake is being eaten.

It might be predicted on this basis that passive voice sentences would take more time to process than their active voice counterparts. However, this is not always the case. Semantic information interacts with syntactic processing and can reduce processing load in cases where meaning can inform syntactic processing. For example, Slobin (1966) used a sentence verification task with reversible and irreversible passives. Sentences were presented along with a picture that in some cases matched the sentence and participants decided if the sentence described the picture. In a reversible passive, either noun could perform the action of the verb; its agent cannot be inferred from semantics. In an irreversible passive, there is only one feasible agent, for example:

A The boy chased the dog; the dog was chased by the boy.

B The boy called the dog; the dog was called by the boy.

Sentence A is reversible: taking the content words 'boy', 'dog' and 'chase', it could be that the dog is chasing the boy or the boy is chasing the dog. But in sentence B there is only one possible interpretation – the dog cannot be calling the boy.

Slobin (1966) found that irreversible passives did not require more processing time than an active voice sentence, whereas reversible passives did. Such data show the interaction of semantic and syntactic processing in sentence comprehension and are consistent with evidence from neuropsychology. Carramazza and Zurif (1976) found that people with Broca's aphasia (see Chapter 12) with impairments consistent with agrammatism could match pictures to irreversible sentences but performed poorly when presented with reversible sentences. This difference suggests that they could use semantic information in irreversible sentences to compensate for the deficit in syntax processing. By contrast, patients with Wernicke's aphasia performed poorly on both tasks.

We conceptualize syntactic processing or mental parsing as building up a phrase structure tree, again reflecting the influence of linguistics. As a sentence is heard or read, the listener constructs a phrase structure that assigns incoming words to a grammatical category on a phrase structure tree (see Figure 13.6), showing the relationships between the words in the sentence.

> Phrase structure tree is a graphic representation of the syntactic structure of a sentence.

We see the processes at work when we look at what happens when the system breaks down. Ambiguous sentences can be used to study parsing errors. Sentences of this type

Garden path sentence is
a grammatically correct but
ambiguous sentence that
biases the reader's initial
parsing.

are sometimes referred to as garden path sentences, because we are led astray (or 'up the garden path') in our initial parsing of the sentence. Bever (1970) provided this much cited example:

'The horse raced past the barn fell.'

The sentence is essentially 'The horse (that was) raced past the barn fell'; the ambiguity arises at 'raced', which is initially parsed as past tense verb – when we arrive at the verb 'fell', we realize an error has been made. Some other examples include 'Fat people eat accumulates' and 'The man who hunts ducks out on weekends.'

The goal of parsing is to assign incoming words to the appropriate role in the sentence as simply and efficiently as possible. Two key strategies used to accomplish this are summarized by Frazier (1987): minimal attachment and late closure. Minimal attach-

Minimal attachment
introduces new items into
the phrase structure using
as few syntactic nodes as
possible.
Late closure attaches
incoming material to the
phrase that is currently
being processed.

ment allows us to create the simplest tree structure that is consistent with the grammar of the language by introducing new items into the phrase structure using as few syntactic nodes as possible. In Bever's (1970) example, 'the horse' is a noun phrase and 'raced' is the main verb in the past tense referring to the noun. We therefore parse 'raced' as the past tense and not the past participle (although there may be some differences across languages; e.g. in Spanish; Cuetos & Mitchell, 1988). Late closure attaches incoming material to the phrase that is currently being processed, as long as that is grammatically permissible, reducing the load on working memory (Frazier, 1987). In other words, the clause we are processing remains open as long as possible, and therefore incoming input is associated with the more recent clause (Altmann, 1998). For example, take the sentence:

'John read the essay Mark wrote in the coffee shop.'

Did the reading of the essay or the writing of the essay take place in the coffee shop? Late closure sees 'coffee shop' attached to 'wrote'.

Serial models such as that of Frazier (1979) propose that parsing is incremental in that we allocate a word to a syntactic role as the word is perceived. Parsing is seen as autonomous and modular in such accounts in that the syntactic analysis is independent of semantic and other factors (Frazier, 1989). The interactive view, by contrast, proposes that semantics can influence syntax, that there is interaction between the levels of language (e.g., Taraban & McClelland, 1988). Grodner et al. (2005) report a range of semantic and contextual influences on parsing. For example, in Bever's 'the horse raced . . .' sentence, lexical frequency affects parsing (see Trueswell, 1996): because 'raced' rarely occurs as a past participle, it is more likely to be parsed as a past tense main verb.

Garden path sentences require the person to revise their initial interpretation of the sentence, as new, conflicting, information is presented. However, this re-analysis does not always produce the 'ideal' sentence structure, and revision of the roles initially assigned to the word may not be consistent, suggesting that structures that are 'good enough', rather than ideal, suffice (Ferreira et al., 2001, p. 3).

The treatment of semantic and syntactic information by the brain is discussed below. For now, we turn our attention to another aspect of language comprehension: understanding written text.

READING

So far in this chapter we have been considering language comprehension as it applies to spoken language. However, much of the language you encounter day to day is written down and it is important to be able to read and understand it (see Box 13.6). We understand written language through reading. Reading is a relatively new development. The oldest ancient writing system dates to the late fourth millennium BCE (Comrie, 2005). It is only within the past century that widespread literacy has been attained, in developed countries at least. The process of learning to read contrasts with learning to speak; children acquire spoken language readily, requiring little by way of 'explicit' instruction. Reading presents more of a challenge and its development differs as a function of features of the script used in the native language. There are vast differences in scripts, in terms of direction of reading, size of symbol repertoire required to read, and the symbolic representation of speech by writing.

Box 13.6 Practical Application: Communicating health guidelines with 'plain English'

In the previous sections, we have seen that ambiguity is inherent in language comprehension, affecting speech perception and understanding of words and sentences. The choice of language used is also important in determining how easy or difficult the comprehension task will be. Banking charge information, insurance company small print and health information have all benefited from a 'plain English' approach, which translates technical, jargon-rich information into a more readily understood form, taking the target audience into account.

The term 'readability' refers to how easily a written document can be read and understood. Various readability formulas have been proposed in order to measure how readily a passage of text can be understood. These generally aim to estimate the education level needed for a reader to understand a text. Some common formulas include the Dale-Chall Formula, Flesch Reading Ease, Flesch-Kincaid Formula, Gunning's Fog Index, and McLaughlin's SMOG (Simple Measure of Gobbledygook) grade. These formulas consider, in various ways, factors such as average sentence length, average word length, word difficulty level, number of syllables, and total number of words. But they cannot take into consideration factors such as context, reading experience and difficulty at the conceptual level. A nonsensical sentence can score highly on a readability measure, if its wording meets certain criteria, but that will not help the reader to understand it.

Irrespective of the difficulties with measuring readability, simplifying language has been shown to aid understanding, particularly within the healthcare context. A study by Michie and Lester (2005) examined whether presenting clinical guidelines in 'plain English' would increase the likelihood that they could be implemented by patients. Eighty-four patients using mental health services received either an original text of the UK's National Institute for Clinical Excellence (NICE) public guidelines for the management of schizophrenia or a 'plain English' version of the same text. The amended text aimed to:

1 increase the degree of specificity by which behaviours were defined;
2 personalize the message;
3 avoid technical language;
4 use active voice verbs;
5 use appropriate numerical information.

Bullet points, headings and key points were used in the amended version. Some examples are shown in Table 13.4. Otherwise, the content and presentation was similar in the two versions.

Table 13.4 Excerpts of text from the original NICE guidelines and the amended 'plain English' version of the text

Original text	Amended text
Also, if you want psychological help, you will need antipsychotic medicines at the same time. Remember, the decision about which medicine to take is best made by you and your doctors together.	You will need to take these medicines if you also want psychological help. You should decide which medicine is best for you with the help of your doctors.
It is also particularly useful if you have symptoms that won't go away and are troubling to you. Cognitive behavioural therapy is also helpful if you are having trouble accepting that you have schizophrenia (sometimes called 'lack of insight'), and it may help if you tend not to take your medicine properly (sometimes called 'poor compliance')	This is particularly useful if you: • have symptoms that won't go away and are troubling you; • are having trouble accepting that you have schizophrenia (sometimes called 'lack of insight'); or • tend not to take your medicine properly (sometimes called 'poor compliance').

Source: Reproduced from Michie, S., & Lester, K. (2005) Words matter: increasing the implementation of clinical guidelines. *Quality and Safety in Health Care, 14*, 367–370 with permission from BMJ Publishing Group Ltd.

Patients who read the 'plain English' guidelines reported stronger intentions to implement the guidelines, more positive attitudes towards the guidelines, and greater perceived behavioural control in terms of using them. There was no difference between the two texts in terms of perceived comprehension, however. These, and other, findings suggest that the style used to communicate healthcare information can affect the likelihood that a patient will understand and be able to implement the advice provided.

WRITING SYSTEMS

Scripts vary across languages in the extent and manner of representation of spoken sounds. All spoken languages have phonemes or basic speech sounds which can be combined in various ways, but written scripts differ markedly in the extent to which, as well as the ways in which, this phonetic information is represented. There are four main types of script:

Logographic scripts represent morphemes or the units of meaning of words. **Syllabic scripts** use a symbol to represent each syllable. **Consonantal scripts** represent the consonants of the language. **Alphabetic scripts** represent the phonemes or sounds in a language.

• Logographic, or ideographic scripts, represent morphemes or the units of meaning of words; for example the Chinese symbol for 'sun' (ri) is 日; the symbol does not map onto the sound 'ri', it represents the meaning 'sun'. We use number words in the same way – the symbol '4' can be read as 'four', or as 'quatre' in French, or 'vier' in German. The symbol '4' is associated with a meaning and not a sound.

• Syllabic scripts use a symbol to represent each syllable.

• Consonantal scripts represent the consonants of the language.

• Alphabetic scripts use letters to represent the phonemes or sounds in a language.

Some writing systems combine elements of these types; for example, Japanese uses both kana (syllabic) and kanji (logographic), and Devanagari, a South Asian language, uses a script with elements of both syllabic and alphabetic systems, an alphasyllabic writing system (e.g., Vaid & Gupta, 2002).

Early writing systems were pictographic. There was a direct pictorial or iconic representation of the meaning of the word, which limited the script to depiction of concrete,

Table 13.5 The word 'dog' as written in several scripts, along with approximate pronunciation in English

Chinese	Japanese kanji	Japanese kana	Hebrew	Cyrillic alphabet (Russian)
狗	犬	イヌ	כלב	собака
gǒu	inu	inu	kelev	sobaka

highly imageable words. Logographic scripts developed from earlier pictographic forms, but the relationship between the symbol and referent became arbitrary (see Table 13.5 for example). Chinese, Korean hanja and Japanese kanji are examples of this type of script and although there may be some phonetic components to the scripts, the individual symbols are not pronounceable in the way that occurs in other scripts. The basic unit of representation in a logographic script is the morpheme.

In syllabic writing, each syllable is represented by a character, so that the precise pronunciation of each symbol is known. In a language with a relatively small number of syllables, this is effective. For example, Japanese has just 69 syllables that need to be represented in a syllabic script, kana (Harris & Coltheart, 1986). But such a script could not be used in English or in other languages with a large set of syllables. (In Japanese, it is supplemented with the morpheme-based kanji script because kana cannot represent homophones, different words with the same pronunciation; kana is used mainly for functional words; Chen et al., 2002.) In consonantal scripts (e.g. Hebrew) letters represent consonants but not vowels, although in some such scripts the vowels might be represented using diacritics (e.g., in Arabic).

The alphabetic writing system is the most dominant across world languages (Comrie, 2005) and its basic unit of representation is the phoneme. Alphabets developed from the Greek system and later split into those based on the Roman script and those based on the Cyrillic script. The grapheme is the written representation of a phoneme. However, a grapheme can consist of more than one letter. In some languages, letters correspond to phonemes (e.g. Serbo-Croatian). These are said to be transparent or shallow orthography languages, because there is a one-to-one correspondence between the letters and sounds. In transparent languages a 'sounding-out' strategy will always produce the correct pronunciation. In opaque or orthographically deep languages by contrast there is not a one-to-one grapheme-to-phoneme relationship; the same sound may be written in a number of ways and the same letter string might be associated with multiple pronunciations. Homophones (e.g. rain, reign) and homographs (e.g. tear – can rhyme with beer or bear; bow – can rhyme with low or cow) require the same sounds to be attached to different spellings or different sounds to be attached to the same spelling respectively. The orthographic depth of the writing system has implications for the models of reading discussed below. It also has implications for reading development; children learning to read a shallow orthography show advantages over those learning a deep orthography (e.g., Frost et al., 1987; Seymour et al., 2003; Spencer & Hanley, 2003). Table 13.6, from Seymour et al. (2003), shows the orthographic depth of some European languages as a function of syllable complexity. The challenges to beginner readers of English reflect both a deep orthography and complex syllabic structure in the language.

> Grapheme is the written representation of a phoneme.
> Transparent or shallow orthography uses a one-to-one correspondence between the letters and sounds.
> Opaque or orthographically deep languages are those where the relationship between letters and sounds is more complex.

Table 13.6 Classification of some European languages according to syllabic complexity and orthographic depth

		Orthographic depth				
		Shallow ————————————————————→ Deep				
Syllabic structure	Simple	Finnish	Greek Italian Spanish	Portuguese	French	
	Complex		German Norwegian Icelandic	Dutch Swedish	Danish	English

Source: Based on Seymour, P. H. K., Aro, M., & Erskine, J. M. (2003). Foundation literacy acquisition in European orthographies. *British Journal of Psychology*, 94, 143–174 (p. 146).

CONTEXT EFFECTS ON VISUAL WORD RECOGNITION

Word superiority effect refers to the finding that a target letter within a letter string is detected more readily when the string forms a word.

In the section on speech perception above, we saw that recognition can occur before the word is fully uttered. Similarly, top-down influences can speed written word recognition – reading is not achieved by reading letter-by-letter until the word is complete. This is illustrated by the word superiority effect, which shows that letters within a letter string are detected more readily if they are presented within a word compared to within a non-word or pseudoword string or in a non-letter array (Reicher, 1969; Wheeler, 1970).

In a typical experiment of this type, a word or non-word stimulus is presented very briefly (25–40 milliseconds) on a computer screen (e.g., WORD). A pattern mask (such as a row of XXXX) follows; then two letters are presented, one of which is the target letter. The participant must choose which letter appeared in a given position (for example, _ _ _*: D or K?). In the forced-choice task, both letter options result in a real word (e.g. WORD or WORK). The effect is relatively unaffected by letter position (Rayner & Clifton, 2002) suggesting parallel processing of letter information rather than left to right letter-by-letter reading. A pseudoword advantage over nonwords has also been reported (e.g, Carr et al., 1978).

Context has a considerable influence on visual word recognition. Meyer and Schvaneveldt (1971) presented subjects with a lexical decision task which incorporated a semantic priming component. Participants had to decide as quickly as possible if a presented letter string was a word. The stimuli were primed by preceding them with a semantically related word in some cases. The semantic prime produced faster word recognition. For example, the word NURSE was recognized faster when primed by DOCTOR than when preceded by the semantically unrelated word BUTTER. Similarly, Zola (1984) examined participants' eye fixations while they read sentences such as:

A Movie theatres must have buttered popcorn to serve their patrons.

B Movie theatres must have adequate popcorn to serve their patrons.

Participants fixate on the word 'popcorn' for longer in sentence B compared to sentence A. They are primed in sentence A by the context provided by the word 'buttered'; this places limits on the (semantically congruous) possibilities for words that will come next, reducing processing effort. The link between the written word and its meaning is explored further in Box 13.7.

Box 13.7 Research Close Up: The Stroop effect

Source: Stroop, J. R. (1935). Studies of interference in serial verbal reactions. *Journal of Experimental Psychology*, *18*, 643–662.

INTRODUCTION

In 1935, J. R. Stroop published a research article describing an effect that continues to form the basis for many diverse experiments today. A typical Stroop colour-naming task requires a participant to name the colour in which a word is printed, when the word is itself a colour term. When the word meaning agrees with the print colour (for example, the word BLUE printed in blue and requiring the response 'blue'), response times are faster than when naming a neutral colour block, a non-word or a neutral word (one that is not associated with a particular colour), an effect called 'Stroop facilitation'. When the word colour and meaning do not concur (e.g., the word RED written in blue ink requiring the response 'blue'), response times are slower than on the neutral condition, an effect known as 'Stroop interference'. Stroop's original experiments, which differ somewhat from the typical Stroop study today (see Table 13.7), are considered here.

Stroop's 1935 paper in the *Journal of Experimental Psychology* is one of the most cited publications in the history of experimental psychology; at the time of writing the paper is listed on the Scopus database as being cited by 5048 articles – since citation counts are a relatively recent development this is likely to underestimate the paper's influence.

Table 13.7 Conditions compared in a typical Stroop task. (Stroop's original experiments did not employ a congruent colour word condition in a colour naming task.)

Congruent condition	Incongruent condition	Neutral condition
Red	Blue	■
Blue	Red	■

METHOD AND RESULTS

In Stroop's study, three experiments explored colour and word naming conditions. In Experiment 1 ($n = 70$), Stroop used five colour stimuli (red, blue, green, brown and purple) to examine the effect of colour on word reading, using a colour-incongruent and a neutral (words in black ink) condition. In this first experiment, no interference was found when reading words from the incongruent colours.

In his second experiment ($n = 100$), Stroop used a colour-naming task – rather than reading words, participants named the colours in which words were printed. Ink colours were incongruent with word meaning, and a neutral condition used solid colour squares. On this task, participants demonstrated a significant interference effect. Colour naming was significantly slower when the colour of the ink was incongruent with word meaning compared to the neutral condition, with a 74 per cent increase in response times. The contrast between the effects in Experiment 1 and Experiment 2 tells us that word reading is more automatic than colour naming (MacLeod & MacDonald, 2000). As MacLeod (1991) described it, 'the basic idea is that processing of one dimension requires much more attention than does processing of the other dimension. Thus, naming the ink color draws more heavily on attentional resources than does reading the irrelevant word. Moreover, reading the word is seen as obligatory, whereas naming the ink color is not. Presumably, this imbalance derives from our extensive history of reading words as opposed to naming ink colors' (p. 188).

Stroop's third experiment ($n = 32$) explored the effects of practice. Participants named ink colours of incongruent words (e.g., given RED in blue ink, respond 'blue') or read words in a series of sessions over eight days, while the colour squares were replaced with a symbol. Interference was found to decrease with practice. In addition, practice was found to interfere with word reading to an extent, an effect known as the reverse Stroop effect.

DISCUSSION

The interference effect itself is robust and has been replicated across dozens of studies, whether employing printed cards, as in Stroop's original work, or using computerized stimulus presentation with precise time recording, and varying colour stimulus and control conditions (see MacLeod, 1991, for a review). The first use of colour-congruent trials was by Dalrymple-Alford and Budayr (1966). The Stroop effect shows that, for proficient readers, word reading is mandatory – even though the participants' task is to name the colour, they cannot avoid reading the word: access to the conflicting meaning creates interference. The Stroop task has been typically associated with activation of anterior cingulate and dorsolateral prefrontal cortex, as well as inferior frontal gyrus, inferior and superior parietal cortex and insula, areas associated with overcoming interference in a cognitive task (see, for example, Nee et al., 2007).

The Stroop effect is also found in non-alphabetical scripts, but neuroimaging studies have shown differential activation in brain regions when reading different writing systems. For example, Coderre et al. (2009) found that the Stroop task activated an area in the left inferior parietal region when participants completed the task in Japanese kana script (syllable-based), but the left inferior frontal gyrus was activated during the same task completed in kanji, a logographic writing system. Coderre et al. suggest that these data reflect differences in how the brain detects and resolves conflict in syllabic and logographic writing systems.

EYE MOVEMENTS

Saccades are fast movements of the eye made when reading or scanning an image. Fixation occurs when the eye settles briefly on a region of interest in a visual scene.

Analysis of eye movements has provided much insight into the processes underlying reading. As we read a line of text, our eyes do not move smoothly from one letter to the next or from one word to the next. Instead, there are some fast movements of the eye, called saccades, with periods in between, called fixations, when the eyes are relatively still. The saccades are very fast, ballistic movements of about 20 to 60 milliseconds duration, with a (relatively) still period of 200 to 250 milliseconds in between (Rayner, 1998). Saccades cover about 7–9 letter spaces (Rayner 1998), or fewer in a logographic writing system (Field, 2003).

The two most robust findings to come from eye movement research, according to Clifton, Staub and Rayner (2007), are, first, that fixation time on a word is reduced if the reader has managed to preview the word prior to fixating it, and, second, that fixation time is reduced for words that are readily identified. Evidence from eye movements shows that we do not just move 'forward' (left to right if reading English), reading each word, nor are all words treated equally (see Rayner, 1998, for a review). Many saccades (about 10–15 per cent according to Rayner, 1998) are regressions. There may also be multiple fixations of the same word (re-fixations) or skipping of words. Content words are fixated more often than are function words (Carpenter & Just, 1983; Rayner & Duffy, 1988). As word length increases, the likelihood that it will be fixated increases (Rayner & McConkie, 1976). Context adds to the efficiency of the process, as a predictable word is more likely to be skipped than a less predictable word (Ehrlich & Rayner, 1981; O'Regan, 1979). Text difficulty affects eye movement; as difficulty increases, the saccade length decreases and the number of regressions increases (e.g., Jacobson & Dodwell, 1979).

Eye movement data have also been informative with regard to processing at the sentence level. The eyes respond predictably to semantic and syntactic anomalies as well as to

Figure 13.7 A hypothetical eye-movement record of a participant reading the sentence 'The shrubs were planted by the greenhouse yesterday'. Each fixation is represented by an asterisk, with the duration of fixation indicated by the number next to it. Time is shown going down the figure. A number of regressive fixations are evident.

Source: Reprinted from Liversedge S. P., & Findlay J. M. (2000) Saccadic eye movements and cognition. *Trends in Cognitive Sciences, 4,* 6–14 with permission from Elsevier.

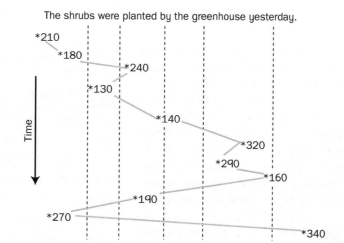

Scan to watch a discussion of texting

parsing errors such as those elicited by garden path sentences (see above), although studies addressing the sentence level have produced more variable findings than those addressing word identification (see Clifton et al., 2007). Box 13.8 examines how eye tracking has been used to examine how people approach reading of new media, such as mobile phone text messaging.

Box 13.8 Research Close Up: Reading and text messaging

Source: Perea, M., Acha, J., & Carreiras, M. (2009). Eye movements when reading text messaging (txt msgng). *The Quarterly Journal of Experimental Psychology, 62,* 1560–1567.

INTRODUCTION

Rsrch shws it dsnt mttr hw mny lttrs u use – it's nly mprtnt u use sm lttrs . . .

There has been much debate in the media around the use of language in mobile phone text (or SMS, Short Message Service) messages, with many commentators suggesting that the conventions of text language bring detrimental effects for writing and literacy, particularly among younger people. Text messages often contain 'textisms', shortened words and other nonstandard spellings (e.g. see Crystal, 2008; Lyddy et al., in press), such as orthographic abbreviations and phonological textisms. Orthographic abbreviations rely on the information provided by consonants, often deleting vowels (e.g., wk, week; pls, please; txt, text; msg, message). Phonological textisms involve sound-based respellings, changing letters and using numbers within words (e.g., c u, see you; 2nite, tonight; u r, you are). But what effect do such textisms have on reading?

METHOD

Perea et al. (2009) used eye-tracking to examine reading of text messages in Spanish. Perea et al. compared sentences containing mostly orthographic abbreviations and sentences with mostly phonological abbreviations with standard text messages in Spanish. The sentences were short in length (at 6.2 words on average, SD = 1.4) and were written in informal language. The abbreviations used in the 'textism' sentences were selected using a Spanish SMS dictionary and were pre-tested for understanding. Twenty-six skilled texters participated. Their eye movements were recorded as they read the sentences, and comprehension was tested intermittently to ensure that participants were reading the sentences fully. Participants pressed a button when they had read each sentence. Seventy-two sentences were presented in total. Some example sentences are presented in Table 13.8.

RESULTS

Perea et al. found a processing cost for sentences containing textisms relative to the control sentences. This processing cost was greater for phonological textisms (e.g., c u 2nite) compared to orthographic textisms (e.g., pls txt). The standard sentences were read significantly faster than the textism sentences. On average, 3.3 words per second were read in the orthographic condition, compared to 3 words per second in the phonological textism condition. By contrast, the respective control conditions produced 5.5 and 5.6 words per second. More fixations were also required in the textism conditions, with on average 6.7 fixations for orthographic sentences, and 7.8 fixations for phonological sentences, compared to 4.8 and 5.3 fixations for their control conditions, respectively. Fixation durations were also longer for the textism conditions compared to the standard sentences. These effects occurred despite the fact that all sentences were easily read by participants.

Table 13.8 Examples of sentences used by Perea et al. (2009)

Condition	Sentence
Orthographic	irmos l cnciert n m mto
Control	iremos al concierto en mi moto
[Translation]	[we'll go to the concert on my bike]
Phonological	akab l kldo d 1 vz
Control	acaba el caldo de una vez
[Translation]	[finish the soup at once]

DISCUSSION

These data show a clear processing cost for text messages using textisms, in Spanish, compared to standard sentences, despite the ease of reading for participants. The greater effect for phonological textisms may be specific to Spanish writing, or to 'shallower' orthographies, or it may be an artefact of the stimuli used here. Perea et al. note that phonological abbreviations of Spanish words tend to involve low-frequency letters. The processing costs observed by Perea et al. may also have been specific to the stimuli used. The textism messages were composed entirely of textisms, with no standard spellings, unlike real text messages, which typically use standard spellings along with textisms (see for example Lyddy et al., in press). Furthermore, many of the sentences used were unlikely to be encountered in real text messages (for example, sentences included 'finish the soup at once'; the sock is stored in the drawer', and 'has anyone seen my suitcase?'). The advantage of such sentences is that they won't have been encountered before in texted form and so prior exposure to such forms is to some extent controlled; however, the disadvantage is that they are therefore not very realistic. These limitations aside, however, the issue of reading costs would seem to warrant further study.

THE DUAL ROUTE MODEL OF READING

Most models of reading are based on studies in which the participants were reading English. Because of the differences in writing systems used around the world, models of reading that are based on a particular script or language may not generalize well to other systems. Written English is orthographically deep; that is, there is not a one-to-one correspondence between written symbols and the sounds represented. To be able to read English, we need to be able to: sound out new words and non-words; and retrieve the pronunciation for words that do not follow the 'rules' for sounding out words from the lexicon.

Words that follow the general rules for converting print to sound could be read either way, by sounding them out or by retrieving the relevant entry for the word in the mental lexicon. This distinction between print–sound rules and lexical entry look-up forms the basis for the dual route model of reading. One version of this is Coltheart et al.'s (2001) dual route cascaded model which proposes three routes for reading (see Figure 13.8). Route 1 allows the conversion of print to sounds, the grapheme-to-phoneme conversion (GPC) route. This allows someone to sound out a word once they have analysed the letters, without necessarily having access to the word in the lexicon. This route is necessary for the reading of unfamiliar or new words (which will have no entry in the lexicon) and can be used to sound out regular words (that is, words that follow the print–sound rules) also. In a language with a deep orthography, this sounding-out strategy will produce errors, as many words in such a language do not follow GPC rules. A second, direct, route, the lexical route, allows reading via word recognition. The word is recognized based on its orthographic features, its entry is found in the lexicon and its meaning is accessed via the semantic system. Thereafter the sound properties of the word are accessed. In Figure 13.8, we also find a third route which bypasses the semantic system. This route accounts for occasions when an irregular word is read correctly when meaning is not available. This last route also accounts for a pattern of deficit observed in some types of acquired dyslexia called non-semantic reading (this is discussed below).

Much evidence for this model comes from data from neuropsychological case studies and these are discussed below. Alternative accounts propose that we do not need two routes for reading. Connectionist accounts such as that of Seidenberg and McClelland (1989) and Plaut et al. (1996), using a single network, produce what might be considered as 'rule-based' or assembly responses as well as dealing with exception words via access.

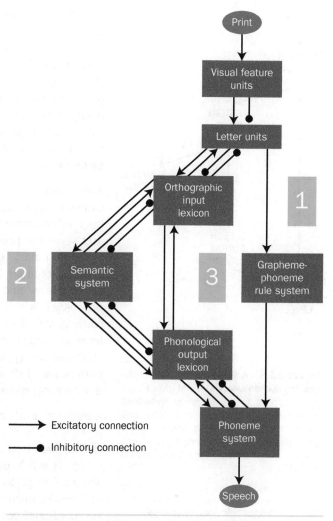

Figure 13.8   The dual route cascaded model of reading. Route 1 allows the conversion of print to sounds, the grapheme-to-phoneme conversion (GPC) route. A second, direct, route, the lexical route, allows reading via word recognition. A third route bypasses the semantic system.

Source: Coltheart, M., Rastle, K., Perry, C., Langdon, R., & Ziegler, J. (2001). DRC: A dual route cascaded model of visual word recognition and reading aloud. *Psychological Review, 108*, 204–256. APA; reprinted with permission.

THE BRAIN AND LANGUAGE COMPREHENSION

NEUROPSYCHOLOGY OF SPEECH COMPREHENSION

The brain area most associated with deficits in language comprehension is Wernicke's area. Affected patients have profound problems with comprehension of even relatively simple sentences (Goodglass, 1993), while Broca's aphasia (see Chapter 12) generally produces comprehension deficits only for sentences with more complex morphosyntactic structures (e.g., see Berndt & Caramazza, 1980). A number of other areas in the brain's left hemisphere which play key roles in language comprehension have been identified.

Grapheme-to-phoneme conversion (GPC) route allows us to sound out words based on letter–sound correspondences.
Lexical or direct route to reading involves the selection of a word from the lexicon.
Non-semantic reading is a pattern of reading deficit whereby the patient can read an irregular word (which cannot be sounded out) and yet cannot access its meaning.

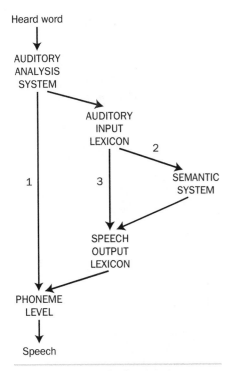

Heard word

AUDITORY
ANALYSIS
SYSTEM

AUDITORY
INPUT
LEXICON

2

1   3

SEMANTIC
SYSTEM

SPEECH
OUTPUT
LEXICON

PHONEME
LEVEL

Speech

Figure 13.9 A three-route model for processing spoken words. The first route allows direct access to the phoneme level from initial auditory analysis. The other two routes are for known words and auditory analysis gives access to the auditory input lexicon where information regarding a known word is stored.

Source: Adapted from Ellis, A. W., & Young, A. W. (1996). *Human cognitive neuropsychology: A textbook with readings*. Hove: Psychology Press.

Pure word deafness is a deficit affecting the ability to recognize speech sounds, while comprehension of non-speech sounds remains intact.
Pure word meaning deafness the patient can repeat back the word, but cannot understand it.

Dronkers et al. (2004) evaluated 64 patients who had suffered left hemisphere strokes affecting language comprehension. Using sub-tests from a receptive language test, the Curtiss-Yamada Comprehensive Language Evaluation (CYCLE-R), they identified five left hemisphere areas that were associated with performance detriments on the test. These areas were the posterior middle temporal gyrus, anterior superior temporal gyrus, superior temporal sulcus and angular gyrus, and mid-frontal cortex in Brodmann's area 46 and area 47. The middle temporal gyrus was also identified as having a key role in language comprehension.

The main types of aphasia were discussed in Chapter 12. Considering comprehension, cases of Wernicke's aphasia have been informative with regard to the distinction between syntactic and semantic processing. In Wernicke's aphasia, content words are problematic but the overall syntactic structure of the sentence, including function words and inflections, remains relatively intact, as does prosody, suggesting relatively independent processes within speech production. Comprehension is profoundly affected in Wernicke's aphasia, and word retrieval problems (anomia), use of made up words (neologisms) and word substitutions (paraphasias) are common (see Chapter 12). The patient has difficulty understanding the language of others, and does not appreciate the errors in his or her own language.

A number of other 'pure' language disorders are of relevance here. Pure word deafness is a deficit affecting the ability to recognize speech sounds, while comprehension of non-speech sounds remains intact. It is a 'pure' disorder in that other aspects of aphasia are absent – the patient can speak and read as normal – and perception of (most) non-speech sounds is intact. Patients have described the sounds they hear as being 'far away' or like words in a foreign language (Albert & Bear, 1974). In pure word meaning deafness, as described by Franklin et al. (1994) for example, the patient can repeat back the word, showing that he or she can access and represent the phonetic sequence in short-term memory, but cannot understand it. The patient may, however, be able to recognize the same word when it is written down. Ellis and Young (1996) suggest a three-route model for processing spoken words (see Figure 13.9) which provides a useful framework for understanding these disorders. A first route allows direct access to the phoneme level from initial auditory analysis; this route would allow us to repeat back a non-word or a foreign word that we do not know. The other two routes are for known words and auditory analysis gives access to the auditory input lexicon where information regarding a known word is stored. We generally can access the semantic system from this point (Route 2) and will therefore understand the word and what it relates to. But we can sometimes bypass semantic access, such that the auditory input lexicon connects directly to speech output, without semantic access (Route 3). In pure word meaning deafness, the patient has access to the auditory input lexicon and can make a judgement that the stimulus is a word but they cannot understand it as there is no access to the semantic system: Route 3 is intact but Route 2 is compromised. By contrast in pure word deafness a problem affects phonemic processing, occurring before access to the auditory input lexicon: Route 1 is damaged. A third pattern predicted by the model suggests a distinction in the treatment of familiar and unfamiliar words. If Route 1 alone is damaged, one might predict a difficulty with repeating unfamiliar strings without a difficulty affecting known words. This pattern has been reported in cases of auditory phonological agnosia (e.g. see Ellis & Young, 1996).

NEUROPSYCHOLOGY OF READING

In the section examining reading above, we saw that the cascaded dual-route model proposes that there are two main routes involved in reading in English: an indirect route involving grapheme-to-phoneme conversion, and a direct lexical route which accesses pronunciation following access to the word's entry in the lexicon and semantic system. A third route is also suggested, which bypasses the semantic system but looks up the written word in the lexicon. Support for these three routes has come from neuropsychological case studies of acquired dyslexia. This involves studying the deficits in reading following brain injury in adults who were able to read normally before the injury; however, the patterns of deficit seen in acquired dyslexia are rarely simple.

Based on the dual-route model, we might predict a double dissociation of function (see Chapter 1), between the two main routes, that is, between the indirect sound-based route and the direct lexical route. This is the pattern seen when we contrast surface and phonological dyslexia. Surface dyslexia is characterized by a deficit in the reading of irregular or exception words, while the reading of regular words is spared (e.g., Marshall & Newcombe, 1973). People with surface dyslexia tend to make over-regularization errors when they try to read exception words; that is, they will read them as they would sound if they followed the rules. For example, they might pronounce 'pretty' to rhyme with 'jetty'. This suggests that they are using their indirect, grapheme-to-phoneme route to read, due to damage to the lexical route. Since the lexical route is required to read exception words, regularization errors are made. Some patients cannot access the meaning of words that they have not been able to pronounce correctly, supporting the model's prediction that phonology is accessed before meaning using the lexical (direct) route. While a dissociation between reading of regular and irregular words is evident here, a range of deficits are evident in surface dyslexia, and so to say that this the pattern of error reflects reading in the absence of a lexical route would be an over-simplification (Patterson et al., 1985).

> Acquired dyslexia refers to reading difficulties following brain injury.
> Surface dyslexia is characterized by a deficit in the reading of irregular words, while the reading of regular words is spared.
> Phonological dyslexia affects non-word reading, but real words can be read.

Scan to watch an animation on 'what is dyslexia?'

People with phonological dyslexia have problems pronouncing non-words or pseudowords but they can read real words (e.g., see Beauvois & Derouesné, 1979), whether regular or irregular. For example, they may be able to read 'rain' but cannot read 'rait'. Visual errors are common; the patient may read the non-word as if it were a real word. Given 'rait' they might read 'rail', 'rite' or 'rat', for example. This pattern suggests an intact lexical route but damaged grapheme-to-phoneme conversion. As Harley (2008) points out, these patterns of deficit are rarely complete and conclusions regarding support of the dual route model must take this into account; no patients have been reported who have a complete inability to read non-words, while words are completely intact, for example. Funnell (1983) reports the case of W.B. who could read no non-words, but he also had a deficit affecting word reading, with performance at about 85 per cent.

Neuropsychological data also support two stages to the lexical route: retrieval of the lemma (see Chapter 12), then access to phonology (Harley, 1995). Reilly (1999) reported an unusually well documented case of temporary dyslexia. A radio presenter, R.H.R., experienced a progressive worsening of dyslexia symptoms when he suffered a seizure while making a live broadcast. He was reading from a script at the time, introducing the topic of the radio programme, and the broadcast continued for just over a minute before the editor cut to another presenter. R.H.R.'s reading errors fell into three broad classes of error (see Reilly, 1999):

1 errors at the orthographic stage prior to lexical access;
2 disruption in lexical access;
3 errors assembling the phonology.

Evidence for a third route from orthography to phonology via the lexicon but not the semantic system comes from a pattern of deficit called non-semantic reading. A few cases have been reported of people who can read irregular words without understanding them (e.g., Coslett, 1991). These cases generally involve dementia, and as access to semantic information is lost it would seem that ability to read the words is retained. As the patients can read irregular words they cannot understand, they must be using the lexical route, yet semantic access is not possible. This supports a third route bypassing semantics (see Figure 13.9).

BRAIN IMAGING AND ELECTROPHYSIOLOGICAL DATA

Electrophysiological studies using event related potentials (ERPs) provide an on-line view of how the brain treats language. ERPs are changes in EEG brain activity that occur in response to a stimulus event. They are collected by means of electrodes placed on an individual's scalp. By time locking EEG activity to stimulus presentation, we can see how the brain responds to particular stimuli. ERPs provide a non-invasive method of observing brain activity and the temporal resolution means that changes are recorded as they occur; this on-line measurement is a valuable addition to experimental methodologies which address an end process but often cannot provide an on-line account.

ERPs have been shown to contain a number of important waves or components. The N400 component is a negative-going potential that occurs approximately 400 milliseconds after the presentation of a triggering stimulus. It has been shown to be associated with the time-course of some aspects of word processing and with semantic processing in particular. Kutas and Hillyard (1980) were the first to show that the N400 is relatively larger when a semantically anomalous word is presented to participants (e.g. 'He spread the warm bread with socks'.) Kutas and Hillyard suggested that the N400 was an 'electrophysiological sign of the "reprocessing" of semantically anomalous information' (p. 203). More recent accounts suggest that the N400 reflects increased processing effort when dealing with semantic information (e.g. Brown and Hagoort, 1993; Holcomb, 1993). Osterhout et al. (1997) provide the following examples of sentences eliciting an N400 wave:

• 'The cats won't bake the food that Mary leaves them.'
• 'I take my coffee with cream and dog.'
• 'A hammer is a bird.'

By contrast the P600 wave occurs when syntactically anomalous words are presented (Osterhout & Holcomb, 1992) and has an onset around 500 milliseconds after presentation of the stimulus. Osterhout et al. (1997) provide the following examples of sentences eliciting a P600 wave:

- 'The cats won't eating the food that Mary leaves them.'
- 'The broker persuaded to sell the stock.'
- 'The elected officials hopes to succeed.'

Figure 13.10 from Osterhout et al. (1997) illustrates the N400 and P600 waves in semantically and syntactically anomalous sentence conditions (the negative ERP component is plotted on the upper part of the graph).

How is reading achieved in orthographically consistent languages? In English, there may be as many as 1120 ways to represent the 40 phonemes in the language, while consistent languages show far less ambiguity in the print–sound mappings – in Italian, for example, 33 graphemes represent the 25 phonemes of the language (see Paulesu et al., 2000) and there is a one-to-one correspondence from print to sound. Paulesu et al. (2000) used positron emission tomography (PET) to examine brain activity while English- or Italian-speaking students read high-frequency regular words in their native language, or non-words. The Italian students were faster to read both words and non-words, an effect that was independent of articulation or naming rates. For both groups, reading of non-words was performed more slowly than reading of words (see also Box 13.8). The PET data reported by Paulesu et al. (2000) identified a number of brain areas activated in common for the two languages: the inferior frontal and premotor cortex, the left hemisphere superior, middle and inferior temporal gyri and fusiform gyrus, and the right superior temporal gyrus. English speakers showed particularly strong activation in the left posterior inferior temporal area and in part of the inferior frontal gyrus, and particularly when reading non-words.

The Italian readers showed greater activation of an auditory area associated with phonological processing, the planum temporale, while reading both words and non-words. These data support commonality in left hemisphere brain structures for reading in both orthographically deep and transparent scripts, with additional activation of specific brain regions that may be orthography-specific.

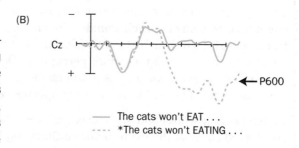
(A)

The cats won't EAT . . .
The cats won't BAKE . . .

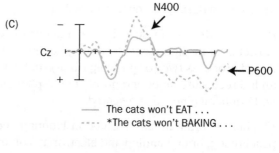
(B)

The cats won't EAT . . .
*The cats won't EATING . . .

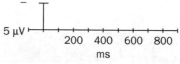
(C)

The cats won't EAT . . .
*The cats won't BAKING . . .

Figure 13.10 The N400 and P600 waves in semantically and syntactically anomalous sentence conditions. The negative ERP component is plotted on the upper part of the graph. An asterisk next to a sentence indicates ungrammaticality. Panel A shows responses to a semantically anomalous word, B shows a syntactically anomalous word and C shows a sentence containing both a semantic and syntactic anomaly, in each case compared to a non-anomalous sentence.

Source: Reprinted from Osterhout, L., McLaughlin, J., & Bersick, M. (1997). Event-related brain potentials and human language. *Trends in Cognitive Sciences, 1,* 203–209, with permission from Elsevier.

Chinese provides an excellent test of this idea of a common network for reading, allowing comparison of the two script types within a single language group. In Chinese a logographic script is used along with an alphabet, pinyin (meaning 'assembling sound'; Chen et al., 2002). Reading non-alphabetic Chinese characters makes little use of letter-sound assembly, while reading pinyin is a process of reading sound from letters. Chen et al. (2002) used fMRI to examine brain activity in Chinese readers exposed to the two types of Chinese script. They found that the alphabetic and non-alphabetic Chinese scripts activated a common brain network, while some script-specific differences were also evident, with activation of the inferior parietal cortex during reading of pinyin and of the fusiform gyrus for Chinese non-alphabetic characters.

Summary

In this chapter we looked at language comprehension. The challenge of language comprehension begins with speech perception. Understanding speech requires us to perceive and interpret input from a continuous stream of speech sounds. The processes involved make use of top-down information (e.g., from context) as well as bottom-up information sources from the speech signal itself. These combine to allow fast and generally accurate perception. Occasional 'slips of the ear' reveal how the cognitive system detects word boundaries, using language-specific features to guide segmentation. We also saw how categorical perception and other properties of the system facilitate perception.

Understanding words and sentences requires lexical access, syntactic and semantic processing. We considered some of the main factors influencing lexical access such as frequency, semantic context, syntactic context and word ambiguity. We also looked at the interaction of semantic and syntactic information during sentence processing.

Reading differs from speech in a number of key ways and differs substantially across languages, particularly in the extent to which phonetic information is represented in the script. The dual route model proposes two (or possibly three) routes for reading; a direct route involving lexical access and an indirect route involving grapheme to phoneme correspondences. Evidence from neuropsychology and brain imaging was presented.

Finally, the brain areas involved in language comprehension were discussed, with data from neuro-psychology, brain imaging and electrophysiology informing our knowledge in this area.

Review questions

1 What can 'slips of the ear' tell us about the processes involved in speech perception?

2 How has evidence from acquired aphasia contributed to our understanding of language comprehension?

3 What do cross-language differences in brain activation during reading tell us about the common processes involved?

4 Does the evidence support a 'dual route' account of reading?

5 How might reading differ in orthographically 'deep' and 'transparent' languages?

FURTHER READING

MacLeod, C. M., & MacDonald, P. A. (2000). Inter-dimensional interference in the Stroop effect: Uncovering the cognitive and neural anatomy of attention. *Trends in Cognitive Sciences, 4*, 383–391.

Mattys, S. L., Melhorn, J. F., & White, L. (2007). Effects of syntactic expectations on speech segmentation. *Journal of Experimental Psychology: Human Perception and Performance, 33*, 960–977.

McQueen, J. M., & Cutler, A. (2001). Spoken word access processes: An introduction. *Language and Cognitive Processes, 16*, 469–490.

Samuel, A. G. (2011). Speech perception. *Annual Review of Psychology, 62*, 49–72.

Thothathiri, M., & Snedeker, J. (2008). Give and take: Syntactic priming during spoken language comprehension. *Cognition, 108*(1), 51–68.

CHAPTER 14:
COGNITION AND EMOTION

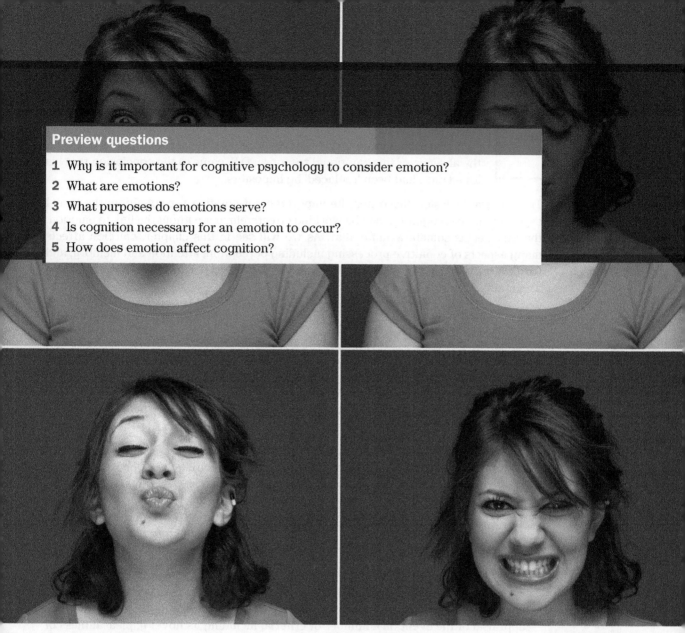

Preview questions

1 Why is it important for cognitive psychology to consider emotion?
2 What are emotions?
3 What purposes do emotions serve?
4 Is cognition necessary for an emotion to occur?
5 How does emotion affect cognition?

INTRODUCTION

In the film *Invasion of the Body Snatchers* (Dir. Don Siegel, 1956), a small-town doctor sees several patients who are convinced that their friends and family members have been replaced by imposters. In the movie, the doctor comes to the realization that these patients are not delusional; in fact the members of the community are being replaced by alien doppelgangers. A delusion of this type is seen in a rare disorder called Capgras syndrome (see Box 2.6 in Chapter 2), which demonstrates the importance of emotion to the act of visual recognition.

Patients with Capgras believe that their loved ones have been replaced by imposters. D.S. was a 30-year-old man who sustained a serious head injury in a car accident and lay in a coma for three weeks. While he experienced a good recovery from his physical injuries, he became convinced that his father and mother were 'imposters'. When asked about his father, D.S. said: 'He looks exactly like my father, but he really isn't. He's a nice guy, but he isn't my father' (Hirrstein & Ramachandran, 1997, p. 438). D.S.'s ability to discriminate faces was unimpaired, but he showed an abnormal

Skin conductance or galvanic skin response (GSR) reflects changes in the skin's ability to conduct electricity in the presence of an emotion-eliciting stimulus.

skin conductance response to faces, in that the magnitude of his response to familiar faces was not greater than for unfamiliar faces. In such cases, it would seem that while the cognitive processes necessary for overt face recognition are intact, brain damage has altered the connection to emotion, such that a familiar face does not produce the typical emotional response. In the absence of this emotional response, D.S. came to the conclusion that his loved ones had been 'replaced' by imposters.

The Capgras delusion illustrates the importance of emotion for cognition: the visual aspects of face recognition may be working effectively, but without the link to emotion, the face seems somehow unfamiliar. As we will see in this chapter, emotion affects many aspects of cognitive processing including perception, attention and memory, and for this reason it is important that cognitive psychology includes emotion as a key aspect of its remit.

WHAT IS AN EMOTION?

Emotion is a fundamental component of human experience, and yet relatively little attention has been given, within psychology, to the scientific study of emotion. Part of the difficulty has been in defining emotion. As Barrett (2006) noted, 'scientists have yet to produce a set of clear and consistent criteria for indicating when an emotion is present and when it is not' (p. 20).

Emotion refers to a number of mental states including anger, joy, and disgust.

The term 'emotion' is used to refer to various mental states that are relatively short-lived and are associated with an eliciting event, be it an environmental trigger (for example, hearing a scream) or a thought (for example, thinking 'Did I leave the oven on?'). They are reactions to a changing and somewhat unpredictable environment and serve to prompt action. Frijda and Scherer (2009; see also Scherer, 2009) suggest the following four key features of emotion, which distinguish the emotions from other affective states such as mood or temperament:

1 Emotions are bounded episodes elicited when an event occurs that is of relevance to an organism's needs, goals, or well-being, where relevance is determined by an appraisal of the event on a number of criteria, including its novelty, pleasantness or unpleasantness and its motivational value.

2 Emotions prepare the organism to act so as to deal with an event.

3 Emotions affect most or all bodily systems such that their functioning can be synchronized for an effective response.

4 Emotions establish control precedence over behaviours, so that actions can be prioritized.

Emotions provide us with essential feedback on the execution of our plans relative to our goals, and allow us to detect, and work to reduce, discrepancies between actual and expected outcomes (Bower, 1992). Emotions such as happiness or pride tell us our goals are supported, while sadness or anger signal that our goals are blocked or unfulfilled (see also Frijda 1986; Oatley & Johnson Laird, 1987). As a bounded episode, an emotion has a clear onset – we can pinpoint when the emotion occurred – and a somewhat fuzzy offset – the emotion dissipates over time (Scherer, 2009). Emotions tend to be intense, and short-lived, preparing us to act. By contract, other affective states are more long-lived. The term 'mood' refers to a more continuous state that is less intense and relatively non-specific compared to emotions – we tend to know the cause of our anger, for example, but will not necessarily know why we are in a bad mood. Moods can be caused by emotions and can be the after-effects of an emotional reaction (Bower, 1992). For example, if you have a disagreement with a friend, you may feel angry, and afterwards remain in a bad mood for some time, even after the initial anger is gone. The term 'affect' is used generically to refer to emotional state or mood (Forgas & Vargas, 1998).

Cognitive psychology has been slow to consider emotion, for two main reasons. First, the traditional view of emotions as irrational, and therefore 'in opposition to' rational thought, has pushed emotion to the sidelines of the cognitive agenda. The dominance of the computer metaphor in cognitive psychology (see Chapter 1) is also relevant here. Second, emotion is not easily studied using the traditional methods of cognitive psychology relying, for example, on self-reports from participants. In recent years, however, research on cognitive topics has increasingly considered emotion, as it has become apparent that emotion and cognition are closely connected, and that we cannot fully understand one without consideration of the other. A cognitive psychology that omits consideration of emotion ignores a fundamental aspect of human cognition.

Some of the key areas of the brain involved in emotion are shown in Figure 14.1. Early neuroscientific studies of the brain and emotion suggested that particular regions of the brain might be linked with

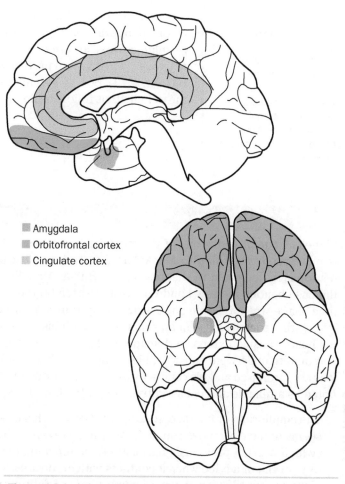

- ■ Amygdala
- ■ Orbitofrontal cortex
- ■ Cingulate cortex

Figure 14.1   Some of the key brain structures involved in emotion.
The figure shows a midsagittal view (top), and a ventral view (bottom) of the human brain.

Source: Adapted from M. L. Kringelbach & E. T. Rolls (2004). The functional neuroanatomy of the human orbitofrontal cortex: Evidence from neuroimaging and neuropsychology, *Progress in Neurobiology*, 72, 341–372.

particular emotions. For example, the amygdala, a structure within the limbic system, has been linked to fear, the insula with disgust, the anterior cingulate cortex with sadness, and the orbitofrontal cortex with anger. However, the mapping of emotion to brain regions is far more complex than this. While the amygdala is traditionally associated with the fear response, for example, in fact fear activates a number of brain regions in addition to the amygdala, and activation in the amygdala occurs in several emotions other than fear. The amygdala shows increased activity for fear, anger, disgust, happiness and sadness (Lindquist et al., 2012). The amygdala is also linked with arousal, with both positive and negative emotion, while emotional valence (that is, whether it is pleasant or unpleasant) is also linked with the orbitofrontal cortex (see Hamann, 2012; Lindquist & Barrett, 2012). Accounts of emotional processing in the brain are therefore moving away from the locationist approach, which aimed to map discrete emotions to specific brain regions, and instead is focusing on networks of interacting brain regions. Meta-analytic studies point to a number of networks of brain regions, including

Amygdala is an almond shaped set of structures located in the medial temporal lobe.
Limbic system consists of the thalamus, hypothalamus, hippocampus and amygdala, and other structures.
Insula is an area hidden within the folds of the cortex, with connections to the cingulate, amygdala, and orbitofrontal cortex, implicated in aspects of emotion, cognition, and action.

Default network is a network of brain regions that is active when a person is not focused on the external environment. **Salience network** is involved in monitoring the external and internal environments to allow detection of salient stimuli.

those associated with the default network (medial prefrontal cortex, medial temporal cortex, ventrolateral prefrontal cortex), salience network (insular cortex, anterior cingulate cortex, amygdala), and frontoparietal network (ventrolateral prefrontal cortex) (Lindquist et al., 2012; Lindquist & Barrett, 2012). Box 14.1 examines the role of the frontal areas in emotion and the deficits that follow brain injury affecting this region.

Box 14.1 When Things Go Wrong: Emotional processing after frontal lobe injury

Phineas Gage provides one of the most famous cases of frontal lobe damage ever reported; the case is mentioned, according to MacMillan (2000), in almost 60 per cent of all textbooks of psychology, neuropsychology, and the neurosciences. But, as MacMillan points out, we know relatively little about the case beyond the few hundred words written by the attending doctor, John Martyn Harlow, at the time. Gage was a reliable and hardworking railroad foreman who in 1848 suffered an accident while excavating rock which sent an iron rod through his left eye socket (Figure 14.2). It exited at the top of his head, causing extensive damage to the frontal cortex. After the injury, Gage's temperament and personality underwent considerable changes and his social behaviour was altered. His decision making was compromised and his conduct was in stark contrast to his behaviour before the injury, when he was noted as a reliable and conservative figure. Harlow (1848, pp. 339–340) wrote this account of Gage:

> The equilibrium or balance, so to speak, between his intellectual faculties and animal propensities, seems to have been destroyed. He is fitful, irreverent, indulging at times in the grossest profanity (which was not previously his custom), manifesting but little deference for his fellows, impatient of restraint or advice when it conflicts with his desires, at times pertinaciously obstinate, yet capricious and vacillating, devising many plans of future operations, which are no sooner arranged than they are abandoned in turn for others appearing more feasible.

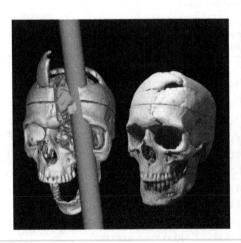

Figure 14.2   Images of Phineas Gage. Left: a three-dimensional computer reconstruction of Gage's skull. Right: The only known image of Phineas Gage. This early photograph had been in the possession of two collectors from Maryland, USA, Jack and Beverly Wilgus, for more than 30 years, before it was identified as Gage. It was identified following comparisons of the image with his life mask and the tamping iron, which are held in the Warren Anatomical Museum.

Source: (L) From Ratiu P., & Talos I.-F. (2004). Images in clinical medicine. The tale of Phineas Gage, digitally remastered. *New England Journal of Medicine, 351,* 23. Copyright © 2004 Massachusetts Medical Society. Reprinted with permission from Massachusetts Medical Society. (R) Wilgus, J., & Wilgus, B. (2009). Face to face with Phineas Gage. *Journal of the History of the Neurosciences, 18,* 340–345.

However, some of the facts of Gage's life are at odds with reports of the case. For example, MacMillan (2000) notes that from early in 1851 until a few months before his death in 1860, Gage would appear to have worked as a stage coach driver, a job that would require a degree of consistency and responsibility that is not generally attributed to him. Did he show recovery of function over time? Or were some of his supposed deficits exaggerated?

There is so much conjecture, fabrication and myth around the Gage case that one cannot be certain how much can be learned from his case about frontal lobe injury and related deficits. Furthermore, Gage's brain was not preserved and so the precise nature of the injury must be inferred from reconstructions and simulations using what is known about the damage to his skull. More recent cases have provided well-documented accounts of frontal lobe injury, although the extreme nature of Gage's injury mean that he is likely to remain the most well-known case and to retain an 'odd kind of fame' (MacMillan, 2000) for some time to come.

A well-documented recent account is that of a man referred to as E.V.R. who was a successful account-ant working with a small company. He was married with two children, and was considered to be a responsible and dependable man. At the age of 35 years, E.V.R. was diagnosed with an orbitofrontal meningioma, a type of brain tumour. He had surgery to remove the tumour, which affected the ventro-medial frontal areas bilaterally. Eslinger and Damasio (1985) tested E.V.R. eight years after his surgery and noted profound and lasting behavioural changes. E.V.R.'s behavioural issues meant that he was no longer capable of fulfilling his personal and professional responsibilities, yet his intelligence was in the superior range (97–99th percentile). Eslinger and Damasio found that E.V.R. successfully completed formal neuropsychological measures and yet his social conduct was profoundly at odds with this pat-tern of intact intellect. In contrast to his behaviour before his illness, E.V.R. entered into ill-advised business ventures and had been declared bankrupt. Having divorced from his wife of over 17 years, he married a prostitute, and was divorced again soon thereafter (Eslinger & Damasio, 1985). He could no longer hold down a job or plan effectively for the future (Damasio et al., 1990). E.V.R. had great difficulty making simple, everyday decisions, such as deciding what restaurant to go to or what clothes to put on in the morning. He would spend an inordinate amount of time going over and over the options, often failing to come to a decision.

E.V.R.'s altered emotional processing is evident from his performance on a skin conductance task. Damasio et al. (1990) showed E.V.R. pictures that would be emotionally arousing (images that typically arouse disgust, such as scenes of mutilated bodies) and neutral pictures. A normal individual shows an elevated skin conductance response to the emotional stimuli. But E.V.R. showed no increase for emotional stimuli. E.V.R. even commented that he had not experienced the kind of feeling he expected, given the content of the images (Damasio et al., 1990). However, when asked to verbally describe the pictures, E.V.R. showed a normal skin conductance response (Damasio et al., 1990), suggesting that the emotional system itself was not the problem. Damasio referred to E.V.R.'s deficit as 'acquired sociopathy' because of the similarity between his emotional reactions post-surgery and those associated with sociopathic disorder.

Some patients, however, show predictably impaired performance on tests of frontal lobe function. Blair and Cipolotti (2000) describe a patient J.S. who was aggressive, did not follow social norms and was reckless regarding others' safety. J.S. had no psychiatric history or history of aggression before an accident which caused bilateral orbito-frontal brain damage. Yet after his injury, he attacked and wounded a hospital staff member and was threatening towards staff and other patients. He showed some bizarre behaviours, riding around the hospital on a gurney for example, and throwing furniture. After the injury, J.S. could not keep a job and his behaviour isolated him from friends and family. While he had an average IQ score (verbal IQ 98, performance IQ 92), he showed impairment on some frontal lobe tests.

Like E.V.R., J.S. showed altered skin conductance responses to emotionally arousing pictures. J.S.'s skin conductance responses can be seen in Table 14.1. The range of responses for healthy controls is

Table 14.1 J.S.'s skin conductance responses (SCRs) to emotionally arousing pictures

	J.S.	Healthy controls
Naturalistic expressions:		
Anger	0.058	0.437 (0.250–0.725)
Sadness	0.055	0.421 (0.246–0.790)
Neutral	0.042	0.134 (0.070–0.273)
Objects:		
Threatening	0.062	0.561 (0.245–1.2)
Neutral	0.109	0.251 (0.076–0.5)

SCRs were recorded 1–3 seconds after stimulus onset. The range of responses for healthy controls is shown in parentheses. In contrast to the controls, J.S.'s responses to emotional stimuli are not significantly greater than for the neutral stimuli.

Source: Based on data from Blair R. J., & Cipolotti, L. (2000) Impaired social response reversal. A case of 'acquired sociopathy'. Brain, 123, 1122–1141.

shown in parentheses. J.S.'s responses were significantly lower than the lowest responding healthy control in each case.

Cases such as these support the notion of a connection between emotional and cognitive processing, particularly in everyday decision making. According to Damasio (1994), people like E.V.R. and J.S., as a result of their injury, no longer experience the emotional input that normally allows us to effectively weigh up response options and come to an effective decision. Such cases demonstrate the key role of emotion in higher cognition, such as decision making, judgement, problem solving, and planning.

The cognitive view of emotions is that they have important immediate and long-term functions that allow us to adapt to a changing environment (Power & Dalgleish, 1997; Levenson, 1994). Before we look at the main cognitive accounts of emotion, let's first consider what makes an emotion.

CORE EMOTIONS

Display rules are social conventions governing how, when and with whom emotions may be expressed.

Emotions are associated with distinctive facial expressions and gestures. While the display of emotion is to some extent culture-dependent and emerges through learning and through the acquisition of social conventions called display rules, there is evidence for a basic set of emotional expressions that is largely consistent across cultures (e.g. see Elfenbein & Ambady, 2002). These arguably correspond to a set of basic or core emotions.

Charles Darwin (1872/1998) proposed that there was an innate and universal set of human emotions with associated facial expressions. This proposal was supported by a series of cross-cultural studies in the 1960s. Paul Ekman and colleagues photographed the emotional facial expressions of the South Fore people of New Guinea, an isolated group unfamiliar with Western culture. If facial expressions and gestures are learned within a culture, then we might expect differences across cultural groups; if they have a biological basis, we would expect less cross-cultural variation. Ekman's research supported a set of basic human emotions, associated with particular facial expressions, that are expressed and recognized in a similar way and in the same contexts, across cultures (e.g. Ekman et al., 1969). Ekman identified the basic emotions as anger, disgust, fear, joy, sadness and surprise, although the South Fore people did not seem to make a clear distinction between fear and surprise. Ekman suggested that in their culture, unexpected events were more likely to be negative, so that fear and surprise tended to co-occur. This research supported an innate basis to the facial expressions for anger, disgust, fear, happiness, and sadness, which correspond to a set of basic or core human goals which are consistent cross-culturally (see Power & Dalgleish, 1997).

However, it should be noted that, while a significant proportion of the Fore sample responded in a manner that was consistent with the Western sample, there was considerable variation in recognition of the emotions. For example, while 82 per cent of the Fore sample recognized happiness, 54 per cent recognized fear, with 25 per cent of the sample mistaking fear for anger. Furthermore, the methodology used in such cross-cultural studies of emotion have been criticized by some. For example, Russell (1994) noted that consistency in responses may be inflated by the use of forced-choice formats (but see also Ekman's, 1994, response). While the balance of evidence would support universality in facial expressions, the degree of universality continues to be debated (see Prinz, 2004).

Other sources support a core set of emotions linked to facial expressions. Blind adults show the same facial emotional expressions as seeing adults, showing that a visual model of facial emotional expressions is not required in order to produce the same expression (Eibl-Eibesfeldt, 1973; Matsumoto & Willingham, 2009). Peleg et al. (2006) showed that adults who were blind from birth showed similar expressions as their family members, suggesting that even the more idiosyncratic aspects of emotional expressions may be inherited. Common facial expressions of emotion are also found in newborn babies, with research suggesting that nature equips the newborn with a 'primal' set of expressions. The primal face of pain, for example, is an expression 'characterized by opening of the mouth, drawing in of the brows, and closing of the eyes' (Schiavenato et al., 2008, p. 460). However, learning also plays a role. For example, infants of depressed mothers, who have reduced facial expressions, show different responses to facial expression than do infants of non-depressed mothers (Field et al., 1998). Of course, facial expressions can be controlled and even faked, so certain aspects of the expression of emotion remain under our control, an issue explored in Box 14.2.

Box 14.2 Practical Application: Reading emotion from faces

In Chapter 12, we saw how an analysis of language can help us to detect when someone is lying. Facial expressions present another means of detecting deception. Emotions are associated with particular facial expressions. When there is no attempt to conceal an emotion, the whole face is typically involved in producing the expression, which can last between 0.5 and 4 seconds. These macroexpressions can be readily identified. However, we also produce microexpressions, much more fleeting expressions that last less than half a second. These are often associated with attempts to conceal emotion, and can therefore be used to detect deception. The term 'emotional leakage' refers to the unintended expression of emotion or a failure to mask an expression.

To the trained eye, and under the right viewing conditions, deceptive expressions can be identified. But under normal circumstances, detecting deception is rather tricky. Ekman and O'Sullivan (1991) showed a videotape of 10 people who were either lying or telling the truth to a large sample of American participants ($N = 509$), including students, psychiatrists, police, judges, personnel from the Secret Service, FBI, CIA, National Security Agency and the Drug Enforcement Agency. Only the Secret Service personnel performed at an above chance level in identifying liars. So how easy is it to fake an emotion and are some emotions easier to fake than others?

Porter and ten Brinke (2008) looked for inconsistent emotional expressions and microexpressions in real and deceptive facial expressions. Participants were videotaped as they looked at disgusting, sad, frightening, happy, and neutral images; they responded on each occasion with a genuine or deceptive (simulated or masked) expression. The videotape was then analysed frame by frame by two trained coders, and emotional expressions including microexpressions and blink rate were examined.

The analysis showed that masked emotions were associated with more inconsistent expressions and an increased blink rate, compared to real emotions. Happiness was the expression most readily faked, with the negative emotions proving more difficult. Inconsistent emotional leakage occurred at some point in all participants. Neutralizing emotions proved more effective than masking them, suggesting that it is easier to appear unemotional rather than having to mask an emotion with a fake emotion. The role of training was apparent in this study: untrained observers proved unable to detect deception.

Might we therefore be able to train people to detect deception from facial expressions? Matsumoto and Hwang (2011) trained participants using a task which embedded full-face microexpressions into a sequence of neutral expressions of the same face. They found that training significantly improved accuracy on the task, an advantage that trained participants retained several weeks later. While the task did not allow a precise replication of real life microexpressions, it does suggest that, with appropriate training, some people might become skilled lie detectors.

Ekman's (1999) list of the characteristics of the basic emotions is shown in Table 14.2. But which are the core or basic emotions? Ekman et al. (1969) listed six basic emotions: anger, disgust, fear, happiness, sadness and surprise. But this list was subsequently expanded; Ekman (e.g. 1999) lists fear, anger, disgust, sadness, and contempt as the 'negative' emotions and amusement, pride, satisfaction, relief and contentment as 'positive'. Frijda (1986) lists the basic emotions as:

- desire
- joy
- pride
- surprise
- distress

- anger
- aversion
- contempt
- fear
- shame.

Table 14.2   The characteristics of the basic emotions

Characteristics that distinguish the basic emotions
1 Distinctive universal signals
2 Distinctive physiology
3 Automatic appraisal, tuned to:
a Distinctive universals in antecedent events
b Distinctive appearance developmentally
4 Presence in other primates
5 Quick onset
6 Brief duration
7 Unbidden occurrence
8 Distinctive thoughts, memories, images
9 Distinctive subjective experience

Source: Based on Ekman, P. (1999). Basic emotions. In T. Dalgleish and M. Power (Eds.) *Handbook of cognition and emotion*. Chichester: John Wiley & Sons.

There is considerable cross-cultural variation in language related to emotion. There are words in English not found in other languages and there are words in other languages not found in English. For example, in German the word 'schadenfreude' refers to a feeling of pleasure derived from someone else's difficulties (several languages have a version of the opposite, such as the Buddhist term 'Mudita'). Polish does not have an exact word for what in English would be called 'disgust' (Wierzbicka, 1986, p. 584). In Japan, 'hagaii' is 'a mood of vulnerable heartache colored by frustration' (Feldman, 2004, p. 269). Tahitians speak of 'musu' (a resistance to unreasonable demands of parents) and 'mehameha', a sensation that occurs in unusual circumstances of perception. Russell (2005) describes it as the kind of feeling one might have in the presence of a ghost. Lutz (1990, p. 206) notes several types of anger in the Ifaluk people of Micronesia:

> There is the irritability that often accompanies sickness (tipmochmoch), the anger that builds up slowly in the face of a succession of minor but unwanted happenings (lingeringer), the annoyance that occurs when relatives have failed to live up to their obligations (nguch), and, finally, there is the frustrated anger that occurs in the face of personal misfortunes and slights which one is helpless to overturn (tang). But each of these emotions is sharply distinguished from the anger which is righteous indignation, or justifiable anger (song), and it is only this anger which is morally approved.

The emerging set of core emotions might therefore have been different if research in the area were dominated by a language other than English. Box 14.3 explores some possible cross-cultural differences in the expression of emotion.

Box 14.3 Research Close Up: Are there cross-cultural differences in emotional expression?

Source: Chentsova Dutton, Y., Chu, J. P., Tsai, J. L., Rottenberg, J., Gross, J. J., & Gotlib, I. H. (2007). Depression and emotional reactivity: Variation among Asian Americans of East Asian descent and European Americans. *Journal of Abnormal Psychology, 116*(4), 776–785.

INTRODUCTION

Research conducted in the West shows that people who are depressed, on average, demonstrate diminished emotional reactivity to both positive and negative stimuli; the terms 'emotional numbness' and 'flattened affect' are often used to describe this reduced response. However, this pattern is not always replicated. Chentsova-Dutton et al. (2007) set out to examine whether these findings generalize to other cultures, by comparing responses of Asian Americans of East Asian descent with those of European Americans.

METHOD

Chentsova-Dutton et al. (2007) compared non-depressed and depressed people of European-American (15 depressed and 15 non-depressed) and Asian-American (12 depressed and 14 non-depressed) backgrounds. The Asian-American group represented a variety of East Asian cultures (Chinese, 42.3 per cent; Korean, 23.1 per cent; Japanese, 15.4 per cent; Southeast Asian, 7.7 per cent; and mixed East Asian background, 11.5 per cent). Participants saw a neutral film (scenery), a sad film (the grieving excerpt from the film *The Champ*) and an amusing film (a segment form the slapstick Mr Bean comedy). The three films ranged from 120–180 seconds in length. A small percentage of participants reported having seen the films before (amusing, 12.5 per cent and sad, 9.1 per cent).

The order of the three film clips was not counterbalanced; the neutral film was always shown first, followed by the sad film, and finally the amusing film was presented. This order was used so that participants would be less likely to complete the experiment in a negative emotional state. Participants' emotional responses were assessed via self-reports during the films, using physiological measures, and by observers' assessments.

RESULTS

The results showed no cultural differences for the neutral and amusing films, but there were differences in reactions to the sad film. The non-depressed European-American participants showed more emotionality as rated by observers and also reported more sadness compared to the depressed participants, who showed the characteristic pattern of reduced emotional reactivity (see Figure 14.3). However, the opposite pattern was found in the Asian-American group. The depressed Asian-Americans showed increased emotional reactivity and reported greater sadness compared to the non-depressed control group. This effect was evident in facial expressions and reports of emotional experience, but no differences in physiological reactivity emerged.

DISCUSSION

The authors concluded that 'although depression may influence particular aspects of emotional reactivity across cultures (e.g. crying), the specific direction of this influence may depend on prevailing cultural norms regarding emotional expression' (p. 776). This is consistent with a 'cultural norm' hypothesis, which holds that depression reduces an individual's ability to regulate their emotional expression in line with cultural norms. While the effect would need to be replicated across a number of contexts, and with larger samples, before strong conclusions would be justified, it would seem that there are implications for the treatment and assessment of depression in different cultural contexts.

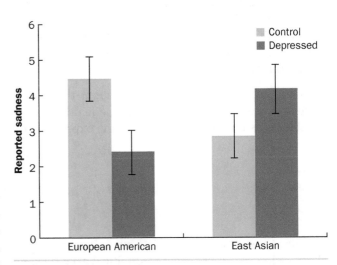

Figure 14.3 **Change scores in reports of sadness during the sad film relative to neutral.** Error bars represent standard errors.

Source: Adapted from Chentsova Dutton, Y., Chu, J. P., Tsai, J. L., Rottenberg, J., Gross, J. J., & Gotlib, I. H. (2007). Depression and emotional reactivity: Variation among Asian Americans of East Asian descent and European Americans. *Journal of Abnormal Psychology, 116*(4), 776–785. APA; reprinted with permission.

THE 'CORE' OF EMOTION

While facial expressions are important to emotion, there is more to an emotion than a particular facial configuration. Power and Dalgleish (1997) note that emotions are characterized by: certain physiological disturbances; changes in facial expression; particular gestures, behaviours, thoughts, beliefs, and desires. But what is at the 'core' of an emotion? Which of the above conditions is necessary for an emotion? Is it useful to deconstruct emotions, that is, to try to break them down into their constituent and defining features? Is there a *sine qua non* for emotion?

Scan to watch
Gerald Clore
discuss emotion

Clore and Ortony (2000) propose that human emotions are characterized by four components:

1 cognitive;

2 motivational-behavioural;

3 somatic;

4 subjective-experiential.

The cognitive component allows us to mentally register the significance of the emotion. This can be conscious or unconscious, and this component is closely associated with appraisal and related processes. We will examine appraisal models of emotion later in this chapter. Appraisal models propose that we monitor our environments for information that is of relevance to us – assessing whether something is good or bad, or a threat, and what resources are available to help us deal with it. For example, imagine a young boy is walking home from school when he hears, close behind him, what seems to be a large growling dog. This is potentially a threat, but appraisal allows context, and available resources, to be considered. For example, if this is an unusual event, the boy may feel afraid. But perhaps that dog growls at the boy every time he passes by, in which case the boy might become angry. Perhaps the boy feels sad for the dog, who he knows is locked behind a gate. The emotion he feels depends on his appraisal of the situation. The degree to which cognition is required in order for an emotion to occur remains contentious, and this issue will be discussed shortly, when we look at the theories examining the relationship between emotion and cognition.

> **Appraisal** refers to the ways in which people interpret or explain to themselves the meaning of events.

The motivational-behavioural component involves our actions in response to the emotion; do we run away or stay and fight when we encounter a threat? The somatic component involves the activation of the autonomic nervous system (ANS) and central nervous system (CNS) and the characteristic physiological responses that occur along with an emotion. The subjective-experiential component involves the actual experience of the emotion for the individual.

> **Autonomic nervous system** is part of the peripheral nervous system and regulates internal organs. **Central nervous system** consists of the brain and spinal cord.

The bodily changes that occur with an emotional state are the most apparent component. On the day of an important examination, you may experience a dry mouth, the palms of your hands might feel clammy, and you may lose your appetite for food. You may look in the mirror and notice that you are pale. As you enter the examination hall, you may feel your heart racing. William James recognized the importance of this component of an emotion when he wrote in the *Principles of Psychology* (1890, p. 379) that 'emotion dissociated from all bodily feeling is inconceivable'.

Emotions are associated with certain changes in the autonomic nervous system, such as increases or decreases in heart rate, respiration and blood flow (e.g. blushing, pallor), vasodilation (widening of blood vessels), piloerection (hairs standing up on skin), sweating, and urinary and gastrointestinal changes, among others (see Frijda, 1986). These physiological changes prepare the animal for action; for example the 'flight or fight' response is associated with fear and the characteristic physiological changes we experience prepare us to flee or to fight (see Table 14.3).

It might therefore seem that physiological changes lie at the core of an emotion. However, similar physiological changes can occur without the experience of emotion, for example, when we exercise or take certain drugs. In addition, there is considerable overlap between the physiological states associated with different emotions and there is debate over whether there is an absolute discriminating factor that can mark one

Table 14.3 Changes in the effects of the autonomic nervous systems associated with some of the emotions

Type	Change	ANS-mediated basis	Emotion
Colouration	Reddening	Vasodilation	Anger
	Blushing	Vasodilation	Embarrassment
	Paling	Vasoconstriction	Fear
Moisture and secretions	Sweating and clamminess	Sweat glands	Fear
	Salivation, drooling	Salivary glands	Disgust
	Foaming	Salivary glands	Anger
	Tearing	Lacrimal glands	Sadness
Protrusions	Piloerection	Muscles fibres at base of hair follicles	Fear, anger
	Blood vessels	Vasodilation	Anger
Eyes' appearance	Constriction	Pupils	Anger
	Dilation	Pupils	Fear
	Bulging	Eyelid muscles	Anger, fear
	Twinkling	Lacrimal glands	Happiness

Source: Adapted from Levenson, R. W. (2004). Blood, sweat, and fears: The autonomic architecture of emotion. In P. Ekman, J. J. Campos, R. J. Davidson, & F. B. M. de Waal (Eds.), *Emotions inside out*. New York: The New York Academy of Sciences.

emotion apart from another, physiologically, although, as we will see shortly neuroscientific approaches are making some progress on this issue.

There is considerable debate over whether an emotional state can be detected based on physiological changes. Ekman reported evidence for distinctive patterns of autonomic nervous system response for anger, fear and disgust (e.g. Ekman et al., 1983; Levenson et al., 1990) but some studies have failed to replicate these patterns. Cacioppo et al. (1993) note that while heart rate is the best available discriminator, 'it too is far from discriminating consistently or fully among the emotions' (p. 125) and therefore 'the cumulative evidence for emotion-specific autonomic patterns remains inconclusive' (p. 132). On the other hand, Rainville et al. (2006) provide evidence for distinct patterns of cardiorespiratory activity associated with the basic emotions. This debate over distinct emotional states has been argued to support the cognitive approach to emotions; if we cannot detect an emotion precisely from somatic changes in the body, then, the argument goes, it must be the cognition that produces the emotion. According to Schacter and Singer (1962) it is only when we evaluate the physiological changes and apply a label to them that we experience a discrete emotion. In other words, cognition is required in order for us to experience a particular emotion. In order to assess whether this is the case, we need to look next at the theoretical accounts of the relationship between emotion and cognition.

THEORIES OF EMOTION AND COGNITION

Theories of the relationship between cognition and emotion basically address a 'chicken-and-egg' type problem: what comes first? Does emotion come first or does cognition, the way we think about a particular event, bring about the emotion? Various theories on the relationship between emotion and cognition have been proposed to address this question. As Scherer (2000) notes, it is difficult to understand the controversies within current theories without considering their historical roots. We begin with two contrasting early theories on the emotion–cognition connection, which continue to influence the field today: The James-Lange theory and the Cannon-Bard theory. We then examine Schachter's influential two-factor theory, which brought aspects of James-Lange and Cannon-Bard together, before considering proponents and opponents of the appraisal theories, which have occupied the dominant theoretical position in the study of emotion since the 1980s, but which use the term 'appraisal' in a number of different ways (Moors et al., 2013) and vary considerably in their detail.

EARLY THEORIES AND THEIR INFLUENCE

1. James-Lange theory

The James-Lange theory holds that the experience of an emotion follows the physiological changes associated with that state. In other words, an emotion arises from bodily feedback: we feel happy *because* we have smiled; we feel fear *because* we have run away, and so forth. William James (1884) argued that 'our feeling of (physiological) changes as they occur is the emotion' (pp. 189–190). In 1885, Carl Lange proposed a similar account independently, and this view became known as the James-Lange theory. The emotion *is* the perception of bodily changes.

While it seems counter-intuitive that the behaviour *causes* the emotion, there is some evidence for the role of the body in altering emotional state. For example, there is some support for the facial feedback hypothesis (Tomkins, 1962, 1963), which states that feedback from the facial muscles can elicit emotion (see Box 14.3). In typical experiments in this area, participants are forced to alter their facial expression and the effect on self-reported emotional state is measured. One of the immediate problems for such studies is this: if participants are faking an expression such as a smile, knowledge of the meaning of that expression, rather that the expression itself, might create the effect. A number of methods have been developed to get around this potential confound. Strack et al. (1988) had participants hold a pen in their mouths in a manner that either inhibited (pursed lips) or engaged (hold with teeth) the muscles for smiling. They found that participants reported more humour in cartoons in the 'smiling' versus 'inhibiting' conditions. Larsen et al. (1992) repeated this procedure with negative emotions, finding higher ratings of sadness following activation of the 'sad' facial muscle configuration. A study by Hennenlotter et al. (2009) made use of their participants' cosmetic use of Botox® injections to investigate what happens when the frown muscles *cannot* be moved. Botox® is a drug made from a toxin produced by the bacterium *Clostridium botulinum* which is used cosmetically for the temporary reduction of frown lines – it acts by reducing the activity of muscles near the injection site. Hennenlotter and colleagues scanned the brains of 38 women while they imitated either sad or angry facial expressions. Half of the women were tested two weeks after they had had injections to their frown muscles; half of the women had not had the cosmetic procedure. Consistent with previous research, Hennenlotter et al. found that imitating an angry or sad expression increased bilateral activity in the amygdala, but in the women who had botox injections, angry expressions were associated with reduced activity in the left amygdala. This provides some support for the notion that feedback from muscle activity can influence emotional experience and concurs with evidence suggesting that expressing an emotion can prolong it (see, for example, Box 14.4). However, it is quite another claim to suggest that such activity is the cause of emotion.

> **Facial feedback hypothesis** proposes that feedback from the facial muscles can influence emotional state.

Box 14.4 Research Close Up: Dispelling the catharsis myth

Source: Bushman, B. (2002) Does venting anger feed or extinguish the flame? Catharsis, rumination, distraction, anger, and aggressive responding. *Personality and Social Psychology Bulletin, 28*(6), 724–731.

INTRODUCTION

People commonly believe that expressing anger will reduce it, that it is healthy to express anger. The 'catharsis myth' is the mistaken idea that aggressive behaviour is an effective means of reducing aggressive feelings. The word catharsis comes from a Greek word meaning 'cleanse' or 'purge'. The catharsis myth has been fuelled by the Freudian-influenced 'hydraulic model' of anger, that is, the idea that anger builds up like pressure and unless it is vented, the person could eventually 'explode' in a destructive rage. A study by Bushman (2002) examined where distraction (directing attention away from the emotion) or rumination (focusing on the anger) works better in order to diffuse anger.

METHOD

Participants ($n = 600$) were told that they were taking part in a study on first impressions and that they would be interacting with a same-sex participant in the study. They were asked to write an essay on a sensitive topic. They then received negative feedback on the essay, supposedly from the participant that they had been paired with. The feedback criticized the style, expression and overall quality of the essay, and included a note that said 'this is one of the worst essays that I have read'. In fact, there was no such other participant, but previous research has shown that this method is effective in making an essay writer angry!

Participants were then assigned to one of three conditions: rumination, distraction or a control group. Participants in the rumination group were encouraged to think about the person who rated their essay while hitting a punch bag. They were even provided with a photo of their alleged critic to help them visualize their target. Participants assigned to the distraction group also hit a punch bag but they were instructed to think about physical fitness while punching the bag. They were shown a photo of a model from a fitness magazine. Those assigned to the control group did not hit a punch bag but just sat quietly while waiting for the next stage of the experiment. Measures of mood and aggression were then conducted for all three groups. In the final stage of the procedure, participants took part in a computerized reaction time task, where they were led to believe that they were competing with the paired participant on another computer. Whoever was slower to respond received a blast of noise; the other participant set the decibel level for that noise. A no-noise option was also offered. Noise intensity and duration were used as measures of aggression. If catharsis is effective at diffusing anger, then we would expect the rumination group to show lower aggression and improved mood.

RESULTS

The results showed that, contrary to the catharsis hypothesis, the rumination group were the angriest group and the most aggressive. One participant in this group became so angry that he punched a hole in the laboratory wall! Those in the distraction group were less angry but they were not less aggressive than the rumination group, showing that just hitting a punch bag while angry, even while thinking of something else, fuels the anger. The control group had the lowest levels of both anger and aggression.

DISCUSSION

While the effects obtained were small to moderate in size, they add to the considerable research literature contradicting the catharsis hypothesis. As Bushman concludes, 'venting to reduce anger is like using gasoline to put out a fire – it only feeds the flame' (p. 729). These findings dovetail with research showing how aggressive behaviour escalates (e.g. see Martens et al., 2007; Martens & Kosloff, 2011) and shows how destructive the pop psychology misconception that expressing anger is healthy might be.

Evaluation

While bodily changes would seem to play an important role in emotional experience, it does not follow that muscle movement *causes* emotional experience. Taken to an extreme this would suggest that we cannot feel an emotion if we cannot experience the physiological response. If we become paralyzed does that mean that we no longer experience emotion? People with spinal cord injuries show minimal effects on emotional processing (Cobos et al., 2004). Similarly, patients who have pure autonomic failure (selective breakdown of neurons, depriving them of bodily feedback) show minor impairments in emotional processing (Heims et al., 2004). People vary considerably in their ability to *detect* visceral changes; the term interoception is used to refer to this ability (Craig, 2002, 2004). For example, some people notice fairly minor changes in heart-rate, while others will not notice minor fluctuations. However, it does not follow that people differ in their emotional experiences depending on how readily they detect these inner changes. Furthermore, sometimes our conscious experience of an emotion precedes the bodily changes that occur; for example, you realize you have said something embarrassing, *then* you blush. Sometimes physiological responses similar to emotion occur without emotion (e.g. when we exercise) – how is it that, in these cases, the physiological response occurs but does not lead to an emotion? And how do we account for the fact that the same changes can bring about different emotional experiences? These problems suggest that visceral changes alone cannot be enough to produce emotion and that the James-Lange theory provides an incomplete account.

2. Cannon-Bard Theory

The shortcomings of the James-Lange theory that we have discussed were noted by Walter Cannon (1927), whose challenge of the James-Lange theory focused on the importance of function. First, Cannon argued that the same physiological state can be associated with different emotions; for example, when we feel fear or anger our heart rate increases; the physiological reaction is similar but the emotion varies considerably. Second, he pointed out that the physiological changes that accompany an emotion can occur without an emotional experience. When we exercise, for example, our hearts race, we may perspire and so on, but we do not feel fear, anger or another emotion, nor do we confuse the physiological reaction with an emotional state. Third, the same bodily changes as occur during emotion occur in different non-emotional states, such as fever, exposure to cold, asphyxia and hypoglycaemia; how is it that this does *not* give rise to an emotion? Fourth, Cannon argued that the conscious experience of emotion occurs quickly, while visceral changes occurred slowly, too slowly to be the cause of emotion. He also noted that physiological changes that are characteristic of emotion can be elicited artificially using adrenalin, but this does not give rise to an emotion. He ascribed a key role to the thalamus, a position developed by Phillip Bard (1934).

The Cannon–Bard account argues that the emotional experience and the physiological changes arise *concurrently* from the stimulus event, in other words that the experience of emotion and the bodily changes are independent. An emotion-provoking event leads to signals being sent simultaneously to the cortex (producing the conscious experience of an emotion) and to the autonomic nervous system (producing the physiological changes).

© stacey-newman/iStock

Evaluation

While Cannon and Bard were incorrect in identifying the thalamus as the key region for the production of emotion, the basic idea of separate cortical and sub-cortical involvement is retained in subsequent theories, including those that propose key involvement of sub-cortical structures (e.g. LeDoux, 1996; Rolls, 1990). While both early theories have their merits and introduced concepts that have been developed by subsequent accounts, both were ultimately lacking. For a full account of emotion, it became important to consider the role of cognition. In the 1960s, an influential account emerged which takes account of the role of physiology posited by the James-Lange, but addresses Cannon's criticism of the need to differentiate between emotion states: Stanley Schachter's two factor theory (see Figure 14.4).

TWO FACTOR THEORY

Scan to watch an animation with an extended explanation of two factor theory

Schachter and Singer's (1962) two factor theory of emotion proposed, as the name suggests, that two factors create the emotion: physiological arousal and our *interpretation* of it. When we experience arousal, we try to work out the basis for the physiological change. If you are standing outside an examination hall, and you notice that your heart is racing and your mouth is dry, you are likely to interpret the reaction as fear or nervousness. If, however, you are driving home and someone in another car cuts you off, you may interpret the same physical responses as anger. By this account, it is our cognitive interpretation of the initially undifferentiated physiological arousal that

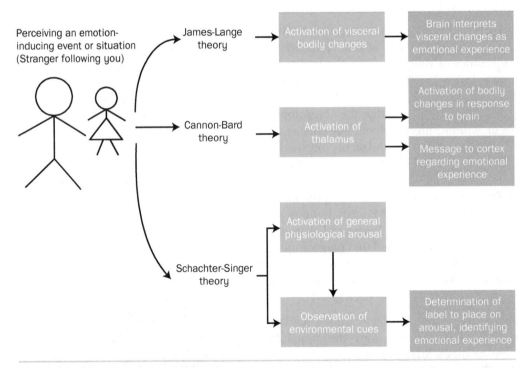

Figure 14.4   Three models of emotion, contrasting the James-Lange, Cannon-Bard and Schachter-Singer accounts. According to the James-Lange account, activation of bodily (visceral) changes (e.g. heart beating faster, sweating) leads directly to the experience of emotion. The Cannon-Bard account by contrast proposed that bodily changes and the experience of emotion occur in parallel. The Schachter-Singer account placed emphasis on the interpretation or appraisal given to the experience, such that bodily changes along with an evaluation of the environment provides a label for the arousal, such that different emotions might be elicited, depending on the evaluation applied.

Source: Adapted from Feldman, R. S. (2004). *Understanding psychology.* New York: McGraw-Hill.

produces the emotion; therefore if either arousal or an interpretation is lacking, the emotion will not occur.

In a study investigating this proposal, Schachter and Singer (1962) injected 174 men with adrenaline (epinephrine) or saline and then placed them in social situations designed to provoke 'anger' or 'euphoria'. Having received their injection, half of the participants waited with an angry confederate and half with a 'manic' one. Participants were misinformed as to the nature of the injection; they were told that the study was testing the effects of a vitamin injection called 'suproxin' on vision. Some participants were told to expect some side-effects, such as trembling or palpitations. Other participants were not informed as to any side-effects. They would therefore be unlikely to attribute any arousal to the adrenaline.

Participants injected with adrenaline who were informed as to the physiological effects did not respond to the attempt to manipulate them into feeling anger or euphoria. But the participants who were injected with adrenaline but *not* told about any physiological effects experienced anger or euphoria, as measured by behavioural and self-report measures, depending on the situation in which they had been placed. Schachter and Singer concluded that, 'given a state of sympathetic activation, for which no immediately appropriate explanation is available, human subjects can be readily manipulated into states of euphoria, anger, and amusement' (p. 396).

Dutton and Aron (1974) provided a more naturalistic test of the role of interpretation. They had an attractive female researcher or a male researcher approach 85 male participants after they had crossed one of two bridges. One was the Capilano suspension bridge near Vancouver, a 230 feet high, 5-foot wide, shaky narrow bridge, constructed from wooden boards lined with cables. The control bridge was a low, sturdy, bridge. This afforded a more naturalistic manipulation of arousal. The researcher asked participants to write a brief story based on a picture from the Thematic Apperception Test and provided a telephone number in case of a need for further clarification regarding the study. Consistent with two-factor theory, participants who had crossed the anxiety-inducing bridge created stories with more sexual content and were more likely to contact the researcher post-study – but only if they had been approached by the female researcher. The results are interpreted in terms of participants misattributing the arousal they experienced on crossing the bridge to attraction rather than to anxiety.

Evaluation

Two factor theory highlighted the importance of attribution or evaluation and as such paved the way for appraisal theories, but it ascribed a key role to physiological arousal and awareness thereof – by this account, arousal is a necessary condition for an emotional state. Some have argued against this position (e.g. Frijda, 1986; Reisenzein, 1983); awareness of bodily arousal may play a role in the intensity of the emotional experience but it is not the cause of the emotion per se. The theory also suggested that any emotion label could be attached to the physiological state: fear could become attraction or anger, based on the available cognitions. The Schachter and Singer study also had a number of methodological limitations; for example, arousal was artificially induced and participants may have been biased by the instruction, or lack thereof, regarding side-effects. Later studies have only partially reproduced Schachter and Singer's findings, with some data suggesting a negative biasing effect of adrenaline (e.g. Mezzacappa et al., 1999; see also Marshall & Zimbardo, 1979).

While specific aspects of Schachter and Singer's theory have been disputed, the idea that interpretation of physiological state is important has had a lasting influence on appraisal theories of emotion. We turn now to two influential theories that have debated the role of appraisal in emotion, and have asked whether cognition is, in fact, necessary for emotion.

AFFECTIVE-PRIMACY: ZAJONC'S THEORY

Robert Zajonc's (1980) affective-primacy (i.e. emotion first) account argues that cognition is not necessary for emotion, and that the two systems can function independently, although he acknowledges that they rarely act independently in everyday life. For Zajonc 'affect and cognition are separate and partially independent systems . . . although they ordinarily function conjointly, affect could be generated without a prior cognitive process' (1980, p. 117). While cognition can influence emotion at a later stage of processing, the initial emotional response can be unaffected by cognition, according to this view. His view is summed up in the subtitle of his 1980 paper: 'preferences needs no inference'. Here, preference, whether or not we like something, is an affective judgement or reaction; essentially it is an emotional response. While cognitive accounts held that affective judgements followed significant information processing, Zajonc argued for the primacy of affect, that is, that an *automatic* affective judgement could be made without cognition (see De Houwer & Hermans, 2010).

Mere exposure effect refers to the tendency for people to develop a preference for a stimulus with repeated exposure to it.

The first source of evidence for this account came from the mere exposure effect (see Kunst-Wilson & Zajonc, 1980). The mere exposure effect demonstrates that people can develop preferences for stimuli through repeated exposure. Bornstein (1989) reviewed 200 studies of the mere exposure effect which used a range of stimuli such as nonsense words, ideographs and pictures. The review concluded that, overall, there was evidence that exposure increases liking for the stimulus at moderate repetition and for short or subliminal exposures. In Kunst-Wilson and Zajonc's (1980) study, participants were presented with 10 irregular octagons, each of which was presented five times for 1 millisecond. Following this exposure phase, the participants were subsequently presented with 10 pairs of octagons for 1 second each. One of the pair was an octagon they had seen before and one of the pair was new. The participant was asked which they preferred. While recognition was close to chance (47 per cent), participants showed a statistically significant *preference* for the stimuli to which they had been previously exposed (60 per cent). Of the 24 participants in this experiment, for 17 of them affective judgements discriminated better between old and new stimuli compared to recognition judgements; for four participants, recognition was superior to affective judgments. This may seem to provide support for emotion (here, in the form of an affective preference) in the absence of cognition (since recognition was at chance), however it may be that cognitive processing had occurred.

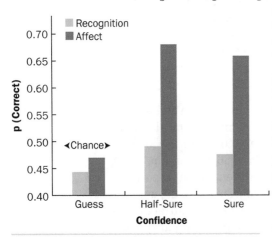

Figure 14.5   The proportion of correct recognition and affective discriminations for responses categorized as guesses, half-sure responses and sure responses.

Source: Kunst-Wilson, W. R., & Zajonc, R. B. (1980). Affective discrimination of stimuli that cannot be recognized. *Science, 207*, 557–558.

The research on the mere exposure effect, and the theories that cite it as support of affective primacy, seem to equate cognition with *conscious* cognition or post-perceptual processing (Lazarus, 1995; Leventhal & Scherer, 1987). In a priming study (see Chapter 5), Murphy and Zajonc (1993) presented participants with neutral stimuli that they were not previously familiar with (written Chinese characters) which were preceded by photos of faces showing either positive (happy face) or negative (angry face) emotions. The priming stimuli (faces) were presented for either 4 milliseconds or for 1 second. The participants' task was to assign a rating to the Chinese character which followed the prime. They were to indicate on a five-point scale whether they thought the character represented a 'good' or a 'bad' concept. For 4 millisecond exposures, the rating assigned to the Chinese character was predicted by the preceding prime; when a happy face came first, the character got a higher liking rating than when an angry face came first. But the effect did not occur when the priming stimulus was presented for one second, presumably because at this duration conscious cognitive processing is possible and we are consciously aware of the prime – its effect on our behaviour can then be moderated. When the faces were clearly visible (consciously perceived), they had no influence on the subsequent ratings. This supports the notion of a fundamental qualitative difference between conscious and unconscious perception, and suggests that our emotions can be affected by unconsciously perceived stimuli. But is this not still cognition?

Evaluation

Other studies have shown low level cognitive effects that mirror affective responses. Mandler et al. (1987) followed Kunst-Wilson and Zajonc's procedure but included two further conditions. During a testing phase, they had participants make judgements regarding which of the pair of shapes was brighter and which was darker. They confirmed Kunst-Wilson and Zajonc's findings in that recognition was at chance (47 per cent), while preference was significantly higher for pre-exposed stimuli (62 per cent). However, they found that judgements of brightness (60 per cent) and darkness (60 per cent) were also significantly more accurate for pre-exposed stimuli, with no differences between the preference, brightness and darkness conditions. This finding weakens the case for affective primacy, because Mandler et al.'s data show both affective (preference) and cognitive (brightness judgement) effects, while conscious recognition remains at chance level. Neuroscientific research further supports cognitive involvement. Elliott and Dolan (1998) showed that the mere exposure effect is associated with activation in the frontal cortical networks and not the amygdala, and studies of patients with lesions affecting the amygdala show that the mere exposure effect is demonstrated even when visual information cannot access the amygdala (Greve & Bauer, 1990), suggesting that emotion is not the basis of the effect.

As Leventhal and Scherer (1987) pointed out, the debate over the primacy of affect versus primacy of cognition was centred on semantic issues and issues of definition, and 'definitional disputes seldom clarify substantive, theoretical points' (p. 3). The debate dominated research for a considerable period of time, and served to focus attention on the role of cognition in emotion, while also raising the profile of emotion among cognitive researchers (see Schorr, 2001, for a historical overview of the influences on appraisal theories).

COGNITIVE PRIMACY: LAZARUS'S THEORY

Richard Lazarus's theory was the first comprehensive appraisal theory, of which there are now many variants. What these theories have in common is summed up by Roseman and Smith (2001): 'Whether emotion is generated in response to perceived, remembered, or imagined events, and by automatic or controlled processing, appraisal theories claim that appraisals start the

> **Appraisal theories** have in common the assertion that emotions result from our interpretations of, or reactions to, events.

emotion process, initiating the physiological, expressive, behavioural and other changes that comprise the resultant emotional state' (p. 7). Lazarus (1982, 1991) argued that cognitive appraisal is fundamental to emotional experience and that you cannot separate out the cognitive aspect of the emotion. He suggested three types of cognitive appraisal:

1 The primary appraisal is an initial assessment of a situation as being positive, negative or threatening, or irrelevant;

2 The secondary appraisal involves an assessment of the resources we have available to us in dealing with the particular situation;

3 Reappraisal involves continual monitoring of the situation until it is resolved.

Note that Lazarus sees cognition and appraisal as involving both conscious and non-conscious processes. For example, he refers to 'two kinds of appraisal processes – one that operates automatically without awareness or volitional control, and another that is conscious, deliberate, and volitional' (Lazarus, 1991, p. 169). Further versions of this account have attempted to show how the different emotions arise from different patterns of appraisal (e.g. Smith & Lazarus, 1993).

Among the sources of data in support of this approach are studies looking at the effect of the way we think about a stimulus on the emotional experience (e.g. Lazarus & Alfert, 1964; Lazarus et al., 1965; Speisman et al., 1964). Speisman et al. (1964) presented participants with film clips of an anxiety-provoking nature. One clip showed a subincision ritual of the aboriginal Arunta tribe of North Central Australia in which an adolescent boy had a piece of flesh cut from his penis. In another film, a workshop accident is shown; a board caught in a circular saw strikes a worker, who crumbles in pain to the floor. These films were accompanied by one of three soundtracks. The voiceover of the 'denial' soundtrack stated that the workshop film involved actors or that the incision was not painful. In the 'intellectualization' condition, the voiceover encouraged the viewer to take a 'health and safety' perspective for the workshop film and encouraged an anthropological perspective for the incision film. The final 'trauma' soundtrack focused on the pain and distress depicted. (The background sounds in horror movies are used to similar effect.) A 'no soundtrack' condition was also included. The participants' physiological stress was measured using skin conductance responses.

Those who heard the trauma voiceover had the largest increases in skin conductance (indicating physiological stress), while lowest effects occurred with the intellectualization soundtrack. The denial soundtrack produced a skin conductance increase marginally greater that the intellectualization condition, and those who heard no soundtrack at all produced increases intermediate between those of the threatening condition and the denial condition. Lazarus and colleagues interpreted these data as showing that our appraisals alter the emotional response to the stimulus. By altering the participants' cognitive appraisal of the events, they altered the stress/emotional response. However, attempts to replicate these studies have met with limited success and one would have to question their generalizability to real life events.

Evaluation

We know that appraisal plays an important role in determining emotion. If you hear a dog growl, what you think about that dog, or about dogs generally, will affect the emotional outcome. If past experience suggests the dog is a threat to you, this will affect the emotional response. On the other hand, if the dog is not a threat, the sound of a growl might merely attract your interest – you may wonder why the dog is growling, whether someone is approaching, for example. Clearly, the appraisal is relevant.

However, what is meant by 'appraisal' is rather vague and Lazarus's assertion that appraisal is involved in non-conscious processing and is *always* involved in emotion would have to be questioned. The survival value of a speedy response to a physical threat suggests a 'faster' route, at least on some occasions.

It may be that sometimes cognition is involved and sometimes not. The multi-level theories (e.g. LeDoux, 1992, 1996) suggest that the Larazus–Zajonc debate is false and that evidence exists to support both views. LeDoux suggests that there are two ways in which an emotion is registered. One is direct, a 'low' route, from the thalamus to the amygdala, and allows very fast responses. This would be important in case of a threat, allowing us to react quickly (e.g. on seeing something move on the ground, which may be a snake). He suggests a second slower route from thalamus via cerebral cortex to amygdala, which allows us to appraise the situation when acting on the emotion.

> **Multi-level theories** of emotion propose that both preattentive and conscious cognitive processes are involved in emotion.

LeDoux's account highlights a key objection to appraisal theories: it is not the idea of appraisal itself that is problematic but the notion that appraisal is always *cognitive* in nature (see Clore & Ortony, 2008, p. 631). But it seems unlikely, however, that any complex emotional experience can occur without cortical involvement.

Subsequent appraisal theories (e.g. Frijda, 1986; Oatley and Johnson Laird, 1987; Ortony et al., 1988; Scherer, 1988) have continued to address the nature of the evaluations that comprise emotions, and make a distinction between undifferentiated physiological responses and fully-fledged emotions, suggesting that 'low-level bodily, hormonal, and affective reactions often get the emotional process started, and that cognitive appraisal processes act like a sculptor, shaping general affective reactions into specific emotions' (Clore & Ortony, 2008, p. 629). This, again, suggests that differentiation is needed between initial automatic, low level or reflexive processes and actual emotional states.

The theoretical approaches to the study of cognition and emotion have served to focus attention on the interrelationships between them and the degree to which cognition is involved in emotion and vice versa. We now turn to this latter issue, the effects of emotion on cognition, or the differences in cognitive processing in the presence of emotion.

EFFECTS OF EMOTION ON COGNITION

At the beginning of this chapter, you read about the case of D.S., a young man who developed the Capgras delusion following a brain injury. This case illustrates the importance of emotion for the process of face recognition, and shows how emotional processing works alongside recognition processes to create meaningful experience. Emotion affects cognition in many ways, and processing of emotional information differs from processing of neutral information. Here, we consider some of the ways in which emotion affects the key processes of attention, perception and memory, focusing in particular on memory.

EMOTION AND ATTENTION

Attentional biases are demonstrated when a participant's attention is selectively directed toward a stimulus. One of the most widely used tasks in the study of attentional biases in participants with depression, anxiety or other disorders is the emotional Stroop task. The emotional Stroop task is a variant of the Stroop colour-naming task (see Chapter 13), in which emotional terms

> **Attentional bias** refers to the tendency for emotional stimuli to capture or draw attention.

take the place of colour terms. In the standard Stroop task, colour terms presented in incongruent colours produce slower response times in a colour naming task than those with congruent colour; for example, it takes longer to respond 'blue' given the word red written in blue ink, compared to the word blue written in blue ink. The effect demonstrates interference from reading in a colour naming task. In the emotional Stroop task, stimuli are chosen with emotional or threatening content. For example, in a study involving participants with a spider phobia (e.g. Lavy et al., 1993; Watts et al., 1986), words such as 'web' and 'hairy' might feature among the stimuli. In the same way as reading interferes with the task of colour naming in the standard Stroop task, the emotional content of the words will take attention from the primary task, disrupting performance.

The effect has been demonstrated in participants with simple phobias, such as spider phobia, but also in generalized anxiety disorder (e.g. Mathews et al., 1995; Mogg et al., 1993), obsessive compulsive disorder (e.g. Foa & McNally, 1986), and post-traumatic stress disorder (e.g. Cassiday et al., 1992). Attentional biases are also evident in those with drug addiction (for an overview see Field et al., 2006). The precise nature of attentional bias in depression continues to be investigated, with conflicting data reported in initial studies in the area (e.g. see MacLeod et al., 1986; Mineka & Sutton, 1992). For example, Mogg et al. (1993) found that anxious participants, but not depressed participants, demonstrated slower colour naming for negative words, supporting a processing bias for negative information in anxiety. On the other hand, Mogg et al. (1995) found that both anxious and depressed participants showed an attentional bias towards negative words, compared to controls. More recently it has become apparent that attentional biases in depression are only evident under specific task conditions, and that depression is associated with deficits in the inhibition of mood-congruent (i.e. negative) material (Joormann et al., 2007).

There are few studies that report emotional Stroop data for non-clinical samples (see Yiend, 2010), but other methods have been used to study the link between emotion and attention in the general population. Lipp and Derakshan (2005) examined attentional bias to fear-relevant animals in undergraduate participants using the attentional probe or dot probe task (MacLeod et al., 1986) with pictures of snakes, spiders, mushrooms, and flowers. In the dot-probe task, two stimuli, one neutral and one emotional (e.g. threatening), are presented on a computer screen, generally for quite a brief exposure duration. A dot probe is then presented in the location of one or other of the stimuli. Participants have to respond to the probe as quickly as they can by pressing a response key. The response time will be affected by the location where the participant had directed his or her attention when the dot appeared. So, for example, if the participant is anxious, his or her attention will have moved toward the threatening stimulus and away from the neutral one. Responses will then be faster when the probe appears in the location of the threatening stimulus compared to trials where the probe appears in the location of the neutral stimulus. One might predict that stimuli such as pictures of fear-relevant animals would attract attention regardless of a participant's trait or state anxiety; it is important for us to be able to act quickly in the presence of a threat.

Consistent with this, Lipp and Derakshan (2005) found that probes that replaced fear-relevant stimuli (snakes and spiders) were associated with faster responses than those that replaced the non-fear-relevant stimuli. This attentional bias was not correlated with self-reported state or trait anxiety. This type of normal bias towards (potentially) threatening information would seem to have an important survival function, one which may have become maladaptive in those with emotional disorders.

Visual search tasks require an active search of a visual array, usually for a particular object or stimulus feature.

The visual search method has also been adapted to study effects of emotion on attention. In the typical procedure, a participant has to detect, as quickly as possible, which one of a group of stimuli is discrepant, for example, a number of faces might be shown, with one facial expression different to the rest. Such studies have shown that pre-attentive visual search is faster for emotional information compared to neutral information (see Yiend, 2010, for a useful review of the literature on emotion and attention). This normal response is also oversensitive in conditions such as anxiety disorders.

EMOTION AND PERCEPTION

Perception and attention are closely related (see Chapters 2 and 3) and it is difficult to tease them apart for the purposes of understanding the effects of emotion on perception. However, a number of studies have addressed the effect of emotion on perception. Phelps et al. (2006) looked at the effect of emotion on early vision. Participants were instructed to look at a fixation point at the centre of a computer screen. A fearful or neutral face appeared briefly (75 milliseconds) on screen. Four stimuli were then presented, one of which was tilted at an angle. Participants simply had to indicate, via button press, the tilt angle (right or left), but the contrast of the stimuli was manipulated. Phelps et al. found that when stimuli were preceded by a fearful face, participants could discriminate the orientation at a lower level of contrast than when stimuli were preceded by a neutral face. Presence of an emotional stimulus heightened contrast sensitivity.

In a second experiment, Phelps et al. asked whether emotion interacts with attention so as to affect early vision. This time, the faces were used as attentional pre-cues, presented either peripherally so as to elicit focused attention or distributed so as to spread attention across the display. The results showed that the effect seen in Experiment 1 was magnified when attention was invoked: peripheral cues produced greater contrast sensitivity than the distributed cues. While the sample sizes in this study were rather small, the facilitative effect on early visual processing was clear.

Similarly, it has been shown that emotion increases participants' field of view (Schmitz et al., 2009). The influence of emotion on perception is therefore seen in even the most basic perceptual processes.

This top-down influence of emotion is also evident for other sensory modalities. Siegel and Stefanucci (2011) induced a negative or neutral mood in participants by having them recount a frightening or neutral experience from their past. They were then presented with a series of short, neutral tones (320 and 640 milliseconds) and asked to rate the loudness and duration of the tones. Siegel and Stefanucci found that loudness perception was influenced by emotion, with participants in a negative mood rating the tones as significantly louder, compared to those in a neutral mood. Consistent with the studies of visual perception, this study suggests a role of emotion in heightening auditory perception, a bias that can be exploited to great effect in horror movie soundtracks. Similar effects have been demonstrated for speech perception (e.g. Wang et al., 2009). These data suggest that the effect that emotion has on perception may be more pervasive than has traditionally been assumed.

EMOTION AND MEMORY

Memory was explored in detail in Chapters 4, 5 and 6. How does emotion affect memory? Everyday experience would suggest that we are more likely to recall emotionally significant events. But are such memories accurate, or, in some circumstances, might emotion have a detrimental effect on memory? William James wrote that 'an experience may be so exciting emotionally as to almost leave a scar on the cerebral tissue' (1890, p. 670). Memory for emotional events is generally better than for events that do not arouse emotions, with both quantitative and qualitative effects (see Kensinger & Schacter, 2010, for an overview). Extreme emotion can have a negative effect on cognition, however.

Flashbulb memories: Effects of emotion

In Chapter 6, you will have read about the idea of a 'flashbulb' memory, that is, a vivid memory for an emotionally significant event that is supposedly called to mind as an exact reproduction of the event, like a 'photographic' memory. Brown and Kulik (1977) argued that a special memory mechanism underlies the vivid experience that is the flashbulb memory. In Chapter 6 we discussed the role of cognitive factors such as rehearsal in the maintenance of flashbulb memories; in this section, we focus on the possible role of emotional factors in flashbulb memories. Events that arouse strong emotions have been studied in order to determine whether a qualitatively distinct kind of memory is involved. For example, participants have been asked about their recollections on hearing about the assassinations of Martin Luther King and President Kennedy (Brown & Kulik, 1977; Winograd & Killinger, 1983), the September 11th 2001 terrorist attacks in the United States (Pezdek, 2003; Talarico & Rubin, 2003), the Hillsborough football stadium disaster in the UK (Wright, 1993; Wright et al., 1998), the resignation of UK prime minister Margaret Thatcher (Conway et al., 1994; Wright et al., 1998) and the assassination of Swedish Prime Minister Olof Palme (Christianson, 1989). People seem to report much detail of their experience of such public events, but is their memory accurate over time, and is there evidence for a 'flashbulb' effect in memory, with an important role for emotion?

In 1989, 96 football supporters were fatally injured at the Hillsborough stadium in England, during the FA Cup semi-final between Liverpool and Nottingham Forest, as a result of overcrowding of a section of the stands. The disaster received extensive coverage on television and in the other media. Wright (1993) examined 247 participants' memories of the disaster two days, one month and five months after the event occurred. While the event was judged by participants to be of more social and emotional significance over time, their memory for detail of the event faded and Wright found that memories were reconstructed and open to bias. In this case, it appears that memory was not like a photograph and did not show a 'flashbulb' effect.

Many studies have shown that while people may report vivid memories for emotional material, such memory is not error-free. Talarico and Rubin (2003) compared participants' memories of first hearing about the terrorist attacks in New York on September 11th 2001 with memory of everyday events. They found that the consistency of the memory for both types of information declined at a similar rate over time. While the emotional intensity of the experience predicted participants' confidence in their memory, it did not predict accuracy. This confidence–accuracy disparity is a major concern in the study of eyewitness memory, because jurors often base their opinion of a credible witness on apparent confidence; unfortunately this does not predict accuracy (Deffenbacher, 1980).

Schmolck et al. (2000) examined students' memories of hearing about the verdict in the O.J. Simpson trial in 1995. (This was a highly publicized trial of a well-known former American footballer, O.J. Simpson, who was tried, and acquitted, on two counts of murder following the deaths of his ex-wife and her friend.) Participants' recall was tested three days, 15 months and 32 months after the event. At 15 months, just 50 per cent of recollections were accurate and by 32 months accuracy had fallen to 29 per cent and the number of errors for particular details rose from 11 per cent to 40 per cent, with many participants showing major distortions of memory. The most common error involved source memory; participants tended to misattribute the source of the information. However, Schmolck et al. also found that the best predictor of later recall accuracy was the strength of the emotional response of the participant at the time the verdict was announced. Similarly, when Conway et al. (1994) examined people's memories of the resignation of the British Prime Minister Margaret Thatcher, they found that the greater emotional reaction of UK citizens over non-citizens was associated with accuracy of memory, even when they controlled for knowledge, rehearsal and perceived importance of the event.

This might suggest that emotional and personally experienced events would be associated with better memory. Personal events are very difficult to study, as by their nature they tend to be individualized and it is difficult to determine accuracy in the absence of a means to corroborate the facts. In diary studies, greater emotional intensity is associated with more detailed subsequent recall of the event (Conway, 1995). We do know, however, that memory for personal experiences is open to bias. Experimental tasks have demonstrated that it is relatively easy to implant false memories, for example, and some people in particular are open to suggestion (e.g. Hyman, Husband & Billings, 1995).

A study by Crombag et al. (1996) demonstrates the relative ease with which a false memory can be reported, under certain circumstances, for an emotionally charged event. On 4 October 1992 an El Al 747 cargo plane crashed into an apartment building in Amsterdam, killing four people on board the plane and 39 people on the ground. The event was widely reported in the media, with initial reports suggesting that over 200 people may have lost their lives. No film footage of the crash exists. Crombag and colleagues used two questionnaires to investigate Dutch participants' memory for the non-existent film footage of the crash. The first questionnaire asked participants if they had seen the film of the crash and, if so, where did they see it. It also asked participants to estimate how long after the crash the plane caught fire. They found that 55 per cent of participants reported having seen the (non-existent) film and most of these participants provided further details, including how long it took for fire to break out. Only 18 per cent of participants reported that they did not remember a film.

A second, modified questionnaire was used with a second group of participants. This second questionnaire asked for additional details such as the angle of the plane as it hit the building, the time taken for fire to break out and where the plane fuselage came to rest after the crash. This time, 66 per cent of participants said that they had seen the film, and many also provided additional details. Crombag and colleagues found that women were more vulnerable to this effect than men, a difference that may be accounted for in part by personality variables (e.g. compliance) rather than differences in memory. Ost et al. (2002) found that higher scores on a self-monitoring scale were associated with an increased likelihood of claiming to have seen a non-existent film; in their study, about 44 per cent of participants reported seeing a (non-existent) film of the car crash in which Diana, Princess of Wales, died. Other studies show similarly high levels of reporting of impossible memories for emotionally charged events. Granhag et al. (2003) found that as many as 55 per cent of their participants claimed to have seen non-existent film footage of the Estonia ferry disaster in 1994, when 852 people lost their lives as the ferry was crossing the Baltic Sea from Tallinn, Estonia, to Stockholm in Sweden.

Self-monitoring describes the extent to which a person is concerned with self-presentation and how others perceive them.

Box 14.5 explores some ways in which questioning can be adapted so as to minimize the risk of error in eyewitness situations.

Box 14.5 Practical Application: The cognitive interview

We have seen in Chapters 5 and 6 how memory can be influenced by questioning. The cognitive interview is one of the most effective ways of reducing the bias that might be introduced when questioning eyewitnesses and may be particularly useful when emotion is a factor. The cognitive interview was developed by psychologists Ed Geiselman and Ron Fisher and has been shown to substantially increase the number of correct details that witnesses provide, with a small increase typically also found, however, for the number of incorrect details. The cognitive interview is based on Tulving's (1983) idea of encoding specificity, that is, the idea that memory is facilitated when there is overlap between the conditions at encoding and those at retrieval (see Chapter 6). The greater the match between the cues available during retrieval and the details encoded during the initial event, the better memory will be. The goal of the cognitive interview is to reinstate aspects of the event during questioning to act as cues for the witness to effectively recall the event. The cognitive interview originally used four techniques designed to aid participants' recall (Geiselman et al., 1984):

1 reinstating the context;
2 reporting everything;
3 recalling the events in different orders;
4 changing perspectives.

Geiselman et al. (1984) showed 89 participants films of (simulated) violent crimes. Each film lasted approximately 4 minutes, and at least one individual in the film was shot and killed. The films, designed for police training purposes, were realistic and emotion-inducing, and scenarios included a bank robbery, an armed robbery at a store, a family dispute, and a warehouse search. Participants were questioned individually, 48 hours after viewing the film, by experienced interviewers. Compared to a standard (control) police interview, a greater number of correct items was produced using the cognitive interview.

Subsequent studies have supported the effectiveness of the cognitive interview. In a meta-analysis of studies conducted over the previous 25 years, Memon et al. (2010) found that the cognitive interview produced better recall compared to structured interviews, while a small increase in the recall of incorrect details was also noted. Memon et al. noted particular gains for older adults using the procedure, with correct details enhanced without observed differences for incorrect details. Memon et al. suggest that this effect is consistent with the environmental support hypothesis, which predicts that older adults rely more on external cues when retrieving information, as opposed to internally generated retrieval strategies, compared to young adults.

Emotion affects our memories for events. Furthermore, the timing and nature of the retrieval task has been shown to be crucial, as has been discussed in Chapters 5 and 6 (see also Boxes 14.5 and 14.6). As the delay between the target event and the memory test increases, people become more likely to err (Loftus et al., 1978). Jelicic et al. (2006) asked participants about their memory of (non-existent) film footage of the assassination of Dutch film director Theo van Gogh. Participants were questioned within 6–8 months of his death. At this time, media reports were frequent, as the trial of the murderer was anticipated. Just 7 per cent of the sample reported seeing footage of the assassination. This study suggests that error is reduced when participants have a good memory for the original event.

When does emotion support memory? Memory for facts would seem to be better when learning is associated with an emotion (Cahill et al., 1995). Emotion-provoking pictures also show a memory advantage, linked to activation of the amygdala. A study by Canli et al. (2000) used fMRI to scan participants' amygdala while they were presented with pictures that were neutral or emotionally negative. After three weeks, participants were given a recognition test and asked to select the pictures they had seen from a set which included pictures they had not seen before. They found increased activation of amygdala bilaterally for pictures that were rated as more emotionally intense, and memory for these pictures was also better. They found that in particular activation of the left amygdala predicted recognition, suggesting an emotion-specific mechanism (see also Hamann et al., 1999). Memory for negative stimuli is generally better than for neutral and even, on some occasions, positive stimuli (Bradley et al., 1992; Ochsner, 2000), consistent with findings from studies of attentional biases (discussed above).

However, on balance, the research suggests that strong negative emotion enhances memory for the central details of an event, but this occurs at the expense of memory for peripheral details, an effect referred to as tunnel memory (see Christianson, 1992; see also Box 14.6). This trade-off between central and peripheral aspects of a witnessed event is evident in the weapons-focus effect, a type of object-salience effect which is demonstrated when witnesses focus on a weapon at the expense of other aspects of the crime (e.g. Loftus et al., 1987; Steblay, 1992). While fewer studies have considered the effect of intense positive emotions – there are fewer public events of a positive nature that have an effect on the average person – it would seem that this tunnel effect of enhanced central details does not apply to the same extent to positive emotions (e.g. Bertnsen, 2002).

> Tunnel memory refers to the enhancement of memory of central details with reduced memory for peripheral details.

Therefore the balance of evidence does not support the 'flashbulb' effect as an indelible memory trace that remains untouched and is recalled without error or bias. However, under many conditions, emotion enhances memory. Levine and Pizarro (2004) provide a useful metaphor – rather than thinking of emotion as writing a record in indelible ink, it is more like a highlighter, increasing the salience of particular aspects of an event in the way a highlighter might be applied during study to a passage of text. They complete the metaphor by suggesting that negative emotion is like a fine highlighter – evidence suggests that it narrows focus so that memory for central aspects of the event might be aided, to the cost of peripheral aspects. Box 14.6 explores this issue further.

Box 14.6 Research Close Up: Emotion effects on memory for a crime – which details suffer?

Source: Houston, K. A., Clifford, B. R., Phillips, L. H., & Memon, A. (2013). The emotional eyewitness: the effects of emotion on specific aspects of eyewitness recall and recognition performance. *Emotion, 13*, 118–128.

INTRODUCTION

Highly emotional situations would seem to have both positive and negative effects on memory, with some accounts suggesting that memory for central details of the event is facilitated, but memory for peripheral details is impaired. But does an eyewitness rely on central or peripheral details of an event when he or she is making a witness identification? A study by Houston et al. aimed to investigate the effects of negative emotion on eyewitness recall and recognition, with a specific focus on memory for the perpetrator, critical incident, victim, and environmental details.

METHOD

Houston et al. examined which aspects of memory for an event would be impaired by emotion. Participants viewed either an emotion-inducing video, which was a crime scenario (a mugging), or a neutral scenario (a conversation). Two staged events were recorded, using the same actors. In both videos, an older woman is seen withdrawing cash from a bank machine. She then walks down a road and into a wooded area. She is approached by a young man. In the crime scenario, the man shouts at the woman and grabs hold of her bag. She shouts back at him and tries to hold onto her bag, but he manages to take it, and runs off. In the other (neutral) scenario, the man approaches the woman and asks her for the time. She turns her arm to look at her watch and her bag falls to the ground. The young man picks up the woman's bag and returns it to her, and runs off to catch a bus.

Having viewed the video, participants ($n = 101$) completed emotion ratings, and following a 20-minute delay they were given a recall sheet and asked to write down all the details they could remember. Details relating to the setting, the critical incident (mugging or bag falling during a conversation), victim, and perpetrator were noted. The dependent variables were the completeness and accuracy of recall. In a second experiment, a similar method was followed but a line-up recognition task was added. Two forms of photographic line-up were shown to 233 participants. In one line-up the target was present, and in the other, the target was absent.

RESULTS

The results of the first experiment showed that the participants who saw the emotion-inducing video could provide more complete descriptions of the perpetrator of the mugging crime, while participants in the neutral condition produced more complete descriptions of the critical incident overall. The more complete descriptions for participants who saw the emotion-inducing video suggest that their attention was focused on the perpetrator of the crime. However, there was no difference between the two groups with regard to accuracy of descriptions of the perpetrator.

Experiment 2 showed that the participants who had seen the emotion-inducing video gave a more complete description of the perpetrator but fewer details regarding his actions, suggesting a narrowing of attention to focus on what the perpetrator looked like. However, those in the emotion condition produced less accurate identifications than their neutral counterparts and they produced a higher rate of false-positive responses in the target-present condition (that is, they were more likely to identify an innocent foil from the line-up when the actual target was present). There was no association between the emotion and line-up decision when the target was absent from the line-up, with no difference between the two groups. The target-absent line-ups produced high rates of false-positive responses overall (that is, incorrectly picking someone from the line-up who was not actually the perpetrator), consistent with other studies.

DISCUSSION

This study shows that participants who had seen an emotion-inducing video could provide a more complete description of the perpetrator than participants who viewed a neutral version of the video. However, the accuracy of the descriptions of the perpetrator did not differ between the two groups, and recognition of the perpetrator in a line-up was found to be impaired for participants who had seen the emotion-inducing video relative to the neutral condition. Of course, witnessing a mugging in real life would be a far more shocking event, and might produce different effects on memory.

Mood congruent memory

Mood congruency refers to the tendency to recall events consistent with current mood state.

Network models of memory treat memories as items related in a network which can affect each other through activation.

There is considerable evidence to suggest a mood congruency effect in memory; that is, when we are in a positive mood we more readily recall positive memories, whereas when in a negative mood, negative memories more easily come to mind (Blaney, 1986; Bower, 1981, 1991). This effect is often explained in terms of network models of memory such as Bower's associative network theory (Bower, 1981). Specific emotions such as anger or sadness, like other concepts, are nodes in a network along with emotion-laden memories. When you are in a sad mood, the 'sad' node in the network is activated and, via its connections, activates related memories. In this way emotion is very much tied in with cognition and memory and imposes a structure on the network of stored relations. Emotions are like other concepts and stored in a semantic network linked to other nodes representing the autonomic responses, behavioural responses, situations that might evoke the emotion and so on. A related effect is mood dependent memory; memory for emotionally neutral material is facilitated when the mood state at encoding matches that at retrieval. This is an example of state-dependent memory. Mood- and state-dependent memory are discussed in Chapter 6.

> **State-dependent memory** refers to the facilitation of memory when the mental or physiological state at encoding and retrieval matches.

Bower (1981) asked participants to keep a diary detailing their moods over a period of one week. A 'happy' or 'sad' mood was then induced (using hypnotic suggestion – a method that is not without its critics) and they were asked to recall events from their diary. A mood congruency effect was noted – if a sad mood had been induced, more sad memories were recalled and if a happy mood was induced more happy memories were recalled. In a similar vein, Eich and Metcalfe (1989) tested the effect of current mood state on learning and subsequent memory. They induced moods in participants by having them listen to classical music that was intended to induce a positive (e.g. Mozart's *Eine Kleine Nachtsmusik*) or negative (e.g. Barber's *Adagio pour Cordes*) mood. Participants were instructed to, at the same time, think of something that made them happy or sad. During the learning phase, 32 triads were presented. Half had the form *category name: category exemplar – target item* (e.g. precious metals: silver – GOLD), and half were of the form *category name: category exemplar – initial letter of target* (e.g. milkshake flavours: chocolate – V). Participants were to generate and state aloud the target item; in the case of 'milkshake flavours: chocolate – V', for example, they were to generate the target 'VANILLA'. On half the trials, instead of generating the item, it was read aloud by the experimenter and the participants simply repeated it back. Memory was then compared for generated or read items.

Memory was tested two days later, when mood was again induced. Participants initially recalled the items aloud, in any order, with no cues or hints given. They were then presented with a list of the 32 targets along with 32 items that had not been presented during the learning phase. Participants had to respond 'old' or 'new' to indicate items that they had encountered during the learning session two days earlier, or not, respectively. The results are shown in Figure 14.6.

The results showed an effect of mood congruence for both 'read' and 'generate' conditions, with a stronger effect for the 'generate' task. This supported Eich and Metcalfe's assertion that mood dependent effects in memory are stronger for internal than for external events. Internal events originate from our own mental processes, as opposed to external events which come to our awareness through the perceptual processes (Eich & Metcalfe, 1989).

If such effects occur for induced moods, do the findings also apply to clinical mood states? Clark and Teasdale (1982) examined the natural mood states of people who were depressed and found that the recall of negative memories increased during periods of low mood, whereas happier memories were relatively more frequent when a more positive mood state prevailed. Similarly, Burke and Matthews (1992) found that, given neutral cues, anxious participants demonstrated a recall bias towards anxiety-related material compared to non-anxious participants.

Some findings do not fit with an associative network model. Emotion-congruent memory has been shown to be stronger for positive than for negative emotions and mood-incongruency effects have also been reported. Parrott and Sabini (1990), for

Figure 14.6 The effect of matching mood on the recall of read or generated target words.

Source: Data from Eich, E., & Metcalfe, J. (1989). Mood dependent memory for internal versus external events. *Journal of Experimental Psychology: Learning Memory and Cognition, 15,* 443–455.

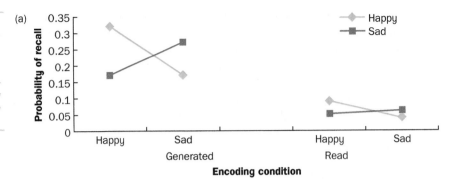

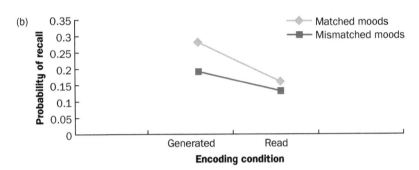

example, found that participants in an unhappy mood recalled more positive memories than participants in a happy mood. Such effects are not predicted by classic network or associative theories and have been explained in terms of the influence of motivational factors, by which a number of mood-regulatory processes kick in to reduce or eliminate negative moods. Isen (1985, 1987) suggested that when someone is in a negative mood state, they are motivated to reduce that state and create a more positive mood. Their attention is therefore focused away from the sources of negative mood; this leads to the retrieval of more positive memories and, one assumes, evokes a positive mood in the person, or at least reduces the negative mood. Forgas (1995) proposed the affect infusion model (AIM), which makes the distinction between motivated processing and constructive processing. Motivated processes use 'highly predetermined and directed information search patterns and require little generative, constructive processing' (p. 40). Motivated processing might be used by someone to regulate their moods and because it accesses previously established goal states and is less susceptible to the effects of current mood. Constructive processing involves a generative processing strategy, using a heuristic or substantive, elaborate, type of processing. According to the model, it is this type of processing that underlies mood congruency effects. By this account, 'affect is unlikely to influence judgments in a mood-congruent direction during direct access or motivated processing; rather, it should have a mood-congruent effect only when heuristic or substantive processing is used' (Forgas, 1995, p. 40).

Thought congruity is the tendency for thoughts and judgements to be consistent with mood state.

The affect infusion model has been applied to studies of thought congruity. Thought congruity refers to the influence of mood state on participants' judgements and decision making. Particularly, positive moods are associated with more positive or lenient thoughts and judgements. For example, risk taking is greater for those in a happy mood (e.g. Chou et al., 2000). AIM is consistent with findings that thought congruity occurs in some contexts, when judgements demand elaborate cognitive processing, while not in others (Sedikides, 1994). Factors such as thought congruity and state-dependent memory have greatly influenced the cognitive approach to clinical states such as depression (see Box 14.7).

Box 14.7 Practical Application: Cognitive behavioural therapy for depression

The cognitive approach to depression focuses on maladaptive thinking habits, errors, biases and depressogenic (meaning 'depression-causing') attributional styles associated with depression. Some theories argue that these thinking styles *cause* depression; others see these thinking styles more as a contributory factor. If such thinking patterns cause or exacerbate depression, then changing these thinking styles should help. This is the basis of cognitive behavioural therapy or CBT. This approach is associated with the work of Aaron Beck and the rational approach of Albert Ellis. The cognitive approach is summed up by Beck et al. (1979, p. 11):

> The cognitive model views the other signs and symptoms of depressive syndrome as a consequence of the activation of the negative cognitive patterns. For example, if the patient incorrectly thinks he is being rejected, he will react with the same negative affect that occurs with actual rejection.

By this account, it's not what happens in our lives that is important, it's how we think about or interpret events that is key. Ellis's ABC concept is useful here (e.g. Ellis & Harper, 1975). According to Ellis, when we experience an Activating Event (A), we interpret or think about the event. Our interpretation of the event leads to a Belief (B) about the event in relation to ourselves and to the world. We then experience Emotional Consequences (C) based on the belief. An error occurs when we infer that A (alone) led to C, rather than recognizing that B led to C (see Figure 14.7).

While all of us can demonstrate this kind of maladaptive thinking occasionally, people who are depressed (or those who will become depressed) think like this generally, according to this account. Beck proposed that, in depression, such thinking applies to the self, the immediate world and the future, a pattern known as the depressive cognitive triad. Beck (1967, 1976) developed cognitive therapy (or cognitive behavioural therapy, CBT) as a method of challenging such maladaptive thinking. The purpose of CBT was to challenge cognitive distortions affecting the depressed person's thinking. Butler et al.'s (2006) review of meta-analyses of CBT efficacy concludes that CBT is 'somewhat superior to antidepressants in the treatment of adult depression' (p. 17).

The cognitive distortions described by Beck are negative automatic thoughts that are habitual, involuntary, and unconstructive, and create systematic logical errors. Depressive thought is, according to Beck, 'schema-driven' (whereby the world is perceived through a depressive schema). But are the thinking patterns of people with depression always distorted and inaccurate? In some (rather limited) circumstances, depressed individuals have been shown to be more accurate than non-depressed individuals. Alloy and Abramson (1979) had participants (a depressed and non-depressed group) rate the degree of control that their responses had over a particular environmental event. On each trial in the task, participants could respond (e.g. press a button) or not respond (e.g. not press). After the response period, a light appeared or did not appear (environmental event). The participants were subsequently asked to rate their control over the outcome (the light coming on). Participants typically tend to overestimate their control over the outcome in such tasks, a pattern referred to as the outcome-density effect (see Allan, 1993) or illusion of control (see Alloy & Abramson, 1979). Alloy and Abramson found that this effect was absent in depressed individuals, who appeared to have a more accurate view of the effect of their responses on the outcome, a pattern they called 'depressive realism' (e.g. Alloy & Ackerman, 1988).

This is a controversial idea and on the balance of evidence currently available one would have to conclude that depressed individuals show a more realistic view of their chances of success, but only when that view matches the depressive schema

Figure 14.7   Ellis's ABC model. This proposes that we suffer emotional consequences not directly from an activating event but from our beliefs about the event. For example, an impending examination (A) might be associated with anxiety (C), but because we hold a belief that we will fail (B). The fear of failure and not the examination itself leads to the anxiety.

with which they are operating. While it is true that depressed individuals have a more accurate view of their own performance and level of control in contingency studies and in chance-determined tasks (Abramson et al., 1978; Klein & Seligman, 1976), it is also the case that depressed individuals *underestimate* the amount of positive feedback (while non-depressed people may overestimate it) in other tasks (see Buckwald, 1977; Moore & Fresco, 2007; Wener & Rehm, 1975). Dunn et al. (2007) showed that depressed participants judged error trials more accurately but correct trials less accurately, for example. Therefore it would seem that the nature of the task is key to the outcome.

There is by now much evidence for the existence of maladaptive thinking styles in depression. However, while much research shows that illogical thoughts are *associated* with depression (e.g. Gara et al., 1993; Haaga et al., 1991), whether such thoughts are the *cause* of depression is less clear.

Summary

In this chapter, we have seen that emotional and cognitive processing are closely connected and that the study of emotion is of central relevance to our understanding of cognitive functioning. Emotion is a fundamental component of human experience. The term 'emotion' refers to various mental states that have an object (they are 'about something') and a valence (they are pleasant or unpleasant) and which are associated with characteristic physiological changes, facial expressions, thoughts, and behaviours. While cognitive psychology has traditionally omitted the study of emotion from its key concerns, data from neuroscientific studies and other sources is showing that emotion is of central importance and must be considered if we are to fully understand cognition.

The cognitive view of emotions is that they have important short- and long-term functions that allow us to adapt in an unpredictable environment. There is evidence for a core set of emotions linked to particular facial expressions that are produced and recognized cross culturally and which would not seem to depend on learning.

Various theories on the relationship between emotion and cognition have been considered in this chapter. These theories address whether, or the extent to which, cognition is required in order for an emotion to occur.

We also looked at the effects of emotion on cognition, particular on memory and on perception and attention. Cognition is affected by emotion in a number of ways and so the confidence with which someone holds a memory does not predict the accuracy of that memory.

Review questions

1 Which theoretical account of the relationship between emotion and cognition best accounts for the evidence?

2 In what ways does emotion impact on cognition?

3 Does emotion help or hinder memory?

4 Are memories for emotional events easily disrupted?

5 Is cognition required for an emotional response?

FURTHER READING

Kensinger, E. A., & Schacter, D. L. (2010). Memory and emotion. In M. Lewis, J. M. Haviland-Jones, & L. Barrett (Eds.) *Handbook of emotion*. New York: Guilford Press.

MacMillan, M. (2000). *An odd kind of fame: Stories of Phineas Gage*. Cambridge, MA: MIT Press.

Memon, A., Meissner, C. A., & Fraser, J. (2010). The cognitive interview: A meta-analytic review and study space analysis of the past 25 years. *Psychology, Public Policy and Law, 16*(4), 340–372.

Porter, S., & ten Brinke, L. (2008). Reading between the lies: Identifying concealed and falsified emotions in universal facial expressions. *Psychological Science, 19*, 508–514.

Yiend, J. (2010). The effects of emotion on attention: A review of attentional processing of emotional information. *Cognition and Emotion, 24*(1), 3–47.

Glossary

Access consciousness includes representations that are broadcast for use in reasoning and control of action and can be reported.

Acquired dyslexia refers to reading difficulties following brain injury.

Action slips involve an action being completed when it was not intended.

Ad hoc categories are categories formed of items that meet a given goal, e.g. the category of 'items to take on a picnic' is ad hoc.

Adversary problems are problems in which the solver has to deal with a rational opponent as in board games.

Affect heuristic involves substituting feelings (positive or negative) for target attributes in decision problems.

Afterimage occurs when vision of an object remains after presentation has ceased. For example, after staring at a bright light.

Algorithm is a problem solving method that is guaranteed to solve but may do so only with high mental load.

Allophones are phonetic variants of the same phoneme.

Alphabetic scripts represent the phonemes or sounds in a language.

Amnesia refers to a pattern of memory loss affecting elements of long-term memory, while short-term memory remains intact.

Amnesic syndrome refers to a pattern of memory loss characterized by impaired long-term memory and spared short-term memory.

Amodal representations are representations that are abstract and do not involve any sensory codes.

Amygdala is an almond shaped set of structures located in the medial temporal lobe.

Anarthria is a disorder affecting the motor function underlying speech.

Anomic aphasia is when the patient has a specific difficulty with word retrieval.

Anterograde amnesia is impairment of memory for events that occurred after the onset of amnesia.

Aphasia is the term given to a group of speech disorders that occur following brain injury.

Appraisal refers to the ways in which people interpret or explain to themselves the meaning of events.

Appraisal theories have in common the assertion that emotions result from our interpretations of, or reactions to, events.

Apraxia is a neurological condition typically resulting from brain damage where a person loses the ability to perform activities that they are physically able and willing to do.

Artificial intelligence is the attempt to program computers to carry out complex tasks such as medical diagnosis, planning, using natural language.

Association is a linkage between mental contents such that activation of one content activates linked content e.g. table → chair

Associative chain theory is a behaviourist theory that explains how sequences of action arise from linking together associations between individual action components.

Atmosphere effect is a tendency to draw conclusions in syllogisms that are over influenced by the form of the premises rather than the logic of the argument.

Attention system is a framework of the human brain containing three different systems for alerting, orienting and the executive function.

Attentional bias refers to the tendency for emotional stimuli to capture or draw attention.

Autobiographical memories are episodic memories for personally experienced events in a person's life.

Autonoetic ('self-knowing') consciousness allows humans to use memory to relive past events and imagine ourselves in the future, from a self-perspective. It is a distinctive aspect of episodic memory.

Autonomic nervous system is part of the peripheral nervous system and regulates internal organs.

Availability heuristic involves judging frequency or probability of events by how easy it is to bring the events to mind.

Backwards propagation is a way of modifying weights on the links between units in a connectionist network, in response to errors, to obtain the desired output.

Basal ganglia are a group of neurons in the base of the forebrain that are connected to cortex and involved in action selection. Disorders of the basal ganglia are related to movement disorders such as Parkinson's disease.

Base rate of an event is the overall probability of the event in a population; so, the base rate of 'engineers' in the UK is the probability that a randomly selected person in the UK will be an engineer.

Basic level categories are categories formed of items that are highly similar and at an intermediate level in a concept hierarchy.

Basilar membrane is a stiff structural element located in the inner ear which contains specialized fluids as well as the hair cells that are key in transducing sound energy into neural impulses.

Belief bias is a tendency to accept invalid but believable conclusions and to reject valid but unbelievable conclusions to arguments.

Binding problem describes the issue that although perception works via analysis of separate perceptual features our subjective experience has all these features bound together.

Binocular rivalry arises when different images are presented simultaneously to the two eyes and results in experiencing seeing one image and then the other alternately.

Bound morpheme is a morpheme that cannot form a word on its own, but forms a word when attached to a free morpheme.

Brainstorming is stimulating the production of unusual ideas, by stressing quantity as against quality and deferment of evaluation of ideas.

Breadth first search is searching a state-action space by generating all possible states from each intermediate state.

Broca's aphasia is an acquired language disorder characterized by non-fluent speech, reduced speech output and problems with grammar processing.

Broca's area is an area located in the left temporal lobe, damage to which is associated with aphasia (speech deficits).

Brodmann areas were developed in 1909 by Korbinian Brodmann, a German neurologist, who divided the brain into approximately 50 regions distinguished by the structural properties of the neuronal architecture.

Capture errors involve a failure to override a routine set of actions; a routine or well-practised action is performed when another action was intended.

Categorical perception is the perception of stimuli on a sensory continuum as falling into distinct categories.

Categorization is a mnemonic strategy involving grouping of items into familiar categories.

Category exemplar tasks are those where participants are given category names one by one and are asked to generate exemplars for each. Some categories will have been encountered during an earlier stage.

Central executive is the component of working memory proposed to control and coordinate the activity of the other components including the phonological loop and the visuo-spatial sketchpad.

Central nervous system consists of the brain and spinal cord.

Central sulcus is a major anatomical landmark on the brain that forms the boundary between parietal cortex and frontal cortex.

Change blindness is the phenomenon where substantial differences between two nearly identical scenes are not noticed when presented sequentially.

Chunking refers to a strategy to improve memory by grouping smaller units together into a larger unit or 'chunk'.

Clause is a part of a sentence containing a subject and verb.

Closed-class words, such as articles, conjunctions, prepositions, remain stable over time and are not added to.

Co-articulation is the tendency for a speech sound to be influenced by sounds preceding or following it.

Cocktail party problem describes how we successfully focus on one speaker in a background of noise and other conversations.

Cognitive psychology is the scientific study of how people and animals process information.

Cognitive sandwich describes the view that perception and action are like slices of bread that surround cognition as the filling of a sandwich.

Common coding is a theory of perception and action production which holds that both production and perception share certain representations of actions in the world.

Communication refers to any means by which information is shared.

Concepts are mental representations of classes of items such as 'cats', 'even numbers', and so on.

Conceptually driven or top-down processes reflect the influence of higher order cognitive processes such as thoughts, beliefs and expectations.

Conduction aphasia is when the patient has a specific difficulty affecting the repetition of speech.

Cones are special neurons in the retina that are sensitive to different coloured light and densely packed to resolve fine image detail.

Confirmation bias, in hypothesis testing, is a tendency to seek out and attend only to information consistent with the hypothesis while ignoring falsifying information.

Conjunction fallacy is the mistaken belief that the conjunction of two events (A and B) is more likely than either one of A or B.

Connectionism is an approach to cognition in terms of networks of simple neuron-like units that pass activation and inhibition through receptor, hidden and output units.

Consonantal scripts represent the consonants of the language.

Content words are words that provide meaning to the sentence; these contrast with function words which do the grammatical work of the sentence.

Context effects occur if memory is better when the external environment at testing is the same as at learning.

Continuity editing describes a filmmaking technique to produce a smooth continuous experience across changes in camera shot.

Corpus callosum is the thick band of nerve fibres that connects the left and right cerebral hemispheres.

Creative in relation to a product is generally defined as novel to the producer of the product and valuable in some way; alternatively, that the product is novel and meets a goal.

Creative synthesis task is a task in which participants have to combine presented shapes to make novel interesting combinations.

Critical incident analysis is gaining information about naturalistic decision making by analysing detailed recalls of recent important decisions.

Crossed aphasia refers to language dysfunction following right hemisphere damage in a right-handed individual.

Cued recall is when a hint or cue is given to task participants to aid recall.

Decay is a process by which information is lost from STM over time.

Decision making is the cognitive process of choosing between alternative possible actions.

Declarative or explicit memory involves conscious recollection of memories such as events, facts, people and places.

Deductive reasoning is drawing logically necessary conclusions from given information.

Default network is a network of brain regions that is active when a person is not focused on the external environment.

Deficient processing view is that massed repetitions lead to deficient processing of the second presentation.

Degrees of freedom of a joint are the number of ways it can move. For example, the shoulder has three (up-down, forward-backward, rotate along axis of bone).

Demand characteristics are the aspects of a research study which convey the hypotheses or aims to the participants and may thereby shape performance.

Deontic rules are rules regarding obligations and typically involve terms such as 'should', 'must', 'ought, 'may' and so on.

Depth first search is searching a state-action space by generating one state only from each intermediate state.

Descriptive approaches aim to describe how decisions are actually taken as against how they should be made. Psychologists focus on the descriptive approach.

Detour problems are problems in which the hill climbing method does not work well, as the solver has to move away from the goal at some stage.

Dichotic listening task is one where different stimuli are presented to each ear.

Digit span refers to the number of digits that can be held is memory and is used as a measure of STM.

Direct perception, also termed event perception and ecological perception, refers to the bottom-up process by which objects and their function are recognized.

Directed forgetting (DF) is memory impairment brought about by instructions to forget some items.

Discourse refers to multi-sentence speech and includes dialogue, conversation and narrative.

Disfluency is a hesitation or disruption to the normal fluency of speech. By contrast, the term 'dysfluency' is used to refer to an abnormal disruption to fluency, such as following brain damage. The use of the prefix 'dys-' signals 'abnormal'.

Displacement is a process by which information coming into STM causes information already held there to be lost.

Display rules are social conventions governing how, when and with whom emotions may be expressed.

Distributed attention is reminiscent of preattentive vision and allows rapid statistical analysis of the entire scene.

Dorsal stream is the visual pathway from occipital cortex to parietal cortex that is involved in locating and guiding how to use an object.

Double dissociation of function arises when, following brain injury, some people do well on one Task 'A' and poorly on a second Task 'B' while others with different brain injuries show the opposite pattern. Then the two tasks are said to be doubly dissociated.

Dual coding hypothesis proposes that concrete words can be encoded both verbally and by means of images representing their meaning; in contrast, abstract words can only be coded verbally. Dual coding is one explanation of why concrete words are easier to remember.

Dual-task paradigm arises when one measures performance on two tasks independently and together. If performance when performed independently and together is equal, then the two tasks do not compete for resources.

Dynamical systems approach to motor control emphasizes interaction between the body and the environment and uses special mathematics that describe how a system's behaviour changes over time.

Dysexecutive syndrome refers to a range of deficits reflecting problems with executive function and control, and often associated with injury to the frontal areas of the brain.

Early selection describes when the filter for attention occurs early in the stream of information processing.

Echoic store is sensory memory specific to auditory stimuli.

Ecological validity is the degree to which the results of a laboratory study can be applied to a real life situation.

Elaborative rehearsal organizes the information so that it can be integrated into LTM.

Electrocortical stimulation of the surface of the cortex allows a surgeon to locate, and avoid damage to, brain regions associated with a particular cognitive function.

Electroencephalography (EEG) is a functional brain imaging method showing waves of electrical activity from scalp recorders.

Embodied cognition holds that cognition is about the experiences arising from a perceptual system tightly linked to an action system rather than the manipulations of abstract representations.

Emotion refers to a number of mental states including anger, joy, and disgust.

Empiricism is the philosophical school which holds that all knowledge comes from experience.

Encoding is the function by which information is coded in a form that allows it to be stored in memory.

Encoding specificity principle is that if the context at recall is similar to the context at encoding then memory will be enhanced.

Encoding variability means that encoding varies with the context at the study period.

Endowment effect is a tendency to over-value a possessed object and to require more money to sell it than to buy it in the first place.

Episodic buffer is the component of working memory proposed for the temporary storage of information integrated from the phonological loop, the visuo-spatial sketchpad and long-term memory into single structures or episodes.

Episodic memory is memory for events, experiences and episodes.

Equilibrium point hypothesis is a theory of motor control that emphasizes how the problem of control can be simplified by taking into account muscle properties.

Essentialism is the view that all members of a given category share some key property.

Event-related potentials (ERPs) are a functional brain imaging method recording electrical activity during repeated stimulus presentations.

Exemplar theories propose that categories are represented purely by stored examples or instances and each example is linked to the category name.

Expected value is the long-term average value of a repeated decision which is determined by the probability and size of the outcome. So if the chance of winning £100 in a gamble is 0.5, then the expected value is £50.

Expertise is the accumulated high level knowledge that allows outstanding performance in complex problem areas.

External attention deals primarily with sensory events external to the body.

Eye tracking involves the measurement of people's eye movements while reading or inspecting a visual scene.

Facial feedback hypothesis proposes that feedback from the facial muscles can influence emotional state.

False memories are inaccurate recollections of events that did not occur, or distortions of events that did occur.

Family resemblance is the tendency for members of a category to be similar to each other but without having any one characteristic in common to all of them.

Feedforward processing describes a bottom-up process where lower levels progressively stimulate higher levels of brain.

Feeling of warmth rating is a rating of how close the solver feels to problem solution, taken at intervals during the solving process.

Feeling-of-knowing is a subjective sense of knowing that we know a word, and is an example of meta-memory – our knowledge about the contents of our memories.

Figural bias is the effect of figure on preferred conclusions.

Firing rates is a term from neurophysiology where the activity of a single cell or group of cells is recorded. A high firing rate indicates great activity of the cell due to sensitivity to the incoming information.

Fixation occurs when the eye settles briefly on a region of interest in a visual scene.

Flashbulb memory is a vivid memory of a dramatic event and of the circumstances in which the event was experienced or heard about.

Fluent aphasia is when the patient's speech is fluent, but not meaningful.

Forgetting refers to processes leading to a loss of ability to retrieve previously learned information.

Forward models are used to predict the relationship between actions and their consequences. Given a motor command the forward model predicts the resulting behaviour of the body and the world.

Four figures of syllogism are the four possible layouts of terms which give four syllogistic figures, i.e. A-B, B-C; B-A, B-C; A-B, C-B; B-A, C-B.

Framing effects arise when irrelevant features of a situation affect the decisions that are made.

Free morpheme is a morpheme that can stand alone as a word.

Free recall is when participants in a task recall the information in any order, without hints or clues to recall.

Frontal eye fields are found in the frontal cortex and are involved with the generation and control of eye movements.

Function words provide grammatical structure that shows how content words relate to each other within a sentence.

Functional fixity is a difficulty in thinking of a novel use for a familiar object.

Functional imaging methods detect brain activity.

Functional Magnetic Resonance Imaging (fMRI) is a method of imaging brain activity that uses oxygenation levels of blood flow and has good temporal and spatial resolution.

Functional reference refers to the use by animals of a specific call to stand for a specific object or threat.

Garden path sentence is a grammatically correct but ambiguous sentence that biases the reader's initial parsing.

Geneplore is a model for creative thinking which stresses the role of a generative and exploratory phase.

Generalizability is the degree to which results are broadly applicable to a wide range of situations.

Geons are the elements of a set of volumetric primitives or shapes that can be recognized from any viewpoint, proposed by Biederman in his recognition by components (RBC) theory.

Gestalt approach to thinking likens problem solving to seeing new patterns; it stresses the role of insight and understanding in problem solving.

Global aphasia is an acquired language disorder involving extreme impairment of language function.

Global workspace theory proposes that consciousness requires interactions across a broad range of brain areas.

Goal-subgoal space is a representation of how an overall problem goal can be broken down into subgoals and sub-subgoals.

Grapheme is the written representation of a phoneme.

Grapheme-to-phoneme conversion (GPC) route allows us to sound out words based on letter–sound correspondences.

Grounded representations are representations that involve sensory-motor codes.

Haptic memory is the sensory memory for stimuli sensed through touch.

Haptic perception is the combination of abilities that allow us to represent the material characteristics of objects and surfaces for recognition.

Heuristic is a problem solving method that often finds a low effort solution but is not guaranteed to solve.

Homographs are words with the same spelling, but more than one meaning and pronunciation.

Homologous in biology means to have the corresponding position, structure and possibly function. It is common to consider across species what anatomical parts are homologous. For brain regions this is important for using data obtained in say monkeys to predict relations in human brain.

Hypothesis generation is deriving possible hypotheses from data for later testing.

Hypothesis testing is assessing hypotheses for truth/falsity against data.

Hypothetico-deductive reasoning is a form of inductive reasoning in which a hypothesis is tested by deducing necessary consequences of the hypothesis and determining whether the consequences are true (supporting the hypothesis) or false (disconfirming or falsifying the hypothesis).

Iconic store is the sensory memory store for visual stimuli.

Ideomotor theory relates how thinking about the results of an action can give rise to producing the action.

Ill-defined problem is a problem in which starting conditions, or actions available or goals are not completely specified.

Imagery is the mental representation of sensory properties of objects – experienced as like perceiving the object but with less vividness than in reality.

Imagination inflation refers to strengthening of a false memory through repeated retrieval.

Inattentional blindness is the failure to notice a clearly visible target due to attention being diverted from the target.

Incidental learning is learning that takes place without any intention to learn.

Incubation is a period in which a problem is set aside; it may be 'immediate', directly after presentation, or 'delayed', after a period of conscious work.

Inductive reasoning is the process of inferring probable conclusions from given information.

An inference rule is a rule for reaching a conclusion given a particular pattern of propositions, e.g. modus ponens which states that given 'If p then q' and 'not q' we can infer 'not p'.

Information processing approach is a metaphor for understanding mental activity, based on computing.

Inner scribe is the component of the visuo-spatial sketchpad, within working memory, that allows spatial processing.

Inner speech refers to the subjective experience of hearing our thoughts, as if 'spoken' by an inner voice, when reading silently for example.

Insight is a restructuring of a problem that makes the solution obvious and understandable.

Insula is an area hidden within the folds of the cortex, with connections to the cingulate, amygdala, and orbitofrontal cortex, implicated in aspects of emotion, cognition, and action.

Interacting images is a mnemonic strategy in which vivid and bizarre images are formed of the items to be recalled, interacting in some way.

Interactive activation is a term used to describe the pattern of network activity generated by excitatory and inhibitory interactions of feature detectors and object representations.

Interference occurs when remembering is disrupted by related memories.

Internal attention deals primarily with our internally generated thoughts, desires and motivations.

Internal representations are mental representations of external objects and events.

Intrusive memories are persistent unwanted memories, e.g., of traumatic events, that frequently come to mind.

Invariance is the principle that choices between alternatives should not be affected by how the options are described.

Invariance problem reflects the variation in the production of speech sounds across speech contexts.

Invariants in vision are properties of the three-dimensional object being viewed that can be derived from any two-dimensional image of the object.

Inverse problem in vision is where there are more than one interpretation of the 3D world given the 2D image information.

Knowledge-lean problems are problems such as puzzles that do not require specialist knowledge.

Knowledge-rich problems are problems that require extensive specialist knowledge.

Language production refers to a number of processes by which we convert a thought into language output, in the form of speech, sign language or writing.

Late closure attaches incoming material to the phrase that is currently being processed.

Late selection describes when the filter for attention occurs late in the stream of information processing. Thus the filter eliminates some information that has already been processed.

Lateralization of function refers to the asymmetric representation of cognitive function in the cerebral hemispheres of humans and higher primates.

Learning refers to processes of acquiring information for mental storage and later use.

Lemma is an abstract word form that contains syntactic and semantic information about the word.

Levels of processing is a theory that better learning results from deeper semantic processing which produces stronger, more elaborated memory traces than superficial level processing.

Lexeme is the basic lexical unit that gives the word's morpho-phonological properties.

Lexical access is the process by which we access stored knowledge about words.

Lexical bias refers to tendency for phonological speech errors to result in real words.

Lexical decision task is a task where participants are presented with a letter string and they must decide whether or not it is a word.

Lexical or direct route to reading involves the selection of a word from the lexicon.

Likelihood principle states that the preferred organization of a perceptual object or event will be the one which is most likely.

Limbic system consists of the thalamus, hypothalamus, hippocampus and amygdala, and other structures.

Linguistic universals are linguistic features said to be found in all languages.

Localist representation is where a single unit represents a particular concept.

Localization is the view that specific mental functions are tied to specific brain areas; this also appears as the modularity hypothesis and may be contrasted with the distributed view, that functions are realized by joint action of many areas.

Logographic scripts represent morphemes or the units of meaning of words.

Long-term memory is the system where information is held for longer periods, and can be accessed when needed.

Long-term potentiation (LTP) is the long-lasting improvement in signal transmission between two neurons that results from stimulating them at the same time.

Loss aversion is a key idea of prospect theory that there is a greater dislike of losing utility than liking for gaining the same degree of utility.

Magnetic resonance imaging is a high-definition method for structural imaging using strong magnetic fields.

Maintenance rehearsal retains information in STM.

Masking refers to reduced perception of a visual stimulus when another stimulus is presented in spatial or temporal proximity to it.

Matching bias, in the four-card task, is choosing the cards mentioned in the rule.

McGurk effect is a perceptual illusion that illustrates the interplay of visual and auditory processing in speech perception.

Memory trace is a mental representation of stored information.

Mental lexicon is our store of knowledge about words and their uses.

Mental maps are mental representations of a spatial layout.

Mental models approach is the view that people tackle logical reasoning problems by forming mental representations of possible states of the world and draw inferences from those representations.

Mental operations are inner actions manipulating mental representations.

Mental representations are inner representations such as an image or a verbal concept of some external reality.

Mere exposure effect refers to the tendency for people to develop a preference for a stimulus with repeated exposure to it.

Metamemory is the ability to monitor and inspect the content of memory. It allows us to know whether we know something.

Method of loci is a mnemonic strategy in which a familiar route is imagined and images of the items to be recalled are linked to landmarks on the route.

Minimal attachment introduces new items into the phrase structure using as few syntactic nodes as possible.

Mirror neurons are neurons with the special property that they represent both the sensory aspects of perceiving actions as well as motor aspects of how to produce the action.

Mnemonic is a learning device used to aid memory.

Mood congruency refers to the tendency to recall events consistent with current mood state.

Mood dependent memory means that memory is better when mood at learning is reinstated at testing.

Morphemes are the meaning units of language.

Morphology is the level of linguistic analysis concerned with morphemes and their role within words.

Motor primitives are the basis set of elemental movements that serve as building blocks for an animal's repertoire of movements.

Motor system includes the components of the central and peripheral nervous systems along with the muscles, joints and bones that enable movement.

Multi-attribute decision problem is a decision task in which the alternatives vary in many dimensions or aspects.

Multi-level theories of emotion propose that both preattentive and conscious cognitive processes are involved in emotion.

Naturalistic decision making refers to making real life decisions in the field.

Negative recency effect reflects poorer memory for list-end items compared to items from earlier input positions, in multi-list recall tasks.

Network models of memory treat memories as items related in a network which can affect each other through activation.

Neuroeconomics is the study of neural processes underlying economic decisions.

Neurolinguistics is the study of the relationship of brain function to language processing.

Neurons are the basic units of the nervous system, principally consisting of a cell, axon and dendrites.

Neuropsychology is the study of psychological effects of brain damage and disease.

Non-adversary problems are problems in which the solver is dealing with inert problem materials with no rational opponent.

Non-declarative or **implicit memory** refers to memory that is not accessed consciously and that we are not able to report verbally. It includes memory which benefits from previous experience but without our awareness of that experience.

Non-fluent aphasia is when the patient's speech output is reduced, laboured, or absent.

Non-plan internal errors occur when the intrusion is external to the planned content of the utterance.

Non-semantic reading is a pattern of reading deficit whereby the patient can read an irregular word (which cannot be sounded out) and yet cannot access its meaning.

Normative approaches attempt to establish ideal ways of deciding that will give the best decision possible. Economists have tended to develop normative models.

Object of a sentence is the word or words that receives the action, or is acted on, by the subject of the sentence.

Onset of a word is the initial phoneme or phonemes. The time follows the onset.

Opaque or **orthographically deep** languages are those where the relationship between letters and sounds is more complex.

Open-class words are content words such as nouns, verbs and adjectives. New words can be added to this class of words.

Optimal control theory of motor control provides a framework for implementing principles that produce movements that optimally satisfy some criterion.

Paired associates learning is a memory task in which participants are presented with pairs of items (typically, words) at study and on test are given the first word and asked to recall the second word in each pair.

Parallel processing is the ability to divide the process of solving a problem into multiple parts and to work simultaneously on each part.

Parapraxes are slips of the tongue or other actions originally thought to reflect unconscious motives.

Parsing is the process by which we assign a syntactic structure to a sentence.

Pegword method is a mnemonic strategy in which to be recalled items are linked by imagery to an already learned sequence list of imagable words.

Perception is our sensory experience of the world.

Permastore involves the long-term retention of content that has been acquired and relearned over a period of time, even if rarely used thereafter.

Perseveration is the inappropriate repetition of an action.

Phenomenal consciousness includes the experiential properties of sensations, feelings and perceptions.

Phoneme is the smallest meaningful sound unit within a language.

Phoneme restoration effect describes the tendency to hear a complete word even when a phoneme has been removed from the input.

Phones are the basic speech sounds.

Phonetics is the study of speech sounds.

Phonological dyslexia affects non-word reading, but real words can be read.

Phonological loop is the component of working memory proposed for temporary storage and manipulation of sound or phonological information. It comprises a short-term phonological store for auditory memory traces and an articulatory rehearsal component to reactivate memory traces.

Phonotactic constraints describe the language-specific sound groupings that occur in a language.

Phonotactic rules stipulate which combinations of sounds are 'permitted' in a language.

Phrase is a group of words referring to a particular idea.

Phrase structure tree is a graphic representation of the syntactic structure of a sentence.

Phrenology was an early form of localization that attempted unsuccessfully to link psychological functions to bumps in the skull taken to reflect growth of brain in specific areas.

Positron emission tomography (PET) is a functional imaging method which uses positron emissions from radioactive glucose to indicate areas of increased blood flow in the brain.

Pragmatics refers to the understanding of the communicative functions of language and the conventions that govern language use.

Preattentive visual processes can simultaneously analyse the entire scene and detect the presence of unique features.

Premises are statements assumed to be true from which conclusions are drawn.

Primacy effect is enhanced recall of items at the start of a list compared to those in the middle.

Priming refers to an implicit memory effect whereby exposure to a stimulus affects a subsequent response.

Proactive interference occurs when previous learning impairs later learning.

Probabilistic classification learning involves learning a set of associations that cannot be readily memorized, and information from across many trials must be used to complete the task.

Problem is a situation in which you have a goal but do not know how to achieve it.

Problem space is an abstract representation of possible states of a problem.

Procedural memory is a type of non-declarative memory involving memory for how to perform skills and actions.

Productivity of language refers to the ability to generate novel utterances.

Progressive deepening is searching a state-action space by using depth first search to a limited depth, When depth limit is reached, search backs up to start and repeats, avoiding previously explored branches and so on until the whole space has been searched up to the initial depth limit. If a solution is not found, increase depth limit, and repeat until the goal is reached.

Propositional reasoning is reasoning about statements connected by logical relations such as 'and' 'or', 'not', 'if'.

Proprioception is the sense of how our limbs are positioned in space.

Prosody is the rhythm, intonation and stress patterns in speech.

Prospect theory is a decision theory stressing relative gains and losses.

Prospective memory allows us to remember to perform certain actions. It has been described as the ability to 'remember to remember'.

Prototype is an ideal example that best represents a category.

Psycholinguistics is the branch of study concerned with the mental processes underlying language comprehension and production.

Pulses involve intentions that are time-locked.

Pure word deafness is a deficit affecting the ability to recognize speech sounds, while comprehension of non-speech sounds remains intact.

Pure word meaning deafness the patient can repeat back the word, but cannot understand it.

Re-enactment is the partial repetition of the internal processes involved in previous perceptions or actions.

Reasoning is the cognitive process of deriving new information from old information.

Recency effect is the tendency, given a list of items to remember, to recall those from the end of the list more readily than items from the middle.

Receptive field of a neuron indicates the physical space that stimulates the neuron. In vision it is the region of visual field to which that neuron is sensitive if stimulated with light.

Recognition is when a task participant must verify if an item is a target.

Recognition primed decision is expert knowledge based decision making in which cues in the situation are recognized as indicating particular actions.

Recollection is the act of recalling something to mind.

Recurrent networks are a type of artificial neural network with connections between units arranged so to obtain a cycle of activation. This design allows a temporal context to be designed into the computation.

Recurrent processing, within a network, involves computations that occur in a cyclic fashion.

Recursion refers to the ability to extend sentences infinitely by embedding phrases within sentences.

Rehearsal refers to a set of processes by which we can act on currently active information.

Repetition priming refers to the finding that repeated exposure to a word leads to faster responses in a lexical decision task.

Representativeness heuristic involves judging frequency or probability of an event or object by how representative or typical it is of its category.

Representativeness increases with the realism and naturalness of the study's materials and tasks.

Restructuring is changing how one represents a problem.

Retrieval induced forgetting (RIF) is an impaired ability to recall some items caused by earlier retrieval of related items.

Retrieval is the function by which information is recollected as needed.

Retroactive interference occurs when later learning impairs memory for earlier learning.

Retrograde amnesia is impairment of memory for events that occurred before the onset of amnesia.

Retrograde facilitation is the beneficial effect on memory of a period of sleep or inactivity following a study period.

Ribot's Law (1881) of retrograde amnesia states that recently formed memories are more susceptible to impairment than are older memories.

Right ear advantage for speech sounds refers to the finding that language sounds are processed more efficiently when presented to the right ear compared to the left.

Risk A decision involves risk if there is a probability that one of the options could lead to negative outcomes for the decision maker.

Risk aversion is avoiding risky choices even when a higher expected value than riskless alternatives.

Risk seeking is a preference for risky choices even when riskless alternatives of higher value are available.

Riskless decisions involve choices where the outcomes of the choices are known with certainty.

Rods are special neurons in the periphery of the retina that are effective in low levels of light and to sense motion.

Saccades are fast movements of the eye made when reading or scanning an image.

Salience network is involved in monitoring the external and internal environments to allow detection of salient stimuli.

Savings is a way of assessing forgetting by comparing trials needed for relearning as against trials required for original learning. If fewer trials are needed for relearning then savings have been demonstrated.

Schema is a framework that represents a plan or a theory, supporting the organization of knowledge.

Segmentation problem refers to detection of distinct words in what is a continuous string of speech sounds.

Self-efficacy is a person's sense of their own competence to complete a certain task or achieve a goal.

Self-monitoring describes the extent to which a person is concerned with self-presentation and how others perceive them.

Semantic memory is memory for facts and knowledge about the world.

Semantics is the study of meaning.

Sensation entails the processes by which physical properties are converted to neural signals.

Sensory memory is a temporary sensory register that allows input from the sensory modalities to be prolonged.

Sentence verification tasks present a sentence frame with a target word, and the participant must decide if the word fits in the frame.

Serial position curve is used to plot recall of a word list such that performance is examined as a function of a word's position in a list.

Set is a tendency to persist with one approach to a problem.

Shadowing is a technique that involves repeating back an auditorily presented message.

Short-term memory is the store where information is temporarily held in an accessible state.

Simulation involves programming computers to solve problems in a similar way to humans.

Simulation is the extended re-enactment of a previous experience.

Single-attribute decision problems involve alternatives that vary in only one dimension.

Skin conductance or galvanic skin response (GSR) reflects changes in the skin's ability to conduct electricity in the presence of an emotion-eliciting stimulus.

Slang describes an informal pattern of speech that is considered to be 'non-standard'.

Slips of the ear occur when we misperceive a word or phrase in speech.

Social cognition refers to the ways in which people make sense of themselves and of others in order to function effectively in a social world.

Social contract theory proposes that rules expressing payment of costs for privileges will be easily solved in 4 card tasks as the correct choices would uncover cheating.

Somatic perception refers to perception of the body through touch and sensing the orientation of limbs in space.

Spacing effect occurs when material studied on many separate occasions is better learned than material studied in one continuous session even if total study times are equal.

Speech perception is the process by which we convert a stream of speech into individual words and sentences.

Spotlight refers to the metaphor of attention where we can think of attention as a spotlight that illuminates locations of interest.

State dependent memory effects occur if memory is better when internal physiological conditions at learning are reinstated at testing.

State-action space is a representation of how problems can be transformed from starting state through intermediate states to the goal.

State-dependent memory refers to the facilitation of memory when the mental or physiological state at encoding and retrieval matches.

Status quo bias is a tendency to prefer the current state of affairs.

Steps are intentions that have a wider time frame in which they can occur.

Stimulus onset asynchrony refers to the time between the onset of a stimulus and the presentation of a mask.

Storage is the function by which information is retained in memory.

Strategies are systematic ways to carry out a cognitive task such as solving a problem.

Structural imaging methods show brain anatomy.

Subject of a sentence is the word or words that gives what the sentence is about or performs the action.

Subjective probability is how likely a person believes an outcome to be irrespective of the objective probability.

Subliminal perception is the case where a stimulus is presented below threshold (e.g. too fast or too dim) but its effects on behaviour can still be measured.

Surface dyslexia is characterized by a deficit in the reading of irregular words, while the reading of regular words is spared.

Syllabic scripts use a symbol to represent each syllable.

Syllogistic reasoning is reasoning about groups/sets using statements connected by logical relations of 'some', 'none', 'all' and 'some not'.

Synaesthesia is an uncommon condition where stimulation of one perceptual modality results in experiencing a percept in a typically unrelated modality, e.g. tasting a sound.

Syntax refers to the rules governing the ways words can be combined to create meaningful sentences.

System 1 is a hypothetical system that carries out rapid intuitive thinking.

System 2 is a hypothetical system that carries out slow deliberate thinking

Think/no-think (TNT) is a memory manipulation in which participants are instructed not to retrieve a memory even when a strong cue is present.

Thinking is a process of mental exploration of possible actions and states of the world.

Thought congruity is the tendency for thoughts and judgements to be consistent with mood state.

Tip-of-the-tongue (TOT) state refers to a temporary inability to access a known word.

Tonal languages use changes in tone to alter the meaning of the word.

Tonotopic map is where the auditory processing of different tones is arranged in an orderly layout in cortex.

Torque is a measure from physics that measures rotational force such as when muscles apply a force for a limb to rotate about a joint centre.

Transcranial magnetic stimulation is a non-invasive method of temporarily exciting or inhibiting cortical areas.

Transparent or **shallow orthography** uses a one-to-one correspondence between the letters and sounds.

Tunnel memory refers to the enhancement of memory of central details with reduced memory for peripheral details.

Two-system view is that there are two modes of thought, System 1 and System 2.

Typicality is the extent to which an object is representative of a category.

Utility is the subjective value of an option.

Utilization behaviour refers to dysfunctional automatic reaching for and use of objects in the environment.

Valid arguments are those in which the conclusions must be true if the premises are true.

Ventral stream is the visual pathway from occipital cortex to temporal cortex that is involved in recognition of the object being viewed.

Verbal learning refers to the area of experimental psychology concerned with how we learn and remember language-based items such as word lists.

Vestibular sensation is the sense of balance and orientation in space.

Viewpoint invariant relationship is any aspect of an object that is preserved no matter the direction from which we view the object.

Visual cache is the component of the visuo-spatial sketchpad, within working memory, that stores visual information.

Visual search tasks require an active search of a visual array, usually for a particular object or stimulus feature.

Visuo-spatial processing is the mental manipulation of visual or spatial information.

Visuo-spatial sketchpad is the component of working memory proposed for the temporary storage and manipulation of visual and spatial information.

Voicing is when speech sounds are produced while the vocal cords are vibrating.

Wechsler Memory Scale is a widely used neurocognitive assessment that measures visual memory, auditory memory, and working memory.

Well-defined problem is a problem in which starting conditions, actions available and goals are all completely specified.

Wernicke-Geschwind model is a simplified model of language function used as the basis for classifying aphasia disorders.

Wernicke's aphasia is a fluent aphasia, characterized by fluent but meaningless output and repetition errors.

Word is the smallest unit of grammar that can be meaningfully produced on its own; it can consist of one or more morphemes.

Word naming tasks require participants to name a word, while response time is measured.

Word superiority effect refers to the finding that a target letter within a letter string is detected more readily when the string forms a word.

Working memory is the system in which information is held and manipulated in order to perform a task.

References

A

Abramson, L. Y., Seligman, M. E. P., & Teasdale, J. (1978). Learned helplessness in humans: Critique and reformulation. *Journal of Abnormal Psychology, 87,* 49–74.

Adams, J. W., & Hitch, G. J. (1998). Children's mental arithmetic and working memory. In C. Donlan (Ed.), *The development of mathematical skills* (pp. 153–173). Hove: Psychology Press.

Adelson, B. (1981). Problem solving and the development of abstract categories in programming languages. *Memory and Cognition, 9,* 422–433.

Aglioti, S., De Souza, J. F., & Goodale, M. A. (1995). Size-contrast illusions deceive the eye but not the hand. *Current Biology, 5,* 679–685.

Ahn, W., Kim, N. S., Lassaline, M. E., & Dennis, M. (2000). Causal status as a determinant of feature centrality. *Cognitive Psychology, 41,* 361–416.

Aitchison, J. (1996). *The seeds of speech: Language origin and evolution.* Cambridge: Cambridge University Press.

Alais, D., & Burr, D. (2004). The ventriloquist effect results from near-optimal bimodal integration. *Current Biology, 14*(3), 257–262.

Albert, M. L., & Bear, D. (1974). Time to understand: A case study of word deafness with reference to the role of time in auditory comprehension, *Brain, 97,* 373–384.

Allan, L. G. (1993). Human contingency judgments: Rule based or associative? *Psychological Bulletin, 114,* 435–448.

Allison, T., Ginter, H., McCarthy, G., Nobre, A. C., Puce, A., Luby, M., *et al.* (1994). Face recognition in human extrastriate cortex.

Journal of Neurophysiology, 71(2), 821–825.

Allison, T., Puce, A., & McCarthy, G. (2000). Social perception from visual cues: Role of the STS region. *Trends in Cognitive Science, 4,* 267–278.

Alloy, L. B., & Abramson, L. Y. (1979). Judgment of contingency in depressed and nondepressed students: Sadder but wiser? *Journal of Experimental Psychology: General, 108,* 441–485.

Alloy, L. B., & Ackerman, L. Y. (1988). Depressive realism: Four theoretical perspectives. In L. B. Alloy (Ed.), *Cognitive processes in depression* (pp. 223–265). New York: Guilford Press.

Allport, D. A. (1980). Attention and performance. In G. Claxton (Ed.), *International library of psychology.* London: Routledge and Kegan Paul.

Allport, D. A. (1983). Language and cognition. In R. Harris (Ed.), *Approaches to language.* Oxford: Pergamon Press.

Allport, D. A., & Funnell, E. (1981). Components of the mental lexicon. *Philosophical Transactions of the Royal Society of London, B295,* 397–410.

Altman, L. K. (1998). *Who goes first?: The story of self-experimentation in medicine.* Berkeley, CA: University of California Press.

Altmann, G. T. M. (1998). Ambiguity in sentence processing. *Trends in Cognitive Sciences, 2,* 146–152.

Anderson, J. R. (2004). *Cognitive psychology and its implications* (6th ed.). New York: Worth.

Anderson, M. C. (2003). Rethinking interference theory: Executive control and the mechanisms of forgetting. *Journal of Memory and Learning, 49,* 415–445.

Anderson, M. C. (2005). The role of inhibitory control in forgetting unwanted memories:

A consideration of three methods. In C. MacLeod & B. Uttl (Eds.), *Dynamic cognitive processes.* Tokyo: Springer Verlag.

Anderson, M. C., & Bell, T. A. (2001). Forgetting our facts: The role of inhibitory processes in the loss of propositional knowledge. *Journal of Experimental Psychology: General, 130,* 544–570.

Anderson, M. C., & Green, C. (2001). Suppressing unwanted memories by executive control. *Nature, 410,* 366–369.

Anderson, M. C., & Neely, J. H. (1996). Interference and inhibition in memory retrieval. In E. L. Bjork & R. A. Bjork (Eds.), *Memory.* San Diego, CA: Academic Press.

Anderson, M. C., Bjork, R. A., & Bjork, E. L. (1994). Remembering can cause forgetting: Retrieval dynamics in long term memory. *Journal of Experimental Psychology: Learning, Memory and Cognition, 20,* 1063–1087.

Anderson, M. C., Ochsner, K. N., Cooper, J., Robertson, E., Gabrieli, S. W., Glover, G. H., *et al.* (2004). Neural systems underlying the suppression of unwanted memories. *Science, 303,* 232–235.

Andics, A., McQueen, J. M., Petersson, K. M., Gal, V., Rudas, G., & Vidnyanszky, Z. (2010). Neural mechanisms for voice recognition. *Neuroimage, 52*(4), 1528–1540.

Anzai, Y., & Simon, H. A. (1979). The theory of learning by doing. *Psychological Review, 86,* 124–140.

Ardila, A. (2010). A review of conduction aphasia. *Current Neurology and Neuroscience Reports, 10,* 499–503.

Ariely, D. (2001). Seeing sets: Representation by statistical properties. *Psychological Science, 12,* 157–162.

Atchley, P., & Andersen, G. J. (1995). Discrimination of speed distributions – sensitivity to statistical properties. *Vision Research, 35*(22), 3131–3144.

Atkeson, C. G., Hale, J. G., Pollick, F. E., Riley, M., Kotosaka, S., Schaal, S., et al. (2000). Using humanoid robots to study human behavior. *IEEE Intelligent Systems & Their Applications, 15*(4), 46–55.

Atkinson, A. P., & Adolphs, R. (2011). The neuropsychology of face perception: Beyond simple dissociations and functional selectivity. *Philosophical Transactions of the Royal Society B-Biological Sciences, 366*(1571), 1726–1738.

Atkinson, R. C., & Shiffrin, R. M. (1968). Human memory: A proposed system and its control processes. In K. W. Spence & J. T. Spence (Eds.), *The psychology of learning and motivation* (Vol. 2, pp. 89–195). New York: Academic Press.

Atwood, M. E., & Polson, P. G. (1976). A process model for water jug problems. *Cognitive Psychology, 8,* 191–216.

Atwood, M. E., Masson, M. E. J., & Polson, P. G. (1980). Further exploration with a process model for water jug problems. *Memory & Cognition, 8,* 182–192.

Averbach, E. A., & Coriell, A. S. (1961). Short-term memory in vision. *Bell Systems Technical Journal, 40,* 309–328.

Awh, E., & Jonides, J. (2001). Overlapping mechanisms of attention and spatial working memory. *Trends in Cognitive Sciences, 5*(3), 119–126.

Awh, E., & Pashler, H. (2000). Evidence for split attentional foci. *Journal of Experimental Psychology-Human Perception and Performance, 26*(2), 834–846.

Awh, E., Jonides, J., & Reuter-Lorenz, P. A. (1998). Rehearsal in spatial working memory. *Journal of Experimental Psychology-Human Perception and Performance, 24*(3), 780–790.

Awh, E., Vogel, E. K., & Oh, S. H. (2006). Interactions between attention and working memory. *Neuroscience, 139*(1), 201–208.

Ayotte, J., Peretz, I., & Hyde, K. (2002). Congenital amusia – A group study of adults afflicted with a music-specific disorder. *Brain, 125,* 238–251.

Ayotte, J., Peretz, I., Rousseau, I., Bard, C., & Bojanowski, M. (2000). Patterns of music agnosia associated with middle cerebral artery infarcts. *Brain, 123,* 1926–1938.

Ayton, P., & Onkal, D. (2005). Effects of ignorance and information on judgments and decisions. Unpublished ms.

B

Baars, B. J. (1988). *A cognitive theory of consciousness.* Cambridge; New York: Cambridge University Press.

Baars, B. J. (1997). *In the theater of consciousness: The workspace of the mind.* New York: Oxford University Press.

Baars, B. J. (2002). The conscious access hypothesis: origins and recent evidence. *Trends in Cognitive Sciences, 6*(1), 47–52.

Baars, B. J., & Motley, M. T. (1974). Spoonerisms: Experimental elicitation of human speech errors. Journal Supplement Abstract Service, Fall 1974. *Catalog of Selected Documents in Psychology.*

Baayen, R. H., Piepenbrock, R., & Gulikers, L. (1995). The CELEX Lexical Database (Release 2) [CD-ROM]. Philadelphia: University of Pennsylvania.

Bachiller, P., Bustos, P., & Manso, L. J. (2008). Attentional selection for action in mobile robots. In J. Aramburo & A. Ramirez-Trevino (Eds.), *Advances in robotics, automation and control.* InTech.

Bachorowski, J. A., & Owren, M. J. (1999). Acoustic correlates of talker sex and individual talker identity are present in a short vowel segment produced in running speech. *Journal of the Acoustical Society of America, 106*(2), 1054–1063.

Baddeley, A. (1993). Holy war or wholly unnecessary? Some thoughts on the 'conflict' between laboratory studies and everyday memory. In G. M. Davies & R. H. Logie (Eds.), *Memory in everyday life.* North-Holland: Elsevier Science Publishers.

Baddeley, A. C., & Lieberman, K. (1980). Spatial working memory. In R. S. Nickerson (Ed.), *Attention and performance* (Vol. 8, pp. 521–539). Hillsdale: Erlbaum.

Baddeley, A. D. (1978). The trouble with levels: A re-examination of Craik and Lockhart's framework for memory research. *Psychological Review, 85,* 139–152.

Baddeley, A. D. (1984). The fractionation of human memory. *Psychological Medicine, 14,* 259–264.

Baddeley, A. D. (1986). *Working memory.* Oxford: Oxford University Press.

Baddeley, A. D. (1992a). Consciousness and working memory. *Consciousness and Cognition, 1,* 3–6.

Baddeley, A. D. (1992b). Working memory. *Science, 255,* 556–559.

Baddeley, A. D. (1996a). The fractionation of working memory. *Proceedings of the National Academy of Sciences of the United States of America, 93,* 13468–13472.

Baddeley, A. D. (1996b). Exploring the central executive. *Quarterly Journal of Experimental Psychology: Human Experimental Psychology, 49*(A), 5–28.

Baddeley, A. D. (1999). *Essentials of human memory.* Hove: Psychology Press.

Baddeley, A. D. (2000). The episodic buffer: A new component of working memory? *Trends in Cognitive Sciences, 4,* 417–423.

Baddeley, A. D. (2003). Working memory: Looking back and looking forward. *Nature Reviews Neuroscience, 4*(10), 829–839.

Baddeley, A. D. (2004). The psychology of memory. In A. D. Baddeley, M. D. Kopelman

& B. A. Wilson (Eds.), *The essential handbook of memory disorders for clinicians* (pp. 1–13). London: Wiley.

Baddeley, A. D. (2007). *Working memory, thought and action.* Oxford: Oxford University Press.

Baddeley, A. D. (2009). Working memory. In A. D. Baddeley, M. W. Eysenck & M. C. Anderson (Eds.), *Memory.* Hove: Psychology Press.

Baddeley, A. D., & Andrade, J. (2000). Working memory and the vividness of imagery. *Journal of Experimental Psychology: General, 129,* 126–145.

Baddeley, A. D., & Hitch, G. (1974). Working memory. In G. H. Bower (Ed.), *The psychology of learning and motivation: Advances in research and theory* (Vol. 8, pp. 47–89). New York: Academic Press.

Baddeley, A. D., & Lieberman, K. (1980). Spatial working memory. In R. Nickerson (Ed.), *Attention and performance, vol. VI,* London: Academic Press.

Baddeley, A. D., & Logie, R. H. (1999). Working memory: The multiple component model. In A. Miyake & P. Shah (Eds.), *Models of working memory: Mechanisms of active maintenance and executive control* (pp. 28–61). New York: Cambridge University Press.

Baddeley, A. D., & Longman, D. J. A. (1978). The influence of length and frequency on training sessions on the rate of learning type. *Ergonomics, 21,* 627–635.

Baddeley, A. D., & Warrington, E. K. (1973). Memory coding and amnesia. *Neuropsychologia, 11,* 159–165.

Baddeley, A. D., & Wilson, B. (1988). Frontal amnesia and the dysexecutive syndrome. *Brain and Cognition, 7,* 212–30.

Baddeley, A. D., Chincotta, D. M., & Adlam, A. (2001). Working memory and the control of action: Evidence from task switching. *Journal of Experimental Psychology: General, 130,* 641–657.

Baddeley, A. D., Grant, S., Wight, E., & Thompson, N. (1975). Imagery and visual working memory. In P. M. Rabbitt and S. Dornic (Eds.), *Attention and performance,* vol. V, London: Academic Press.

Baddeley, A. D., Lewis, V. J., & Vallar, G. (1984). Exploring the articulatory loop. *Quarterly Journal of Experimental Psychology, 36,* 233–252.

Baddeley, A. D., Papagno, C., & Vallar, G. (1988). When long-term learning depends on short-term storage. *Journal of Memory and Language, 27,* 586–595.

Baddeley, A. D., Thomson, N., & Buchanan, M. (1975). Word length and the structure of short-term memory. *Journal of Verbal Learning and Verbal Behavior, 14,* 375–589.

Bahrick, H. P. (1983). The cognitive map of a city: Fifty years of learning and memory. In G. H. Bower (Ed.), *The psychology of learning and motivation, 17.* New York: Academic Press.

Bahrick, H. P. D. (1984). Fifty years of language attrition: Implications for programmatic research. *Modern Language Journal, 68,* 105–118.

Bahrick, H. P., Bahrick, P. O., & Wittlinger, R. P. (1975). Fifty years of memory for names and faces: A cross-sectional approach. *Journal of Experimental Psychology: General, 104,* 54–75.

Bahrick, H. P., Hall, L. K., & Berger, S. A. (1996). Accuracy and distortion in memory for high school grades. *Psychological Science, 7,* 265–271.

Baker, C. (2006). *Foundations of bilingual education and bilingualism.* 4th ed. Clevedon: Multilingual Matters.

Baker, C., & Prys Jones, S. (1998). *Encyclopedia of bilingualism and bilingual education.* Clevedon: Multilingual Matters.

Balota, D. A., & Chumbley, J. I. (1984). Are lexical decisions a good measure of lexical access? The role of word frequency in the neglected decision stage. *Journal of*

Experimental Psychology; Human Perception and Performance, 10, 340–357.

Banaji, M. R., & Crowder, R. (1989). The bankruptcy of everyday memory. *American Psychologist, 44,* 1185–1193.

Banbury, S. P., Macken, W. J., Tremblay, S., & Jones, D. M. (2001). Auditory distraction and short-term memory: phenomena and practical implications. *Human Factors, 43*(1), 12–29.

Banks, W. P. (2002). On timing relations between brain and world. *Consciousness and Cognition, 11,* 141–143.

Bard, E. G., Shillcock, R. C., & Altmann, G. T. M. (1988). The recognition of words after their acoustic offsets in spontaneous speech: Effects of subsequent context. *Perception & Psychophysics, 44,* 395–408.

Bard, P. (1934). Emotion. I. The neuro-humoral basis of emotional reactions In C. Murchison (Ed.), *A handbook of general experimental psychology.* Worcester: Clark University.

Baron, J. (1994). Nonconsequentialist decisions. *Behavioral and Brain Sciences, 17,* 1–42.

Baron, J., & Jurney, J. (1993). Norms against voting for coerced reform. *Journal of Personality and Social Psychology, 64,* 347–355.

Baron, J., & Ritov, I. (1993). Intuitions about penalties and compensation in the context of tort law. *Journal of Risk and Uncertainty, 7,* 17–33.

Barrett, H. C., & Kurzban, R. (2006). Modularity in cognition: Framing the debate. *Psychological Review, 113,* 628–647.

Barrett, L. F. (2006). Solving the emotion paradox: Categorization and the experience of emotion. *Personality and Social Psychology Review, 10,* 20–46.

Barsalou, L. W. (1983). Ad hoc categories. *Memory and Cognition, 11,* 211–227.

Barsalou, L. W. (1985). Ideals, central tendency, and frequency of instantiation as determinants of graded

structure in categories. *Journal of Experimental Psychology: Learning, Memory and Cognition, 11,* 629–654.

Barsalou, L. W. (1999). Perceptual symbol systems. *Behavioral and Brain Sciences, 22*(4), 577660+.

Barsalou, L. W. (2003). Situated simulation in the human conceptual system. *Language and Cognitive Processes, 18,* 513–562.

Barsalou, L. W. (2008). Grounded cognition. *Annual Review of Psychology, 59,* 617–645.

Bartha, L., & Benke, T. (2003). Acute conduction aphasia: An analysis of 20 cases. *Brain and Language, 85,* 93–108.

Bartlett, F. C. (1932). *Remembering: A study in experimental and social psychology.* Cambridge: Cambridge University Press.

Bartolomeo, P. (2002). The relationship between visual perception and visual mental imagery: A re-appraisal of the neuropsychological evidence. *Cortex, 38,* 357–378.

Barton, M. E., & Komatsu, L. K. (1989). Defining features of natural kinds and artifacts. *Journal of Psycholinguistic Research, 18,* 433–447.

Basden, B. H., & Basden, D. R. (1996). Directed forgetting: further comparisons of the item and list methods. *Memory, 4,* 633–653.

Basden, B. H., Basden, D. R., & Gargano, G. J. (1993). Directed forgetting in implicit and explicit memory tests: a comparison of methods. *Journal of Experimental Psychology: Learning, 19,* 603–616.

Bassetti, C., Vella, S., Donati, F., Wielepp, P., & Weder, B. (2000). SPECT during sleepwalking. *Lancet, 356*(9228), 484–485.

Bauer, R. M. (1984). Autonomic recognition of names and faces in prosopagnosia – A neuropsychological application of the guilty knowledge test. *Neuropsychologia, 22*(4), 457–469.

Baumann, O., & Belin, P. (2010). Perceptual scaling of voice identity: Common dimensions for different vowels and speakers. *Psychological Research-Psychologische Forschung, 74*(1), 110–120.

Baumeister, R. F. (1984). Choking under pressure – self-consciousness and paradoxical effects of incentives on skillful performance. *Journal of Personality and Social Psychology, 46*(3), 610–620.

Baumeister, R. F., & Showers, C. J. (1986). A review of paradoxical performance effects – Choking under pressure in sports and mental tests. *European Journal of Social Psychology, 16*(4), 361–383.

Baumgartner, T., Lutz, K., Schmidt, C. F., & Jancke, L. (2006). The emotional power of music: How music enhances the feeling of affective pictures. *Brain Research, 1075,* 151–164.

Bavelas, J., Gerwing, J., Sutton, C., & Prevost, D. (2008). Gesturing on the telephone: Independent effects of dialogue and visibility. *Journal of Memory and Language, 58*(2), 495–520.

Baxendale, S. (2004). Memories aren't made of this: Amnesia at the movies. *British Medical Journal, 329,* 1480–1483.

Bayley, P. J., Frascino, J. C., & Squire, L. R. (2005). Robust habit learning in the absence of awareness and independent of the medial temporal lobe, *Nature, 436,* 550–553.

Bear, M. F., Connors, B. W., & Paradiso, M. A. (2007). *Neuroscience: Exploring the brain.* 3rd Ed., Philadelphia, PA: Lippincott, Williams, Wilkins.

Beaman, C. P. (2010). Working memory and working attention: What could possibly evolve? *Current Anthropology, 51,* s1, s27–s38.

Beardsworth, T., & Buckner, T. (1981). The ability to recognize oneself from a video recording of one's movements without seeing one's body. *Bulletin of the Psychonomic Society, 18*(1), 19–22.

Beauchamp, M. S., & Martin, A. (2007). Grounding object concepts in perception and action: Evidence from fMRI studies of tools. *Cortex, 43*(3), 461–468.

Beauvois, M. F., & Derouesné, J. (1979). Phonological alexia: Three dissociations. *Journal of Neurology, Neurosurgery, & Psychiatry 42,* 1115–1124.

Beck, A. T. (1976). *Cognitive therapy and the emotional disorders.* New York: Meridian.

Beck, A. T. (1991). Cognitive therapy: A 30-year retrospective. *American Psychologist, 46,* 368–375.

Beck, A. T., Rush, A. J., Shaw, B. F., & Emery, G. (1979). *Cognitive therapy of depression.* New York: Guilford.

Becker, A. (2006). A review of writing model research based on cognitive processes. In A. S. Horning & A. Becker (Eds.), *Revision: History, theory, and practice,* Parlor Press, pp. 25–49.

Begg, I. & Harris, G. (1982). On the interpretation of syllogisms. *Journal of Verbal Learning and Verbal Behaviour 21,* 595–620.

Belin, P., Zatorre, R. J., Lafaille, P., Ahad, P., & Pike, B. (2000). Voice-selective areas in human auditory cortex. *Nature, 403*(6767), 309–312.

Belin, P., Fecteau, S., & Bedard, C. (2004). Thinking the voice: Neural correlates of voice perception. *Trends in Cognitive Sciences, 8*(3), 129–135.

Bentin, S., McCarthy, G., & Wood, C. C. (1985). Event related potentials, lexical decision and semantic priming, *Electroencephalography and Clinical Neurophysiology, 60,* 343–355.

Berent, I., Steriade, D., Lennertz, T., & Vaknin, V. (2007). What we know about what we have never heard: Evidence from perceptual illusions. *Cognition, 104,* 591–630.

Berndt, R. A., & Caramazza, A. (1980). A redefinition of the syndrome of Broca's aphasia:

implications for a neuropsychological model of language. *Applied Psycholinguistics, 1,* 225–278.

Bernstein, N. A. (1967). *The co-ordination and regulation of movements.* New York: Pergamon.

Berntsen, D. (2002). Tunnel memories for autobiographical events: Central details are remembered more frequently from shocking than from happy experiences. *Memory & Cognition, 30,* 1010–1020.

Berscheid, E. H. (1990). Contemporary vocabularies of emotion. In B. S. Moore & A. Isen (Eds.), *Affect & Social Behavior* (pp. 22–38). New York: Cambridge University Press.

Bertelson, P., & Radeau, M. (1981). Cross-modal bias and perceptual fusion with auditory-visual spatial discordance. *Perception & Psychophysics, 29*(6), 578–584.

Bertrand, M. Karlan, D., Mullainathan, S., Shafir, E., & Zinman, B. (2005). What's psychology worth? A field experiment in the consumer credit market. *National Bureau for Economic Research Working Paper No.11892.*

Best, C. T. (1988). The emergence of cerebral asymmetries in early human development: A literature review and a neuroembryological model. In D. L. Molfese & S. J. Segalowitz (Eds.), *Brain lateralization in children: Developmental implications* (pp. 5–34). New York: Guilford Press.

Bever, T. G. (1970). The cognitive basis for linguistics structures. In J. R. Hayes (Ed.), *Cognition and the development of language.* New York: Wiley.

Bialystok, E., Craik, F. I. M., Green, D. W., & Gollan, T. H. (2009). Bilingual minds. *Psychological Science in the Public Interest, 10,* 89–129.

Bialystok, E., Craik, F., & Luk, G. (2008). Cognitive control and lexical access in younger and older bilinguals. *Journal of Experimental Psychology: Learning, Memory and Cognition, 34*(4), 859–873.

Biederman, I. (1987). Recognition-by-components

– A theory of human image understanding. *Psychological Review, 94*(2), 115–147.

Biederman, I., & Gerhardstein, P. C. (1995). Viewpoint-dependent mechanisms in visual object recognition – Reply to Tarr and Bulthoff (1995). *Journal of Experimental Psychology-Human Perception and Performance, 21*(6), 1506–1514.

Biederman, I., Rabinowitz, J. C., Glass, A. L., & Stacy, E. W., Jr. (1974). On the information extracted from a glance at a scene. *Journal of Experimental Psychology, 103*(3), 597–600.

Biggs, J. B., Kember, D., & Leung, D. Y. P. (2001). The revised two factor study process questionnaire: R-SPQ-2F. *British Journal of Educational Psychology, 71,* 133–149.

Binder, J. R., Frost, J. A., Hammeke, T. A., Bellgowan, P. S. F., Springer, J. A., Kaufman, J. N., et al. (2000). Human temporal lobe activation by speech and nonspeech sounds. *Cerebral Cortex, 10*(5), 512–528.

Binford, T. O. (1981). Inferring surfaces from images. *Artificial Intelligence, 17*(1–3), 205–244.

Birbaumer, N., Ramos Murguialday, A., & Cohen, L. (2008). Brain-computer interface in paralysis. *Current Opinion in Neurology, 21,* 634–638.

Birnbaum, I. M., Parker, E. S., Hartley, J. T., & Noble, E. P. (1978). Alcohol and memory: Retrieval processes. *Journal of Verbal Learning and Verbal Behavior, 17,* 325–35.

Bjork, R. A. (1972). Theoretical implications of directed forgetting. In A. W. Melton & E. Martin (Eds.), *Coding processes in human memory.* (pp. 217–235). Washington, DC: Winston & Sons.

Bjork, R. A. (1970). Positive forgetting: The non-interference of items intentionally forgotten. *Journal of Verbal Learning and Verbal Behavior, 9,* 255–268.

Bjork, R. A., Bjork, E. L., & Anderson, M. C. (1998). Varieties of goal directed forgetting. In J. M. Golding &

C. M. MacLeod (Eds.), *Intentional forgetting: Interdisciplinary approaches.* Mahwah, NJ: Erlbaum.

Blair, R. J., & Cipolotti, L. (2000). Impaired social response reversal: A case of 'acquired sociopathy'. *Brain, 123,* 1122–1141.

Blaney, P. H. (1986). Affect and memory: A review. *Psychological Bulletin, 99,* 229–246.

Blanken, G., Dittmann, J., & Wallesch, C.-W. (2002). Parallel or serial activation of word forms in speech production? Neurolinguistic evidence from an aphasic patient. *Neuroscience Letters, 325,* 72–74.

Blasing, B., Calvo-Merino, B., Cross, E. S., Jola, C., Honisch, J., & Stevens, C. J. (2012). Neurocognitive control in dance perception and performance. *Acta Psychologica, 139*(2), 300–308.

Bliss, J. C., Crane, H. D., Mansfield, P. K., & Townsend, J. T. (1966). Information available in brief tactile presentations. *Perception and Psychophysics, 1,* 273–283.

Block, N. (1995). On a confusion about a function of consciousness. *Behavioral and Brain Sciences, 18*(2), 227–247.

Bloom, K. L., & Schuell, J. T. (1981). Effects of massed and distributed practice on the learning and retention of second language vocabulary. *Journal of Educational Research, 74,* 245–248.

Blum, H. (1973). Biological shape and visual science. *Journal of Theoretical Biology, 38*(2), 205–287.

Blumsteinm, D. T., Davitian, R., & Kaye, P. D. (2010). Do film soundtracks contain nonlinear analogues to influence emotion? *Biology Letters, 6,* 751–754.

Bock, J. K. (1986). Syntactic persistence in language production. *Cognitive Psychology, 18,* 355–387.

Bock, J. K., & Garnsey, S. M. (1998). Language processing. In W. Bechtel & G. Graham (Eds.), *A companion to cognitive science* (pp. 226–234). Malden: Blackwell.

Bock, K., & Levelt, W. J. M. (1994). Language production: Grammatical encoding. In M. A. Gernsbacher (Ed.), *Handbook of psycholinguistics* (pp. 945–984). London: Academic Press.

Boden, M. A. (2004). *The creative mind, 2nd revised edition.* London: Routledge.

Bond, Z. S., & Garnes, S. (1980). Misperception of fluent speech. In R. A. Cole (Ed.), *Perception and production of fluent speech.* Hillsdale: Erlbaum.

Bongaerts, T., Planken, B., & Schils, E. (1995). Can late starters attain a native accent in a foreign language: A test of the critical period hypothesis. In D. Singleton & Z. Lengyel (Eds.), *The age factor in second language acquisition* (pp. 30 –50). Clevedon: Multilingual Matters.

Bonhannon, J. N., III. (1988). Flashbulb memories for the Space Shuttle disaster: A tale of two theories. *Cognition, 29,* 179–196.

Bonneau, J., Preibusch, S., & Anderson, R. (2012). A birthday present every eleven wallets? The security of customer-chosen banking PINs. In *FC 2012, 16th International Conference on Financial Cryptography,* 1 March.

Boomer, D. S. & Laver, J. D. M. (1968). Slips of the tongue. *British Journal of Disorders of Communication, 3*(1), 1–12.

Borghi, A. M. (2005). Object concepts and action. In D. Pecher & R. A. Zwaan (Eds.), *Grounding cognition: The role of perception and action in memory, language, and thinking.* Cambridge: Cambridge University Press.

Born, J., Rasch, B., & Gais, S. (2006). Sleep to remember. *Neuroscientist, 12,* 410–424.

Bornstein, M. H. (1989). *Maternal responsiveness: Characteristics and consequences.* San Francisco: Jossey-Bass.

Boroditsky, L. (2001). Does language shape thought? Mandarin and English speakers' conceptions of time. *Cognitive Psychology, 43,* 1–22.

Boroditsky, L. (2010). Lost in translation, *Wall Street Journal*, 30 July.

Boroditsky, L., & Ramscar, M. (2002). The roles of body and mind in abstract thought. *Psychological Science*, *13*, 185–188.

Botvinick, M. M. (2008). Hierarchical models of behavior and prefrontal function. *Trends in Cognitive Sciences*, *12*(5), 201–208.

Botvinick, M. M., & Plaut, D. C. (2002). Representing task context: proposals based on a connectionist model of action. *Psychological Research*, *66*(4), 298–311.

Bouchard, T. J. Jr., & Hare, M. (1970). Size, performance and potential in brainstorming groups. *Journal of Applied Psychology*, *54*, 51–55.

Bousefield, W. A. (1953). The occurrence of clustering in recall of randomly arranged associates. *Journal of General Psychology*, *49*, 229–240.

Bouvier, S. E., & Engel, S. A. (2006). Behavioral deficits and cortical damage loci in cerebral achromatopsia. *Cerebral Cortex*, *16*(2), 183–191.

Bowden, E. M., & Jung-Beeman, M. (2003). Aha! Insight experience correlates with solution activation in the right hemisphere. *Psychonomic Bulletin Review*, *10*, 730–737.

Bower, G. H. (1970). Imagery as a relational organizer in associative learning. *Journal of Verbal Learning and Verbal Behavior*, *9*, 529–533.

Bower, G. H. (1981). Mood and memory. *American Psychologist*, *36*, 129–148.

Bower, G. H. (1991). Mood congruity of social judgements. In J. P. Forgas (Ed.), *Emotion and social judgements* (pp. 31–53). Oxford: Pergamon.

Bower, G. H. (1992). How might emotions affect learning? In F. A. Christianson (Ed.), *The handbook of emotion and memory: Research and theory* (pp. 3–32). Hillsdale, NJ: Lawrence Erlbaum.

Bower, G. H., & Karlin, M. B. (1974). Depth of processing pictures of faces and recognition memory. *Journal of Experimental Psychology*, *103*, 751–757.

Bower, G. H., Clark, M. C., Lesgold, A. M., & Winzenz, D. (1969). Hierarchical retrieval schemes in recall of categorised word lists. *Journal of Verbal Learning and Verbal Behavior*, *8*, 323–343.

Boye, M., Gunturkun, O., & Vauclair, J. (2005). Right ear advantage for conspecific calls in adults and subadults, but not infants, California sea lions (Zalophus californianus): hemispheric specialization for communication?, *European Journal of Neuroscience*, *21*, 1727–173.

Bracewell, R. J. (1974). *Interpretation factors in the four card selection task*. Paper presented at the Selection Task Conference, Trento, Italy, April 17–19.

Bradley, M. M., Greenwald, M. K., Petry, M. C., & Lang, P.J. (1992). Remembering pictures: Pleasure and arousal in memory. *Journal of Experimental Psychology: Learning, Memory, and Cognition*, *18*, 379–390.

Braine, M. D. S., Reiser, B. J., & Rumain, B. (1984). Some empirical justification for a theory of natural propositional logic. In G. H. Bower (Ed.), *The psychology of learning and motivation*. Vol. 18. New York: Academic Press.

Bramham, C. R., & Srebo, B. (1989). Synaptic plasticity in the hippocampus is modulated by behavioral state. *Brain Research*, *493*, 74–86.

Braun, A. R., Balkin, T. J., Wesensten, N. J., Carson, R. E., Varga, M., Baldwin, P., et al. (1997). Regional cerebral blood flow throughout the sleep-wake cycle – An (H2O)-O-15 PET study. *Brain*, *120*, 1173–1197.

Brázdil, M., Marecek, R., Urbánek, T., Kašpárek, T., Mikl, M., Rektor, I., & Zeman, A. (2012). Unveiling the mystery of déjà vu: The structural anatomy of déjà vu. *Cortex*, *48*(9), 1240–1243.

Breazeal, C. L. (2004). *Designing sociable robots*. Cambridge: MIT Press.

Bregman, A. S. (1990). *Auditory scene analysis: The perceptual organization of sound*. Cambridge, MA: MIT Press.

Breiman, L., Friedman, J. H., Olshen, R. A., & Stone, C. J. (1993). *Classification and regression trees*. New York: Chapman Hall.

Brener, R. (1940). An experimental investigation of memory span. *Journal of Educational Psychology*, *26*, 467–483.

Brenner, E., & Smeets, J. B. J. (1996). Size illusion influences how we lift but not how we grasp an object. *Experimental Brain Research*, *111*(3), 473–476.

Brewer, W. F. (1996). What is recollective memory? In D. C. Rubin (Ed.), *Remembering our past: Studies in autobiographical memory* (pp. 19–66). New York: Cambridge University Press.

Brewer, W. F. (1999). Bartlett's concept of the schema and its impact on theories of knowledge representation in contemporary cognitive psychology. In A. Saito (Ed.), *Bartlett, culture and cognition*. (pp. 69–89). Hove: Psychology Press.

Brewer, W. F., & Treyens, J. C. (1981). Role of schemata in memory for places. *Cognitive Psychology*, *13*, 207–230.

Brigham, J. C. (2002). Face identification: Basic processes and developmental changes. In M. L. Eisen, J. A. Quas & G. S. Goodman (Eds.), *Memory and suggestibility in the forensic interview* (pp. 115–140). New Jersey: Erlbaum.

Brigham, J. C., Bennett, L. B., Meissner, C. A., & Mitchell, T. L. (2007). *The influence of race on eyewitness memory*. New Jersey: Lawrence Erlbaum.

Broadbent, D. E. (1958). *Perception and communication*. London: Pergamon.

Broadbent, D. E. (1971). *Decision and stress*. London: Academic Press.

Broadbent, D. E. (1975). The magic number seven after fifteen years. In A. Kennedy &

A. Wilkes (Eds.), *Studies in long-term memory* (pp. 3–18). New York: John Wiley & Sons.

Broadbent, D. E. (1982). Task combination and selective intake of information. *Acta Psychologica*, *50*(3), 253–290.

Broadbent, D. E., & Broadbent, M. H. P. (1987). From detection to identification – Response to multiple targets in rapid serial visual presentation. *Perception & Psychophysics*, *42*(2), 105–113.

Broca, P. (1861). Remarques sur le siège de la faculté du langage articulé suivies d'une observation d'aphémie. *Bulletins de la Société Anatomique de Paris*, *6*, 330.

Brooks, L. R. (1967). The suppression of visualization by reading. *Quarterly Journal of Experimental Psychology*, *19*, 289–299.

Brooks, L. R. (1968). Spatial and verbal components of the act of recall. *Canadian Journal of Psychology*, *22*, 349–368.

Brown, A. S. (1991). A review of the tip-of-the-tongue experience. *Psychological Bulletin*, *109*, 204–223.

Brown, A. S. (2002). Consolidation theory and retrograde amnesia in humans. *Psychonomic Bulletin & Review*, *9*, 403–425.

Brown, A. S. (2003). A review of the déjà vu experience. *Psychological Bulletin*, *129*, 394–413.

Brown, A. S. (2004a). The déjà vu illusion. *Current Directions in Psychological Science*, *13*, 256–259.

Brown, A. S. (2004b). *The déjà vu experience*. New York: Psychology Press.

Brown, A. S., & Marsh, E. J. (2010). Digging into déjà vu: Recent research findings on possible mechanisms. In B. H. Ross (Ed.), *The psychology of learning and motivation*, Vol. 53 (pp. 33 –62). Burlington: Academic Press.

Brown, C. M., & Hagoort, P. (1993). The processing nature of the N400: Evidence from masked priming. *Journal of Cognitive Neuroscience*, *5*, 34 –44.

Brown, G. D. A. (1984). A frequency count of 190,000 words in the London-Lund Corpus of English Conversation. *Behavioural Research Methods Instrumentation and Computers, 16*(6), 502–532.

Brown, R., & Kulik, J. (1977). Flashbulb memories. *Cognition, 5*, 73–99.

Brown, R., & McNeill, D. (1966). The 'tip of the tongue phenomenon'. *Journal of Verbal Learning and Verbal Behavior, 5*, 325–337.

Brown, R. M., & Robertson, E.M. (2007). Off-line processing: reciprocal interactions between declarative and procedural memories. *The Journal of Neuroscience, 27*(39), 10468–75.

Bruce, K. R., & Pihl, R. O. (1997). Forget 'drinking to forget': Enhanced consolidation of emotionally charged memory by alcohol. *Experimental Clinical Psychopharmacology, 5*, 242–50.

Bruce, V., & Young, A. (1986). Understanding face recognition. *British Journal of Psychology, 77*, 305–327.

Bruno, N. (2001). When does action resist visual illusions? *Trends in Cognitive Sciences, 5*(9), 379–382.

Buccino, G., Vogt, S., Ritzl, A., Fink, G. R., Zilles, K., Freund, H. J., et al. (2004). Neural circuits underlying imitation learning of hand actions: An event-related fMRI study. *Neuron, 42*(2), 323–334.

Buchwald, A. M. (1977). Depressive mood and estimates of reinforcement frequency. *Journal of Abnormal Psychology, 86*, 443–446.

Buckingham, H. W. (1981). Explanations for the concept of apraxia of speech. In M. T. Sarno (Ed.), *Acquired aphasia* (pp. 271–302). New York: Academic Press.

Buckner, R. L., Andrews-Hanna, J. R., & Schacter, D. L. (2008). The brain's default network: anatomy, function and relevance to disease. *Annals of the New York Academy of Science, 1124*, 1–38.

Bugelski, B. R., Kidd, E., & Segmen, J. (1968). Image as a mediator in one-trial paired associate learning. *Journal of Experimental Psychology, 76*, 69–73.

Bulevich, J. B., Roediger, H. L., Balota, D. A., & Butler, A. C. (2006). Failures to find suppression of episodic memories in the Think/No-Think paradigm. *Memory, & Cognition, 34*, 1569–1577.

Buonomano, D. V., & Karmarkar, U. R. (2002). How do we tell time? *Neuroscientist, 8*, 42–51.

Burgess, N., & Hitch, G. J. (2005). Computational models of working memory: Putting long-term memory into context. *Trends in Cognitive Science, 9*, 535–541.

Burgess, P. W., Dumontheil, I., Gilbert, S. J., Okuda, J., Schölvinck, M. L., & Simons, J. S. (2007). On the role of rostral prefrontal cortex (area 10) in prospective memory. In M. Kliegel, M. A. McDaniel & G. O. Einsten (Eds.), *Prospective memory: Cognitive, neuroscience, developmental and applied perspectives*. Hillsdale: Erlbaum.

Burke, M., & Matthews, A. (1992). Autobiographical memory and clinical anxiety. *Cognition and Emotion, 6*, 23–35.

Burnett, M., & Kleiman, D. (2005). *Perfect passwords: Selection, protection, authentication.* Boston, MA: Syngress Publishing.

Bushman, B. (2002). Does venting anger feed or extinguish the flame? Catharsis, rumination, distraction, anger, and aggressive responding. *Personality and Social Psychology Bulletin, 28*(6), 724–731.

Butler, A. C., Chapman, J. E., Forman, E. M., & Beck, A. T. (2006). The empirical status of cognitive-behavioral therapy: A review of meta-analyses. *Clinical Psychology Review 26*, 17–31.

Butters, N. (1984). Alcoholic Korsakoffs syndrome: An update. *Seminars in Neurology, 4*, 226–244.

Butterworth, B. (1980). Evidence from pauses in speech. In B. Butterworth (Ed.), *Language production, Volume 1. Speech and talk.* (pp. 155–176). London: Academic Press.

Byrne, R. M. J. (1989). Suppressing valid inferences with conditionals. *Cognition, 31*, 61–83.

Byrne, R. W., & Russon, A. E. (1998). Learning by imitation: A hierarchical approach. *Behavioral and Brain Sciences, 21*(5), 667–684.

C

Cacioppo, J. T., Klein, D. J., Berntson, G. G., & Hatfield, E. (1993). The psychophysiology of emotion. In R. Lewis & J. M. Haviland (Eds.), *The handbook of emotion* (pp. 119–142). New York: Guilford Press.

Cahill, L., Babinsky, R. Markowitch, H. J., & McGaugh. J. L. (1995). The amygdala and emotional memory. *Nature, 377*, 295–296.

Calder, A. J., & Young, A. W. (2005). Understanding the recognition of facial identity and facial expression. *Nature Reviews Neuroscience, 6*(8), 641–651.

Calvo-Merino, B., Glaser, D. E., Grezes, J., Passingham, R. E., & Haggard, P. (2005). Action observation and acquired motor skills: An fMRI study with expert dancers. *Cerebral Cortex, 15*(8), 1243–1249.

Calvo-Merino, B., Grezes, J., Glaser, D. E., Passingham, R. E., & Haggard, P. (2006). Seeing or doing? Influence of visual and motor familiarity in action observation. *Current Biology, 16*(19), 1905–1910.

Calvo-Merino, B., Jola, C., Glaser, D. E., & Haggard, P. (2008). Towards a sensorimotor aesthetics of performing art. *Consciousness and Cognition, 17*(3), 911–922.

Canli, T., Zhao, Z., Brewer, J., Gabrieli, J. D. E., & Cahill, L. (2000). Activation in the human amygdala associates event-related arousal with later memory for individual emotional experience. *Journal of Neuroscience, 20*, RC99, 1–5.

Cannon, W. B. (1927). The James-Lange theory of emotions. *American Journal of Psychology, 39*, 115–124.

Caplan, D. (1987). *Neurolinguistics and linguistic aphasiology.* New York: Cambridge University Press.

Caplan, D., & Hildebrandt, N. (1988). *Disorders of syntactic comprehension.* Cambridge, MA: MIT Press.

Caplan, D., Alpert, N., & Waters, G. (1998). Effects of syntactic structure and prepositional number on patterns of regional cerebral blood flow. *Journal of Cognitive Neuroscience, 10*, 541–552.

Carey, D. P. (2001). Do action systems resist visual illusions? *Trends in Cognitive Sciences, 5*(3), 109–113.

Carlston, D. L. (2011). Benefits of student-generated note packets: A preliminary investigation of SQ3R implementation. *Teaching of Psychology, 38*, 142–146.

Carpenter, P. A., & Just, M. A. (1983). What your eyes do while your mind is reading. In K. Rayner (Ed.), *Eye movements in reading: Perceptual and language processes.* New York: Academic.

Carr, T. H., Davidson, B. J., & Hawkins, H. L. (1978). Perceptual flexibility in word recognition: Strategies affect orthographic computation but not lexical access. *Journal of Experimental Psychology: Human Perception and Performance, 4*, 674–690.

Carramazza, A., & Zurif, E. (1976). Dissociations of algorithmic and heuristic processes in sentence comprehension: Evidence from aphasia. *Brain and Language, 3*, 572–582.

Caspers, S., Zilles, K., Laird, A. R., & Eickhoff, S. B. (2010). ALE meta-analysis of action observation and imitation in the human brain. *Neuroimage, 50*(3), 1148–1167.

Cassiday, K. L., McNally, R. J., & Zeitlin, S. B. (1992).

Cognitive processing of trauma cues in rape victims with posttraumatic stress disorder. *Cognitive Therapy and Research, 16,* 28395.

Casscells, W., Schoenberger, A., & Grayboys, T. (1978). Interpretation by physicians of clinical laboratory results. *New England Journal of Medicine, 299,* 999–1000.

Castel, A. D., Pratt, J., & Drummond, E. (2005). The effects of action video game experience on the time course of inhibition of return and the efficiency of visual search. *Acta Psychologica, 119*(2), 217–230.

Cattaneo, L., Sandrini, M., & Schwarzbach, J. (2010). State-dependent TMS reveals a hierarchical representation of observed acts in the temporal, parietal, and premotor cortices. *Cerebral Cortex, 20*(9), 2252–2258.

Cattell, J. M. (1888). 'Psychometrische untersuchungen', *Philosophische Studien, 4,* 241–250.

Ceraso, J., & Provitera, A. (1971). Sources of error in syllogistic reasoning. *Cognitive Psychology, 2,* 400–410.

Chalmers, A. F. (1978). *What is this thing called science?* Milton Keynes: Open University Press.

Chalmers, D. J. (1996). *The conscious mind: In search of a fundamental theory.* New York: Oxford University Press.

Chambers, D., & Reisberg, D. (1985). Can mental images be ambiguous? *Journal of Experimental Psychology: Human Perception and Performance, 11,* 317–328.

Chambers, D., & Reisberg, D. (1992). What an image depicts depends on what an image means. *Cognitive Psychology, 24,* 145–174.

Chapman, C. E. (1994). Active versus passive touch – Factors influencing the transmission of somatosensory signals to primary somatosensory cortex. *Canadian Journal of Physiology and Pharmacology, 72*(5), 558–570.

Chapman, L. J., & Chapman, A. P. (1959). Atmosphere effect re-examined. *Journal of*

Experimental Psychology, 58, 220–226.

Charness, N. (1989). Expertise in chess and bridge. In D. Klahr & K. Kotovsky (Eds.), *Complex information processing: the impact of H. A. Simon.* Hillsdale, NJ: Lawrence Erlbaum.

Chartrand, J.-P., Peretz, I., & Belin, P. (2008). Auditory recognition expertise and domain specificity. *Brain Research, 1220,* 191–198.

Chase, W. G., & Simon, H. A. (1973). Perception in chess. *Cognitive Psychology, 4,* 55–81.

Chater, N., & Oaksford, M. (2001). Human rationality and the psychology of reasoning. where do we go from here? *British Journal of Psychology, 92,* 193–216.

Chen, Y., Fu, S., Iversen, S. D., Smith, S. M., & Matthews, P. M. (2002). Testing for dual brain processing routes in reading: a direct contrast of Chinese character and pinyin reading using fMRI. *Journal of Cognitive Neuroscience, 14*(7), 1088–1098.

Chen, Z-Y., Cowell, P. E., Varley, R., & Wang, Y.-C. (2009). A cross-language study of verbal and visuospatial working memory span. *Journal of Clinical and Experimental Neuropsychology, 31,* 385–391.

Cheney, D. L., & Seyfarth, R. M. (2005). Constraints and preadaptations in the earliest stages of language evolution. *Linguistic Review, 22,* 135–159.

Cheng, P. C.-H. (1996). Scientific discovery with law encoding diagrams. *Creativity Research Journal, 9,* 145–162.

Cheng, P. W., & Holyoak, K. J. (1985). Pragmatic reasoning schemas. *Cognitive Psychology, 17,* 391–416.

Cherry, E. C. (1953). Some experiments on the recognition of speech, with one and with two ears. *The Journal of the Acoustical Society of America, 25*(5), 975–79.

Chi, M. T. H., Glaser, R., & Rees, E. (1982). Expertise in problem solving. In R. J. Sternberg (Ed.), *Advances in the psychology of human*

intelligence, Vol.1, Hillsdale, NJ: Lawrence Erlbaum.

Chiel, H. J., & Beer, R. D. (1997). The brain has a body: adaptive behavior emerges from interactions of nervous system, body and environment. *Trends in Neurosciences, 20*(12), 553–557.

Chierchia, G. (2001). Linguistics and language. In R. A. Wilson & F. C. Keil (Eds.), *The MIT encyclopedia of the cognitive sciences,* pp. xci–cviii. Cambridge, MA: MIT Press.

Chincotta, D., & Hoosain, R. (1995). Reading rate, articulatory suppression and bilingual digit span. *European Journal of Cognitive Psychology, 7,* 201–211.

Chincotta, D., & Underwood, G. (1996). Mother tongue, language of schooling and bilingual digit span, *British Journal of Psychology, 87,* 193–208.

Chomsky, N. (1980). *Rules and representations.* Oxford: Blackwell.

Chomsky, N. (1957). *Syntactic structures.* The Hague: Mouton.

Chomsky, N. (1965). *Aspects of the theory of syntax.* Cambridge, MA: MIT Press.

Chong, S. C., & Treisman, A. (2003). Representation of statistical properties. *Vision Research, 43*(4), 393–404.

Chou, K. L., Lee, T. M. C., & Ho, A. H. Y. (2007). Does mood state change risk taking tendency in older adults. *Psychology and Aging, 22,* 310–318.

Christianson, S. A. (1989). Flashbulb memories: Special but not so special. *Memory and Cognition, 17,* 435–443.

Christianson, S. A. (1992). Emotional stress and eyewitness memory: A critical review. *Psychological Bulletin, 112,* 284–309.

Christoff, K., Gordon, A., & Smith, R. (2008). The role of spontaneous thought in human cognition. In O. Vartanian and D. R. Mandel (Eds.), *Neuroscience of decision making.* New York: Psychology Press.

Chubb, C., Nam, J. H., Bindman, D. R., & Sperling, G. (2007). The three dimensions of human visual sensitivity to first-order contrast statistics. *Vision Research, 47*(17), 2237–2248.

Chun, M. M. (2011). Visual working memory as visual attention sustained internally over time. *Neuropsychologia, 49*(6), 1407–1409.

Chun, M. M., Golomb, J. D., & Turk-Browne, N. B. (2011). A taxonomy of external and internal attention. *Annual Review of Psychology, 62,* 73–101.

Cienki, A., & Müller, C. (2008). Metaphor, gesture, and thought. In R. W. Gibbs (Ed.), *The Cambridge handbook of metaphor and thought* (pp. 483–501). Cambridge: Cambridge University Press.

Claparede, E. (1911/ 1950). Recognition and me-ness. In D. Rapaport (Ed.), *The organization and pathology of thought: Selected sources* (pp. 58–75). New York: Columbia University Press. Originally published 1911.

Clark, A. (1997). *Being there: Putting brain, body, and world together again.* Cambridge, MA; London: MIT Press.

Clark, D. M., & Teasdale, J. D. (1982). Diurnal variation in clinical depression and accessibility of memories of positive and negative experiences. *Journal of Abnormal Psychology, 91,* 87–95.

Clark, E. V. (2003). *First language acquisition.* Cambridge: Cambridge University Press.

Clark, H. H., & Clark, E. V. (1977). *Psychology and language: An introduction to psycholinguistics.* New York: Harcourt Brace Jovanovich.

Clark, H. H., & Fox Tree, J. E. (2002). Using uh and um in spontaneous speaking. *Cognition, 84,* 73–111.

Clark, J. J., & Yuille, A. L. (1990). *Data fusion for sensory information processing systems.* Boston: Kluwer Academic.

Clifton, C., Jr., Staub, A., & Rayner, K. (2007). Eye movements in reading words and sentences. In R. Van

Gompel, M. Fisher, W. Murray, and R. L. Hill (Eds.), *Eye movement research: A window on mind and brain* (pp. 341–372). Oxford: Elsevier.

Clore, G. L. (1992). Cognitive phenomenology: Feelings and the construction of judgment. In L. L. Martin & A. Tesser (Eds.), *The construction of social judgment* (pp. 133–164). Hillsdale, NJ: Lawrence Erlbaum.

Clore, G. L., & Ortony, A. (2000). Cognition in emotion: Always, sometimes, or never? In L. Nadel, R. Lane & G. L. Ahern (Eds.), *The cognitive neuroscience of emotion*. New York: Oxford University Press.

Cobos, P., Sánchez, M., Pérez, N., & Vila, J. (2004). Effects of spinal cord injuries on the subjective component of emotions. *Cognition and Emotion, 18*, 281–287.

Coderre, E. L., Filippi, C. G., Newhouse, P. A., & Dumas, J. A. (2008). The Stroop Effect in Kana and Kanji scripts in native Japanese speakers: An fMRI study. *Brain and Language, 107*(2), 124–132.

Coenen, A. M. L., & Van Luijtelaar, E. L. J. M. (1997). Effects of benzodiazepines, sleep and sleep deprivation on vigilance and memory. *Acta Neurologica Belgica, 97*, 123–129.

Cohen, A. J. (2001). Music as a source of emotion in film. In P. Juslin & J. Sloboda (Eds.), *Music and emotion: Theory and research* (pp. 249–272). Oxford: Oxford University Press.

Cohen, L. J. (1981). Can human irrationality be experimentally demonstrated? *Behavioral and Brain Sciences, 4*, 317–331.

Cohen, N. J., & Squire, L. R. (1981). Retrograde amnesia and remote memory impairment. *Neuropsychologia, 19*, 337–356.

Colchester, A., Kingsley, D., Lasserson, D. et al. (2001). Structural MRI volumetric analysis in patients with organic amnesia: 1. Methods and comparative findings across diagnostic groups. *Journal of Neurology & Psychiatry, 71*, 13–22.

Cole, L. E. (1953). *Human behavior: Psychology as a bio-social science.* Yonkers-On-Hudson, NY: World Book Company.

Cole, M., Gay, J., Glick, J., & Sharp, J. (1971). *The cultural context of learning and thinking: An exploration in experimental anthropology.* New York: Basic Books.

Colle, H. A., & Welsh, A. (1976). Acoustic masking in primary memory. *Journal of Verbal Learning and Verbal Behavior, 15*, 17–32.

Coltheart, M., Rastle, K., Perry, C., Langdon, R., & Ziegler, J. (2001). DRC: A dual route cascaded model of visual word recognition and reading aloud. *Psychological Review, 108*, 204–256.

Comrie, B. (2005). Writing systems. In M. Haspelmath, M. S. Dryer, D. Gil & B. Comrie (Eds.), *The World atlas of language structures* (pp. 568–571). Oxford: Oxford University Press.

Comrie, B. (1989). *Language universals and linguistic typology.* Oxford: Blackwell.

Connor, S. (2000). *Dumbstruck: A cultural history of ventriloquism.* Oxford: Oxford University Press.

Connors, E., Miller, N., Lundregan, T., & McEwan, T. (1996). *Convicted by juries, exonerated by science: Case studies in the use of DNA evidence to establish innocence after trial*: National Institute of Justice.

Constable, A., Stackhouse, J., & Wells, B. (1997). Developmental word-finding difficulties and phonological processing: The case of the missing handcuffs. *Applied Psycholinguistics, 18*, 507–536.

Conway, M. A. (1992). A structural model of autobiographical memory. In M. A. Conway, H. Spinnler & W. A. Wagenaar (Eds.), *Theoretical perspectives on autobiographical memory* (pp. 167–194). Dordrecht, The Netherlands: Kluwer Academic Publishers.

Conway, M. A. (1995). *Flashbulb memories.* Hillsdale, NJ: Erlbaum.

Conway, M. A. (2009). Episodic memories. *Neuropsychologia, 47*(11), 2305–13.

Conway, M. A., Anderson, S. J., Larsen, S. F., Donnelly, C. M., McDaniel, M. A., et al. (1994). The formation of flashbulb memories. *Memory and Cognition, 22*, 326–343.

Conway, M. A., Cohen, G., & Stanhope, N. (1992). Very long-term memory for knowledge acquired at school and university. *Applied Cognitive Psychology, 6*, 467–482.

Cooke, S. F., & Bliss, T. V. (2006). Plasticity in the human central nervous system. *Brain, 129*, 1659–1673.

Cooney, J. W., & Gazzaniga, M. S. (2003). Neurological disorders and the structure of human consciousness. *Trends in Cognitive Sciences, 7*(4), 161–165.

Cooper, R. P., & Shallice, T. (2000): Contention scheduling and the control of routine activities. *Cognitive Neuropsychology, 17*, 297–338.

Cooper, R. P., Schwartz, M. F., Yule, P., & Shallice, T. (2005). The simulation of action disorganisation in complex activities of daily living. *Cognitive Neuropsychology, 22*(8), 959–1004.

Copeland, D. E., & Radvansky, G. A. (2001). Phonological similarity in working memory. *Memory and Cognition, 29*, 774–776.

Corballis, M. C. (1994). Split decisions: problems in the interpretation of results from commissurotomized subjects. *Behavioral Brain Research, 64*(1–2), 163–172.

Corballis, M. C. (2003). From mouth to hand gesture: speech and the evolution of right handedness. *Behavioral & Brain Sciences, 26*, 199–260.

Corkin, S. (2002). 'What's new with the amnesic patient H.M.?' *Nature Reviews Neuroscience, 3*(2), 153–160.

Cornell, T. L., Fromkin, V. A., & Mauner, G. (1993). A linguistic approach to language processing in Broca's aphasia: A paradox resolved. *Current Directions in Psychological Science, 2*, 47–52.

Coslett, H. B. (1991). Read but not write 'idea': Evidence for a third reading mechanism. *Brain and Language, 40*, 425–443.

Cosmides, L. (1989). The logic of social exchange: Has natural selection shaped how humans reason? Studies with the Wason selection task. *Cognition, 31*, 187–276.

Cosmides, L., & Tooby, J. (1996). Are humans good intuitive statisticians after all? Rethinking some conclusions from the literature on judgment under uncertainty. *Cognition, 58*, 1–73.

Cowan, N. (1984). On short and long auditory stores. *Psychological Bulletin, 96*, 341–370.

Cowan, N. (1988). Evolving conceptions of memory storage, selective attention, and their mutual constraints within the human information processing system. *Psychological Bulletin, 104*, 163–191.

Cowan, N. (1995a). *Attention and memory: An integrated framework.* New York: Oxford University Press.

Cowan, N. (1995b). Verbal working memory: A view with a room. *American Journal of Psychology, 108*, 123–155.

Cowan, N. (1998). Visual and auditory working memory capacity. *Trends in Cognitive Sciences, 2*, 77–78.

Cowan, N. (1999). An embedded-processes model of working memory. In A. Miyake & P. Shah (Eds.), *Models of working memory: Mechanisms of active maintenance and executive control* (pp. 62–101). Cambridge: Cambridge University Press.

Cowan, N. (2008). Sensory memory. In H. L. Roediger, III (Ed.), & J. Byrne (Vol. Ed.), *Cognitive psychology of memory: Vol. 2. Learning and memory: A comprehensive reference* (pp. 23–32). Oxford: Elsevier.

Cowan, N. (2010). The magical mystery four: How is working memory capacity limited, and why? *Current Directions in Psychological Science, 19*, 51–57.

Cowan, N., Beshin, N., & Della Sala, S. (2004).Verbal recall in amnesiacs under conditions of diminished retroactive interference. *Brain*, *27*, 825–834.

Cowan, N., Morey, C. C., & Chen, Z. (2007). The legend of the magical number seven. In S. Della Sala (Ed.), *Tall tales about the mind & brain: Separating fact from fiction* (pp. 45–59). Oxford: Oxford University Press.

Craig, A. D. (2002). How do you feel? Interoception: The sense of the physiological condition of the body. *Nature Reviews Neuroscience*, *3*, 655–666.

Craig, A. D. (2004). Human feelings: Why are some more aware than others? *Trends in Cognitive Sciences*, *8*, 239–241.

Crick, F. (1994). *The astonishing hypothesis: The scientific search for the soul.* New York: Scribner.

Crick, F. (1995). *The astonishing hypothesis: The scientific search for the soul.* London: Touchstone.

Craik, F. I. M. (1970). The fate of primary memory items in free recall. *Journal of Verbal Learning and Verbal Behavior*, *9*, 143–148.

Craik, F. I. M. (1986). A functional account of age differences in memory. In F. Klix and H. Hagendorf (Eds.), *Human memory and cognitive capabilities: Mechanisms and performances* (pp. 409–422). Amsterdam: Elsevier Science Publishers, North-Holland.

Craik, F. I. M. (2002). Levels of processing: Past, present . . . and future. *Memory*, *10*, 305–318.

Craik, F. I. M., & Lockhart, R. S. (1972). Levels of processing: A framework for memory research. *Journal of Verbal Learning and Verbal Behavior*, *11*, 671–684.

Craik, F. I. M., & Tulving, E. (1975). Depth of processing and the retention of words in episodic memory. *Journal of Experimental Psychology: General*, *104*, 268–294.

Crombag, H. F. M., Wagenaar, W. A., & van

Koppen, P. J. (1996). Crashing memories and the problem of 'source monitoring'. *Applied Cognitive Psychology*, *10*, 95–104.

Cross, E. S., Hamilton, A. F., & Grafton, S. T. (2006). Building a motor simulation de novo: Observation of dance by dancers. *Neuroimage*, *31*(3), 1257–1267.

Crowder, R. G. (1976). *Principles of learning and memory*. Hillsdale, NJ: Erlbaum.

Cruse, D., Chennu, S., Chatell, C., Bekinschtein, T. A., Fernandez-Espejo, D., Pickard, J. D., Laureys, S., & Owen, A. M. (2011). Bedside detection of awareness in the vegetative state: A cohort study. *The Lancet*, September, 2011 Online issue, http://dx.doi.org/10.1016/S0140-6736(11)61224-5.

Crystal, D. (1997). *The Cambridge encyclopaedia of language*, 2nd ed. Cambridge: Cambridge University Press.

Crystal, D. (1998). *Language play*. Harmondsworth: Penguin.

Crystal, D. (2000). *Language death*. Cambridge: Cambridge University Press.

Crystal, D. (2008). *Txtng: The Gr8 Db8*. Oxford: Oxford University Press.

Cubelli, R., & Della Sala, S. (2008). Flashbulb memories: special but not iconic. *Cortex*, *44*, 908–909.

Cuetos, F., & Mitchell, D. C. (1988). Cross-linguistic differences in parsing: Restrictions on the use of the Late Closure strategy in Spanish. *Cognition*, *30*, 73–105.

Curtiss, S. (1977). *Genie: A psycholinguistic study of a modern-day 'wild child'.* Boston: Academic Press.

Curtiss, S. (1981). Dissociations between language and cognition: Cases and implications. *Journal of Autism and Developmental Disorders*, *2*, 15–30.

Cushing, S. (1994). *Fatal words: Communication clashes and aircraft crashes.* Chicago: University of Chicago Press.

Cutler, A., & Butterfield, S. (1992). Rhythmic cues to speech segmentation: Evidence

from juncture misperception. *Journal of Memory and Language*, *31*, 218–236.

Cutler, A., & Carter, D. M. (1987). The predominance of strong initial syllables in the English vocabulary. *Computer Speech, & Language*, *2*, 133–142.

Cutler, A., & Norris, D. G. (1988). The role of strong syllables in segmentation for lexical access. *Journal of Experimental Psychology: Human Perception and Performance*, *14*, 113–121.

Cutler, A., & Norris, D. (1979). Monitoring sentence comprehension. In W. E. Cooper & E. T. C. Walker (Ed.), *Sentence processing: Psycholinguistic studies presented to Merill Garrett* (pp. 113–134). Hillsdale, NJ: Erlbaum.

Cutler, A., Dahan, D., & van Donselaar, W. (1997). Prosody in the comprehension of spoken language: A literature review. *Language and Speech*, *40*, 141–210.

Cutler, A., Mehler, J., Norris, D. G., & Segui, J. (1986). The syllable's differing role in the segmentation of French and English. *Journal of Memory and Language*, *25*, 385–400.

Cutler, A., Mehler, J., Norris, D. G., & Segui, J. (1992). The monolingual nature of speech segmentation by bilinguals. *Cognitive Psychology*, *24*, 381–410.

Cutting, J. E. (2005). Perceiving scenes in film and in the world. In J. D. Anderson & B. F. Anderson (Eds.), *Moving image theory: Ecological considerations* (pp. 9–27). Carbondale, IL: University of Southern Illinois Press.

Cutting, J. E., & Kozlowski, L. T. (1977). Recognizing friends by their walk – Gait perception without familiarity cues. *Bulletin of the Psychonomic Society*, *9*(5), 353–356.

Cutting, J. E., DeLong, J. E., & Nothelfer, C. E. (2010). Attention and the evolution of Hollywood film. *Psychological Science*, *21*(3), 432–439.

Cuttler, C., & Graf, P. (2007). Sub-clinical compulsive

checkers' prospective memory is impaired. *Journal of Anxiety Disorders*, *21*, 338–352.

Cytowic, R. E. (2003). *The man who tasted shapes* (MIT Press edition with new afterword, 2003. ed.). Cambridge, MA: MIT Press.

D

Da Costa Pinto, A. (1991). Reading rates and digit span in bilinguals: The superiority of mother tongue. *International Journal of Psychology*, *26*, 471–483.

Dahan, D. (2010). The time course of interpretation in speech comprehension. *Current Directions in Psychological Science*, *19*(2), 121–126.

Dakin, S. C., & Watt, R. J. (1997). The computation of orientation statistics from visual texture. *Vision Research*, *37*(22), 3181–3192.

Dalrymple-Alford, E. C., & Budayr, B. (1966). Examination of some aspects of the Stroop Color-Word Test. *Perceptual and Motor Skills*, *23*, 1211–1214.

Damasio, A. (1994). *Descartes' error: Emotion, reason and the human brain.* New York: G.P. Putnam.

Damasio, A. R. (2000). A second chance for emotion. In R. D. Lane & L. Nadel (Eds.), *Cognitive neuroscience of emotion*. New York and Oxford: Oxford University Press.

Damasio, A. R., Tranel, D., & Damasio, H. (1990). Individuals with sociopathic behavior caused by frontal damage fail to respond autonomically to social stimuli. *Behavioural Brain Research*, *41*, 81–94.

Damasio, A., Tranel, D., & Damasio, H. (1992). Verbs but not nouns: Damage to left temporal cortices impairs access to nouns but not verbs, *Society for Neuroscience Abstracts*, *18*, 387.

Danquah, A. N., Farrell, M. J., & O'Boyle, D. J. (2008). Biases in the subjective timing of perceptual events: Libet *et al.* (1983) revisited. *Consciousness and Cognition*, *17*, 616–627.

Darwin, C. (1998). *The expression of the emotions in man and animals* (3rd ed.) New York: Oxford University Press.

Darwin, C. J., Turvey, M. T., & Crowder, R. G. (1972). An auditory analogue of the Sperling partial report procedure: Evidence for brief auditory store. *Cognitive Psychology, 3,* 255–267.

Davidson, R. J. (2003). Seven sins in the study of emotion: Correctives from affective neuroscience. *Brain and Cognition, 52,* 129–132.

Dayan, E., Casile, A., Levit-Binnun, N., Giese, M. A., Hendler, T., & Flash, T. (2007). Neural representations of kinematic laws of motion: Evidence for action-perception coupling. *Proceedings of the National Academy of Sciences of the United States of America, 104*(51), 20582–20587.

De Groot, A. D. (1965). *Thought and choice in chess.* The Hague: Mouton.

De Groot, A. M. B., & Van Hell, J. G. (2005). The learning of foreign language vocabulary. In J. F. Kroll & A. M. B. de Groot (Eds.), *Handbook of bilingualism: Psycholinguistic approaches* (pp. 9–29). New York: Oxford University Press.

De Neys, W. (2006). Automatic-heuristic and executive-analytic processing in reasoning: Chronometric and task considerations. *Quarterly Journal of Experimental Psychology, 59,* 1070–1110.

De Ruiter, J. P. (2000). The production of gesture and speech. In D. McNeill (Ed.), *Language and gesture* (pp. 284–311). Cambridge: Cambridge University Press.

De Ruiter, J. P., Mitterer, H., & Enfield, N. J. (2006). Projecting the end of a speaker's turn: A cognitive cornerstone of conversation. *Language, 82,* 515–535.

de Vries *et al.,* (2010). Electrical stimulation of Broca's area enhances implicit learning of an artificial grammar. *Journal of Cognitive Neuroscience, 22,* 2427–2436.

De Houwer, J., & Hermans, D. (2010). Do feelings have a mind of their own? In J. De Houwer & D. Hermans (Eds.), *Cognition and emotion: Reviews of current research and theories* (pp. 38–65). Hove: Psychology Press.

Defeyter, M. A., & German, T. B. (2003). Acquiring an understanding of design: evidence from children's insight problem solving. *Cognition, 89,* 133–115.

Deffenbacher, K. A. (1980). Eyewitness accuracy and confidence: Can we infer anything about their relationship? *Law and Human Behavior, 4,* 243–260.

Deffenbacher, K. A., Bornstein, B. H., Penroad, S. A., & McGorty, E. K. (2004). A meta-analytic review of the effects of high stress on eyewitness memory. *Law and Human Behavior, 28,* 687–706.

Dell, G. S. (1986). A spreading activation theory of retrieval in sentence production. *Psychological Review, 93,* 283–321.

Dell, G. S. (1995). Speaking and misspeaking. In L. Gleitman & M. Liberman (Eds.), *Invitation to cognitive science, Part I, Language.* Cambridge, MA: MIT Press.

Dell, G. S., & O' Seaghdha, P. G. (1991). Mediated and convergent lexical priming in language production: A comment on Levelt *et al. Psychological Review, 98,* 604–614.

Dell, G. S., & Reich, P. A. (1981). Stages in sentence production: An analysis of speech error data. *Journal of Verbal Learning & Verbal Behavior, 20,* 611–629.

Dell, G. S., Burger, L. K., & Svec, W. R. (1997). Language production and serial order: A functional analysis and a model. *Psychological Review, 104,* 123–147.

Della Sala, S., Gray, C., Baddeley, A. D., Allamano, N., & Wilson, L. (1999). Pattern span: A tool for unwelding visuo-spatial memory. *Neuropsychologia, 37,* 1189–1199.

Dennett, D. C. (1987). *The intentional stance.* Cambridge, MA: MIT Press.

Dennett, D. C. (1992). *Consciousness explained.* London: A. Lane.

Derwinger, A., Neely, A. S., & Bäckman, L. (2005). Design your own memory strategies! Self-generated strategy training versus mnemonic training in old age: An 8-month follow-up. *Neuropsychological Rehabilitation, 15*(1), 37–54.

Deutsch, J. A., & Deutsch, D. (1963). Attention – Some theoretical considerations. *Psychological Review, 70*(1), 80–90.

Dewaele, J. M. (2009). The cognitive perspective: The age factor. In K. Knapp & B. Seidlhofer (Eds.), *Handbook of foreign language communication and learning* (pp. 279–306). Berlin: Mouton De Gruyter.

Dewar, M., Della Sala, S., Beschin, N., & Cowan, N. (2010). Profound retroactive interference in anterograde amnesia. What interferes? *Neuropsychology, 24,* 357.

Dewar, M., Fernandez Garcia, Y., Cowan, N., & Della Sala, S. (2009). Delaying interference enhances memory consolidation in amnesic patients. *Neuropsychology, 23,* 627–634.

Dewar, M. T., Cowan, N., & Della Sala, S. (2007). Forgetting due to retroactive interference: A fusion of Muller and Pilzecker's (1900). early insights into forgetting and recent research on anterograde amnesia. *Cortex, 43,* 616–634.

Dhami, M. K. (2003). Psychological models of professional decision making. *Psychological Science, 14,* 175–180.

Dhami, M. K., & Ayton, P. (2001). Bailing and jailing the fast and frugal way. *Journal of Behavioral Decision Making, 14,* 141–168.

Diedrichsen, J., Shadmehr, R., & Ivry, R. B. (2010). The coordination of movement: optimal feedback control and beyond. *Trends in Cognitive Sciences, 14*(1), 31–39.

Dijiksterhuis, A., & Meurs, T. (2006). Where creativity resides: The generative power of unconscious thought. *Consciousness and Cognition, 15,* 135–146.

Dijiksterhuis, A., & Nordgren, L. F. (2006). A theory of unconscious thought. *Perspectives on Psychological Science, 1,* 95–109.

Dijkstra, A. (2005). Bilingual visual word recognition and lexical access. In J. F. Kroll & A. De Groot (Eds.), *Handbook of bilingualism: Psycholinguistic approaches* (pp. 178–201). Oxford: Oxford University Press.

Dillon, P. C., Graham, W. K., & Aidells, A. L. (1972). Brainstorming on a 'hot' problem: Effects of training and practice on individual and group performance. *Journal of Applied Psychology, 56,* 487–490.

Dipellegrino, G., Fadiga, L., Fogassi, L., Gallese, V., & Rizzolatti, G. (1992). Understanding motor events – A neurophysiological study. *Experimental Brain Research, 91*(1), 176–180.

Dittrich, W. H. (1993). Action categories and the perception of biological motion. *Perception, 22*(1), 15–22.

Dittrich, W. H., Troscianko, T., Lea, S. E. G., & Morgan, D. (1996). Perception of emotion from dynamic point-light displays represented in dance. *Perception, 25*(6), 727–38.

Dobbs, D. (2005). Fact or phrenology? *Scientific American Mind, 16,* 24–31.

Dodds, R. A., Ward, T. B., & Smith, S. M. (2003). A review of the experimental literature on incubation in problem solving and creativity. In M. A. Runco (Ed.), *Creativity research handbook* (Vol. 3). Cresskill, NJ: Hampton Press.

Donald, M. (1991). *Origins of the modern mind: Three stages in the evolution of culture and cognition.* Cambridge, MA: Harvard University Press.

Donald, T. W. (1999). Preconditions for the evolution of protolanguages. In M. C. Corballis & I. Lea (Eds.), *The descent of mind* (pp. 355–365). Oxford: Oxford University Press.

Downing, P. E. (2000). Interactions between visual working memory and selective attention. *Psychological Science, 11*(6), 467–473.

Doyle, A. C. (1887). A study in scarlet. *Beeton's Christmas Annual 1887*. London: Ward Lock.

Drews, F. A., Pasupathi, M., & Strayer, D. L. (2008). Passenger and cell phone conversations in simulated driving. *Journal of Experimental Psychology: Applied, 14*(4), 392–400.

Driver, J. (1996). Enhancement of selective listening by illusory mislocation of speech sounds due to lip-reading. *Nature, 381*(6577), 66–68.

Dronkers, N. F. (1996). A new brain region for coordinating speech articulation. *Nature, 384*, 159–161.

Dronkers, N. F., Plaisant, O., Iba-Zizen, M. T., & Cabanis, E. A. (2007). Paul Broca's historic cases: High resolution MR imaging of the brains of Leborgne and Lelong. *Brain, 130*, 1432–1441.

Dronkers, N. F., Wilkins, D. P., Van Valin, R. D., Redfern, B. B., & Jaeger, J. J. (2004). Lesion analysis of the brain areas involved in language comprehension. *Cognition, 92*, 145–177.

Dryer, M. S. (2005). Order of subject, object, and verb. In M. Haspelmath, M. S. Dryer, D. Gil & B. Comrie (Eds.), *The world atlas of language structures*. Oxford: Oxford University Press.

Dudai, Y. (2004). The neurobiology of consolidation, or, how stable is the engram? *Annual Review of Psychology, 55*, 51–86.

Dunbar, K. (1993). Concept discovery in a scientific domain. *Cognitive Science, 17*, 397–434.

Dunbar, K., & Fugelsang, J. (2005). Scientific thinking and reasoning. In K. J. Holyoak & R. G. Morrison (Eds.), *The Cambridge handbook of thinking and reasoning*. New York: Cambridge University Press.

Duncan, J. (1984). Selective attention and the organization of visual information. *Journal of Experimental Psychology-General, 113*(4), 501–517.

Duncan, S., & Barrett, L. F. (2007). Affect as a form of cognition: A neurobiological analysis. *Cognition and Emotion, 21*, 1184–1211.

Duncker, K. (1945). On problem solving. *Psychological Monographs, 58*, 1–113.

Dunn, B. D., Dalgleish, T., Lawrence, A. D., & Ogilvie, A. D. (2007). The accuracy of self-monitoring and its relationship to self-focused attention in dysphoria and clinical depression. *Journal of Abnormal Psychology, 116*, 1–15.

Dunn, B. D., Dalgleish, T., & Lawrence, A. D. (2006). The somatic marker hypothesis: A critical evaluation. *Neuroscience Biobehavioral Reviews, 30*, 239–71.

Dunnette, M. D., Campbell, J., & Jaastad, K. (1963). The effects of group participation on brainstorming effectiveness for two industrial samples. *Journal of Applied Psychology, 47*, 10–37.

Dunning, D., & Perretta, S. (2002). Automaticity and eyewitness accuracy: A 10 to 12 second rule for distinguishing accurate from inaccurate positive identification. *Journal of Applied Psychology, 87*(5), 951–962.

Dutton, D. G. and Aron, A. P. (1974). Some evidence for heightened sexual attraction under conditions of high anxiety. *Journal of Personality and Social Psychology, 30*, 510–517.

Durgin, F. H., Baird, J. A., Greenburg, M., Russell, R., Shaughnessy, K., & Waymouth, S. (2009). Who is being deceived? The experimental demands of wearing a backpack. *Psychonomic Bulletin & Review, 16*(5), 964–969.

Durgin, F. H., Klein, B., Spiegel, A., Strawser, C. J., & Williams, M. (2012). The social psychology of perception experiments: Hills, backpacks, glucose and the problem of generalizability. *Journal of Experimental Psychology: Human Perception and Performance, 38*, 1582–1595.

E

Easterbrook, J. A. (1959). The effect of emotion on cue utilization and the organization of behavior. *Psychological Review, 66*(3), 183–201.

Easton, R. D., & Moran, P. W. (1978). A quantitative confirmation of visual capture of curvature. *Journal of General & Psychology, 98*(1st Half), 105–112.

Ebbinghaus, H. (1885). *Memory: A contribution to experimental psychology*. Translated by Henry A. Ruger, & Clara E. Bussenius (1913). Originally published in New York by Teachers College, Columbia University.

Edwards, A., Elwyn, G. J., Covey, E., M., & Pill, R. (2001). Presenting risk information – a review of the effects of 'framing' and other manipulations on patient outcomes. *Journal of Health Communication, 6*, 61–82.

Edwards, T., Kingston, K., Hardy, L., & Gould, D. (2002). A qualitative analysis of catastrophic performances and the associated thoughts, feelings, and emotions. *Sport Psychologist, 16*(1), 1–19.

Efron, R. (1970a). Effects of stimulus duration on perceptual onset and offset latencies. *Perception & Psychophysics, 8*, 231–234.

Efron, R. (1970b). The minimum duration of a perception. *Neuropsychologia, 8*, 57–63.

Efron, R. (1970c). The relationship between the duration of a stimulus and the duration of a perception. *Neuropsychologia, 8*, 37–55.

Egly, R., Driver, J., & Rafal, R. D. (1994). Shifting visual-attention between objects and locations – Evidence from normal and parietal lesion subjects. *Journal of Experimental Psychology-General, 123*(2), 161–177.

Ehrlich, S. F., & Rayner, K. (1981). Contextual effects on word perception and eye movements during reading. *Journal of Verbal Learning and Verbal Behaviour, 20*, 641–655.

Eibl-Eibesfeldt, I. (1973). The expressive behaviour of the deaf-and-blind born. In M. von Cranach & I. Vine (Eds.), *Social communication and movement*. New York: Academic Press.

Eich, E. (1995). Searching for mood dependent memory. *Psychological Science, 6*, 67–75.

Eich, J. E. (1980). The cue-dependent nature of state-dependent retention. *Memory and Cognition, 8*, 157–173.

Eich, E., & Metcalfe, J. (1989). Mood dependent memory for internal versus external events. *Journal of Experimental Psychology: Learning Memory and Cognition, 15*, 443–455.

Eichenbaum, H. (2010). Long-term potentiation. *Corsini Encyclopedia of Psychology*, 1–2.

Eimas, P. D., & Corbit, J. D. (1973). Selective adaptation of linguistic feature detectors. *Cognitive Psychology, 4*, 99–109.

Eimas, P. D., Siqueland, E. R., Jusczyk, P. W., & Vogorito, J. (1971). Speech perception in infants. *Science, 171*, 303–306.

Einstein, O., & McDaniel, M. (2005). Prospective memory: Multiple retrieval processes. *Current Directions in Psychological Science, 14*, 286–290.

Einstein, O., McDaniel, M., Thomas, R., Mayfield, S., Shank, H., Morrisette, N., & Breneiser, J. (2005). Multiple processes in prospective memory retrieval: Factors determining monitoring versus spontaneous retrieval. *Journal of Experimental Psychology, 134*, 327–342.

Ekman, P. (1999). Basic emotions. In T. Dalgleish and M. Power (Eds.) *Handbook of cognition and emotion*. Chichester: John Wiley & Sons.

Ekman, P., & O' Sullivan, M. (1991). Who can catch a liar?

American Psychologist, 46, 913–920.

Ekman, P., Levenson, R. W., & Friesen, W. V. (1983). Autonomic nervous system activity distinguishes among emotions. *Science, 221*, 1208–1210.

Ekman, P., Sorenson, E. R., & Friesen, W. V. (1969). Pan-cultural elements in facial displays of emotion. *Science, 164*, 86–88.

Ekstrand, B. R. (1972). To sleep, perchance to dream (about why we forget). In C. P. Duncan, L. Sechrest & A. W. Melton (Eds.), *Human memory: Festschrift for Benton J. Underwood*. New York: Appleton Century Crofts.

Elfenbein, H. A., & Anbady, N. (2002). Is there an in group advantage in emotion recognition? *Psychological Bulletin, 128*(2), 243–249.

Ellenbogen, J. M., Hulbert, J. C., Stickgold, R., Dinges, D. F., & Thompson-Schill, S. L. (2006). Interfering with theories of sleep and memory: sleep, declarative memory, and associative interference. *Current Biology, 16*, 1290–1294.

Elliott, D., Helsen, W. F., & Chua, R. (2001). A century later: Woodworth's (1899) two-component model of goal-directed aiming. *Psychological Bulletin, 127*(3), 342–357.

Elliott, R., & Dolan, R. J. (1998). The medial prefrontal cortex in depression. In D. Ebert & K. P. Ebmeier (Eds.), *New models for depression*. Basel: Karger.

Elliot, R., Newman, A. L., Longe, O. A., & Deakin, J. F. (2003). Differential response patterns in the striatum and orbitofrontal cortex to financial reward in humans: A parametric functional magnetic resonance imaging study. *Journal of Neuroscience, 23*, 303–307.

Ellis, A., & Harper, R. A. (1975). *A new guide to rational living*. Englewood Cliffs, NJ: Prentice-Hall.

Ellis, A. W., & Young, A. W. (1996). *Human cognitive neuropsychology: A textbook with readings*. Hove: Psychology Press.

Ellis, A. W., Miller, D., & Sin, G. (1983). Wernicke's aphasia and normal language processing: A case study in cognitive neuropsychology. *Cognition, 15*, 111–144.

Ellis, H. D., & Lewis, M. B. (2001). Capgras delusion: a window on face recognition. *Trends in Cognitive Sciences, 5*(4), 149–156.

Ellis, H. D., Luaute, J. P., & Retterstol, N. (1994). Delusional misidentification syndromes. *Psychopathology, 27*(3–5), 117–120.

Ellis, H. D., Whitley, J., & Luaute, J. P. (1994). Delusional misidentification. The three original papers on the Capgras, Fregoli and intermetamorphosis delusions. (Classic Text No. 17). *History of Psychiatry, 5*(17 Pt 1), 117–146.

Ellis, J. (1988). Memory for future intentions: Investigating pulses and steps. In M. M. Gruneberg, P. Morris & R. N. Sykes (Eds.), *Practical aspects of memory: Current research and issues, Vol. 1: Memory in everyday life* (pp. 371–376). Chichester: John Wiley.

Ellis, J. A., & Cohen, G. (2008). Memory for intentions, actions and plans. In G. Cohen, & M. A. Conway (Eds.), *Memory in the real world*. 3rd ed. (pp. 141–172). Hove: Psychology Press.

Ellis, N. C., & Hennelly, R. A. (1980). A bilingual word-length effect: Implications for intelligence testing and the relative ease of mental calculation in Welsh and English. *British Journal of Psychology, 71*, 289–318.

Ellsworth, P. C. (2005). Legal reasoning. In K. J. Holyoak & R. G. Morrison (Eds.), *The Cambridge handbook of thinking and reasoning*. New York: Cambridge University Press.

Elman, J. L. (1990). Finding structure in time. *Cognitive Science, 14*(2), 179–211.

Elman, J. L., & McClelland, J. L. (1988). Cognitive penetration of the mechanisms of perception: Compensation for coarticulation of lexically restored phonemes. *Journal of Memory and Language, 27*, 143–165.

Engle, R. W. (2002). Working memory capacity as executive attention. *Current Dircetions in Psychological Science, 11*, 19–23.

Engle, R. W., & Conway, A. R. A. (1998). Working memory and comprehension. In R. H. Logie & K. J. Gilhooly (Eds.), *Working memory and thinking*. Hove: Psychology Press.

Engle, R. W., & Oransky, N. (1999). The evolution from short-term to working memory: Multi-store to dynamic models of temporary storage. In R. Sternberg (Ed.), *The nature of human cognition*. Cambridge, MA: MIT Press.

Entwistle, N. (1987). *Understanding classroom learning*. London: Hodder and Stoughton.

Erdelyi, M. H. (1974). A new look at the New Look: Perceptual defense and vigilance. *Psychological Review, 81*, 1–25.

Ericsson, K. A. (1999). Creative expertise as superior reproducible performance: innovative and flexible aspects of expert performance. *Psychological Inquiry, 10*, 329–333.

Ericsson, K. A. (2003). Exceptional memorizers: Made, not born. *Trends in Cognitive Sciences, 7*, 233–235.

Ericsson, K. A., & Chase, W. G. (1982). Exceptional memory. *American Scientist, 70*, 607–615.

Ericsson, K. A., & Kintsch, W. (1995). Long-term working memory. *Psychological Review, 102*, 211–245.

Ericsson, K. A., & Simon, H. A. (1993). *Protocol analysis: Verbal reports as data*. Cambridge, MA: MIT Press.

Ericsson, K. A., Delaney, P. F., Weaver, G., & Mahadevan, R. (2004). Uncovering the structure of a mnemonist's superior 'basic' memory capacity. *Cognitive Psychology, 49*, 191–237.

Ericsson, K. A., Krampe, R. T. and Tesch-Rohmer, C. (1993). The role of deliberate practice, *Psychological Review, 100*, 363–406.

Eriksen, C. W., & St James, J. D. (1986). Visual-attention within and around the field of focal attention – A zoom lens model. *Perception & Psychophysics, 40*(4), 225–240.

Eriksen, C. W., & Yeh, Y. Y. (1985). Allocation of attention in the visual-field. *Journal of Experimental Psychology-Human Perception and Performance, 11*(5), 583–597.

Erman, L. D., & Lesser, V. R. (1980). 'The HEARSAY-II speech understanding system: a tutorial'. In W. Lea (Ed.), *Trends in speech recognition*. Englewood Cliffs, NJ: Prentice-Hall.

Ernst, M. O., & Banks, M. S. (2002). Humans integrate visual and haptic information in a statistically optimal fashion. *Nature, 415*(6870), 429–433.

Eslinger, P. J., & Damasio, A. R. (1985). Severe disturbance of higher cognition after bilateral frontal lobe ablation: Patient EVR. *Neurology, 35*, 1731–1741.

Esposito, A., & Marinaro, M. (2007). What pauses can tell us about speech and gesture partnership. In A. Esposito, M. Bratanic, E. Keller & M. Marinaro (Eds.), *Fundamentals of verbal and nonverbal communication and the biometric issue* (Vol. 18, pp. 45–57). Amsterdam: IOS Press.

Esposito, A., Esposito, D., Refice, M., Savino, M., & Shattuck-Hufnagel, S. (2007). Preliminary investigation of the relationships between gestures and prosody in Italian. In A. Esposito, M. Bratanic, E. Keller & M. Marinaro (Eds.), *Fundamentals of verbal and nonverbal communication and the biometric issue* (Vol. 18, pp. 65–74). Amsterdam: IOS Press.

Estes, W. K. (1972). An associative basis for coding and organization in memory. In A. W. Melton & E. Martin (Eds.), *Coding processes in human memory*: V. H. Winston, & Sons.

Evans, J. St. B. T. (1977). Linguistic factors in reasoning.

Quarterly Journal of Experimental Psychology, 29, 297–306.

Evans, J. St. B. T. (1984). Heuristic and analytic processes in reasoning. *British Journal of Psychology, 75*, 451–458.

Evans, J. St. B. T. (1993). Relevance and reasoning. In S. E. Newstead & J. St B. T. Evans (Eds.), *Current directions in thinking and reasoning*. Hove: Lawrence Erlbaum.

Evans, J. St. B. T. (2003). In two minds: Dual process accounts of reasoning. *Trends in Cognitive Sciences, 7*, 454–459.

Evans, J. St. B. T. (2008). Dual processing accounts of reasoning, judgment, and social cognition. *Annual Review of Psychology, 59*, 255–278.

Evans, J. St. B. T., & Curtis-Holmes, J. (2005). Rapid responding increases belief bias: Evidence for the dual process theory of reasoning. *Thinking & Reasoning, 11*, 382–389.

Evans, J. St. B. T., & Lynch, J. S. (1973). Matching bias in the selection task. *British Journal of Psychology, 64*, 391–397.

Evans, J. St. B. T., Barston, J. L., & Pollard, P. (1983). On the conflict between logic and belief in syllogistic reasoning. *Memory & Cognition, 11*, 295–306.

Eysenck, M. W. (1978). Levels of processing – Critique. *British Journal of Psychology, 69*, 157–169.

Eysenck, M. W., & Calvo, M. G. (1992). Anxiety and performance – the processing efficiency theory. *Cognition & Emotion, 6*(6), 409–434.

Eysenck, M. W., Derakshan, N., Santos, R., & Calvo, M. G. (2007). Anxiety and cognitive performance: Attentional control theory. *Emotion, 7*(2), 336–353.

F

Farah, M. J. (1990). *Visual agnosia : disorders of object recognition and what they tell us about normal vision.* Cambridge, MA: MIT Press.

Farah, M. J., & Hammond, K. M. (1988). Mental rotation and orientation-invariant object recognition: Dissociable processes. *Cognition, 29*, 29–46.

Farah, M. J., Hammond, K. M., Levine, D. N., & Calvanio, R. (1988a). Electrophysiological evidence for a shared representational medium for visual images and visual percepts. *Journal of Experimental Psychology: General, 117*, 248–257.

Farah, M. J., Hammond, K. M., Levine, D. N., & Calvanio, R. (1988b). Visual and spatial mental imagery: Dissociable systems of representation. *Cognitive Psychology, 20*, 439–462.

Fasolo, B., McClelland, G. H., & Lange, K. A. (2005). The effect of site design and interattribute correlations on interactive web-based decisions. In C. P. Haugtved, K. Machleit & R. Yalch (Eds.) *Online consumer psychology: understanding and influencing behaviour in the virtual world.* (pp. 325–344). Mahwah, NJ: Lawrence Erlbaum.

Favreau, J. (Writer). (2008). *Iron Man.* USA: Paramount Pictures.

Feldman, A. G. (1966). Functional tuning of nervous system with control of movement or maintenance of a steady posture. 2. Controllable parameters of muscles. *Biophysics-USSR, 11*(3), 565.

Feldman, A. G. (1986). Once more on the equilibrium-point hypothesis lambda-model for motor control. *Journal of Motor Behavior, 18*(1), 17–54.

Feldman, A. G., & Latash, M. L. (2005). Testing hypotheses and the advancement of science: Recent attempts to falsify the equilibrium point hypothesis. *Experimental Brain Research, 161*(1), 91–103.

Feldman, M. H. (1971). Physiological observations in a chronic case of 'locked-in' syndrome. *Neurology, 21*, 459–478.

Feldman, R. S. (2004). *Understanding psychology* (7th ed.). New York: McGraw-Hill.

Ferreira, F. (2003). Prosody. In L. Nadel (Ed.), *Encyclopedia of cognitive science* (pp. 762–768). London: Macmillan Reference Ltd.

Ferreira, F., Christianson, K., & Hollingworth, A. (2001). Misinterpretations of garden-path sentences: Implications for models of sentence processing and reanalysis. *Journal of Psycholinguistic Research, 30*, 3–20.

Ferri, S., Kolster, H., Jastorff, J., & Orban, G. A. (2013). The overlap of the EBA and the MT/V5 cluster. *NeuroImage, 66*, 412–425.

Ferris, C. F., Kulkarni, P., Sullivan, J. M., Harder, J. A., Messenger, T. L., & Febo, M. (2005). Pup suckling is more rewarding than cocaine: Evidence from functional magnetic resonance imaging and three-dimensional computational analysis. *The Journal of Neuroscience, 25*, 149–156.

Fiedler, K. (1988). The dependence of the conjunction fallacy on subtle linguistic factors. *Psychological Research, 50*, 123–129.

Field, J. (2003). *Psycholinguistics: A resource book for students.* Routledge.

Field, M., Mogg, K., & Bradley, B. P. (2006). Attention to drug-related cues in drug abuse and addiction: component processes. In R. Wiers & A. Stacy (Eds.), *Handbook of implicit cognition and addiction.* Thousand Oaks, CA: Sage.

Field, T., Pickens, J., Fox, N. A., Gonzalez, & Nawrocki, T. (1998). Facial expression and EEG responses to happy and sad face/voices by 3-month-old infants of depressed mothers. *British Journal of Developmental Psychology, 16*, 486–494.

Fillmore, M. T., Kelly, T. H., Rush, C. R., & Hays, L. (2001). Retrograde facilitation of memory by triazolam: Effects on automatic processes. *Psychopharmacology, 158*, 314–321.

Finke, R. A. (1989). *Principles of mental imagery.* Cambridge, MA: MIT Press.

Finke, R. A., Ward, T. B., & Smith, S. M. (1992). *Creative cognition: Theory, research, applications.* Cambridge, MA: MIT Press.

Finucane, M. L., Alhakami, A., Slovic, P., & Johnson, S. M. (2000). The affect heuristic in judgments of risks and benefits. *Journal of Behavioral Decision Making, 13*, 1–17.

Finucane, M. L., Peters, E., & Slovic, P. (2003). Judgment and decision making: the dance of affect and reason. In S. L. Schneider & J. Shanteau (Eds.), *Emerging perspectives on judgment and decision research.* Cambridge: Cambridge University Press.

Fiske, S. T. (2010). Venus and Mars or down to Earth: Stereotypes and realities of gender differences. *Perspectives on Psychological Science, 5*(6), 688–692.

Flach, R., Knoblich, G., & Prinz, W. (2004). Recognizing one's own clapping: The role of temporal cues. *Psychological Research-Psychologische Forschung, 69*(1–2), 147–156.

Flash, T., & Handzel, A. A. (2007). Affine differential geometry analysis of human arm movements. *Biological Cybernetics, 96*(6), 577–601.

Flash, T., & Hochner, B. (2005). Motor primitives in vertebrates and invertebrates. *Current Opinion in Neurobiology, 15*(6), 660–666.

Flash, T., & Hogan, N. (1985). The coordination of arm movements – An experimentally confirmed mathematical-model. *Journal of Neuroscience, 5*(7), 1688–1703.

Fleck, J. I., & Weisberg, R. W. (2004). The use of verbal protocols as data: An analysis of insight in the candle problem. *Memory and Cognition, 32*, 990–1006.

Flower, L., Hayes, J. R., Carey, L., Schriver, K., & Stratman, J. (1986). Detection, diagnosis, and the strategies of revision. *College Composition and Communication, 37*, 16–55.

Foa, E. B., & McNally, R. J. (1986). Sensitivity to feared stimuli in obsessive-compulsives: A dichotic listening analysis. *Cognitive Therapy and Research, 10*, 477–485.

Fodor, J. A. (1983). *The modularity of mind: An essay on faculty psychology.* Cambridge, MA: MIT Press.

Fodor, J. A. (1998). *Concepts: Where cognitive science went wrong.* Oxford: Clarendon Press.

Fodor, J. A. (1999). Let your brain alone. *London Review of Books, 21*, 19.

Foer, J. (2011). *Moonwalking with Einstein: The art and science of remembering everything.* New York: Penguin Books.

Foer, J. (2011). Secrets of a Mind-Gamer: How I trained my brain and became a world-class memory athlete. *New York Times*, 15 February. http://www.nytimes.com/interactive/2011/02/20/magazine/mind-secrets.html

Fogassi, L., Ferrari, P. F., Gesierich, B., Rozzi, S., Chersi, F., & Rizzolatti, G. (2005). Parietal lobe: From action organization to intention understanding. *Science, 308*(5722), 662–667.

Ford, M. (1995). Two modes of mental representation and problem solution in syllogistic reasoning. *Cognition, 54*, 1–71.

Forgas, J. P. (1982). Reactions to life dilemmas: Risk taking, success and responsibility attribution. *Australian Journal of Psychology, 34*, 25–35.

Forgas, J. P. (1995). Mood and judgment: The Affect Infusion Model (AIM). *Psychological Bulletin, 117*, 39–66.

Forgas, J. P., & Vargas, P. (1998). Affect and behavior inhibition: The mediating role of cognitive processing strategies. *Psychological Inquiry, 9*, 205–210.

Forster, J., Friedman, R., Butterbach, E. M., & Sassenberg, K. (2005). Automatic effects of deviancy cues on creative cognition. *European Journal of Social Psychology, 35*, 345–259.

Forster, K. I. (1979). Levels of processing and the structure of the language processor. In W. E. Cooper & E. Walker (Eds.), *Sentence Processing: Psycholinguistic essays presented to Merrill Garrett.* Hillsdale, NJ: Erlbaum.

Forster, K. I. (1989). Basic issues in lexical processing. In W. Marslen-Wilson (Ed.), *Lexical representation and process* (pp. 75–107). Cambridge, MA: MIT Press.

Forster, K. I., & Davis, C. (1984). Repetition priming and frequency attenuation in lexical access. *Journal of Experimental Psychology: Learning, Memory, and Cognition, 10*, 680–698.

Foss, D. J. (1969). Decision processes during sentence comprehension: Effects of lexical item difficulty and position upon reaction times. *Journal of Verbal Learning and Verbal Behavior, 8*, 457–462.

Foss, D. J. (1970). Some effects of ambiguity upon sentence comprehension. *Journal of Verbal Learning and Verbal Behavior, 9*, 699–706.

Foster, D. H., & Gilson, S. J. (2002). Recognizing novel three-dimensional objects by summing signals from parts and views. *Proceedings of the Royal Society of London Series B-Biological Sciences, 269*(1503), 1939–1947.

Fougnie, D., & Marois, R. (2006). Distinct capacity limits for attention and working memory – Evidence from attentive tracking and visual working memory paradigms. *Psychological Science, 17*(6), 526–534.

Fox Tree, J. E. (1995). The effects of false starts and repetitions on the processing of subsequent words in spontaneous speech. *Journal of Memory and Language, 34*, 709–738.

Franconeri, S. L., Alvarez, G. A., & Enns, J. T. (2007). How many locations can be selected at once? *Journal of Experimental Psychology-Human Perception and Performance, 33*(5), 1003–1012.

Franklin, S., Howard, D., & Patterson, K. (1994). Abstract word meaning deafness. *Cognitive Neuropsychology, 11*, 1–34.

Franz, V. H. (2001). Action does not resist visual illusions. *Trends in Cognitive Sciences, 5*(11), 457–459.

Frauenfelder, U. H., Scholen, M., & Content, A. (2001). Bottom-up inhibition in lexical selection: Phonological mismatch effects in spoken word recognition, *Language and Cognitive Processes, 16*, 583–607.

Frazier, L. (1979). *On comprehending sentences: Syntactic parsing strategies.* Indiana University Linguistics Club.

Frazier, L. (1987). Sentence processing. In M. Coltheart (Ed.), *Attention and performance volume 12. The psychology of reading* (pp. 559–586). Hillsdale NJ: Erlbaum.

Frazier, L. (1989). Against lexical generation of syntax. In W. D. Marslen-Wilson (Ed.), *Lexical representation and process.* Cambridge, MA: MIT Press.

Freud, S. (1900/1976). *The interpretation of dreams.* London: Hogarth.

Freud, S. (1922). *Introductory lectures on psycho-analysis.* London: George Allen, & Unwin.

Freud, S. (1924/1938 1975). *The psychopathology of everyday life.* Harmondsworth: Penguin.

Frijda, N. H. (1986). *The emotions.* Cambridge: Cambridge University Press.

Frijda, N. H., & Scherer, K. R. (2009). Emotion definition (psychological perspectives). In D. Sander & K. R. Scherer (Eds.), *Oxford companion to emotion and the affective sciences* (pp. 142–143). Oxford: Oxford University Press.

Frith, U., & Frith, C. D. (2003). Development and neurophysiology of mentalizing. *Philosophical Transactions of the Royal Society B-Biological Sciences, 358*(1431), 459–473.

Fromkin, V. (1971). The non-anomalous nature of anomalous utterances. *Language, 51*, 696–719.

Fromkin, V., Krashen, S., Curtiss, S., Rigler, D., & Rigler, M. (1974). The development of language in genie: A case of language acquisition beyond the 'critical period'. *Brain and Language, 1*, 81–107.

Fromkin, V., Rodman, R., & Hyams, N. (2007). *An Introduction to Language.* 8th ed. Thomson/Wadsworth.

Fromkin, V., Rodman, R., & Hyams, N. (2010). An introduction to language, 9th ed. Wadsworth Cengage Learning.

Frost, R., Katz, L., & Bentin, S. (1987). Strategies for visual word recognition and orthographical depth: A multilingual comparison. *Journal of Experimental Psychology: Human Perception and Performance, 13*, 104–115.

Fugelsang, J., Stein, C., Green, A., & Dunbar, K. (2004). Theory and data interactions of the scientific mind: Evidence from the molecular and the cognitive laboratory. *Canadian Journal of Experimental Psychology, 58*, 132–141.

Funnell, E. (1983). Phonological processes in reading: New evidence form acquired dyslexia. *British Journal of Psychology, 74*, 159–180.

Fusser, F., Linden, D. E. J., Rahm, B., Hampel, H., Haenschel, C., & Mayer, J. S. (2011). Common capacity-limited neural mechanisms of selective attention and spatial working memory encoding. *European Journal of Neuroscience, 34*(5), 827–838.

G

Gainotti, G. (2000). What the locus of brain lesion tells us about the nature of the cognitive defect underlying category-specific disorders: A review. *Cortex, 36*, 539–559.

Galifret, Y. (2006). Visual persistence and cinema? *C.R. Biologies, 329*, 369–385.

Gallace, A., Tan, H. Z., & Spence, C. (2006). The failure to detect tactile change: a tactile analog of visual change blindness, *Psychonomic Bulletin and Review, 13*, 300–303.

Gallese, V., Fadiga, L., Fogassi, L., & Rizzolatti, G. (1996). Action recognition in the premotor cortex. *Brain*, *119*, 593–609.

Gallese, V., Gernsbacher, M. A., Heyes, C., Hickok, G., & Iacoboni, M. (2011). Mirror neuron forum. *Perspectives on Psychological Science*, *6*(4), 369–407.

Galotti, K. M. (2007). Decision structuring in important real-life choices. *Psychological Science*, *18*, 320–325.

Galotti, K. M., Baron, J., & Sabini, J. P. (1986). Individual differences in syllogistic reasoning: Deduction rules or mental models? *Journal of Experimental Psychology: General 115*, 16–25.

Gandour, J., Ponglorpisit, S., Khunadorn, F., Dechongkit, S. (1992). Lexical tones in Thai after unilateral brain damage. *Brain and Language*, *43*, 275–307.

Ganis, G., Thompson, W. L., & Kosslyn, S. (2004). Brain areas underlying visual mental imagery and visual perception: An fMRI study. *Cognitive Brain Research*, *20*, 226–241.

Gara, M. A., Woolfolk, R. L., Cohen, B. D., Goldston, R. B., Allen, L. A., & Novalany, J. (1993). Perception of self and other in major depression. *Journal of Abnormal Psychology*, *102*, 93–100.

Gardner, H. (1985). *The mind's new science*. New York: Basic Books.

Gardner, W. L., Gabriel, S., & Lee, A. (1999). 'I' value freedom, but 'we' value relationships: Self-construal priming mimics cultural differences in judgment. *Psychological Science*, *10*, 321–326.

Garling, T., Kirchler, E., Lewis, A., & van Raaj, F. (2010). Psychology, financial decision making and, financial crises. *Psychological Science in the Public Interest*, *10*, 1–47.

Garnham, A., Shillock, R. C., Brown, G. D., Mill, A. I. D., & Culter, A. (1981). Slips of the tongue in the London-Lund Corpus of spontaneous conversation. In G. Brown & A. Cutler (Eds.), *Slips of the tongue and language*

production (pp. 251–263). The Hague: Mouton.

Garrett, M. F. (1975). The analysis of sentence production. In G. Bower (Ed.) *The psychology of learning and motivation* (volume 9, pp. 133–177). New York: Academic Press.

Garrett, M. F. (1980). Levels of processing in sentence production. In B. Butterworth (Ed.), *Language production, volume 1, Speech and talk* (pp. 177–220). London: Academic Press.

Garrett, M. F. (1982). Production of speech: observations from normal and pathological language use. In A. W. Ellis (Ed.), *Normality and pathology in cognitive function* (pp. 19–76). London: Academic Press.

Garrett, M. F. (1992). Disorders of lexical selection. *Cognition*, *42*, 143–180.

Gaskell, M. G., & Marslen-Wilson, W. D. (1997). Integrating form and meaning: a distributed model of speech perception. *Language and Cognitive Processes*, *12*, 613–56.

Gathercole, S. E., & Baddeley, A. D. (1989). Evaluation of the role of phonological STM in the development of vocabulary in children: A longitudinal study. *Journal of Memory & Language*, *28*, 200–213.

Gathercole, S. E., Hitch, G. J., Service, E., & Martin, A. J. (1997). Short-term memory and long-term learning in children. *Developmental Psychology*, *33*, 966–979.

Gauthier, I., Tarr, M. J., Moylan, J., Skudlarski, P., Gore, J. C., & Anderson, A. W. (2000). The fusiform 'face area' is part of a network that processes faces at the individual level. *Journal of Cognitive Neuroscience*, *12*(3), 495–504.

Gawande, A. A., Gawande, A. A., Studdert, D. M., Drav, J., Brennan, T. A., & Zinner, M. J. (2003). Risk factors for retained instruments and sponges after surgery. *New England Journal of Medicine*, *348*, 229–235.

Gazzaniga, M. S. (1981). 1981 Nobel prize for physiology or medicine. *Science*, *214*(4520), 517–518.

Gazzaniga, M. S. (1983). Right hemisphere language following brain bisection: A 20-year perspective. *American Psychologist*, *38*(5), 525–537.

Gazzaniga, M. S. (2005). Forty-five years of split-brain research and still going strong. *Nature Reviews Neuroscience*, *6*(8), 653–659.

Gazzaniga, M. S., Bogen, J. E., & Sperry, R. W. (1965). Observations on visual perception after disconnexion of the cerebral hemispheres in man. *Brain*, *88*(2), 221–236.

Gazzaniga, M. S., & Sperry, R. W. (1967). Language after section of the cerebral commissures. *Brain*, *90*, 131–148.

Gebhard, J. W., & Mowbray, G. H. (1959). On discriminating the rate of visual flicker and auditory flutter. *The American Journal of Psychology*, *72*(4), 521–529.

Geiselman, R. E., Fisher, R. P., Firstenberg, I., Hutton, L. A., Sullivan, S. J., Avetissian, I. V., & Prosk, A. L. (1984). Enhancement of eyewitness memory: An empirical evaluation of the cognitive interview. *Journal of Police Science & Administration*, *12*, 74–80.

Geisler, W. S., & Kersten, D. (2002). Illusions, perception and Bayes. *Nature Neuroscience*, *5*(6), 508–510.

Gelman, S. A., & Wellman, H. (1991). Insides and essences: Early understandings of the non-obvious. *Cognition*, *38*, 213–244.

Gentner, T. Q., Fenn, K. M., Margoliash, D., & Nusbaum, H. C. (2006). Recursive syntactic pattern learning by songbirds. *Nature*, *440*, 1204–1207.

Gepshtein, S., Seydell, A., & Trommershauser, J. (2007). Optimality of human movement under natural variations of visual-motor uncertainty. *Journal of Vision*, *7*(5).

German, T. B., & Barrett, H. C. (2005). Functional fixity in a technologically sparse

culture. *Psychological Science*, *16*, 1–5.

Gibson, J. J. (1962). Observations on active touch. *Psychological Review*, *69*(6), 477–491.

Gibson, J. J. (1979). *The ecological approach to visual perception*. Boston: Houghton Mifflin.

Giese, M. A., & Poggio, T. (2003). Neural mechanisms for the recognition of biological movements. *Nature Reviews Neuroscience*, *4*(3), 179–192.

Gigerenzer, G. (1993). The bounded rationality of probabilistic mental models. In K. I. Manktelow & D. E. Over (Eds.), *Rationality: Psychological and philosophical perspectives*. London: Routledge.

Gigerenzer, G. (2007). *Gut feelings*. London: Allen Lane.

Gigerenzer, G., & Hug, K. (1992). Domain specific reasoning: Social contracts, cheating, and perspective change. *Cognition*, *43*, 127–171.

Gigerenzer, G., Todd, P. M., & ABC Research Group (1999). *Simple heuristics that make us smart*. Oxford: Oxford University Press.

Gilhooly, K. J. (2005). Working memory and strategies in reasoning. In M. J. Roberts & E. J. Newton (Eds.), *Methods of thought: Individual differences in reasoning strategies*. Hove: Psychology Press.

Gilhooly, K. J., & Falconer, W. (1974). Concrete and abstract terms and relations in testing a rule. *Quarterly Journal of Experimental Psychology*, *26*, 355–359.

Gilhooly, K. J., Fioratou, E., & Henretty, N. (2010). Effects of think-aloud in verbal and spatial insight and non-insight problems. *British Journal of Psychology*, *101*, 81–93.

Gilhooly, K. J., Fioratou, E., Anthony, S., & Wynn, V. (2007). Divergent thinking: Strategies and executive involvement in generating novel uses for familiar objects. *British Journal of Psychology*, *98*, 611–625.

Gilhooly, K. J., Georgiou, G., Garrison, J., Reston, J., &

Sirota, M. (2012). Don't wait to incubate: Immediate versus delayed incubation in divergent thinking. *Memory & Cognition, 40*(6), 966–975.

Gilhooly, K. J., Logie, R. H., Wetherick, N. E., & Wynn, V. (1993). Working memory and strategies in syllogistic reasoning tasks. *Memory and Cognition, 21*, 115–124.

Gilhooly, K. J., Logie, R. H., & Wynn, V. (1999). Syllogistic reasoning tasks, working memory and skill. *European Journal of Cognitive Psychology, 11*, 473–498.

Gilhooly, K. J., Logie, R. H., & Wynn, V. (2002). Syllogistic reasoning tasks and working memory: Evidence from sequential presentation of premises. *Current Psychology, 21*, 111–120.

Glancy, G. D., Bradford, J. M., & Fedak, L. (2002). A comparison of R. v. Stone with R. v. Parks: Two cases of automatism. *Journal of the American Academy of Psychiatry and the Law, 30*(4), 541–547.

Glanzer, M., & Razel, M. (1974). The size of the unit in short-term storage. *Journal of Verbal Learning & Verbal Behavior, 12*, 114–131.

Glaze, J. A. (1928). The association value of nonsense syllables. *Journal of Genetic Psychology, 35*, 255–269.

Glenberg, A. M., & Kaschak, M. P. (2003). The body's contribution to language. *The Psychology of Learning and Motivation, 45*, 93–126.

Glenberg, A. M. (1977). Influences of retrieval process on the spacing effect in free recall. *Journal of Experimental Psychology: Human Learning and Memory, 3*, 282–294.

Glover, S. (2004). Separate visual representations in the planning and control of action. *Behavioral and Brain Sciences, 27*, 3–78.

Glucksberg, S., & Cowan, G. N. (1970). Memory for nonattended auditory material. *Cognitive Psychology, 1*, 149–156.

Godden, D. R., & Baddeley, A. D. (1975). Context-dependent memory in two

natural environments: On land and underwater. *British Journal of Psychology, 66*, 325–332.

Godden, D. R., & Baddeley, A. D. (1980). When does context influence recognition memory? *British Journal of Psychology, 71*, 99–104.

Goel, V. (2005). Cognitive neuroscience of deductive reasoning. In K. J. Holyoak & R. G. Morrison (Eds.), *The Cambridge handbook of thinking and reasoning.* New York: Cambridge University Press.

Goel. V., & Dolan, R. J. (2004). Differential involvement of left prefrontal cortex in inductive and deductive reasoning. *Cognition, 93*, B109–21.

Goel, V., Buchelm, C., Rith, C., & Olan, J. (2000). Dissociation of mechanisms underlying syllogistic reasoning. *Neuroimage, 12*, 504–514.

Goh, W. D., & Lu, S. H. X. (2012). Testing the myth of encoding-retrieval match. *Memory & Cognition, 40*, 28–39.

Goldberg, R. F., Perfetti, C. F., & Schneider, W. (2006). Perceptual knowledge retrieval activates sensory brain regions. *Journal of Neuroscience, 26*, 4917–4921.

Goldin-Meadow, S. (1982). The resilience of recursion: A study of a communication system developed without a conventional language model. In E. Wanner & L. R. Gleitman (Eds.), *Language acquisition: The state of the art.* New York: Cambridge University Press.

Goldin-Meadow, S. (2003). *Hearing gesture: How our hands help us think.* Cambridge, MA: Belknap Press of Harvard University Press.

Goldin-Meadow, S., & Mylander, C. (1990). The role of parental input in the development of a morphological system. *Journal of Child Language, 17*, 527–563.

Goldin-Meadow, S., Nusbaum, H., Kelly, S. D., & Wagner, S. (2001). Explaining math: Gesturing lightens the

load. *Psychological Science, 12*(6), 516–522.

Goldman-Eisler, F. (1968). *Psycholinguistics: Experiments in spontaneous speech.* London: Academic Press.

Goldman-Rakic, P. S. (1992). Working memory and the mind. *Scientific American, 267*, 110–117.

Goldstein, D. G., & Gigerenzer, G. (2002). Models of ecological rationality: The recognition heuristic. *Psychological Review, 109*, 75–90.

Gollan, T. H., & Acenas, L. R. (2004). What is a TOT? Cognate and translation effects on tip-of-the-tongue states in Spanish-English and Tagalog-English bilinguals. *Journal of Experimental Psychology: Learning, Memory, and Cognition, 30*(1), 246–269.

Gomila, T., & Calvo, P. (2008). Directions for an embodied cognitive science: Toward an integrated approach. In P. Calvo & T. Gomila (Eds.), *Handbook of cognitive science: An embodied approach* (pp. 1–25). Amsterdam: Elsevier Science.

Gonzalez, J., Barros-Loscertales, A., Pulvermuller, F., Meseguer, V., & Sanjuan, A. (2006). Reading cinnamon activates olfactory brain regions. *Neuroimage, 32*, 906–912.

Goodale, M. A., & Milner, A. D. (1992). Separate visual pathways for perception and action. *Trends in Neurosciences, 15*(1), 20–25.

Goodglass, H. (1993). *Understanding aphasia.* San Diego, CA: Academic Press.

Goodglass, H., & Geschwind, N. (1976). Language disorders (aphasia). In E. C. Carterette & M. P. Friedman (Eds.), *Handbook of perception, volume vii: Language and speech.* New York: Academic Press.

Goodrich, M. A., & Schultz, A. C. (2007). Human-robot interaction: A survey. *Foundations and Trends in Human-Computer Interaction, 1*(3), 203–275.

Gorman, M. E. (1986). How the possibility of error affects falsification on a task that models scientific problem solving. *British Journal of Psychology 77*, 85–96.

Gosseries, O., Bruno, M.-A., Vanhaudenhuyse, A., Laureys, S., & Schnakers, C. (2008/2009). Consciousness in the locked-in syndrome. In S. Laureys & G. Tononi (Eds.), *The neurology of consciousness: Cognitive neuroscience and neuropathology.* New York: Academic Press.

Gough, P. M., Nobre, A. C., & Devlin, J. T. (2005). Dissociating linguistic processes in the left inferior frontal cortex with transcranial magnetic stimulation. *The Journal of Neuroscience, 25*(35), 8010–8016.

Goulden, R., Nation, P., & Read, J. (1990). How large can a receptive vocabulary be? *Applied Linguistics, 11*, 341–363.

Graf, P., & Grondin, S. (2008). Time perception and time-based prospective memory. In J. Glicksohn & M. S. Myslobodsky (Eds.), *Timing the future: The case for a time-based prospective memory* (pp. 1–24). New Jersey: World Scientific.

Graf, P., & Schacter, D. L. (1985). Implicit and explicit memory for new associations in normal and amnesic subjects. *Journal of Experimental Psychology: Learning, Memory, and Cognition, 11*, 501–518.

Graf, P., & Schacter, D. L. (1987). Selective effects of interference on implicit and explicit memory for new associations. *Journal of Experimental Psychology: Learning, Memory, and Cognition, 13*, 45–53.

Graf, P. Squire. L. R., & Mandler, G. (1984). The information that amnesic patients do not forget. *Journal of Experimental Psychology: Learning, Memory, and Cognition, 10*, 164–178.

Grafton, S. T., Fadiga, L., Arbib, M. A., & Rizzolatti, G. (1997). Premotor cortex activation during observation and naming of familiar tools. *Neuroimage*, 6(4), 231–236.

Granhag, P. A., Strömwall, L. A., & Billings, J. F. (2003). 'I'll never forget the sinking ferry!' How social influence makes false memories surface. In M. Vanderhallen, G. Vervaeke, P. J. van Koppen & J. Goethals (Eds.), *Much ado about crime. Chapters on psychology and law* (pp. 129–140). Brusses: Politeia.

Green, A. J. K., & Gilhooly, K. J. (1990). Individual differences and effective learning procedures: The case of statistical computing. *International Journal of Man-Machine Studies, 33*, 97–119.

Green, C. S., & Bavelier, D. (2003). Action video game modifies visual selective attention. *Nature, 423*(6939), 534–537.

Green, C. S., & Bavelier, D. (2006a). Effect of action video games on the spatial distribution of visuospatial attention. *Journal of Experimental Psychology: Human Perception and Performance, 32*(6), 1465–1478.

Green, C. S., & Bavelier, D. (2006b). Enumeration versus multiple object tracking: The case of action video game players. *Cognition, 101*(1), 217–245.

Green, C. S., & Bavelier, D. (2007). Action-video-game experience alters the spatial resolution of vision. *Psychological Science, 18*(1), 88–94.

Green, K. P., Kuhl, P. K., Meltzoff, A. N., & Stevens, E. B. (1991). Integrating speech information across talkers, gender, and sensory modality: Female faces and male voices in the McGurk effect. *Perception & Psychophysics, 50*, 524–536.

Greenberg, D. L. (2007). Comment on 'Detecting awareness in the vegetative state'. *Science, 315*, 1221b.

Greenberg, J. H. (1963). Some universals of grammar with particular reference to the order of meaningful elements. In J. H. Greenberg, *Universals of Language* (pp. 58–90). Cambridge, MA: MIT Press.

Greenberg, J. H. (Ed.) (1978). *Universals of human language.* Stanford, CA: Stanford University Press.

Greene, R. L. (1989). Spacing effects in memory: Evidence for a two process account. *Journal of Experimental Psychology: Learning, Memory and Cognition, 15*, 371–377.

Greenfield, P. M. (2005). Paradigms of cultural thought. In K. J. Holyoak & R. G. Morrison (Eds.), *The Cambridge handbook of thinking and reasoning.* New York: Cambridge University Press.

Greenfield, P. M., DeWinstanley, P., Kilpatrick, H., & Kaye, D. (1994). Action video games and informal education: Effects on strategies for dividing visual attention. *Journal of Applied Developmental Psychology, 15*(1), 105–123.

Greve, K. W., & Bauer, R. M. (1990). Implicit learning of new faces in prosopagnosia: An application of the mere-exposure paradigm. *Neuropsychologia. 28*, 1035–1041.

Grice, H. P. (1957). 'Meaning'. *Philosophical Review, 66*(3).

Grice, H. P. (1975). Logic and conversation. In P. Cole & J. Morgan (Eds.), *Syntax and semantics, volume 3 Speech acts* (pp. 41–58). New York: Academic Press.

Griggs, R. A., & Cox, J. R. (1982). The elusive thematic-materials effect in Wason's selection task. *British Journal of Psychology, 73*, 407–420.

Grodner, D., Gibson, E., & Watson, D. (2005). The influence of contextual contrast on syntactic processing: Evidence for strong-interaction in sentence comprehension. *Cognition, 95*, 275–296.

Grodzinsky, Y., & Santi, A. (2008). The battle for Broca's region. *Trends in Cognitive Sciences, 12*(12), 474–480.

Groeger, J. A. (1999). Expectancy and control: Perceptual and cognitive aspects of the driving task. In P. A. Hancock (Ed.), *Human performance and ergonomics.* San Diego, CA: Academic.

Groome, D. (1999). *An introduction to cognitive psychology: Processes and disorders.* Hove: Psychology Press.

Grosjean, F. (1980). Spoken word recognition processes and the gating paradigm. *Perception and Psychophysics, 28*, 267–283.

Grosjean, F. (1985). The recognition of words after their acoustic offset: Evidence and implications. *Perception and Psychophysics, 38*, 299–310.

Grosjean, F. (2008). *Studying bilinguals.* Oxford: Oxford University Press.

Grosjean, F., & Gee, J. (1987). Prosodic structure and spoken word recognition. *Cognition, 25*, 135–155.

Gross, R. G., & Grossman, M. (2008). Update on apraxia. *Current Neurology and Neuroscience Reports, 8*(6), 490–496.

Grossman, E. D., & Blake, R. (2002). Brain areas active during visual perception of biological motion. *Neuron, 35*(6), 1167–1175.

Grueter, M., Grueter, T., Bell, V., Horst, J., Laskowski, W., Sperling, K., et al. (2007). Hereditary prosopagnosia: The first case series. *Cortex, 43*(6), 734–749.

Grüter, T., Grüter, M., & Carbon, C. C. (2008). Neural and genetic foundations of face recognition and prosopagnosia. *Journal of Neuropsychology, 2*, 79–97.

Gunns, R. E., Johnston, L., & Hudson, S. M. (2002). Victim selection and kinematics: A point-light investigation of vulnerability to attack. *Journal of Nonverbal Behavior, 26*, 129–158.

Gurney, D. J., Pine, K. J., & Wiseman, R. (2013). The gestural misinformation effect: Skewing eyewitness testimony through gesture. *American Journal of Psychology, 126*, 301–314.

H

Haaga, D. A., Dyck, M. J., & Ernst, D. (1991). Empirical status of cognitive theory of depression. *Psychological Bulletin, 110*, 215–236.

Haber, R. N., & Standing, L. G. (1969). Direct measures of short-term visual storage. *Quarterly Journal of Experimental Psychology, 21*, 43–54.

Hacking, I. (1975). *The emergence of probability: A philosophical study of early ideas about probability, induction and statistical inference.* Cambridge: Cambridge University Press.

Haggard, P. (2001). The psychology of action. *British Journal of Psychology, 92*, 113–128.

Haggard, P. (2005). Conscious intention and motor cognition. *Trends in Cognitive Sciences, 9*(6), 290–295.

Haggard, P., & Eimer, M. (1999). On the relation between brain potentials and the awareness of voluntary movements. *Experimental Brain Research, 126*(1), 128–133.

Hagoort, P., & Brown, C. M. (2000). ERP effects of listening to speech compared to reading: The P600/SPS to syntactic violations in spoken sentences and rapid serial visual presentation. *Neuropsychologia, 38*, 1531–1549.

Haken, H., Kelso, J. A. S., & Bunz, H. (1985). A theoretical-model of phase-transitions in human hand movements. *Biological Cybernetics, 51*(5), 347–356.

Hall, T. (1970). *Carl Friedrich Gauss: A biography.* Cambridge, MA: MIT Press.

Hamann, S. B. (2012). Mapping discrete and dimensional emotions onto the brain: Controversies and consensus, *Trends in Cognitive Neurosciences, 16*, 458–466.

Hamann, S. B., Ely, T., Grafton, S., & Kilts, C. (1999). Amygdala activity related to enhanced memory for pleasant and aversive stimuli, *Nature Neuroscience, 2*, 289–293.

Hamann, S. B., Ely, T. D., Hoffman, J. M., & Kilts, C. D. (2002). Ecstasy and agony: Activation of the human amygdala in positive and negative emotion. *Psychological Science, 13*, 35–141.

Hampton, J. A. (1979). Polymorphous concepts in semantic memory. *Journal of Verbal Learning and Verbal Behavior, 18*, 441–461.

Hampton, J. A. (1981). An investigation of the nature of abstract concepts. *Memory and Cognition, 9*, 149–156.

Hancock, P. J. B., Bruce, V., & Burton, A. M. (2000). Recognition of unfamiliar faces. *Trends in Cognitive Sciences, 4*(9), 330–337.

Handzel, A., & Flash, T. (1999). Geometric methods in the study of human motor control. *Cognitive Studies, 6*, 1–13.

Harley, T. A. (1995). *The psychology of language.* Hove: Psychology Press.

Harley, T. A. (2008). *The psychology of language*, 3rd ed. Hove: Psychology Press.

Harley, T. A. (2010). *Talking the talk: Language, psychology and science.* Hove: Psychology Press.

Harlow, J. M. (1848). Passage of an iron rod through the head. *Boston Medical and Surgical Journal, 39*, 389–393. (Republished in *Journal of Neuropsychiatry and Clinical Neuroscience 11*, 281–283).

Harrington, J., Palethorpe, S., & Watson, C. I. (2000a). Does the Queen still speak the Queen's English?, *Nature, 407*, 927–928.

Harrington, J., Palethorpe, S., & Watson, C. I. (2000b). Monophthongal vowel changes received pronunciation: An acoustic analysis of the Queen's Christmas broadcasts. *Journal of the International Phonetic Association, 30*, 63–78.

Harris, C. M., & Wolpert, D. M. (1998). Signal-dependent noise determines motor planning. *Nature, 394*(6695), 780–784.

Harris. M., & Coltheart, M. (1986). *Language processing in children and adults: An introduction.* London: Routledge.

Hassin, R. R., Bargh, J. A., Engell, A., & McCulluch, K. C. (2009). Implicit working memory. *Consciousness and Cognition, 18*, 665–678.

Haugeland, J. (1998). *Having thought: Essays in the metaphysics of mind.* Cambridge, MA: Harvard University Press.

Haxby, J. V., Hoffman, E. A., & Gobbini, M. I. (2000). The distributed human neural system for face perception. *Trends in Cognitive Sciences, 4*(6), 223–233.

Hay, J. C., Pick, H. L., & Ikeda, K. (1965). Visual capture produced by prism spectacles. *Psychonomic Science, 2*(8), 215–216.

Hayes, J. R. (1996). A new framework for understanding cognition and affect in writing. In C. M. Levy & S. Ransdell (Eds.), *The science of writing* (pp. 1–27). Mahwah, NJ: Lawrence Erlbaum.

Hayes, J. R., & Flower, L. S. (1980). *Identifying the organization of writing processes*, In L. W. Gregg & E. R. Steinberg (Eds.), *Cognitive processes in writing* (pp. 3–30). Hillsdale, NJ: Lawrence Erlbaum.

Haynes, J. D., & Rees, G. (2005). Predicting the orientation of invisible stimuli from activity in human primary visual cortex. *Nature Neuroscience, 8*(5), 686–691.

Hayward, W. G. (2003). After the viewpoint debate: Where next in object recognition? *Trends in Cognitive Sciences, 7*(10), 425–427.

Head, H., & Holmes, G. (1911). Sensory disturbances from cerebral lesions. *Brain, 34*, 102–254.

Heath, C., Larrick, R. P., & Klayman, J. (1998). Cognitive repairs: How organizational practices can compensate for individual shortcomings. In B. M. Staw & L. L. Cummings (Eds.), *Research in organizational behaviour.* (Vol. 20, pp. 1–37). Greenwich, CT: JAI Press.

Hebb, D. O. (1949). *The organization of behavior: A neuropsychological theory.* New York: Wiley.

Heider, F., & Simmel, M. (1944). An experimental study of apparent behavior.

American Journal of Psychology, 57, 243–259.

Heims, H. C., Critchley, H. D., Dolan, R., Mathias, C. J., & Cipolotti, L. (2004). Social and motivational functioning is not critically dependent on feedback of autonomic responses: Neuropsychological evidence from patients with pure autonomic failure. *Neuropsychologia, 42*, 1979–1988.

Heiser, M., Iacoboni, M., Maeda, F., Marcus, J., & Mazziotta, J. C. (2003). The essential role of Broca's area in imitation. *European Journal of Neuroscience, 17*(5), 1123–1128.

Helmholtz, H. (1896). *Vortrage und Reden. Vol. 1.* Braunschweig: Vieweg.

Helmholtz, H. V., & Southall, J. P. C. (1962). *Helmholtz's treatise on physiological optics.* New York: Dover Publications.

Henderson, J. M., & Hollingworth, A. (1999). The role of fixation position in detecting scene changes across saccades. *Psychological Science, 10*(5), 438–443.

Henderson, L. (1972). Spatial and verbal codes and the capacity of STM. *Quarterly Journal of Experimental Psychology, 24*, 485–495.

Henle, M. (1962). On the relation between logic and thinking. *Psychological Review 69*, 366–378.

Hennenlotter, A., Dresel, C., Castrop, F., Ceballos Baumann, A., Wohlschlager, A., & Haslinger, B. (2009). The link between facial feedback and neural activity within central circuitries of emotion: New insights from botulinum toxin-induced denervation of frown muscles. *Cerebral Cortex, 19*(3), 537–542.

Hertel, P. T., & Calcaterra, G. (2005). Intentional forgetting benefits from thought substitution. *Psychonomic Bulletin & Review, 12*, 484–489.

Hertwig, R., & Gigerenzer, G. (1999). The 'conjunction fallacy' revisited: How intelligent inferences look like reasoning errors. *Journal of Behavioral Decision Making, 12*, 275–305.

Heyes, C. (2011). Automatic imitation. *Psychological Bulletin, 137*(3), 463–483.

Hickok, G., & Hauser, M. (2010). (Mis)understanding mirror neurons. *Current Biology, 20*(14), R593–594.

Hicks, J. L., & Starns, J. J. (2004). Retrieval-induced forgetting occurs in tests of item recognition. *Psychonomic Bulletin & Review, 11*, 125–130.

Higuchi, S., Holle, H., Roberts, N., Eickhoff, S. B., & Vogt, S. (2011). Imitation and observational learning of hand actions: Prefrontal involvement and connectivity. *Neuroimage.*

Hilts, P. J. (1995). *Memory's ghost: The nature of memory and the strange tale of Mr. M.* New York: Simon & Schuster.

Himberg, T., & Thompson, M. R. (2011). Learning and synchronising dance movements in South African songs – Cross-cultural motion-capture study. *Dance Research, 29*(2), 305–328.

Hinrichs, J. V., Ghoneim, M. M., & Mewaldt, S. P. (1984). Diazepam and memory: Retrograde facilitation produced by interference reduction. *Psychopharmacology, 84*, 158–162.

Hirstein, W., & Ramachandran, V. S. (1997). Capgras syndrome: A novel probe for understanding the neural representation of the identity and familiarity of persons. *Proceedings of The Royal Society, Biological Sciences, 264*(1380), 437–444.

Hirstein, W., & Sifferd, K. (2011). The legal self: Executive processes and legal theory. *Consciousness and Cognition, 20*(1), 156–171.

Hiscock, M. (1988). Behavioral asymmetries in normal children. In D. L. Molfese & S. J. Segalowitz (Eds.), *Brain lateralization in children: Developmental implications* (pp. 85–169). New York: Guilford.

Hitch, G. J., & Fergusen, J. (1991). Prospective memory for future intentions. *European Journal of Cognitive Psychology, 3*, 285–295.

Ho, C., Reed, N., & Spence, C. (2007). Multisensory in-car warning signals for collision avoidance. *Human Factors, 49*(6), 1107–1114.

Hockett, C. F. (1960). The origin of speech. *Scientific American, 203*, 88–96.

Hodge, F. S., Colton, R. H., & Kelley, R. T. (2001). Vocal intensity characteristics in normal and elderly speakers. *Journal of Voice, 15*, 503–511.

Hoff, E. (2005). *Language development*. 3rd ed. Wadsworth.

Hoffman, B. (2010). 'I think I can, but I'm afraid to try': The role of self-efficacy beliefs and mathematics anxiety in mathematics problem-solving efficiency. *Learning and Individual Differences, 20*(3), 276–283.

Hoffman, B., & Schraw, G. (2009). The influence of self-efficacy and working memory capacity on problem-solving efficiency. *Learning and Individual Differences, 19*, 91–100.

Holcomb, P. J. (1988). Automatic and attentional processing: An event-related brain potential analysis of semantic priming. *Brain and Language, 35*, 66–85.

Holcomb, P. J. (1993). Semantic priming and stimulus degradation: Implications for the role of the N400 in language processing. *Psychophysiology, 30*, 47–61.

Holcombe, A. O. (2009). Seeing slow and seeing fast: Two limits on perception. *Trends in Cognitive Sciences, 13*(5), 216–221.

Holding, D. (1970). Guessing behaviour and the Sperling store. *Quarterly Journal of Experimental Psychology, 22*, 248–256.

Holding, D. H. (1979). The evaluation of chess positions. *Simulation and Games, 10*, 207–221.

Holding, D. H. (1985). *The psychology of chess*. Hillsdale, NJ: Lawrence Erlbaum.

Holding, D. H., & Reynolds, J. R. (1982). Recall or evaluation of chess positions

as determinants of chess skill. *Memory and Cognition, 10*, 237–242.

Holt, N. et al. (2012). *Psychology: The science of mind and behaviour*. Maidenhead: McGraw-Hill.

Hommel, B., Musseler, J., Aschersleben, G., & Prinz, W. (2001). The theory of event coding (TEC): A framework for perception and action planning. *Behavioral and Brain Sciences, 24*(5), 849–878.

Hoosain, R. (1984), Experiments on digit span in the Chinese and English languages. In H. S. R. Kao & R. Hoosain (Eds.), *Psychological studies of the Chinese language* (pp. 23–28). Hong Kong: Chinese Language Society.

Hoosain, R., & Salili, F. (1987). Language differences in pronunciation speed for numbers, digit span and mathematical ability, *Psychologia, 30*, 34–38.

Hostetter, A. B., & Alibali, M. W. (2008). Visible embodiment: Gestures as simulated action. *Psychonomic Bulletin & Review, 15*(3), 495–514.

Houston, S. (2011). The methodological challenges of research into dance for people with Parkinson's. *Dance Research, 29*(2), 329–351.

Hubal, R., Mitroff, S. R., Cain, M. S., Scott, B., & DeWitt, R. (2010). *Simulating a vigilance task: Extensible technology for baggage security assessment and training*. Paper presented at the Technologies for Homeland Security (HST), 2010 IEEE International Conference.

Hubbard, E. M., & Ramachandran, V. S. (2005). Neurocognitive mechanisms of synesthesia. *Neuron, 48*(3), 509–520.

Hubel, D. H., & Wiesel, T. N. (1959). Receptive fields of single neurones in the cat's striate cortex. *Journal of Physiology-London, 148*(3), 574–591.

Hubel, D. H., & Wiesel, T. N. (1962). Receptive fields, binocular interaction and functional architecture in cat's

visual cortex. *Journal of Physiology-London, 160*(1), 106–&.

Huddleston, R., & Pullum, G. K. (2002). The Cambridge Grammar of the English Language. Cambridge: Cambridge University Press.

Hulme, C., Thomson, N., Muir, C., & Lawrence, A. (1984). Speech rate and the development of short-term memory. *Journal of Experimental Child Psychology, 38*, 241–253.

Humphrey, N. (2002). *The uses of consciousness the mind made flesh: Essays from the frontiers of psychology and evolution* (pp. 65–85). Oxford: Oxford University Press.

Humphreys, G. W., & Forde, E. M. E. (1998). Disordered action schema and action disorganisation syndrome. *Cognitive Neuropsychology, 15*(6–8), 771–811.

Humphreys, G. W., & Riddoch, M. J. (1987). *To see but not to see a case study of visual agnosia*. London: Erlbaum.

Hurley, S. L. (1998). *Consciousness in action*. Cambridge, MA: Harvard University Press.

Huxley, T. H. (1896). *Methods and results: Collected Essays* (Vol. 1). New York: Appleton.

Hyman, I. E., Jr., & Pentland, J. (1996). The role of mental imagery in the creation of false childhood memories. *Journal of Memory and Language, 35*, 101–117.

Hyman, I. E., Boss, S. M., Wise, B. M., McKenzie, K. E., & Caggiano, J. M. (2010). Did you see the unicycling clown? Inattentional blindness while walking and talking on a cell phone. *Applied Cognitive Psychology, 24*, 597–607.

Hyman, I. E., Husband, T. H., & Billings, F. J. (1995). False memories of childhood experiences. *Applied Cognitive Psychology, 9*, 181–197.

Hymes, D. (1972). On communicative competence. In J. B. Pride & J. Homes (Eds.), *Sociolinguistics*. Harmondsworth: Penguin.

I

Ingram, J. (2007). *Neurolinguistics*. Cambridge: Cambridge University Press.

Intons-Peterson, M. J. (1983). Imagery paradigms: How vulnerable are they to experimenter expectations. *Journal of Experimental Psychology: Human Perception and Performance, 9*, 394–412.

Intraub, H. (1997). The representation of visual scenes. *Trends in Cognitive Sciences, 1*, 217–221.

Intraub, H., Gottesman, C. V., & Bills, A. (1998). Effects of perceiving and imagining scenes on memory for pictures. *Journal of Experimental Psychology: Learning, Memory, and Cognition, 24*, 186–201.

Intraub, H., Gottesman, C. V. Willey, E. V., & Zuk, I. J. (1996). Boundary extension for briefly glimpsed photographs: Do common perceptual processes result in unexpected memory distortions? *Journal of Memory and Language, 35*, 118–134.

Isen, A. M. (1985). The asymmetry of happiness and sadness in effects on memory in normal college students. *Journal of Experimental Psychology: General, 114*, 388–391.

Ishai, A., Pessoa, L., Bikle, P. C., & Ungerleider, L. G. (2004). Repetition suppression of faces is modulated by emotion. *Proceedings of the National Academy of Sciences of the United States of America, 101*, 9827–9832.

Itti, L., & Koch, C. (2001). Computational modelling of visual attention. *Nature Reviews Neuroscience, 2*(3), 194–203.

Iverson, P., Kuhl, P. K., Akahane-Yamada, R., Diesch, E., Tohkurae, Y., Kettermann, A., & Siebert, C. (2003). A perceptual interference account of acquisition difficulties for non-native phonemes. *Cognition, 87*, B47–B57.

Izard, C. (1977). *Human emotions*. New York: Plenum Press.

J

Jackson, F. (1982). Epiphenomenal qualia. *Philosophical Quarterly*, *32*(127), 127–136.

Jacobs, D. W. (2003). What makes viewpoint-invariant properties perceptually salient? *Journal of the Optical Society of America a-Optics Image Science and Vision*, *20*(7), 1304–1320.

Jacobs, N., & Garnham, A. (2007). The role of conversational hand gestures in a narrative task. *Journal of Memory and Language*, *56*(2), 291–303.

Jacobson, J. Z., & Dodwell, P. C. (1979). Saccadic eye movements during reading. *Brain and Language*, *8*(3), 303–314.

James, W. (1884). What is an emotion? *Mind*, *9*, 188–205.

James, W. (1890). *The principles of psychology*. (2 vols.). New York: Henry Holt.

Jamison, K. (1993). *Touched with fire: Manic-depressive illness and the artistic temperament*. New York: Free Press/Macmillan.

Jang, S. H., & Pollick, F. E. (2011). Experience influences brain mechanisms of watching dance. *Dance Research*, *29*(2), 352–377.

Jastorff, J., & Orban, G. A. (2009). Human functional magnetic resonance imaging reveals separation and integration of shape and motion cues in biological motion processing. *Journal of Neuroscience*, *29*(22), 7315–7329.

Jastrow, J. (1899). The mind's eye. *Popular Science Monthly*, *54*, 299–312.

Jay, T. B., & Danks, J. H. (1977). Ordering of taboo adjectives. *Bulletin of the Psychonomic Society*, *9*, 405–408.

Jazayeri, M., & Shadlen, M. N. (2010). Temporal context calibrates interval timing. *Nature Neuroscience*, *13*(8), 1020–U1152.

Jeannerod, M. (1984). The timing of natural prehension movements. *Journal of Motor Behavior*, *16*(3), 235–254.

Jeannerod, M., Arbib, M. A., Rizzolatti, G., & Sakata, H. (1995). Grasping objects – The cortical mechanisms of visuomotor transformation. *Trends in Neurosciences*, *18*(7), 314–320.

Jeffries, R., Polson, P. G., Razran, L., & Attwood, M. E. (1977). A process model for missionaries-cannibals and other river crossing problems. *Cognitive Psychology*, *9*, 412–420.

Jelicic, M., Smeets, T., Candel, I., van Suijdam, M., & Merckelbach, H. (2006). No, I don't remember seeing video footage of the killing of Theo van Gogh! Misinformation manipulations do not always elicit false memories. In D. Canter (Series Ed.), & K. Nixon (Vol. ed.), *Forensic recall and eyewitness testimony* (pp. 21–25). London: IA-IP Publishing.

Jelicic, M., Smeets, T., Peters, M. J. V., Candel, I., Horselenberg, R., & Merckelbach, H. (2006). Assassination of a controversial politician: Remembering details from another non-existent film. *Applied Cognitive Psychology*, *20*, 591–596.

Jelinek, L., Moritz, S., Heeren, D., & Naber, D. (2006). Everyday memory functioning in obsessive-compulsive disorder. *Journal of the International Neuropsychological Society*, *12*, 746–749.

Jenkins, J. G., & Dallenbach, K. M. (1924). Oblivescence during sleep and waking. *American Journal of Psychology*, *35*, 605–612.

Johansson, G. (1973). Visual-perception of biological motion and a model for its analysis. *Perception & Psychophysics*, *14*(2), 201–211.

Johnson, K., & Shiffrar, M. (2013). People watching: Social, perceptual and neuropsychological studies of body. *Perception*. Oxford University Press.

Johnson-Laird, P. N. (1975). Models of deduction. In R. C. Falmagne (Ed.), *Reasoning: Representation and process* (pp. 7–54). Hillsdale, NJ: Lawrence Erlbaum.

Johnson-Laird, P. N. (1983). *Mental models*. Cambridge: Cambridge University Press.

Johnson-Laird, P. N. (1999). Deductive reasoning. *Annual Review of Psychology*, *50*, 109–135.

Johnson-Laird, P. N. (2006). *How we reason*. Oxford: Oxford University Press.

Johnson-Laird, P. N. (2008). *How we reason*. Oxford. Oxford University Press.

Johnson-Laird, P. N., & Bara, B. G. (1984). Syllogistic inference. *Cognition*, *16*, 1–61.

Johnson-Laird, P. N., & Byrne, R. M. J. (1991/1993a). *Deduction*. Hove: Lawrence Erlbaum.

Johnson-Laird, P. N., & Steedman, M. (1978). The psychology of syllogisms. *Cognitive Psychology*, *10*, 64–99.

Johnson-Laird, P. N., Byrne, R. M. J., & Schaeken, W. (1992). Propositional reasoning by model. *Psychological Review*, *90*, 418–439.

Johnson-Laird, P. N., Byrne, R. M. J., & Schaeken, W. (1994). Why models rather than rules give a better account of propositional reasoning: A reply to Bonatti and to O'Brien, Braine and Yang. *Psychological Review*, *101*, 734–739.

Johnson-Laird, P. N., Legrenzi, P., & Legrenzi, M. S. (1972). Reasoning and a sense of reality. *British Journal of Psychology*, *63*, 395–400.

Johnson-Laird, P. N., Mancini, J. L., & Gangemi, A. (2006). A hyper-emotion theory of psychological illnesses. *Psychological Review*, *113*, 822–841.

Johnston, R. A., & Edmonds, A. J. (2009). Familiar and unfamiliar face recognition: A review. *Memory*, *17*(5), 577–596.

Jones, G. (2003). Testing two theories of insight. *Journal of Experimental Psychology: Learning, Memory and Cognition*, *29*, 1017–1027.

Jones Leonard, B., McNaughton, B. L., & Barnes, C. A. (1987).

Suppression of hippocampal synaptic activity during slow-wave sleep. *Brain Research*, *425*, 174–177.

Jonides, J., Smith, E. E., Koeppe, R. A., Awh, E., Minoshima, S., & Mintun, M. A. (1993). Spatial working memory in humans as revealed by PET. *Nature*, *363*, 623–625.

Joo, S. J., Shin, K., Chong, S. C., & Blake, R. (2009). On the nature of the stimulus information necessary for estimating mean size of visual arrays. *Journal of Vision*, *9*(9), 1–12.

Joormann, J., Yoon, K. L., & Zetsche, U. (2007). Cognitive inhibition in depression. *Applied and Preventive Psychology*, *12*, 128–139.

Jordan, M. I. (1986). *Serial order: A parallel distributed approach*. Institute for Cognitive Science, University of California, San Diego.

Jordan, M. I. (1997). Chapter 25 Serial order: A parallel distributed processing approach. In J. W. Donahoe & V. Packard Dorsel (Eds.), *Neural-network models of cognition* (pp. 471–495). Amsterdam: Elsevier Science.

Jordan, M. I., & Rumelhart, D. E. (1992). Forward models – Supervised learning with a distal teacher. *Cognitive Science*, *16*(3), 307–354.

Jost, A. (1897). Die assoziationsfestigkeit in ihrer abhangigheit von der verteilung der wiederholungen. *Zeitschrift fur Psychologie*, *14*, 436–472.

Jung-Beeman, M., Bowden, E. M., Haberman, J., Frymiare, J. L., Arambel-Liu, S., Greenblatt, R., Reber, P. J., & Kounios, J. (2004). Neural activity when people solve verbal problems with insight. *PLoS Biology*, *2*, 0500–0510.

Jusczyk, P. W. (1999). How infants begin to extract words from speech. *Trends in Cognitive Science*, *3*, 323–328.

Jusczyk, P. W., & Aslin, R. N. (1995). Infants' detection of speech patterns of words in fluent speech. *Cognitive Psychology*, *29*, 1–23.

Jusczyk, P. W., Houston, D. M., & Newsome, M. (1999).

The beginnings of word segmentation in English learning infants. *Cognitive Psychology, 39,* 159–207.

Juslin, P. N., & Laukka, P. (2003). Communication of emotions in vocal expression and music performance: Different channels, same code? *Psychological Bulletin, 129*(5), 770–814.

K

Kahneman, D. (1973). *Attention and effort.* Englewood Cliffs, NJ: Prentice-Hall.

Kahneman, D. (2003). A perspective on judgment and choice: Mapping bounded rationality. *American Psychologist, 58,* 697–720.

Kahneman, D. (2011). *Thinking, fast and slow.* London: Allen Lane.

Kahneman, D., & Tversky, A. (1979). Prospect theory: An analysis of decision under risk. *Econometrica, 47,* 263–291.

Kahneman, D., & Tversky, A. (1984). Choices, values and frames. *American Psychologist, 39,* 341–350.

Kahneman, D., Knetsch, J. L., & Thaler, R. H. (1990). Experimental tests of the endowment effect and the Coase theorem. *Journal of Political Economy, 98,* 1325–1348.

Kalenine, S., Buxbaum, L. J., & Coslett, H. B. (2010). Critical brain regions for action recognition: Lesion symptom mapping in left hemisphere stroke. *Brain, 133*(11), 3269–3280.

Kalat, J. W. (2007). *Biological psychology.* Cengage Learning.

Kaminski, J., Call, J., & Fischer, J. (2004). Word learning in a domestic dog: Evidence for 'fast mapping'. *Science, 304*(5677), 1682–1683.

Kaminski, J., Tempelmann, S., Call, J., & Tomasello, M. (2009). Domestic dogs comprehend human communication with iconic signs. *Developmental Science, 12*(6), 831–837.

Kane, M. J., Brown, L. H., McVay, J. C., Silvia, P. J., Myin-Germeys, I., & Kwapil, T. R. (2007). For whom the mind wanders, and when: An experience-sampling study of working memory and executive control in daily life. *Psychological Science, 18,* 614–621.

Kanwisher, N., McDermott, J., & Chun, M. M. (1997). The fusiform face area: A module in human extrastriate cortex specialized for face perception. *Journal of Neuroscience, 17*(11), 4302–4311.

Katayama, M., & Kawato, M. (1993). Virtual trajectory and stiffness ellipse during multijoint arm movement predicted by neural inverse models. *Biological Cybernetics, 69*(5–6), 353–362.

Kato, P. M. (2010). Video games in health care: Closing the gap. *Review of General Psychology, 14*(2), 113–121.

Kawato, M. (1999). Internal models for motor control and trajectory planning. *Current Opinion in Neurobiology, 9*(6), 718–727.

Kawato, M., & Gomi, H. (1992). A computational model of 4 regions of the cerebellum based on feedback-error learning. *Biological Cybernetics, 68*(2), 95–103.

Keither, M. (2005). Repetition priming modulates category-related effects on event-related potentials: Further evidence for multiple cortical semantic systems. *Journal of Cognitive Neuroscience, 17,* 199–211.

Kellogg, R. T. (1999). Multiple systems of working memory in writing. In M. F. Crété & E. Espéret (Eds.), *Writing and learning to write at the dawn of the 21st century: Proceedings of the 1998 Writing Conference.* Poitiers: LaCo-CNRS, University of Poitiers.

Kelly, S., Byrne, K., & Holler, J. (2011). Raising the ante of communication: Evidence for enhanced gesture use in high stakes situations. *Information, 2,* 579–593.

Kelso, J. A. S. (1984). Phase-transitions and critical-behavior in human bimanual coordination. *American Journal of Physiology, 246*(6), 1000–1004.

Kelso, J. A. S. (1995). *Dynamic patterns: The self-organization of brain and behavior.* Cambridge, MA: MIT Press.

Kemp, S., Wilkinson, K., Caswell, H., Reynders, H., & Baker, G. (2008). The base rate of Wada test failure. *Epilepsy & Behaviour, 13,* 630–633.

Kendon, A. (2004). *Gesture: Visible action as utterance.* Cambridge: Cambridge University Press.

Kenealy, P. M. (1997). Mood-state-dependent retrieval: The effects of induced mood on memory reconsidered. *Quarterly Journal of Experimental Psychology, 50A,* 290–317.

Kennedy, W. G., Bugajska, M. D., Harrison, A. M., & Trafton, J. G. (2009). 'Like-me' simulation as an effective and cognitively plausible basis for social robotics. *International Journal of Social Robotics, 1,* 181–194.

Kentridge, R. W., Heywood, C. A., & Weiskrantz, L. (1999). Attention without awareness in blindsight. *Proceedings of the Royal Society of London Series B-Biological Sciences, 266*(1430), 1805–1811.

Kerr, D. S., & Murthy, U. S. (2004). Divergent and convergent idea generation in teams: A comparison of computer-mediated and face-to-face communication. *Group Decision and Negotiation, 13,* 381–399.

Kilner, J. M. (2011). More than one pathway to action understanding. *Trends in Cognitive Sciences, 15*(8), 352–357.

Kimura, D. (1967). Functional asymmetry of the brain in dichotic listening. *Cortex, 3,* 163–178.

Kingston, J. A., & Lyddy, F. (2013). Self-efficacy and short-term memory capacity as predictors of proportional reasoning. *Learning and Individual Differences, 26,* 185–190.

Kirchner, H., & Thorpe, S. J. (2006). Ultra-rapid object detection with saccadic eye movements: Visual processing speed revisited. *Vision Research, 46*(11), 1762–1776.

Kita, S., & Ozyurek, A. (2003). What does cross-linguistic variation in semantic coordination of speech and gesture reveal?: Evidence for an interface representation of spatial thinking and speaking. *Journal of Memory and Language, 48*(1), 16–32.

Klatzky, R. L. (1980). *Human memory: Structures and processes* (2nd ed.). San Francisco: Freeman.

Klatzky, R. L., Lederman, S. J., & Metzger, V. A. (1985). Identifying objects by touch – An expert system. *Perception & Psychophysics, 37*(4), 299–302.

Klatzky, R. L., Pellegrino, J. W., McCloskey, B. P., & Doherty, S. (1989). Can you squeeze a tomato? The role of motor representations in semantic sensibility judgments. *Journal of Memory and Language, 28,* 56–77.

Klauer, S. G., Dingus, T. A., Neale, V. L., Sudweeks, J. D., & Ramsey, D. J. (2006). *The impact of driver inattention on near-crash/crash risk: An analysis using the 100-car naturalistic driving study data.* Washington, DC: National Highway Traffic Safety Administration.

Klein, D. C., & Seligman, M. E. P. (1976). Reversal of performance deficits and perceptual deficits in learned helplessness and depression. *Journal of Abnormal Psychology, 85,* 11–26.

Klein, G. (1998/1999). *Sources of power: How people make decisions.* Cambridge, MA: MIT Press.

Klein, G., Wolf, S., Militello, L., & Zsambok, C. (1995). Characteristics of skilled option generation in chess. *Organizational Behavior and Human Decision Processes., 62,* 63–69.

Klein, R. M. (1988). Inhibitory tagging system facilitates visual-search. *Nature, 334*(6181), 430–431.

Klein, R. M. (2000). Inhibition of return. *Trends in Cognitive Sciences, 4*(4), 138–147.

Klein, S. B., & Loftus, J. (2002). Memory and temporal experience: The effects of episodic memory loss on an amnesic patient's ability to remember the past and imagine the future. *Social Cognition*, *20*, 353–379.

Klein, W., & Perdue, C. (1997). The basic variety (or: couldn't natural languages be much simpler?). *Second Language Research*, *13*(4), 301–347.

Klinger, E., & Cox, W. M. (1987). Dimensions of thought flow in everyday life. *Imagination, Cognition and Personality*, *7*, 105–128.

Knight, A., Underhill, P. A., Mortenson, H. M., & Zhivotovsky, L. A. (2003). African Y chromosome and mtDNA divergence provides insight into the history of click languages. *Current Biology*, *13*, 464–473.

Knoblich, G., & Flach, R. (2003). Action identity: Evidence from self-recognition, prediction, and coordination. *Consciousness and Cognition*, *12*(4), 620–632.

Knoblich, G., Ohlsson, S., Haider, H., & Rhenius, D. (1999). Constraint relaxation and chunk decomposition in insight problem solving. *Journal of Experimental Psychology: Learning, Memory and Cognition*, *25*, 1534–1556.

Knowlton, B., Squire, L., & Gluck, M. (1994). Probabilistic classification learning in amnesia. *Learning and Memory*, *1*, 106–120.

Ko, S. J., Judd, C. M., & Blair, I. V. (2006). What the voice reveals: Within- and between-category stereotyping on the basis of voice. *Personality and Social Psychology Bulletin*, *32*(6), 806–819.

Koch, C. (2004). *The quest for consciousness: A neurobiological approach*. Denver, CO: Roberts and Co.

Koch, C., & Ullman, S. (1985). Shifts in selective visual-attention – Towards the underlying neural circuitry. *Human Neurobiology*, *4*(4), 219–227.

Koechlin, E. (2008). The cognitive architecture of the human lateral prefrontal cortex. In P. Haggard, Y. Rossetti, & M. Kawato (Eds.), *Attention and Performance XXII: Sensorimotor foundations of higher cognition*. Oxford: Oxford University Press.

Koh, R. Y. I., Park, T., Wickens, C. D., Ong, L. T., & Chia, S. N. (2011). Differences in attentional strategies by novice and experienced operating theatre scrub nurses. *Journal of Experimental Psychology: Applied*, *17*(3), 233–246.

Kohler, W. (1925). *The mentality of apes*. New York: Harcourt Brace.

Kohler, E., Keysers, C., Umilta, M. A., Fogassi, L., Gallese, V., & Rizzolatti, G. (2002). Hearing sounds, understanding actions: Action representation in mirror neurons. *Science*, *297*(5582), 846–848.

Kolers, P. A., & Roediger, H. L. (1984). Procedures of mind. *Journal of Verbal Learning and Verbal Behavior*, *23*, 425–449.

Kolk, H. (2007). Variability is the hallmark of aphasic behaviour: Grammatical behaviour is no exception. *Brain and Language*, *101*, 99–102.

Konen, C. S., Behrmann, M., Nishimura, M., & Kastner, S. (2011). The functional neuroanatomy of object agnosia: A case study. *Neuron*, *71*(1), 49–60.

Kong, J., Gollub, R. L., Webb, J. M., Vangel, M. G., & Kwong, K. (2007). Test-retest study of fMRI signal change evoked by electro-acupuncture stimulation. *NeuroImage*, *34*, 1171–1181.

Kopelman, M. D., Lasserson, D., Kingsley, D., Bello, F., Rush, C., Stanhope, N., Stevens, T., Goodman, G., Heilpern, G., Kendall, B., & Colchester, A. (2001). Structural MRI volumetric analysis in patients with organic amnesia, 2: Correlations with anterograde memory and executive tests in 40 patients. *Journal of Neurology, Neurosurgery and Psychiatry*, *71*, 23–28.

Kopelman, M. D., Thomson, A., Guerrini, I., Marshall, E. J. (2009). The Korsakoff syndrome: Clinical aspects, psychology and treatment. *Alcohol and Alcoholism*, *44*(2), 148–154.

Kording, K. P. (2007). Decision theory: What 'should' the nervous system do? *Science*, *318*(5850), 606–610.

Kording, K. P., & Wolpert, D. M. (2006). Bayesian decision theory in sensorimotor control. *Trends in Cognitive Sciences*, *10*(7), 319–326.

Koriat, A., & Goldsmith, M. (1996). Memory metaphors and the real life/ laboratory controversy: Correspondence versus storehouse conceptions of memory. *Behavioral and Brain Sciences*, *19*, 167–187.

Kosslyn, S. M. (1973). Scanning visual images: Some structural implications. *Perception and Psychophysics*, *14*, 90–94.

Kosslyn, S. M., & Thompson, W. L. (2003). When is early visual cortex activated during visual mental imagery? *Psychological Bulletin*, *129*, 723–746.

Kosslyn, S. M., Ball, T. M., & Reiser, B. J. (1978). Visual images preserve metric spatial information: Evidence from studies of image scanning. *Journal of Experimental Psychology: Human Perception and Performance*, *4*, 56–60.

Kosslyn, S. M., Thompson, W. L., Kim, I. J., & Alpert, N. M. (1995). Topographical representations of mental images in primary visual cortex. *Nature*, *378*, 496–498.

Kovacs, I., & Julesz, B. (1994). Perceptual sensitivity maps within globally defined visual shapes. *Nature*, *370*, 644–646.

Kozlowski, L. T., & Cutting, J. E. (1977). Recognizing sex of a walker from a dynamic point-light display. *Perception & Psychophysics*, *21*(6), 575–580.

Kramer, A. F., & Hahn, S. (1995). Splitting the beam: Distribution of attention over noncontiguous regions of the visual field. *Psychological Science*, *6*(6), 381–386.

Krauss, M. (1992). The world's languages in crisis. *Language* 68, 1–42.

Krauss, R. M., Chen, Y., & Gottesman, R. F. (2000). Lexical gestures and lexical access: A process model. In D. McNeill (Ed.), *Language and gesture* (pp. 261–283). Cambridge: Cambridge University Press.

Kringelbach, M. L. (2004). Emotion. In R. L. Gregory (Ed.), *The Oxford companion to the mind*, 2nd ed. (pp. 287–290). Oxford: Oxford University Press.

Kringelbach, M. L., & Rolls, E. T. (2004), The functional neuroanatomy of the human orbitofrontal cortex: Evidence from neuroimaging and neuropsychology, *Progress in Neurobiology*, *72*, 341–372.

Kroll, J. F., & Dussias, P. E. (2004). The comprehension of words and sentences in two languages. In T. Bhatia & W. Ritchie (Eds.), *The handbook of bilingualism*. Cambridge: Blackwell.

Kroos, C., Herath, D. C., & Stelarc. (2011). From robot arm to intentional agent: The Articulated Head. In S. Goto (Ed.), *Advances in robotics, automation and control* (pp. 215–240). InTech.

Kübler, A., Kotchoubey, B., Kaiser, J., Wolpaw, J. R., Birbaumer, N. (2001). Brain-computer communication: Unlocking the locked in. *Psychological Bulletin*, *127*(3), 358–375.

Kucera, H., & Francis, W. N. (1967). *Computational analysis of present-day American English*. Providence: Brown University Press.

Kuhl, P. K. (1993). Early linguistic experience and phonetic perception: Implications for theories of developmental speech perception. *Journal of Phonetics*, *21*, 125–139.

Kuhl, P. K., & Miller, J. D. (1978). Speech perception by the chinchilla: Identification functions for synthetic VOT stimuli. *Journal of the*

Acoustical Society of America, 63, 905–917.

Kuhn, G., Tatler, B. W., Findlay, J. M., & Cole, G. G. (2008). Misdirection in magic: Implications for the relationship between eye gaze and attention. *Visual Cognition, 16*(2–3), 391–405.

Kunst-Wilson, W. R., & Zajonc, R. B. (1980). Affective discrimination of stimuli that cannot be recognized. *Science, 207*(4430), 557–558.

Kusumi, T. (2006). Human metacognition and the déjà vu phenomenon. In K. Fujita & S. Itakura (Eds.), *Diversity of cognition: Evolution, development, domestication, and pathology.* Kyoto: Kyoto University Press.

Kutas, M., & Hillyard, S. A. (1980). Reading senseless sentences: Brain potentials reflect semantic incongruity. *Science, 207,* 203–205.

Kvavilashvili, L. (1987). Remembering intention as a distinct form of memory. *British Journal of Psychology, 78,* 507–518.

Kvavilashvili, L., & Ellis, J. (2004). Ecological validity and twenty years of real life/laboratory controversy in memory research: A critical (and historical) review. *History and Philosophy of Psychology, 6,* 59–80.

L

Labate, A., & Gambardella, A. (2013). Comment on Brázdil (2012) 'Unveiling the mystery of dèjà-vù: The structural anatomy of dèjà-vù'. *Cortex, 49,* 1162.

Laberge, D. (1983). Spatial extent of attention to letters and words. *Journal of Experimental Psychology-Human Perception and Performance, 9*(3), 371–379.

Laberge, D., & Brown, V. R. (1987). Comparison of moving-spotlight and gradient models of attention. *Bulletin of the Psychonomic Society, 25*(5), 349–349.

Lacquaniti, F., Terzuolo, C., & Viviani, P. (1983). The law relating the kinematic and figural aspects of drawing movements. *Acta Psychologica, 54*(1–3), 115–130.

Ladefoged, P. (1993). *A course in phonetics.* (3rd ed.). New York: Harcourt Brace Jovanovich.

Lakoff, G., & Johnson, M. (1980). *Metaphors we live by.* Chicago: University of Chicago Press.

Lamberty, G. J., Beckwith, B. E., & Petros, T. V. (1990). Posttrial treatment with ethanol enhances recall of prose narratives. *Physiology and Behavior, 48,* 653–58.

Lamme, V. A. F. (2003). Why visual attention and awareness are different. *Trends in Cognitive Sciences, 7*(1), 12–18.

Lamme, V. A. F., & Roelfsema, P. R. (2000). The distinct modes of vision offered by feedforward and recurrent processing. *Trends in Neurosciences, 23*(11), 571–579.

Landy, D., & Goldstone, R. L. (2007). How abstract is symbolic thought? *Journal of Experimental Psychology-Learning Memory and Cognition, 33*(4), 720–733.

Landy, M. S., Maloney, L. T., Johnston, E. B., & Young, M. (1995). Measurement and modeling of depth cue combination – in defense of weak fusion. *Vision Research, 35*(3), 389–412.

Lang, P. J. (1988). What are the data of emotion? In V. Hamilton, G. H. Bower, & N. H. Frijda (Eds.), *Cognitive perspectives on emotion and motivation* (pp. 173–191). New York: Kluwer Academic/Plenum Press.

Lange, J., & Lappe, M. (2006). A model of biological motion perception from configural form cues. *Journal of Neuroscience, 26*(11), 2894–2906.

Larkin, J. H. (1978). Problem solving in physics: Structure, process and learning. In J. M. Scandura & C. J. Brainerd (Eds.), *Structural/process models of complex human behavior.* The Netherlands: Sijthoff & Noordhoff.

Larsen, R. J., Kasimatis, M., & Frey, K. (1992). Facilitating the furrowed brow: An unobtrusive test of the facial feedback hypothesis applied to unpleasant affect. *Cognition and Emotion, 6,* 321–338.

Lashley, K. (1929). *Brain mechanisms and intelligence.* Chicago: University of Chicago Press.

Lashley, K. S. (1951). The problem of serial order in behavior. In L. A. Jeffress (Ed.), *Cerebral mechanisms in behavior.* New York: Wiley.

Latash, M., & Zatsiorsky, V. (2001). *Classics in movement science.* Champaign: Human Kinetics.

Latinus, M., & Belin, P. (2011). Human voice perception. *Current Biology, 21*(4), R143-R145.

Laurienti, P. J., Burdette, J. H., Maldjian, J. A., & Wallace, M. T. (2006). Enhanced multisensory integration in older adults. *Neurobiology of Aging, 27*(8), 1155–1163.

Lavie, N. (1995). Perceptual load as a necessary condition for selective attention. *Journal of Experimental Psychology-Human Perception and Performance, 21*(3), 451–468.

Lavie, N. (2005). Distracted and confused? Selective attention under load. *Trends in Cognitive Sciences, 9*(2), 75–82.

Lavy, E., van den Hout, M. A., & Arntz, A. (1993). Attentional bias and facilitated escape: A pictorial test. *Advances of Behaviour Research and Therapy, 15,* 279–289.

Laws, K. R., Leeson, V. C., & McKenna, P. J. (2006). Domain specific deficits in schizophrenia. *Cognitive Neuropsychiatry, 11,* 537–556.

Lazarus, R. S. (1966). *Psychological stress and the coping process.* New York: McGraw-Hill.

Lazarus, R. S. (1982). Thoughts on the relations between emotion and cognition. *American Psychologist, 37,* 1019–1024.

Lazarus, R. S. (1995). Vexing research problems inherent in cognitive-mediational theories of emotion – and some solutions. *Psychological Inquiry, 6,* 183–196.

Lazarus, R. S. (1991). *Emotion and adaptation.* New York: Oxford University Press.

Lazarus, R. S., & Alfert, E. (1964). The short-circuiting of threat by experimentally altering cognitive appraisal, *Journal of Abnormal and Social Psychology, 69,* 195–205.

Lazarus, R. S., Opton, E. M., Nomikos, M. S., & Rankin, N. O. (1965). The principle of short-circuiting of threat: Further evidence. *Journal of Personality, 33,* 622–635.

Lea, S. E. G., & Dittrich, W. H. (2000). What do birds see in moving video images? In J. Fagot (Ed.), *Picture perception in animals.* Psychology Press.

Leaper, C., & Ayres, M. (2007). A meta-analytic review of moderators of gender differences in adults' talkativeness, affiliative, and assertive speech. *Personality and Social Psychology Review, 11,* 328–363.

Leaper, C., & Smith, T. E. (2004). A meta-analytic review of gender variations in children's language use: Talkativeness, affiliative speech, and assertive speech. *Developmental Psychology, 40,* 993–1027.

Le Brun. Y., & Leleux, C. (1986). Central communication disorders in deaf signers. In J. Nespolous, P. Perrott, & A. R. Lecours (Eds.), *The biological foundation of gestures: Motor and semiotic aspects* (pp. 255–269). Hillsdale, NJ: Erlbaum.

Le Doux, J. E. (1992). Brain mechanisms of emotion and emotional learning. *Current Opinion in Neurobiology, 2*(2): 191–197.

Le Doux, J. E. (1996). *The emotional brain.* New York: Simon and Schuster.

Le Doux, J. E. (2000). Emotion circuits in the brain. *Annual Review of Neuroscience, 23,* 155–184.

Lederman, S. J., & Klatzky, R. L. (1986). Exploratory hand movements and object perception. *Bulletin of the Psychonomic Society, 24*(5), 322–322.

Lederman, S. J., & Klatzky, R. L. (2009). Haptic perception: A tutorial. *Attention Perception*

& Psychophysics, 71(7), 1439–1459.

Lee, L. F., & Horowitz, I. A. (1997). Enhancing juror competence in a complex trial, *Applied Cognitive Psychology*, 11, 305–314.

Lee, S. H., Blake, R., & Heeger, D. J. (2007). Hierarchy of cortical responses underlying binocular rivalry. *Nature Neuroscience*, 10(8), 1048–1054.

Legrenzi, P., & Umilta, C. (2011). *Neuromania: On the limits of brain science*. Oxford: Oxford University Press.

Legrenzi, P., Girotto, V., & Johnson-Laird, P. N. (2003). Models of consistency. *Psychological Science*, 14, 131–137.

Lehrer, J. (2008). The eureka hunt: Why do good ideas come to us when they do? *The New Yorker*, July 28, 40–45.

Lenneberg, E. H. (1967). *Biological foundations of language*. London: Wiley.

Leopold, D. A., & Logothetis, N. K. (1996). Activity changes in early visual cortex reflect monkeys' percepts during binocular rivalry. *Nature*, 379(6565), 549–553.

Levelt, W. J. M. (1989). Working models of perception; five general issues. In B. A. S. Elsendorn & H. Bouma (Eds.), *Working models of perception* (pp. 489–503). London: Academic Press.

Levelt, W. J. M. (1992). Accessing words in speech production: Stages, processes and representations. *Cognition*, 42, 1–22.

Levelt, W. J. M. (1999). Models of word production. *Trends in Cognitive Sciences*, 3(6), 223–232.

Levelt, W. J. M. (2001). Spoken word production: A theory of lexical access. *Proceedings of the National Academy of Sciences*, 98(23). 13464–513.

Levelt, W. J. M., Roelofs, A. P. A., & Meyer, A. S. (1999). A theory of lexical access in speech production. *Behavioral and Brain Sciences*, 22(1), 1–37.

Levenson, R. W. (1994). Human emotions: A functional view. In P. Ekman & R. J.

Davidson (Eds.), *The nature of emotion: Fundamental questions* (pp. 123–126). New York: Oxford University Press.

Levenson, R. W. (2004). Blood, sweat, and fears: The autonomic architecture of emotion. In P. Ekman, J. J. Campos, R. J. Davidson & F. B. M. de Waal (Eds.). *Emotions inside out*. New York: The New York Academy of Sciences.

Levenson, R. W., Ekman, P., & Friesen, W. V. (1990). Voluntary facial action generates emotion-specific autonomic nervous system activity. *Psychophysiology*, 27, 363–384.

Leventhal, H., & Scherer, K. R. (1987). The relationship of emotion to cognition: A functional approach to semantic controversy. *Cognition and Emotion*, 1, 3–28.

Levin, D. T., & Simons, D. J. (1997). Failure to detect changes to attended objects in motion pictures. *Psychonomic Bulletin, & Review*, 4(4), 501–506.

Levin, D. T., & Simons, D. J. (2000). Perceiving stability in a changing world: Combining shots and integrating views in motion pictures and the real world. *Media Psychology*, 2(4), 357–380.

Levine, L. J., & Pizarro, D. A. (2004). Emotion and memory research: A grumpy overview. *Social Cognition*, 22, 530–554.

Levy, B. J., & Anderson, M. C. (2008). Individual differences in the suppression of unwanted memories: The executive deficit hypothesis. *Acta Psychologica*, 127, 623–635.

Levy, R. (2008). Expectation-based syntactic comprehension. *Cognition*, 106, 1126–1177.

Lewis-Peacock, J. A., Drysdale, A. T., Oberauer, K., & Postle, B. R. (2012). Neural evidence for a distinction between short-term memory and the focus of attention. *Journal of Cognitive Neuroscience*, 24, 61–79.

Leyton, M. (1987). Symmetry-curvature duality. *Computer Vision Graphics and Image Processing*, 38(3), 327–341.

Li, X. B., & Basso, M. A. (2008). Preparing to move increases the sensitivity of superior colliculus neurons. *Journal of Neuroscience*, 28(17), 4561–4577.

Liberman, A. (2009). The etymology of 'brain' and cognates. *The Nordic Journal of English Studies*, 8, 45–59.

Liberman, A. M., Cooper, F. S., Shankweiler, D. S., & Studdert-Kennedy, M. (1967). Perception of the speech code. *Psychological Review*, 74, 1967, 431–461.

Liberman. A. M., Harris, K. S. Hoffman, H. S., & Griffith, B. C. (1957). The discrimination of speech sounds within and across phoneme boundaries. *Journal of Experimental Psychology*, 54, 358–368.

Libet, B. (1985). Unconscious cerebral initiative and the role of conscious will in voluntary action. *Behavioral and Brain Sciences*, 8(4), 529–539.

Libet, B. (2002). The timing of mental events: Libet's experimental findings and their implications. *Consciousness and Cognition*, 11, 291–299.

Libet, B., Gleason, C. A., Wright, E. W., & Pearl, D. (1983). Time of unconscious intention to act in relation to onset of cerebral activity (Readiness-*Potential*), Brain, 106, 623–642.

Lichtenstein, S., Slovic, P., Fischhoff, B., Layman, M., & Coombes, B. (1978). Judged frequency of lethal events. *Journal of Experimental Psychology: Human Learning and Memory*, 4, 551–578.

Lindquist, K., A., & Barrett, L. F. (2012). A functional architecture of the human brain: Insights from emotion. *Trends in Cognitive Sciences*, 16, 533–540.

Lindquist, K. A., Wager, T. D., Kober, H., Bliss-Moreau, E., & Barrett, L. F. (2012). The brain basis of emotion: A meta-analytic review. *Behavioral and Brain Sciences*, 35(3), 121–43.

Lindsay, R. C. L., & Wells, G. L. (1985). Improving eyewitness identifications from lineups – simultaneous versus sequential lineup presentation.

Journal of Applied Psychology, 70(3), 556–564.

Lindsay, R. C. L., Mansour, J. K., Bertrand, N. K., & Whaley, E. I. (2011). Face recognition in eyewitness memory: Face perception and recognition in eyewitness memory. In A. Calder, G. Rhodes, M. Johnson, J. Haxby & J. Keane (Eds.), *The handbook of face perception*. Oxford: Oxford University Press.

Lindstrom, M. (2011). You love your iPhone, literally. *New York Times*, September 30.

Linn, L. (1954). Psychological implications of the 'activating system.' *American Journal of Psychiatry*, 110, 61–65.

Linton, M. (1978). Real-world memory after six years: An in vivo study of very long-term memory. In M. M. Gruneberg, P. E. Morris & R. N. Sykes. (Eds.), *Practical aspects of memory* (pp. 69–76). London: Academic Press.

Lipnicki, D. M., & Byrne, D. G. (2005). Thinking on your back: Solving anagrams faster when supine than when standing. *Brain Research: Cognitive Brain Research*, 24, 719–722.

Lipp, O. V., & Derakshan, N. (2005). Attentional bias to pictures of fear relevant animals in a dot probe task. *Emotion*, 5(3), 365–369.

Lipshitz, R., Klein, G., Orasanu, J., & Salas, E. (2001). Taking stock of naturalistic decision making. *Journal of Behavioral Decision Making*, 14, 331–352.

Lisman, S. A. (1974). Alcoholic 'blackout': State dependent learning? *Archive of General Psychiatry*, 30, 46–53.

Lister, R. G., Eckardt, M. J., & Weingartner, H. (1987). Ethanol intoxication and memory: Recent developments and new directions. In M. Galanter (Ed.), *Recent developments in alcoholism*, Vol. 5. New York: Plenum.

Littlemore, J. (2009). *Applying cognitive linguistics to second language learning and teaching*. Basingstoke: Palgrave Macmillan.

Locke, J. (1690/2004). *An essay concerning human*

understanding. London: Penguin.

Loewenstein, G. F., Weber, E. U., Hsee, C. K., & Welch, E. S. (2001). Risk as feelings. *Psychological Bulletin, 127,* 267–286.

Loftus, E. F. (1980). *Memory.* Reading, MA: Addison-Wesley.

Loftus, E. F. (1997). Creating false memories. *Scientific American, 277,* 70–75.

Loftus, E. F. (1975). Leading questions and the eyewitness report. *Cognitive Psychology, 7,* 560–572.

Loftus, E. F. (1993). The reality of repressed memories. *American Psychologist, 48,* 518–537.

Loftus, E. F., & Palmer, J. C. (1974). Reconstruction of automobile destruction: An example of the interaction between language and memory. *Journal of Verbal Learning and Verbal Behavior, 13,* 585–589.

Loftus, E. F., & Zanni, G. (1975). Eyewitness testimony: The influence of the wording of a question. *Bulletin of Psychonomic Society, 5,* 86–88.

Loftus, E. F., Loftus, G. R., & Messo, J. (1987). Some facts about weapon focus. *Law and Human Behavior, 11,* 55–62.

Loftus, E. F., Miller, D. G., & Burns, H. J. (1978). Semantic integration of verbal information into a visual memory. *Human Learning and Memory, 4,* 19–31.

Logie, R. H. (1995). *Visuo-spatial working memory.* Hove: Lawrence Erlbaum.

Logothetis, N. K. (1998). Single units and conscious vision. *Philosophical Transactions of the Royal Society B-Biological Sciences, 353*(1377), 1801–1818.

Logothetis, N. K., & Sheinberg, D. L. (1996). Visual object recognition. *Annual Review of Neuroscience, 19,* 577–621.

Longo, M. R., Azanon, E., & Haggard, P. (2010). More than skin deep: Body representation beyond primary somatosensory cortex. *Neuropsychologia, 48*(3), 655–668.

Loula, F., Prasad, S., Harber, K., & Shiffrar, M. (2005).

Recognizing people from their movement. *Journal of Experimental Psychology-Human Perception and Performance, 31*(1), 210–220.

Luchins, A. W. (1942). Mechanization in problem solving: The effect of Einstellung. *Psychological Monographs, 54.*

Lung, C. T., & Dominowski, R. L. (1985). Effects of strategy instructions and practice on nine-dot problem solving. *Journal of Experimental Psychology: Learning, Memory and Cognition, 11,* 804–811.

Luria, A. R. (1971). Towards the problem of the historical nature of psychological processes. *International Journal of Psychology, 6,* 259–272.

Lutz, C. (1990). Morality, domination and understandings of 'justifiable anger' among the Ifaluk. In G. Semin & K. Gergen (Eds.), *Everyday understanding* (pp. 204–226). London: Sage.

Lyddy, F., Farina F., Hamey, J., Farrell, L., & Kelly O'Neill, N. (2014, in press). An analysis of language in university students' text messages. *Journal of Computer Mediated Communication.*

Lynch, M. A. (2004). Long-term potentiation and memory. *Physiology Review, 84*(1): 87–136.

M

MacFarland, D. (1999). *Animal behaviour.* Harlow: Longman.

Macfarlane, D. A. (1930). The role of kinesthesis in maze learning. *University of California Publications in Psychology, 4,* 277–305.

Macgregor, J. N., Ormerod, T. C., & Chronicle, E. P. (2001). Information processing and insight: A process model of performance on the nine-dot and related problems. *Journal of Experimental Psychology: Learning, Memory and Cognition, 27,* 176–201.

Mack, A., & Rock, I. (1998). *Inattentional blindness.* Cambridge, MA: MIT Press.

MacKay, D. G. (1987). *The organization of perception and*

action: A theory for language and other cognitive skills. New York: Springer-Verlag.

Macknik, S. L., King, M., Randi, J., Rabbins, A., Teller, Thompson, J., & Martinez-Conde, S. Attention and awareness in stage magic: Turning tricks into research. *Nature Reviews Neuroscience, 9*(11), 871–879.

Maclay, H., & Osgood, C. E. (1959). Hesitation phenomena in spontaneous English speech. *Word, 15,* 19–44.

MacLeod, C. (1991). Half a century of research on the stroop effect: An integrative review. *Psychological Bulletin, 109,* 163–203.

MacLeod, C., Mathews, A., & Tata, P. (1986). Attentional bias in emotional disorders. *Journal of Abnormal Psychology, 95*(1), 15–20.

MacLeod, C. M., & MacDonald, P. A. (2000). Inter-dimensional interference in the Stroop effect: Uncovering the cognitive and neural anatomy of attention. *Trends in Cognitive Sciences, 4,* 383–391.

MacLin, O. H., MacLin, M. K., & Malpass, R. S. (2001). Race, arousal, attention, exposure, and delay – An examination of factors moderating face recognition. *Psychology Public Policy and Law, 7*(1), 134–152.

MacMillan, M. (2000). *An odd kind of fame: Stories of Phineas Gage.* Cambridge, MA: MIT Press.

MacNeilage, P. F. (1998). The frame/content theory of evolution of speech production. *Behavioral and Brain Sciences, 21,* 499–511.

Maddieson, I. M. (1984). *Patterns of sounds.* Cambridge: Cambridge University Press.

Maguire, E. A., Valentine, E. R., Wilding, J. M., & Kapur, N. (2003). Routes to remembering: The brains behind superior memory. *Nature Neuroscience, 6,* 90–95.

Mahon, B. Z., & Caramazza, A. (2008). A critical look at the embodied cognition hypothesis and a new proposal for grounding conceptual content.

J Physiol Paris, 102(1–3), 59–70.

Maier, N. R. F. (1931). Reasoning in humans II: The solution of a problem and its appearance in consciousness. *Journal of Comparative Psychology, 12,* 181–194.

Malt, B. C. (1990). Features and beliefs in the mental representation of categories. *Journal of Memory and Language, 29,* 289–315.

Malt, B. C. (1994). Water is not H2O. *Cognitive Psychology, 27,* 41–70.

Malt, B. C., & Smith, E. E. (1982). The role of familiarity in determining typicality. *Memory & Cognition, 10,* 69–75.

Mamassian, P., & Landy, M. S. (2010). It's that time again. *Nature Neuroscience, 13*(8), 914–916.

Mamassian, P., Landy, M. S., & Maloney, L. T. (2002). Bayesian modelling of visual perception. In R. P. N. Rao, B. A. Olshausen, & M. S. Lewicki (Eds.), *Probabilistic models of the brain: Perception and neural function.* Cambridge, MA: MIT Press.

Mandler, G. (1967). Organization and memory. In K. W. Spence & J. T. Spence (Eds.), *The psychology of learning and motivation* (Vol. 1, pp. 327–372). New York: Academic Press.

Mandler, G. (1984). *Mind and body: Psychology of emotion and stress.* New York: Norton.

Mandler, G., & Pearlstone, Z. (1966). Free and constrained concept learning and subsequent recall. *Journal of Verbal Learning and Verbal Behavior, 5,* 126–131.

Mandler, G., Nakamura, Y., & Shebo-Van Zandt, B. J. (1987). Nonspecific effects of exposure on stimuli that cannot be recognized. *Journal of Experimental Psychology: Learning, Memory & Cognition, 13,* 646–648.

Mann, R. E., Cho-Young, J., & Vogel-Sprott, M. (1984). Retrograde enhancement by alcohol of delayed free recall performance. *Pharmacology and Biochemistry of Behavior, 20,* 639–42.

Mann, S., Vrij, A., & Bull, R. (2004). Detecting true lies: Police officers' ability to detect suspects' lies. *Journal of Applied Psychology, 89*, 137–149.

Manns, J. R., Hopkins, R. O., & Squire, L. R. (2003). Semantic memory and the human hippocampus. *Neuron, 38*, 127–133.

Mapelli, D., & Behrmann, M. (1997). The role of color in object recognition: Evidence from visual agnosia. *Neurocase, 3*, 237–247.

Marcus, S. L. and Rips, L. J. (1979). Conditional reasoning. *Journal of Verbal Learning and Verbal Behaviour* 18, 199–233.

Markovits, H. (1988). Conditional reasoning, representation, empirical evidence on a concrete task. *Quarterly Journal of Experimental Psychology, 45A*, 133–148.

Marr, D. (1982). *Vision: A computational investigation into the human representation and processing of visual information.* San Francisco: W.H. Freeman.

Marsh, R. L., Hicks, J. L., & Landau, J. D. (1998). An investigation of everyday prospective memory. *Memory & Cognition, 24*, 633–643.

Marshall, G. D. and Zimbardo, P. G. (1979). Affective consequences of inadequately explained physiological arousal. *Journal of Personality and Social Psychology, 37*, 970–988.

Marshall, J. C. and Newcombe, F. (1973). Patterns of paralexia: A psycholinguistic approach. *Journal of Psycholinguistic Research, 2*, 175–199.

Marslen-Wilson, W. D. (1990). Activation, competition, and frequency in lexical access. In G. T. M. Altmann (Ed.), *Cognitive models of speech processing: Psycholinguistics and computational perspectives* (pp. 148–172). Cambridge, MA: MIT Press.

Marslen-Wilson, W. D., & Tyler, L. K. (1980). The temporal structure of spoken language understanding, *Cognition, 8*, 1–71.

Martens, A., & Kosloff, S. (2011). Evidence that killing escalates within-subjects in a bug-killing paradigm. *Aggressive Behavior*, doi: 10.1002/ab.21412.

Martens, A., Kosloff, S. Greenberg, J., Landau, M. J., & Schmader, T. (2007). Killing begets killing: Evidence from a bug-killing paradigm that initial killing fuels subsequent killing. *Personality and Social Psychology Bulletin, 33*(9), 1251–1264.

Martin, A., & Caramazza, A. (2003). Neuropsychological and neuroimaging perspectives on conceptual knowledge: An introduction. *Cognitive Neuropsychology, 20*, 195–212.

Martinez-Trujillo, J. C., & Treue, S. (2004). Feature-based attention increases the selectivity of population responses in primate visual cortex. *Current Biology, 14*(9), 744–751.

Mathews, A., Mogg, K., Kentish, J., & Eysenck, M., (1995). Effects of psychological treatment on cognitive bias in generalised anxiety disorder Effect of psychological treatment on cognitive bias in generalized anxiety disorder. *Behaviour Research and Therapy, 33*(3), 293–303.

Matsumoto, D., & Hwang, H. (2011). Evidence for training the ability to read microexpressions of emotion. *Motivation and Emotion, 35*(2), 181–191.

Matsumoto, D., & Willingham, B. (2009). Spontaneous facial expressions of emotion of congenitally and noncongenitally blind individuals. *Journal of Personality and Social Psychology, 96*, 1–10.

Massaro, D. W. (1975). Backward recognition masking. *Journal of the Acoustical Society of America, 58*(5), 1059–1065.

Massaro, D. W. (1994). Psychological aspects of speech perception: Implications for research and theory. In M. Gemsbacher (Ed.), *Handbook of Psycholinguistics* (pp. 219–63). New York: Academic Press.

Massaro, D. W. (2001). Speech perception. In N. M. Smeiser & P. B. Baltes (Eds.), *International encyclopaedia of social and behavioural sciences* (pp. 14870–5). Amsterdam: Elsevier.

Massaro, D. W., & Cohen, M. (1983). Phonological context in speech perception. *Perception and Psychophysics, 34*, 338–348.

Mast, F. W., & Kosslyn, S. (2002). Visual mental images can be ambiguous: Insights from insights from individual differences in spatial transformation abilities. *Cognition, 81*, 57–70.

Masters, R. S. W. (1992). Knowledge, knerves and know-how – The role of explicit versus implicit knowledge in the breakdown of a complex motor skill under pressure. *British Journal of Psychology, 83*, 343–358.

Mattar, A. A. G., & Gribble, P. L. (2005). Motor learning by observing. *Neuron, 46*(1), 153–160.

Mattys, S. L., Melhorn, J. F., & White, L. (2007). Effects of syntactic expectations on speech segmentation. *Journal of Experimental Psychology: Human Perception and Performance, 33*, 960–977.

Maule, J., & Villejoubert, G. (2007). What lies beneath: reframing framing effects. *Thinking and Reasoning, 13*, 25–44.

May, J., Calvo-Merino, B., deLahunta, S., McGregor, W., Cusack, R., Owen, A. M., *et al.* (2011). Points in mental space: An interdisciplinary study of imagery in movement creation. *Dance Research, 29*(2), 404–432.

Mayer, E., & Rossion, B. (2007). Prosopagnosia. In O. Godefroy & J. Bogousslavsky (Eds.), *The behavioral and cognitive neurology of stroke* (pp. 315–334). Cambridge: Cambridge University Press.

Mayer, J. S., Bittner, R. A., Nikolic, D., Bledowski, C., Goebel, R., & Linden, D. E. J. (2007). Common neural substrates for visual working memory and attention. *Neuroimage, 36*(2), 441–453.

Mazzoni, G., & Mamon, A., (2003). Imagination can create false memories. *Psychological Science, 14*, pp. 186–8.

McAdams, C. J., & Maunsell, J. H. R. (1999). Effects of attention on orientation-tuning functions of single neurons in macaque cortical area V4. *Journal of Neuroscience, 19*(1), 431–441.

McCarley, J. S., Kramer, A. F., Wickens, C. D., Vidoni, E. D., & Boot, W. R. (2004). Visual skills in airport-security screening. *Psychological Science, 15*(5), 302–306.

McClelland, J. L., & Elman, J. L. (1986). The TRACE model of speech perception. *Cognitive Psychology, 18*, 1–86.

McClelland, J. L., & Rumelhart, D. E. (1981). An interactive activation model of context effects in letter perception.1. An account of basic findings. *Psychological Review, 88*(5), 375–407.

McClelland, J. L., Mirman, D., & Holt, L. L. (2006). Are there interactive processes in speech perception. *Trends in Cognitive Sciences, 10*, 363–369.

McCloskey, M. E., & Glucksberg, S. (1978). Natural categories: Well defined or fuzzy sets? *Memory and Cognition, 6*, 462–472.

McClure, S. M., Laibson, D. I., Loewenstein, G., & Cohen, J. D. (2004). Separate neural systems value immediate and delayed monetary rewards. *Science, 306*, 503–507.

McClure, S. M., Li, J., Tomlin, D., Cypert, K. S., Latane, M. M., & Montague, P. R. (2003). Neural correlates of behavioral preference for culturally familiar drinks. *Neuron, 44*, 379–387.

McGeoch, J. A., & Nolen, M. E. (1933). Studies in retroactive inhibition. IV. Temporal point of interpolation and degree of retroactive inhibition. *Journal of Comparative Psychology, 15*, 407–417.

McGeoch, J. A., & McDonald, W. T. (1931). Meaningful relation and retroactive inhibition. *American Journal of Psychology, 43*, 579–588.

McGurk, H., & MacDonald, J. (1976). Hearing lips and seeing voices. *Nature, 264*(5588), 746–748.

McKay, L. S., Simmons, D. R., McAleer, P., Marjoram, D., Piggot, J., & Pollick, F. E. (2012). Do distinct atypical cortical networks process biological motion information in adults with Autism Spectrum Disorders? *Neuroimage, 59,* 1524–1533.

McManus, I. C., Richards, P., Winder, B. C., & Sproston, K. A. (1998). Clinical experience, performance in final examinations, and learning style in medical students: A prospective study. *British Medical Journal, 316,* 345–350.

McNeill, D. (1992). *Hand and mind: What gestures reveal about thought.* Chicago: University of Chicago Press.

McNeill, D. (2005). *Gesture and thought.* Chicago: University of Chicago Press.

McNeill, D., & Duncan, S. D. (2000). Growth points in thinking-for-speaking. In D. McNeill (Ed.), *Language and gesture* (pp. 141–161). Cambridge: Cambridge University Press.

McQueen, J. M., & Cutler, A. (2001). Spoken word access processes: An introduction. *Language and Cognitive Processes, 16,* 469–490.

McQueen, J. M., Norris, D., & Cutler, A. (1994). Competition in spoken word recognition: Spotting words in other words. *Journal of Experimental Psychology: Learning, Memory, and Cognition, 20,* 621–638.

McQueen, J. M., Otake, T., & Cutler, A. (2001). Rhythmic cues and possible-word constraints in Japanese speech segmentation. *Journal of Memory and Language, 45,* 103–132.

Meadow, A., Parnes, S. J., & Reese, H. (1959). Influence of brainstorming instruction and problem sequence on a creative problem solving test. *Journal of Applied Psychology, 43,* 413–416.

Medin, D. L. (1989). Concepts and conceptual structure. *American Psychologist, 44,* 1469–1481.

Medin, D. L., & Ortony, A. (1989). Psychological essentialism. In S. Vosniadou & A. Ortony (Eds.), *Similarity and analogical reasoning.* Cambridge: Cambridge University Press.

Meissner, C. A., & Brigham, J. C. (2001). Thirty years of investigating the own-race bias in memory for faces – A meta-analytic review. *Psychology Public Policy and Law, 7*(1), 3–35.

Melzack, R. (1990). Phantom limbs and the concept of a neuromatrix. *Trends in Neurosciences, 13*(3), 88–92.

Melzack, R. (1992). Phantom limbs. *Scientific American, 266*(4), 120–126.

Memon, A., & Wright, D. B. (1999). Eyewitness testimony and the Oklahoma bombing. *The Psychologist, 12,* 292–295.

Memon, A., Meissner, C. A., & Fraser, J. (2010). The cognitive interview: A meta-analytic review and study space analysis of the past 25 years. *Psychology, Public Policy and Law, 16*(4), 340–372.

Mendes, M., Schwaninger, A., & Michel, S. (2011). *Does the application of virtually merged images influence the effectiveness of computer-based training in x-ray screening.* Paper presented at the Security Technology (ICCST), 2011 IEEE International Carnahan Conference.

Mendes, S. (Writer). (1999). *American Beauty:* Dreamworks SKG.

Merckelbach, H., Merten, T., & Lilienfeld, S. O. (2011). A skeptical look at a remarkable case report of 'overnight' amnesia. *Skeptical Inquirer,* Volume 35.3, May/June 2011.

Meringer, R., & Mayer, K. (1895). *Versprechen und Verlesen: Eine psychologisch-linguistiche Studie* (Mistakes in speech and reading: A psychological and linguistic study). Stuttgart: Gùschense Verlagsbuchhandlung.

Metcalfe, J., & Dunlosky, J. (2008). Metamemory. In H. L. Roediger, III (Ed.), *Cognitive psychology of memory. Vol. 2 of Learning and memory: A comprehensive reference* (pp. 349–362). Oxford: Elsevier.

Metcalfe, J., & Weibe, D. (1987). Intuition in insight and non-insight problem solving. *Memory and Cognition, 15,* 238–46.

Meyer, D. E., & Schvaneveldt, R. W. (1971). Facilitation in recognizing pairs of words: Evidence of a dependence between retrieval operations. *Journal of Experimental Psychology, 90,* 227–234.

Mezzacappa, E. S., Katkin, E., & Palmer, S. N. (1999). Epinephrine, arousal, and emotion: A new look at two-factor theory. *Cognition and Emotion, 13*(2), 181–199.

Michie, S., & Lester, K. (2005). Words matter: increasing the implementation of clinical guidelines. *Quality and Safety in Health Care, 14,* 367–370.

Michotte, A. É. (1946). *La perception de la causalité.* Louvain: Institut supérieur de philosophie.

Michotte, A. É. (1963). *The perception of causality.* New York: Basic Books.

Michotte, A., Thinès, G., Costall, A., & Butterworth, G. (1990). *Michotte's experimental phenomenology of perception.* Hillsdale, NJ: L. Erlbaum.

Miller, G. A. (1956). The magical number seven, plus or minus two. *The Psychological Review, 63,* 81–97.

Miller, G. A. (1962). *Psychology: The science of mental life.* Harmondsworth: Hutchinson.

Miller, G. A. (1968). *The psycholinguists. In the psychology of communication seven essays.* Harmondsworth: Penguin.

Miller, G. A. (1977). *Spontaneous apprentices.* New York: Seabury Press.

Miller, G. A., Galanter, E., & Pribram, K. H. (1960). *Plans and the structure of behavior.* New York: Holt, Rinehart, & Winston.

Miller, J. L., & Jusczyk, P. W. (1989). Seeking the neurobiological bases of speech perception. *Cognition, 33,* 111–137.

Miller, N., Lowit, A., & O'Sullivan, H. (2006). What makes acquired foreign accent syndrome foreign? *Journal of Neurolinguistics, 19,* 385–409.

Milner, B. (1963). Effects of different brain lesions on card sorting. *Archives of Neurology, 9,* 100–110.

Milner, B., Corkin, S., and Teuber, H-L (1968). Further analysis of hippocampal amnesic syndrome – 14-year follow-up study of H. M. *Neuropsychologia, 6*(3), 215–230.

Minami, H., & Dallenbach, K. M. (1946). The effects of activity upon learning and retention in the cockroach. *Periplaneta Americana. American Journal of Psychology, 59,* 1–58.

Mineka, S., & Sutton, S. K. (1992). Cognitive biases and the emotional disorders, *Psychological Science 3,* 65–69.

Miozzo, M., & Caramazza, A. (1997). On knowing the auxiliary of a verb that cannot be named: Evidence for the independence of grammatical and phonological aspects of lexical knowledge. *Journal of Cognitive Neuroscience, 9,* 160–166.

Mitroff, I. I. (1974). *The subjective side of science.* Amsterdam: Elsevier.

Moen, I. (1991). Functional lateralisation of pitch accents and intonation in Norwegian. *Brain and Language, 41,* 538–554.

Mogg, K., Bradley, B. P., Williams, R. (1995). Attentional bias in anxiety and depression: The role of awareness. *British Journal of Clinical Psychology, 34,* 17–36.

Mogg, K., Bradley, B. P., Williams, R., & Mathews, A. (1993). Subliminal processing of emotional information in anxiety and depression. *Journal of Abnormal Psychology, 102,* 304–311.

Molfese, D. L., & Betz, J. C. (1988). Electrophysiological indices of the early development of lateralization for language and cognition and their implications for predicting later development. In D. L. Molfese & S. J. Segalowitz (Eds.), *Brain lateralization in children* (pp. 171–190). New York: Guilford Press.

Monrad-Krohn, G. H. (1947). Dysprosody or altered 'melody of language'. *Brain, 70,* 405–415.

Moody, T. (1994). Conversations with zombies. *Journal of Consciousness Studies, 1,* 196–200.

Moore, M. T., & Fresco, D. M. (2007). Depressive realism and attributional style: Implications for individuals at risk for depression. *Behavior Therapy, 38,* 144–154.

Moors, A., Ellsworth, P. C., Scherer, K. R., & Frijda, N. H. (2013). Appraisal theories of emotion: State of the art and future development. *Emotion Review, 5,* 119–124.

Moran, A. (2012). *Sport and exercise psychology: A critical introduction.* 2nd ed. Hove: Psychology Press.

Moran, J., & Desimone, R. (1985). Selective attention gates visual processing in the extrastriate Cortex. *Science, 229*(4715), 782–784.

Moray, N. (1959). Attention in dichotic-listening – Affective cues and the influence of instructions. *Quarterly Journal of Experimental Psychology, 11*(1), 56–60.

Moray, N., Bates, A., & Barnett, T. (1965). Experiments on the four-eared man. *Journal of the Acoustical Society of America, 38,* 196–206.

Morgan, C. A., Hazlett, G., Baranoski, M., Doran, A., Southwick, S., & Loftus, E. (2007). Accuracy of eyewitness identification is significantly associated with performance on a standardized test of face recognition. *International Journal of Law and Psychiatry 30,* 213–223.

Moritz, S., Jacobsen, D., Willenborg, B., Jelinek, L., Fricke, S. (2006). A check on the memory deficit hypothesis of obsessive-compulsive checking. *European Archives of Psychiatry and Clinical Neuroscience, 256,* 82–86.

Morris, P. E. (1979). Strategies for learning and recall. In M. M. Gruneberg & P. E. Morris (Eds.), *Applied problems in memory.* London: Academic Press.

Morris, P. E. (1992). Theories of memory. In M. M. Gruneberg & P. E. Morris (Eds.), *Aspects of memory: The practical aspects.* London: Routledge.

Morrison, J. B., & Tversky, B. (1997). Body schemas. *Proceedings of the Meetings of the Cognitive Science Society* (pp. 525–529). Mahwah, NJ: Erlbaum.

Morton, J. (1970). A functional model of memory. In D. A. Norman (Ed.), *Models of human memory.* New York: Academic Press.

Morton, J. (1979). Word recognition. In J. Morton & J. C. Marshall (Eds.), *Psycholinguistics Volume 2 – Structures and processes.* London: Paul Elek.

Morton, J., & Patterson, K. E. (1980). A new attempt at an interpretation or an attempt at a new interpretation. In M. Coltheart, K. E. Patterson & J. C. Marshall (Eds.), *Deep dyslexia* (pp. 91–118). London: Routledge & Kegan Paul.

Morton, N., & Morris, R. G. (1995). Image transformation dissociated from visuospatial working memory. *Cognitive Neuropsychology, 12,* 767–791.

Moseley, C. (2007). *Encyclopedia of the world's endangered languages.* London: Routledge.

Moyer, R. S. (1973). Comparing objects in memory: Evidence suggesting and internal psychophysics. *Perception and Psychophysics, 13,* 180–184.

Mueller, C. W., Lisman, S. A., & Spear, N. E. (1983). Alcohol enhancement of human memory: Tests of consolidation and interference hypotheses. *Psychopharmacology, 80,* 226–230.

Mukamel, R., Ekstrom, A. D., Kaplan, J., Iacoboni, M., & Fried, I. (2010). Single-neuron responses in humans during execution and observation of actions. *Current Biology, 20*(8), 750–756.

Muller, G. E., & Pilzecker, A. (1900). Experimentelle Beitrage zur Lehre vom Gedachtnis [Experimental contributions to the science of memory]. *Zeitschrift fur Psychologie. Erganzungsband, 1,* 1–300.

Münsterberg, H. (1916). The *photoplay: A psychological study.* New York.

Murdoch, B. E. (2009). *Acquired speech and language disorders.* London: John Wiley and Sons.

Murphy, G. L., & Medin, D. (1985). The role of theories in conceptual coherence. *Psychological Review, 92,* 289–316.

Murphy, S. T., & Zajonc, R. B. (1993). Affect, cognition, and awareness: Affective priming with optimal and suboptimal stimulus exposures. *Journal of Personality & Social Psychology, 64*(5), 723–739.

Murray, D. J. (1965). Vocalization-at-presentation and immediate recall, with varying presentation-rates. *Quarterly Journal of Experimental Psychology, 17,* 41–56.

Murray, D. J. (1988). *A history of Western psychology* (2nd ed.). Englewood Cliffs, NJ: Prentice Hall.

Mynatt, C. R., Doherty, M. E., & Tweney, R. D. (1977). Confirmation bias in a simulated research environment: An experimental study of scientific inference. *Quarterly Journal of Experimental Psychology, 29,* 85–95.

Mynatt, C. R., Doherty, M. E., & Tweney, R. D. (1978). Consequences of confirmation and disconfirmation in a simulated research environment. *Quarterly Journal of Experimental Psychology, 30,* 395–406.

N

Nachev, P., & Husain, M. (2007). Comment on 'Detecting awareness in the vegetative state'. *Science, 315,* 1221a.

Nagy, W. E. and Anderson, R. C. (1984). How many words are there in printed English? *Reading Research Quarterly, 19,* 304–330.

Nairne, J. S. (2002). The myth of the encoding-retrieval match. *Memory, 10,* 389–395.

Nairne, J. S. (2010). Adaptive memory: Evolutionary constraints on remembering. *Psychology of Learning & Motivation, 53,* 1–32.

National Safety Council (2010). *Understanding the distracted brain: Why driving while using hands-free cell phones is risky behavior.* National Safety Council.

Nauta, W. J. H. (1971). The problem of the frontal lobe: A reinterpretation. *Journal of Psychiatric Research, 8,* 167–187.

Naveh-Benjamin, M., & Ayres, T. J. (1986). Digit span, reading rate, and linguistic relativity. *Quarterly Journal of Experimental Psychology, 38A,* 739–751.

Navon, D. (1984). Resources – A theoretical soup stone. *Psychological Review, 91*(2), 216–234.

Navon, D., & Miller, J. (2002). Queuing or sharing? A critical evaluation of the single-bottleneck notion. *Cognitive Psychology, 44*(3), 193–251.

Nee, D. E., Wager, T. D., & Jonides, J. (2007). Interference resolution: Insights from a meta-analysis of neuroimaging tasks. *Cognitive, Affective & Behavioral Neuroscience, 7,* 1–17.

Neisser, U. (1967). *Cognitive psychology.* Englewood Cliffs, NJ: Prentice-Hall.

Neisser, U. (1976). *Cognition and reality: Principles and implications of cognitive psychology.* San Francisco: W.H. Freeman.

Neisser, U. (1978). Memory: what are the important questions? In M. M. Gruneberg, P. E. Morris & R. N. Sykes (Eds.), *Practical aspects of memory.* London: Academic Press.

Neisser, U. (1981). John Dean's memory: A case study. *Cognition, 9*(1), 1–22.

Neisser, U. (1982). Snapshots or benchmarks? In U. Neisser (Ed.), *Memory observed: Remembering in natural contexts.* San Francisco: W.H. Freeman.

Neisser, U. (1988). Time present and timaqe past. In M. M. Gruneberg, P. E. Morris, & R. N. Sykes (Eds.), *Practical aspects of memory: Current research and issues (vol. 2)*. Chichester: Wiley.

Neisser, U., & Becklen, R. (1975). Selective looking – Attending to visually specified events. *Cognitive Psychology, 7*(4), 480–494.

Newell, A. (1980). Physical symbol systems. *Cognitive Science, 4*, 135–183.

Newell, A., Shaw, J. C., & Simon, H. A. (1958). Elements of a theory of human problem solving. *Psychological Review, 65*, 151–166.

Newstead, S. E., & Griggs, R. A. (1983). Drawing inferences from quantified statements: A study of the square of opposition. *Journal of Verbal Learning and Verbal Behaviour, 22*, 535–546.

Newtson, D. (1973). Attribution and unit of perception of ongoing behavior. *Journal of Personality and Social Psychology, 28*(1), 28–38.

Nickerson, R. S., Perkins, D. N., & Smith, E. E. (1985). *The teaching of thinking*. Hillsdale, NJ: Lawrence Erlbaum.

Nijstad, B. A., Stroebe, W., & Lodewijkx, H. F. N. (2003). Production blocking and idea generation: Does blocking interfere with cognitive processes? *Journal of Experimental Social Psychology, 39*, 531–548.

Noë, A. (2004). *Action in perception*. Cambridge, MA: MIT Press.

Nooteboom, S. (2010). Monitoring for speech errors has different functions in inner and overt speech. In M. Everaert, T. Lentz, H. De Mulder & O. Nilsen (Eds.), *The linguistic enterprise: From knowledge of language to knowledge in linguistics* (pp. 231–234). Amsterdam: John Benjamins.

Nooteboom, S. G., & Quené, H. (2008). Self-monitoring and feedback: A new attempt to find the main cause of lexical bias in phonological speech errors. *Journal of Memory and Language, 58*, 837–861.

Norman, D. A. (Ed.) (1970). *Models of human memory*. New York: Academic Press.

Norman, D. A. (1981). Categorization of action slips. *Psychological Review, 88*, 1–15.

Norman, D. A., & Bobrow, D. G. (1975). Data-limited and resource-limited processes. *Cognitive Psychology, 7*(1), 44–64.

Norman, D. A., & Shallice, T. (1986). Attention to action. Willed and automatic control of behaviour. In R. J. Davidson, G. E. Schwartz & D. Shapiro (Eds.), *Consciousness and self-regulation*, New York: Plenum Press.

Norris, D., McQueen, J. M., & Cutler, A. (2000). Merging information in speech recognition: Feedback is never necessary. *Behavioral & Brain Sciences, 23*, 299–370.

Nunez, R. (2004). Do real numbers really move? Language, thought, and gesture: The embodied cognitive foundations of mathematics. *Embodied Artificial Intelligence, 3139*, 54–73.

Nussbaum (2001). *Upheavals of thought: The intelligence of emotions*. Cambridge: Cambridge University Press.

O

Oaksford, M., & Chater, N. (1994). A rational analysis of the selection task as optimal data selection. *Psychological Review, 101*, 608–631.

Oaksford, M., & Chater, N. (2003). Optimal data selection: Revision, review and re-evaluation. *Psychonomic Bulletin & Review, 10*, 289–318.

Oatley, K., & Johnson-Laird, P. N. (1987). Towards a cognitive theory of emotions. *Cognition and Emotion, 1*, 29–50.

Oberauer, K. (2002). Access to information in working memory: Exploring the focus of attention. *Journal of Experimental Psychology: Learning, Memory, and Cognition, 28*, 411–421.

Oberauer, K., Weidenfeld, A., & Hornig, R. (2004). Logical reasoning and probabilities: A comprehensive test of Oaksford and Chater (2001). *Psychonomic Bulletin & Review, 11*, 521–527.

Obler, L. K., & Gjerlow, K. (1999). *Language and the brain*. Cambridge: Cambridge University Press.

O'Brien, D. P., Braine, M. D. S., & Yang, Y. (1994). Propositional reasoning by mental models? Simple to refute in principle and in practice. *Psychological Review, 101*, 701–704.

Ochsner, K. N. (2000). Are affective events richly recollected or simply familiar? The experience and process of recognizing feelings past. *Journal of Experimental Psychology: General, 129*, 242–261.

O'Connell, D., & Kowal, S. (2004). The history of research on the filled pause as evidence of the written language bias in linguistics (Linell, 1982). *Journal of Psycholinguistic Research, 33*, 459–474.

O'Craven, K. M., Downing, P. E., & Kanwisher, N. (1999). fMRI evidence for objects as the units of attentional selection. *Nature, 401*(6753), 584–587.

Ohlsson, S. (1992). Information processing explanations of insight and related phenomena. In M. T. Keane & K. J. Gilhooly (Eds.), *Advances in the psychology of thinking*. London: Harvester-Wheatsheaf.

Okada, T., & Simon, H. A. (1997). Collaborative discovery in a scientific domain. *Cognitive Science, 21*, 109–141.

Oliva, A., & Torralba, A. (2001). Modeling the shape of the scene: A holistic representation of the spatial envelope. *International Journal of Computer Vision, 42*(3), 145–175.

Olsson, A., & Ochsner, K. N. (2008). The role of social cognition in emotion. *Trends in Cognitive Sciences, 12*(2), 65–71.

Oppenheim, G. M., & Dell, G. S. (2010). Motor movement matters: The flexible abstractness of inner speech. *Memory & Cognition, 38*, 1147–1160.

O'Regan, J. K. (1979). Saccades size control in reading: Evidence for the linguistic control hypothesis. *Perception and Psychophysics, 25*, 501–509.

Ormerod, T. C., MacGregor, J. N., & Chronicle, E. P. (2002). Dynamics and constraints in insight problem solving. *Journal of Experimental Psychology: Learning, Memory and Cognition, 28*, 791–799.

O'Rourke, T. B., & Holcomb, P. J. (2002). Electrophysiological evidence for the efficiency of spoken word processing. *Biological Psychology, 60*(2–3), 121–150.

Ortmann, A., Gigerenzer, G., Borges, B., & Goldsten, D. G. (2008). The recognition heuristic: A fast and frugal way to investment choice? In C. R. Plott & V. L. Smith (Eds.), *Handbook of experimental economics results*. Amsterdam: Elsevier/ North Holland.

Ortony, A., Clore, G. L., & Collins, A. (1988). *The cognitive structure of emotions*. Cambridge: Cambridge University Press.

Osborn, A. F. (1958). *Applied imagination*. New York: Scribners.

Ost, J., Vrij, A., Costall, A., & Bull, R. (2002). Crashing memories and reality monitoring: Distinguishing between perceptions, imaginations and 'false memories'. *Applied Cognitive Psychology, 16*, 125–134.

Osterhout, L., & Holcomb, P. J. (1992). Event related potentials elicited by syntactic anomaly. *Journal of Memory and Language, 31*, 785–806.

Osterhout, L., McLaughlin, J., & Bersick, M. (1997). Event-related brain potentials and human language. *Trends in Cognitive Sciences, 1*, 203–209.

Ostry, D. J., & Feldman, A. G. (2003). A critical evaluation of the force control hypothesis in motor control. *Experimental Brain Research, 153*(3), 275–288.

Owen, A. M., Coleman, M. R., Boly, M., Davis, M. H., Laureys, S., Jolles, D., & Pickard, J. D. (2006). Detecting awareness in the vegetative state. *Science, 313*, 1402.

Owen, A. M., Coleman, M. R., Boly, M. Davis, M. H., Laureys, S., Jolles, D., & Pickard, J. D. (2007). Response to comments on 'Detecting awareness in the vegetative state'. *Science, 315*, 1221c.

P

Page, M. P. A. (2006). What can't functional neuroimaging tell the cognitive psychologist? *Cortex, 42*, 428–443.

Paivio, A. (1965). Abstractness, imagery, and meaningfulness in paired associates learning. *Journal of Verbal Learning and Verbal Behaviour, 4*, 32–38.

Paivio, A. (1969). Mental imagery in associative learning and memory. *Psychological Review, 76*, 241–263.

Paivio, A. (1971). *Imagery and verbal processes*. New York: Holt, Rinehart & Winston.

Paivio, A. (1975). Perceptual comparisons through the mind's eye. *Memory and Cognition, 3*, 635–647.

Paivio, A. (1983). The empirical case for dual coding. In J. C. Yuille (Ed.), *Imagery, memory and cognition* (pp. 307–322). Hillsdale, NJ: Erlbaum.

Parker, E. S., Birnbaum, I. M., Weingartner, H., Hartley, J. T., Stillman, R. C., & Wyatt, R. J. (1980). Retrograde enhancement of human memory with alcohol. *Psychopharmacology, 69*, 219–222.

Parker, E. S., Cahill, L., & McGaugh, J. L. (2006). A case of unusual autobiographical remembering. *Neurocase, 12*, 35–49.

Parker, E. S., Morihisa, J. M., Wyatt, R. J., Schwartz, B. L., Weingartner, H., & Stillman, R. C. (1981). The alcohol facilitation effect on memory: A dose-response study. *Psychopharmacology, 74*, 88–92.

Parkin, A. J. (1997). *Memory and amnesia: An introduction*, 2nd ed. Oxford: Blackwell.

Parkin, A. J., & Leng, N. R. C. (1993). *Neuropsychology of the amnesic syndrome*. Hillsdale, NJ: Erlbaum.

Parkin, A. J., & Leng, N. R. C. (1993). *Neuropsychology of the amnesic syndrome*. Hove: Lawrence Erlbaum.

Parnes, S. J., & Meadow, A. (1963). Development of individual creative talent. In C. W. Taylor & F. Barron (Eds.), *Scientific creativity: Its recognition and development*. New York: J. Wiley.

Parrott, W. G., & J. Sabini, J. (1990). Mood and memory under natural conditions: Evidence for mood incongruent recall. *Journal of Personality and Social Psychology, 59*, 321–336.

Patterson, K. E., Marshall, J. C., & Coltheart, M. (Eds.) (1985). *Surface dyslexia*. London: Erlbaum.

Paulesu, E., McCrory, E. Fazio, F. Menoncello, L., Brunswicte, N., Cappa, S. F. . . . Frith, U. (2000). A cultural effect on brain function. *Nature Neuroscience, 3*(1), 91–96.

Pavlas, D., Rosen, M. A., Fiore, S. M., & Salas, E. (2008). *Using visual attention video games and traditional interventions to improve baggage screening*. Paper presented at the Proceedings of the Human Factors and Ergonomics Society Annual Meeting 2008.

Payne, J. (1976). Task complexity and contingent processing in decision making: an information search and protocol analysis. *Organisational Behavior and Human Performance, 16*, 366–387.

Payne, J., Huddleston, R., & Pullum, G. K. (2010). The distribution and category status of adjectives and adverbs. *Word Structure, 3*, 31–81.

Payne, J. W., Bettman, J. R., & Johnson, E. J. (1993). *The adaptive decision maker*. Cambridge: Cambridge University Press.

Payne, J. W., Bettman, J. R., & Johnson, E. J. (1988). Adaptive strategy selection in decision making. *Journal of Experimental Psychology: Learning, Memory and Cognition, 14*, 534–552.

Peelen, M. V., Wiggett, A. J., & Downing, P. E. (2006). Patterns of fMRI activity dissociate overlapping functional brain areas that respond to biological motion. *Neuron, 49*(6), 815–822.

Peirce, C. S., & Jastrow, J. (1884). On small differences of sensation. *Memoirs of the National Academy of Sciences, 3*(1), 73–83.

Peleg, G., Katzir, G., Peleg, O., Kamara, M., Brodsky, L., Hel-Or, H., Keren, D., & Nevo, E. (2006). Hereditary family signature of facial expression. *Proceedings from the National Academy of Sciences, 103*, 15921–15926.

Pentland, A. (2007). Social signal processing. *Signal Processing Magazine, 24*(4), 108–111.

Perea, M., Acha, J., & Carreiras, M. (2009). Eye movements when reading text messaging (txt msgng). *The Quarterly Journal of Experimental Psychology, 62*, 1560–1567.

Peretz, I., Ayotte, J., Zatorre, R. J., Mehler, J., Ahad, P., Penhune, V. B., et al. (2002). Congenital amusia: A disorder of fine-grained pitch discrimination. *Neuron, 33*(2), 185–191.

Pessoa, L., & Ungerleider, L. G. (2004). Top-down mechanisms for working memory and attentional processes. In M. S. Gazzaniga (Ed.), *The cognitive neurosciences* (3rd ed., pp. 919–930). Cambridge, MA: MIT Press.

Petersen, M. R., Beecher, M. D., Zoloth, S. R., Moody, D. B., & Stebbins, W. C. (1978). Neural lateralization of species-specific vocalizations by Japanese macaques (Macaca fuscata). *Science, 202*, 324–327.

Petersen, S. E., & Posner, M. I. (2012). The attention system of the human brain: 20 years after. *Annual Review of Neuroscience, 35*, 73–89.

Peterson, L. R., & Johnson, S. T. (1971). Some effects of minimizing articulation on short-term memory. *Journal of Verbal Learning and Verbal Behavior* 10, 346–354.

Peverly, S. T. (2006). The importance of handwriting speed in adult writing. *Developmental Neuropsychology, 29*(1), 197–216.

Pezdek, K. (2003). Event memory and autobiographical memory for the events of September 11, 2001. *Applied Cognitive Psychology, 17*, 1033–1045.

Phelps, E. A., Ling, S., & Carrasco, M. (2006). Emotion facilitates perception and potentiates the perceptual benefit of attention. *Psychological Science, 17*, 292–299.

Phillips, J. K., Klein, G., & Sieck, W. R. (2004). Expertise in judgment and decision making: A case for training intuitive decision skills. In D. J. Koehler & N. Harvey (Eds.), *Blackwell handbook of judgment and decision making*.

Phillips, M. R., McAuliff, B. D., Kovera, M. B., & Cutler, B. L. (1999). Double-blind photoarray administration as a safeguard against investigator bias. *Journal of Applied Psychology, 84*(6), 940–951.

Pijlaarsdam, G., H. Van den Bergh, M. Couzijn (Eds.) (1996). *Theories, models & methodology in writing*. Amsterdam: Amsterdam University Press.

Pillutla, M. M., & Murningham, J. K. (1996). Unfairness, anger and spite: Emotional rejections of ultimatum offers. *Organizational Behavior and Human Decision Processes, 68*, 208.

Pinker, S. (1994). *The language instinct*. Harmondsworth: Penguin.

Pizlo, Z. (2001). Representation and recognition in vision. *Journal of Mathematical Psychology, 45*(2), 402–409.

Plaisier, M. A., Tiest, W. M. B., & Kappers, A. M. L. (2008). Haptic pop-out in a hand sweep.

Acta Psychologica, 128(2), 368–377.

Platchias, D. (2010). *Phenomenal consciousness: Understanding the relation between neural processes and experience.* Durham: acumen.

Platt, J. R. (1964). Strong inference. *Science, 146,* 347–353.

Plaut, D. C., McClelland, J. L., Seidenberg, M. S., & Patterson, K. (1996). Understanding normal and impaired word reading: Computational principles in quasi-regular domains. *Psychological Review, 103,* 56–115.

Plazzi, G., Vetrugno, R., Provini, F., & Montagna, P. (2005). Sleepwalking and other ambulatory behaviours during sleep. *Neurological Sciences, 26,* S193–S198.

Plihal, W., & Born, J. (1997). Effects of early and late nocturnal sleep on declarative and procedural memory. *Journal of Cognitive Neuroscience, 9,* 534–47.

Plihal, W., & Born, J. (1999). Effects of early and late nocturnal sleep on priming and spatial memory. *Psychophysiology, 36,* 571–582.

Plummer, C., Kleinitz, A., Vroomen, P., & Watts, R. (2007). Of Roman chariots and goats in overcoats: The syndrome of Charles Bonnet, *Journal of Clinical Neuroscience, 14,* 709–714.

Pockett, S., & Miller, A. (2007). The rotating spot method of timing subjective events. *Consciousness and Cognition, 16,* 241–254.

Poincare, H. (1908). *Science et Methode.* Paris: Flammarion.

Poincare, H. (1929). *The foundations of science.* New York: Science House.

Poizner, H., Bellugi, U., & Iragui, V. (1984). Apraxia and aphasia for a visual-gestural language. *American Journal of Physiology, 246,* R868–R883.

Poldrack, R. A. (2006). Can cognitive processes be inferred from neuroimaging data? *Trends in Cognitive Science, 19,* 59–63.

Police and Criminal Evidence Act (1984). *Code D* (2010). https://www.gov.uk/government/uploads/system/uploads/attachment_data/file/117600/pace-code-d-2011.pdf

Pollack, I., & Pickett, J. M. (1964). The unintelligibility of excerpts from conversations. *Language & Speech, 6,* 165–171.

Pollick, F. E., & Sapiro, G. (1997). Constant affine velocity predicts the 1/3 power law of planar motion perception and generation. *Vision Research, 37*(3), 347–353.

Pollick, F. E., Kay, J. W., Heim, K., & Stringer, R. (2005). Gender recognition from point-light walkers. *Journal of Experimental Psychology-Human Perception and Performance, 31*(6), 1247–1265.

Pomerantz, J. R., & Kubovy, M. (1986). Theoretical approaches to perceptual organization: Simplicity and likelihood principles. In K. R. Boff, L. Kaufman & J. P. Thomas (Eds.), *Handbook of perception and human performance: Volume H. Cognitive processes and performance* (pp. 36.31–36.46). New York: Wiley.

Popper, K. R. (1959). *The logic of scientific discovery.* London: Hutchinson.

Popper, K. R. (1968). Plato. In D. L. Sills (Ed.). *International encyclopedia of the social sciences.* New York: Macmillan & Free Press.

Porter, S., & ten Brinke, L. (2008). Reading between the lies: Identifying concealed and falsified emotions in universal facial expressions. *Psychological Science, 19,* 508–514.

Posner, M. I. (1980). Orienting of attention. *Quarterly Journal of Experimental Psychology, 32,* 3–25.

Posner, M. I., & Cohen, Y. (1984). Components of visual orienting. In H. Bouma & D. Bouwhuis (Eds.), *Attention and performance Vol. X* (Vol. 10, pp. 531–556). Hillsdale, NJ: Erlbaum.

Posner, M. I., & Keele, S. W. (1970). Retention of abstract ideas. *Journal of Experimental Psychology, 77,* 353–363.

Posner, M. I., & Petersen, S. E. (1990). The attention system of the human brain. *Annual Review of Neuroscience, 13,* 25–42.

Postman, L., Stark, K., & Henschel, D. M. (1969). Conditions of recovery after unlearning. *Journal of Experimental Psychology, 82,* 1–24.

Potter, J. M. (1980). What was the matter with Dr. Spooner? In V. Fromkin (Ed.), *Errors in linguistic performance: Slips of the tongue, ear, pen, and hand* (pp. 13–34). New York: Academic Press.

Potter, M. C., & Levy, E. I. (1969). Recognition memory for a rapid sequence of pictures. *Journal of Experimental Psychology, 81*(1), 10–15.

Power, M., & Dalgleish, T. (1997). *Cognition and emotion: From order to disorder.* Hove: Psychology Press.

Prasad, S., Loula, F., & Shiffrar, M. (2005). The visual analysis of actions performed by the self and others. *Journal of Cognitive Neuroscience,* 249–249.

Prinz, J. (2004). Which emotions are basic? In D. Evans & P. Cruse (Eds.), *Emotion, evolution and rationality* (pp. 69–88). Oxford: Oxford University Press.

Prinz, W. (1997). Perception and action planning. *European Journal of Cognitive Psychology, 9*(2), 129–154.

Proffitt, D. R. (2006). Embodied perception and the economy of action. *Perspectives on Psychological Science, 1*(2), 110–122.

Provini, F., Tinuper, P., Bisulli, F., & Lugaresi, E. (2011). Arousal disorders. *Sleep Medicine, 12,* S22–S26.

Pylyshyn, Z. W. (1973). What the mind's eye tells the mind's brain: A critique of mental imagery. *Psychological Bulletin, 80,* 1–24.

Pylyshyn, Z. W. (1981). The imagery debate: Analogue media versus tacit knowledge. *Psychological Review, 88,* 16–45.

Pylyshyn, Z. W. (1984). *Computation and cognition.* Cambridge, MA: MIT Press.

Pylyshyn, Z. W. (2002). Mental imagery: In search of a theory. *Behavioral and Brain Sciences, 5,* 157–238.

R

Radvansky, G. (2006). *Human memory.* New York: Pearson.

Raichle, M. E., & Snyder, A. Z. (2007). A default model of brain function: A brief history of an evolving idea. *NeuroImage, 37,* 1083–1090.

Rainville, P., Bechara, A., Naqvi, N. H., & Damasio, A. R. (2006). Basic emotions are associated with distinct patterns of cardiorespiratory activity. *International Journal of Psychophysiology, 6.*

Ramachandran, V. S., & Hirstein, W. (1998). The perception of phantom limbs – The D. O. Hebb lecture. *Brain, 121,* 1603–1630.

Rao, R. P. N., Zelinsky, G. J., Hayhoe, M. M., & Ballard, D. H. (2002). Eye movements in iconic visual search. *Vision Research, 42*(11), 1447–1463.

Rapp, B., & Goldrick, M. (2000). Discreteness and interactivity in spoken word production. *Psychological Review, 107,* 460–499.

Rasmussen, T., & Milner, B. (1977). The role of early left-brain injury in determining lateralization of cerebral speech functions. *Ann N Y Acad Sci, 299,* 355–69.

Ratcliff, R., & McKoon, G. (1986). More on the distinction between episodic and semantic memories. *Journal of Experimental Psychology: Learning, Memory, and Cognition, 12,* 312–313.

Ratneshwar, S., Barsalou, L. W., Pechmann, C., & Moore, M. (2001). Goal-derived categories: Roles of personal and situational goals in category representation. *Journal of Consumer Psychology, 10,* 147–157.

Raymond, J. E., Shapiro, K. L., & Arnell, K. M. (1992). Temporary suppression of visual processing in an Rsvp task – An attentional blink. *Journal of Experimental Psychology-Human Perception and Performance, 18*(3), 849–860.

Rayner, K. (1998). Eye movements in reading and information processing: Twenty years of research. *Psychological Bulletin, 124,* 372–422.

Rayner, K., & Clifton, C., Jr. (2002). Language processing. In D. Medin (Vol. Ed.) *Stevens handbook of experimental psychology, Third Edition: Volume 2 Memory and cognitive processes* (pp. 261–316). New York: John Wiley and Sons.

Rayner, K., & Duffy, S. A. (1988). On-line comprehension processes and eye movements in reading. In M. Daneman, G. E. MacKinnon, & T. G. Waller (Eds.), *Reading research: Advances in theory and practice (Vol. 6).* New York: Academic Press.

Rayner, K., & McConkie, G. W. (1976). What guides a reader's eye movements? *Vision Research, 16,* 829–837.

Rayner, K., Pollatsek, A., & Reichle, E. D. (2003). Eye movements in reading: Models and data. *Behavioral and Brain Sciences, 26,* 507–526.

Rea, C. P., & Modigliani, V. (1985). The effect of expanded v. massed practice on the retention of multiplication facts and spelling lists. *Human Learning, 4,* 11–18.

Reason, J. (1979). Actions not as planned: The price of automatization. In G. Underwood & R. Stevens (Eds.), *Aspects of consciousness* (pp. 67–89). London: Academic Press.

Reason, J. (1990). *Human error.* New York: Cambridge University Press.

Reason, J. (2000). The Freudian slip revisited. *The Psychologist, 13*(12), 10–11.

Recanzone, G. H. (2003). Auditory influences on visual temporal rate perception. *Journal of Neurophysiology, 89*(2), 1078–1093.

Reed, S. K. (1972). Pattern recognition and categorization. *Cognitive Psychology, 3,* 382–407.

Reed, S. K., & Friedman, M. P. (1973). Perceptual and conceptual categorization. *Memory & Cognition, 1,* 157–163.

Reggev, N., Zuckerman, M., & Maril, A. (2011). Are all judgments created equal? An fMRI study of semantic and episodic metamemory predictions. *Neuropsychologia, 49,* 1332–42.

Reicher, G. M. (1969). Perceptual recognition as a function of meaningfulness of the stimulus material. *Journal of Experimental Psychology, 81,* 274–280.

Reilly, R. G. (1999). A case study of transient dyslexia. *Brain and Language, 70*(3), 336–346.

Reinmann, R. (1999). The role of external representations in distributed problem solving. *Learning and Instruction, 9,* 411–418.

Reisenzein, R. (1983). The Schachter theory of emotion: Two decades later *Psychological Bulletin, 94,* 239–264.

Reitman, W. R. (1976). Skilled perception in Go: Deducing memory structures from inter-response times. *Cognitive Psychology, 8,* 336–356.

Renoult, L., Davidson, P. S. R., Palombo, D. J., Moscovitch, M., & Levine, B. (2012). Personal semantics: At the crossroads of semantic and episodic memory. *Trends in Cognitive Sciences, 16,* 550–558.

Rensink, R. A. (2002). Change detection. *Annual Review of Psychology, 53,* 245–277.

Rensink, R. A., ORegan, J. K., & Clark, J. J. (1997). To see or not to see: The need for attention to perceive changes in scenes. *Psychological Science, 8*(5), 368–373.

Reynolds, D., Jola, C., & Pollick, F. E. (2011). Dance research electronic-introduction dance and neuroscience-new partnerships. *Dance Research, 29*(2), 260–269.

Reynolds, J. H., & Desimone, R. (2003). Interacting roles of attention and visual salience in V4. *Neuron, 37*(5), 853–863.

Reynolds, J. H., & Heeger, D. J. (2009). The normalization model of attention. *Neuron, 61*(2), 168–185.

Ribot, T. R. (1882). *Diseases of memory.* New York: Appleton & Co.

Rips, L. J. (1989). Similarity, typicality and categorisation. In F. C. Keil & R. A. Wilson (Eds.), *Explanation and cognition.* Cambridge, MA: MIT Press.

Rips, L. J., & Collins, A. (1993). Categories and resemblance. *Journal of Experimental Psychology: General, 122,* 468–486.

Ritov, I., & Baron, J. (1990). Reluctance to vaccinate: Omission bias and ambiguity. *Journal of Behavioral Decision Making, 3,* 263–277.

Rizzolatti, G., Fadiga, L., Fogassi, L., & Gallese, V. (1996). Premotor cortex and the recognition of motor actions. *Cognitive Brain Research, 3,* 131–141.

Rizzolatti, G., & Sinigaglia, C. (2010). The functional role of the parieto-frontal mirror circuit: Interpretations and misinterpretations. *Nature Reviews Neuroscience, 11*(4), 264–274.

Rizzolatti, G., Fogassi, L., & Gallese, V. (2001). Neurophysiological mechanisms underlying the understanding and imitation of action. *Nature Reviews Neuroscience, 2*(9), 661–670.

Roberson, D., Davidoff, J., & Braisby, N. (1999). Similarity and categorisation: Neuropsychological evidence for a dissociation in explicit categorisation tasks. *Cognition, 71,* 1–42.

Robson, J. G. (1980). Neural images: The physiological basis of spatial vision. In C. S. Harris (Ed.), *Visual coding and adaptability.* Hillsdale, NJ: Lawrence Erlbaum.

Roediger, H. L., & Karpicke, J. D. (2006a). Test-enhanced learning: Taking memory tests improves long term retention. *Psychological Science, 17,* 249–255.

Roediger, H. L., & Karpicke, J. D. (2006b). The power of testing memory: Basic research and implications for educational practice. *Perspectives on Psychological Science, 1,* 181–201.

Roediger, H. L., Bergman, E. T., & Meade, M. L. (2000). Repeated reproduction from memory. In A. Saito (Ed.), *Bartlett, cognition and culture* (pp. 115–134). London: Routledge.

Roediger, H. L., Marsh, E. J., & Lee, S. C. (2002). Varieties of memory. In D. L. Medin & H. Pashler (Eds.), *Stevens' handbook of experimental psychology*, 3rd ed., Volume 2: *Memory and cognitive processes* (pp. 1–41). New York: John Wiley & Sons.

Roediger, H. L., Weldon, M. S., & Challis, B. H. (1989). Explaining dissociations between implicit and explicit measures of retention: A processing account. In H. L. Roediger & F. I. M. Craik (Eds.), *Varieties of memory and consciousness: Essays in honour of Endel Tulving* (pp. 3–14). Hillsdale, NJ: Erlbaum.

Roediger, H. L., & Guynn, M. J. (1996). Retrieval processes. In E. L. Bjork & R. A. Bjork (Eds.), *Memory.* San Diego, CA: Academic Press.

Roland, P. E., & Friberg, L. (1985). Localization of cortical areas activated by thinking. *Journal of Neurophysiology, 53,* 1219–1243.

Rolls, E. T. (1990). A theory of emotion, and its application to understanding the neural basis of emotion. *Cognition and Emotion, 4,* 161–190.

Rolls, E. T. (1998). *The brain and emotion.* Oxford: Oxford University Press.

Rosch, E. (1973). On the internal structure of perceptual and semantic categories. In T. E. Moore (Ed.), *Cognitive development and the acquisition of language* (pp. 111–144). New York: Academic Press.

Rosch, E. (1975). Cognitive representations of semantic categories. *Journal of Experimental Psychology: General, 104,* 192–233.

Rosch, E. (1978). Principles of categorization. In E. Rosch & B. B. Lloyd (Eds.), *Cognition and categorization.* Hillsdale, NJ: Lawrence Erlbaum.

Rosch, E., & Mervis, C. B. (1975). Family resemblance:

Studies in the internal structure of categories. *Cognitive Psychology, 7*, 573–605.

Rosch, E., Mervis, C. B., Gray, W. D., Johnson, D. M., & Boyes-Braem, P. (1976). Basic objects in natural categories. *Cognitive Psychology, 8*, 382–439.

Roseman, I. J., & Smith, C. A. (2001). Appraisal theory. In K. Scherer, A. Schorr & T. Johnstone (Eds.), *Appraisal processes in emotion: Theory, methods, research*. Oxford: Oxford University Press.

Rosenbaum, D. A. (2005). The cinderella of psychology – The neglect of motor control in the science of mental life and behavior. *American Psychologist, 60*(4), 308–317.

Rosenbaum, D. A. (2006). *Human motor control*. San Diego: Academic Press/ Elsevier.

Rosenbaum, D. A., Loukopoulos, L. D., Meulenbroek, R. G. J., Vaughan, J., & Engelbrecht, S. E. (1995). Planning reaches by evaluating stored postures. *Psychological Review, 102*(1), 28–67.

Rosenbaum, D. A., Meulenbroek, R. J., Vaughan, J., & Jansen, C. (2001). Posture-based motion planning: Applications to grasping. *Psychological Review, 108*(4), 709–734.

Rosenblum, L. D., Gordon, M. S., & Jarquin, L. (2000). Echolocating distance by moving and stationary listeners. *Ecological Psychology, 12*(3), 181–206.

Ross, B. H., & Landauer, T. K. (1978). Memory for at least one of two items: Test and failure of several theories of spacing effects. *Journal of Verbal Learning and Verbal Behavior, 17*, 669–680.

Ross, J., & Lawrence, K. A. (1968). Some observations on memory artifice. *Psychonomic Science, 13*, 107–108.

Rossion, B., Gauthier, I., Tarr, M. J., Despland, P., Bruyer, R., Linotte, S., et al. (2000). The N170 occipito-temporal component is delayed and enhanced to inverted faces but not to inverted objects: An electrophysiological account of face-specific processes in the human brain. *Neuroreport, 11*(1), 69–74.

Roth, A. E. (1995). Bargaining experiments. In J. H. Kagel & A. E. Roth (Eds.), *Handbook of experimental economics*. Princeton, NJ: Princeton University Press.

Roth, W. M. (2000). From gesture to scientific language. *Journal of Pragmatics, 32*(11), 1683–1714.

Rubin, D. C., & Wenzel, A. E. (1996). One hundred years of forgetting: A quantitative description of retention. *Psychological Bulletin, 103*, 734–760.

Rumelhart, D. E., & McClelland, J. L. (1982). An interactive activation model of context effects in letter perception. 2. The contextual enhancement effect and some tests and extensions of the model. *Psychological Review, 89*(1), 60–94.

Rumelhart, D. E., & Norman, D. A. (1982). Simulating a skilled typist – A study of skilled cognitive-motor performance. *Cognitive Science, 6*(1), 1–36.

Russell, A., Penny, L., & Pemberton, C. (1995). Speaking fundamental frequency changes over time in women: A longitudinal study. *Journal of Speech, Language, and Hearing Research, 38*, 101–109.

Russell, J. A. (1994). Is there universal recognition of emotion from facial expression? A review of the cross-cultural studies. *Psychological Bulletin, 115*(1), 102–141.

Russell, J. A. (2003). Core affect and the psychological construction of emotion. *Psychological Review, 110*(1), 145–172.

Russell, J. A. (2005). Emotion in human consciousness is built on core affect. *Journal of Consciousness Studies, 12*, 26–42.

Rylander, G. (1939). *Personality changes after operations on the frontal lobes*. Copenhagen: E. Munksgaard.

Ryle, G. (1949). *The concept of mind*. Chicago: University of Chicago Press.

Rymer, R. (1992). A silent childhood. *The New Yorker*, April 13 & 20.

S

Saberi, K., & Perrott, D. R. (1999). Cognitive restoration of reversed speech. *Nature, 398*, 760.

Sacks, H., Schegloff, E. A., & Jefferson, G. (1974). A simplest systematics for the organization of turn-taking for conversation. *Language, 50*, 696–735.

Sacks, O. (2007). A neurologist's notebook: The abyss. *Music and amnesia. The New Yorker*, September 24.

Sacks, O. W. (1997). *The island of the colorblind*. New York: A. A. Knopf.

Saffran, E. M., & Marin, O. S. M. (1975). Immediate memory for word lists and sentences in a patient with deficient auditory short-term memory. *Brain and Language, 2*, 420–433.

Sahraie, A., Trevethan, C. T., MacLeod, M. J., Murray, A. D., Olson, J. A., & Weiskrantz, L. (2006). Increased sensitivity after repeated stimulation of residual spatial channels in blindsight. *Proceedings of the National Academy of Sciences of the United States of America, 103*(40), 14971–14976.

Salthouse, T. A. (1990). Working memory as a processing resource in cognitive aging. *Developmental Review, 10*, 101–124.

Samanez-Larkin, G. R., Gibbs, S. E. B., Khanna, K., Nielsen, L., Carstensen, L. L., & Knutson, B. (2007). Anticipation of monetary gain but not loss in healthy older adults. *Nature Neuroscience, 10*, 787–791.

Samanez-Larkin, G. R., Kuhnen, C. M., Yoo, D. J., & Knutson, B. (2010). Variability in nucleus accumbens activity mediates age-related suboptimal financial risk taking. *The Journal of Neuroscience, 30*, 1426–1434.

Samson, D., & Pillon, A. (2003). A case of impaired knowledge for fruit and vegetables. *Cognitive Neuropsychology, 20*, 373–400.

Samuel, A. G. (1997). Lexical activation produces potent phonemic percepts. *Cognitive Psychology, 32*, 97–127.

Samuel, A. G., & Kat, D. (2003). Inhibition of return: A graphical meta-analysis of its time course and an empirical test of its temporal and spatial properties. *Psychonomic Bulletin & Review, 10*(4), 897–906.

Samuelson, W., & Zeckhauser, R. (1988). Status quo bias in decision making. *Journal of Risk and Uncertainty, 1*, 7–59.

Sanfey, A. G., Rilling, J. K., Aronson, J. A., Nystrom, L. E., & Cohen, J. D. (2003). The neural basis of economic decision-making in the ultimatum game. *Science, 300*, 1755–1758.

Santhouse, A. M., Howard, R. J., & Fffytche, D. H. (2000). Visual hallucinatory syndromes and the anatomy of the visual brain. *Brain, 123*, 2055–2064.

Sarason, I. G. (1984). Stress, anxiety, and cognitive interference – Reactions to tests. *Journal of Personality and Social Psychology, 46*(4), 929–938.

Sarkamo, T., Tervaniemi, M., Soinila, S., Autti, T., Silvennoinen, H. M., Laine, M., et al. (2009). Cognitive deficits associated with acquired amusia after stroke: A neuropsychological follow-up study. *Neuropsychologia, 47*(12), 2642–2651.

Saunders, J., & MacLeod, M. D. (2006). Can inhibition resolve retrieval competition through the control of spreading activation? *Memory & Cognition, 34*, 307–322.

Scarborough, D. L., Cortese, C., & Scarborough, H. S. (1977). Frequency and repetition effects in lexical memory. *Journal of Experimental Psychology: Human Perception and Performance, 3*, 1–17.

Schaal, S., Mohajerian, P., & Ijspeert, A. (2007). Dynamics

systems vs. optimal control – A unifying view. *Computational Neuroscience: Theoretical Insights into Brain Function, 165*, 425–445.

Schacter, D. L. (1987). Implicit memory: History and current status. *Journal of Experimental Psychology: Learning, Memory, & Cognition, 13*, 501–518.

Schacter, D. L. (1999). The seven sins of memory. *American Psychologist, 54*(3), 182–203.

Schachter, S., & Singer, J. E. (1962). Cognitive, social and physiological determinants of emotional state. *Psychological Review, 69*, 379–399.

Schachter, S., Christenfeld, N., Ravina, B., & Bilous, F. (1991). Speech disfluency and the structure of knowledge. *Journal of Personality and Social Psychology, 60*, 362–367.

Schenkman, B. N., & Nilsson, M. E. (2010). Human echolocation: Blind and sighted persons' ability to detect sounds recorded in the presence of a reflecting object. *Perception, 39*(4), 483–501.

Scherer, K. R. (1988). Criteria for emotion-antecedent appraisal: A review, in V. Hamilton, G. H. Bower & N. H. Frijda (Eds), *Cognitive perspectives on emotion and motivation* (pp. 89–126). Dordrecht: Kluwer.

Scherer, K. R. (2000). Psychological models of emotion. In J. Borod (Ed.). *The neuropsychology of emotion* (pp. 137–162). Oxford: Oxford University.

Scherer, K. R. (2009). Emotions are emergent processes: They require a dynamic computational architecture, *364*(1535), 3459–3474.

Schiavenato, M., Byers, J. F., Scovanner, P., McMahon, J. M. et al. (2008). Neonatal pain facial expression: Evaluating the primal face of pain. *Pain, 138*(2), 460–471.

Schlickum, M. K., Hedman, L., Enochsson, L., Kjellin, A., & Fellander-Tsai, L. (2009). Systematic video game training in surgical novices improves performance in virtual reality endoscopic surgical simulators:

A prospective randomized study. *World Journal of Surgery, 33*(11), 2360–2367.

Schlittmeier, S. J., & Hellbrück, J. (2009). Background music as noise abatement in open-plan offices: A laboratory study on performance effects and subjective preferences. *Applied Cognitive Psychology, 23*(5), 684–697.

Schlottmann, A., Ray, E. D., Mitchell, A., & Demetriou, N. (2006). Perceived physical and social causality in animated motions: Spontaneous reports and ratings. *Acta Psychologica, 123*(1–2), 112–143.

Schmidt, R. C., Carello, C., & Turvey, M. T. (1990). Phase-transitions and critical fluctuations in the visual coordination of rhythmic movements between people. *Journal of Experimental Psychology-Human Perception and Performance, 16*(2), 227–247.

Schmitz, T. W., De Rosa, E., & Anderson, A. K. (2009). Opposing influences of affective state valence on visual cortical encoding. *Journal of Neuroscience, 29*, 7199–7207.

Schmolck, H., Buffalo, E. A., & Squire, L. R. (2000). Memory distortions develop over time: Recollections of the O. J. Simpson trial verdict after 15 and 32 months. *Psychological Science, 11*, 39–45.

Schneider, W., & Shiffrin, R. M. (1977). Controlled and automatic human information processing: I. Detection, search, and attention. *Psychological Review, 84*, 1–66.

Scholl, B. J., & Tremoulet, P. D. (2000). Perceptual causality and animacy. *Trends in Cognitive Sciences, 4*(8), 299–309.

Schooler, J. W., Ohlsson, S., & Brooks, K. (1993). Thoughts beyond words: When language overshadows insight. *Journal of Experimental Psychology: General, 122*, 166–183.

Schorr, A. (2001). Subjective measurements in appraisal research: Present state and future perspectives. In

K. R. Scherer, A. Schorr & T. Johnstone (Eds.), *Appraisal processes in emotion: Theory, methods, research. Series in affective science.* Oxford: Oxford University Press.

Schroyens, W. (2010). A critical review of thinking about what is true, possible, and irrelevant in reasoning from from or reasoning about conditional propositions. *Journal of Cognitive Psychology, 325*, 2016–2021.

Schwaninger, A. (2004). *Increasing efficiency in airport security screening.* Paper presented at the Proceedings of AVSEC World 2004.

Schwartz, M. F. (2006). The cognitive neuropsychology of everyday action and planning. *Cognitive Neuropsychology, 23*(1), 202–221.

Schwartz, M. F., Reed, E. S., Montgomery, M., Palmer, C., & Mayer, N. H. (1991). The quantitative description of action disorganization after brain-damage – A case-study. *Cognitive Neuropsychology, 8*(5), 381–414.

Scorsese, M. (Writer). (1976). *Taxi Driver.* USA: Columbia Films.

Scott, S. H. (2004). Optimal feedback control and the neural basis of volitional motor control. *Nature Reviews Neuroscience, 5*(7), 534–546.

Scott, S. K., McGettigan, C., & Eisner, F. (2009). A little more conversation, a little less action: Candidate roles for motor cortex in speech perception. *Nature Reviews Neuroscience, 10*, 295–302.

Scoville, W. B., & Milner, B. (1957). Loss of recent memory after bilateral hippocampal lesions. *Journal of Neurology, Neurosurgery, & Psychiatry, 20*(1), 11–21.

Searle, J. (2013). Theory of mind and Darwin's legacy. *Proceedings of the National Academy of Sciences, 110*, 10343–10348.

Searle, J. R. (1983). *Intentionality: An essay in the philosophy of mind.* Cambridge: Cambridge University Press.

Sedikides, C. (1994). Incongruent effects of sad

mood on self-conception valence: It's a matter of time. *European Journal of Social Psychology, 24*, 161–172.

Seidenberg, M. S., & McClelland, J. L. (1989). A distributed, developmental model of word recognition and naming. *Psychological Review, 96*, 523–568.

Seifert, C. M., Meyer, D. E., Davidson, N., Patalano, A. L., & Yaniv, I. (1995). Demystification of cognitive insight: Opportunistic assimilation and the prepared mind perspective. In R. J. Sternberg & J. E. Davidson (Eds.), *The nature of insight.* Cambridge, MA: MIT Press.

Selfridge, O. G. (1958). *Pandemonium: A paradigm for learning.* Paper presented at the Proceedings of the Symposium on the Mechanisation of Thought Processes, London.

Sells, S. B. (1936). The atmosphere effect: An experimental study of reasoning. *Archives of Psychology, 29*, 3–72.

Sells, S. B., & Koob, H. F. (1937). A classroom demonstration of 'atmosphere effect' in reasoning. *Journal of Educational Psychology, 72*, 197–200.

Service, E. (1992). Phonology, working memory, and foreign language learning. *Quarterly Journal of Experimental Psychology, 45A*, 21–50.

Seyfarth, R. M., Cheney, D. L., et al. (1980). Monkey responses to three different alarm calls: Evidence of predator classification and semantic communication. *Science,* (4471), 801–803.

Seymour, P. H. K., Aro, M., & Erskine, J. M. (2003). Foundation literacy acquisition in European orthographies. *British Journal of Psychology, 94*, 143–174.

Shadmehr, R., & Krakauer, J. W. (2008). A computational neuroanatomy for motor control. *Experimental Brain Research, 185*(3), 359–381.

Shaffer, D. M., McManama, E., Swank, C., & Durgin, F. H. (2013). Sugar and space? Not the case: Effects of low blood glucose on slant estimation are mediated by beliefs. *i-Perception, 4,* 147–155.

Shah, P., & Miyake, A. (1996). The separability of working memory resources for spatial thinking and language processing: An individual differences approach. *Journal of Experimental Psychology: General, 125,* 4–27.

Shallice, T. (2002). Fractionation of the supervisory system. In D. T. Stuss & R. Knight (Ed.), *Principles of frontal lobe functions.* New York: Oxford University Press.

Shallice, T., & Butterworth, B. (1977). Short-term memory impairment and spontaneous speech. *Neuropsychologia, 15,* 729–735.

Shallice, T., & Burgess, P. W. (1991). Deficits in strategy application after frontal lobe damage in man, *Brain, 114,* 727–741.

Shallice, T., & Warrington, E. K. (1970). Independent functioning of verbal memory stores: A neuropsychological study. *Quarterly Journal of Experimental Psychology, 22,* 261–273.

Shallice, T., & Warrington, E. K. (1974). The dissociation between long-term retention of meaningful sounds and verbal material. *Neuropsychologia, 12,* 553–555.

Shankweiler, D., & Studdert-Kennedy, M. (1967). Identification of consonants and vowels presented to the left and right ears. *Quarterly Journal of Experimental Psychology, 19,* 59–63.

Shapiro, L. (2004). *The mind incarnate.* Cambridge, MA: MIT Press.

Shapiro, L. (2007). The embodied cognition research programme. *Philosophy Compass, 2*(2), 338–346.

Shaywitz, B. A., Shaywitz, S. E., Pugh, K. R., Constable, R. T., Skudlarski, P., Fulbright, R. K., Bronen, R. A., Fletcher, J. M., Shankweiler, D. P., Katz, L., & Gore, J. C. (1995). Sex differences in the functional organization of the brain for

language. *Nature, 16*(373), 607–9.

Shea, C. H., Kovacs, A. J., & Panzer, S. (2011). The coding and inter-manual transfer of movement sequences. *Front Psychol, 2,* 52.

Sheen, M., Kemp, S., & Rubin, D. C. (2001). Twins dispute memory ownership: A new false memory phenomenon. *Memory & Cognition, 29,* 779–788.

Shepard, R. N., & Metzler, J. (1971). Mental rotation of three-dimensional objects. *Science, 171,* 701–703.

Sheppard, J. P., Raposo, D., & Churchland, A. K. (2013). Dynamic weighting of multisensory stimuli shapes decision-making in rats and humans. *Journal of Vision, 13,* 1–19.

Shergill, S. S., Samson, G., Bays, P. M., Frith, C. D., & Wolpert, D. M. (2005). Evidence for sensory prediction deficits in schizophrenia. *American Journal of Psychiatry, 162*(12), 2384–2386.

Shimamura, A. P. (1992), Organic amnesia. In L. R. Squire (Ed.), *Encyclopedia of learning and memory* (pp. 30–35). New York: Macmillan.

Shin, Y. K., Proctor, R. W., & Capaldi, E. J. (2010). A review of contemporary ideomotor theory. *Psychological Bulletin, 136*(6), 943–974.

Shipley, T. (1964). Auditory flutter-driving of visual flicker. *Science, 145*(3638), 1328–1330.

Shipley, T. F. (2008). An invitation to an event. In T. F. Shipley & J. M. Zacks (Eds.), *Understanding events: From perception to action.* Oxford: Oxford University Press.

Siegel, E. H., & Stefanucci, J. K. (2011). A little bit louder now: Negative affect increases perceived loudness. *Emotion, 11,* 1006–1011.

Silk, T. J., Bellgrove, M. A., Wrafter, P., Mattingley, J. B., & Cunnington, R. (2010). Spatial working memory and spatial attention rely on common neural processes in the intraparietal sulcus.

Neuroimage, 53(2), 718–724.

Simmons, W. K., & Barsalou, L. W. (2003). The similarity-in-topography principle: Reconciling theories of conceptual deficits. *Cognitive Neuropsychology, 20,* 451–486.

Simon, A. (2004). A third view of the black box: Cognitive coherence in legal decision making. *University of Chicago Law Review, 71,* 511–586.

Simon, A., Pham, L. B., Quang, A., & Holyoak, K. J. (2001). The emergence of coherence over the course of decision making. *Journal of Experimental Psychology: Learning, Memory, and Cognition, 27,* 1250–1260.

Simon, H. A. (1956). Rational choice and the structure of environments. *Psychological Review, 63,* 129–138.

Simon, H. A. (1966). Scientific discovery and the psychology of problem solving. In R. G. Colodny (Ed.), *Mind and cosmos: Essays in contemporary science and philosophy.* Pittsburgh, PA: University of Pittsburgh Press.

Simon, H. A. (1978). Rationality as process and product of thought. *American Economic Association, 68,* 1–16.

Simons, D. J., & Chabris, C. F. (1999). Gorillas in our midst: Sustained inattentional blindness for dynamic events. *Perception, 28*(9), 1059–1074.

Singleton, D. (2001). Age and second language acquisition. *Annual Review of Applied Linguistics, 21,* 77–89.

Sinha, P., Balas, B., Ostrovsky, Y., & Russell, R. (2006). Face recognition by humans: Nineteen results all computer vision researchers should know about. *Proceedings of the IEEE, 94*(11), 1948–1962.

Sivak, M. (1996). The information that drivers use: Is it indeed 90% visual? *Perception, 25*(9), 1081–1089.

Skaggs, E. B. (1925). Further studies in retroactive inhibition. *Psychological Monographs.* (Whole No.161), *34,* 1–60.

Skaggs, E. B. (1933). A discussion on the temporal

point of interpolation and degree of retroactive inhibition. *Journal of Comparative Psychology, 16,* 411–414.

Skinner, B. F. (1938). *The behavior of organisms.* New York: Appleton.

Slepian, M. L., Weisbuch, M., Rutchick, A. M., Newman, L. S., & Ambady, N. (2010). Shedding light on insight: Priming bright ideas. *Journal of Experimental Social Psychology, 46,* 696–700.

Slobin, D. I. (1966). Grammatical transformations and sentence comprehension in childhood and. adulthood. *Journal of Verbal Learning and Verbal Behavior, 5,* 219–227.

Sloman, S. A. (1996). The empirical case for two systems of reasoning. *Psychological Bulletin, 119,* 3–22.

Slovic, P., Finucane, M., Peters, E., & MacGregor, D. G. (2002). The affect heuristic. In T. Gilovich, D. Griffin & D. Kahneman (Eds.), *Heuristics and biases.* New York: Cambridge University Press.

Slovic, P., Fischhoff, B., & Lichtenstein, S. (1982). Response mode, framing, and information processing effects in risk assessment. In R. Hogarth (Ed.), *New directions for methodology of social and behavioural science: Question framing and response consistency.* San Francisco: Jossey-Bass.

Smalley, N. S. (1974). Evaluating a rule against possible instances. *British Journal of Psychology, 65,* 293–304.

Smith, C. A., & Lazarus, R. S. (1993). Appraisal components, core relational themes, and the emotions. *Cognition and Emotion, 7,* 233–296.

Smith, L., & Gilhooly, K. (2006). Regression versus fast and frugal models of decision making: The case of prescribing for depression. *Applied Cognitive Psychology, 20,* 265–274.

Smith, S. M., & Rothkopf, E. Z. (1984). Contextual enhancement and distribution of practice in the classroom. *Cognition & Instruction, 1,* 341–358.

Smith, S. M., Brown, H. O., Toman, J. E. P., & Goodman, L. S. (1947). The lack of cerebral effects of D-tubocurarine chloride, *Anesthesiology, 8,* 1–14.

Smith, T. J. (2010). Film (cinema) perception. In E. B. Goldstein (Ed.), *Encyclopedia of perception.* Los Angeles: Sage.

Smith, T. J., & Henderson, J. M. (2008). Edit blindness: The relationship between attention and global change blindness in dynamic scenes. *Journal of Eye Movement Research, 2,* 1–17.

Smyth, M. M. (1996). Interference with rehearsal in spatial working memory in the absence of eye movements. *Quarterly Journal of Experimental Psychology Section a-Human Experimental Psychology, 49*(4), 940–949.

Smyth, M. M., & Pelky, P. L. (1992). Short-term retention of spatial information. *British Journal of Psychology, 83,* 359–374.

Solomon, K. O., & Barsalou, L. W. (2001). Representing properties locally. *Cognitive Psychology, 43,* 129–169.

Solomon, K. O., & Barsalou, L. W. (2004). Perceptual simulation in property verification. *Memory and Cognition, 32,* 244–259.

Song, J. J. (2001). *Linguistic typology: Morphology and syntax* (Longman Linguistics Library). Harlow: Longman.

Soto, D., Heinke, D., Humphreys, G. W., & Blanco, M. J. (2005). Early, involuntary top-down guidance of attention from working memory. *Journal of Experimental Psychology-Human Perception and Performance, 31*(2), 248–261.

Speisman, J. C., Lazarus, R. S., Mordkoff, A., & Davison, L. (1964). Experimental reduction of stress based on ego-defense theory. *Journal of Abnormal and Social Psychology, 68*(4), 367–380.

Spence, C., & Ho, C. (2008). Crossmodal information processing in driving. In C. Castro & L. R. Hartley (Eds.), *Human factors of visual and cognitive performance in driving* (pp. 187–200). Boca Raton: CRC Press.

Spencer, L., & Hanley, J. R. (2003). The effects of orthographic consistency on reading development and phonological awareness: Evidence from children learning to read in Wales. *British Journal of Psychology, 94,* 1–28.

Sperling, G. (1960). The information available in brief visual presentations. *Psychology Monographs, 74,* 1–29.

Sperry, R. W. (1952). Neurology and the mind-body problem. *American Scientist, 40*(2).

Sperry, R. W. (1974). Lateral specialization in the surgically separated hemispheres. In F. O. Schmitt & F. G. Worden (Eds.), *Neuroscience 3rd Study Program* (pp. 5–19). Cambridge, MA: MIT Press.

Spiers, H. J., Maguire, E. A., & Burgess, N. (2001). Hippocampal amnesia. *Neurocase, 7,* 357–382.

Spitzer, H., Desimone, R., & Moran, J. (1988). Increased attention enhances both behavioral and neuronal performance. *Science, 240*(4850), 338–340.

Sporer, S. L., Penrod, S., Read, D., & Cutler, B. (1995). Choosing, confidence, and accuracy: A meta-analysis of the confidence–accuracy relation in eyewitness identification studies. *Psychological Bulletin, 118,* 315–327.

Spranca, M., Minsk, E., & Baron, J. (1991). Omission and commission in judgment and choice. *Journal of Experimental Psychology, 27,* 76–105.

Springer, S., & Deutsch, G. (1989). *Left brain, right brain,* New York: W.H. Freeman.

Squire, L. R. (1986). The neuropsychology of memory dysfunction and its assessment. In I. Grant & K. Adams (Eds.), *Neuropsychological assessment of neuropsychiatric disorders* (pp. 268–299). New York: Oxford University Press.

Squire, L. R. (1987). *Memory and brain.* New York: Oxford University Press.

Squire, L. R. (1992). Declarative and nondeclarative memory: Multiple brain systems supporting learning and memory. *Journal of cognitive neuroscience, 4,* 232–243.

Squire, L. R. (1993). The organization of declarative and nondeclarative memory. In T. Ono, L. R. Squire, M. Raichle, D. Perrett & M. Fukuda (Eds.), *Brain mechanisms of perception and memory: From neuron to behavior* (pp. 219–227). New York: Oxford University Press.

Squire, L. R. (2004). Memory systems of the brain: A brief history and current perspective. *Neurobiology of Learning and Memory, 82,* 171–177.

Squire, L. R. (Ed.) (2008). *The encyclopedia of neuroscience.* San Diego: Elsevier.

Squire, L. R. (2009). The legacy of patient H. M. for neuroscience. *Neuron, 61,* 6–9.

Squire, L. R., & Moore, R. Y. (1979). Dorsal thalamic lesion in a noted case of chronic memory dysfunction. *Annals of Neurology, 6,* 503–506.

Squire, L. R., & Slater, P. C. (1978). Anterograde and retrograde memory impairment in chronic amnesia. *Neuropsychologia, 16,* 313–322.

Squire, L. R., & Zola, S. M. (1996). Structure and function of declarative and nondeclarative memory systems. *Proceedings of the National Academy of Sciences of the United States of America, 93,* 135–215.

Squire, L. R., Clark, R. E., & Knowlton, B. J. (2001). Retrograde amnesia. *Hippocampus, 11,* 50–55.

Stanovich, K. E. (1999). *Who is rational? Studies in individual differences in reasoning.* Mahwah, NJ: Erlbaum.

Stanovich, K. E., & West, R. F. (2000). Individual differences in reasoning: Implications for the rationality debate. *Behavioral and Brain Sciences, 23,* 645–665.

Steblay, N. M. (1992). A meta-analytic review of the weapon focus effect. *Law and Human Behavior, 16,* 413–24.

Stefanacci, L., Buffalo, E. A., Schmolck, H., & Squire, L. R. (2000). Profound amnesia after damage to the medial temporal lobe: A neuroanatomical and neuropsychological profile of patient E. P. *Journal of Neuroscience, 20,* 7024–7036.

Stein, M. B., Forde, D. R., Anderson, G., & Walker, J. R. (1997). Obsessive-compulsive disorder in the community: An epidemiologic survey with clinical reappraisal. *American Journal of Psychiatry, 154,* 1120–1126.

Stemberger, J. P. (1985). An interactive activation model of language production. In A. W. Ellis (Ed.), *Progress in the psychology of language* (pp. 143–186). London: Erlbaum.

Sternad, D., Dean, W., & Schaal, S. (2000). Interaction of rhythmic and discrete pattern generaators in single-joint movements. *Human Movement Science, 19,* 627–664.

Stewart, L., von Kriegstein, K., Warren, J. D., & Griffiths, T. D. (2006). Music and the brain: Disorders of musical listening. *Brain, 129,* 2533–2553.

Stigler, J. W., Lee, S. Y., & Stevenson, H. W. (1986). Digit memory in Chinese and English: Evidence for a temporally limited store. *Cognition, 23,* 1–20.

Stock, A., & Stock, C. (2004). A short history of ideo-motor action. *Psychological Research-Psychologische Forschung, 68*(2–3), 176–188.

Storms, G. (2004). Exemplar models in the study of natural language concepts. *Psychology of Learning and Motivation, 42,* 1–39.

Storms, G., De Boeck, P., & Rus, W. (2000). Prototype and exemplar-based information in natural language categories. *Journal of Memory and Language, 42,* 51–73.

Strack, F., Martin, L., & Stepper, S. (1988). Inhibiting and facilitating conditions of the human smile: A nonobtrusive test of the facial feedback hypothesis. *Journal of Personality and Social Psychology, 54*, 768–777.

Strayer, D. L., & Johnston, W. A. (2001). Driven to distraction: Dual task studies of simulated driving and conversing on a cellular phone. *Psychological Science, 12*, 6, 462–466.

Stroop, J. R. (1935). Studies of interference in serial verbal reactions. *Journal of Experimental Psychology, 18*, 643–662.

Studdert-Kennedy, M. (1974). The perception of speech. In T. A. Sebeok (Ed.), *Current trends in linguistics Vol. 12: Linguistics and adjacent arts and sciences*, The Hague: Mouton.

Studdert-Kennedy, M. (1975). Dichotic studies: Two questions. *Brain and Language, 2*, 123–130.

Suddendorf, T., & Corballis, M. C. (2008). Episodic memory and mental time travel. In E. Dere, J. P. Huston & A. Easton (Eds.), *Handbook of episodic memory research*, Vol. 18 (pp. 31–42). Amsterdam: Elsevier.

Suetomi, T., & Kido, K. (1997). *Driver behavior under a collision warning system– A driving simulator study.* SAE Technical Paper 970279, doi: 10.4271/970279.

Sugase, Y., Yamane, S., Ueno, S., & Kawano, K. (1999). Global and fine information coded by single neurons in the temporal visual cortex. *Nature, 400*(6747), 869–873.

Sumit, A., Driscoll, J. C., Gabaix, X., & Laibson, D. (2009). The age of reason: financial decisions over the life-cycle with implications for regulation. *Brookings Papers on Economic Activity, 2*, 51–117.

Sunderland, A., Harris, J. E., & Baddeley, A. D. (1983). Do laboratory tests predict everyday memory? *Journal of Verbal Learning and Verbal Behaviour, 22*, 341–357.

Sutherland, S. (1998). Book reviews: Feature selection. *Nature, 392*, 350.

Sweetser, E. E. (1998). Regular metaphoricity in gesture: Bodily-based models of speech interaction. In B. Caron (Ed.), *Actes du 16e Congres International des Linguists.* New York: Elsevier.

Swinnen, S. P. (2002). Intermanual coordination: From behavioural principles to neural-network interactions. *Nature Reviews Neuroscience, 3*(5), 350–361.

Swinney, D. (1979). Lexical access during sentence comprehension: (Re) consideration of context effects. *Journal of Verbal Learning and Verbal Behavior, 18*, 645–659.

T

Taft, M., & Hambly, G. (1986). Exploring the cohort model of spoken word recognition. *Cognition, 22*, 259–282.

Talarico, J. M., & Rubin, D. C. (2003). Confidence, not consistency, characterizes flashbulb memories. *Psychological Science, 14*, 455–461.

Tambovtsev, Y., & Martindale, C. (2007). Phoneme frequencies follow a yule distribution. *SKASE Journal of Theoretical Linguistics, 4*(2), 1–11.

Tanaka, A., Koizumi, A., Imai, H., Hiramatsu, S., Hiramoto, E., & de Gelder, B. (2010). I feel your voice: Cultural differences in the multisensory perception of emotion. *Psychological Science, 21*, 1259–62.

Taplin, J. E. (1971). Reasoning with conditional sentences. *Journal of Verbal Learning and Verbal Behaviour, 10*, 219–225.

Taraban, R., & McClelland, J. L. (1988). Constituent attachment and thematic role assignment in sentence processing: Influences of content-based expectations. *Journal of Memory & Language, 27*, 597–632.

Tarr, M. J., & Bulthoff, H. H. (1995). Is human object recognition better described by geon structural descriptions or by multiple views – Comment on Biederman and Gerhardstein (1993). *Journal of*

Experimental Psychology-Human Perception and Performance, 21(6), 1494–1505.

Tarr, M. J., & Bulthoff, H. H. (1998). Image-based object recognition in man, monkey and machine. *Cognition, 67*(1–2), 1–20.

Tatler, B. W., Wade, N. J., Kwan, H., Findlay, J. M., & Velichkovsky, B. M. (2010). Yarbus, eye movements, and vision. *1*(1), 7–27.

Taylor, D. W., Berry, P. C., & Block, C. H. (1958). Does group participating when using brainstorming facilitate or inhibit creative thinking? *Administrative Science Quarterly, 3*, 23–47.

Technical Working Group for Eyewitness Evidence. (1999). *Eyewitness evidence: A guide for law enforcement.* Washington, DC: United States Department of Justice, Office of Justice. Programs.

Teti, D. M., Gelfand, D. M., Messinger, D. S., & Isabella, R. (1995). Maternal depression and the quality of early attachment: An examination of infants, preschoolers, and their mothers. *Developmental Psychology, 31*, 364–376.

Teuber, H.-L., Milner, B., & Vaughan, H. G. (1968). Persistent anterograde amnesia after stab wound of the basal brain. *Neuropsychologia, 6*, 267–282.

Thaler, R. (1980). Towards a positive theory of consumer choice. *Journal of Economic Behavior and Organization, 1*, 39–60.

Thomas, J. C. Jr. (1974). An analysis of behavior in the hobbits-orcs problem. *Cognitive Psychology, 6*, 257–269.

Thompson, J. C., & Baccus, W. (2012). Form and motion make independent contributions to the response to biological motion in occipitotemporal cortex. *NeuroImage, 59*, 625–634.

Thompson, R. G., Moulin, C. J. A., Conway, M. A., & Jones, R. W. (2004). Persistent déjà vu: A disorder of memory. *International Journal of Geriatric Psychiatry, 19*, 906–907.

Thomson, D. M., & Tulving, E. (1970). Associative encoding and retrieval: Weak and strong cues. *Journal of Experimental Psychology, 86*, 255–262.

Thorndike, E. L. (1898). *Animal intelligence.* New York: Macmillan.

Thorndike, E. L., & Lorge, I. (1944). *The teacher's word book of 30,000 words.* New York: Teachers College, Columbia University.

Thorpe, S., Fize, D., & Marlot, C. (1996). Speed of processing in the human visual system. *Nature, 381*(6582), 520–522.

Thothathiri, M., & Snedeker, J. (2008). Give and take: Syntactic priming during spoken language comprehension. *Cognition, 108*(1), 51–68.

Tipper, S. P., Driver, J., & Weaver, B. (1991). Object-centered inhibition of return of visual-attention. *Quarterly Journal of Experimental Psychology Section a-Human Experimental Psychology, 43*(2), 289–298.

Tollestrup, P. A., Turtle, J. W., & Yuille, J. C. (1994). Actual victims and witnesses to robbery and fraud: An archival analysis. In D. F. Ross, J. D. Reed & M. P. Taylor (Eds.), *Adult eyewitness testimony: Current trends and developments.* New York: Wiley.

Tolman, E. C. (1948). Cognitive maps in animals and man. *Psychological Review, 55*, 189–208.

Tomkins, S. S. (1962). *Affect, imagery, consciousness: Vol. 1, The positive affects.* New York: Springer.

Tononi, G., & Koch, C. (2008). The neural correlates of consciousness – An update. *Year in Cognitive Neuroscience 2008*(1124), 239–261.

Tooby, J., & Cosmides, L. (2009). Conceptual foundations of evolutionary psychology. In Rosenberg and Arp (Eds.), *Philosophy of biology.* New York: J.Wiley.

Torralba, A., Oliva, A., Castelhano, M. S., & Henderson, J. M. (2006). Contextual guidance of eye movements and attention in real-world scenes: The role of global features in object search. *Psychological Review, 113*(4), 766–786.

Towse, J. N., & Hitch, G. J. (2007). Variation in working memory due to normal development. In A. R. A. Conway, C. Jarrold, M. J. Kane, A. Miyake & J. N. Towse (Eds.), *Variation in working memory* (pp. 109–133). New York: Oxford University Press.

Treiman, R., Clifton, C., Jr., Meyer, A. S., & Wurm, L. H. (2003). Language comprehension and production. In A. F. Healy & R. W. Proctor (Eds.), *Experimental psychology. Volume 4* (pp. 527–547). New York: Wiley.

Treisman, A. (1964). Monitoring and storage of irrelevant messages in selective attention. *Journal of Verbal Leaning and Verbal Behavior, 3*, 449–459.

Treisman, A. M. (1964). Selective attention in man. *British Medical Bulletin, 20*, 12–16.

Treisman, A. M. (2006). How the deployment of attention determines what we see. *Visual Cognition, 14*(4–8), 411–443.

Tremoulet, P. D., & Feldman, J. (2000). Perception of animacy from the motion of a single object. *Perception, 29*(8), 943–951.

Triandis, H. (1989). Cross-cultural studies of individualisn and collectivism. *Nebraska Symposium on Motivation, 37*, 41–133.

Trickey, S., & Topping, K. J. (2004). Philosophy for children: A systematic review. *Research Papers in Education, 19*, 363–278.

Troje, N. F. (2002). Decomposing biological motion: A framework for analysis and synthesis of human gait patterns. *Journal of Vision, 2*(5), 371–387.

Trommershauser, J., Landy, M. S., & Maloney, L. T. (2006). Humans rapidly estimate expected gain in movement planning. *Psychological Science, 17*(11), 981–988.

Trueswell, J. C. (1996). The role of lexical frequency in syntactic ambiguity resolution. *Journal of Memory and Language, 35*, 566–585.

Tucker, M., & Ellis, R. (1998). On the relations between seen objects and components of potential actions. *Journal of Experimental Psychology-Human Perception and Performance, 24*(3), 830–846.

Tuckey, M., & Brewer, N. (2003). How schemas affect eyewitness memory over repeated retrieval attempts. *Applied Cognitive Psychology, 17*, 785–800.

Tukey, D. D. (1986). A philosophical and empirical analysis of subject's modes of inquiry in Wason's 2-4-6 task. *Quarterly Journal of Experimental Psychology, 38A*, 5–34.

Tulving, E. (1972). Episodic and semantic memory. In E. Tulving & W. Donaldson (Eds.), *Organisation of memory* (pp. 381–403). New York: Academic Press.

Tulving, E. (1983). *Elements of episodic memory*. Oxford: Oxford University Press.

Tulving, E. (1985). Memory and consciousness. *Canadian Psychologist, 25*, 1–12.

Tulving, E. (1999). Study of memory: processes and systems. In J. K. Foster & M. Jelicic (Eds.), *Memory: Systems, process, or function?* (pp. 11–30). New York: Oxford University Press.

Tulving, E. (2002). Episodic memory: From mind to brain. *Annual Review of Psychology, 53*, 1–25.

Tulving, E. (2004). Episodic memory: From mind to brain. *Revue Neurologique, 160*, S9–S23.

Tulving, E. (2007). 'Are there 256 different kinds of memory?'. In J. S. Nairne (Ed.), *The foundations of remembering: Essays in honor of Henry L. Roediger, III* (pp. 39–52). New York: Psychology Press.

Tulving, E., Schacter, D. L., & Stark, H. A. (1982). Priming effects in word-fragment completion are independent of recognition memory. *Journal of*

Experimental Psychology: Learning, Memory, and Cognition, 8(4), 336–342.

Turing, A. M. (1950). Computing machinery and intelligence. *Mind, 59*, 433–460.

Turvey, M. T. (1990). Coordination. *American Psychologist, 45*(8), 938–953.

Tversky, A. (1972). Elimination by aspects: A theory of choice. *Psychological Review, 79*, 281–299.

Tversky, A., & Kahneman, D. (1974). Judgment under uncertainty: Heuristics and biases. *Science, 125*, 1124–1131.

Tversky, A., & Kahneman, D. (1980). Causal schemata in judgments under uncertainty. In M. Fishbein (Ed.), *Progress in social psychology*. Hillsdale, NJ: Lawrence Erlbaum.

Tversky, A., & Kahneman, D. (1981). The framing of decisions and the psychology of choice. *Science, 211*, 453–458.

Tversky, A., & Kahneman, D. (1983). Extensional vs. intuitive reasoning: The conjunction fallacy in probability judgment. *Psychological Review, 90*, 293–315.

Tversky, A., & Kahneman, D. (1992). Advances in prospect theory: Cumulative representation of uncertainty. *Journal of Risk and Uncertainty, 5*, 297–323.

Tversky, B. (2011). Visualizing thought. *Topics in Cognitive Science, 3*(3), 499–535.

U

Ucros, C. G. (1989). Mood state-dependent memory: A meta-analysis. *Cognition & Emotion, 3*, 139–167.

Ullman, S., Vidal-Naquet, M., & Sali, E. (2002). Visual features of intermediate complexity and their use in classification. *Nature Neuroscience, 5*(7), 682–687.

Uman, M. A. (1986). *All about lightning*. Dover Publications.

Underwood, B. J. (1957). Interference and forgetting. *Psychological Review, 64*, 49–60.

Ungerleider, L. G., & Mishkin, M. (1982). Two

cortical visual systems. In D. Ingle, M. A. Goodale, & R. J. W. Mansfield (Eds.), *Analysis of visual behavior* (pp. 549–586). Cambridge, MA: MIT Press.

Uno, Y., Kawato, M., & Suzuki, R. (1989). Formation and control of optimal trajectory in human multijoint arm movement – Minimum torque-change model. *Biological Cybernetics, 61*(2), 89–101.

V

Vaid, J., & Gupta, A. (2002). Exploring word recognition in a semi-alphabetic script: The case of Devanagari. *Brain and Language, 81*, 679–690.

Vaidya, C. J., Gabrieli, J. D. E., Keane, M. M., & Monti, L. A. Perceptual and conceptual memory processes in global amnesia. *Neuropsychology, 9*, 580–591.

Vallacich, J. S., Dennis, A. R., & Connolly, T. (1994). Idea generation in computer based groups: A new ending to an old story. *Organisational Behavior and Decision Processes, 7*, 448–467.

Van Petten, C., Coulson, S., Rubin, S., Plante, E., & Parks, M. (1999). Timecourse of word identification and semantic integration in spoken language. *Journal of Experimental Psychology: Learning, Memory, and Cognition, 25*, 394–417.

Van Rullen, R., & Thorpe, S. J. (2001). Is it a bird? Is it a plane? Ultra-rapid visual categorisation of natural and artifactual objects. *Perception, 30*(6), 655–668.

Van Tonder, G. J. (2006). Order and complexity in naturalistic landscapes. In L. Albertazzi (Ed.), *Visual thought: The depictive space of perception* (pp. 257–301). Amsterdam: Benjamin Press.

Van Tonder, G. J., Lyons, M. J., & Ejima, Y. (2002). Visual structure of a Japanese Zen garden – The mysterious appeal of a simple and ancient composition of rocks is unveiled. *Nature, 419*(6905), 359–360.

Vangeneugden, J., Pollick, F., & Vogels, R. (2009). Functional differentiation of macaque visual temporal cortical neurons using a parametric action space. *Cerebral Cortex, 19*(3), 593–611.

Vanlancker, D. R., Kreiman, J., & Cummings, J. (1989). Voice perception deficits – neuroanatomical correlates of phonagnosia. *Journal of Clinical and Experimental Neuropsychology, 11*(5), 665–674.

Veling, H., & Van Knippenberg, A. (2004). Remembering can cause inhibition: Retrieval induced inhibition as a cue independent process. *Journal of Experimental Psychology: Learning, Memory, & Cognition, 30*, 315–318.

Velmans, M. (2009). *Understanding consciousness*, 2nd Ed. London: Routledge/Psychology Press.

Vera, A. H., & Simon, H. A. (1993). Situated action: A symbolic interpretation. *Cognitive Science, 17*, 7–48.

Vernon, D., Hofsten, C. v., & Fadiga, L. (2010). *A roadmap for cognitive development in humanoid robots.* from http://dx.doi.org/10.1007/978-3-642-16904-5 MIT Access Only

Vernon, P. E. (1970). *Creativity.* Harmondsworth: Penguin.

Vertes, R. P., & Eastman, K. E. (2000). The case against memory consolidation in REM sleep. *Behavioral and Brain Sciences*, 867–876.

Vigliocco, G., Antonini, T., & Garrett, M. F. (1997). Grammatical gender is on the tip of Italian tongues. *Psychological Science, 8*, 314–317.

Vinciarelli, A., Pantic, M., & Bourlard, H. (2009). Social signal processing: Survey of an emerging domain. *Image and Vision Computing, 27*(12), 1743–1759.

Viviani, P., & Cenzato, M. (1985). Segmentation and coupling in complex movements. *Journal of Experimental Psychology-Human Perception and Performance, 11*(6), 828–845.

Viviani, P., & Stucchi, N. (1992). Biological movements

look uniform – Evidence of motor-perceptual interactions. *Journal of Experimental Psychology-Human Perception and Performance, 18*(3), 603–623.

Vogt, S. (1995). On relations between perceiving, imagining and performing in the learning of cyclical movement sequences. *British Journal of Psychology, 86*, 191–216.

Vogt, S., & Thomaschke, R. (2007). From visuo-motor interactions to imitation learning: Behavioural and brain imaging studies. *Journal of Sports Sciences, 25*(5), 497–517.

Vogt, S., Buccino, G., Wohlschlager, A. M., Canessa, N., Shah, N. J., Zilles, K., Eickhoff, S. B., Freund, H-J., Rizzolattl, G., & Fink, G. R. (2007). Prefrontal involvement in imitation learning of hand actions: Effects of practice and expertise. *Neuroimage, 37*(4), 1371–1383.

Von Frisch, K. (1962). Dialects in the language of the bees. *Scientific American, 207*, 79–87.

Voyles, R., & Adams, J. A. (2011). Editorial: Security, search and rescue robotics. *Journal of Intelligent Robot Systems, 64*, 3–6.

Vrecko, S. (2010). Neuroscience, power and culture: An introduction. *History of the Human Sciences, 23*, 1–10.

Vrij, A. (2000). *Detecting lies and deceit: The psychology of lying and the implications for professional practice.* New York: John Wiley.

Vrij, A. (2004). Why professionals fail to catch liars and how they can improve. *Legal and Criminological Psychology, 9*, 159–181.

Vrij, A., & Mann, S. (2001). Telling and detecting lies in a high-stake situation: The case of a convicted murderer. *Applied Cognitive Psychology, 15*, 187–203.

Vrij, A., Edward, K., & Bull, R. (2001). People's insight into their own behaviour and speech content while lying. *British Journal of Psychology, 92*, 373–389.

Vrij, A., Granhag, P. A., & Porter, S. (2010). Pitfalls and opportunities in nonverbal and verbal lie detection. *Psychological Science in the Public Interest, 11*, 89–121.

Vul, E., Harris, C., Winklielan, P., & Pashler, H. (2009). Puzzlingly high correlations in fMRI studies of emotion, personality, and social cognition. *Perspectives on Psychological Science, 4*, 274–290.

W

Wachowicz, F., Stevens, C. J., & Byron, T. P. (2011). Effects of balance cues and experience on serial recall of human movement. *Dance Research, 29*(2), 450–468.

Wallas, G. (1926). *The art of thought.* London: Jonathan Cape.

Wallentin, M. (2009). Putative sex differences in verbal abilities and language cortex: A critical review. *Brain & Language, 108*, 175–183.

Wang, J., Nicol, T., Skoe, E., Sams, M., & Kraus, N. (2009). Emotion modulates early auditory response to speech. *Journal of Cognitive Neuroscience, 21*(11), 2121–2128.

Wansink, B. (1994). Advertising's impact on category substitution. *Journal of Marketing Research, 31*, 505–515.

Wansink, B., & Ray, M. L. (1996). Advertising strategies to increase usage frequency. *Journal of Marketing, 60*, 3146.

Ward, G. (2001). A critique of the working memory model. In J. Andrade (Ed.), *Working memory in perspective* (pp. 219–239). Hove: Psychology Press.

Ward, J. (2008). *The frog who croaked blue: Synesthesia and the mixing of the senses.* London: Routledge.

Warren, D., Welch, R., & McCarthy, T. (1981). The role of visual-auditory 'compellingness' in the ventriloquism effect: Implications for transitivity among the spatial senses. *Perception & Psychophysics, 30*, 557–564.

Warren, R. M., & Obusek, C. J. (1971). Speech perception and phonemic restorations. *Perception & Psychophysics, 9*, 358–362.

Warren, R. M., & Warren, R. P. (1970). Auditory illusions and confusions. *Scientific American, 223*, 30–36.

Warrington, E. K., & Mccarthy, R. (1983). Category specific access dysphasia. *Brain, 106*, 859–878.

Warrington, E. K., & Shallice, T. (1972). Neuropsychological evidence of visual storage in short-term memory tasks. *The Quarterly Journal of Experimental Psychology, 24*, 30–40.

Warrington, E. K., & Shallice, T. (1984). Category specific semantic impairments. *Brain, 107*, 829–853.

Warrington, E. K., Logue, V., & Pratt, R. T. (1972). The anatomical localisation of selective impairment of auditory verbal short-term memory. *Neuropsychologia, 9*, 377–387.

Was, C. A., & Woltz, D. J. (2007). Re-examining the relationship between working memory and comprehension: The role of available long-term memory. *Journal of Memory and Language, 56*, 86–102.

Wason, P. C. (1960). On the failure to eliminate hypotheses in a conceptual task. *The Quarterly Journal of Experimental Psychology, 12*, 129–140.

Wason, P. C. (1966). Reasoning. In B. M. Foss (Ed.), *New horizons in psychology.* Harmondsworth: Penguin.

Wason, P. C. (1968). Reasoning about a rule. *Quarterly Journal of Experimental Psychology, 20*, 273–281.

Wason, P. C. (1969). Regression in reasoning? *British Journal of Psychology 60*, 471–480.

Wason, P. C., & Evans, J. St. B. T. (1975). Dual processes in reasoning? *Cognition, 3*, 141–154.

Wason, P. C., & Johnson-Laird, P. N. (1970). A conflict between selecting and evaluating information in an inferential task. *British*

Journal of Psychology, 61, 509–515.

Wason, P. C., & Johnson-Laird, P. N. (1972). *Psychology of reasoning: Structure and content.* London: Batsford.

Wason, P. C., & Shapiro, D. (1971). Natural and contrived experience in a reasoning problem. *Quarterly Journal of Experimental Psychology, 23,* 63–71.

Watson, J. B. (1913). Psychology as the behaviorist views it. *Psychological Review, 20,* 158–177.

Watts, F. N., McKenna, F. P., Sharrock, R., & Trezise, L. (1986). Colour naming of phobia-related words. *British Journal of Psychology, 77,* 97–108.

Waugh, N. C., & Norman, D. A. (1965). Primary memory. *Psychological Review, 72,* 89–104.

Weaver, C. A. III. (1993). Do you need a 'flash' to form a flashbulb memory? *Journal of Experimental Psychology: General, 122,* 39–46.

Weber, N., Brewer, N., Wells, G. L., Semmler, C., & Keast, A. (2004). Eyewitness identification accuracy and response latency: The unruly 10–12 second rule. *Journal of Experimental Psychology: Applied, 10,* 139–147.

Wegner, D. M. (1994). Ironic processes of mental control. *Psychological Review, 101*(1), 34–52.

Wegner, D. M. (1997). When the antidote is the poison: Ironic mental control processes. *Psychological Science, 8*(3), 148–150.

Weiner, K. S., & Grill-Spector, K. (2012). The improbable simplicity of the fusiform face area. *Trends in Cognitive Sciences, 16*(5), 251–254.

Weingartner, H. J., Sirocco, K., Curran, V., & Wolkowitz, O. (1995). Memory facilitation following the administration of the benzodiazepine triazolam. *Experimental Clinical Psychopharmacology, 3,* 298–303.

Weisberg, R. W. (1994). Genius and madnesss? A quasi-experimental test of the hypothesis that manic depression increases creativity. *Psychological Science, 5,* 361–367.

Weisberg, R. W. (2006). *Creativity: Understanding innovation in problem solving, science, invention and the arts.* New York: J. Wiley.

Weisberg, R. W., & Alba, J. W. (1981). An examination of the alleged role of 'fixation' in the solution of several 'insight' problems. *Journal of Experimental Psychology: General, 110,* 169–192.

Welch, G. B., & Burnett, C. T. (1924). Is primacy a factor in association-formation. *American Journal of Psychology, 35,* 396–401.

Welch, R. B., & Warren, D. H. (1980). Immediate perceptual response to intersensory discrepancy. *Psychological Bulletin, 88*(3), 638–667.

Welch, R. B., Duttonhurt, L. D., & Warren, D. H. (1986). Contributions of audition and vision to temporal rate perception. *Perception & Psychophysics, 39*(4), 294–300.

Wells, G. L., & Loftus, E. F. (2003). Eyewitness memory for people and events. In A. M. Goldstein (Ed.), *Handbook of psychology.* Vol. 11, *Forensic psychology* (pp. 149–160). New York: John Wiley.

Wells, G. L., & Olson, E. A. (2003). Eyewitness testimony. *Annual Review of Psychology, 54,* 277–295.

Wells, G. L., Small, M., Penrod, S. J., Malpass, R. S., Fulero, S. M., & Brimacombe, C. A. E. (1998). Eyewitness identification procedures: Recommendations for lineups and photospreads. *Law and Human Behavior, 22,* 603–647.

Wells, H. G. (1908). *First and last things.* London.

Wener, A. E., & Rehm, L. (1975). Depressive affect: A test of behavioral hypotheses. *Journal of Abnormal Psychology, 84,* 221–227.

Wernicke, C. (1874). *Der aphasische symtomemcomplex.* Breslau Poland: M. Cohn und Weigert.

Wertheimer, M. (1945). *Productive thinking.* New York: Harper and Row.

Wetherick, N. E., & Gilhooly, K. J. (1990). Syllogistic reasoning: Effects of premise order. In K. Gilhooly, M. T. G. Keane, R. Logie & G. Erdos (Eds.), *Lines of thought: Reflections in the psychology of thinking,* Vol. 1. London: John Wiley.

Weylman, S. T., Brownell, H. H., & Gardner, H. (1988). 'It's what you mean, not what you say': Pragmatic language use in brain-damaged patients. In F. Plum (Ed.), *Language, communication, and the brain* (pp. 229–243). New York: Raven Press.

Whaley, C. P. (1978). Word-nonword classification time. *Journal of Verbal Learning and Verbal Behavior, 17,* 143–54.

Wheaton, L. A., & Hallett, M. (2007). Ideomotor apraxia: A review. *Journal of the Neurological Sciences, 260*(1–2), 1–10.

Wheeler, D. D. (1970). Processes in word recognition. *Cognitive Psychology, 1,* 59–85.

Whitaker, H. (1982). Levels of impairment in disorders of speech. In R. Malatesha & L. Hartlage (Eds.), *Neuropsychology and Cognition – Volume 1: Proceedings of the NATO Advanced Study Institute on Neuropsychology and Cognition,* The Hague: Martinus Nijhoff Publishers.

White, A. (2004). *What happened? Alcohol, memory blackouts and the brain.* Downloaded from http://pubs.niaaa.nih.gov/publications/arh27-2/186-196.htm

Whorf, B. (1956). The relation of habitual thought and behavior to language. In J. B. Carroll (Ed.), *Language, thought and reality: Selected writings of Benjamin Lee Whorf* (pp. 134–59). Cambridge, MA: MIT Press.

Wickelgren, W. A. (1969). Context-sensitive coding associative memory and serial order in (speech) behavior. *Psychological Review, 76*(1), 1–15.

Wickens, C. D. (1980). The structure of attentional resources. In R. S. Nickerson (Ed.), *Attention and performance* (Vol. 8, pp. 239–257). Hillsdale: Erlbaum.

Wickens, C. D. (1992). *Engineering psychology and human performance* (2nd ed.). New York: Harper Collins.

Wickens, C. D. (2002). Multiple resources and performance prediction. *Theoretical Issues in Ergonomic Science, 3,* 159–177.

Wierzbicka, A. (1986). Human emotions: Universal or culture-specific? *American Anthropologist, 88*(3), 584–594.

Wilgus, J., & Wilgus, B., Face to face with Phineas Gage. *Journal of the History of Neurosci*ences, *18,* 340–345, 2009.

Wilkins, A. J., & Baddeley, A. D. (1978). Remembering to recall in everyday life: An approach to absentmindedness. In M. M. Gruneberg, P. E. Morris & R. N. Sykes (Eds.), *Practical aspects of memory.* London: Academic Press.

Wilkins, M. (1928). The effect of changed material on ability to do formal syllogistic reasoning. *Archives of Psychology, 16,* 83.

Williams, L. E., & Bargh, J. A. (2008). Experiencing physical warmth promotes interpersonal warmth. *Science, 222,* 606–607.

Willingham, D. (2002). Allocating student study time. *American Educator,* Summer. www.aft.org/newspubs/periodicals/ac/summer2002

Wilson, M. (2002). Six views of embodied cognition. *Psychonomic Bulletin & Review, 9*(4), 625–636.

Wilson, M., Smith, N. C., & Holmes, P. S. (2007). The role of effort in influencing the effect of anxiety on performance: Testing the conflicting predictions of processing efficiency theory and the conscious processing hypothesis. *British Journal of Psychology, 98,* 411–428.

Winkler, R. (2005). The need for speed. *New York Times*, 13 November.

Winograd, E. (1988). Some observations on prospective remembering. In M. M. Gruneberg, P. E. Morris & R. N. Sykes (Eds.), *Practical aspects of memory: Current research and issues* (pp. 348–353). Chichester: Wiley.

Winograd, E., & Killinger, W. A. (1983). Relating age at encoding in early childhood to adult recall: Development of flashbulb memories. *Journal of Experimental Psychology General, 112*, 413–422.

Wirth, M., et al. (2011). Effects of transcranial direct current stimulation (tDCS) on behaviour and electrophysiology of language production. *Neuropsychologia, 49*(14), 3989–3998.

Wiseman, R., & Greening, E. (2005). 'It's still bending': Verbal suggestion and alleged psychokinetic metal bending. *British Journal of Psychology, 96*, 115–127.

Wit, J. K., Kemmerer, D., Linkenauger, L., & Culham, J. (2010). A functional role for motor simulation in identifying tools. *Psychological Science OnlineFirst*, published on July 16, 2010 as doi:10.1177/0956797610378307

Wittgenstein, L. (1953). *Philosophical investigations.* Oxford: Basil Blackwell.

Wixted, J. T. (2004). The psychology and neuroscience of forgetting. *Annual Review of Psychology, 55*, 235–269.

Wixted, J. T. (2010). The role of retroactive interference and consolidation in everyday forgetting. In S. Della Sala (Ed.), *Forgetting.* Hove: Psychology Press.

Wolfe, J. M. (1994). Guided Search 2.0 – A revised model of visual-search. *Psychonomic Bulletin & Review, 1*(2), 202–238.

Wolfe, J. M., Võ, M. L. H., Evans, K. K., & Greene, M. R. (2011). Visual search in scenes involves selective and nonselective pathways. *Trends in Cognitive Sciences, 15*(2), 77–84.

Wolpert, D. M., & Ghahramani, Z. (2000). Computational principles of movement neuroscience. *Nature Neuroscience, 3*(11), 1212–1217.

Wolpert, D. M., & Kawato, M. (1998). Multiple paired forward and inverse models for motor control. *Neural Networks, 11*(7–8), 1317–1329.

Wolpert, D. M., Shergill, S. S., Bays, P. M., & Frith, C. D. (2003). Two eyes for an eye: The neuroscience of force escalation. *Science, 301*(5630), 187–187.

Woodman, G. F., & Vogel, E. K. (2008). Selective storage and maintenance of an object's features in visual working memory. *Psychonomic Bulletin & Review, 15*(1), 223–229.

Woods, A. J., Philbeck, J. W., & Danoff, J. V. (2009). The various perceptions of distance: An alternative view of how effort affects distance judgments. *Journal of Experimental Psychology: Human Perception, & Performance, 35*, 1104–1117.

Woods, A. T., & Newell, F. N. (2004). Visual, haptic and cross-modal recognition of objects and scenes. *Journal of Physiology-Paris, 98*(1–3), 147–159.

Woodworth, R. S. (1899). The accuracy of voluntary movement. *Psychological Review, 3*(Suppl 13), 1–119.

Woodworth, R. W., & Schlosberg, H. (1954). *Experimental psychology,* 3rd ed. London: Methuen.

Worthen-Chaudhari, L. C. (2011). New partnerships between dance and neuroscience: Embedding the arts for neurorecovery. *Dance Research, 29*(2), 469–496.

Wright, B., & Garrett, M. (1984). Lexical decision in sentences: Effects of syntactic structure. *Memory & Cognition, 12*(1), 31–45.

Wright, D. B. (1993). Recall of the Hillsborough disaster over time: systematic biases of 'flashbulb' memories. *Applied Cognitive Psychology, 7*, 129–138.

Wright, D. B., Gaskell, G. D., & O'Muircheartaigh, C. A. (1998). Flashbulb memory assumptions: Using national surveys to explore cognitive phenomena. *British Journal of Psychology, 36*, 443–456.

Wright, G. (1984). *Behavioural decision theory.* Harmondsworth: Penguin Books.

Wright, S. (1954). The death of Lady mondegreen. *Harper's Magazine 209*(1254), 48–51.

Y

Yan, J., & Blackwell, A. (2004). Password memorability and security: Empirical results. *IEEE Security, & Privacy, 2*(5), 25–31.

Yarbus, A. L. (1967). *Eye movements and vision.* New York: Plenum Press.

Yiend, J. (2010). The effects of emotion on attention: A review of attentional processing of emotional information. *Cognition and Emotion, 24*(1), 3–47.

Young, A., & Ellis, H. D. (1989). *Handbook of research on face processing.* Amsterdam: North Holland.

Z

Zacks, J. M., & Tversky, B. (2001). Event structure in perception and conception. *Psychological Bulletin, 127*(1), 3–21.

Zacks, J. M., Speer, N. K., Swallow, K. M., Braver, T. S., & Reynolds, J. R. (2007). Event perception: A mind-brain perspective. *Psychological Bulletin, 133*(2), 273–293.

Zajonc, R. B. (1980). Feeling and thinking: Preferences need no inferences. *American Psychologist, 35*, 151–175.

Zakay, D. (1985). Post-decisional confidence and conflict experienced in a choice process. *Acta Psychologica, 58*, 75–80.

Zatorre, R. J., Halpern, A. R., Perry, D. W., Meyer, E., & Evans, A. C. (1996). Hearing in the mind's ear: A PET investigation of musical imagery and perception. *Journal of Cognitive Neuroscience, 8*, 29–46.

Zeki, S. (1991). Cerebral akinetopsia (visual-motion blindness) – A review. *Brain, 114*, 811–824.

Zeki, S. (2001). Artistic creativity and the brain. *Science, 293*(5527), 51–52.

Zeki, S. (2003). *Inner vision: An exploration of art and the brain.* Oxford: Oxford University Press.

Zheng, K., Glas, D. F., Kanda, T., Ishiguro, H., & Hagita, N. (2011). How many social robots can one operator control? *HRI '11: Proceedings of the 6th ACM/IEEE International Conference on Human-Robot Interaction* (pp. 379–386).

Zola, D. (1984). Redundancy and word perception during reading. *Perception and Psychophysics, 36*, 277–284.

Name Index

Subject Index

Page numbers for definitions are shown in **bold**

Page numbers for boxes are followed by letters showing box type
pa Practical Applications
rcu Research Close Up
tgw When Things Go Wrong